CULTURAL PSYCHOLOGY

Steven J. Heine

UNIVERSITY OF BRITISH COLUMBIA

W. W. NORTON

NEW YORK | LONDON

For Nariko, Seiji, and Kokoro

W.W. Norton & Company has been independent since its founding in 1923, when William Warder Norton and Mary D. Herter Norton first published lectures delivered at the People's Institute, the adult education division of New York City's Cooper Union. The Nortons soon expanded their program beyond the Institute, publishing books by celebrated academics from America and abroad. By mid-century, the two major pillars of Norton's publishing program—trade books and college texts—were firmly established. In the 1950s, the Norton family transferred control of the company to its employees, and today—with a staff of four hundred and a comparable number of trade, college, and professional titles published each year—W.W. Norton & Company stands as the largest and oldest publishing house owned wholly by its employees.

Copyright © 2008 by W. W. Norton & Company, Inc.

Editor: Jon Durbin
Managing Editor, College: Marian Johnson
Project Editor: Sarah Mann
Production Manager: Jane Searle
Editorial Assistants: Alexis Hilts and Robert Haber

Composition by Matrix.
Manufacturing by The Maple-Vail Book Group—Binghamton.
Book design by Jo Anne Metsch.

Library of Congress Cataloging-in-Publication Data
Heine, Steven J.
Cultural psychology / Steven J. Heine.—1st ed.
     p. cm.
Includes bibliographical references and index.
ISBN: 978-0-393-92573-9 (pbk.)
1. Ethnopsychology. I. Title.
GN502.H45 2008
155.8′2—dc22

                    2007027192

     W. W. Norton & Company, Inc., 500 Fifth Avenue, New York, N.Y. 10110
                    www.wwnorton.com
     W. W. Norton & Company Ltd., Castle House, 75/76 Wells Street, London W1T 3QT

                    2 3 4 5 6 7 8 9 0

About the Author

Steven J. Heine (Ph.D. University of British Columbia) is Professor of Psychology and Distinguished University Scholar at the University of British Columbia. His research focuses on the role of culture in people's motivations to view themselves positively. He has published over thirty articles and written nine book chapters, including "Culture and Motivation" in the *Handbook of Cultural Psychology*. He received the Distinguished Scientist Early Career Award for Social Psychology from the American Psychological Association in 2003 and the Early Career Award from the International Society of Self and Identity in 2002. He lives with his family in Vancouver.

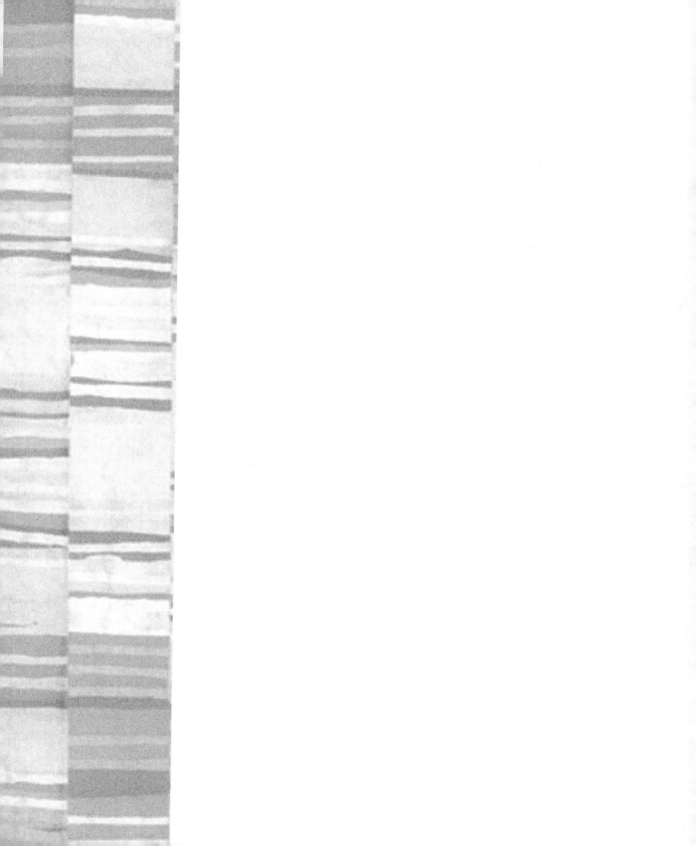

Contents in Brief

Preface xv

1 Culture and Human Nature 1

2 Cultural Evolution 43

3 Methods for Studying Culture and Psychology 92

4 Development and Socialization 136

5 Self and Personality 176

6 Motivation 227

7 Morality, Religion, and Justice 273

8 Emotions 311

9 Cognition and Perception 355

10 Mental and Physical Health 408

11 Interpersonal Attraction, Close Relationships, and Groups 462

12 Living in Multicultural Worlds 508

Glossary G-1
References R-1
Credits C-1
Name Index N-1
Subject Index S-1

Contents

Preface   xv

1 **Culture and Human Nature**   1
    A Psychology for a Cultural Species   1
       What is Culture?   3
    Is Culture Unique to Humans?   5
       Cultural Learning   7
       Theory of Mind   9
       Why Are Humans Adept at Cultural Learning?   17
    Psychological Universals and Variability   23
       Is the Mind Independent from, or Intertwined with, Culture?   23
       Case Study: The Sambia   27
       Psychological Universals and Levels of Analysis   30
       The Psychological Database Is Largely Western   34
    Where Does Cultural Psychology Come From?   36
    You Are a Product of Your Own Culture   40
    Summary   42

2 **Cultural Evolution**   43
    Where Does Cultural Variation Come From?   46
       Ecological and Geographic Variation   46
    How Do Ideas Catch On?   54
       Parallels Between Biological and Cultural Evolution   56
    Factors that Cause Ideas to Spread   62
    How Have Cultures Been Changing?   70
       Cultures Are Becoming Increasingly Interconnected   70
       Many Cultures Are Becoming More Individualistic   72
       People in Many Cultures Are Becoming More Intelligent   76

In the Face of Change, How Do Cultures Persist?   81
    Cultural Innovations Build on Previous Structures   83
    Early Conditions Have Disproportionate Influence on Cultural
    Evolution   85
    Pluralistic Ignorance   88
Summary   91

3 Methods for Studying Culture and Psychology   92
Considerations for Conducting Research Across Cultures   94
    What Cultures Should We Study?   94
    Making Meaningful Comparisons Across Cultures   96
    Conducting Cross-Cultural Research with Surveys   101
    Conducting Cross-Cultural Research with Experiments   113
    Conducting Cross-Cultural Research with Multiple Methods   116
Some Methods Particular to the Study of Culture   117
    Situation Sampling   117
    Cultural Priming   120
    Culture-Level Measures   121
    The Challenge of Unpackaging   123
    Case Study: The Culture of Honor in the Southern United
    States   126
Summary   135

4 Development and Socialization   136
Universal Brains Develop into Culturally Variable Minds   137
Sensitive Periods for Cultural Socialization   138
    Sensitive Periods for Language Acquisition   139
    Sensitive Periods for Acquiring Culture   144
Cultural Differences in Psychological Processes Emerge with
Age   146
What Kinds of Childhood Experiences Differ Across
Cultures?   148
    Sleeping Arrangements   148
    Individualistic Versus Collectivistic Orientations   154
    Attachment Styles   156
    Noun Biases   159
Difficult Developmental Transitions   162
    The Terrible Twos   162

Adolescent Rebellion   164
Socialization Through Education   166
  Case Study: East Asians and Math Education   170
Summary   175

5   **Self and Personality**   176
  Who Am I?   177
  Independent Versus Interdependent Views of Self   182
  Individualism and Collectivism   187
  Beyond Individualism and Collectivism   189
  A Note on Heterogeneity of Individuals and Cultures   190
  Gender and Culture   191
  Some Other Ways That Cultures Differ in the
  Self-Concept   198
    Self-Consistency   198
    Self-Awareness   207
  Implicit Theories Regarding the Nature of the Self   214
  Personality   217
    The Five Factor Model of Personality   219
  Summary   226

6   **Motivation**   227
  Motivations for Self-Enhancement and Self-Esteem   228
  Motivations for Face and Self-Improvement   239
  Religion and Achievement Motivation   242
  Agency and Control   250
    Primary and Secondary Control   252
    Making Choices   257
  Motivations to Fit In or to Stick Out   266
  Summary   272

7   **Morality, Religion, and Justice**   273
  Universalism, Evolutionism, and Relativism   276
  Ethnocentrism and Interpreting Cultural Variability   279
  Kohlberg's Stages of Moral Development   281
    Cross-Cultural Evidence for Kohlberg's Model   284
  Ethics of Autonomy, Community, and Divinity   285

Ethic of Community   286
   Gemeinschaft and Gesellschaft Relations   287
   Ethic of Community in India   288
Ethic of Divinity   293
Culture Wars   295
Emotions and Moral Violations   299
The Morality of Thoughts   302
Culture and Distributive Justice   306
Summary   310

8 Emotions   311
   What Is An Emotion?   313
      The James-Lange Theory of Emotions   313
      The Two-Factor Theory of Emotions   315
      The Role of Appraisals in Emotions   319
   Does Emotional Experience Vary Across Cultures?   322
      Emotions and Facial Expressions   323
      Displaying Emotions Versus Experiencing Them   330
      Cultural Display Rules   331
      Facial Feedback Hypothesis   334
      Cultural Variation in Intensity of Emotional Experience   336
   Emotion and Language   339
   Cultural Variation in Kinds of Emotional Experiences   342
   Cultural Variation in Subjective Well-Being and Happiness   344
   Conclusions Regarding Cultural Variation in Emotions   352
   Summary   354

9 Cognition and Perception   355
   Analytic and Holistic Thinking   358
   Attention   361
   Understanding Other People's Behaviors   370
      The Fundamental Attribution Error   371
   Reasoning Styles   375
   Toleration of Contradiction   378
   Talking and Thinking   383
   Explicit Versus Implicit Communication   389
   Linguistic Relativity   392

How We Understand Humans' Place in the World   404
Summary   406

10 Mental and Physical Health   408
  Mental Health   410
    What is a Psychological Disorder?   410
  Culture-Bound Syndromes   412
    Eating Disorders   413
    Koro   415
    Amok   417
  Universal Syndromes   419
    Depression   419
    Social Anxiety Disorder   423
    Suicide   426
    Schizophrenia   429
  Physical Health   432
  Biological Variability of Humans   432
    Genetic Variation Across Populations   432
    Acquired Physical Variation Across Cultures   435
  Culture and Health   442
    Socioeconomic Status and Health   442
    Ethnicity and Health   450
  Medicine and Culture   453
  Summary   460

11 Interpersonal Attraction, Close Relationships, and Groups   462
  Interpersonal Attraction   463
    Other Bases of Interpersonal Attraction   469
    Similarity-Attraction Effect   471
  Close Relationships   474
    Friends and Enemies   474
    Love   479
  Groups   487
    Relations With Ingroups and Outgroups   487
    Bases of Group Identification   491
    The Four Elementary Forms of Relationships   494
    Working With Others   497
  Summary   506

12 Living in Multicultural Worlds   508

Difficulties in Studying Acculturation   511

What Happens When People Move to a New Culture?   512

Changes in Attitudes Toward the Host Culture   512

Who Adjusts Better?   516

Some Pitfalls of Acculturation   526

Multicultural People   528

Evidence for Blending   528

Frame-Switching   531

Different but Often Unequal   542

Summary   546

Glossary   G-1

References   R-1

Credits   C-1

Name Index   N-1

Subject Index   S-1

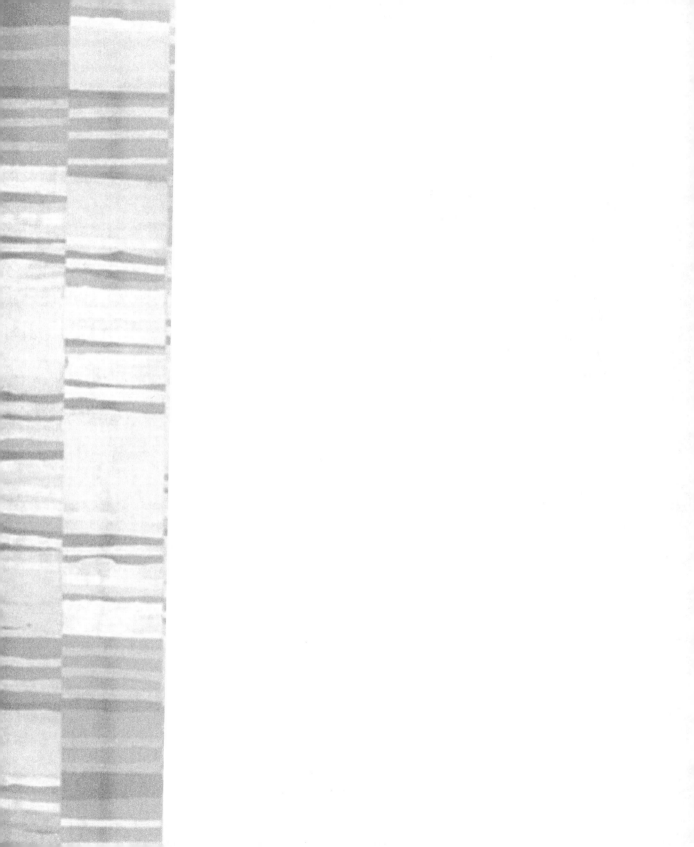

Preface

My own quest to become a cultural psychologist began upon graduating with a BA in psychology and, not knowing what to do with it, moving to a small town in Japan to teach English and, hopefully, figure out what I might do with my life. I thought I had been an attentive student in my psychology classes, and I had learned much about how people think. Imagine, then, my surprise upon moving to rural Japan and discovering that much of what I thought I understood about human nature didn't seem to explain how my new friends and colleagues thought and behaved. I went through a series of cross-cultural misunderstandings and gaffes before I came to realize that my ideas about human nature were just plain wrong—they may have explained the nature of North Americans, but they weren't so useful outside that cultural context. This seemed interesting because from what I learned in my psychology classes, people *should* think in the same ways everywhere. So it was on the basis of many embarrassing cross-cultural misunderstandings that I decided to become a cultural psychologist. This book, too, is a product of those same kinds of misunderstandings.

Cultural psychology, as a field, is largely a new discipline, and it continues to produce striking findings that challenge psychologists' understanding of human nature. In contrast to much conventional wisdom, this new field has been revealing that culture shapes how people's minds operate—sometimes in profound ways. The past couple of decades have been an exciting time, as an abundance of new research continues demonstrate that culture is not just a thin veneer covering the universal human mind. Rather, this research has begun to show just how deeply cultural influences penetrate our psychology and shape the ways that people think. The research underscores how human thoughts occur within cultural contexts, and shows that different cultural contexts can lead to fundamentally different ways of thinking.

For the past several years I have very much enjoyed teaching students about the exciting discoveries coming out of this new field. However, there wasn't really an undergraduate textbook covering the fascinating theories and findings that cultural psychologists were discussing. Without a textbook, teaching a course in cultural psychology usually meant having students read the original journal articles describing these new ideas. This made for stimulating classroom discussions, but it also meant that my courses on cultural psychology were typically limited to small seminars for senior students. I discussed this problem with cultural psychologists at other universities, and many said they were in the same situation. Cultural psychology had become a tremendously interesting and important discipline, and had rapidly developed a rich theoretical and empirical foundation unique from other approaches that considered the influences of culture. But at that point, the field lacked an undergraduate textbook that could be used in large lecture classes, and consequently, very few students were learning about it. I reluctantly came to the realization that the quickest way that I could start teaching larger cultural psychology classes was to write a textbook myself. Alas, it hasn't been so quick (over four years in the making), as I failed to appreciate just how much new and significant research was being conducted. And even now, after sending the final version to the presses, there is much new and fascinating work that I unfortunately wasn't able to include in time for the deadline.

I sought to write a book focused on what I have found most interesting about the field of cultural psychology. Toward this end, I have written the chapters around some provocative key questions with which cultural psychologists are still struggling. For example, one theme that arises repeatedly throughout the book is the question of how similar the psychologies of people from different cultures are. That human brains are largely the same everywhere, yet their experiences diverge widely, makes this a difficult and important question. Some other fundamental questions I address include: Where does culture come from? How are humans similar to and different from other animals? What are the many different ways to be human?

I also endeavored to integrate much cultural diversity into the topics discussed here: The text considers research findings from every populated continent, including many investigations of subsistence cultures around the world, as well as explorations of variance between ethnic groups within countries. I also wrote the chapters to provide a strong emphasis on experimental research throughout, while also paying particular attention to observation studies and ethnographies. I think it's important to gain a sense of the varieties of ways that we can go about studying culture. I also wanted to highlight how culture underlies all aspects of human psychology, so I have attempted to explore the role of culture across many disciplines both within psychology (e.g., clinical, cognitive, developmental, social, and personality psychology), and outside psychology (e.g., anthropology, evolutionary biology, linguistics, sociology). Finally, students will find many detailed examples throughout the book that show how cultural psychologists' theorizing and research is relevant to their lives. Hopefully, the combination of these ingredients will yield an interesting and educational experience for the readers.

I was very fortunate to receive an enormous amount of support in writing this book. First, this book would not exist without the sage guidance, clear-eyed vision, and unflagging encouragement and optimism on the part of my editor, Jon Durbin, and the rest of the terrific staff at W. W. Norton & Company. I also want to thank Sarah Mann at W. W. Norton, who served as the project editor. She made some highly helpful comments along the way, while pulling together all the disparate pieces that have made this into a fine book. I am also indebted to the extremely thoughtful and helpful reviewers' comments from Jon Haidt, Ashleigh Merrit, Dick Nisbett, and Julie Spencer-Rodgers. In particular, Beth Morling went far beyond the call of duty to show me how almost every manuscript page could be greatly improved pedagogically. Students should be very thankful to her that they are not now reading the book as I had originally written the first draft.

This book benefited from several discussions over the years with my formal mentors, Darrin Lehman and Shinobu Kitayama, from whom I learned how to become a cultural psychologist, as well as from informal mentors who have educated me from afar, such as Dov Cohen, Hazel Markus, Dick Nisbett, and Paul Rozin. Also, many conversations at cafeterias, in hallways, and on ski lifts with my current cultural psychology colleagues at UBC, Joe Henrich, Ara Norenzayan, and Mark Schaller, developed many of the ideas discussed in the book. Several chapters of this text also benefited from the feedback of many readers, including Emma Buchtel, Edith Chen, Ilan Dar-Nimrod, Takeshi Hamamura, Greg Miller, Andrew Ryder, Janet Werker, and Katie Yoshida, as well as from the many undergraduates who sat as willing and patient guinea pigs as I tried out various drafts of the chapters with

them in class. These readers all offered excellent advice—the book would be
a stronger product would I have taken it better.

STEVEN J. HEINE
Vancouver, British Columbia
June, 2007

CULTURAL
PSYCHOLOGY

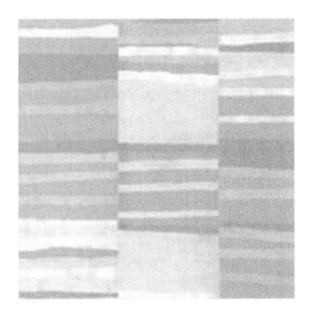

Culture and Human Nature

Humans are an interesting bunch. If a team of alien biologists arrived at our planet and tried to catalog all the different species here, they would no doubt notice how peculiar we humans are. In many ways, we would seem to be ill adapted to survive. We're not particularly strong, we're not very fast, we don't have sharp teeth or claws, and we don't even have a furry coat to keep us warm. Furthermore, we don't ensure the survival of our species through rampant reproduction, like rabbits. The alien biologists must wonder what kind of strange beasts we are. The odds would certainly seem stacked against us. Yet despite the apparent disadvantages that humans have compared to other species, the alien biologists would notice that we've populated more parts of the world, in more diverse ecologies, using a broader range of subsistence systems and social arrangements, than any other species. And our numbers keep growing. How is it that humans have come to be so successful?

Were these alien biologists very keen, though, they might note that we humans do have one adaptation that compensates for all that we lack. Humans have culture. We rely on culture more than any other species, and it is our reliance on culture that has allowed us to succeed in such diverse environments. And this reliance on culture has important and profound implications for our thoughts and behaviors. Cultural psychology is the field that studies those implications.

A Psychology for a Cultural Species

One does not need to take a course on cultural psychology to recognize that humans are a cultural species. This fact is immediately evident whenever you travel to a different country or meet people from different cultural backgrounds. In many ways, people from different cultures live their lives differently; they

"You seem familiar, yet somehow strange—are you by any chance Canadian?"

speak different languages, have different customs, eat different foods, have different religious beliefs, have different child-rearing practices, and so on. Cultural psychology is not original in highlighting the many obvious ways that people's experiences differ around the planet. The unique contribution of cultural psychology, and the main thesis of this book, is that people from different cultures also differ in their psychology. One theme that will be returned to throughout this book is the notion that *psychological processes are shaped by experiences*. Because people in different cultures have many different experiences, we should then expect differences in many ways that they think. As you read through this book I encourage you to examine the kinds of experiences that you have had and the ways that you think, in contrast to the descriptions that are provided of people from other cultures.

Although experiences shape psychological processes, they clearly do not determine them. Psychological processes are constrained and afforded by the neurological structures that underlie them. And because the biology of the brain is virtually identical around the world, people from all cultures share the same constraints and affordances of the universal human brain. Herein lies a challenge for making sense of virtually all cross-cultural studies in psychology. To what extent should ways of thinking look similar around the world because people share a universal brain, and to what extent should they look different because people have divergent experiences? Providing an answer to this question is not always straightforward as some ways of thinking do appear to be highly similar around the world whereas others appear strikingly different. This tension between *universal and culturally variable psychologies* is another theme that will be addressed throughout this book. As you read through the various descriptions of psychological phenomena covered in this book I encourage you to ask yourself whether the evidence suggests that the phenomena are universal or culturally variable.

This chapter will provide an overview of how culture is considered by psychologists. We will explore questions such as how humans evolved the capacities to engage in cultural learning, how culture shapes the ways we think, how we can understand ways of thinking as being culturally universal or variable, and how the field of cultural psychology came to be.

What Is Culture? This book investigates the relations between culture and the ways that people think and, as such, it's necessary to clearly define culture. The question of what culture is has been debated among anthropologists, sociologists, and psychologists for decades, and there is no single consensual answer that applies to all fields. Some people have focused on the symbolic aspects of culture, some have attended to the physical artifacts of culture, and some have emphasized the habits that are contained in culture.

In this book, I use the term "culture" to mean two different things. First, I'll use the term to indicate a particular kind of *information*. Specifically, I'll use culture to mean any kind of information that is acquired from other members of one's species through social learning that is capable of affecting an individual's behaviors (see Richerson & Boyd, 2005). In other words, culture is any kind of idea, belief, technology, habit, or practice that is acquired through learning from others. Humans are therefore a cultural species as people have a great deal of "culture" that fits this definition.

Second, I'll use the term "culture" to indicate a particular *group of individuals*. Cultures are people who are existing within some kind of shared context. People within a given culture are exposed to many of the same cultural ideas. They might attend the same cultural institutions, engage in similar cultural practices, see the same advertisements, read the same newspapers, and have conversations with each other on a day-to-day basis.

There are a few challenges with thinking about groups of people as constituting cultures. First, as you can see from the above definition, the boundaries of cultures are not always clear-cut. For example, an individual might be exposed to cultural ideas that emerge from distant locations, such as those from their immigrant parents, experiences that they have while traveling, advertisements that they see from multinational firms, or ideas that they learn from watching a foreign movie. Cultural boundaries are thus not distinct. Although we can never be certain that we have identified a clear cultural boundary that separates two or more samples, a shorthand practice that is used in many studies described in this book is to look at nationality as a very rough indicator of culture. For example, Italians may be compared with Germans, although one would be unable to ensure that every member of the Italian group was exposed to exclusively Italian cultural messages. The fluid nature of cultural boundaries weaken researchers' abilities to find differences between cultures, but when such differences are found, despite the fluid nature of the boundaries, this is powerful evidence that cultures do differ in their psychological tendencies.

A second challenge, as will be described in the next chapter, is that cultures also change over time, and some shared cultural information disappears as new habits replace the old (although much cultural information persists across time as well). Cultures are thus not static entities but are dynamic and ever-changing.

Last, and perhaps the most important challenge in considering cultures as groups of people, there is much variability among individuals that belong to the same culture. People inherit distinct temperaments (they are born with predispositions toward having certain kinds of personality traits, abilities, and attitudes), they each belong to a unique collection of various social groups (e.g., Jason grew up on Oak street, attended King George elementary school, often met with his extended family of several cousins, played on the Maple Grove junior soccer team, was in the band at Carnegie High School, and was a founding member of the *Perspectives* school newspaper that he worked on for three years), and they each have had a unique history of individual experiences that has shaped their views. Hence, all of these individual differences lead some people to reflexively embrace certain cultural messages, staunchly react against other cultural messages, and largely ignore some other cultural messages. Individuals are nothing if not variable, and the findings that are identified in the studies reported in this book do not apply equally to all members of cultures—the studies reflect average tendencies within cultural groups. So to say that Italians are more emotionally expressive than Germans would mean that, on average, Italians score higher on some measure of emotional expressiveness than do Germans, yet there is also an enormous degree of individual variation that includes some extremely expressive Germans and some quite unexpressive Italians. Cultural membership does not determine individual responses.

In this latter sense, the term "culture" refers to dynamic groups of individuals that share a similar context, are exposed to many similar cultural messages, and contain a broad range of different individuals who are affected by those cultural messages in divergent ways.

Is Culture Unique to Humans?

It is not controversial to say that humans are a cultural species. What is more controversial, however, is to ask whether humans are unique in being a cultural species. This question is controversial, in part, because of the lack of consensus regarding a definition for culture. A different way of defining culture than what I have provided above is to say that culture refers to some kind of symbolic coding—that is, of having a set of signals, icons, and words that refer to something else that most members of that culture recognize. If we accept this definition, then, yes, humans are the only species that have culture because no other species has symbolic coding (Deacon, 1997). But this is a rather unsatisfying and circular definition in that we are defining culture in terms of what is uniquely human (i.e., having symbolic coding), and then concluding that culture is therefore unique to humans.

The definition of culture that I provided earlier is much broader, and it avoids this problem of circularity. That is, are humans unique in being able to learn information from other members of their species through social transmission? If we accept this definition, then, no, humans are by no means the only species that have culture. There are many clear examples of cultural learning in the animal kingdom. Perhaps the most famous example of cultural learning in animals is the case of a very clever female macaque named "Imo" on a small island off of Japan (Kawamura, 1959). One day Imo was given some pieces of sweet potato, and she went to some nearby water to wash the sand off of them before she ate them. Within 3 months, Imo's mother and a couple of her playmates also started washing their potatoes. Three years later, 40% of the other macaques in Imo's troupe were washing their potatoes. It appears that potato-washing became a strategy that was invented by Imo, learned by those around her, and then subsequently became part of the cultural repertoire of a subgroup of macaques living in the same troupe.

Another example of cultural learning can be seen in chimpanzees. Chimps love to eat termites—they're very nutritious and apparently (to chimps, at least) delicious. The challenge, however, is to figure out a way to get these tiny snacks out from the large rock-hard mounds that they live in. Chimps from Mt. Assirik in Senegal have been shown to use tools to extract termites from their mounds. Specifically, they take a twig, peel the bark from it, and then stick the twig into a termite mound to fish out the termites. Chimps from Gombe National Park in Tanzania also use tools to extract termites, but they do so in a different way. These chimps also peel bark from twigs, but unlike the Senegalese chimps, they use the bark to fish out the termites (Whiten et al., 1999). These behaviors appear to be learned behaviors that are culturally transmitted from one generation of chimps to another. At least two different cultures of chimps have thus formed—the twig-fishers versus the bark-fishers. Actually, at this point, a total of 39 different specific behaviors have been identified that distinguish some troupes of chimps from others, including the ways that they clean their bodies with leaves, attract attention from others by slapping branches, and use objects to tickle themselves (Whiten et al., 1999). One can thus speak of different cultures of chimpanzees.

Culture is evident not only in other primate species, who are our closest animal relatives. Elephants, too, appear to engage in culture learning. In 1919, some citrus farmers requested that officials annihilate a local population of

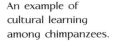

An example of cultural learning among chimpanzees.

140 elephants in the South African park of Addo. A skilled hunter was hired who went about killing off the elephants one by one. After about a year there were only a couple of dozen elephants remaining, and these elephants were eventually given sanctuary somewhere else. Those remaining elephants, after seeing the majority of their herd exterminated, not surprisingly came to respond extremely aggressively to humans. The descendants of this original herd still exist and are reported to be among the most dangerous elephants in Africa. None of the original herd that was attacked in 1919 would still be alive, yet their defensive behavior appears to have been passed on to their offspring, even though none of their offspring themselves have been hunted (Douglas-Hamilton & Douglas-Hamilton, 1975). A culture of aggressive elephants was thus formed and this culture has been passed down through a number of generations. This aggressive elephant culture parallels the aggressive human cultures that we see today in cultures that have experienced generations of continuing warfare (e.g., the Sambia of New Guinea or the Yanomamo of Brazil).

Likewise, many instances of rather complex cultural learning have been identified among dolphins and whales, both in terms of feeding strategies and in vocalizations (for a review see Rendell & Whitehead, 2001). Furthermore, it is not in just the most intelligent species that we see evidence for cultural learning. For example, pigeons appear to learn specific food acquisition strategies from other pigeons (Lefebvre & Giraldeau, 1994). Even guppies have shown evidence of learning from others (Lachlan, Crooks, & Laland, 1998). Some forms of cultural learning are thus evident across a broad swath of the animal kingdom.

Cultural Learning. Humans, then, are not unique in being able to engage in cultural learning. However, humans do seem to stand out in contrast to other animals in the extent of their cultural learning skills. Although many species of animals have been shown to be able to learn cultural information, none of the nonhuman species seem to be very good at it. For example, although the Japanese macaques were able to learn Imo's technique of washing potatoes, they didn't learn it very well. It took years for the potato washing to get learned by others, and many of the macaques never figured it out. In contrast, humans frequently learn new information from each other, and often with only a single exposure to it. Many aspects of human cultures are shared by nearly every member of the culture; for example, dialects, some cultural practices, and specific tools are often so widespread in a particular culture that they are accessible to virtually everyone from that culture. So the cultural learning by the macaques and of other animals at least seems to be very slow compared to the kinds of cultural learning evidenced by humans.

Furthermore, humans seem to be unique among other species in *whom* they choose to imitate. There is no indication, for example, that macaques who are learning a new skill like potato-washing choose which macaques to imitate. Any model that they regularly encounter appears to be equally likely to be imitated. In contrast, there is much evidence to suggest that humans are quite particular about whom they choose to imitate. Humans are especially concerned with detecting "prestige"—that is, they seek others who have skills and are respected by others, and they try to imitate what these individuals are doing (Henrich & Gil-White, 2001). Imitating prestigious others is a very efficient way of cultural learning. Rather than picking someone at random to imitate, and perhaps ending up learning from models who don't really know what they are doing, individuals are more likely to learn successfully if they target those people who are especially talented. If you want to learn how to be a successful golfer a good place to start would be to watch what Tiger Woods does, rather than watching someone like me, who couldn't golf to save his life. Identifying signs of prestige and then imitating people who displayed those signs were skills that were likely selected for in the course of human evolution. Those of our ancestors who did this were more likely to acquire the highly useful cultural knowledge that gave them a survival advantage compared with those who did not. Moreover, in trying to learn a skill from others it isn't always clear what particular behaviors are responsible to achieve success. For example, is Tiger Woods's phenomenal golfing success due to the way he holds his golf club, the way he studied his idol Jack Nicklaus, the weights that he lifts, or the advice he took from his father? Because it is not clear what the critical behaviors for success are, individuals would fare best by having a general imitating mechanism, by which they are attracted to prestigious individuals, whom they observe and try to imitate, regardless of what they are doing. Advertisers of course capitalize on this general imitating mechanism that we have inherited, and they will use prestigious people like Tiger Woods to sell us products that don't seem to have anything to do with the source of their prestige. For example, Tiger Woods appears in commercials for American Express credit cards, Asahi coffee, Wheaties breakfast cereal, and Buick automobiles—none of which would appear to be relevant to his golf skills. Our general imitating mechanism leads us to want to do everything that prestigious people do, even if we often end up copying the wrong behaviors. This strategy should increase the likelihood that we learn the skills that really do lead to success.

Humans' unusually sophisticated cultural learning skills rest on two key capacities: the ability to consider the perspective of others, and the ability to communicate with language. These are described below.

"Which celebrities do this type of yoga?"

Theory of Mind. Another feature of the ways that humans engage in cultural learning appears to be unique, or nearly unique, among humans compared with other animal species. When humans learn from others they are able to take on the perspectives of those others. Humans have what is known as a **theory of mind**. A theory of mind means that people understand that others have minds that are different from their own, and thus that other people have perspectives and intentions that are different from their own. For example, a 2-year-old child will point to a toy that he wants, indicating that he understands that his mother is not aware of where the toy is, and that he is also motivated to share this information about the toy's location with his mother. The child understands that his mother has different thoughts in her head than he does. This understanding of others' intentional states is evident in humans across all cultures, and it tends to develop at a fairly similar rate across cultures (Callaghan et al., 2005). Such a theory of mind is not evident in most other species, and even in our closest genetic relatives, chimpanzees, the evidence is somewhat mixed (Povinelli, Perilloux, Reaux, & Bierschwale, 1998; Tomasello, Kruger, & Ratner, 1993). Specifically, although chimpanzees that are trained by humans do appear to be able to take on the perspective of others (e.g., Savage-Rumbaugh, McDonald, Sevcik, Hopkins, & Rubert, 1986), chimpanzees in the wild show far less evidence. For example, chimpanzees in the wild do not point to outside objects, they do not hold objects up to show them to others, they do not bring others to locations so that they can observe things there, they do not actively offer objects to other individuals by holding them out, and they do not intentionally teach other individuals new behaviors (Tomasello, 1999). Furthermore, chimpanzees do not appear to strive to share their experiences and activities with others of their own kind (Tomasello, Carpenter, Call, Behne, & Moll, 2005). The points about what specifically wild chimpanzees can and cannot do continue to be debated in the literature (de Waal, 2001; Tomasello et al., 1993; Whiten, 1998), and it is difficult to say conclusively what is the full extent of their capabilities. What we can say confidently, however, is that human abilities and motivations to imagine the perspectives and intentions of others (as well as to share their own perspectives and intentions with others), are far superior to those of chimps and other animals. And this difference in ability and motivation to consider the intentions of others has important consequences for cultural learning.

If individuals are able and motivated to understand the intentions of others, then this provides an important step in being able to fruitfully engage in cultural learning. For example, imagine seeing someone use a tool, such as using a stick, to knock some out-of-reach bananas off a shelf. If one is able to appreciate the intentions of the other, he or she is likely to think, "Oh, Bonzo over there wants to get those bananas. He's using that stick in his hand to reach up and knock them off the shelf." By appreciating what Bonzo is trying to do with the stick, the individual can internalize the goals of Bonzo and be better able to reproduce them. When given the chance, the individual is likely to try to use the stick to get some out-of-reach bananas for himself, and use it in the way that Bonzo did. This would be an example of one kind of cultural learning known as **imitative learning**. In imitative learning the learner internalizes something of the model's goals and behavioral strategies (Tomasello et al., 1993; Tomasello, 1999). Tomasello and colleagues argue that chimpanzees have such a difficult time taking on the perspective of others that instead of engaging in imitative learning, they tend to focus on the object itself. By watching Bonzo try to knock the bananas down with a stick they come to learn that the stick can be used to knock down bananas. That is, they learn that the stick affords such banana-knocking strategies. When they then have the opportunity, they try to figure out for themselves how they could use the stick to knock down some bananas. This kind of learning is an example of a second kind of cultural learning known as **emulative learning**. In emulative learning, the learning is focused on the environmental events that are involved—how the use of one object could potentially effect changes in the state of the environment. The key difference between emulative learning and imitative learning is that emulative learning does not require imitating a model's behavioral strategies. An emulative learner is only focusing on what the model appears to be doing, rather than what the model *intends* to accomplish.

Emulative learning can be a very clever and creative form of learning. The individual has to use creative insight to imagine how an object could be used to solve a particular problem. Consider the following study: chimpanzees and 2-year-old human children were compared with how they learned a novel task (Nagell, Olguin, & Tomasello, 1993). Researchers presented the children with a rake-like tool and a desired object (some food for the chimpanzees or a toy for the children) that was kept out of reach. The chimpanzees and children observed the model use the rake to get access to the out-of-reach object in one of two ways. In one condition, the chimpanzees and children observed the model use the rake in the most effective way. That is, the rake was turned upside down with the teeth pointing up, and this provided a wide tool that could easily be used to drag the object toward them. In a second condition, a different group of chimpanzees and children observed the model use the rake in a rather ineffective way. The rake was dragged with the teeth side down (see Figure 1.1). Although it was possible to drag the object toward them like this, it was less effective as the object sometimes slid between the teeth. After watching the model, the chimpanzees and children had the chance to use the rake themselves to get the object. The children showed evidence of true imitative learning, in that they tried to do precisely what the model had done. They used the rake in the same way that

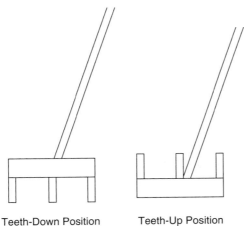

Teeth-Down Position   Teeth-Up Position

FIGURE 1.1

The two rake positions that were possible for the chimpanzee and 2-year-old participants.

the model had, even though this meant that in the "teeth-down" condition, they had a more difficult time getting the object. Chimpanzees, in contrast, showed evidence for emulative learning. Regardless of how the model had used the rake, the chimpanzees used the rake in the most effective "teeth-up" position. They thus seemed to notice that the rake could be used to get the object, and then they figured out for themselves, very creatively, that the rake would be most effective if it was used to drag the object with the teeth up. A number of other studies provide evidence that chimpanzees and other primates tend to solve problems with emulative learning rather than imitative learning (e.g., Custance, Whiten, & Fredman, 1999; Tomasello, 1996).

So whose actions would appear to be smarter in this case—the actions of the chimpanzee or those of the 2-year-old? Well, if we looked at the effectiveness of the behavior, the chimpanzee's strategy of holding the rake teeth down is going to be more successful for obtaining the bananas. This is a critical point: Emulative learning can be a very effective and intelligent kind of learning. However, although emulative learning is often very effective, and in the study above it allowed for a more successful strategy than imitation learning, it has one critical drawback. Emulative learning does not allow for cultural information to accumulate, a point to which we'll return later.

Language Facilitates Cultural Learning. Sophisticated cultural learning is possible, in part, because humans have a theory of mind. A second related adaptation that fostered humans' abilities to engage in cultural learning is language. Being able to communicate with others is enormously important for conveying cultural information. Language allows ideas to be communicated without having to be visually demonstrated. Through language people can question, clarify, persuade, describe, direct, and explain—they can directly manipulate the thoughts in others' minds. Language makes it possible for people to convey their beliefs, intentions, and complex thoughts, and this facilitates the coordination of behavior among individuals living in groups. Language is thus integral to human cultural learning. Consider, for example, the cultural learning that you are engaging in by reading this book. How well do you think you could learn the ideas of cultural psychology that are covered in this book if you did not have language? Perhaps there are some key pictures that might be able to vaguely illustrate some points. Or if your instructor was particularly skilled at gesturing, maybe he or she could get across the gist of some other points. But the vast majority of the material in this book would simply be impossible to communicate without language. Cultural ideas are most successfully transmitted through language.

Similar to the evidence for cultural learn-ing in animals, contrasting the language abil-ities of other species with those of humans reveals that although some species have some features of language, none have the rich abil-ities of humans. Some animals have small vocabularies of specific calls; for example, vervet monkeys make different calls to alert their conspecifics of threats such as eagles and snakes (Cheney & Seyfarth, 1990). Domesti-cated chimpanzees and gorillas have been taught a number of words of sign language (e.g., Savage-Rumbaugh et al., 1986); how-ever, they do not use these to communicate

The emergence of language

in the ways that humans do (Pinker, 1994). Moreover, no species has shown clear evidence for grammar or syntax, although the full linguistic capabilities of whales remains somewhat unknown. In contrast, humans from all cul-tures, even those from cultures that appear to quite simple or "primitive," have remarkably complex grammar and syntax, and they all have rich vocab-ularies. Humans have far more sophisticated ways to communicate their ideas than any other primate species.

In sum, humans differ from their nearest primate relatives both in terms of their abilities to have a rich theory of mind and to have an extensive lan-guage. These two adaptations, which likely evolved in tandem, allow humans to learn from each other in ways that other species cannot. They allow for individuals to learn cultural information from each other in highly precise ways. And this high-precision cultural learning provided humans with a truly unique advantage over other species that has profound implications: human cultural learning is cumulative.

Cumulative Cultural Evolution. The one way that human cultures stand head and shoulders above the rest of animal cultures is that the cultures of humans are cumulative. That is, after an initial idea is learned from others, it can then be modified and improved upon by other individuals. The cul-tural information thus grows in complexity, and often in utility, over time. This process is called the **ratchet effect** (Tomasello et al., 1993). Like a ratchet, which can go forward, but does not slip backward, cultural infor-mation can continue to accumulate without losing the earlier information. A modified practice is learned by others, who then add their own modifications, and these modifications accumulate over time. To have cumulative cultural evolution you need creative invention, which we often can observe among many species, such as when a clever chimpanzee first figured out how to fish termites out of their mounds with a twig. In addition, however, you need reliable and faithful social transmission. The newly invented tool or practice needs to be replicated veridically enough that others have a solid foundation upon which to build any future innovations. This kind of high-fidelity social transmission requires accurate imitative learning and sophisticated communication. No other species of animals has been shown to have any evidence for significant cumulative cultural evolution. In other species, the learning and retention of cultural knowledge is so poor that they are unable to build on each other's discoveries. New generations of chimps are likely not any better at fishing out termites than were their ancestors, millions of years ago. There is just too much slippage in their ratchets.

Here is an example of cumulative cultural evolution. Imagine that you need to pound something, and you have to create something that would help you with the pounding. It probably wouldn't be all that difficult for you to fashion yourself a rudimentary hammer. If you were to build yourself a hammer, you would probably think about how you could put a heavy flat object on the end of a stick, and to fashion something like the kinds of hammers that you see for sale at Home Depot. You would likely be able to create a fairly effective hammer—one that was surely more effective than the stones that chimpanzees use to crack open nuts, and which frequently bruise their fingers. However, you might not realize that your creation of this simple invention is possible only because of your reliance on millions of years of accumulated cultural information. Figure 1.2 shows the history of hammers that has been obtained from the archaeological record. Our hominid ancestors were using simple stones and suffering the concomitant bruised fingers for millions of years before someone figured out how to attach the stone to a stick. There were several iterations, spread out over many millennia, before people started to make the kind of hammer that you're probably most familiar with today. The hammer in your toolbox was thus not invented from scratch. It is the current end product of a very long series of inventions, adaptations, and modifications. The idea of how to make a hammer might strike you as incredibly obvious. But this is because you have grown up in a world that included the cultural ideas of hammers, and you have been influenced by them through cultural learning. For millions of years our hominid ances-

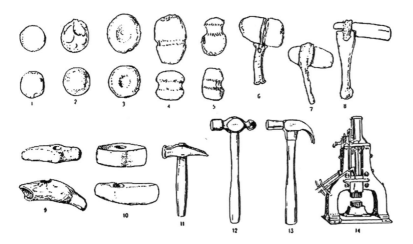

FIGURE 1.2

The evolution of the hammer, from the archaeological record to modern times (Hough, 1922).

tors were going about smashing rocks together and bruising their fingers because the idea of tying the rock to the end of a stick never occurred to them. And remember, this is just the simple hammer! Think about all the accumulated innovations and ideas that went into creating all the other tools around you, such as the technology used in computers, cell phones, or airplanes.

The tools that we use are all the most recent product of many years, if not millennia, of accumulated cultural innovations. And these innovations grow at exponential rates, as they come to accumulate faster with the growing number of potential models to imitate from, and the increasing amount of information and technologies that new innovations can be built on. For example, archaeologists estimate that up until 100,000 years ago, major technological innovations appeared at the rate of approximately .0015 per thousand years. From that time until 40,000 years ago, the rate increased to about 0.05 innovations per thousand years. Then, from that time until 12,000 years ago the rate of change increased to .55 innovations per thousand years. And from 12,000 years ago to 9,000 years ago, which coincided with the birth of agriculture, the rate of change increased sharply to about 5.2 innovations per thousand years (Lenski & Lenski, 1987). From that time on, cultural innovations have progressed at an exponential rate. The U.S. Patent and Trademark Office now issues more than 500 patents each day! Take the example of the computer. The speed at which accumulated cultural innovations appear in the computer is captured in Moore's Law. As the "law" states, the data density (e.g., the number of transistors on integrated circuits) that can be built into computers doubles approximately every 18 months. This means that if you are about to buy a computer, you can get one that will be approximately twice as powerful if you can wait for another 18 months. This also means that the computers sold today are approximately one million times more powerful than the ones that were sold 30 years ago. Each innovation in computer technology is built on accumulated cultural knowledge. As more and more cultural ideas are available, there is a larger foundation on which to build new ideas. Ideas beget other ideas, and culture accumulates.

Cumulative cultural innovations are not limited to physical tools. A cultural idea, say democracy, also represents the accumulation of ideas and innovations spread out over human history. This book will also make the argument that psychological mechanisms can undergo cumulative cultural evolution as well. One example is mathematical reasoning. You can likely easily engage in mathematical reasoning that involves addition, multiplication, and fractions. If you're especially talented, you might even be able to figure out problems involving quadratic equations, probability, calculus, irrational numbers, or matrix algebra. We were not born with the innate capacity to reason about numbers in these ways, and this is evident as people from some cultures are incapable of even counting numbers past 3 or so, or of estimating the amount of rather small quantities (we'll explore this more in Chapter 9, Cognition and Perception). Rather, these different kinds of mathematical reasoning strategies can be understood as cultural products that have become more and more complex as people have added innovations to earlier ways of thinking about numbers. This kind of cultural evolution is not possible unless cultural learning is of the highest fidelity, when individuals are able to understand a model's intentions, mimic them, and then, only when the model's behaviors are successfully imitated, build on them to allow for cultural evolution. We'll discuss more about how cultures evolve in the next chapter.

The fact that humans uniquely have cumulative culture is an important point. Unlike other species, then, we do not just live in physical worlds. In addition to the physical characteristics of our environment, we exist within worlds that consist of valuable cultural information that has accumulated over history: *cultural worlds* (Luria, 1928). Humans are a cultural species that exists within environments that importantly include shared ideas. We are born into these worlds, and we are constantly learning, and being influenced by, the shared ideas that make up our cultures. Coming to understand why people behave and think in the ways that they do means that we need to also consider the kinds of cultural information that people encounter in their daily lives.

Why Are Humans Adept at Cultural Learning? The abilities to speak and have a theory of mind were key adaptations for cultural learning, and these have allowed humans to develop so much of what we think of as uniquely human. They are largely what distinguish us from our chimpanzee ancestors. What is it about the human brain that facilitated these abilities? How did we evolve the capacities to become cultural animals?

You and Your Big Brain. The high-fidelity cultural learning and sophisticated language skills that are uniquely possessed by humans would seem to depend on considerable cognitive resources. Indeed, humans do have quite enormous brains. Our brain size, as determined by the **encephalization quotient,** which is the ratio of the brain weight of an animal to that predicted for a comparable animal of the same body size, is approximately 4.6. That is, our brain is about four to five times larger than that of other mammals our size. This large brain, however, does not come without costs. Brains require an enormous amount of energy to operate. You can think of the big brain in your skull as being akin to a massive, gas-guzzling jet engine, that consumes about 16% of all of your basal metabolism. That is, if you were to eat a dozen eggs, the energy from two of those eggs would be devoted solely to keeping your brain operating (and to thinking about this question), leaving just 10 of the eggs to take care of the rest of your body. This is a lot of energy intake, especially as our brains constitute only about 2% of our body weight. In contrast, the average mammal gets by with much less energy— only 3% of their basal metabolism is used by their brains. Some other mammals, such as marsupials, get by with the equivalent of a rubber-band powered gizmo, that uses up only about 1% of their basal metabolism (Aiello & Wheeler, 1995; Richerson & Boyd, 2005), leaving them with a lot of other resources to take care of the rest of their physical needs. Given the huge operating costs for large brains, there must have been some significant selective advantage for humans to get them.

Humans aren't the only species with large brains (although, ahem, ours are the largest in terms of the encephalization quotient [Martin, 1981]—that is, except for the very tiny, yet remarkably big-brained, shrews). Our closest evolutionary ancestors, primates, also have quite large brains. Indeed, non-human primates have encephalization quotients that average about 1.9, with our closest relatives, chimpanzees, scoring about 2.5 (Aiello & Wheeler, 1995). We can perhaps come to understand why human brains became so large if we first consider how primates got their big brains.

How primates' brains got to be so much larger than those of other mammals has been a matter of some debate. Let's explore a number of the theories that have been proposed to explain how particular aspects of primates' lives would have exerted selection pressures that would have favored large brains. One such theory rests on the observation that many primates eat a lot of fruit. There are good reasons to eat fruit. Fruit is rich in vitamins, carbohydrates, and calories, and fruits tend to be available in concentrated patches. The challenge with having a diet based on fruit, however, is that fruit is ripe for only brief periods at a time. To live off a diet of fruit you need to keep in mind where the various fruit trees are located and when they would likely be bearing ripe fruit. Perhaps the selection for big brains in primates was driven by the need for cognitive abilities that would help them keep a mental map of the short-lived and patchily distributed fruit that was around them (Clutton-Brock & Harvey, 1980). Those primates who had better skills at remembering where the fruit was would have been more likely to eat well and to have surviving offspring than those who were stumbling about aimlessly trying to find some ripe bananas.

A second theory regarding the relevance of the diet of primates has also been offered to account for the evolution of primate brains. A number of primate species rely on food sources that require a fair bit of ingenuity to access them. For example, some primate food sources include nuts and seeds encased in hard shells that need to be cracked open, tubers that need to be dug up, and termites that need to be fished out of their mounds. These "extractive" food sources are often worth pursuing as they tend to be rich in protein and energy. Perhaps the cognitive skills needed to allow primates to extract these valuable foods served as the selective force for larger brains (Parker & Gibson, 1977). Those primates who were smart enough to figure out how to open the nuts and get themselves a nutritious meal would have had more surviving offspring than those who were left to eat less nutritious food.

A third theory to account for primates' big brains is the complexity of primates' social worlds. Most species of primates live in complex social groups.

There are clear power hierarchies within these groups, and individuals form various relationships and alliances with each other that are often communicated through their regular grooming activities. Within these groups there are conflicts, power struggles, and opportunities for cooperation, nepotism, and reciprocity. To function well in a highly social community one must be able to outmaneuver others within it, and this requires attending to a highly complex series of relations. Perhaps it was the great cognitive demands inherent in social living that led to the evolution of large primate brains (Humphrey, 1976). This theory has become known as the **social brain hypothesis** (Dunbar, 1998). Those primates who were most successful at navigating the intricate and elaborate webs of social relationships would have been more likely to attract mates, secure resources, and protect themselves and their offspring from dangers than those who were left to fend for themselves.

Psychologists do more than just armchair theorizing, and the value of theories is ultimately judged by assessing which theories are most consistent with the available evidence. The above three competing theories were evaluated to see which one was best able to account for the evolution of primates' large brains (Dunbar, 1992). To do this, researchers calculated the ratio of the volume of the neocortex (the outermost layer of the brain that is concerned with higher functions, such as sensory perception, motor control, and conscious thought) to the volume of the rest of the brain. This is known as the **neocortex ratio**, and it has been used as a proxy measure of intelligence, as the most notable way that primates' brains differ from those of other mammals is that their neocortexes are larger. Furthermore, much research conducted with functional magnetic resonance imaging (fMRI) has revealed that problem solving tends to be focused in the neocortex. Researchers compared the neocortex ratios across a number of different primate species, while attending to variables relevant to the three competing hypotheses. Namely, the percentage of fruit in the diets of each of the primate species was calculated; the foraging styles of the different primate species were categorized as being either focused on extractive or nonextractive foods; and the average group size that the different primate species lived in was calculated. The three graphs plotting these three variables against neocortex ratios are shown in Figure 1.3. Each of the dots in the figures indicates a different genus of primates.

First, looking at Figure 1.3a, we can see the relation between neocortex size and the percentage of fruit in the diets of various primate species. The

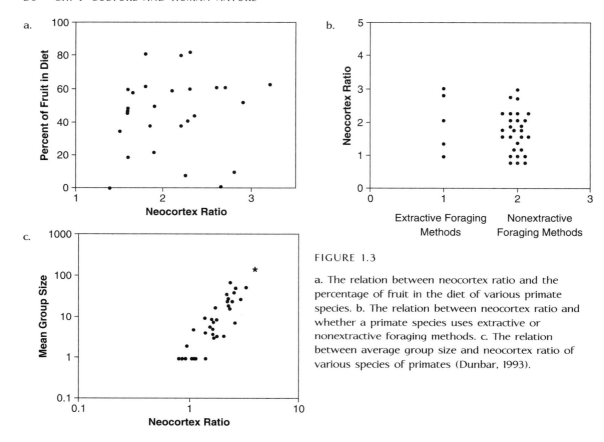

FIGURE 1.3

a. The relation between neocortex ratio and the percentage of fruit in the diet of various primate species. b. The relation between neocortex ratio and whether a primate species uses extractive or nonextractive foraging methods. c. The relation between average group size and neocortex ratio of various species of primates (Dunbar, 1993).

individual primate species are pretty much scattered randomly across the graph, indicating that these two variables are uncorrelated. There is little support here for the notion that the cognitive skills required to find ripe fruit drove the evolution of primate brains.

Second, Figure 1.3b tests whether the average neocortex ratio is larger for those primates that engaged in extractive foraging strategies than it is for those primates who used nonextractive techniques. Overall, there was little difference in neocortex ratio between these two groups. This analysis thus failed to provide support for the notion that the challenges of obtaining hard to extract foods is what selected for primate intelligence.

Third, as can be seen in Figure 1.3c, there is a rather clear relation between neocortex ratio and average group size for the different species of primates. Those primates that lived in larger social groups tended to have larger neocortex ratios. This is consistent with the notion that the complexities of social living selected for cognitive skills that allowed individual primates to successfully navigate their social worlds. The social brain hypothesis is thus the best supported account for why primates got their large brains. Indeed, there is much other evidence that some species of primates are able to attend to rather complex social relationships. For example, in one study researchers placed speakers around the jungle where vervet monkeys lived and they played back the recorded distress calls of juvenile monkeys (Cheney & Seyfarth, 1990). Not only did the mothers of those distressed juveniles react, showing that the mothers recognized the sound of their offspring's voices, but the other females also reacted; they reacted by looking at the juvenile's mother, indicating that they too recognized the sound of the voice as belonging to that mother's offspring. Primates tend to be highly social animals, and this requires considerable cognitive skills.

The Magic Number of 150. What does this suggest for humans? Dunbar (1993) reasoned that if humans could be added to the data in Figure 1.3.c (look at the little star in the top right of the graph), we could estimate the average group size within which humans evolved. If we plotted humans on the figure based on their large neocortex ratio, taking into account the relation between neocortex ratio and average group size, we could estimate that the average size of human ancestral populations should be 147.8, or approximately 150 people. By this reasoning, humans should have evolved in groups that averaged about 150 members, and this should have led to the cognitive capacity to keep track of approximately 150 relations. But clearly, most people in industrialized societies live in communities that are larger than 150. Greater Vancouver, which is where I live, has a population of over 2,000,000. However, it is important to remember that large populations are a relatively recent phenomenon. Before the onset of agriculture about 10,000 years ago, humans everywhere lived in small subsistence societies. Dunbar (1993) surveyed the ethnographic accounts of present-day subsistence societies and found that although people can live in overnight camps as small as 30–35 people, and tribes can typically number around 1,500–2,000 people, the average size of clans turns out to be 148.4. Clans have a number of social properties that are similar to the groups that characterize monkeys and apes (Dunbar, 1996), and they likely reflect the primary social unit of most subsistence populations. Furthermore, given the estimated birth rate of ancestral humans, 150 is about the number of living descendants (including all the wives, husbands, and children) that you would expect an ancestral human couple to produce after four generations.

Dunbar (1996) further provides some anecdotal evidence that many modern groups function best with around 150 members. For example, Hutterite communities—Hutterites are a fundamentalist Christian sect living in the Dakotas and in the Prairie provinces of Canada—divide into new communities whenever a community reaches the size of 150. Their reasoning is that peer pressure is a powerful means of social control up until the size of 150, but beyond that some kind of institutionalized structure is necessary to regulate behavior, because in larger groups people start to become strangers to each other. Gore Associates, the successful corporation that makes Gore-Tex fabric, has a similar philosophy. They build a new plant whenever the number of employees at a given plant gets larger than 150, because they feel that the company can work best when "unruly behavior (can be) controlled on the basis of personal loyalties and direct man-to-man contacts" (Gladwell, 2000, p. 186). In sum, much evidence supports the notion that humans evolved the cognitive capacities to function best in groups of around 150 people. Any groups that are smaller than this lose the advantages of large numbers, and any groups that are larger than 150 become too unwieldy to manage without some kind of formal institutional structure.

What does this social brain hypothesis suggest for understanding how humans became cultural animals? If the hypothesis is correct, then the primary forces that drove the evolution of the costly human brain were associated with our being able to attend to, and accurately understand, the intentions and activities of a reasonably large group of individuals with whom we regularly interacted. That is, humans evolved to participate in complex social environments with all of the opportunities that these environments afforded for cultural acquisition. Thinking about it this way suggests that humans did not just evolve biologically to the point that they could cross over a magic threshold and become cultural beings. Rather, the ability to engage in cultural learning itself was a selective force that has shaped human evolution since we last shared common ancestors with other primates (Richerson & Boyd, 2005). As the anthropologist Clifford Geertz (1973) put it, culture was a central "ingredient" to human evolution. We evolved to depend on cultural learning. Those of our ancestors who were best able to engage in cultural learning were the ones most likely to have surviving offspring. Culture and the biology of our brain are thus inextricably bound. Humans evolved to be a cultural species.

Psychological Universals and Variability

In the following chapters of this book there will be much focus on numerous psychological processes, many of which were hitherto viewed (either implicitly or explicitly) as human universals, which emerge in quite different ways across cultures. For example, in Chapter 9, Cognition and Perception, we'll cover how Westerners and East Asians differ in terms of the kind of reasoning they apply to solving the same problem.

The fact that psychological processes vary importantly across cultures raises a difficult question: How can we understand the workings of the human mind when it apparently works in different ways in different contexts? Arguments for cultural variability in psychological processes are controversial, and this controversy reveals the differing underlying assumptions that are embraced by many psychological researchers.

Is the Mind Independent from, or Intertwined with, Culture? Richard Shweder, who is viewed by many to be the father of the modern incarnation of cultural psychology, argues that much of the field of psychology (what he calls "general psychology") inherently assumes that the mind operates under a set of natural and universal laws that are independent from content or context (Shweder, 1990). He argues that the guiding assumption of general psychology is one captured in the lyrics of a song by Paul McCartney and Stevie Wonder: "People are the same wherever you go." Surely, in many ways people really are the same wherever you go, and some researchers have attempted to document the many ways that people's thinking can be said to be the same across all cultures. For example, in all cultures people speak a language using between 10 and 70 phonemes, they all smile when they are happy, they all have a word for the color "black," they are all disgusted at the idea of incest between parents and children, and they all understand the number 2. A list of all the human universals that have been documented can be found in a 12-page chapter in a fascinating book (Brown, 1991). The study of human universals is a highly interesting, albeit enormously challeng-ing, enterprise that tells us a great deal about human nature. We can learn much about how the mind works by identifying the universal and invariant ways that it operates.

However, in many important ways people are *not* the same wherever you go. For example, in some languages pronouns can be dropped while in oth-ers they cannot, people in some cultures bite their tongues when they are embarrassed whereas people in other cultures do not, some languages do not have a word for blue, people in some cultures are disgusted at the idea of incest between cousins whereas people in other cultures are not, and in some cultures people do not understand the number 5. The study of human vari-ability is also a very interesting and challenging enterprise that greatly informs our understanding of human nature and of the ways that the mind operates.

If you have taken a course on introductory psychology before, think back to the questions that were investigated in that course. Was it a course pri-marily on what all humans share in common with their psychology, or was it primarily a course on the ways that some people think differently from others? Shweder argues that general psychologists, perhaps as captured in your intro psychology course, tend to be more captivated by arguments about human universality than about cultural variability. This interest in universal-ity, Shweder proposes, arises because general psychologists tend to conceive of the mind as a highly abstract central processing unit (CPU) that operates independently of the content that it is thinking about or of the context within which it is thinking. The underlying goal of general psychology, as Shweder sees it, is to provide glimpses of the CPU operating in the raw so that we can understand the set of universal and natural laws that govern human thought. Context and content are viewed as unwanted noise that cloud our ability to perceive the functioning of the CPU, and thus elaborate experi-ments are conducted in the highly controlled environment of the laboratory to provide the purest view of the CPU. The computer metaphor here is no accident; indeed, the CPUs in computers do largely function independently of content and context. The mind as computer is a metaphor that has been embraced so strongly within general psychology that many of the theories could equally be applied to computers as to human brains.

According to this perspective of general psychology, important cultural variation in ways of thinking cannot exist because cultures merely provide variations in context and content that lie *outside* the operations of the underlying CPU. If cultural differences do appear in psychological studies, this universalist perspective would suggest that they must reflect the contamination of various sources of noise, such as translation errors, or the differences in familiarity that people have with being in psychological experiments. They could not reflect differences in the CPU because it is universally the same across all contexts. General psychology would argue, then, that virtually all of human psychology is universally experienced in similar ways.

In contrast, an assumption that tends to be embraced by cultural psychologists is that in many ways the mind does *not* operate independently of what it is thinking about. According to this view, thinking is not merely the operation of the universal CPU; thinking also involves interacting with the content that one is thinking about and participation in the context within which one is doing the thinking. Cultural psychologists would argue that to fully understand the mind it is important to consider, say, whether one is thinking about food, weapons, sexual partners, or sacred rituals. It is critical to consider whether one's behaviors increase one's status within the community, violate a law, demonstrate affection to one's child, or are consistent with religious doctrine. Furthermore, the ways that people will think about these kinds of behaviors will be influenced by the very specific and particular ways that cultural knowledge shapes their understanding of those behaviors. As humans are cultural beings, their actions, thoughts, and feelings are immersed in cultural information, and this information renders these actions, thoughts, and feelings to be *meaningful* (see Bruner, 1990, for an in-depth discussion). That is, these actions, thoughts, and feelings come to relate to other things beyond them.

For example, the simple act of an American college student going out to have a cappuccino might come to mean for that student a chance to quench her thirst, a demonstration that she has quit her diet, an effort to wake herself up so she can study, or an opportunity to pursue a romantic partner. The identical action can come to take on different meanings, and the potential meanings that are available are influenced by the cultural context within which they occur. For example, in some other cultural contexts it is not viewed as appropriate for women to go to coffee shops on their own, people do not strive for ideal body weights that are less than what they currently have, it can be seen as sinful to seek artificial stimulants to provide you with energy, or romantic relationships are typically arranged by family members rather than sought out by individuals themselves. That is, the same array of meanings that may be derived from the experience of an American college student going to a coffee shop are not available in all cultures, and, instead, other arrays of meaning are available there. Humans seek meaning in their actions, and the shared ideas that make up cultures provide the kinds of meanings that people can derive from their experiences.

Many cultural psychologists would argue that to the extent that people in one culture are often faced with a particular cultural idea (e.g., the belief that it is good for children to become independent from their parents at a young age), they will think a great deal about that idea, creating a rich network of thoughts, behaviors, and feelings that surround it. These networks of information will be activated whenever people encounter something that reminds them of this idea, be it a conversation that they hear, a memory of what has happened in the past, the situation they are in, or their impressions that others around them are concerned with this idea. If people consider these networks of information often enough, they should become chronically activated, such that these networks of information readily come to mind and become prioritized ahead of other networks of information that are less likely to be activated. Because cultures differ in the ideas their members frequently encounter, they will also differ in the networks of thoughts, actions, and feelings that are most accessible to them. In this way, culture comes to shape the ways we think.

Many cultural psychologists would thus view as ultimately misguided the goal of general psychology to understand the mind after it has been stripped clear of the noise of content and context. Because human thought is sustained by the meaning that people pursue, any efforts to bleach out this meaning to more clearly reveal the underlying CPU would only distort and misrepresent what the mind actually is. Humans are so embedded in their cultural worlds that they are always behaving as cultural actors, and their thoughts are always sustained by the meanings that are derived from their cultures. There are no occasions when people step outside of their cultural meaning systems and start to think instead like the universal human (see Geertz, 1973, for a rich elaboration of this); our thoughts are forever bound up in our own cultural meaning systems.

Many cultural psychologists would argue that culture cannot be separated from the mind because culture and mind make each other up. Cultures emerge from the interaction of the various minds of the people that live within them, and cultures then, in turn, shape the ways that those minds operate.

For example, consider this question: What is a weed? Obviously, a weed is a plant, and plants have an objective existence that is independent of what people think about them. However, a weed is a particular kind of plant—it's a plant that we do not want in our garden. A weed could be crabgrass or dandelion, or it could even be a rose or the sapling of a mighty oak if it was growing in the wrong place. Because weeds represent unwanted plants we can say that a weed doesn't fully come into existence as a weed unless there is a person who doesn't want it (see Shweder, 1990). Weeds require people to become weeds. On the other hand, one aspect of our lives is that we live in a cultural world that includes the idea of not wanting weeds to grow in places that they shouldn't. Our cultural worlds, in part, also require weeds in order to be complete as we know them. Weeds and people thus are inextricably bound. In the same way, cultures are dependent on the minds of the people within them, and people's minds are dependent on the cultures in which they exist. And because cultures often do differ in dramatic ways in terms of their practices, institutions, symbols, artifacts, beliefs, and values, the ways that people from different cultures think, act, and feel should also vary in important ways. Cultural psychologists thus expect to find significant differences in the psychological processes among people from various cultures. Much of the remaining chapters in this book will elaborate on those differences.

Case Study: The Sambia. Discussions of cultural differences in psychological processes are often quite controversial. The controversy seems to rest on the contrasting views of the mind inherent in the perspective of "general psychology" (i.e., the mind operates independently of content and context) and cultural psychology (i.e., the mind is shaped by content and context). I have had countless discussions and debates with other psychologists about various cultural differences in ways of thinking. In many instances we disagree about whether the observed cultural difference reflects a deep difference in the ways that people from various cultures think (which is usually the position that I take) or whether it represents a superficial difference of no significance or is the product of some kind of bias in the experimental design (which is often the position that my opponent takes). In many of these instances, we can have a good debate as the evidence is such that there is room to interpret it in either way. People who have received psychological training are often rather resistant to accepting the ideas of real cultural differences in ways of thinking, and I anticipate that many of the readers of this book will be similarly resistant. As an initial effort to demonstrate that psychological differences between cultures can run deep I describe here a case study of the Sambia (for a more detailed exploration, see the ethnography by Herdt, 2006). It represents one of the more dramatic instances of a cultural difference that is covered in this book.

The Sambia live perched up in an expansive valley high up a mountain range, over a mile above sea level, in the eastern highlands of Papua New Guinea. Their environment is one of the least accessible places on the planet. Until a few decades ago, they had been a ferocious warring people, engaged in constant battles with neighboring tribes in the valley. Today, they are largely peaceful, and they exist by hunting and cultivating taro gardens and pandanus nut groves. However, one cultural practice has persisted since their warring days: their initiation practices to transform young boys into men.

The Sambia believe that femaleness is an innate natural essence, whereas maleness is a tenuous essence that must be explicitly cultivated. Boys are viewed as existing in the female world, hanging out with their mothers, and doing what are viewed as female tasks, such as babysitting and weeding. Boys are believed to be polluted from their mother's wombs, and they are seen as too dependent on their mothers for protection and warmth. Their feminized position is highlighted as they wear the same type of grass apron as females. The men are often quite openly hostile to the boys, taunting them by saying "Go back to your mother where you belong!"

As a former warrior tribe, the Sambia viewed as crucial a process for boys to become masculinized, and the Sambia had lengthy initiation procedures to rid boys of their feminine habits and transform them into brave and fighting men. Much of that initiation ritual involves painful practices, such as piercing the septum of the boy's nose and thrashing the boys with sticks. The Sambia are not unique in having such initiation rituals: indeed, throughout history many warrior societies have had similar initiations to recruit and train male warriors. The goal of the initiation is to give boys a sense of power, which is termed *jerungdu*. *Jerungdu* is physical strength and is viewed as the supreme essence of maleness. However, boys are believed to be born without any *jerungdu*. They must acquire it. And they acquire it through semen. Semen is viewed as the physical basis of *jerungdu*. Without semen, a boy has no *jerungdu*, and he has no masculinity. However, the male body is believed to be incapable of manufacturing semen—it must be acquired. And it is acquired by the boys through years of ritualized homosexuality. From the age of around 7 boys regularly ingest semen by performing daily oral sex on adolescent boys and men. Around the age of 15, they stop ingesting semen from others, switch roles, and start providing semen to younger boys, who perform fellatio on them. They usually get married after the age of 17 or so, and after a few years of marriage, men typically have children, and at that point their sexual practices become exclusively heterosexual. Each time a man ejaculates he loses semen and *jerungdu*, but once he is a man he is capable of topping it up by ingesting some white tree sap. Hence, the sex life of a Sambian man tracks an arc of exclusively homosexual behaviors from the age of 7 until they are married, a period of bisexual behaviors (sex with their wives, and oral sex with younger boys) from the time they are married until they enter fatherhood, and then exclusive heterosexual behaviors after that. In contrast, Sambian females do not have any similar cult of ritualized homosexuality—they remain exclusively heterosexual.

Sambian views of sexuality and sexual identity contrast sharply with those of Western society. Sexual orientation tends to be viewed as a lifestyle among Westerners—a lifestyle that affects how people view themselves and even shapes the activities that people pursue and the people with whom they associate. Whereas Westerners might identify themselves as homosexual, bisexual, or heterosexual, every Sambian male proceeds through all of these stages in sequence. Homosexuality and bisexuality are minority types of sexuality

A Sambian initiate is tested by sucking a flute in preparation for his transformation into manhood.

among Westerners, yet among Sambian men, homosexuality, bisexuality, and heterosexuality are universal and natural stages in life. They serve as behaviors rather than as a basis of Sambian identity. Moreover, among Sambian men, it is heterosexuality that is held in disdain as contact with women is viewed to be especially contaminating and draining of a man's *jerungdu*.

I include this rather dramatic contrast between the Sambia and Western culture to make two points. First, the distinctiveness of the Sambian initiation rituals underscores how humans live in cultural worlds. Our actions are fraught with meaning, and this meaning is derived from particular cultural experiences. A Sambian father *desires* to rid his 7-year-old son of the contaminating feminine influence of his mother, and he *wants* his son to perform oral sex on a married man as a means to toughen him up. However startling and bizarre the Sambian initiation practices may be to us, they carry deep meaning for the Sambians, and Sambians have a rich set of thoughts and emotions that are associated with these practices that people who are not socialized in Sambian contexts do not. We cannot fully understand the psychological experiences of Sambians without considering the cultural contexts in which their actions occur.

Second, the Sambian sexual practices raise an important question: What aspects of sexuality are human universals? Sexual orientation serves as a key basis of identity in the West, and the rights of gays and lesbians remain among the most politically contentious topics, especially in the United States. The Sambia do not have the construct of sexual orientation. This suggests that as biologically grounded as our sexual motives are, they do become shaped by specific cultural beliefs and practices.

Psychological Universals and Levels of Analysis. The American poet Mark Van Doren made this observation about human nature: "There are two statements about human beings that are true: that all human beings are alike, and that all are different. On those two facts all human wisdom is founded." With this profound statement Van Doren has identified the issue that underlies the enterprise of cultural psychology.

When we consider culture and psychology we have two contrasting views. One view is that psychological processes are essentially the same everywhere, and the other is that psychological processes emerge differently across cultural contexts. It would seem that it should be straightforward to demonstrate which view is better supported by the evidence; all you would need to do would be to measure some psychological variables across a number of different cultures, and if the result tends to look the same everywhere, the general psychologists would win, whereas if the results look substantially different, the cultural psychologists would claim victory. However, the controversy continues because it is difficult to agree upon what kinds of evidence would be best suited to test a question of universality.

For example, consider the question of marriage. Is it culturally universal? The answer to this depends on what you mean by marriage. If you mean the kind of marriage that is common in Western cultures in which a man and a woman fall in love and agree to share their lives exclusively with each other until either one of them dies or they get divorced, then marriage is *not* universal, as there are many cultures in which people do not form such relationships (Ford & Beach, 1951). On the other hand, you could instead consider marriage in a more abstract sense, where there is some kind of formal arrangement in which men and women stay together in an enduring relationship (whether there be multiple women per man or multiple men per woman, and whether there were feelings of love prior to the marriage), with public recognition of exclusive sexual access among those who are married, and these relationships are centered around the rearing of children. Here, we could say that marriage is a cultural universal as there are relationships in most cultures that fit this more abstract definition (Goodenough, 1970). One eternal source of controversy in discussing human universals, then, is whether the phenomena under question are posed in particular, concrete terms, or in more general, abstract terms. The level of abstraction that one entertains will influence the success that one has in identifying evidence for universality. At more abstract levels there is often more evidence for universals; however, at more abstract levels the phenomena under question are often too abstract to be of much utility. This tension between universal and culturally specific psychologies will be evident in many of the topics that we discuss in this book.

A second reason that it is not straightforward to settle controversies regarding whether certain psychological processes are universal is because there are a number of different levels by which we can consider evidence for universality. A hierarchical framework has been proposed for considering whether particular psychological phenomena or cognitive tools are universal (Norenzayan & Heine, 2005). Figure 1.4 depicts a decision tree by which we can determine the level of universality that best fits a given psychological process. The existence of this hierarchy of levels of universality underscores the com-

FIGURE 1.4

The decision tree for determining the degree of universality in a psychological process (Norenzayan & Heine, 2005).

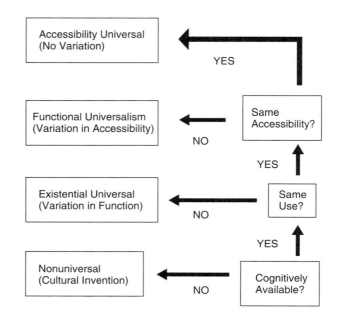

plexity of discussions of whether a psychological process can be said to be universal.

First, we can think of different psychological phenomena as cognitive tools. Just as a hammer is used for pounding nails, we can think of specific cognitive tools, such as a quantity estimator, of having the purpose of estimating quantities. The strongest case for universality can be made when it could be said that a given cognitive tool *exists in all cultures, is used to solve the same problem* across cultures, and *is accessible to the same degree* across cultures. This level of universality is termed an **accessibility universal**. There are likely many accessibility universals, although few have been documented thus far in psychological research. The best candidates would be those psychological phenomena that emerge very early in infancy or are shared across species. For example, social facilitation—the tendency for individuals to do better at well-learned tasks and worse at poorly learned ones, when in the presence of others—has been shown to occur in both insects and humans (e.g., Zajonc, Heingartner, & Herman, 1969). It would be surprising if this tendency varied significantly across cultures, and indeed, there is thus far no evidence for any cultural variability. Likewise, a folk understanding of the laws of physics (e.g., an understanding that objects cannot just disappear), is evident among infants at a very early age, and thus also likely reflects accessibility universals (e.g., Baillargeon & DeVos, 1991).

The second level of universality is termed a **functional universal**. Here, a cognitive tool *exists in multiple cultures*, it i*s used to solve the same problem* across cultures, yet it *is more accessible to people from some cultures than others*. In the case of functional universals, the cognitive tool serves the same function everywhere, although it may not be used that much in some cultures. For example, one large-scale investigation explored whether people from a variety of different subsistence societies around the world tended to punish those who acted unfairly, even if that punishment was costly for the individual to mete out (Henrich et al., 2006). Such costly punishment was evident in all 15 societies that were investigated: apparently costly punishment is meted out in response to unfair behavior universally—such punishment thus serves a similar function. However, there was also considerable variation in the amount that each of the societies was willing to punish offenders. For example, among the Tsimane of Bolivia, participants spent up to 28% of their earnings to punish others who were unfair. In contrast, among the Gusii of Kenya, participants spent over 90% of their earnings in an effort to punish unfair others. The costly punishment of others is thus not accessible to the same degree across cultures and thus fails the test of an accessibility universal. Some other examples of functional universals that will be discussed later in this book include certain kinds of categorization rules (e.g., Norenzayan, Smith, Kim, & Nisbett, 2002), attachment styles (e.g., Grossmann, Grossmann, Spangler, Suess, & Unzner, 1985), an attraction to similarity (e.g., Heine & Renshaw, 2002), and the role of negative affect in depression (e.g., Kleinman, 1982). Many of the cross-cultural studies summarized in this textbook are testing whether a phenomenon meets the standards of functional universals.

If a psychological process fails the test of an accessibility universal and of a functional universal, then it may qualify as an **existential universal**. Here, a cognitive tool *is said to exist in multiple cultures*, although the tool *is not necessarily used to solve the same problem*, nor *is it equally accessible* across cultures. That is, the cognitive tool is latently present, although it might be used to achieve different ends across cultures. For example, Westerners tend to find experiences with success to be motivating and experiences with failure to be demotivating (e.g., Feather, 1966). In contrast, East Asians tend to show the opposite pattern, whereby they work harder after failures than after successes (Heine et al., 2001; Hoshino-Browne & Spencer, 2000; Oishi & Diener, 2003). Intrinsic motivations to do one's best are present in both cultural groups; however, experiences with successes and failures are not equally likely

People trained to use an abacus perform calculations differently from those who are not.

to lead to such motivations across cultures. Increased persistence in the face of failure thus fails the test of functional universals and can be said to be example of an existential universal.

The fourth level in the hierarchy reflects an absence of universality and is termed, appropriately enough, a **nonuniversal**. Cognitive tools that are nonuniversals *do not exist in all cultures* and can be said to be cultural inventions. An example of this is abacus reasoning. An abacus is a calculation tool that is used in some parts of the Middle East and in Asia. People from cultures where they are trained to use the abacus think about numbers differently from those who are from cultures that do not use the abacus—they tend to favor the odd-even distinction, they think in base units of fives, and they make a particular pattern of errors not seen in non-abacus users (Miller & Paredes, 1996). The cognitive tools associated with abacus reasoning can be said to be nonexistent in people who have not been trained in them. Much of numerical reasoning appears to be a nonuniversal (Carey, 2004; Gordon, 2004), in that some of the cognitive tools involved seem to be present only among those who have been raised in cultures that use them. There are rather few nonuniversals that have been identified in the cross-cultural literature.

The Psychological Database Is Largely Western. At this point, we know very little about the extent to which many psychological processes are universal. This is largely due to the inescapable fact that in many cases we don't yet have the data that would allow us to test the question of whether a phenomenon is universal. The vast majority of psychological studies that have been conducted thus far have largely been limited to explorations of the minds of people living in Western cultures. For example, a recent review summarized every paper that was ever published in the most prestigious and influential journal of social and personality psychology, the *Journal of Personality and Social Psychology* (Quinones-Vidal, Lopez-Garcia, Penaranda-Ortega, & Tortosa-Gil, 2004). Ninety-two percent of the papers published there were conducted by authors at North American institutions. A full 99% of the articles were conducted by authors at Western institutions. This fact is perhaps even more startling in that social psychology is the field of psychology that is arguably the most interested in the effects of context on the mind. Indeed, other fields of psychology do not fare any better in their coverage of the topic of culture (Hansen, 2005). This itself reflects an interesting, and as of yet unexplained, cultural psychological finding: Why are Westerners, especially North Americans, so much more interested in psychology than the rest of the world? At many North American institutions the most popular student major is psychology, whereas in many universities around the world psychology is not even offered as a topic of study. For some reason, North Americans appear to be more fascinated with psychological questions than those from much of the rest of the world. Why do you think it is that you are taking a course on psychology? Can you identify any cultural reasons that have resulted in your sitting here and reading this book?

If it wasn't bad enough that the psychological database on the functioning of the human mind is limited to people from a handful of the world's cultures, it is even more problematic that the samples of participants in those studies are not even representative of Westerners more generally. The sampling method that has become standard in cognitive, social, personality, and some research in clinical psychology is to recruit participants from undergraduate psychology classes (Sears, 1986). What ways do you think undergraduate psychology students are different from the rest of the population? Undergrad psychology students make for a very thin slice of humanity, and a rather unusual slice at that, from which to make generalizations about human nature. An unfortunate fact is that for many of the psychological phenomena that have been studied, the entire relevant database has been based on North American psychology undergraduates. This does not place us in good stead for knowing whether the phenomena are equally strong elsewhere or whether they might be limited to certain cultural populations.

What, then, is perhaps the strongest evidence for Shweder's contention that general psychology does not concern itself with content or context is the fact that psychology has adopted a sampling methodology that itself largely ignores questions about the generalizability of its findings. The extremely narrow samples employed by most psychologists make good sense if the mind really does exclusively operate according to universal laws. To the extent this is true, then any person's mind is as good as anyone else's for revealing its universal nature. If minds are universally similar, you might as well study the most conveniently accessible ones. There is no need to be off trekking through the highlands of New Guinea to recruit study participants if their minds are functioning identically to those of Western college students, who can be enticed to participate with some extra course credit or a few dollars.

The cost of this sampling method for psychology has become more and more evident as cross-cultural studies have been conducted. As you'll see as you read the remaining chapters of this book, for many of the phenomena that psychologists have studied, and many of the theories that have been generated, the findings simply do not replicate in some other cultures. When non-Western samples are included in psychological studies the mind often reveals itself in dramatically different ways. These culturally divergent findings have made the question of what is human nature a difficult one indeed.

Where Does Cultural Psychology Come From?

The study of culture in psychology is not new. Indeed, the person who is widely seen as the father of psychology as a discipline, and who created the world's first psychological laboratory in 1879, Wilhelm Wundt, was himself a cultural psychologist. Wundt became famous for introducing experimental methods into the study of psychology and launching the field as a science. What is less well known, however, is that he wrote a 10-volume tome entitled *Volkerpsychologie,* or *Elements of Folk Psychology* (1921), which roughly captures much of the inquiry of modern-day cultural psychologists. Wundt's contributions to the study of experimental psychology were enormously influential to all fields of psychology; however, his ideas about cultural psychology were largely ignored by the field.

Since Wundt's early contributions, the study of culture in psychology has had a number of revivals, although it was never fully embraced by mainstream psychology until recently. One of the more enduring developments occurred in the former Soviet Union, where developmental psychologists Vygotsky, Luria, and Leontiev developed what became known as the **Russian cultural-historical school**. This school of thought argued that people interact with their environments through the "tools" or human-made ideas that have been passed to them across history. According to this view, all of human thought is sustained and expressed through accumulated human-made ideas as it is practiced in day-to-day activities (e.g., Luria, 1928; Vygotsky, 1929, 1978). These ideas have been developed and extended more recently by a number of researchers (e.g., Cole, 1996; Cole, Gay, Glick, & Sharp, 1971; Rogoff, 2003; Scribner & Cole, 1981; Wertsch, 1998) and have influenced much of cultural psychology.

Starting just prior to World War II and continuing for a couple of decades was a period when a number of anthropologists and personality psychologists worked together in an interdisciplinary enterprise that was known as "Culture and Personality Studies." Ruth Benedict wrote a book in 1934, *Patterns of Culture,* that is often seen as one of the prototypic exemplars of the enterprise. In this book she argued that culture was for populations what personality was for individuals, and these ideas were elaborated and critiqued by subsequent scholars. This collaboration among psychologists and anthropologists attracted some of the most influential figures across the disciplines and led to a great outpouring of research. However, in the 1950s the enterprise ultimately met an ignoble demise as it was criticized for not attending sufficiently to individual variation within cultures and for being unable to develop a strong and coherent research program (Levine, 2001).

The field of social psychology started out to be very much in the tradition of cultural psychology. A guiding tenet of the field, as espoused by one of the most influential social psychologists, Solomon Asch, was that social psychology "stood for the belief that no psychology can be complete that fails to look directly at man as a social being" (Asch, 1959, p. 364). However, the ascendancy of the experimental method in social psychology often was paralleled by an effort to exert greater experimental control over the study of social nature. For example, the study of the social relations that people have with members of other groups tends not to look at people's actual relationships, but instead it is usually investigated by creating random and artificial groups (e.g., Hamilton & Gifford, 1976; Tajfel, 1970), and the study of people's attraction toward each other is typically investigated by having people evaluate fictitious strangers that they never meet (e.g., Byrne, Clore, & Worchel, 1966) or by being exposed to inanimate stimuli (e.g., Zajonc, 1968). Much of the recent growth in cultural psychology has occurred among social psychologists, in an effort to more forcefully consider the influence of one's social relations on thought.

Psychology was dominated by the perspective of behaviorism in the early to mid-part of the 20th century in which the mind came to be viewed as largely irrelevant to psychological research. Rather, the concern then was with observable behaviors that could be influenced through conditioning of simple stimulus-response relations. In the 1950s psychology entered what became known as the "cognitive revolution," as researchers rejected the tenets of behaviorism and began to focus on the meaning that people created through their encounters with the world. One of the leading architects of the cognitive revolution, Jerome Bruner, however, argued that soon after the revolution began it became distracted from its initial vision by becoming more concerned with computer metaphors for understanding the functions of the mind (Bruner, 1990). Meaning became replaced with information, and meaning-making with information processing. Bruner argues that cultural psychology has picked up the torch that was originally carried by the cognitive revolution and has again addressed how people derive meaning from their worlds.

In addition to the various subfields and trends that have explored the relations between culture and psychology over the past century, a number of individual researchers have persistently wrestled with this topic. Some of the key figures who delved into the psychological study of culture in the 1960s, 1970s, and 1980s include John Berry, Michael Bond, Michael Cole, Roy D'Andrade, Ken Gergen, Patricia Greenfield, Geert Hofstede, Walter Lonner, Sylvia Scribner, Marshall Segall, and Harold Stevenson. The tremendous research efforts of these people, along with those of many other cross-cultural psychologists, played a key role in setting the stage for cultural psychology to be reintroduced to mainstream psychology as a new and revolutionary way of thinking about the mind.

The most recent reincarnation of cultural psychology, and its most impactful, appeared when a number of seminal papers and books were published nearly simultaneously. In 1989 Harry Triandis, who had been conducting leading work in culture and psychology for decades, wrote a highly influential article in which he argued that there were a number of cultural dimensions and aspects of the self-concept by which much of the observed variation across cultures could be understood. In 1990 Jerome Bruner published a book arguing that human psychology could only be properly understood by considering the meaning that people derived from their encounters with their worlds. In that same year, an edited book by Stigler, Shweder, and Herdt contained a number of key articles that provided exemplars for how culture could be incorporated into psychological research. That same book also included an article by Richard Shweder that provided a theoretical foundation for the psychological study of culture. In that paper, Shweder made cogent arguments that mind and culture mutually constituted each other, and thus needed to be studied together. One year later, in 1991, Hazel Markus and Shinobu Kitayama published a landmark article that has since become the most cited paper in cultural psychology. In that paper, they made the case that many psychological processes, such as cognitions, emotions, and motivations, can all be viewed through the lens of the self-concept. They then demonstrated that researchers can come to understand and predict cultural differences in many psychological processes by attending to the ways that the self-concept is shaped differently across cultures. These four seminal works, building on the groundwork provided by earlier forays into the study of psychology and culture and buttressed by the many papers that emerged in subsequent years, have led to the foundation of a new field of psychology.

Hence, although people have been conducting cultural psychological research for some time, they have been relatively few in number and their contributions had managed to be largely ignored by much of mainstream psychology. It has been less than two decades since cultural psychology began to be taken seriously by much of mainstream psychology. In that time, we have seen some of the more prestigious psychology departments build programs in cultural psychology, and we have witnessed an explosion of research on the topic.

In doing the research for this book I have consistently had two thoughts: first, there has been a flood of excellent research in cultural psychology in these past two decades. Indeed, so much has come out over this time that it has been hard for me to keep up. Second, despite this enormous flood of research, many key questions about the relation between culture and psychology have yet to be investigated. There are large gaps in our knowledge base waiting to be filled regarding how culture influences psychology. In particular, much of the world's cultures remain unexplored frontiers in terms of psychological testing. In all likelihood, psychologists will be grappling with cultural psychological research for many decades to come.

You Are a Product of Your Own Culture

On reading ethnographies or cross-cultural experiments involving "exotic" people it is not difficult to appreciate that culture affects other people. Somehow, though, it is far more difficult to appreciate how culture influences us. We don't speak with a discernible accent—only people from other places do. Although we can't hear our own accents, they are plainly evident to people who speak other languages or dialects. This point holds more generally to culture: For the most part, our cultures remain invisible to us, although everyone else can see them. As the anthropologist Clyde Kluckhohn remarked, "It would hardly be fish who discovered the existence of water" (1949, p. 11). Our own thoughts and behaviors appear natural to us as we really don't know how we could think and behave otherwise. However, people from many other cultures around the world would be quite surprised to learn about the things that you do. For example, when people from around the world learn about North American cultural practices, it is not uncommon to hear, "They put their babies in cages when they sleep!" "They talk to young children as if they were psychotherapists, asking them to explore their feelings." "Couples feel oddly compelled to keep reassuring themselves that they love each other, even when they call their partners from the office!" "They send their elderly parents off to institutions instead of caring for them themselves!"

In many ways we don't really come to understand our own cultures until we see them in contrast to other cultures. One perspective that I hope you gain from reading this book is a greater appreciation for your own culture. Just like people from the most exotic and remote cultures on the planet, the ways that you think and behave are guided by particular cultural experiences that you have had.

Furthermore, our values too are shaped by our cultural experiences. We are socialized to think of particular ways of doing things to be good and moral—usually, the very ways that are common within our own cultures. As

"Why is it so wet?"

such, culturally normative behavior comes to be seen as natural, and deviations from that natural path often tend to be viewed as less desirable or even
immoral. This leads to people to be victims of **ethnocentrism**—that is, we
often judge people from other cultures by comparing them to the standards
of our own culture. Our cultures ultimately socialize us to be ethnocentric
as we are socialized to value normative cultural behaviors. As you'll see, learning about other cultures can sometimes be provocative as we confront other
ways of doing things that go against our own cultural values. These experiences too should help you to gain a new perspective on how your culture
has influenced you.

SUMMARY

Humans are unique in the animal kingdom for being so dependent on cultural learning. While other animals are capable of creative kinds of learning such as emulative learning, there is scant evidence for imitative learning in other species, as they lack the rich theory of mind that would enable them to understand the perspective of others well. Likewise, humans are unique in having complex language capabilities. Language greatly facilitates cultural learning by allowing communication among individuals. A theory of mind and sophisticated language skills are necessary for cultural accumulation, whereby cultural innovations build upon ones that are already learned. Other species do not appear to have any appreciable degrees of cultural accumulation.

Much of the human brain, particularly the regions that differ appreciably in size from those of other mammals, appear to have been selected for primarily to solve social problems. Hence, it appears that humans' social worlds played a large role in the evolution of our capacities, and the capacity for cultural learning is one that has been significant.

Cultural psychology can be contrasted with much of "general" psychology in that it views the mind and culture to be ultimately inseparable. The guiding assumption is that psychological processes are influenced by the content that is being processed, and the context within which it is processed. With this view, people who participate in different contexts should be expected to think differently.

Controversy continues for whether a given psychological process is universal to all cultures or is specific to certain cultures. These arguments are controversial because the evidence for the universality of a process will often depend on the level of abstraction by which that process is considered. Furthermore, there are four different levels of universality of psychological processes, listed in order of increasing universality: nonuniversals, existential universals, functional universals, and accessibility universals.

The extent of universality that exists for most psychological processes is still unclear. This is largely because the database for psychological research has generally been limited to North American undergraduates in psychology classes. Much recent research has found that when other populations are investigated the findings often look quite different across cultures.

Cultural psychology is not new, as there have been a number of attempts to study culture's influences on ways of thinking throughout the history of psychology. The more recent reincarnation of the field started in the early 1990s and has been the most influential. The past two decades have produced an enormous amount of research but at the same time have raised many more unanswered questions.

Cultural Evolution

There are many behaviors that you distinctly avoid engaging in, as they are considered to be "bad manners." However, many of those manners that you are aware of have not emerged to address universal human problems but instead are the result of cultural learning. This fact becomes clear when we consider how manners vary across cultures. For example, when you enter a Japanese house it is good manners to remove your shoes, point them toward the door, and put on a pair of slippers, which are to be removed when you enter a room with a tatami mat, or are to be exchanged for a pair of special "toilet slippers" upon entering the restroom. And, I can testify from personal experience, it's a guaranteed show-stopper if you ever forget to remove the toilet slippers when you sit down to eat at the dining table. In contrast, for many Americans, shoes only come off when they are taking a shower or going to bed. Manners differ across cultures as people are socialized to different sets of norms and customs.

The evidence for the cultural foundation of manners is even stronger when we consider how manners have changed over time. The German sociologist Norbert Elias, in his classic work *The Civilizing Process* (1939/1994), argues that Western Europe, and likewise other modernizing cultures, have been transformed as the manners of the aristocracy slowly trickled down to govern the behavior of the lower classes as well. People became "civilized," as a growing set of rules and norms came to regulate the behaviors of people across all classes of society. Elias provides a sampling of many of these manners, some of which I describe below.

Consider the maxim offered in a 15th-century German book of table manners: "It is unseemly to blow your nose in the tablecloth." Today this advice remains equally sound, but now it somehow goes without saying. You can't help wondering who were the runny-nosed readers that the author had in mind when he wrote this useful piece of guidance. Blowing your nose was

"Not so loud, sweetie. We're in Europe."

a common topic in older manners books, and one's technique was seen to indicate one's status. As a 16th-century Dutch manners book stated: "To blow your nose on your hat or clothing is rustic, and to do so with the arm or elbow befits a tradesman; nor is it much more polite to use the hand, if you immediately smear the snot on your garment. It is proper to wipe the nostrils with a handkerchief, and to do this while turning away if more honourable people are present." Here we can see how what was formerly the etiquette for only the upper classes came to govern the manners for all classes of people.

A section in Elias's book entitled "On Spitting" reveals too how much current manners have diverged from the past. Advice from the Middle Ages recommended: "Do not spit into the basin when you wash your hands, but beside it," or "Do not spit across the table in the manner of hunters." By the 18th century, spitting etiquette had progressed from the norms of the Middle Ages. Advice included the following: "Frequent spitting is disagreeable. When it is necessary you should conceal it as much as possible, and avoid soiling either persons or their clothes, no matter who they are." By the late 19th century, however, spitting was far less tolerated, although still very common: "Spitting is at all times a disgusting habit. I need say nothing more than— never indulge in it." As the centuries passed, greater and greater care was placed on acting in so-called civilized ways.

One reason manners have changed over time is because people's views of what is healthy have also changed. For example, in the 16th century it was viewed as unhealthy to refrain from either spitting or from passing wind. These behaviors have become less tolerated as it is no longer considered healthy to engage in them. And some differences in manners of the past simply reflect changing norms that are quite arbitrary as to what is considered polite. For example, medieval eating etiquette prescribed, "You should always eat with the outside hand; if companion sits on your right, eat with your left hand." A 16th-century recommendation said, "If a serviette is given, lay it

In past centuries, spittoons were regular fixtures in many public locations in the United States, so that people could spit indoors without making a mess. This is the luxurious lobby of the Brown Palace Hotel in Denver, Colorado taken around 1900. The vessel at the front of the picture is a spittoon, signifying a very different attitude toward spitting than is present in the United States today.

on your left shoulder or arm." A 19th-century manners book offered the following: "I may hint that no epicure ever yet put knife to apple, and that an orange should be peeled with a spoon." These table manners appear as arbitrary as the current Western norms for salad forks to be on the far left of the plate, for soup to precede a main course, or for wine to be served in glasses that are held by the stem.

These transformations in manners over time are instances of an obvious fact: cultures change. Behavior considered polite a few centuries ago would not necessarily be appropriate today. Standards of politeness, as well as many other cultural norms, have changed over generations. Cultures continue to evolve, and your parents likely participated in a quite distinct culture when they were your age from what you do today, even if they grew up in the same neighborhood as you. Cultures are not monolithic and frozen entities but are fluid and constantly evolving as new ideas emerge and conditions change. Hence, it is important to keep in mind that the studies discussed in this book in which different cultures are contrasted represent a snapshot in time, and the findings very well might not hold for later generations.

In this chapter we will explore where cultural variation comes from and how cultures are able to both change and persist over time. The fact that cultures do often change and evolve, and that psychological processes likewise change and evolve, underscores a theme in this book—that experiences shape our psychology. But before we can understand how cultural experiences come to shape the ways we think, we first must understand how cultures come to be.

Where Does Cultural Variation Come From?

There are few questions more challenging in the social sciences than the question of what causes cultural variation. It has been considered from a variety of different disciplines outside of psychology, and we will consider some of those perspectives in this chapter. It is immediately apparent that cultures around the world vary, often tremendously, in their practices, social structures, diets, economic systems, technologies, religious beliefs, and, as this book argues, their psychology. Why cultures vary in these ways defies any single answer—rather, we can come to understand cultural variation by considering a variety of different forces that come into play.

"I don't know how it started, either. All I know is that it's part of our corporate culture."

Ecological and Geographic Variation. One way that we can consider how cultural variation comes to be is to consider the ecologies within which people live. By the late Pleistocene era (about 20,000 years ago), humans had already settled in a more diverse range of physical environments than any other species. And it is quite obvious that these different environments affect the ways that people go about living their daily lives. Some of the ways that physical environments affect culture are quite direct. For example, there are no large indigenous mammals in Hawaii, and native Hawaiians do not have any hunting traditions. This contrasts sharply with the !Kung of the Kalahari who live in an environment surrounded by large animals and who derive much of their caloric intake by hunting them. The kinds of foods that are available within a given ecology will affect the kinds of foraging behaviors that people will engage in.

These ecological differences can have some more indirect effects on cultures as well. Different physical ecologies do not just affect the diets of people; the different foraging behaviors can also come to affect how the societies are structured and the values that people come to adopt. For example, cultural variation in sex roles can arise from the different ecologies within which people live (Gilmore, 1990). In those cultures in which the environment is harsh and requires courage and physical prowess to secure a living (e.g., in places where large game is hunted, or risky deep-sea fishing is performed), cultures of masculinity that value strength and toughness of males are more likely to emerge. For example, on the South Pacific island of Truk, traditionally men had to go on dangerous deep-sea fishing expeditions to secure food for their families. At the same time, the Trukese greatly value masculinity, and this is made manifest by young men engaging in frequent violent drunken melees with knives and clubs. In contrast, in cultures in which the environment is more benign and food is plentiful and more easily acquired, then more androgynous sex roles will more likely emerge (see Cohen, 2001). For example, in Tahiti, men do not hunt; the shallow lagoons provide ample fishing without needing to venture into more treacherous waters; and the rich volcanic soils allow for the easy harvesting of taro, cassava, coconuts, and fruit. There is virtually no warfare or feuding in Tahiti, and there is little evidence that masculinity is a matter of much concern for Tahitians. In general, a survey of the norms for masculinity across diverse ecological contexts led one anthropologist to conclude that "the harsher the environment and the scarcer the resources, the more manhood is stressed as the inspiration and the goal. The correlation could not be more clear, concrete, or compelling" (Gilmore, 1990, p. 224). The physical environments that we live in shape the array of lifestyles that are possible. How much do you think your own culture is the way that it is because of the physical environment around you?

Small Differences Can Have Large Effects. Sometimes what might seem to be small variations in ecologies can lead to dramatically different cultures, especially as they unfold over time. Consider the following historical event: In 1532, Francisco Pizarro, leading a group of 168 Spanish soldiers, met with the Incan emperor Atahuallpa in the Peruvian highland town of Cajamarca. At the time the Incans were the largest and most advanced state in the Americas, and Atahuallpa was surrounded by 80,000 soldiers when Pizarro met with him. Within the day, Pizarro's men had succeeded in capturing the emperor, and had killed about 7,000 of his soldiers. In a series of other similarly lopsided battles, Pizarro and his small band of soldiers continued on their rampage, and ultimately the Spaniards conquered the Incan empire. Jared Diamond, in his Pulitzer Prize–winning book on cultural and geographic variability, *Guns, Germs, and Steel* (1997), raises some simple yet profound questions about this event. How was it that Pizarro and his vastly outnumbered band of soldiers succeeded in overthrowing the Incan empire? Why didn't the Incans defeat Pizarro, or why didn't the Incans go over to conquer the Spanish in Europe instead?

These questions can be addressed by looking both at proximal and distal causes. **Proximal causes** are those that have direct and immediate relations with their effects. At a proximal level, the Spaniards had the political organization that drew on the experiences of thousands of years of written history, and oceangoing ships that allowed them to reach the Americas. They had steel swords and steel armor, and guns that easily bested the stone clubs, sling shots, and quilt armor of the Incans. The Spaniards also had horses, which allowed them to outmaneuver and overtake the Incans who were all on foot. Furthermore, the Incan empire at the time was divided because of a smallpox epidemic that had been spread across the Americas by the first Spanish explorers and had decimated the population. These proximal advantages are largely what led to Pizarro's conquest of Atahuallpa.

However, these Spanish advantages over the Incans just push the questions back further. Why did the Spaniards have the technologies, the horses, and the long written history that the Incans didn't have? Why did the Spanish germs kill the Incans—and not the reverse? To address these questions we need to consider the distal causes. **Distal causes** are those initial differences that lead to effects over long periods of time, and often through indirect relations. Diamond proposes that rather subtle differences in the geography of Eurasia and the Americas can importantly help in addressing why the Spanish defeated the Incans. First, in a region labeled the "Fertile Crescent," straddling the Middle East from Iran up to Turkey and over to Egypt, there existed a unique collection of plant (i.e., wheat, barley, peas, lentils) and animal species (i.e., sheep, goats, pigs, donkeys, and cows) that were especially suitable for domestication. These species ultimately provided the basis for the development of Western agriculture, and no other region in the world has had as many plant or animal species that are suitable for domestication. Furthermore, these domesticated species quickly spread both East and West as there were populated areas that shared a similar latitude and hence, a similar climate to that of the Fertile Crescent (in contrast, agricultural developments by the Mayans in Mexico were unlikely to reach the Incans in Peru because the regions are far apart in terms of latitude and climate). This difference exists because the major continental axis of Eurasia runs east to west, whereas the major continental axes of the Americas and Africa run north to south (Figure 2.1). The birth of agriculture allowed people to adopt sedentary lifestyles, in which they would benefit from creating tools and artifacts as they wouldn't have to carry them all the time. Also, agriculture allowed for enough food production that some people could devote their activities to non–food producing tasks, such as working to create various tools and innovations.

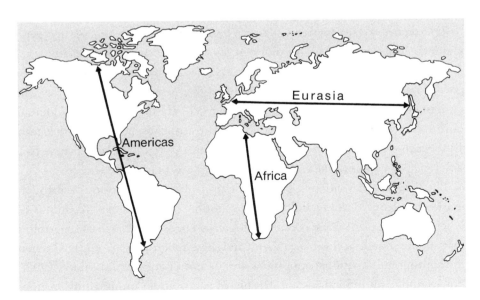

FIGURE 2.1

The major continental axes (Diamond, 1997).

These benefits, together with the greater exchange of ideas permitted by the denser populations in Eurasia, allowed for inventions such as steel, ships, and writing systems to emerge much earlier in Eurasia than in the Americas.

Second, the domestication of various animal species in the Fertile Crescent caused humans in Eurasia to live in close proximity with animals for thousands of years. Living close to animals led many diseases that originated in animal species (e.g., measles, tuberculosis, smallpox, and influenza) to cross over and infect humans as well. Furthermore, the settlements in Eurasia became more densely populated because of the food surplus provided by agriculture, so any contagious diseases that were caught by one person were likely to spread to many others as well. Diamond proposes that thousands of years of dense populations living among livestock in Eurasia led to the development of many diseases over the centuries that the survivors ultimately developed resistance to. These diseases would later prove to be enormously virulent when they were introduced to people in the Americas, where the population had not developed resistances to them. In sum, Diamond proposes that minor geographical differences in the availability of easy-to-domesticate species of plants and animals, and the position of Eurasia, stretching for thousands of miles from east to west along the same latitude and climate, allowed people in Eurasia to develop complex societies, writing systems, tools, weapons, and resistance to deadly germs much earlier than other parts of the globe. Diamond's thesis is a powerful argument that cultural differences can importantly originate in geographical differences.

Transmitted Versus Evoked Culture. The above arguments suggest that geographical differences lead to different cultural responses—for example, a dependence on food sources that are obtained through bravery leads to a greater respect for bravery and masculinity. There are two ways that we can understand how geography can contribute to cultural variation. Cultural norms can arise as direct responses to features of the ecology, or they can arise because of learning from other individuals. As you'll soon see, these two different bases of cultural variability are not always clearly separable.

The first way that different geographies can affect cultural norms is through **evoked culture**. Evoked culture is the notion that all people, regardless of where they are from, have certain biologically encoded behavioral repertoires that are potentially accessible to them, and these repertoires are engaged when the appropriate situational conditions are present (Tooby & Cosmides, 1992). For example, all individuals are capable of acting in an intimidating manner when they or their offspring are being threatened by others. The capacity to act in an intimidating way is universally present; however, it is evoked among some people only when they find themselves or their loved ones under threat. Some cultural variation can thus be understood as the result of universal domain-specific psychological responses being activated in response to specific conditions.

One example of an evoked cultural difference can be seen in cross-cultural variation in the importance of physical attractiveness in selecting a mate. Everything else held constant, people from around the world prefer mates who are more physically attractive. One important reason for our attraction to physically attractive mates, according to evolutionary reasoning, is that physically attractive people are less likely to be infected by parasites (parasitic infections can cause asymmetry and blemishes, which tend to be viewed as unattractive), and are thus, on average, healthier. Because our ancestors who were attracted to healthy mates had more surviving offspring than those who were attracted to unhealthy mates, humans have inherited preferences for attractive mates.

However, there are many other characteristics that we find attractive in mates aside from their physical beauty, such as their intelligence, kindness, sense of humor, and so on. In many contexts these other characteristics can come to be valued more than physical attractiveness. This would especially be true in contexts in which there was little variability in the health of our potential mates. If there is little variability in the health of potential mates, then physical attractiveness is a less useful basis for selecting a mate. However, if people are living in an environment where there are pronounced threats from various parasites (such as those causing leprosy, malaria, boils, or syphilis), then it should be more important to select physically attractive mates to better ensure that one will have surviving offspring. Supporting this reasoning, the prevalence of various parasites in 29 different cultures, as well as the importance that people in those cultures placed on physical attractiveness in choosing mates, were assessed in one study (Gangestad, Haselton, & Buss, 2006). The study revealed that the more parasites there were prevalent in a culture, the more people emphasized the physical attractiveness of potential mates. This finding suggests that we all have the potential to value physical attractiveness; however, this motivation for selecting attractive mates is most strongly activated when we are in an environment where the health of our mates is less certain. Variation in geography—in this case, in terms of parasite prevalence—differentially evokes universal aspects of our psychology. Evoked culture is thus tied to particular geographic environments: When one moves to a new environment, new behavioral responses should be evoked.

A second way that geography leads to cultural variation is that people come to learn about particular cultural practices through social learning or by modeling others who live near them. This is known as **transmitted culture**. For example, if you observe your neighbor planting wheat seeds, and notice the benefits that she earned for doing so, you might adopt this cultural practice for yourself. The vast majority of the cultural differences that are discussed through this book can be best understood in terms of the results of transmitted culture. Although transmitted culture typically begins in a particular geographic area (as we are more likely to learn from those people with whom we interact regularly), it does not necessarily stay bound to a particular geography. Unlike evoked culture, transmitted culture can travel with people when they move to new environments. People can bring their transmitted ideas with them, and cultures can spread past their initial set of geographic conditions.

Often, however, the distinction between evoked and transmitted culture is not clear-cut. A particular behavioral script (e.g., a heightened preference for attractive mates) might be activated by a specific situational variable (e.g., prevalence of parasites); however, if that behavioral script becomes a norm, then that norm might be learned by others, and thus transmitted to future generations. These cultural norms can continue to be transmitted even in contexts where the initial situational variable (e.g., prevalence of parasites) is no longer present. Indeed, it would seem that transmitted culture is always involved in maintaining cultural norms, even when evoked cultural responses are also present (e.g., Norenzayan, 2006).

Ecological variation and evoked culture represent important reasons underlying cultural variability. However, there is much more to cultural variation than just variation in ecologies. For example, consider two cultures, the Dinka and the Nuer, that coexist in the marshlands of southern Sudan. These cultures have coexisted in the same region for over a century, and they live a migratory existence where they grow millet and corn in the wet season and move about to let their cattle graze in the dry season. However, despite the fact that people from these two cultures live in the same ecology, share a similar technology, raise similar crops and livestock, and descend from the same ancestors from about a thousand years ago, their cultures are different in a number of pronounced ways. The Nuer maintain larger herds of cattle

Striking differences between the Dinka (top) and the Nuer (bottom) of southern Sudan highlight the limits of geography's influence on culture.

and rely largely on milk from their herds, whereas the Dinka regularly slaughter their herds and rely on the meat. The Dinka tribal memberships are based on who lives next to whom in the wet season, whereas the Nuer base kinship on the male line. Furthermore, the Nuer tribes are far larger and more militarily powerful than the Dinka. The Nuer also have very costly and inflexible dowry payments that are incurred when daughters are married, whereas the Dinka have small and flexible payments. The same geography thus results in quite different cultural practices (see Richerson & Boyd, 2005, for a review).

Likewise, the limits of ecological variation on culture are evident in a landmark study by the anthropologist Robert Edgerton (1971), who contrasted culture against ecology. Edgerton studied four East African tribes (the Sebei, Pokot, Kamba, and Hehe) that each had multiple communities that lived in different ecological settings. For example, some communities from all four of the tribes lived in moist highlands where they subsisted largely through farming, whereas other communities from each of the four tribes lived in dry lowlands where they subsisted largely through herding. Edgerton contrasted the attitudes of these various communities. If people's attitudes are largely a product of ecology, then the communities that farmed should show attitudes that are largely similar, and should appear different from the communities that herded. In contrast, if people's attitudes are largely the product of transmitted culture, then the different communities within each tribe should show attitudes that are quite similar to each other, and different from the attitudes of the other tribes, regardless of whether they lived in farming regions or in herding regions. Edgerton found that for the majority of attitudes, tribal affiliation was a better predictor of people's attitudes than was their primary means of subsistence (see Richerson & Boyd, 2005, for a review). Again, these findings demonstrate that although ecology is a key component of cultural variation, much cultural variation is transmitted in ways that are largely independent of ecology.

Understanding cultural variability thus requires us to look both at the evoked culture that originates in the surrounding geography, and the transmitted culture that spreads the norms that develop. An important question to consider then is why are some ideas transmitted whereas others are not.

How Do Ideas Catch On?

It was the worst natural disaster in U.S. history. After Hurricane Katrina slammed into New Orleans in the summer of 2005 and damaged the levees holding back the waters of Lake Pontchartrain, the city began to fill up like a bathtub. Over 1,500 people were killed in the flooding and property damage was estimated to be about $75 billion. Over the next several days, as assistance was ineffective and slow in coming, the news reported many extremely disturbing events coming out of New Orleans. Rescue helicopters were being shot at, a 7-year-old rape victim was found with a slit throat, sharks were swimming in the floodwaters, gang rapes and gang violence was rampant, and the Convention Center and Superdome were live-in morgues, stacked with dozens of dead bodies, with people murdering each other inside. The world recoiled in shock at the violence and chaos of the aftermath of Katrina. However, as reporters researched the origins of the stories that were being reported, it turned out that virtually none of them were true. Some were based on exaggerations (one person was murdered in the Superdome, and a total of 10 people died while at the Convention Center and Superdome); however, most of the stories circulated turned out to be completely fabricated—false rumors that arose in the chaos of the aftermath (Welch, 2005).

Rumors are of course not limited to Katrina. Rumors arise in all kinds of situations, particularly in times of war or disaster. For example, in the Second World War, people were fed a daily ration of rumors, the majority of which were simply untrue. There were rumors that thousands of soldiers' bodies had washed ashore at various towns (the town names varied), that crab meat packed by the Japanese contained ground glass, and that the entire American Pacific Fleet was destroyed at Pearl Harbor (Knapp, 1944). Rumors are fueled by a lack of information, creating an environment where facts can be extremely valuable, and their spread is fanned by strong emotional feelings.

The study of rumors is informative as it can indicate what kinds of ideas come to be spread and become common within a culture. Cultural evolution requires that certain ideas are passed on to others (i.e., people must be motivated to share some information), and those ideas are selectively retained (i.e., people recall that information out of the barrage of information that they are exposed to each day). Cultures change when ideas become widely shared among their populations. The study of cultural evolution is an important and rapidly growing enterprise, although it has proven to be a challenging topic to study.

There are two models for understanding how cultural ideas spread. The first model considers that the spread of ideas through populations is similar to the way genes replicate; the second suggests that the spread of ideas through populations is similar to the way diseases spread. To better understand both of these models we first need to discuss the processes of biological evolution, which is common to both models.

Parallels Between Biological and Cultural Evolution. Many aspects of cultural evolution can be informed by looking at the processes of biological evolution (Collard, Shennan, & Tehrani, 2005; Mesoudi, Whiten, & Laland, 2006). Biological evolution occurs when certain genes become more common in populations than they were in the past. It operates through two related mechanisms. The first is **natural selection**. Natural selection is the evolutionary process that occurs when the following three conditions are present: (1) There is individual variability among members of a species on certain traits (e.g., some antelopes can run faster than other antelopes); (2) those traits are associated with different survival rates (e.g., faster antelopes are better able to outrun predators than slower antelopes); and (3) those traits have a hereditary basis (e.g., the offspring of faster antelopes tend to be faster than the offspring of slower antelopes). If all three of these are present, with enough time, you will have natural selection. With each new generation the proportion of faster antelopes in the population will increase, and ultimately the species will change over time. However, the ecological world is extremely complex, and there are numerous trade-offs involved with respect to any given trait. For example, faster antelopes might require more calories to support their additional muscle mass, and when food is scarce, slower antelopes, who are in need of fewer calories, would have a survival advantage over the faster antelopes. It is the balance of all the selective pressures that a species faces in a given environment that affects which individual members will survive to pass on their genes to the next generation.

The second mechanism for biological evolution is **sexual selection**. Sexual selection operates in ways very similar to those of natural selection; however, the focus here is not so much on the survival of individuals but on their reproductive success. If the gist of natural selection can be captured in the expression "the survival of the fittest," then the gist of sexual selection can be captured in the expression "the fecundity of the sexiest." Those individuals who can best attract a mate—or, more accurately, who can best attract the healthiest mate—will be the most likely to have surviving offspring. Consider the peacock. Those males with the largest and most brightly colored tails are more likely to win the affections, and the future offspring, of the highly discerning peahens. This is true even though a large colorful tail would seem to be a survival *disadvantage* for the peacock—it would be an easily spotted signal to all predators indicating that he can't fly very well. However, this survival disadvantage is outweighed by the reproductive advantage of being able to attract all of those discerning peahens. Peahens prefer outlandishly large and colorful tales to short drab ones because the tails advertise the peacock's health. Only a healthy peacock, with a good genetic constitution, is able to produce such a glorious tail, and thus peahens who are attracted to this signal of the male's health and mate with him will probably have healthy offspring, who will likewise be more successful at attracting their own mates in the future. Sexual selection is thus a mechanism that determines which traits will come to be desired by sexual partners.

These two kinds of selective mechanisms for biological evolution have parallels in cultural evolution. Some ideas are more likely to persist across time than others—they have long survival rates. And some ideas are more likely to attract adherents than others—they reproduce more. As ideas persist across time and become more common in a population, we have the beginning of the cultural evolution of norms. For example, as described at the beginning of the chapter, specific cultural norms for appropriate table manners have become more common from generation to generation in Western culture. Like fast-running antelopes or peacocks with brightly colored tails, cultural norms for not spitting at the table or for not blowing your nose in the tablecloth have had a selective advantage over the norms for engaging in these behaviors. Note, importantly, that "selection" for cultural evolution is not tied to genes. Certain ideas or norms are more likely to be retained or shared compared with other ideas or norms.

Biological evolution and cultural evolution are not identical processes, however. Genes can

"What's the matter? Not puffy enough for you?

only be passed vertically from parents to offspring, and the evolution of genes is an enormously slow and gradual process that occurs across many, many generations, as the percentage of individuals carrying certain genetic variants slowly changes over time. In contrast, a cultural idea can pass horizontally from one person to anyone else, it can be transmitted to many people in an instant (e.g., think of how quickly attitudes toward flying changed on September 11, 2001), and people can elaborate on, change, and extend the cultural ideas quickly as they learn them. Cultural evolution can thus often occur at extremely rapid speeds, such as when we see a new fad take off, a political revolution sparked by perceptions of an unjust event, or broad societal changes that occur as a result of the introduction of a new technology, such as the Internet.

Ideas as Replicators. Biological evolution is possible because it involves replicators that are able to make copies of themselves. Genes are the replicators in biological evolution, and these replicators need to possess a few characteristics in order to be successful (see Dawkins, 1976, for further discussion). First, replicators should be relatively stable and long-lasting entities and shouldn't dissolve or fall apart readily, as otherwise there would be nothing left to replicate. That is, successful replicators need to have a certain degree of **longevity**. Genes have remarkable longevity and typically last the lifetime of a cell (although old egg cells, for example, can develop anomalous chromosomes over time). Second, replicators should do their replicating as accurately as possible. When organisms reproduce, their genes are copied to their offspring. It would be extremely problematic if that copying produced many errors, such that offspring received very different sets of genes from what their parents had. Good replicators require the copying to be of extremely high **fidelity**. However, the copying of genes, accurate as it is, is not perfect. Of the approximately 3 billion base pairs of nucleotides that constitute the 25,000 or so genes that were copied from your parents' sperm and egg cells that ultimately united and grew into you, copying errors produced mutations, on average, in about four of your genes (Leroi, 2003). Mutations are a necessary part of evolution, as mutations provide the variety of potential genes that allows for differential selection. However, if too many of the nucleotides that were copied from your parents' DNA were mutations, or if any of those copying errors resulted in particularly harmful mutations, you would not be able to survive long enough to produce surviving offspring yourself, and replication would no longer be possible. Hence, high-fidelity copying is important for successful replication. Third, good replicators will produce many copies of themselves. Those replicators that are especially fecund and produce many copies of themselves will come to be more common in future generations than those replicators that rarely reproduced. **Fecundity** is thus another important feature of replicators. In biological evolution this is determined by the number of offspring an individual organism has.

Cultural evolution can also be seen as involving replicators that possess longevity, fidelity, and fecundity. Richard Dawkins (1976) proposed that there could be a cultural equivalent to genes which he termed **memes**. Memes are the smallest units of cultural information that can be faithfully transmitted. Some examples of memes are tunes, catch-phrases, ways of making hammers, scientific theories, table manners, and iPods. Whereas genes are instructions for making proteins, which are stored in our chromosomes and are replicated through reproduction, memes are instructions for particular ways of behaving or speaking, which are storied in our brains or in written texts or in objects and are replicated through communication or imitation (see Blackmore, 1999).

As with genes, successful memes should be of sufficient longevity if they are to be faithfully transmitted. An idea that is in your head for only a few seconds, for example, is unlikely to be transmitted to others. Successful memes are also highly fecund. Those memes that were especially popular and were transmitted many times over would be more likely to become an important thread in the cultural fabric than a meme that was rarely ever passed on to another. Ideally, memes too would have high copying fidelity, where the same idea would be copied more or less accurately each time it was reproduced.

This last point about copying fidelity exposes a weakness about the idea that memes are cultural equivalents of genes. First, random copying errors or mutations are the source of genetic variability that allows genes, and ultimately species, to evolve over time. Cultural evolution, in contrast, grows from innovations that are typically not random copying errors but are usually consciously planned innovations. The basis of variability in genes and memes is thus fundamentally different.

Furthermore, in many ways, cultural transmission does not appear to be of very high fidelity. A stark example of this is evident in the game "Telephone" in which a person whispers a message to someone, and that person, in turn, whispers it to another, and so on, until the last person receives the message. The reason that Telephone can be a fun game is that typically the message that the last person received is quite different from the initial message that was delivered, as there were many copying errors at each link. However, often the gist of the message does survive all the retellings fairly well, although many of the tangential details get lost or transformed. To the extent that the gist of the message can be seen as the central meme of the message, then the fidelity of the transmission might not be so problematic after all. However, the analogy of memes as replicating units that are like genes is weakened if we can't specify precisely what aspects of messages constitute memes. For example, if a tune is a meme, then what about half a tune? Is that a meme too? Are single melodies, bars, or notes also memes? Many scholars have called into question the utility of the concept of memes for understanding cultural evolution because of the difficulty in specifying precisely what memes are. Whereas genes can be precisely identified (they are those portions of DNA that encode discrete proteins), memes remain interesting analogies or metaphors that have thus far not been explicitly identified or even consensually recognized. Nonetheless, despite these difficulties with the idea of replicating ideas or memes, many researchers have tried to understand cultural evolution by considering the ways that ideas pass on from person to person (for a thorough discussion of the parallels between biological and cultural evolution see Mesoudi et al., 2006).

Importantly, memes do not have to be adaptive (i.e., result in more surviving offspring) to become common, unlike evolutionary processes with genes. Many cultural ideas spread even though they are quite maladaptive. Consider the cultural practice among the Fore of New Guinea of engaging in ritualized cannibalism, in which the Fore honor their dead by consuming parts of their bodies. This practice became popular even though it often leads to the development of the degenerative disease called *kuru* among its practitioners—a disease that has killed more than 2,000 Fore (Durham, 1991). The fact that an idea can catch on, even though the individuals who follow this idea may be more likely to die, demonstrates how the forces of cultural evolution occur in terms that are independent from the processes of biological evolution. The power of cultural evolution is so great that ideas can spread even if as many as 50% of those who follow the ideas lose their lives from doing so (Cavalli-Sforza & Feldman, 1981). One does not have to look hard through history to find many examples of extremely harmful ideas that nonetheless quickly spread through populations (such as National Socialism in the 1930s and 1940s in Germany or the Cultural Revolution in the 1960s and 1970s in China).

Epidemiology of Ideas. A variant on the "ideas as replicators" approach to understanding cultural evolution is the **epidemiology of ideas** (Sperber, 1996). Epidemiology is the branch of medicine that is concerned with the distribution of diseases among populations. In the case of cultural evolution, the epidemiological view considers the distribution of ideas in a particular population and explores the features of ideas that facilitate or inhibit the likelihood that an idea will be passed on. In contrast to efforts to understand cultural evolution through replicators like memes, proponents of the epidemiological view argue that there is no direct replication of ideas. Rather, for an idea to spread from one individual to another, the epidemiological view proposes the following steps: First, an individual (the inventor) has a mental representation of an idea in her mind. Second, another individual (the imitator), who learns about this idea from the first person, then creates a mental representation of the idea in his own head. The idea does not transmit directly from inventor to imitator; rather, the gist of the idea is communicated to the imitator, and then the imitator re-creates the idea anew. The mental representation of the imitator is different from that of the inventor because it is constrained by the imitator's own idiosyncratic ways of thinking (which are termed "biases"). However, because people share so many common features in the ways they think, they share many similar biases, and thus people's imitating tends to be quite accurate. However, the epidemiological view maintains that true replication of ideas is not occurring. Each individual recreates his or her own reasonable facsimile of what was learned from the other.

For example, imagine that a person creates a new invention designed to remove the seeds from strawberries. She then shows her invention to a friend. The friend, impressed with this new invention that he has seen, goes home to build his own strawberry seeder. However, he only recalls the gist of what he was shown. He creates his own idiosyncratic strawberry seeder, based on the mental representation that he has of the one that he originally saw. His mental representation of the strawberry seeder consists of what he recalls seeing plus his own unique ideas. And the imitator's strawberry seeder might then be imitated by someone else. In this way, ideas spread from person to person, but the ideas are always created anew by each individual, and there is much individual variation from person to person. According to this view, cultural evolution is a process that is clearly distinct from biological evolution, as there is no true replication going on. Both the ideas as replicators approach and the epidemiological approach are theories for understanding cultural evolution, and thus far, there is no consensus as to which approach has more explanatory power.

Factors That Cause Ideas to Spread

Regardless of whether one thinks of cultural evolution as occurring through the replication of memes or through the spread of individually created mental representations, both views assume that ideas spread and ultimately evolve. Now we need to consider the question of what makes an idea likely to spread. Why do some ideas spread like wildfire, whereas other ideas never leave the inventor? Understanding what motivates individuals to communicate and remember ideas is key to understanding how ideas spread across populations.

Communicable Ideas Spread. For ideas to spread, they need to have some way of moving from one person's head to another. The most direct way for this to occur is through language; however, some ideas might be more likely to be communicated than others. For example, some ideas are difficult to summarize succinctly, some ideas might seem to be less useful or pertinent, and some ideas might be deemed too socially undesirable for people to express them to others. These kinds of ideas would seem to be less likely to spread than ones people were eager to communicate to others.

One way to investigate culturally shared ideas has been to look at the stereotypes that people have of certain cultural groups (Schaller, Conway, & Tanchuk, 2002). These stereotypes vary tremendously from place to place and across historical time. For example, in the 19th century, a relatively common stereotype in the United States about the Irish was they were obese, wasteful, and violent drug-abusing monkeys, as depicted in the cartoon on the next page. Today, the circumstances of Irish in the United States have improved so much that it is hard to believe that these crude kinds of stereotypes about them ever existed. This reflects how negative stereotypes about cultures tend to be motivated beliefs that stem from particular circumstances, such as a conflict over resources (e.g., new Irish immigrants competing for low-paying jobs with poorer Americans), the remnants of historical conflicts (e.g., the centuries-old struggles between the UK and Ireland), disenfranchisement, and ignorance about a group's cultural practices.

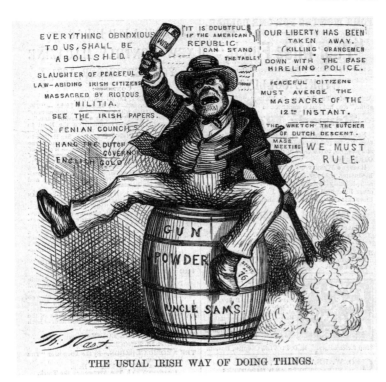

THE USUAL IRISH WAY OF DOING THINGS.

Anti-Irish prejudice was common throughout the United States in the late 19th century, as shown in this cartoon published in 1871.

Stereotypes can thus be seen to reflect shared ideas that people have in particular cultural contexts about some specific cultural groups. It would seem, then, that the content of stereotypes would be influenced by the kinds of ideas that people were most likely to communicate. If some ideas were rarely communicated about various ethnic groups then they were less likely to become part of any shared stereotypes that might exist. In one study participants were asked to consider how characteristic a number of trait words were for what they believed others thought about certain ethnic groups (Schaller et al., 2002). Participants were asked what they believed *others* thought because, in general, people are more willing to discuss the contents of stereotypes that they think other people have than they are to discuss the contents of stereotypes that they have—people usually don't like to admit that they think about others in stereotypical ways. Also, participants were asked how likely they were to use those traits in describing other people that they knew. The researchers found that for relatively common ethnic groups in Vancouver (e.g., people of European, Chinese, and East Indian descent), people said that the trait words that were the most characteristic of the shared stereotypes were also the words that were most commonly used to communicate information about others. In contrast, for less common ethnic groups in Vancouver (e.g., those with smaller local populations, such as First Nations tribes), there was no correlation between the communicability of traits and the likelihood that they were characteristic of stereotypes, as people apparently rarely discussed these less common groups. That is, culturally shared stereotypes tend to be formed based on the kinds of traits that people are most likely to communicate, and for the kinds of groups that people are most likely to be talking about.

Of course, when you communicate your ideas, not everyone is equally likely to be your communication partner. Quite simply, we are far more likely to communicate ideas with people we see regularly than with those we rarely or never meet. Because of this obvious fact, people tend to be more influenced by the ideas of those with whom they regularly interact. **Dynamic social impact theory** posits that individuals come to influence each other, and they do so primarily in terms of how often the individuals interact, which ultimately leads to clusters of like-minded people that are separated by geography—cultures, in other words (Latané, 1996). Dynamic social impact theory is thus one account for the origin of culture: Norms develop among those who communicate with each other regularly. For example, there is clear evidence of people sharing many similarities with those who cluster around them in terms of dialect, crime rate, self-concepts, attitudes toward alcohol, product consumptions, lifestyles, and music preferences (Harton & Bourgeois, 2004; Mark, 1998; Plaut, Markus, & Lachman, 2002; Weiss, 1994). Political attitudes, for instance, show a great deal of clustering. If you consider the election map of the November 2004 American presidential election, support for Bush and Kerry was not randomly distributed across the nation. Rather, support for the candidates emerged in clear-cut geographic clusters, indicating how people's political preferences were regularly influenced by their neighbors, coworkers, and the local media that they watched (Figure 2.2).

One study investigated how ideas spread in accordance with predictions from dynamic social impact theory (Cullum & Harton, in press). Students' attitudes were surveyed at the beginning of the year and then at later points throughout the school year. The researchers kept track of the individuals who were the students' roommates, housemates, and residence hallmates over that time. In the vast majority of cases, the assignments to rooms, houses, and residence halls was conducted randomly. Over the course of the year, stu-

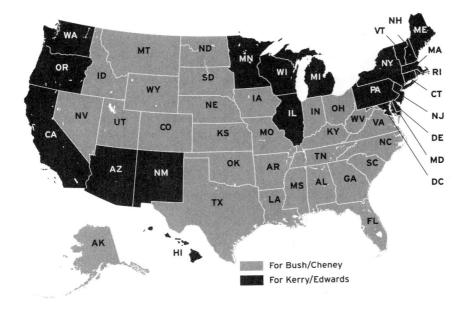

FIGURE 2.2

In the 2004 American presidential election, Bush's support was strongest in the South, the Midwest, and the West, while much of Kerry's support came from the Northeast, the Great Lakes region, and the West Coast.

dents came to have attitudes that were similar to the attitudes of the people with whom they shared a common living space. This change in attitudes was especially true of those attitudes that participants viewed to be personally important at the beginning of the semester, and, consequently, were discussed most with their peers over time. Attitudes came to be quite similar within houses and dining halls, but remained different between houses and dining halls. In effect, the researchers documented the formation of some microcultures within people's living quarters. Cultures thus emerge when people communicate with those around them, and people are most likely to communicate information that is personally relevant to them. Can you identify any microcultures that might have developed around you and your friends?

Emotional Ideas Spread. When I was a child going trick or treating on Halloween, my mother had a rule that she had to inspect all of the candy before we were allowed to eat it. Anything that was not wrapped or was in an opened package was confiscated, for fears that a nasty neighbor had inserted razor blades in it, or had spiked it with poison. This seemed like a reasonable precaution at the time, as we had all heard many tales of children who had been killed from such booby-trapped candy. *Newsweek* published an article in 1975, right before Halloween, that warned, "In recent years, several children have died and hundreds have narrowly escaped injury from razor blades, sewing needles, and shards of glass purposefully put into their goodies by adults." However, in a study of every single reported Halloween incident since 1958, there were reports of only two deaths—both of which were caused by the unfortunate children's parents rather than by sadistic strangers (Best & Horiuchi, 1985). In only a few incidents had children received minor cuts from sharp objects in candy bags (the most serious injury of all was one requiring 11 stitches), but the large majority of the reports were hoaxes enacted either by the children or by their parents seeking to extort money through lawsuits and insurance scams. There was little evidence that children were endangered by taking candy from strangers; the problems seemed to stem largely from kids taking candy from their dysfunctional parents.

So if booby-trapped Halloween candies are such rare events, how did fears of them ever lead to the beliefs that several children had been killed by them? Such stories are just one of many different kinds of urban or **contemporary legends** that have spread through various cultures. Contemporary legends are simply fictional stories that are told in modern societies as though they are true. Of concern to psychologists are the reasons these legends spread (Heath, Bell, & Sternberg, 2001).

One reason is that they have informational value. If children really are potentially at risk from booby-trapped candy, it is important to receive this information. The spread of rumors and legends thus can be seen to fuel a desire that people have for information, even if the information they receive might not always be accurate (e.g., Allport & Postman, 1947; Knapp, 1944). It is highly adaptive for people to communicate potentially useful information to each other.

Heath et al. (2001) proposed that rumors and legends are more likely to spread when they can evoke a shared emotional reaction among people. People appear motivated to share emotions with others because this allows people to connect with others. Social interactions should be facilitated to the extent that people feel their partners are experiencing similar feelings as themselves. Rumors or legends that spark strong feelings should thus facilitate a sense of shared connection with others. Heath and colleagues investigated this hypothesis by creating a number of variants on some contemporary legends to see whether participants felt motivated to pass the stories on to others. For example, one story that participants read referred to a man who found a dead rat inside a soda bottle. One group of participants read a variant of the story that was designed to elicit in readers only a *small* amount of emotion (disgust, in this case). It went like this:

> *"Before he drank anything he saw that there was a dead rat inside."*

A second version of the story was designed to lead to a *moderate* degree of emotional response in the readers.

> *"About halfway through he saw that there was a dead rat inside."*

And a third version of the story was written so that it should create a *strong* emotional response. Brace yourself.

> *"He swallowed something lumpy and saw that*
> *there were pieces of a dead rat inside."*

Each participant read a total of 12 stories, varying in their emotional impact, and they were then asked a number of questions about their reactions to the stories and whether they would be willing to pass the story along to others. A variety of features of the stories increased people's willingness to pass along the stories. In terms of informational features, people were more motivated to spread the stories if they were plausible and they felt the stories would cause them to change their behaviors—that is, people were motivated to communicate stories that contained potentially useful information. Furthermore, the more emotion the stories elicited (i.e., the more interesting, joyful, contemptible, and disgusting they were), the more likely people were to say they would pass them on. In addition to the informational value of the stories, then, people are motivated to pass on stories that convey a lot of emotion. Emotional ideas are more likely to spread through a culture than are unemotional ones.

Minimally Counterintuitive Ideas Persist. One source of evolution of cultural ideas is evident in religions and myths around the world. For example, almost every culture has a creation myth—a story for how the world came to be. The Fulani believe that the world was created from a drop of milk; according to Japanese mythology, the world was created from brine dripping from the tip of the Jewel-spear of Heaven; Judeo–Christian beliefs state that

God created the heavens and the earth in six days. It is not possible for all of these conflicting creation myths to be literally true, and it may be that none of these beliefs are literally true, so religions and myths can be considered as cultural ideas that successfully catch on and spread through cultures. What influences the extent to which particular myths or beliefs come to be shared across a population?

Atran and Norenzayan (2004) propose that not all stories are equally memorable. Rather, the kinds of stories that are especially likely to persist in our memories are ones that contain a few **minimally counterintuitive ideas**. "Minimally counterintuitive" means statements that are surprising and unusual in the sense that they violate our expectations, but are not too outlandish. In the case of a religious text, such as the Bible, the vast majority of the text describes rather ordinary events, and those ordinary events are interspersed with occasional "counterintuitive" events, such as a talking bush, a virgin birth, or miracles such as water turned into wine. Atran and Norenzayan propose that such kinds of narratives—mostly ordinary, intuitive events sprinkled with the occasional counterintuitive idea—will be the most likely to persist in our memories and survive many retellings. One demonstration of this found that participants who were asked to remember and retell Native American folk tales remembered approximately 92% of minimally counterintuitive items, but only 71% of intuitive ones (Barrett & Nyhof, 2001; also see Boyer & Ramble, 2001). The minimally counterintuitive ideas were recalled better than intuitive ideas.

Atran and Norenzayan tested their hypothesis by providing participants with sets of statements that included many two- and three-word statements that varied in their intuitiveness. Participants were later asked to recall the statements they had read. Some statements were designed to be intuitive (e.g., a chanting man), some were designed to be minimally counterintuitive (e.g., a melting grandfather), and some were designed to be maximally counterintuitive (e.g., a squinting wilting brick). Participants were later asked to recall the events. Immediately after learning the statements participants tended to have the best recall for the intuitive statements, and the worst recall for the maximally counterintuitive ones. However, this initial preferential memory for intuitive statements did not seem to last. Participants were contacted again, one week later, and were asked to recall what they had learned. Participants had the best recall for those sets of statements that were mostly intuitive, but also contained a few minimally counterintuitive ones. That is, sets of ideas

The Grimms' tale of "The Donkey Lettuce" failed to catch on as well as some of their other stories.

that were largely intuitive, with the occasional counterintuitive idea interspersed, were the most memorable after a long period of time.

Likewise, another study explored the kinds of statements that were included in folk tales by the Grimm Brothers. Some of these folk tales have been quite successful and have become part of the cultural landscape. For example, it is quite likely that you are familiar with the story of "Little Red Riding Hood." However, some of the other folk tales by the Grimm Brothers have been much less successful. For example, you likely have never heard of their story "The Donkey Lettuce." One study investigated 42 different folk tales by the Grimm Brothers and had trained raters count the number of counterintuitive elements in each of the tales (e.g., talking mirrors, a house made of gingerbread; Norenzayan, Atran, Faulkner, & Schaller, 2006). The researchers then did a search on Google for the number of times each of the folk tales was listed. The results indicated that the most successful folk tales (i.e., the ones with the most Google hits) tended to have between two and three counterintuitive elements in the story. In contrast, the least successful folk tales had a broad range of counterintuitive elements, ranging from zero to six, and no clear pattern was discernible among the unpopular stories. Again, there was evidence that narratives that are largely intuitive but contain a couple of violations of expectations end up being the most memorable. The secret to a good story thus appears to be one that, for the most part, is a tale of everyday expected events, with the occasional unexpected element.

How Have Cultures Been Changing?

The notion that cultures evolve does not just refer to the distant past. Cultures are always evolving, and they continue to change today. How have cultures been evolving over recent decades?

Cultures Are Becoming Increasingly Interconnected. Different cultures have always been in contact with each other, and there have always been trade, intermarriage, political alliances, immigration, and a sharing of ideas and technologies across cultures. However, as a series of technological innovations have occurred both in terms of reducing the costs of transportation and of easing the process of long-distance communication, cultures have become far more interconnected than ever before. These increasing interconnections between cultures allow ideas that emerge in one culture to have an influence on people in other cultures, thereby hastening the process of cultural evolution. What happens tomorrow in Paris, then, is not just a matter for Parisians and the French but is something that can potentially affect people all over the world.

Furthermore, in many ways, these interconnections among cultures are resulting in the formation of a global culture. Many large companies are now global entities that have outgrown their cultural boundaries. For example, Sony, IKEA, and Exxon each do more than three-quarters of their business outside their respective home countries of Japan, Sweden, and the United States (Barber, 1995). Across much of the world today, people are drinking the same Starbucks coffee, using the same Microsoft software, and driving the same Toyotas. Much of popular culture also transcends national borders. MTV is available in 71 countries around the world, and thus people everywhere are exposed to the same kinds of themes that are conveyed in many music videos, such as embracing freedom, defying authority, celebrating youth, and promoting sexuality (Barber, 1995). Hollywood movies too are watched the world over. In a typical year, between 9 and 10 of the top 10 grossing movies in countries such as Argentina, Kazakhstan, the Philippines, Russia, and South Africa are Hollywood productions (Rosenthal, 2004), communicating largely American cultural values. Likewise, the Internet is allowing cultural information to be shared across national boundaries without people ever having to leave their homes. Does globalization mean that we are destined to all become citizens of a homogenous world culture?

Probably not, because this trend toward globalization is simultaneously paralleled by an opposing trend toward increasing tribalism, such as the dissolution of many former Eastern bloc countries into smaller and more culturally distinct nations, the independence movement for Quebec to separate from Canada, and Muslim fundamentalists battling Muslim secularists throughout the Mideast and South Asia. As Michael Ignatieff stated, "The key narrative of the new world order is disintegration of states" (Ignatieff, 1994, p. 5). The title of a popular book by political scientist Benjamin Barber (1995), *Jihad vs. McWorld*, nicely encapsulates these coexisting forces of motivations for cultural distinctiveness appearing alongside motivations for global homogeneity. In his book, Barber argues that as cultures around the world are penetrated by global companies and largely American popular culture, one common reaction has been for people to reject the globalizing force in an effort to return to the traditional cultures of their past. Sometimes these nationalistic sentiments are wrapped in religious overtones, and sometimes they are expressed violently, as a jihad, or holy war.

Likewise, while different cultures around the world are exposed to the same global products and popular culture, there is increasing cultural heterogeneity within the borders of many countries, as many nations receive immigrants from around the world. Ethnically diverse locations such as New York, Singapore, Sydney, and Toronto in many ways are microcosms of the world at large, each having many distinct ethnic enclaves coexisting within their own boundaries. Somewhat paradoxically, then, there are trends toward cultural homogeneity at a global level and toward cultural heterogeneity at a more local level. Interconnections between culture thus do not just breed homogeneity but also serve to underscore cultural differences. How do you think people's ways of thinking are affected as the world becomes more interconnected? This is a topic that we'll explore in Chapter 12, Living in Multicultural Worlds.

Many Cultures Are Becoming More Individualistic. One important dimension of culture that will be discussed and contrasted throughout this book is individualism versus collectivism. Cultures that are **individualistic** include a variety of practices and customs that encourage individuals to prioritize their own personal goals ahead of those of the collective, and consider how they are distinct from others (Triandis, 1989). For example, some practices common in individualistic cultures include the tracking of children at school, college-age children being encouraged to move out of their parents' homes, meritocratic pay at the office, employees being given individual offices or cubicles, and people choosing to put their elderly relatives in retirement homes. In contrast, cultures that are **collectivistic** include many cultural practices, institutions, and customs that encourage individuals to place relatively more emphasis on collective goals—specifically, the goals of one's ingroups. For example, collectivistic cultures often include cultural practices such as children sleeping with their parents, classes of school children being promoted together to the next grade regardless of the performance of some individual children, marriages being arranged by parents, companies compensating their employees on the basis of how long they have been employed, and extended families living under one roof. As you'll see later in several chapters of this book, the dimension of individualism and collectivism is important for understanding many cultural differences in a wide variety of different psychological processes.

Although an analysis of contemporary cultures around the world reveals how much cultures vary in the degree to which they can be considered individualistic or collectivistic (see Chapter 5, Self and Personality, for more on this), it is important to remember that cross-cultural comparisons make contrasts at a single point in time. We can also consider how cultures have changed across time, and such analyses reveal much about how some cultures are becoming more individualistic over recent decades.

In his best-selling book, *Bowling Alone* (2000), political scientist Robert Putnam made the case that social life in the United States has changed considerably since the 1960s. As he argued, up until the 1960s, people were more socially engaged and civically active than they have been in recent years. This societal transformation is evident in a wide variety of different social measures. Compared with the early 21st century, people in the 1960s were far more likely to entertain at home, be members of the Parent-Teacher Association, belong to a union, have dinner together as a family, hang out at bars or nightclubs, play cards, socialize with neighbors, hold a position in a club or organization, and trust each other. Perhaps the most symbolic change, as captured in the title of Putnam's book, is how Americans have come to bowl differently. Bowling remains the most popular competitive sport in America, and bowlers far outnumber participants in other sports such as softball, golf, soccer, or jogging. However, in previous decades the most common way to bowl was to belong to a league, where a group of friends formed a team that met on a weekly basis to bowl, share some beer and conversation, and maintain social ties. For example, in 1964 there were 84 men and 46 women league bowlers for every 1,000 adults. In 1997, the last year data were available, there were only 22 men and 18 women league bowlers per 1,000 adults, and this number continues to drop. People are still bowling (in 1996 approximately 1 out of every 3 Americans bowled that year, a larger number of people than those who voted in the 1998 congressional elections); however, unlike in the past, the vast majority of them did not bowl as part of a league. Americans are less likely to participate in formal groups than they did in the past. They are spending more time by themselves, and they are participating in fewer organizational activities. These changes have been occurring gradually over the past few decades. Importantly, however, they appear to be generational changes. For the most part, people who are over the age of 60 are as socially engaged as those who were over the age of 60 in past decades. Older Americans do not appear to be any less socially engaged. In contrast, it is the younger generations of Americans who have come to differ the most from previous generations of young Americans. That is, younger Americans appear to be more individualistic, on average, than their parents, and as the American population slowly becomes replaced with people who were born in more recent decades, the culture changes accordingly.

A key question to consider here is why are we seeing these changes? What is causing Americans to become more individualistic? Putnam has looked at a number of sources of evidence and has reached some interesting conclusions. First, there have been increasing pressures of time and money that have competed with people's time for being socially engaged. Many surveys reveal that Americans feel more financially pressed than before, even though real incomes have been rising, and time pressures have increased as two-career families have become more common. However, this is only a small piece of the puzzle—Putnam estimates its contribution to explaining American's increasing individualism to be only 10%. A second small contributor (also estimated at around 10%) is the increasing suburbanization of America, which results in people spending more time in their cars and in their homes and being less likely to run into friends and neighbors during the day. A larger culprit (approximately 25%) behind the transformation that Putnam identifies is electronic entertainment, especially television, which leads people to isolate themselves and engage in more passive ways of entertaining themselves. Interestingly, Putnam documents how the younger generations even watch TV differently from the way their parents and grandparents did, as they are more likely to turn the TV on even if there is nothing in particular that they had in mind to watch; the older generations are more likely to watch TV only when there is a particular show that they want to see. And the largest cause of this cultural change remains the most difficult to identify directly. Approximately half of the variance behind the increasing individualism rests with the different lifestyles between the younger and older generations. It is not altogether clear what causes the older generations to watch television differently from the younger ones, or for the older generations to be more socially connected than the younger ones, but Putnam proposes that living through World War II is a key factor in this generational shift. World War II united the country for a common cause more than any event since, and Putnam suggests that this critical episode changed all of those who experienced it, making them embedded in their social groups, with a sense of shared fate, that subsequent generations have not felt. Whether this single transformational experience is largely behind the dramatic generational changes in social engagement is not clear; however, at this point it is the single variable that has the most empirical support.

This trend of increasing individualism is not solely an American event. Indeed, if Putnam is correct in identifying the key culprits behind this cultural transformation as television, not having a recent national unifying event such as World War II, and to a lesser extent, increasingly suburban lifestyles and women entering the workforce, then we would expect that there would be trends of increasing individualism wherever these usual suspects are found—that is, in most industrialized and developing cultures. For example, Hamamura (2006) identified some variables to indicate changes in individualism, and he found that Japan has also shown increasing individualism over the past few decades. Hamamura looked at changes in people's ratings of col-

This cover illustration from the *New Yorker* magazine contrasting Thanksgiving dinners in 1942 and 2006 captures Putnam's arguments about cultural change in the United States.

lectivistic values (e.g., values for family and religion) and individualistic values (e.g., self-interest, the pursuit of happiness), as well as demographic changes such as the average size of households and the divorce rate. Over the past 50 years, according to these indicators, Japan has become far more individualistic. Hamamura also looked at a similar set of indicators among Americans and, like Putnam, found clear evidence that individualism has been increasing there as well. It appears that individualism has been increasing at a comparable rate in Japan as in the United States, although there remains a sizable gap in individualism between the two cultures at every point in time.

That both Japan and the United States are showing increases in individualism, and given the worldwide trend toward increasing globalization discussed earlier, it is likely that similar cultural changes are also evident in other industrialized cultures.

These changes raise the question of whether these trends will continue in the future. Is the world destined to become an increasingly individualistic environment? If technology continues to provide leisure that is socially isolating, if people continue to have too many commitments in their work and commuting to have time to be socially engaged, and if there are no more events such as World War II to lead citizens to feel a common fate with their compatriots, then this trend very well might continue for some time. Alternatively, perhaps there is a maximum degree of individualism that people can comfortably tolerate, and on reaching that point people might react and begin to reject cultural practices that decrease their social engagement. However, it is useful to remember that it was not clear before the 1960s that cultures would become increasingly individualistic, and I suspect that we are not very adept at being able to identify the future cultural changes that will occur over the next several decades.

Furthermore, as you'll see in many studies discussed throughout this book, although Japan and the United States have both become more individualistic over past decades, there are still pronounced cultural differences in their psychologies. Likewise, striking cultural differences remain in many psychological phenomena among people from cultures around the world. Despite recent growth in individualistic tendencies worldwide, cultures today remain importantly different in many ways that impact the ways we think. We'll have much to learn as cultures from around the world continue to evolve in front of us.

People in Many Cultures Are Becoming More Intelligent. One of the most remarkable findings regarding cultural change is that people seem to be getting smarter. On average, across all cultures for which there is adequate longitudinal data, people in the current generation have higher IQ scores than those from earlier generations. This trend has been dubbed the "Flynn effect" after the researcher who first identified it. A review of changes in IQ scores in 14 nations revealed that the average increase in IQ was between 5 and 25 points per generation (Flynn, 1987). Subsequent research has revealed that the pattern extends to other countries as well (Flynn, 1994). These are not trivial changes. IQ is reported in standardized scores, with a mean of 100 and a standard deviation of 15. This means that if the performance of a given sample is standardized, only about 2% have IQ scores below 70 (which is often viewed as a cutoff for a classification of mental retardation), and only about 2% have IQ scores over 130 (which is often viewed as a cutoff for being classified as "gifted"). IQ has been increasing at a rate of approximately 6 points per decade in many countries around the world. If this trend could be extended further into the past (a big if), this means that a person who is tested with an IQ of only 70 today (and is thus in the bottom 2% of the population of her contemporary peers) would be about as smart as a person who was tested with an IQ of 130 a century ago (and thus would have been in the top 2% of her peers back then). These massive gains in IQ remain controversial as people debate what IQ tests really measure.

The measurement of intelligence is one of the most contentious issues in psychology. When asked for a definition of "intelligence" the standard answer by many psychologists is to demur and say that intelligence is what intelligence tests measure. This tautological answer reflects the difficulty in identifying a universal definition of intelligence. Is one's ability to construct a kayak out of driftwood and sealskin, and use it to hunt a walrus in the darkness of an Arctic winter, a good measure of intelligence? Arguably yes, and if so, we would expect that Inuit hunters would score far higher on this intelligence test than would people from other cultural contexts. Is one's ability to solve algebraic puzzles a good measure of intelligence? This is also arguably yes, and again we would expect better performance among those who have participated in contexts with much algebraic learning. It is exceedingly difficult to conceive of intelligence outside a particular cultural context, and this makes it challenging to understand what the pattern of increasing IQ scores across generations is telling us.

As a further challenge to understanding what the Flynn effect means, not all measures of "intelligence" have been showing the same increases over time. The one striking exception to the general pattern of increasing IQ scores has been the findings that scores on the Scholastic Aptitude Test (SAT) have been *decreasing* in the United States over past decades. One argument for why SAT scores have been falling is that the SAT measures acquired knowledge: In particular, the verbal component of the SAT measures a good deal of difficult vocabulary. There is much evidence that people are reading less and are gaining more information from TV, the Internet, and computer games than in previous generations. Although TV viewing might prompt certain kinds of learning (more about this later), it does not allow for much development of vocabulary as most TV communicates at about a fourth-grade vocabulary level (Healy, 1990). If people are not reading as much today as they did in past generations, and are not developing as large a vocabulary, then their verbal SAT scores would go down (Greenfield, 1998). Some other commonly used IQ tests, such as the Wechsler, the Otis, and the CTMM, have shown moderate gains over time. However, the IQ test that shows the largest amount of increase across time is the Raven's Matrices, which was originally developed as a "culture-free" measure of IQ, as it doesn't require any specific cultural knowledge or language skills. An example of the type of questions on the test is included below (Figure 2.3; answer is at the end of the chapter). To answer the question, the test taker must choose which of the six numbered alternatives best fits into the bottom right corner of the matrix. Raven's Matrices is thus often viewed as the purest measure of intelligence, although the fact that cultures of recent decades score higher on it than those cultures of past decades reveals that it is by no means "culture-free" (see Greenfield, 1998, for more discussion on this). Performance on the Raven's Matrices involves basic problem-solving skills and this is where people seem to be making the most increases. Why would that be?

A number of different accounts have been proposed for this increase in IQ. One argument is that IQ is a proxy for health, as one can develop a fully

FIGURE 2.3

A simulated item from the Raven's Matrices IQ test.

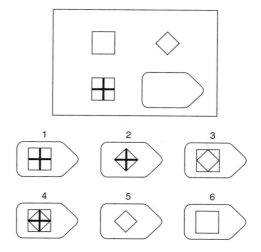

functioning mind only with adequate nutrition. Hence, it follows that as dietary nutrition has improved around the world, accordingly so has IQ (Lynn, 1989). However, evidence for improvements of nutrition around the world do not closely parallel those of IQ gains, rendering this account incapable of explaining much of the global increase in IQ (Flynn, 1999).

Another argument is that the world is becoming a far more complex place than it used to be, and navigating it successfully requires much learning and practice with demanding problem-solving tasks, which ultimately influences one's intelligence. One indicator of the increasing complexity of the world is represented in the amount of education that is necessary to get a good job. Of men born in 1890 in the United States, only 27% of them had more than an eighth-grade education, and only 9% of them had any schooling after high school (Goldin, 1998; only male data are provided, as at this time relatively few women entered the workforce). In contrast, according to the 2000 census, the percentage of Americans between the ages of 25 and 34 (both men and women) who had more than an eighth-grade education was approximately 95%; 58% had some schooling after high school, and approximately 7% have post-graduate degrees (U.S. Census Bureau, 2000). The percentage of 25-year-olds with a bachelor's degree has increased consistently across decades (see Figure 2.4). Similar trends hold for post-graduate degrees: for example, the number of PhDs granted per year at Canadian universities increased by 64% from 1988 to 1998 (Statistics Canada, 2001). Whereas most

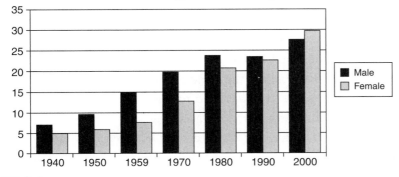

FIGURE 2.4

The percentage of the U.S. population with at least a Bachelor's degree has steadily increased over the past century, with particularly notable increases among women.

adults got by with less than an eighth-grade education in the early part of the 20th century, today, most adults get by with some college education, and an ever-growing proportion are getting post-graduate degrees. As the world becomes increasingly complex, succeeding in it requires understanding in a broader array of domains, and this is facilitated by education. Most likely, this trend toward increasing average levels of education will continue for some time. Importantly, however, the increasing number of years of higher education by itself cannot account for the overall increase in IQ as IQ has also been rising among those who do not go on to higher education.

Another argument for the effect that increasing complexity has on people's growing intelligence comes from an unlikely source: pop culture. The key proponent of this view, Steven Johnson, argues that popular culture has become progressively more complex and challenging over the past half century (Johnson, 2005). For example, he notes that television dramas of the 1950s, such as the police drama *Dragnet*, consisted of a single story line that Sergeant Joe Friday pursued from the beginning scene to the very end. Each scene built on the subsequent one, and the viewer had to follow only one story. Watching *Dragnet* was not a very challenging exercise and, arguably, did little in developing one's intelligence. In contrast, Johnson argues that since that time many of the programs on television have become steadily more complex. For example, the hit HBO drama *The Sopranos* involves more than 20 recurring characters who are typically involved in about a dozen different story lines per episode, some of which are connected to events that happened in previous seasons. Likewise, many other shows, such as *24*, *West Wing*, and *ER*, are equally complex. To be sure, there is still no shortage of mindless offerings on television today (case in point: *Dancing with the Stars*). However, Johnson makes a good case that the average program broadcast today has grown progressively more complex than the average programs of previous generations, and that even the mindless offerings of today's programs are more complex than the mindless ones of the 1950s. Furthermore, electronic entertainment is not limited to television, and there has been an evolution in the complexity of video games as well. I grew up playing *Space Invaders*, a game in which one could choose between moving left or moving right while shooting at a grid of descending blobs (aliens, I guess) before they shot you. There is no comparison between the complexity of *Space Invaders* and the complexity of many video games today, such as *Half-Life*, *Civilization*, or *Zelda*. For example, Johnson notes that the game *Grand Theft*

Auto III has a walk-through, which explains how to play the game, that is 53,000 words long—about one-third the length of this textbook. In addition to the visceral thrills of shooting at opponents or trying to run over them, playing video games involves a lot of problem-solving skills and very complex plots. The increasing complexity of popular games and television programs shows that people are demanding greater challenges from their entertainment. If Johnson's thesis is correct, the complexity of our entertainment is making us smarter, and that is leading us to demand more challenging entertainment, which further develops our problem-solving skills.

In sum, in every culture for which there are good longitudinal data on intelligence tests, IQ scores have been rising over past decades, in particular for tests from the Raven's Matrices. As of yet, there is no widely accepted explanation for this increase, but it most certainly reflects some kind of change in the cultural environments in which people are participating.

In the Face of Change, How Do Cultures Persist?

As discussed above, cultures are highly fluid and continue to change across time. Perhaps the more remarkable fact, then, is that even with this fluidity, cultures also have an enduring tendency to persist over time. That is, once cultural habits get established, many of them remain entrenched across generations, despite the great amount of change that those generations encounter. The notion that cultures can persist over time is central to many of the key theories that are discussed later in this book (e.g., see Nisbett & Cohen, 1996; Nisbett, Peng, Choi, & Norenzayan, 2001; Weber, 1904/1992). These theories propose that cultures have surprising abilities to retain much of their shape and many of their characteristics across centuries.

There is much evidence that cultures persist a great deal across time (see Cohen, 2001; Richerson & Boyd, 2005). For example, in medieval Italy the northern regions had a number of egalitarian institutions (e.g., guilds, neighborhood associations) whereas the southern regions did not. During that time the south of Italy was ruled by Norman kings in an autocratic manner that engendered much corruption and distrust among families. A highly centralized Italian state was created in the 1870s, and the same laws and reforms were applied across all of Italy. However, since then, northern Italian regions have built powerful and competent regional government organizations, whereas the southern regions have made comparatively little progress and remain the least civic regions of the country (Putnam, Leonardi, & Nanetti, 1993). Regional differences in Italy today thus mirror the differences that were present 800 years ago.

An example of cultural persistence for a psychological characteristic can be seen by contrasting people from various countries around the world with the descendants of immigrants to the United States from those same countries. For example, how similar are the experiences of Swedes living in Sweden to the experiences of Swedish Americans? Does the culture of one's ancestors shape how people think today? One domain in which this question has been explored is with respect to **subjective well-being**. Subjective well-being is the feeling of how satisfied one is with one's life. There is much evidence for striking cultural variability in the average levels of subjective well-being reported by people from different countries. For example, among European nations, Scandinavian nations score particularly high in their citizens' average level of well-being, whereas eastern European nations score rather low, and many central European nations fall in between. We'll return to discuss and make sense of cultural differences in subjective well-being in Chapter 8, Emotions. How well are these cultural differences in subjective well-being preserved in the descendants of immigrants to the United States from those countries? This question was explored by contrasting the well-being scores of people who were born in America and who reported a single ethnic identity with the average well-being scores of various countries around the world (Rice & Steele, 2004). The research revealed two notable things. First, there was much less variability among the various American samples than among the samples from different countries around the world. Not surprisingly, people who were born and raised in the United States share many similar cultural experiences, and this leads them to have somewhat similar well-being scores. Second, despite the fact that the range of well-being scores among the American samples was much narrower than that of the international samples, there was still a clear pattern among the American samples. There was a strikingly large positive correlation (r = .62) between the average well-being scores for American ethnic groups and the well-being scores for the countries from which those ethnic groups were originally descended. That is, Americans of Scandinavian descent tended to have the highest well-being scores, followed by Americans of central European descent, and followed by Americans of eastern European descent. Furthermore, this pattern remained even after statistically controlling for any variation in socioeconomic status, age, education, and a number of other variables. Apparently, people learn cultural traditions from their families that affect their well-being and these are passed down through the generations, even after their ancestors have moved to the United States. The ways that people think thus are not just due to the influence of the mainstream culture with which they interact, but they are also influenced by cultural traditions of their ancestors, some of which might date back many generations. This is a striking example of cultural persistence.

Cultural Innovations Build on Previous Structures. Why should aspects of culture persist across time, especially as people from those cultures face new challenges, technological innovations, and historical changes? An exploration of the biological evolution of species can illuminate one reason that cultural elements have a tendency to persist. The evolution of new species is constrained by traits of the ancestors from which those species evolved. For example, bats are small mammals that evolved a number of particular adaptations, including wings. The wings did not grow out of nothing, rather, bats' wings emerged from a series of gradual adaptations over the evolutionary record as their forelimbs became more and more adapted to flight until they became fully functioning wings and rather useless arms. It was a far more straightforward process to have a series of incremental adaptations leading arms to evolve into wings than it would have been for wings to have somehow grown, say, out of the backs of bats. This underscores a critical point about biological evolution: Adaptations are constrained by previously existing structures. If you were to design a flying mammal from scratch you might very well want to create a bat that had both wings *and* arms. A bat with arms would appear to be a more effective bat as it could carry its prey or hold its offspring. But with evolution you don't start from scratch; you are always making very small adjustments to a preexisting set of circumstances, and those circumstances influence the evolutionary path that is followed.

Likewise, cultures do not emerge out of a vacuum. The thread of every cultural innovation must be woven into an existing web of beliefs and practices. The culture of 21st-century America grew out of the culture of 20th-century America, which grew out of the culture of the 19th century, and so on. Along the way, American culture evolved from the cultures of the first settlements and adapted to a set of emerging ideas, technological innovations,

Although Japanese baseball has the same rules as American baseball, it has been shaped by traditional Japanese attitudes about self-discipline.

continuing migrations of people, and responses to a series of particular historical events. We can be confident that 22nd-century American culture will in many ways be different from 21st-century American culture. However, these future changes will be modifications to the preexisting cultural foundation rather than a new culture cut from whole cloth, and in many ways one can confidently predict that 22nd-century America will remain distinctively American. Existing cultural habits influence and constrain the evolution of new cultural habits.

For example, consider the game of Japanese baseball. Baseball was imported into Japan from the United States in the late 19th century. Japanese and American baseball use the same rulebook; however, as former Los Angeles Dodger Reggie Smith said after playing his first season as a Tokyo Giant, "This isn't baseball; it only looks like it." Robert Whiting (1990) describes the many differences between Japanese and American baseball in his book, *You Gotta Have Wa*. Indigenous Japanese sports were traditionally the martial arts (e.g., sumo, kendo, judo, karate)—activities dedicated to self-discipline and the refinement of the human spirit. Baseball was a foreign import to Japan that was grafted onto this existing culture, and the echoes of the indigenous sports remain. For example, training camp for professional baseball in the United States starts in the spring, and consists of 3 to 4 hours of practice a day, typically in a southern locale such as Florida, with much time for swimming and golf in between. In contrast, Japanese training camp is held in the frigid winter; players typically are on the field for 7 hours, run approximately 10 miles a day, and then return to the dormitory for strategy sessions and indoor workouts. As Warren Cromartie, a former player for the Montreal Expos and Tokyo Giants, stated when describing Japanese training camp, "It makes boot camp look like a church social." Also, in comparison with its American counterpart, Japanese baseball involves far more plays in which the individual makes a sacrifice for the benefit of the team, such as the sacrifice bunt, and teams work to prevent members of the other team from losing face, such as avoiding three pitch strikeouts or extremely lopsided victories. Even though the games are played by the same set of rules, Japanese and American baseball reflect the respective cultural backgrounds from which they have evolved.

Early Conditions Have Disproportionate Influence on Cultural Evolution. Because cultures evolve from their past circumstances, the early conditions of a culture matter a great deal with respect to how cultures subsequently evolve. Just as if you were to start off on a long journey by foot, the direction that you took in your first few steps would determine your path more than the direction that you took in your last few steps, the early conditions of a culture likewise have greater influence in shaping a culture's long-term evolution than do later conditions. The critical role of early conditions is one important reason that cultural differences can persist across time. Although people from cultures from around the world are encountering many similar experiences in this age of globalization, each culture is following a path with a distinctive origin. These distinctive origins preserve many cultural differences across time.

We can see much evidence for the significance of early settlements by contrasting different regions within the United States that were settled by different populations (for an excellent discussion of this see Fischer, 1989). For example, in the 17th century, Boston was settled largely by Puritans whereas Philadelphia was settled largely by Quakers. Although these were both Protestant sects that shared many similarities, there were also some key differences in the views of Puritans and Quakers. Puritanism emphasized the importance of applying one's wealth and social position to community goals, and respect for authority. Furthermore, many of the original Puritans who first settled in Massachusetts were highly educated intellectuals (including over 100 graduates from Oxford and Cambridge), and they felt that their dream to form a utopian society could emerge only from an educated population. In contrast, Quakerism placed more emphasis on pragmatic concerns, individual equality, and tolerance. The sociologist Digby Baltzell (1979) argues that the differences in these early settlements have led to distinct cultural contrasts between Boston and Philadelphia that continue to this day. For example, the two oldest and most prestigious schools in the two cities, Harvard and the University of Pennsylvania, have reflected their respective origins. Harvard was originally built on a liberal arts curriculum, emphasized public service, and received tremendous community and financial support. In contrast, the University of Pennsylvania emphasized a more utilitarian curriculum with medical, business, and engineering schools dominating the university; public service received relatively little emphasis (an example is how few political leaders have graduated from the University of Pennsylvania); and the school received little community or financial support from a Quaker culture that had little trust in the value of higher education. Likewise, Baltzell argues that Boston's culture has maintained an elitism and a respect for authority that trace to its Puritan roots, whereas Philadelphia's culture has remained distrustful of authority and hard to govern, yet tolerant of diversity. Despite the fact that only a small minority of citizens in Boston or Philadelphia today are direct descendants of their cities' original Puritan and Quaker ancestors, and relatively few continue to practice Puritan or Quaker faiths, the cultures of both cities have continued to persist since they were first founded by European settlers. All people who were subsequently born in, or immigrated to, Boston and Philadelphia have needed to adjust themselves to the prevailing cultural traditions, and this has perpetuated the distinctive cultures.

Researchers have tried to isolate the effects of initial conditions on the development of cultural norms by studying changing norms in the laboratory. In one study, participants entered a completely dark room in groups of four people (Jacobs & Campbell, 1961). These four people were tested to see whether they would form any kind of microculture that persisted across time. Their task was to look at a small light on the opposite wall and to report how far they thought the light moved. The light was actually attached to the wall, so any perceived movement was entirely illusory and a product of the **autokinetic effect**. The autokinetic effect is caused by the involuntary saccadic movements of our eyes which, in the dark, create the illusion of movement. The task was set up so that people reported out loud how much they saw the light move. The first person to report was a confederate of the experiment, and he reported that the light had moved 16 inches, which is considerably more than the amount of movement that the average person tested alone reports (mean of 3.8 inches). There is much ambiguity in this task, so people tend to conform to other people's reported judgments—in this way, norms develop among groups with regard to how much they believe the light is moving. After the confederate reported 16 inches most of the other members of the group also begin to "see" the light move at about 16 inches. In sum, a microculture is produced where four people have adapted to a norm of seeing the light move about 16 inches. At the end of the trial, in which everyone has reported how much he or she saw the light move, one person would leave the room (the first person to leave the room was the confederate) and be replaced by a new participant. After four trials, then, the group has a completely different membership from what it had started with, as all four members would have been replaced with new people. This continues on for 11 generations, resulting in a total of 11 different microcultures of four people each, with each microculture having a slightly different membership from the previous one. The experimenters wanted to see how long the confederate's initial report would continue to influence the subsequent participants. Although the estimates began to gradually drift toward the mean of the control group (i.e., 3.8 inches), the influence of the confederate's judgment persisted for five generations after he or she had left. Even though there were no longer any members from the original group who had been exposed to the confederate's rather large estimate, people continued to see the light as moving more than those who were tested by themselves. Initial conditions thus do indeed influence later generations, although their effects can diminish over time. A weakness of this particular study is that these experimental "cultures" are very different from ones in real life, as in them a few strangers have only the most limited of interactions with regard to an unusual task and for a short period of time. One would expect that the effects of initial conditions would persist more if people participated in the cultures for a longer period of time, as they do in real life.

Initial conditions thus have lasting effects on cultural norms. Sometimes, these small variations in the early stages of the development of a culture can have a cascading influence that comes to shape aspects of a culture that are quite far removed from the initial conditions. For example, research on dynamical systems (a branch of mathematics) maintains that very minute differences at the beginning of a process can ultimately lead to an enormous effect much further down the line (for a thorough review see Cohen, 2001). The prototypical example of a dynamical system is the "butterfly effect"—the notion that a butterfly flapping its wings on the Great Wall of China can ultimately lead to a tornado over Texas (Gleick, 1987). Small changes in initial conditions can sometimes have far-reaching consequences. This also remains true for cultures. Consider the example that Harry Triandis provides for the cultural consequences of the existence of tsetse flies in parts of Africa.

> Because the flies decimate the herds, it is difficult to keep cattle. With no herds it is difficult for babies to obtain milk. As a result, mothers feed their infants their own milk. Since women do not lactate if they become pregnant, this results in a long postpartum sex taboo—women are not supposed to have sex with their husbands for three years after giving birth. But, then, what will the men do? That makes polygyny functional! In turn, polygyny results in children's sleeping in the same bed with their mothers until they are quite old. Male children thus become very attached to their mothers and so do not learn the male roles very well. To overcome this, the cultures develop severe initiation ceremonies that clearly separate the "child" from the "adult" male. (Triandis, 1994, p. 23)

According to this proposed chain of events, gender roles and the nature of initiation ceremonies are all determined by the presence of tiny tsetse flies! Small causes can lead to large effects much later on. However, given the complexity of cultures it remains impossible to confidently predict all the effects that will emerge from a single variable, such as the presence of tsetse flies.

Pluralistic Ignorance. Here is an interesting finding: Students at Princeton stated that they believed that most others at their school approved of the large quantities of alcohol that were regularly consumed at campus events. However, that same survey revealed that most students themselves said that they were not so comfortable with the amount of alcohol being consumed (Prentice & Miller, 1996). If people were accurate in assessing others' feelings toward alcoholic consumption, then we would expect that people's self-assessments averaged across the sample would be similar to the average of their assessments of other people's feelings toward alcohol. That there was a difference indicates a bias: Why would people assume that others have more liberal attitudes toward heavy drinking than they themselves do?

This is an example of pluralistic ignorance, and this is a mechanism that further leads to cultural persistence. **Pluralistic ignorance** is the tendency for people to collectively misinterpret the thoughts that underlie other people's behaviors. Often we try to figure out how others are thinking, but really, all we have to go on is what people tell us or observations of how they behave. We can be pretty accurate in inferring others' thoughts when people's statements or behaviors accurately reflect their private thoughts. For example, if I tell you I don't like olives, it would be quite reasonable for you to assume that my private feelings toward olives are similarly negative. I have no reason to mislead you about my feelings for olives. However, in other kinds of situations, people's behaviors and statements are not accurate reflections of their thoughts. Some kinds of behaviors or statements are socially desirable—that is, others think more positively of us if we say desirable things. People are likely to make socially desirable statements as they wish to maintain a positive impression. In the case of the Princeton students, people assumed that their own private thoughts of being uncomfortable with the amount of alcoholic consumption were more conservative than their fellow students' opinions. This bias exists because people apparently feel it is socially undesirable to publicly express that their classmates are drinking too much, so such thoughts are rarely stated publicly. On the other hand, thoughts that it is fun to drink to excess appear to be more socially desirable and are more regularly stated, which yields a false impression of a consensus that students like to drink to abandon. Because some thoughts are more likely to be publicly expressed than others, people come to collectively misrepresent what other people's true feelings are.

Interestingly, the precise opposite case of pluralistic ignorance existed in the U.S. in the early 20th century. During that time Prohibition was in effect, a legal ban on the public sale and consumption of alcohol. Prohibition never had majority support, but it *seemed* to have public support as few people were willing to publicly argue in favor of keeping alcohol legal, apparently because open support of alcohol was socially undesirable at that time. Once polls were conducted and clear evidence was collected on the strength of anti-Prohibition feelings, the pluralistic ignorance was eliminated and Prohibition came to an abrupt end (Katz & Schnack, 1938). Other examples of pluralistic ignorance that currently exist in college student samples are that people believe their peers are more interested in "hooking up" than they are (Lambert, Kahn, & Apple, 2003), and that people believe others hold more politically correct beliefs than they do (Van Boven, 2000). These biases exist because it tends to be socially desirable on some college campuses to talk about hooking up and to espouse politically correct views.

Pluralistic ignorance is relevant to cultural persistence because people are influenced by what they *believe* other people feel rather than by what other people *actually* feel. If I think that I'm the only one who is uncomfortable about the amount of drinking on campus, then I am likely to be shy about expressing my concern and may go along with others and drink excessively myself, thereby further contributing to the misconception and perpetuating the drinking culture. Through the mechanisms of pluralistic ignorance a culture that includes the practice of heavy drinking on campus can thus come to persist even when a majority of people privately do not endorse the practice themselves.

Furthermore, people's willingness to openly discuss certain topics is not just a matter of social desirability. In some cultural contexts, particularly those with totalitarian governments, there can be significant risks for openly discussing some topics. It is likely that in such contexts there will be even less congruence between what people say and what they privately think, and thus there should be greater degrees of cultural persistence (Cohen, 2001). A disturbing example of pluralistic ignorance was identified by Hannah Arendt in her controversial analysis of the rise of National Socialism in Germany (Arendt, 1964). Arendt viewed the extensive German cooperation with National Socialism to be caused not by evil motives but by thoughtlessness and mass conformity (Cohen, 2001). In Nazi Germany it seemed safer to go along with the fascist crowd than to risk speaking publicly against the growing horrors. As long as everyone else seemed to be in support of the actions of the Third Reich, people collectively convinced each other that they were pursuing the right tack, and the culture persisted until it met an abrupt and violent end in World War II.

The correct answer to the Ravens Matrix item (p. 78) is 2.

SUMMARY

Cultures are not fixed entities but continually evolve over time. Norms that were common a generation ago are not necessarily common any more.

Cultures vary, and it is challenging to understand where the variation comes from. One source of variation is from the geographic environment. Different environments afford different subsistence patterns, and these can lead to different cultural practices. Sometimes what might appear to be minor geographic variants can lead to large cultural differences.

Cultural variability emerges through one of two mechanisms. Transmitted culture is the process by which one learns a cultural idea from another. Evoked culture is the notion that some behavioral responses are universally available to people, but they only become engaged when appropriate triggering conditions are present.

Cultural evolution occurs when ideas change across time. There are many similarities between biological evolution and cultural evolution and they are analogous. Biological evolution is possible because it involves replicators (genes) that have longevity, fecundity, and fidelity. One theory holds that cultural evolution has replicators that are called memes, which also have longevity and fecundity, although there is poor fidelity with their replication. The epidemiological perspective argues that cultural ideas do not replicate, but individuals re-create their own mental representations of ideas when they learn of them.

Cultural ideas are most likely to spread if they are communicated, if they involve strong emotions, and if the ideas are largely intuitive, with a few unexpected elements.

In the past few decades, many cultures have been changing around the world in similar ways. There is evidence that cultures are becoming more interconnected, that individualism is growing in industrialized countries, and that average IQ levels have been increasing.

Although cultures are always changing, many elements and patterns persist over time. Cultural evolution involves changes to preexisting conditions, so early conditions of a culture can have a large influence on how cultures evolve over time. Pluralistic ignorance is one mechanism that also leads cultures to persist across time.

3

Methods for Studying Culture and Psychology

What do you do if you want to study how culture influences the ways that people think? Consider what happened when the cultural psychologist Patricia Greenfield tried to study the psychology of the Zinacantecans, an indigenous people living in Mexico. She wanted to interview the Zinacantecans to find out about their experiences in textile production (see Greenfield, 1997). She went about interviewing the Zinacantecans using the same kinds of surveys that have been validated many times with Western, largely college-educated, populations. But these same surveys didn't work so well with the Zinacantecans. One implicit understanding that is involved with survey methodology is that each of the questions is independent; the different questions do not necessarily take on the form of a conversation. Researchers rely on this convention, and the result of it is that one standard methodological technique used in survey research is to ask participants a number of items that vary slightly about the same issue. A measure of extraversion, for example, typically does not have just one item but more often a dozen or more items that all assess the extent to which one acts in extraverted ways. There are psychometric benefits for asking people similar questions over and over again (this reduces concerns with random error, and ensures that people's responses are with respect to the underlying construct and not to various tangential aspects of each item). Zinacantecans, however, approached Greenfield's survey with an expectation that their interaction would follow their conversational norms: that is, when you give an answer to someone's question, the questioner then doesn't just ignore your answer and go ahead and ask another question that sounds almost the same as before. Greenfield found that her standard, ordinarily methodologically sound, interview technique just seemed to make her Zinacantecan participants angry, as if they couldn't understand how she could be so stupid as to keep asking the same question over and over again!

As this one example demonstrates, psychologists are often in a difficult position. Our object of study is the mind, which, fascinating as it is to study, is a black box that doesn't reveal itself to us readily. It is extremely challenging to collect sound and compelling evidence for psychological phenomena, as these are by nature elusive, abstract, and invisible. With current technology we still know strikingly little about how specific psychological phenomena are produced and represented in the brain (although we are making great progress).

Consider the challenge of trying to understand our own thought processes. It would seem that if anyone should know about what's going on inside someone's head, it would be the owner of that head. However, much of our own psychological experience occurs completely beyond our awareness. For example, research has revealed that we often don't really know how we feel (Schacter & Singer, 1962), what we have remembered (Loftus, 1993), whether we've enjoyed a task (Festinger, 1957), or the reasons we like something (Nisbett & Wilson, 1977). It is for these reasons that experimental psychologists rarely investigate psychological processes by asking their subjects directly about their experiences. People are usually able to come up with answers to such questions, answers that they often are quite convinced are true, but research reveals, in many situations, that people's answers can be outright wrong.

If we don't have good access to our own psychological experiences, consider how much more difficult it is to try to discern someone else's psychological experiences. What is your roommate thinking about right now? What did she mean when she said that your fashion sense was "unique"? Has she really forgiven you for the time she thought you were flirting with her boyfriend? We're often skating on thin ice in trying to confidently assess what is going on in the minds of others. The problem for cultural psychologists is that these difficulties are multiplied many times over when trying to understand the minds of people from another culture.

The goal of this chapter is to learn how to design studies to study culture and psychology. How can we go about investigating how people think in cultures that are different from our own? Below I list some methodological concerns that are inherent in the study of people from other cultures (see Cohen, in press, for a more detailed review). Although some of these concerns seem particularly daunting, you'll see that, with appropriate consideration, creativity, and efforts, we are able to surmount them, gathering compelling data that give us a very nice perspective on what exactly is going on in the heads of people from other cultures.

The study of culture and psychology touches clearly on the two central themes that guide this book. First, the goal of many cultural studies is either to demonstrate similarities across cultures in the ways that people think (thereby reflecting universal psychological tendencies) or to demonstrate cultural differences (thereby reflecting culturally shaped psychological tendencies). Second, for those ways of thinking in which cultural differences emerge, many studies are designed with the express purpose of understanding how people's different experiences in their cultures resulted in their different ways of thinking. How do people's experiences shape the ways that they think?

Considerations for Conducting Research Across Cultures

Studying people from other cultures involves some issues that are unique compared with those involved in studying people from one's own culture. Because the study of culture's influence on psychological processes cuts across virtually all subfields of human psychology, researchers often utilize methods that are commonly used in the study of those subfields. For example, people studying culture and personality tend to rely on the methods of the personality psychologist, the study of culture and cognition utilizes methods from the field of cognitive psychology, the study of culture and mental health borrows from the methods of clinical psychology, and so on. Each of these methods has its own strengths and weaknesses. As David Funder (2007) emphasizes, psychological data are only clues, and clues are always ambiguous. The problem for cultural psychologists is that not only do they inherit the standard ambiguities of whatever methods they adopt from other subfields of psychology, but that many of these methods create further ambiguities when they are applied to the study of people from other cultures (Cohen, in press). In this chapter I will describe various strategies by which researchers can improve their ability to assess the psychological states of people from other cultures.

What Cultures Should We Study? There are thousands of different cultures around the world. How can one go about deciding which ones to study? In general, it's not recommended to employ a "shotgun" method to studying cultures and to randomly select the cultures that you are studying. Although such an approach might reveal some unexpected cultural differences, it can be very difficult to interpret the results if there is no theory guiding the selection of the cultures. Rather, you will more likely find meaningful and easy-to-interpret results if you let your research question guide your choice of your research samples.

One common approach for selecting cultures is to choose samples based on a theoretical variable that you are investigating. For example, if you are interested in exploring how collectivism shapes the ways people view their relationships, then your research would fare well by selecting cultures that clearly differ in terms of their collectivism. If you contrast how people view their relationships between two cultures that vary in their degree of collectivism, and you find a significant cultural difference, then you would have some preliminary evidence to suggest that collectivism shapes how people view their relationships. You could then follow up that research with some other strategies that are discussed later in this chapter. Alternatively, if you found no difference in terms of how people view their relationships between two cultures that vary in their collectivism, then this would suggest that collectivism and people's views of relationships are unrelated. One good way to choose your samples, then, is to look for cultures that vary on a specific theoretical dimension of interest, such as collectivism.

Sometimes you might be interested in exploring the degree of universality of a particular psychological finding. Is a particular way of thinking peculiar to North American culture, or does it characterize the way of thinking of humans everywhere? A good first step would be to select two cultures that vary greatly on as many theoretically relevant dimensions as possible, such as language, geography, philosophical traditions, level of education, or social practices. If there is similarity in a particular psychological process between two cultures that are maximally different, then this would be compelling evidence that there is a high degree of universality for that process. For example, as we discussed in Chapter 1, humans are unique in developing a rich theory of mind, and they do so at a young age. Is the development of a rich theory of mind a product of having participated in a complex industrialized culture, or is this something that emerges in all human contexts? One study explored this question by examining how two sets of children did on a measure of a "theory of mind," contrasting Western children with Baka children, members of a pygmy people who live in the rainforests of southeast Cameroon (Avis & Harris, 1991). The Baka are nonliterate hunter-gatherers with little or no exposure to Western philosophical ideas, so the Baka and Western children represent sharply divergent cultural contexts. Despite this great difference between the cultures, children performed extremely similarly on the experimental tasks, suggesting that the development of a theory of mind is highly similar across the world—it is a good example of an accessibility universal. The researchers were able to make a convincing case for the universality of a theory of mind by selecting cultures that differed maximally from each other.

Making Meaningful Comparisons Across Cultures. After one has selected the cultures to study, it is critical that the researcher design a study so that the results can be meaningfully interpreted. What kinds of steps should a researcher take to ensure that the research findings provide a fair contrast of the cultures under study?

Develop Some Knowledge About the Cultures Under Study. For the most part, psychologists in many other fields have one key advantage over cultural psychologists in that they are studying people who are usually from their own culture and thus are likely to think in ways similar to themselves. They can thus rely on a healthy dose of introspection, everyday observations, and their intuitions to guide their development of theories and hypotheses. Cultural psychologists, in contrast, are often studying people who are of a different culture from that of the researcher, and it is not always clear how much the researcher's own experiences would generalize to the people she is studying. Consider the following example described by Richard Shweder (1997, p. 155), regarding what can happen if researchers study a culture with which they lack familiarity.

> A team of psychologists from Scandinavia was doing comparative research [on] variations in the "universal" family meal. They wired ahead to a prominent local psychologist in this rural area of India and asked him to arrange for a family meal. . . . Being civil and polite, he did so, without ever telling them that in rural India there is no such thing as a family meal. The Scandinavian research team spent a few days in the area. The local psychologist convinced some family to sit down at a table together and food was served and they were filmed. But everyone was uncomfortable. Avoidance relationships were being

violated. People kept getting up from the table and leaving. No one ever explained to the visitors that family meals should not be presumed to be part of some universal grid. They returned home, coded the materials, and made some sort of inference about what was going on, without really ever understanding what was really going on.

The moral of this story is to make sure you know something about what you are studying! In this example, it is difficult to draw any meaningful conclusions about Indian family meals because they don't really exist in the context they were studied. Had the researchers had more knowledge about the culture they were studying prior to investigating it, they would have been able to conduct their research in a far more effective way. Thus, what should always be the initial step in studying people from other cultures is to first learn something about the culture under study. A little bit of knowledge can go a long way in avoiding costly and embarrassing mistakes.

One can learn about another culture in a variety of ways. Perhaps the simplest way is to read existing texts and ethnographies about the culture under study. Ethnographies usually contain rich descriptions of a culture, or a particular situation or group of people within a culture, derived from extensive observation and interaction by an anthropologist. We can learn an extraordinary amount from the rich cultural detail provided in ethnographies. Moreover, in most cases the kinds of data derived from ethnographies is complementary to the kinds of data that are collected by the more empirical and hypothesis-driven methods of psychologists—such as the methods that I describe in the other chapters of this book. Given the challenges inherent in studying psychology within another culture it would seem that researchers would be at a distinct disadvantage if they did not have access to the vivid cultural detail that is provided in ethnographies. However, learning about a culture through books and ethnographies limits you to learning about the ideas that the author felt were relevant, and this might not shed too much light on the phenomena that you are interested in studying. Moreover, much of what is described through ethnographic observation is information that is filtered through the ethnographer's own peculiar set of beliefs, biases, and values. There are many instances in which two ethnographers describe the same culture in strikingly different ways (e.g., Freeman, 1983; Mead, 1928).

Another approach is to find a collaborator who is from the culture that you are studying and who is interested in pursuing the same research with you. The more involved your collaborator is in the project, the more likely you are to avoid the situation that happened to the researchers studying the Indian family dinner. Much research in cultural psychology is conducted in collaboration between people who are from the cultures they are studying. For example, the study of cultural psychology received a tremendous boost when the American social psychologist Hazel Markus compared notes with the Japanese social psychologist Shinobu Kitayama and realized that there were significant and meaningful gaps in the ways that the self-concept appeared in their respective cultures (Markus & Kitayama, 1991). Much important cross-cultural research would likely never be conducted if researchers did not collaborate across cultures.

Alternatively, another effective strategy is to immerse yourself in another culture to learn it firsthand. This is an excellent way to gain a rich understanding of another culture, but it can be very time-consuming and costly. In my own case, much of my cross-cultural research has explored ways of thinking in Japan, and this research has been enormously aided by the experiences that I had living in Japan for two years prior to starting graduate school, and again living there as a researcher while I was conducting many of the studies. To this day, my research plans are still shaped by things that I observed while living in Japan. There is no substitute for firsthand experience.

Some combination of the above strategies is probably the optimal way to learn about other cultures. It can take much time to develop a rich understanding of a culture; however, such efforts to ensure that one's research is culturally informed are important for conducting successful studies.

Contrasting Highly Different Cultures Versus Similar Cultures. Are there any special considerations that need to be taken when contrasting cultures that are especially different? It might not seem obvious to you, but if you are reading this book in a course at a college or university, you are engaging in a set of culturally learned skills about acquiring knowledge. You are considering the information in this textbook from a variety of different culturally learned perspectives: You might critique some of the ideas presented here, you might try to memorize some in order to do well on an exam, you might expect to discuss the ramifications of these ideas with your instructor in class. You have learned how to go about considering and studying academic topics in textbooks. There are many cultures around the world that do not have formal systems of education, and we would expect that people from such cultures wouldn't respond to this textbook in the same way that you do. As much as I would like to think that what I have written here is universally relevant and important, I imagine that in much of the world people wouldn't have much use for this book other than using it to start a fire.

There are also culturally learned skills regarding completing surveys or participating in psychological studies. By now you have participated in countless surveys in your life; for example, when a marketing research firm calls your house, when you evaluate your instructor at the end of your courses, or when you fill out the registration card after purchasing some computer software. These kinds of experiences are common in industrialized cultures everywhere. Through such experiences you have gained much implicit knowledge about the survey process. For example, your experiences have led you to understand that when people ask your opinion on a survey they are not doing so to start a dispute with you; they are interested in your own unique opinion and they expect you to give an answer that is not necessarily the same as what your father thinks; your responses will be kept anonymous; and your response will not be met with some kind of reward or punishment based on how much the researcher agrees with you. This kind of implicit understanding of survey research by those surveyed is a prerequisite for researchers to be able to collect survey or questionnaire data. It would be meaningless to compare responses from people who have this understanding with those of respondents who did not. Hence, although the standard survey methodologies are useful for conducting cross-cultural research among people of industrialized societies who have comparable experiences, they are not of much use when exploring subsistence societies that don't share these kinds of research experiences.

Recall the difficulties Greenfield (1997) was having trying to apply survey methodology when studying Zinacantecan girls. If we are to make meaningful comparisons across cultures, our participants must understand our questions or situations in equivalent ways. Having one's methods perceived in identical ways across different cultures is termed **methodological equivalence**. A variety of statistical techniques are applied to cross-cultural studies of survey data to increase such equivalence. However, when the cultures are not comparably familiar with the research setting, ensuring methodological equivalence is a more challenging endeavor, and we have to adapt our procedures so that they are understandable in each culture we study, which sometimes results in our using a slightly different procedure in each culture

(Triandis, 1994). Some experimental control is lost when we use different procedures in the different cultures that we are comparing. There is an unavoidable trade-off in experimental control versus comparable meaning when studying extremely diverse cultures.

Because of the challenges inherent in creating methodologically equivalent studies across cultures, the vast majority of cross-cultural research has been conducted between industrialized societies: By far, the most common comparisons are between North Americans and East Asians. When cultures are similar in their familiarity with research settings we can often use the same methods between cultures. Likewise, studying college students from different cultures also lends itself to making meaningful comparisons, as students the world over tend to be familiar with many of the kinds of procedures used in psychological studies (and college students tend to be an easily accessible sample for most university researchers). Most of the studies covered in this book were conducted with such samples.

However, there can be some pronounced costs to cross-cultural studies that focus solely on targeting university students in industrialized societies. What kinds of problems do you think emerge when psychologists overemphasize students in their samples? First, there is a significant problem with **generalizability**—do the findings generalize to populations other than the samples that were studied? It is not always clear how well findings that emerge from college students will generalize to nonstudent populations. It is possible that the cultural differences exist only between student populations but might not exist between other populations, such as between elementary school children, or between elderly populations. We are less able to confidently generalize our results if we do not have much evidence from a diverse range of samples.

Second, there is a problem with the **power** of the studies. Power refers to the capability of your study to detect an effect (which is usually a cross-cultural difference in studies of culture) to the extent that such an effect really exists. Power reflects the quality of the design of your study—is your study designed so that it is sensitive enough to identify the anticipated effect? It is possible that one's hypothesis is correct but that the study has insufficient power to be able to provide support for it. In cross-cultural studies you can think of culture as the **independent variable** (i.e., the variable that is varied or manipulated), and if researchers contrast two similar cultures, they would not have as much variance in their independent variable than if they had compared two very dissimilar cultures. The more variance there is in the independent variable, the more likely one should be to detect an effect in the **dependent variable** (i.e., the variable that you measure). Students from industrialized societies share many similar experiences, so a failure to find cultural differences in a phenomenon between such populations (e.g., Japanese versus American students) does not necessarily mean that the phenomenon is not influenced by culture; it could instead mean that you don't have a powerful enough contrast to be able to detect the influences of culture. Comparisons of more divergent cultures (such as Americans versus a traditional hunting and gathering society) might reveal pronounced differences in the phenomenon. In this way, a comparison between students of industrialized societies is a rather conservative, and less powerful, investigation of the effects of culture. If cultural differences emerge with such similar samples we can often assume that the effects of culture would be at least as pronounced with more divergent samples.

Conducting Cross-Cultural Research with Surveys. One of the most common ways of conducting cross-cultural research is to employ surveys. That is, participants are asked for their responses to a series of questions, usually presented in the format of an anonymous questionnaire. There are several unique challenges to conducting survey research across cultures, which I describe below.

Translation of Questionnaire Items. One rather obvious challenge that is unique to studying cultural differences in psychology is that the research participants and the researchers often speak different languages. If you've ever traveled in a place where you don't speak the local language, and the locals don't speak your language, you've probably discovered how hard it can be sometimes to get even a concrete question answered, such as "Where is the nearest bank machine?" When dealing with topics that are far less concrete, such as emotions, values, narratives, or personality traits, these communication difficulties become even more problematic.

One potential solution for comparing cultures that you might consider is that you could avoid the difficulties associated with translating by keeping all of your materials in the original language, such as English, and only studying people who are bilingual with English and their native language. This avoids the costs and challenges associated with translating the materials; however, can you think of any problems that such a strategy entails for learning about how culture affects how people think? First, your participants will likely have poorer English skills than your translators. Our data would be meaningless if our participants did not have the requisite language skills to understand what was being asked of them. Second, one has to be concerned about whether those in a culture who have good English capabilities are representative of their cultures. It is likely that respondents from a non-English-speaking, non-Western culture who are fluent in English have had more exposure to Western things and ideas and might be more Westernized than their non-English-speaking compatriots. This would decrease the likelihood of finding cultural differences that might exist more generally in the population. Moreover, there is another problem in giving bilingual respondents materials in English and comparing their answer with those of native English speakers. As we'll see in Chapter 12, Living in Multicultural Worlds, the language that we're thinking in can greatly affect the way we're thinking. Much research has found that bilingual participants respond differently when tested in their native language and in their second language (Bond, 1983; Ross, Xun, & Wilson, 2002). For example, Sussman and Rosenfeld (1982) observed that when speaking their native languages, Venezuelans sit closer to each other than do Japanese, and Americans fall in between. However, when the participants conversed in English, they all sat about the same distance from each other, regardless of culture. Apparently, when people are responding in English, they start thinking in ways that are more characteristic of native English speakers. In general, a minimal step to take for providing a strong test of whether cultural differences exist is to translate the materials (e.g., Berry & Dasen, 1974; Cole & Scribner, 1974).

However, translating psychological materials is not as easy a task as you might expect. One demonstration of how intertwined culture and psychology are is that many psychological terms do not have equivalents in other languages. For example, there are emotion words from many languages that do not have an equivalent counterpart in English (e.g., *amae* in Japanese, *schadenfreude* in German, *fago* in Ifaluk). Likewise, many English psychological terms have no direct translation into another language: for example, there is no direct translation of the term "self-esteem" into Chinese (Miller, Wang, Sandel, & Cho, 2002). Questions such as "Do you have high self-esteem?" or "Do you regularly experience *amae*?" for example, will yield dubious results in some cultures. To allow for meaningful cross-cultural comparisons it's crucial that we ask questions that have comparable meaning across cultures.

Having an accurate translation of your psychological materials is a necessary precondition for doing good cross-cultural research. Given this necessity, it's crucial that researchers be extra cautious to ensure that their materials are translated well. How can we go about ensuring that we get a good translation? My favored approach is to be sure that at least one of the primary investigators on a project is fully bilingual in the languages that are being compared. This person is then in a very good position to assess whether the materials are capturing the subtle nuances of the intentions of the research questions. Psychological meanings are complex and many of the nuances can easily be lost in translation unless a translator has a rich understanding of what the questions are asking. A bilingual investigator will be able to compare the translated materials with the originals and will be in a good position to assess whether the translations are accurate. In the field of professional translations

The Perils of Translation: Examples of Translations Gone Wrong	
Chinese hotel	Notice: Please don't accept strangler's invitation, so as not to be cheated.
Chinese store	Please don't touch yourself. Let us help you to try out.
Cambodian hotel	Wishing you "Bong Voyage."
Hong Kong bathroom	For keeping the toilet clean and tidy, please dump at the dust bin.
Japanese street	When carrying a parasol, please be careful to get in the way of other people around you.
Japanese drug store	We make up prescriptions.
Bucharest hotel lobby	The lift is being fixed for the next day. During that time we regret that you will be unbearable.
Paris hotel elevator	Please leave your values at the front desk.
Athens hotel	Visitors are expected to complain at the office between the hours of 9 and 11 am daily.
Japanese hotel	You are invited to take advantage of the chambermaid.
Paris dress shop	Dresses for street walking.
German campground	It is strictly forbidden on our black forest camping site that people of different sex, for instance, men and women, live together in one tent unless they are married with each other for that purpose.
Hotel bar in Tokyo	Special cocktails for the women with nuts.
Soviet weekly newspaper	There will be a Moscow Exhibition of Arts by 15,000 Soviet Republic painters and sculptors. These were executed over the past two years.
Majorcan shop	Here speeching American.

Samples from Lederer, 1987, and www.engrish.com.

this is the most commonly used method (Wilss, 1982). This process is further improved if a number of the primary investigators are bilingual so that they can discuss any of the most problematic translations in order to resolve them through consensus. There will always be a number of problematic phrases or words that require discussion between the translators and the investigators to ensure that the literal meaning is captured and that the translations do not sound awkward or unnatural.

In many instances, however, it's impossible for researchers to secure collaborators who are both fluent in the languages of interest and intimately involved with the project. In this situation the researcher is somewhat at the mercy of the translators. It's a bit too much of a blind leap of faith to hope that whatever translator has been hired has captured the nuances of the meanings included in the materials. A strategy that can reduce the size of this leap of faith is to use the **back-translation** method (e.g., Brislin, 1970). Here's how it works. Imagine that you want to compare Americans and Indonesians, you've developed all of your materials in English, and you need to have them translated into Indonesian. You would hire one translator to translate the original English materials into Indonesian. You would then hire another translator to translate the translated Indonesian materials back into English. You would then have two different English versions of your materials (the original one and the back-translated one), and you would carefully compare these two. There are likely to be some differences between the two English versions. The researcher would then discuss the problematic places with the two translators and, through a series of back and forth discussions, reach a consensus among the two translators for how to alter the materials (either the English version, the Indonesian version, or both) so that they would be equivalent. One weakness with the back-translation method is that it might result in a very unnatural or hard to understand translation, even though the literal meaning is preserved. For example, idioms such as "it's a piece of cake," "beat around the bush," or "let the cat out of the bag" might be preserved word for word in a back-translation, but these expressions would likely be completely unintelligible in the other language.

In sum, reliable and valid cultural differences are more likely to be found with well-translated materials. Because cross-cultural comparisons are meaningful only if participants understand the materials in the same way, it's always important to get the best translation possible, even though securing a good translation might be very time-consuming and costly.

Response Biases. Once you have a translation of your materials that you are confident with, you are ready to start recruiting participants to complete your survey. However, interpreting and comparing survey responses from people of different cultures is far more challenging than interpreting those from within a single culture. Below I describe some of these challenges and potential solutions for surmounting them.

Moderacy and Extremity Biases. Often psychological materials present participants with statements, and the participants indicate their agreement by choosing a number from a scale—for example, a scale that runs from 1 (Strongly Disagree) to 7 (Strongly Agree). However, there is a tendency for people from different cultures to vary in terms of how likely they are to express their agreement in a moderate fashion—that is, by choosing an item close to the midpoint of the scale (e.g., choosing a 5 on a 7-point scale), or to express their agreement in an extreme fashion—that is, by choosing an item close to the end of the scale (e.g., choosing a 7 on a 7-point scale). The former is known as a **moderacy bias** and the latter as an **extremity bias**. There is considerable cultural variation on this dimension. African-Americans and Hispanic-Americans tend to give more extreme responses than do Americans of European descent (Bachman & O'Malley, 1984; Hui & Triandis, 1989). For example, a Hispanic respondent might be more likely to indicate his agreement with a statement such as "I am impulsive" by circling a 6 on a 1 to 7 scale, whereas a non-Hispanic who possessed the same degree of impulsivity might indicate his agreement by circling a 5. The Hispanic participant's response thus appears more extreme than that of non-Hispanic because of a habitual way of responding to questions, even though they do not differ in their actual degree of impulsivity. Likewise, East Asians tend to be more moderate in their responses than do European-Americans (Chen & Stevenson, 1995; Zax & Takahashi, 1967). Furthermore, East Asians show a greater moderacy bias when they complete the materials in their native language than when they complete them in English (Kuroda, Hayashi, & Suzuki, 1986). Moderacy and extremity biases are response styles as they affect how an individual responds to an item *independent of the content* of the item. Such response styles are problematic for cultural comparisons because if cultures vary in how people respond to questions, this is going to affect any conclusions that we can draw when comparing average scores across cultures.

Moderacy and extremity biases can be controlled for in certain situations. One simple strategy is that you can avoid providing participants with a set of responses that has a middle answer. For example, rather than having people indicate their answers on a 7-point scale, you could have them respond with a simple "Yes/No" format. Because there is no middle response option, you do not need to be concerned that some cultural groups might be more likely to select it. However, this approach might not provide you with a sensitive enough measure to detect nuanced differences in opinion across individuals.

If you are interested in assessing how people feel across a broad range of items or content domains, you might consider "standardizing" your data before conducting cross-cultural comparisons (e.g., Bond, 1988). In standardization, each participant's scores are first averaged, and then the individual items are assessed with respect to how much they deviate from the participant's own personal average. The standardized scores (also known as Z-scores) indicate how participants respond to each item compared with their typical way of responding. The participants' responses are no longer kept in the original metric, such as the 1 to 7 scale that was written in the questionnaire, but are now expressed in terms of the number of standard deviations by which they depart from the participant's own personal average. Standardizing dramatically alters one's data, but it preserves the individual's own pattern of responses. It shows us which items the individual agreed with most and which items the individual disagreed with most. It allows us to compare the patterns of responses across individuals or across cultures by statistically forcing everyone to have a uniform response style, thereby eliminating the problems with moderacy and extremity biases. However, there is an important catch: Standardizing assumes that the average level of response is identical across cultures (that is, everyone's scores are forced to have an average Z score of 0). This assumption might not be especially problematic when we are looking for patterns of responses across a broad array of different measures—for example, if we provide people with an inventory of many different personality traits. It might not be unreasonable to assume in this case that everyone has about the same amount of personality but it just varies in which traits are more pronounced in each person. However, if we are comparing individuals or cultures on just a few different constructs we cannot confidently assume that people share the same average response. For example, consider what would happen if we wanted to compare cultures on a 10-item measure of talkativeness. We might be concerned about moderacy and extremity biases so we would first standardize our data. However, this standardization statistically forces every individual to have the identical level of talkativeness: Everyone's average response is set to a Z score of 0. Standardization could thus not tell us which culture was more talkative, as the two cultures would be equated at the same level of talkativeness. Standardizing is a powerful statistical tool, but it does alter our dataset, and sometimes in problematic ways, depending on the comparisons we are trying to make. It is only appropriate when we are interested in cultural differences in the pattern of responses and is not appropriate when we want to compare the average level of responses across cultures in a single measure.

Acquiescence Bias. People also differ in the extent to which they tend to agree with statements they encounter. Some people might be more prone to agree with any item they read, whereas others might be prone to disagree with them. A tendency to agree with most statements is known as an **acquiescence bias** and is an issue for cross-cultural comparisons. Imagine that you're interested in assessing people's feelings toward the current U.S. administration's foreign policy. Individuals are presented with several items that ask them to evaluate different aspects of the government's foreign policy, and then a total approval score is calculated by summing up their answers to the individual questions. You can imagine that people who tend to agree with almost any statement would score quite high on this foreign policy approval measure, even if they were not a big fan of the government's policies. They could earn a high score simply because they find most statements agreeable, regardless of the content. This bias would make it very hard to compare the individual's true degree of approval with that of another person who tends to find most statements to be disagreeable, regardless of content.

The acquiescence bias is a problem for cross-cultural research because cultures differ in their tendencies to agree with items (e.g., Grimm & Church, 1999; Marin, Gamba, & Marin, 1992; Ross & Mirowsky, 1984). Much work has revealed that East Asians tend to have a relatively holistic way of looking at the world (something that we'll return to in Chapter 9, Cognition and Perception), and one consequence of this is that there are more possible truths in a holistic world. That is, to the extent that the world is an interconnected place that is always changing, which is how it appears with a holistic point of view, then most statements have some truth in them. For example, the statements "I am introverted" and "I am extraverted" both contain some truth if one takes on a holistic perspective. In some situations a person may feel introverted, and in some he might feel extraverted, so these are both truths, and a holistic person would endorse both of them (e.g., Choi & Choi, 2002). If people in some cultures have a predisposition to see the truth in more statements than those in another culture, this will lead to cultural differences in responses, independent from the content of the items. This is known as an "acquiescence bias." It is the tendency to agree or to acquiesce to a relatively large range of statements.

There is a straightforward solution to the acquiescence bias that is commonly applied when researchers construct trait measures. Typically, half of the items in a measure are designed to be reverse-scored; that is, they are written so that agreeing with them indicates an opinion opposite to that measured in the construct. For example, if we were to measure self-esteem we would want to ensure that half of our items indicated low self-esteem (e.g., I feel like a failure), and half indicated high self-esteem (e.g., I have many great talents.) One's total self-esteem score would be calculated by first reverse-scoring the responses for the items written in the direction of low self-esteem (i.e., on a 7-point scale, we would need to change the 7's to 1's, the 6's to 2's, the 5's to 3's and leave the 4's as 4's), and then summing all of these together with the items written in the direction of high self-esteem. By ensuring that half the items are reverse-scored, any acquiescing tendency would be cancelled out as the individual would be agreeing with items that both increase their total score (the positively worded items) and items that decrease their total score (the negatively worded items), thereby neutralizing the effects of this bias. Alternatively, standardizing the data would also neutralize acquiescence biases; however, standardization can be problematic as described above.

Reference-Group Effects. Consider another problem with comparing survey results across cultures. Imagine that you're interested in comparing height across cultures. One straightforward approach would be to ask people in different cultures to rate themselves on a scale of 1 to a 7 for a statement such as "I am tall," and then to compare the responses between the cultures. If more people agreed with this statement in Culture A than in Culture B we might be tempted to conclude that we have found evidence that people are taller in Culture A than in Culture B. But there is a problem with this conclusion. And the problem is that statements such as "I am tall" do not have the same meaning in all contexts. For example, among the Pygmies of central Africa the average height for men in the shortest tribe is 4′ 9″ (Cavalli-

The average Pygmy is considerably shorter than the average Dutch. This makes it problematic to assess height by asking people whether they are tall, as the Pygmies will likely compare themselves to a shorter standard than the Dutch will.

Sforza & Cavalli-Sforza, 1995). The average height of men in the Netherlands, in contrast, is just over 6 feet (Gould, 1999). A Pygmy man of 5′ 6″ might likely agree with the statement that he is tall, because he is tall by Pygmy standards. In contrast a Dutch man of 5′ 6″ likely would not agree with the statement that he is tall, because by Dutch standards he is not. The problem in comparing cultures with these kinds of statements, then, is that people in different cultures are using different standards to answer the questions. As much research in social psychology has revealed, people tend to evaluate themselves by comparing themselves with others—similar others (Festinger, 1954). This point is critical for cross-cultural research because people from different cultures tend to evaluate themselves by comparing themselves to *different reference groups*, and thus, to different standards. This is a problem for cross-cultural research because usually we are interested in assessing cultures by a single standard. This is known as the **reference-group effect** (Heine, Lehman, Peng, & Greenholtz, 2002; Peng, Nisbett, & Wong, 1997). Research has shown that reference-group effects are potentially problematic whenever we are comparing cultures on how much they agree with statements with subjective response formats. One classic example of the reference-group effect was a study that found African-American soldiers in the northern United States were less satisfied than those in the South because they compared themselves primarily to civilian African-Americans who were better off in the North than in the South (Stouffer, Suchman, DeVinney, Star, & Williams, 1949). In this situation, the reference-group effect leads one to make the exact opposite conclusion (i.e., southern African-American soldiers were better off than northern ones) than a more objective comparison would indicate.

One technique for correcting the problems associated with the reference-group effect is to avoid subjective measures that might have different standards in the groups being compared. Instead, one is often better off using more concrete measures that will be perceived more similarly across cultures. Measures can be made more concrete by either changing the content of the item or by changing the response format. For example, a statement such as "I am helpful" can be interpreted quite differently depending on a culture's standards for what kinds of behaviors are perceived to be helpful. In contrast, a statement such as "If a friend of mine needed help with his studies, I would be willing to cancel my own plans to help him" is more concrete in describing the situation in terms of what kind of help is needed and what kinds of sacrifices are made. The more concrete the scenario, the less likely it is that people from different cultures would interpret the meaning of the terms differently. However, more concrete scenarios also tend to be more specific (e.g., one could be helpful in situations other than helping a friend study). To ensure that you are adequately covering the range of helpful behaviors you would want to create a number of items that indicated helping behaviors. Past research reveals that more concrete items better capture cultural differences than more subjective ones (e.g., Choi et al., 2002; Heine et al., 2001; Peng et al., 1997; Takemura, Yuki, Kashima, & Halloran, 2004). Also, you could make your questions more concrete by altering the response format. Some response formats are quite subjective, such as indicating one's endorsement by choosing a number from a scale that ranges from "Strongly Disagree" to "Strongly Agree." This format is subjective in that respondents are able to determine for themselves what kind of agreement corresponds to "Strongly Agree" (e.g., Biernat & Manis, 1994). A more concrete response option would be to provide some quantitative descriptions, such "At least once a day," or "10–20% of the time," which do not provide much room for different interpretations. Likewise, one can reduce the range of interpretations for an item by asking participants to make a forced choice between two or more response alternatives, for example, "Which of these two responses would you be more likely to choose if you were in such a situation?" This removes concerns with reference-group effects as people are no longer answering the question by comparing themselves to some imagined standard, but they are comparing two or more response options and are making their choice from them. Efforts to change response formats in this way have been shown to improve the validity of cross-cultural comparisons as well (Peng et al., 1997).

Some other kinds of measures are well protected from reference-group effects. For example, many cross-cultural studies have employed behavioral measures that do not rely on people's understanding of how they compare against others (e.g., Sussman & Rosenfeld, 1982; Vandello & Cohen, 2003). For example, Levine and Norenzayan (1999) investigated the pace of life in 31 cultures by examining behavioral measures. They calculated the pace of life by timing how long it took people to walk a certain distance on a busy street, by checking how accurate the clocks were in banks, and by timing how long it took a postal worker to sell them a stamp. These measures appear reliable in that they are better correlated with other measures relevant to the pace of life than are self-report measures (see Heine, Buchtel, & Norenzayan, 2007). Likewise, physiological measures are especially protected from reference-group concerns (Cohen, Nisbett, Bowdle, & Schwarz, 1996). For example, one study investigated the autonomic nervous system responses of the Minangkabau of West Sumatra (Levenson, Ekman, Heider, & Friesen, 1992). While physiological measures are often difficult and costly to obtain, especially in remote cultures, they are especially powerful for cross-cultural

"Could you walk a little faster, buddy? This is New York."

study as they occur independently of the various response biases that challenge questionnaire work.

Deprivation Effects. Consider the results of the following study that investigated values in 38 different countries around the world (Schwartz, 1994). One question asked how much people valued "enjoying life" and "pleasure." The findings showed that East Germans scored the third highest of all the countries on this dimension, and Italians scored the second lowest (Schwartz, 1994). Another study found that Americans value "humility" more than Chinese, whereas Chinese value "choosing one's own goals" more than Americans (Peng et al., 1997). Do these findings fit with the stereotypes that you have for these cultures? Evidence from a variety of other sources stands in conflict with these findings from the value measures. Why do Italians rate "pleasure" as so unimportant compared to other nationalities when they simultaneously have developed a lifestyle that emphasizes good food, leisurely breaks in cafes, opera, art, and long summer vacations?

The disconnect that is sometimes observed between self-report measures of values and other indicators is a challenge for cross-cultural investigations. One way to make sense of this disconnect is to consider what people *actually* have in contrast to what they would *like to* have. Consider the question, "How much do you value personal safety?" Clearly, personal safety is of importance to everyone, everywhere. But it would seem that people start thinking about their personal safety more, and would be more willing to make sacrifices in order to secure it, in situations where their personal safety is most at risk. It is when your safety is vulnerable that you are likely most concerned with it, and at other times you might be quite willing to forget about it. The problem with this for measuring values across cultures is that we might expect that in cultures where there is chronically *less* personal safety that people express valuing it *more*. This is known as the **deprivation effect**, and it poses a serious challenge to the investigation of values (Peng et al., 1997). It can thus be problematic to make inferences about a culture from the values that people endorse the most. There is no straightforward technique to correct for the deprivation effect other than to investigate whether the results from self-report measures of values converge with the results from other sources of evidence regarding values. The existence of the deprivation effect forces us to be cautious in interpreting what is valued in different cultures.

As you can see, there are several methodological challenges that make it difficult to compare subjective questionnaire responses across cultures.

Although there are some strategies to reduce the impact of these challenges, which I described above, cross-cultural comparisons of means of questionnaires remain potentially problematic. My own personal view of these kinds of comparisons (which is admittedly more critical than that of most other researchers) is that we should be very cautious of accepting any cultural differences that are identified by comparing means across subjective questionnaire measures unless the patterns converge with findings from other methodologies.

Although the use of subjective self-report measures makes it problematic to compare average scores *across* cultures, these measures can be extremely useful for identifying individual differences *within* a culture. For example, Americans who score high on a measure of extraversion can be assumed to be more extraverted than Americans who score low on the same measure. Because the within-culture validity of subjective self-report measures is preserved, these measures are extremely useful for identifying correlations between different constructs within cultures—for example, investigating whether extraversion and self-esteem are related. These measures work fine within cultures because cultural members tend to *share the same response biases and reference groups*. On the other hand, subjective self-report measures do not work as well between cultures because the members from the different cultural groups potentially have *different response styles and reference groups*, thereby obscuring the comparisons.

Conducting Cross-Cultural Research with Experiments. In addition to standard survey methods, much psychological research in cultural psychology employs the experimental method. The experiment is a powerful methodological tool that can reveal much that straightforward questionnaires are not always able to do. Many psychologists get quite excited about a nice experimental design because of their confidence that it allows us to draw inferences about the findings. In general, the experiment is the method of choice for psychological research. Most of the research examples in this textbook are derived from the experimental method.

The experimental method involves the manipulation of an independent variable and a measurement of the influence that this manipulation had on a dependent variable. It allows researchers to be confident in their exploration of the relation between the independent variable and the dependent variable because all other extraneous influences can be held constant. If the only aspect of the study that varies is the independent variable then we can be confident that any differences in the dependent variable must be due to that independent variable. The independent variable can be said to *cause* the change in the dependent variable. Such experimental control greatly increases the power of our investigations.

In cross-cultural studies, one important independent variable—one's cultural background—is *not* manipulated because it can't be. This means that comparisons of cultures are not true experiments but are quasi-experiments. However, even though this one independent variable is beyond the experimenter's ability to control, there are many other independent variables that can be manipulated to give cross-cultural researchers a great deal of experimental control in their studies.

There are two kinds of manipulations of independent variables that can be performed in psychological research. One kind is a **between-groups** manipulation, in which different groups of participants receive different levels of the independent variable. The groups that receive each level of the independent variable are referred to as "conditions." Between-groups manipulations require random assignment such that each participant has an equal chance of being assigned to any given condition. Random assignment ensures that the participants in the different conditions are statistically equivalent at the beginning of the study. Any differences in their responses, or behaviors, that are observed must be due to the independent variable, as this is the only thing that differs systematically between the experimental conditions. For example, let's imagine that we're interested in exploring whether people are more persuaded by fast-talking salespeople or by slow-talking salespeople. In this case, each participant would be randomly assigned to listen to either a fast-talking salesperson or a slow-talking one and we would measure their persuasion and compare these across conditions.

A second kind of manipulation is a **within-groups** manipulation. In this case, each participant receives more than one level of the independent variable. Within-groups manipulations do not involve random assignment because *every* participant receives all the levels of the independent variable. In other words, each participant is assigned to all of the conditions. Let's return to our earlier example of exploring persuasion by fast- and slow-talking salespeople. To manipulate the independent variable, talking speed, with a within-subjects design, we would first assess participants' persuasion by a fast-talking salesperson and then by slow-talking salesperson. One factor that is important in within-groups designs is to provide participants with different orders of the conditions. If we want to be certain that people respond to the fast-talkers differently from the slow-talkers we want to rule out the possibility that people are differently persuaded by whatever salesperson they encounter first compared with the salesperson that they encounter second. Hence, we would have one group of participants hear the fast-talking salesperson before the slow-talking one, and another group would hear the slow-talking salesperson before the fast-talking one. Then we would be able to explore whether the order of the conditions affected people's responses (the astute reader might notice that in this hypothetical study the order of the conditions is a between-groups manipulation). Because all participants are included in both the fast-talking and slow-talking conditions, we can again be confident that any differences in the responses of participants to the conditions are due solely to the independent variable and not to other factors.

The experimental method is not limited to laboratory situations but can also be utilized in questionnaire research (questionnaires can include different conditions too). A clear virtue of manipulating independent variables in cultural research is that it can provide us with a comparison that is not limited by the response biases associated with questionnaire research that are described above. As you now know, these response biases influence how participants respond to self-report items, making it problematic to compare mean scores directly across cultures as we end up comparing apples to oranges. However, if we can make comparisons *within* cultures, or within individuals, which the experimental method allows, these response biases are no longer a concern, as the comparison is across groups that *share a response bias*. The experimental method, then, allows us to get back to comparing apples with apples, despite the response biases that people have.

For example, imagine that you are interested in investigating how Jamaicans and Indians view people with high status. A nonexperimental method would simply ask individuals to rate a particular high-status person on a number of traits. Let's imagine that this showed that, on average, the Jamaicans evaluated the high-status person more positively than did the Indians. However, because of the various response biases described above, we would not be able to confidently assess whether this finding reflected different attitudes toward the high-status person or different response biases.

In contrast, an experimental approach would include more than one condition. In one condition, participants would rate the high-status person. In a second condition, participants would evaluate a person of moderate social status. And, perhaps, in a third condition participants would evaluate a person of low-social status. Now we are able to compare how the different individuals were evaluated *within* the cultures. That is, we can see, for example, whether Indians evaluated the high-status person significantly more positively than either the low- or moderate-status person. This will allow us to see how big an impact status has on Indians' evaluations. Note that this kind of analysis is protected from the response biases described above, because even if Indians and Jamaicans have different reference groups, moderacy biases, or acquiescence norms, we are explicitly comparing Indians with Indians, so these response biases are not affecting our comparisons. Once we have determined the impact of status within each culture, we can then compare the magnitude of this impact *between* cultures. The experimental method changes our between-culture comparison from one of comparing the *magnitude of means* across cultures (which is problematic) to one of comparing the *pattern of means* across cultures (which is fine). The experimental method is an excellent solution for correcting the methodological challenges in cultural research. Many of the studies in cultural psychology with greatest impact have employed this method.

Conducting Cross-Cultural Research with Multiple Methods. A key point to realize about research is that no single study is perfect. Every study has potential methodological shortcomings or alternative theoretical explanations. In fact, one important skill that students learn in graduate school in psychology is precisely how to come up with alternative explanations for virtually any study they encounter. This is viewed as a good exercise in critical thinking. To the extent that compelling alternative accounts can be offered, we become less confident in the conclusions of the study. Just because there are alternative explanations for every study does not mean that every study is worthless. Each study still provides us with a valuable perspective; however, no single study can provide us with a complete picture.

Because of this fact, a more compelling case is always made when researchers utilize multiple methods in their research. If a finding is observed with one method, it is good practice for the researcher to try to replicate it with a different kind of method. The more divergent the methods across the different studies, the more compelling a convergent set of findings would be. If each study provides one perspective, we're going to have a more complete picture if we can consider it from multiple perspectives. Researchers tend to get especially excited about multiple studies with divergent methods, as this kind of approach is largely resistant to alternative accounts because any alternative explanation that is offered must apply to all the different methods that were explored. We rely on the principle of **Occam's Razor**. This principle states that any theory should make as few assumptions as possible, eliminating, or "shaving off," any extraneous assumptions. All else held equal, then, Occam's Razor maintains that the simpler theory is more likely to be correct. Hence, if a researcher conducts four studies on a topic, each using different methods, and these results all converge with his predictions, the researcher's own account would be more compelling than an account that offered four separate alternative explanations for each of his studies. A single explanation is more parsimonious and more likely to be correct than four separate explanations. Multiple methods are important for all kinds of scientific research, but they are especially so in cultural psychology because of the methodological challenges involved (e.g., Triandis, McCusker, & Hui, 1990).

Some Methods Particular to the Study of Culture

Surveys, experiments, and multiple methods are not specific to cultural psychology but are characteristic of the ways we test hypotheses in all of psychology, and the sciences, more generally. There are some methods, however, that lend themselves especially well to the study of cultural psychology.

Situation Sampling. One inherent shortcoming about cross-cultural research is that we're unable to manipulate our participants' cultural background. From a scientific point of view the ideal way to conduct a cross-cultural experiment would be to assign cultures to our participants. That is, we would need to take newly born infants who did not have any cultural experiences and randomly assign some of them to be raised in, say, an American cultural condition and some others to be raised in a Bolivian cultural condition, and a third group would be assigned to a "control" condition that was raised without any culture at all. Everything else would be kept completely constant throughout their lives. Then we could measure whatever dependent variable interested us. If we found any differences we could be certain that they were due to the different cultural experiences that our participants had. This would be an ideal cross-cultural experiment for determining the influence of culture, and, I must confess, I sometimes fantasize about running studies like this because of all that we could learn. For obvious ethical and practical reasons, however, we cannot go around enculturating people into different cultural worlds. Because of these limitations we usually resort to contrasting individuals who have grown up in different cultures.

One methodological technique provides us with a practical, and ethical, way of getting one step closer to my fantasized experimental methodology (Kitayama, Markus, Matsumoto, & Norasakkunkit, 1997; Morling, Kitayama, & Miyamoto, 2002). Called situation sampling, this methodology utilizes the fact that cultures do not affect us in the abstract; they affect us in particular, concrete ways. You can think of your day as consisting of a series of situations that you've experienced. You woke up, you stumbled into the shower to clean yourself, you had a shouting match with your roommate over an apparent missing bottle of conditioner, you received a phone call from a furniture store telling you that the sofa you ordered was going to be delayed, and so on. The ways in which our cultures affect us is that they provide us with particular kinds of situations that we encounter on a regular basis. In different cultures, people regularly encounter a different collection of situations. It is our experiences in these culturally shaped situations that lead us to adopt habitual ways of thinking about ourselves and our worlds.

The underlying idea of the situation-sampling methodology is that if we can see how people respond to situations that are regularly experienced by people in another culture, we can get a viewpoint into how cultures shape our ways of thinking. The situation-sampling method involves a two-step process. First, participants from at least two cultures are asked to describe a number of situations that they have experienced in which something specific has happened. For example, in one study, Japanese and American participants were asked to list situations in which their self-esteem had either increased or decreased (Kitayama et al., 1997). In the second step, different groups of participants are asked to participate in the study. This second set of participants is provided with a list of the situations that have been generated by the first set of participants, and they are asked to imagine how they would have felt if they had been in those situations themselves. In the above study, this second set of participants was asked to indicate how much they thought their self-esteem would have increased or decreased had they been in those specific situations. Importantly, in this second stage, participants are provided with situations that have been generated by *both* of the comparison cultures.

That is, American participants think about how they would feel both in the situations generated by other Americans and in situations generated by Japanese, and vice versa for the Japanese participants. In this way, we can get an idea for how Americans and Japanese would respond if they were participating in the other group's cultural worlds. It is similar to being an exchange student in the other culture. We can get a viewpoint into how Japanized Americans and Americanized Japanese behave, thereby learning a great deal about the ways culture shapes our psychology.

This methodology allows the researcher to do a number of kinds of analyses. First, the researcher can explore features of the situations that were listed in step one. Was one kind of situation more commonly listed in one culture than the other, or were there consistent features that appeared more often in one culture's situations than in the other's? For example, the above study found that Japanese listed more situations than Americans in which their self-esteem decreased, whereas Americans listed more situations than Japanese where their self-esteem increased. This suggests that self-esteem decreasing situations are more common in Japanese cultural experiences and that self-esteem increasing situations are more common in American cultural experiences. We will explore the reasons behind this particular cultural difference when we discuss self-esteem in Chapter 6, Motivation.

Second, the researcher can explore whether there are cultural differences in the ways people from different cultures respond to the situations in step two. If, regardless of the situation that participants imagine, people in one culture indicate that they would consistently respond differently from people in the other culture, this suggests that there are learned cultural experiences that have become habitualized by people such that they govern people's reactions across all kinds of situations. For example, in the above study, Japanese participants indicated that their self-esteem would increase less than that of Americans in the self-esteem increasing situations, and that their self-esteem would decrease more than that of Americans in the self-esteem decreasing situations. This suggests that Japanese are habitually more attentive to situations that afford opportunities for self-criticism, whereas Americans are habitually more attentive to situations that allow people to boost the positivity of their self-views.

Third, the situation sampling methodology allows the researcher to explore whether the cultural origin of the situations that participants listed in step one are responded to differently by participants in step two. To the extent that situations from one culture are consistently responded to differently from situations from another culture, this would suggest that the two cultures provide participants with different kinds of experiences. For example, in the above study, both American and Japanese participants in step two reported that their self-esteem would decrease more when they responded to Japanese-made self-esteem decreasing situations than when they responded to American-made ones. Likewise, both Americans and Japanese reported that their self-esteem would increase more when they responded to American-made self-esteem increasing situations than to Japanese-made ones. This suggests that the kinds of experiences people encounter in the United States are especially conducive to boosting self-esteem, whereas the kinds of experiences people regularly encounter in Japan lead people to be especially self-critical. These three different kinds of analyses that are afforded by the situation-sampling methodology allow us to identify both the kinds of cultural experiences people regularly encounter in different cultures and the habitual responses they tend to develop. It is a powerful methodological tool, although the two-step procedure makes it a time-consuming technique to use.

Cultural Priming. Situation sampling is not the only method that we have to come closer to the idealized goal of being able to manipulate culture. Another technique involves the "priming" or activation of cultural ideas within participants. Priming works by making certain ideas more accessible to participants, and to the extent that those ideas are associated with cultural meaning systems, we can investigate what happens when people start to think about certain cultural ideas.

Although cultures differ quite profoundly in ways of thinking that are common, for the most part it appears that these differences are ones of degree rather than of kind. That is, there are some ways of thinking that might be more uncommon in Culture A than in Culture B; however, those ways of thinking are likely still present to a limited degree in Culture A as well. There are a few exceptions to this pattern (i.e., there are ways of thinking that only appear to emerge with certain cultural experiences—nonuniversals; Norenzayan & Heine, 2005), but in general, most of the psychological processes that have been studied thus far are at least existential universals that exist in varying degrees across cultures.

For example, one way of thinking that varies across cultures is the extent to which one views oneself as distinct from others (independent) or as connected with others (interdependent). In Chapter 5, Self and Personality, we'll explore this way of thinking in more detail, but suffice it for now to say that cultures vary in the extent to which they habitually think of themselves in either of these two ways. One study demonstrated that thoughts about independent aspects of the self are more characteristic of Americans than of Chinese, and thoughts of interdependent aspects of the self are more characteristic of Chinese than Americans (Trafimow, Triandis, & Goto, 1991). The researchers hypothesized that people could be led to consider more independent aspects of themselves if thoughts about people's distinctness could be activated in their minds; likewise, people could be led to consider more interdependent aspects of themselves if thoughts about people's relations were activated. American and Chinese participants were asked to think either of how they were different from others (an independence prime) or how they were similar to their family and friends (an interdependence prime). Then participants were asked to describe themselves in an open-ended survey. Interestingly, when Chinese participants encountered the independence prime, their self-descriptions became more similar to the ways that Americans typically describe themselves, and when Americans encountered the interdependence prime, their self-descriptions became more similar to the ways that Chinese typically describe themselves. In other words, when cultural ideas are activated that are more common in another culture people start thinking in ways that are more similar to the thinking of people from other cultures. Much recent research has explored how a wide variety of different ways to prime cultural ideas in people's minds can effectively lead people to think and act in culturally distinct ways (e.g., Hong, Morris, Chiu, & Benet-Martinez, 2000; Kuhnen, Hannover, & Schubert, 2001; Lee, Aaker, & Gardner, 2000). We'll return more to priming methods when we consider the minds of bicultural people in Chapter 12, Living in Multicultural Worlds.

Culture-Level Measures. The goal of much research in cultural psychology is to assess how cultures affect people's thinking, and the most common way of pursuing this goal is to measure people's thoughts in an effort to see the effects of culture. However, before we can be confident that the psychological processes that we're investigating have been influenced by culture it's important that we have a confident understanding of what the cultures are like in the first place. That is, we need a way to measure cultures.

For the most part, psychologists tend to be interested in data that allow us to test hypotheses. The kinds of methods we've been discussing thus far have been with regard to collecting data to test hypotheses about people, but how can we collect data that allow us to test hypotheses about culture? In principle, the data should be similar in nature to those of psychological hypothesis testing in that they should be (1) objective and capable of being replicated by others and (2) quantifiable so that we can conduct statistical analyses to determine whether our hypotheses are supported. The challenge is to appropriate the kinds of methods that psychologists have mastered for the study of people and apply these to the study of cultures.

Cultural psychologists have used such empirical methods to investigate the kinds of cultural messages to which individuals are habitually exposed. The cultural messages that we encounter are highly relevant to cultural psychologists as they reflect the ideas that are communicated to individuals by participating in their cultures. A careful analysis of the messages that people are exposed to on a regular basis will provide us with a nice perspective on the ways that cultures influence their members.

We encounter a barrage of cultural messages from all kinds of different sources as we go about our daily lives. A first step in studying these messages is to focus our investigation on an identifiable and quantifiable subset of them. A variety of different domains of cultural messages lend themselves well to this kind of investigation. Past research has explored cultural messages in domains as diverse as magazine advertisements (Han & Shavit, 1994), laws (Cohen, 1996), newspaper articles (Morris & Peng, 1994), fairy tales (Doyle & Doyle, 2001) and children's stories (McClelland, 1961), sports coverage (Markus, Uchida, Omoregie, Townsend, & Kitayama, 2006), and personal ads (Parekh & Beresin, 2001). As an illustration, consider some research that contrasted working-class and upper-middle-class Americans (Snibbe & Markus, 2005). The researchers reasoned that they could identify the different cultural messages these two groups were exposed to by attending to the lyrics of the music they most commonly listened to. Their surveys revealed that country music was more popular among working-class folks whereas rock music was more commonly listened to by upper-middle-class folks. Exploring the lyrics from songs of these two genres, then, will provide us with a window on the kinds of cultural messages that working-class and upper-middle-class Americans commonly encounter while driving to work.

A second step to take when studying cultural messages is to derive a specific hypothesis that we would like to test. For example, the researchers in the above study were interested in testing the hypothesis that working-class individuals were more commonly exposed to messages emphasizing resilience whereas upper-middle-class individuals were more in contact with messages that called for carving one's own unique path. This hypothesis can be tested by exploring whether such messages really are more common in the different genres of music.

Last, we need to come up with a way to transform our raw data (in this case, the actual song lyrics) into quantifiable data that lend themselves to a test of our hypothesis. This transformation involves coding the data, that is, deriving a set of categories that are consistent with particular cultural messages—for example, whether the messages emphasize something relevant to resilience (e.g., rebelling against authority) or uniqueness (e.g., being unique or talented). Coders who are trained to identify the different categories then go through the raw data in search of instances of specific cultural messages that fit into the different categories. Unfortunately, many coding decisions are quite subjective and on occasion the decisions are not obvious. To ensure that the coders' individual biases are not overly influencing the results, a couple of safeguards can be introduced: First, the coders can be kept blind to the hypotheses being tested—for example, in the above study the coders would not know that the researchers are expecting that resilience categories would be more common in country than in rock music lyrics. Keeping the coders blind prevents their motivation to get good results from leaking into the subjective decisions they have to make. Second, multiple coders are employed, and some, or all, of the raw data are coded by more than one individual. Then, the experimenters can check to see whether the different coders are making the same decisions. If the different coders are making different decisions, this means that the data are not reliable and the coders need more training about the boundaries of the different categories. Once the coders have reached a consensus for all the decisions they have made, the data are considered reliable and can be statistically analyzed. For example, in the above study, analyses did indeed reveal that country music lyrics convey more messages about resilience and rock music lyrics more messages about uniqueness (see Figure 3.1).

The Challenge of Unpackaging. Many cross-cultural psychological studies find pronounced differences between cultures, and these differences reveal to us that there are ways in which people from different cultures have divergent experiences that affect their psychologies. Finding a cultural difference

FIGURE 3.1

Country music
listeners hear
different cultural
messages than rock
music listeners.

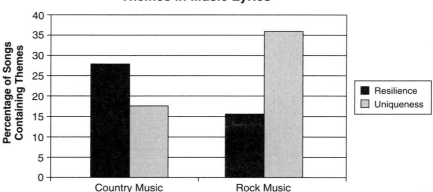

represents an important first step in understanding how culture influences psychological processes as it shows that the psychological process under study is grounded in cultural experiences. However, a cultural difference by itself does not tell us *which* cultural experiences sustain it. There are myriad ways in which cultures differ from each other. Which of these ways are relevant to understanding the psychological process at hand? This question belies a particular challenge to cultural research. Cultures appear to us as "packaged" (Whiting, 1976); that is, participating in a culture means that one is exposed to a broad network of practices and meanings that are presented to the individual as a whole. We are not able to separate the individual cultural practices and meanings from each other as they are always wrapped up together, as if in a package. If we are to deepen our understanding of how cultures and minds are intertwined we need to "unpackage" the cultural differences to reveal the specific cultural experiences or variables that relate to the cultural difference. **Unpackaging** cultural findings means identifying the underlying variables that give rise to the cultural difference.

For example, consider the finding that Japanese scored higher than Americans on a measure of embarrassability (Singelis, Bond, Lai, & Sharkey, 1999). Why might we expect this cultural difference? Which of the multitude of cultural differences between Japanese and Americans can account for this difference? Is it because many Japanese take baths together with their parents until they reach puberty that they become more habitually embarrassed? Is it because American schools encourage children to express their own opinions more that they become less embarrassed? We could go on and on coming up with potential cultural explanations. The key to advancing our understanding would be to discover *which* cultural experiences are relevant.

How would one go about unpackaging the observed cultural differences in embarrassability? The first step would be to let a theory guide the researchers' search for potential underlying cultural variables. Much other research has revealed that Japanese tend to have more interdependent views of self than Americans (Markus & Kitayama, 1991), something we'll return to in Chapter 5, Self and Personality, and the researchers reasoned that a concern with interdependence and how one relates with close others might lead one to become more easily embarrassed. The next step in the unpackaging process of this study is to demonstrate that Japanese really do have more interdependent views of self than Americans. Indeed, this is what the researchers found. So now there is evidence that Japanese score higher than Americans on both embarrassability and on interdependence. The third necessary step in the unpackaging process is to demonstrate that the observed cultural differences in interdependence relate to the observed differences in embarrassability. In the case of this study, the researchers' approach for exploring this was to correlate people's embarrassability scores and their interdependence scores within each culture. They found that these two variables were significantly related within both Japanese and American cultures. That is, those Japanese who were more interdependent reported feeling the most easily embarrassed, and likewise for Americans. The cultural difference in embarrassability has thus been successfully unpackaged. Unpackaging does not mean that you have necessarily identified *all* the variables behind a cultural difference, or even the most powerful variable. It does show you, however, that the variable you identified is at least partly responsible for the observed cultural difference.

Unpackaging cultural differences is a powerful analytical tool. It's a tool by which we can use cultural differences themselves to shed light on the nature of underlying processes. Discovering cultural differences increases not only our understanding of how culture and psychology are interrelated, but also our understanding of the psychological processes themselves. If the above study hadn't first identified the cultural difference in embarrassability, we might never have learned about the important relationship between embarrassability and interdependence. Knowing about this relation enables us to better understand the nature of embarrassability by focusing our exploration on the aspects of interdependence that lead to heightened embarrassment.

Similar to how neuroscientists often study the cognitive deficits of people with brain injuries as a tool for discovering what parts of the brain are associated with what kinds of cognitive abilities, cultural psychologists can also learn more about particular psychological phenomena by identifying cultures that engage in these phenomena relatively more or less than other cultures. Learning about the minds of people from other cultures helps us to understand our own minds better as well.

Case Study: The Culture of Honor in the Southern United States. In many things we learn, the best educational device is a good example. I can think of no better way to learn about how to conduct cross-cultural psychological research than to read about a research program conducted by some of the most skilled methodological craftsmen.

Richard Nisbett and Dov Cohen (Cohen et al., 1996; Cohen, Vandello, Puente, & Rantilla, 1999; Nisbett, 1993; Nisbett & Cohen, 1996) launched a large-scale investigation of an intriguing cultural difference that they had noticed: Why does the U.S. South seem so much more violent than the North? Their observation that the South is an especially violent place is not new. Early in the country's settlement a number of observers noted that the U.S. South seemed to have a penchant for violent activities and outbursts (Gastil, 1989; Tocqueville, 1835/1969). From the 18th century on, the South has had a greater number of lynchings, sniper attacks, feuds, homicides, and duels than the North (Fischer, 1989; Gastil, 1989; Nisbett & Cohen, 1996). The South also has had more tolerance for other aggressive pursuits. In the colonial days in the South, there were many gruesome reports of "no holds-barred" fights, where participants resorted to eye-gouging and biting off noses and ears (Fischer, 1989), and there was participation in violent games such as "gander-pulling" (where the object of the game was to ride by on horseback and try to yank the head off a live, greased goose hanging upside-down from a tree; Fischer, 1989) or "purring" (where the goal was to kick your opponent in the shins until he lost his grip on your shoulder; McWhiney, 1988). While this was going on, the Puritans in New England were inventing baseball. Furthermore, from colonial times to the present, the South has historically been more tolerant of corporal punishment of children, capital punishment, and gun ownership, and has been more supportive of the United States engaging in wars compared with the North (see Cohen, 1996, for a review). How can we make sense of this greater tolerance for violence in the South than in the North?

Many others have noticed this cultural difference in the United States, and a number of explanations have been offered. For example, the South's higher rates of violence have been attributed to the more uncomfortably hot temperatures (people tend to become more frustrated and violent when the weather is uncomfortable; Anderson, 1989), the greater poverty (people might resort to more drastic, and potentially violent, attempts to improve their quality of life if they can't afford the bare necessities), and the longer history of slavery (treating some people inhumanely might have led to a greater tolerance for violent behavior more generally; e.g., Tocqueville, 1835/1969). Nisbett and Cohen's own explanation is unique, and it might strike you as rather bizarre. They argue that there have historically been more herders in the South (i.e., people raising cows, pigs, and sheep) than in the North and this has given rise to a violent **culture of honor** that has continued to persist until this day. A culture of honor is one in which people (especially men) strive to protect their reputation through aggression. This is admittedly an unusual explanation for the regional differences in violence, and when we encounter these kinds of extraordinary claims we require extraordinary evidence to be convinced. Nisbett and Cohen tried to marshal the kind of compelling evidence necessary to support such an unusual hypothesis, and I highlight their research program as an exemplary way to study cultural psychology.

The famous multi-generational feud between the Hatfields (pictured above) and the McCoys started with the reputed theft of a single pig.

Before considering Nisbett and Cohen's methodological approach, let's first explore why herders should be expected to be more violent. Imagine you're a herder and your family's wealth is tied up in the 10 pigs you own. One night, while you're sleeping, someone comes by and opens up the pen and steals all your pigs. Now you're in trouble, as your family's wealth has literally vanished overnight. In contrast, imagine you're a farmer with a field full of wheat. There isn't much thieves can do—they're probably not going to stick around to harvest your crops for you. In sum, herders face a particular kind of threat that farmers do not: Their wealth is portable. This threat is exacerbated because herding tends to be practiced on rather marginal land, which can't support large populations, making it very difficult to police. Herders would seem to live a rather precarious existence indeed.

What is one to do if one's livelihood can be easily stolen and there isn't much of a police force around to guard it? Nisbett and Cohen propose that you'll fare better if you can develop a reputation as someone who maintains his sense of honor. In this case, others come to think of you as someone who is likely to respond with violence when people try to take advantage of you. Of course, if you wait until someone steals your herd before you demonstrate that you're not someone to be messed with, this would be too late. You'd want to develop this reputation beforehand, and a good way to do so would be to show that you are prepared to respond with violence to any threat to your honor—for example, if someone insults you or makes a pass at your girlfriend. Note that Nisbett and Cohen's rationale here is not limited to herders in the United States, but to herders everywhere. And they discuss some evidence that this kind of culture of honor develops in other places where there has historically been a lot of herding—for example, the Scotch-Irish borderlands of Britain (from which the first settlers of the South came; Fischer, 1989), many countries in the Middle East (recall the violent rhetoric of Saddam Hussein, and his threats that the United States would drown in its own blood), and some traditional societies in Africa (Galaty & Bonte, 1991).

That, in a nutshell, is Nisbett and Cohen's theory. Now what kind of evidence could they collect to make a convincing case of it? The particular strength of their research program, as you'll see, is in using a wide array of different methods to test their hypothesis.

One kind of evidence they gathered was *archival data* (see Nisbett & Cohen, 1996). Archival data exist in accumulated documents or records of a culture. Although there is not much of an archival database out there on attitudes toward violence in general, there is an extremely detailed database on police records of homicides. If the South's violence is due to a culture of honor, we shouldn't expect that all kinds of homicide would be higher in the South than in the North. Rather, specifically *argument-related murders*, in which people are compelled to defend their honor, should be higher. Nisbett and Cohen show that, overall, this pattern is true; however, the pattern is especially pronounced when you contrast the rural South with the rural North. It is in the rural South where culture of honor norms should persist more strongly, as they are that much closer to the traditional herding cultures from which these norms originated. Furthermore, within the rural U.S. South the homicide rate is over twice as large in the hills and dry plains where livestock are raised than in the moist plains where farming is practiced. This finding by itself lends support to the culture of honor explanation for southern violence over the other competing hypotheses. Because the herding regions do not differ much from the farming regions in terms of either income or temperature, the hypotheses that the South is more violent because of its poverty or high temperatures loses plausibility. And because, prior to the Civil War, slaves were far more numerous in the farming regions (which are heavily labor dependent) than they were in the herding regions, the South's history with slavery can also not explain why the homicide rate is higher in the herding regions than in the farming regions of the South. This is one piece of evidence for Nisbett and Cohen's culture of honor explanation.

Another kind of evidence that they recruited was *survey data* (see Cohen & Nisbett, 1994). They contacted people by phone who lived in either the South or North and asked them to respond to some attitude items and some scenarios regarding the appropriateness of violence. Southerners were more likely than Northerners to agree that a man has the right to kill a person to defend his family or house. However, Southerners were not more likely than Northerners to agree with statements about violence in general. Southerners were only more likely than Northerners to have more positive attitudes toward violence when it related to defending their families or honor. Respondents were also asked to imagine that a guy named Fred was in a variety of different scenarios in which some bad things happened to him. In one version, they were told to imagine that Fred's 16-year-old daughter was sexually assaulted. Respondents were asked whether they felt that Fred would be "extremely justified" to go out and shoot the assailant; 23% of northern respondents agreed with this, compared with 47% of Southerners. Again, the regional differences were evident only for scenarios that involved defending one's family or honor. Score another point for Nisbett and Cohen.

Nisbett and Cohen aspired to get some *physiological measures* to support the idea that Southerners responded with violence to insults. One thing we've learned from physiological research is that when people are ready to aggress, their testosterone levels rise (e.g., Mazur, 1985). Nisbett and Cohen reasoned that if the culture of honor theory was correct, you should see evidence of testosterone rising in Southerners but not in Northerners following an insult. The challenge for Nisbett and Cohen, then, was to find a good way to insult people in an experimentally controlled situation. Here's what they did (see Cohen et al., 1996, for a more detailed description): Participants (who were all non-Hispanic white male students at the University of Michigan who had grown up either in the North or the South) came into the lab. Half were randomly assigned to an "insult condition" and were instructed to walk down a room between a wall and a long a row of tables to pick up a questionnaire to fill out. Along the way they encountered a confederate of the experimenter, posing as a rather uptight research assistant, busily digging in the open drawer of a file cabinet, which blocked the participants' path. The confederate looked rather frustrated that he had to close the file drawer to let the participant by, and the participant passed him and picked up his questionnaire. But on his way back, the participant discovered that the confederate had the file drawer open again and again was blocking his path. This time the confederate looked thoroughly ticked off at being interrupted once more. He slammed the door shut, bumped his shoulder into the participant as he walked by, and said "asshole!" Before the startled participant had the chance to react the confederate exited through a door marked "Photo Lab" that locked behind him (which was a good thing, as some participants tried to go after him). The insult had been delivered and the hapless participant was left alone to stew in his juices. The other half of the participants were in a control condition in which they were never insulted by the confederate. The dependent variable in this study was the change in participant's testosterone level throughout the experiment. The participants were asked to give saliva samples at various times through the experiment under a false explanation that the study was about task performance and blood sugar levels. The experimenters analyzed participants' testosterone level as it was meas-

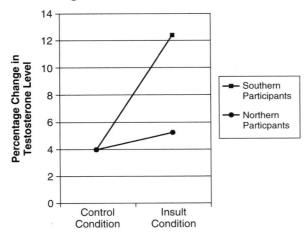

FIGURE 3.2

Whereas Northerners appear rather unaffected by insults, Southerners show a large increase in testosterone levels following an insult.

ured both before and several minutes after the insult, and it was compared between Northerners and Southerners. Here's what was found.

As Figure 3.2 shows, Southerners who had been insulted showed a sharp spike in their testosterone level. The insult made them angry and poised to aggress. In contrast, Northerners did not show a significant difference in their testosterone level between the two conditions. They had little reaction to the insult. Indeed, other measures showed that the Northerners found the insult to be quite humorous, apparently as it reflected a problem with the confederate. The Southerners showed clear signs of anger, as in a culture of honor a challenge to one's honor is a problem for oneself. This is further evidence for Nisbett and Cohen's theory.

The kinds of data that are perhaps most exciting for many psychologists are *behavioral measures*. Ultimately, we're interested in the kinds of things people do; however, behavioral measures are usually extremely difficult to get. They're especially challenging in studies of aggression, as one thing that is not acceptable is for your participants to leave your experiment with their experimental credit and a black eye. How can you measure aggression in a way in which no one actually gets hurt? Being creative methodologists, Cohen and colleagues (1996) figured that they could tap into aggressive behaviors by staging a game of "chicken" with the participant. They ran another study using the same "asshole" manipulation described above. After the participants had been insulted (or not, for those in the control condition), they were told that they had to proceed to another laboratory for the next part of the study. The way to the other lab was through a narrow hallway that had a row of tables along either side. Once the participant had started his trek down the hallway the experimenter signaled for a second confederate to begin his role. This confederate was chosen for his role because of his physical characteristics. Namely, he was 6′ 3″, weighed 250 pounds, and played on the offensive line of his college football team. His instructions were clear: Walk toward the participant at a quick pace and be sure *not* to give way. The participant thus had the choice of either stepping aside or being flattened by this oncoming freight train. The dependent measure was how close the participant got to this second confederate before yielding way. As Figure 3.3 shows, there was a clear cultural difference. Northerners showed no significant difference in their behaviors between the insult and control conditions. Southerners, in contrast, showed a pronounced difference. When they were not insulted they yielded much earlier than the northern subjects did—perhaps showing some of that famous southern hospitality. When they had been insulted, in stark contrast, they went right up to the face of the second confederate. This is a

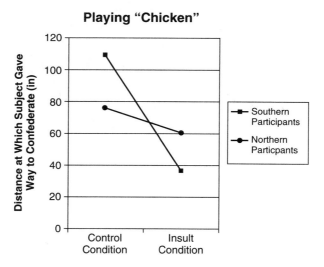

FIGURE 3.3

When they have not been insulted, Southerners yield to an oncoming person earlier than Northerners do. But when insulted, Southerners are more likely than Northerners to confront an oncoming person.

clear example of the culture of honor. It is interesting that they showed this aggressive stance even though the second confederate had never insulted them. The desire to show that one was a tough guy and not to be messed with was active in their minds and carried over to their interactions with a new person. This is yet another piece of evidence in support of Nisbett and Cohen's theory.

Another way to test the theory of the culture of honor is to see if there are regional differences in people's tolerance for insult-related aggression out in the real world. Cohen and Nisbett (1997) conducted a *field experiment* to test this hypothesis. Field experiments are experiments that are conducted outside the laboratory in the real world, with participants who are typically not aware that they are in a study. The real advantage of the field experiment is that we can be confident we are observing patterns that generalize to the real world and are not just limited to the artificial confines of the laboratory. Cohen and Nisbett conducted their study by mailing out letters to employers around the United States. Some of these offices were in the North, and some were in the South. The letters specified that the applicant, a 27-year-old male who was fresh out of prison, was looking for a job. However, there were two different versions of these letters. In an "honor letter" condition, the applicant explained that he had served time for manslaughter, because he had killed a man who had slept with his girlfriend and had teased him about it publicly. The applicant described how he had told the victim to "take it back, or else"—meaning the public insult—and when it wasn't taken back, he had grabbed a pipe and killed the victim in anger. In a "control letter" condition, the applicant explained that he had served time for stealing a car. The dependent variable of interest was the warmth of the letter that the employer sent in return. As might be expected from what we've seen thus far, the southern employers were more sympathetic to the applicant in the "honor letter" condition than the northern employers, but there were no regional differences in warmth in the "control letter" condition. The culture of honor appears to be still operating in the South. This is yet another demonstration in favor of Nisbett and Cohen's account for the greater violence in the U.S. South.

Nisbett and Cohen have conducted a number of other studies using diverse methodologies that further converge to support their hypothesis, but I think you've gotten the point by now, so I won't go into those. Why their research program is so compelling is that they were able to find support for their hypotheses from such a diverse range of methods. No single study is perfect, not Nisbett and Cohen's, or anyone else's. Alternative explanations exist for virtually any given study. However, when you utilize a diverse range of methods and continually find convergent evidence for your hypotheses, these alternative explanations fall by the wayside. You might wonder, for example, how representative were the southern students who were attending classes at the University of Michigan of Southern culture in the testosterone study. That would be a good point, and it's a valid challenge to that study. However, that point cannot account for the findings in the field experiment or in the archival evidence. Unless there is an alternative explanation that can account for the results in *all* of the experiments, we're left to accept the one explanation that can account for all the findings. That is, the U.S. South has a culture of honor that leads people (particularly white men) to respond aggressively to insults or threats to their honor, and this seems to be associated with the herding background of the South's initial European settlers. This doesn't mean that other competing theories that might arise in the future don't warrant our attention; however, unless they are consistent with the wide array of findings presented here they'll pale in comparison to Nisbett and Cohen's theory. As noted before, research across cultures is particularly prone to methodological challenges, raising many alternative explanations for each study, and because of this a multiple-method approach is especially valuable in cultural psychology. Our confidence in a theory increases with the number of different ways a researcher can provide support for it.

SUMMARY

Cross-cultural psychological research presents a set of unique methodological challenges. As a first step, it is crucial to learn something about the culture you are studying. Also, it is important to ensure that there is methodological equivalence between the cultures that you are comparing.

In survey research a variety of issues pose validity problems for comparisons of cultures, particularly for questionnaires with subjective questions. These include problems inherent in translating materials, response biases such as moderacy and extremity biases, acquiescence biases, reference-group effects, and deprivation effects. There are some methodological and analytic strategies to deal with most of these problems; however, the best solution would seem to be to avoid comparisons of means of questionnaire responses whenever possible.

The experiment provides a method that transcends the methodological shortcomings in comparisons of means across cultures. Furthermore, any scientific investigation is improved when multiple methods are adopted in the search for convergent findings.

There have been many methodological developments that are particular to the study of culture. An inherent limitation of cross-cultural research is that the primary independent variable, culture, cannot be manipulated by the experimenter because our participants arrive at our experiments already enculturated. Two methods that approximate experimental manipulations of cultural background are the situation-sampling and cultural priming techniques. Cultures can also be studied directly, either through quantitative analyses or the presence of particular cultural variables.

Cultural differences beg for explanations, and the "unpackaging" method allows for the identification of other psychological processes that relate to the cultural differences that have been observed. Unpackaging allows cultural psychological studies not only to significantly advance our investigation of the cultures under study, but also to provide an added level of explanation for why psychological processes operate as they do in a given culture.

4

Development and Socialization

Culture shapes many of the norms that govern our behavior. Take the question of interpersonal space. When you have a conversation with someone you stand a certain distance from the person. There's quite a range of distances that would allow for a functional conversation. You could communicate fine if you were just one foot away, and you could also communicate fine if you were 15 feet away. However, people usually don't use the full range of possible distances from their partners when they have conversations. Rather, within a culture there is usually an implicitly understood "appropriate" conversation distance that people unconsciously adopt. If someone starts off a conversation that is at either too great or too small a distance, usually people will adjust where they are standing until they have reestablished the appropriate distance, and these adjustments occur for the most minor deviations from the norm. Furthermore, these appropriate distances vary across cultures. For example, in Venezuela the typical conversation distance is 32 inches, in the United States it is 35 inches, and in Japan it is 40 inches (Sussman & Rosenfeld, 1982). Venezuelans prefer closer conversational distances, and Japanese prefer wider conversational distances, compared with Americans.

Upon learning about this cultural difference, or any of the others covered in this book, you might ask this: How did Venezuelans come to prefer closer interpersonal spaces and Japanese to prefer more distant interpersonal spaces than Americans? How did cultures get inside people's heads in the first place? There seem to be at least two distinct possibilities for the origins of these cultural differences. One is that Venezuelans, Japanese, and Americans were born that way. That is, Venezuelans tend to have more of an inherited genetic predisposition to prefer closer interpersonal distances, and Japanese have inherited tendencies to prefer greater interpersonal distances, whereas Americans were born preferring intermediate interpersonal distances. Although it is theoretically possible that the genes underlying inherited psychological traits are not distributed equally across the globe, there is as yet no psychological evidence to support this hypothesis, and this explanation is challenged by acculturation research that finds weaker cultural differences among those who have moved to other cultures (e.g., Heine & Lehman, 2004).

The second possibility to account for such cultural differences is that people of different cultural backgrounds come into the world with rather similar genetic temperaments, yet interact with different environments as they grow up. According to this perspective, it is their early experiences with their environments that lead Venezuelans to prefer closer interpersonal distances, Japanese to prefer greater interpersonal distances, and Americans to prefer intermediate distances. That is, people acquire their cultures through socialization. The field of cultural psychology hinges on this second explanation.

This chapter explores how people come to be socialized into particular cultural worlds. How do people acquire culture? How do child-rearing experiences differ around the world? This chapter addresses the two guiding themes of this book: first, how universal predispositions become shaped in culturally specific ways, and second, how people's experiences, particularly when they are infants and children, come to influence the ways they think.

Universal Brains Develop into Culturally Variable Minds

The starting assumption of cultural psychology is that we are all cultural beings. One key adaptation that enabled humans to distinguish themselves from their proto-chimpanzee ancestors was the ability to learn and accumulate cultural information so well. This adaptation allowed humans to learn the requisite technologies and skills to stake out a successful existence in such diverse environments as the ice-encased Arctic hinterland, the thick Amazonian jungle, the parched Kalahari desert, and the dog-eat-dog corporate world of Wall Street. Without this ability to learn cultural information so well we would likely still be competing with our distant chimpanzee relatives over territorial rights to some termite mounds. The ability to acquire culture knowledge has allowed us to succeed in an amazingly diverse array of environments.

The key point about cultural knowledge and skills is that they are not in our heads from the beginning. This contrasts with other important kinds of knowledge and skills that we see in other species. Salmon do not have to be taught how to find their way back from the ocean to the stream where they were born. That knowledge is instinctual. Cats do not need to be taught to go into their hunting position when they hear something rustle in the grass. These kinds of skills are hard-wired, although certain environmental experiences might be necessary to trigger them. In contrast, we are not born with the knowledge of how to hunt a seal with a handmade kayak and harpoon, catch a howler monkey with a poisoned blowdart, collect the morning dew in emptied ostrich egg shells, or close a seven-figure advertising deal with a multinational firm on Madison Avenue. We must learn these skills, and we have certain biological potentials that enable us to learn them so well. We come into this world cultureless, but we are prepared to adjust to and seize meaning from any environment with which we are presented.

That people from different cultures come into this world so similarly yet end up having such different life experiences attests to the powerful role that socialization occupies in influencing who we become. As the cultural anthropologist Clifford Geertz (1973) famously asserted, "we all begin with the natural equipment to live a thousand kinds of life but end in the end having lived only one" (p. 45). This suggests that fundamentally our nature is that of a cultural being. Our universal biological foundation is shaped by our experiences, such that we are able to thrive in an extremely broad array of cultural environments. Who we are is importantly influenced by the cultural worlds into which we are socialized. And all humans have been socialized into some kind of cultural environment that influences how they perceive and understand themselves and their worlds.

Sensitive Periods for Cultural Socialization

It would seem that if humans evolved as cultural beings, we should see evidence that our brains are preprogrammed to learn cultural meaning systems. One such source of evidence would be an indication that there is a sensitive period for being enculturated. A sensitive period is a period of time in an organism's development that allows for the relatively easy acquisition of a set of skills. If an organism misses that chance to acquire those skills, it would have a difficult time doing so later after the sensitive period has expired. Sensitive periods provide evidence that an organism is preprogrammed to learn something by suggesting that the acquisition of some kinds of skills occurs because a set of biological constraints is present during the sensitive period but weakens with maturation (Newport, 1991). Sensitive periods highlight the presence of those biological constraints that allow for easy learning. If the skills that are to be acquired will increase the likelihood of survival for that individual throughout his or her lifespan, then we should see signs that the individual has a biological disposition to learn those skills.

Sensitive Periods for Language Acquisition. Have you ever learned a second language? How easy was it for you to speak the new language flawlessly? Likely, the success of your experiences depends on how old you were when you started to learn the new language.

How people go about acquiring languages is the question that has attracted the vast majority of research on sensitive periods in humans. Language ability is a hallmark human characteristic, and although there are rudimentary language skills in some other species (Seyfarth, Cheney, & Marler, 1980), no other species is as dependent on their language skills or has as complex a language system as humans. It is easy to imagine how language skills provided a survival advantage to humans. Being able to describe to others where the dangers are, to coordinate each other's behaviors to increase the success of a hunt, to discover and share the precise social dynamics that are occurring among your allies and competitors, and to say the right things so that you can attract a mate—all of these advantages suggest that those humans who were able to communicate most effectively were more likely to produce surviving offspring than those who were not. Because language skills confer such an obvious evolutionary advantage, there should be evidence of a sensitive period for language acquisition.

One source of evidence for a sensitive period of language acquisition is with respect to people's abilities to discriminate among different sounds. Humans are capable of producing, recognizing, and using approximately 150 phonemes in communication; however, no language uses more than 70 of them (Brown, 1991). This means that many phonemes that are used in various languages around the world are not used in other languages. Interestingly, people are not able to discriminate easily between some phonemes that are not in their own language. For example, the Japanese language does not have separate phonemes for the sounds "la" and "ra." Likewise, the Japanese language does not have a phoneme for "va," although it does have a phoneme for the closely related sound of "ba." Consequently, an adult who was exposed only to the Japanese language cannot perceive the differences between "la"s and "ra"s, or between "ba"s and "va"s—phonemes that sound obviously different to English speakers. To native Japanese-speaking adults who never learned English as a child, the words "rubber" and "lover" sound the same, a fact that has surely led to some embarrassing cross-cultural misunderstandings!

So how do English speakers learn to distinguish between sounds that sound the same to Japanese speakers? Research with infants suggests that young infants can discriminate among all the phonemes that humans are able to produce. We come into this world able to recognize all kinds of different sounds. However, when we learn a language, it is functional to perceive sounds categorically. That is, it's easier to understand an utterance if we can recognize that any sound that falls within a particular range is a "la," and that any sound that falls within a slightly different range is a "ra." If we did not perceive sounds categorically we would have a most difficult time understanding the sounds that we heard. As we are exposed to a language we begin to categorize sounds in ways that are used by that language. And this begins early in life—very early. Within the first year of life children already begin to lose the ability to distinguish between closely related sounds that are not in their own language. For example, as Figure 4.1 shows, native English-speaking children of 6–8 months of age can reliably distinguish between two sounds from the Hindi language, but 10–12-month-old native English speakers cannot (Werker & Tees, 1984). Even 4-day-old infants already begin to show a preference for the rhythm of sounds from their own language over other languages (Mehler, Jusczyk, & Lambertz, 1988). Humans appear to come into this world ready to attend to the sounds that they hear communicated in language and to separate this from all the other noises that they encounter. The universal human ability of being able to distinguish all possible phonemes gets whittled down to the ability to perceive and categorize only the phonemes are heard during the critical window of language development.

This research suggests that we are biologically prepared to attend to human speech as soon as we come into this world. And this preference for speech (we are not especially attentive to many other kinds of sound as babies; Vouloumanos & Werker, 2004) predisposes us to start picking up languages at an early age. However, in the process of learning a language our brains

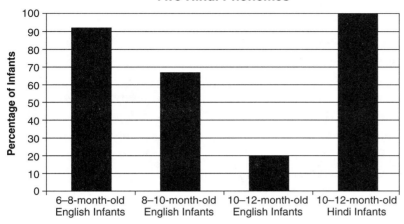

FIGURE 4.1

Although very young infants in English-speaking households can distinguish between two Hindi phonemes, older infants being raised by English speakers can no longer do so.

need to organize the sounds and other features of our languages so they can recognize them. Early in life (before puberty) our brains are especially plastic for organizing themselves in response to language input. Later on, however, our brains are not as flexible. Because of this, humans are better at acquiring and mastering languages early in life (both first and second languages, although adults may initially outstrip children when they begin to learn a second language; Johnson & Newport, 1989), but this capacity declines with age, especially with respect to aspects such as accent and grammar (Lenneberg, 1967; Newport, 1991). For example, deaf children who first learn sign language late in childhood do not learn it as well as either deaf children who learn it earlier in childhood or children who become deaf later in childhood and learn sign language as their second language (Mayberry, 1993).

This sensitive period for language acquisition has been exploited by the militaries of various countries throughout history. In many wars the militaries have used words, called shibboleths, which are peculiar to a language, and that those who learned the language late in life have a difficult time pronouncing. For example, in World War II the American military would ask people with Japanese appearance to pronounce the word "Lollapalooza" as a way of identifying whether the person grew up speaking English, and thus was unlikely to be a Japanese spy. Those Japanese who learned English later in life typically mangled the pronunciation. Likewise, Nazi spies were ferreted out from various European nations by being asked to pronounce words that were difficult for a native German speaker to say, thus betraying that they had not learned the languages as a child.

The differences in language competence can be quite striking among members of a family who were of different ages at the time they immigrated to a new country. For example, Henry Kissinger, former secretary of state of the United States, was 15 when his family moved to this country from Germany. His younger brother, Walter, was 14 at the time. After decades of living in the United States Henry's English always preserved a thick German accent. Walter, on the other hand, speaks with no German accent whatsoever. When asked why his brother still spoke with an accent Walter replied, "Because Henry doesn't listen!" However little Henry may have listened, a more likely explanation for his German accent is that he started learning English after his sensitive period for acquiring languages was for the most part closed. It is much more difficult to master a language if you start learning it after the sensitive period has expired.

Another source of evidence for this sensitive period in language acquisition comes from studies of bilingual individuals' brains. In these studies, people are placed in functional magnetic resonance imaging (fMRI) scanners to see which parts of their brain are active while they are listening to different languages. For bilinguals who learned their second language later in life, one part of the brain is active when they hear their second language and another when they hear their native language (both parts are in Broca's area). In contrast, bilinguals who learned their second language early in life showed activation in the same part of the brain, regardless of whether they were hearing their second language or their native one (Kim, Relkin, & Lee, 1997; also see Chee et al., 1999). This is evidence that early in life the language center of the brain is quite flexible at attuning itself to various kinds of linguistic input. After the sensitive period starts to close, however, those regions of the brain are no longer as capable of being restructured to accommodate the new language (also see related work by Perani, Paulesu, & Galles, 1998).

The most compelling kind of evidence that one could gather to test whether humans have a sensitive period for language acquisition would be to experimentally raise some children with no language input until they were 15 or so, and then try to teach the unfortunate subjects a language and measure their performance. You'll be happy to know that psychologists don't run

Genie, at the time of her discovery (left), and the so-called Wild Boy of Aveyron (right).

these kinds of experiments. However, there are a few tragic instances of children whose real-life situations have mirrored this horrific thought experiment. In 1800 in France, someone found a 12-year-old boy who had apparently lived in the wild for most of his life. This wild boy of Aveyron, as he was called, was coached to speak for several years by a teacher. This coaching had little success, however, and the boy was able to learn to speak only two words: "milk," and "ohmyGod." Indeed, he never developed into a fully functioning adult and was able to live only "a kind of vegetative life, sunk in inaccessible torpor, capable only of detached and half-articulate sounds, or silent from an absence of ideas" (Newton, 2002, p. 101).

A more recent instance was an appalling case of child abuse. A young Californian girl, named Genie, was raised alone in silence, either tethered to a potty chair or confined to a cagelike crib until the age of 13. Poor Genie's vocabulary at the time of discovery in 1970 consisted of two words: "stopit," and "nomore." Many people were involved in Genie's rehabilitation, including various scientists and foster parents. However, despite her considerable intelligence, Genie never developed any mastery over grammar or syntax (although she did develop a good-sized vocabulary). A poignant example of one of her sentences as an adult was "Think about Mama love

Genie" (Newton, 2002, p. 27). Despite decades of exposure to her only language, Genie has not been able to attain the grammatical competence of a 5-year-old. These tragic instances lack the rigorous experimental control that would allow us to draw firm conclusions, and it is clearly possible that the children's language difficulties might have stemmed from the hard times they experienced rather than their isolation. Nonetheless, these case studies are very much in line with what you would expect from efforts to learn a first language after the sensitive period had ended.

The tragic stories of the Aveyron boy and Genie, as well as the volumes of research on language acquisition, demonstrate that we all come into the world with similar language learning capabilities, yet some of us have those capabilities directed toward learning English, and others toward learning Hindi or any other of the more than three thousand languages spoken on the planet. We are born biologically prepared to learn a language, and our early experiences determine how our minds process the different kinds of human speech we later encounter. We are socialized to understand different languages. English speakers do not have English-speaking genes, and Hindi speakers do not have Hindi-speaking genes. They differ in their experiences—importantly, their early experiences—and this leads their minds to process the linguistic input that they are hearing in greatly different ways.

Sensitive Periods for Acquiring Culture. Learning a language is a necessary aspect of being socialized into a particular culture. As the linguist Edward Sapir put it, "Language is a great force of socialization, probably the greatest that exists" (Mandelbaum, 1951, p. 15). Language and culture are both meaning systems that we acquire through our social interactions, and they depend greatly on each other. Some would say that language is a part of culture—the communicating function of culture. Because learning a language and being socialized in a culture are so closely intertwined, we should expect some similarities between language acquisition and cultural acquisition more generally. Is there a sensitive period for acquiring cultural knowledge?

Measuring the acquisition of culture, unfortunately, is much less straightforward than measuring the acquisition of language. I've always been rather envious of linguists because languages around the world are different in such concrete ways that they are easy to measure. Each language has its own grammar, accent, syntax, morphology, and vocabulary. Cultures are far less tangible to study than languages. Whereas it's easy to determine whether someone has mastered a particular language, it's not as straightforward to determine whether someone has mastered a particular culture. An inability to distinguish between the words "rubber" and "lover," for example, is a pretty reliable indicator that one is not a native English speaker. It is much more challenging to identify ways of understanding the world that can indicate whether one has acquired a particular cultural meaning system. How could we investigate whether people have a sensitive period for acquiring culture?

Despite the various methodological challenges involved, the anthropologist Yasuko Minoura (1992) launched a large-scale investigation to see whether there was a sensitive period for learning culture. She targeted Japanese-born children who had moved to the United States at different ages along with their parents. Minoura reasoned that if there was a sensitive period for learning cultures, then people who moved from Japan at different ages would have different understanding of American and Japanese ways. She interviewed her participants, and developed an elaborate coding system to assess how well people had acquired various cognitive, behavioral, and emotional domains of Japanese and American culture. For example, she asked people whether they preferred the company of Japanese or American friends. Her results are quite intriguing.

Judging from the answers that people gave, it seems that people appear to be internalizing cultural meaning systems from birth; however, after 9 years of age some permanence emerges in the retention of learned cultural meanings. That is, those participants who moved to the United States before the age of 9 reported becoming largely "Americanized," and felt relatively distant from their Japanese heritage. It seems that before these individuals were 9 years old, their cultural meaning systems were plastic enough that their Japanese selves could be largely erased and replaced with American ones. In contrast, those who moved to the United States when they were between the ages of 9 and 15 still retained some Japanese cultural sensibilities but also felt reasonably comfortable with American ways, but not to the extent of those who had moved at a younger age. It would appear that during this window people's minds are still plastic enough to learn a new cultural meaning system fairly well; however, their earlier acquired Japanese selves have a sense of permanence. Those who moved to the United States after the age of 15, however, were never able to fully embrace American culture, particularly with respect to their emotional experiences. Although they could learn what was considered to be appropriate behavior, and they could act quite competently in those ways, they reported that it didn't always feel natural. There was something that seemed more comfortable to them about Japanese cultural ways. Those people who left Japan after the age of 15 appear to continue to see the world through Japanese cultural lenses. Just as people who learn a second language after puberty often maintain an indelible accent from their mother tongue, it seems that people who learn a second culture later on often preserve an echo of the emotional repertoire of their mother culture (also see McCauley & Henrich, 2006; Tsai, Ying, & Lee, 2000).

Although more research is necessary to draw firm conclusions, this developmental sequence of culture-learning that Minoura identified is quite similar in timing to people's ability to acquire a second language (Johnson & Newport, 1989). Moreover, in Minoura's study the variable that correlated most strongly with American cultural mastery was English language ability. Those who mastered English especially well also felt the most at home in the United States. Cultural acquisition and language acquisition may be inextricably intertwined as they both involve efforts to extract meaning from the social environment. Humans appear to have a sensitive window when they are especially adept at attending to the meanings provided by their social environments and at organizing their lives around these meanings.

Cultural Differences in Psychological Processes Emerge with Age

Because humans are born cultureless and acquire their culture as they are socialized, it follows that cultural differences in psychological processes should become more pronounced with age. Young children from different cultures should appear relatively more similar to each other (although, as you'll soon see, there are still some cultural differences even among toddlers) than should older children, because younger children have been socialized less deeply into their cultures. Likewise, the most pronounced cultural differences should emerge for adults, as they have had much more time for their minds to be shaped by cultural experiences.

Conducting studies across different age groups is inherently challenging, and few studies have done this in different cultures. However, the few that have been done nicely highlight how people become socialized to think in culturally divergent ways. For example, consider people's beliefs about how the future will unfold. One way is to extrapolate linearly from the recent past to the present and on to the future. For example, the Euro was worth approximately $.90 U.S. in 2002, $1.10 in 2003, and $1.20 in 2004. What will the Euro be worth in 2010? If we assume that the pattern of change continues linearly then the Euro should be worth approximately $1.80 in 2010. However, change can also occur nonlinearly. Indeed, the Euro was worth approximately $.95 U.S. in 1999, .90 in 2000, and .88 in 2001. The pattern of the Euro thus changed from a currency that was decreasing in value relative to the U.S. dollar to one that was increasing in value.

Some research reveals that East Asians and North Americans differ in how they expect the future to unfold (Ji, 2005). For example, North Americans are more likely to expect that trends will continue in the same direction as they have in the past. East Asians, in contrast, are more likely to expect that change will be nonlinear, and that an increasing trend will soon be followed with a decreasing trend. This cultural difference has been explained in terms of cultural differences in dialectical ways of thinking, which we will explore in more detail in Chapter 9, Cognition and Perception.

When are these cultural differences in perceptions of trends evident between Chinese and Canadians? In one study, children, aged 7, 9, and 11, were brought into the laboratory (Ji, 2005). The children read a number of scenarios about a past state of affairs (e.g., they read about a child who was always sad) and they were asked to predict a future state of affairs (e.g., how would the child feel tomorrow). The Chinese and Canadian 7-year-olds tended to respond quite similarly. In contrast, the Chinese 9-year-old children were more likely to expect a reversal of the trends compared with the Canadian 9-year-olds, and this cultural difference became slightly more pronounced among 11-year-olds (see Figure 4.2). Chinese and Canadian 7-year-olds are more similar in terms of their thoughts about the future than are 9- and 11-year-olds. With age, people from different cultures diverge in their psychological experiences. These kinds of developmental patterns showing cultural differences increasing with age have been identified for a number of phenomena: explanations of others' behaviors (Miller, 1984; see Chapter 9, Cognition and Perception), social loafing (Gabrenya, Wang, & Latane, 1985; see Chapter 11, Interpersonal Attraction, Close Relationships, and Groups), and tendencies to focus on positive aspects of the self (Falbo, Poston, Triscari, & Zhang, 1997; see Chapter 6, Motivation).

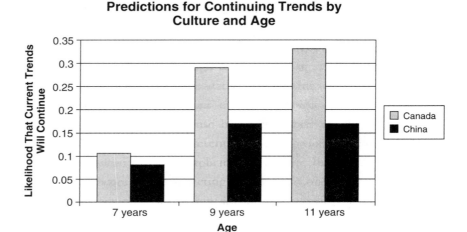

FIGURE 4.2

Seven-year-old Chinese and Canadian children make similar predictions about the future. As the children age, however, Canadian children come to expect more consistent trends than Chinese children.

What Kinds of Childhood Experiences Differ Across Cultures?

Acquiring a culture is thus a developmental process and people are socialized into their respective cultural worlds by participating in specific cultural practices and institutions. The more one has engaged in such practices, the more one's ways of thinking will become habitualized to respond to those practices. What are some specific childhood experiences that vary across cultures?

Sleeping Arrangements. The first decision that every new parent must make is, "Where do we put the baby?" This seemingly simple decision can tell us a lot about one's cultural values, and it largely influences the kind of environment in which the baby is going to start its life. And people from different cultures make this decision in strikingly different ways.

If you grew up in a European-descent North American household, odds are that your parents made this decision in one particular way. It is quite likely that your parents set aside a room in their house, perhaps decorating it with pastel colors and scenes of romping bunny rabbits or alphabet letters, and put a crib in it for you to sleep in. That is, there is a cultural norm widely shared among many European-descent North American families that the "right way" to bring up children is to provide them with their own private rooms to grow up in, often starting the day that they return from the hospital.

As "right" as this way seems to many European-descent North Americans, people from many other cultural backgrounds have a very different view. For example, in a study of 136 societies, infants in two-thirds of these groups slept in the same bed as their mothers; in the majority of the other cases, infants slept in the same room as their mothers but in a different bed (Whiting, 1964). American parents were the only ones in a survey of 100 societies who created a separate room for the baby to sleep in (Burton & Whiting, 1961). In many societies, children continue to sleep in the same bed as their parents, or sometimes grandparents, until they are well into their primary school years. Furthermore, this practice of "co-sleeping" is also quite common in other subcultures in the United States—for example, among African-Americans, Asian-Americans, and Hispanics. The practice of people sleeping separately in their own beds has not yet been identified in a single subsistence society around the world. For example, among the Efe, a hunting and gathering culture from Zaire, it is not unusual for their small leaf huts to include the sleeping bodies of parents, their children, a grandparent, and a visitor, with their limbs all tangled together in one snoring mass (Worthman & Melby, 2002). Providing separate sleeping quarters for the baby, so common in much of North America, is a rather unusual cultural practice throughout the world.

One thing that I learned upon becoming a parent is the extent to which parenting decisions are moralized by others. That is, people tend to evaluate the decisions of parents as either "good" or "bad," and parents go through a lot of grief trying to ensure that they are raising their child in the best possible way. And this tendency to moralize parenting decisions clearly extends to the decision of whether parents should allow their child to co-sleep with them. For example, America's most famous infant sleep expert, Dr. Richard Ferber, had the following to say about co-sleeping in his 1985 book: "if you find that you actually prefer to sleep with your infant, you should consider your own feelings very carefully." Dr. Ferber also states that "even if you and your child seem happy about his sharing your bed at night, and even if he seems to sleep well there, in the long run this habit will probably not be good for either of you." The moralization of co-sleeping is even more evident when we consider some guidance that is provided on this topic by advice columnists Ann Landers and Prudence:

Dear Ann Landers: I have three children, ages 2, 3, and 5. Here's my problem: All three end up in my bedroom during the night. Usually I know they are there, but I sleep right through it. . . . I'm newly divorced and there, is no man in my bed, so the kids aren't disturbing anyone. . . . My mother tells me I must make the kids sleep in their own rooms. She says sometimes children who want to sleep with their parents need to be taken to a psychologist because their behavior indicates deeper problems. What do you say? Is it that big a deal when they are so young?
—Wondering

Dear Wondering: Usually, I tell parents to keep the kids out of their bed at night, but in your case I suspect the divorce has made them insecure. Talk to your pediatrician about the way to wean these kids away from this habit. You really do need professional guidance. . . . Good luck, dear. You have your hands full. (January 14, 1992; reported in Shweder, Jensen, & Goldstein, 1995)

Dear Prudence: I am writing you about a rather bizarre situation. My wife and I have been together for nearly 13 years. Things were great until the birth of our second child, a daughter, in 1998. Since the day our daughter came home, she has slept in our bed. The year before last we even bought a new, larger home so that our daughter would have her own bedroom. This improved nothing; our daughter still sleeps in our bed, and I have been retired to the family room couch. I love my wife and my daughter, but I am alone. I complain, only to be told that our daughter—nearly 7!—will be in her own room soon. At times these debates become loud, at which point I am told I am selfish and must not care about our daughter. I know that I am not selfish or uncaring. I am, however, considering a divorce. It is not something I want, but I no longer wish to live like a guest in my own home.
—Lost and lonely

Dear Lost: Something obviously happened in year six of your marriage that made your wife decide she had reached her sexpiration date. Not only does she have a 7-year-old chastity belt, but no kid in the second grade belongs in her mother's bed. The emotional turmoil for this child should be immeasurable. You certainly have the patience of a saint—a celibate one, at that—but you must now insist she see a counselor or mediator with you. If her problems cannot be dealt with, you will, indeed, have to divorce. . . .
—Prudie, promptly.
(June 2, 2005, *Slate*)

As you can see, issues of children co-sleeping with parents are not seen as a matter of personal choice; rather, they are seen as behaviors that reflect the moral value of the parents. Making the "wrong" choice in where you let your child sleep is something that suggests that you need "professional guidance," or is something that will cause the child "immeasurable emotional turmoil," indicates the reaching of a "sexpiration date," and necessitates divorce. Parenting decisions, and the ways that others in the culture respond to them, reflect the underlying values of a culture.

Why do you think European-descent North Americans are so much more likely than most of the rest of the world to view co-sleeping as a morally bad parenting decision? One possibility is that co-sleeping is something that you do only if you don't have enough space in your home to give the children their own rooms. Perhaps the big wide open spaces of the North American continent allowed the room to let children have their own privacy, whereas much of the rest of the world can't afford the luxury of having that much real estate, given higher population densities. Perhaps people in other cultures would also think it is better parenting to give their children their own private rooms, and the only thing preventing them from doing so is that their houses are not big enough.

Although the availability of space is an issue that must be relevant to the question of why people co-sleep, it is not the only issue. Consider the following study: Researchers approached people living in Chicago and in Orissa, India, and asked them how they would arrange the sleeping arrangements for a hypothetical family that consisted of seven members: a father (f), mother (m), three sons aged 15, 11, and 8 (s15, s11, s8), and two daughters aged 14 and 3 (d14, d3) (Shweder et al., 1995). The participants were asked to imagine a variety of different space situations. In one case they have to figure out where everyone would sleep in a house that has only one room (that decision was easy), in another the house has two rooms, three rooms, and so on up to seven rooms. There are many different ways that you can arrange the families in the different room combinations.

For example, in a house with three rooms there are 301 possible ways that you can divide up the sleeping arrangements of this hypothetical seven-member family. However, people do not see all of these 301 ways as equally appropriate. Rather, people in the different cultures tended to favor just a handful of possible solutions. When asked to divide up the family into these three rooms people in the two cultures tended to reach quite different solutions. For example, here are two possible solutions: The 3-year-old daughter can be put in the same room as the mother and father, the 14-year-old daughter can share a room with the 8-year-old son, and the 15-year-old and 11-year-old sons can be together. A second arrangement is to put the father in a room with the 8-year-old son, put the 15-year-old and 11-year-old sons together, and put the mother in a room with both the 3-year-old and 14-year-old daughters. These two arrangements were viewed as the best three-room solution by 47% of the Indian respondents (see Figure 4.3). In stark contrast, not a single American participant viewed either of these as the best three-room solution. Rather, 88% of the Americans considered this the best solution: The father and mother are put in one room, the two daughters share a room, and the three sons share a room. The Indians saw this arrangement as best 47% of the time (there were a number of other different arrangements that were viewed as best by a few participants). Given the same resources, the Indians and Americans tended to come up with different solutions.

The different sleeping arrangements that were preferred between the two cultures tells us much about the underlying values of the cultures. The Indians seemed to be guided by four moral principles in deciding which sleeping arrangements were appropriate. The most important principle they adhered to was entitled "**incest avoidance**." That is, post-pubescent members of the family of the opposite sex should not sleep in rooms together. The second most important principle for the Indians was "**protection of the vulnerable**." According to this principle, young children who are needy and vulnerable should not be left alone at night. The principle that was third

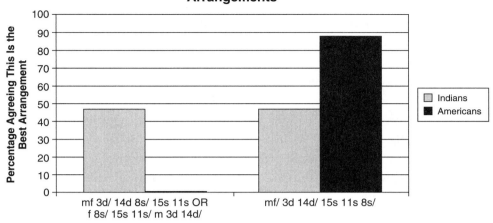

FIGURE 4.3

The two different sleeping arrangements on the left of the graph are often considered desirable by Indians, but they were not rated as desirable by any Americans. In contrast, the sleeping arrangement on the right of the graph is preferred by more Americans than Indians.

most important for the Indians was **"female chastity anxiety."** This principle holds that unmarried post-pubescent women should always be chaperoned to protect them from engaging in any sexual activity that would be viewed as shameful. The last principle to guide the Indians' decisions was **"respect for hierarchy,"** in which post-pubescent boys are conferred social status by allowing them to not have to sleep with parents or young children.

The decisions made by Americans, in contrast, were governed by a rather different set of principles. The Americans were similar to the Indians in that they also viewed incest avoidance as the most important principle in deciding about sleeping arrangements. Indeed, incest avoidance is often discussed as a cultural universal whose breach has serious consequences, both in terms of destroying family relations and in potentially producing offspring that suffer from recessive genetic disorders (Westermarck, 1922). Two other moral principles were adhered to by Americans. The second most important principle for them was the **"sacred couple,"** in which participants believed that married couples should be given their own space for emotional intimacy and sexual privacy. This principle, prized by many Westerners, is violated in many cultures. For example, a review by Whiting and Whiting (1979) found that in 42% of herding and agricultural societies the husbands and wives slept in separate rooms. The third most important principle for Americans was the **"autonomy ideal,"** a belief that young children who are needy and vulnerable should learn to be self-reliant and able to take care of themselves.

In sum, with the exception of a shared concern about avoiding potentially incestuous situations, different cultural values guided the Indians and the Americans in deciding about sleeping arrangements. Americans strive to protect the privacy of the married couple and encourage the development of independence among their children. In stark contrast, Indians prefer to keep their young children and post-pubescent daughters from being alone, and try to offer older boys the deference of not having to sleep with their parents or younger siblings. A simple decision about sleeping arrangements can tell us a lot about a culture's values.

North American children and children from many other cultures would thus appear to have very different early experiences. How do you think these different sleeping arrangements affect children's socialization? It would seem that North American children live in an environment where they are by themselves from a very early age and must cry out to their parents when they have needs to be taken care of. Children from many other cultures, in contrast, may live in an environment where their mother is always around—often, as in many cultures, the children are literally carried by their mother throughout the day. Mothers do not need to be called to, as they are always present to respond to the child's needs. Furthermore, the cultural variability in children's social worlds is not just limited to the nearness of their mothers. In many cultures around the world, children are raised in far closer proximity with various others than are Western children. For example, whereas Scottish children spend more time with physical objects than they do with other people, the precise opposite pattern is evident among Nigerian children (Agiobu-Kemmer, 1984). The social worlds of young children differ dramatically around the world, and children are thus learning very different ideas about how to perceive themselves and their relations with others (see Rothbaum, Weisz, Pott, Miyake, & Morelli, 2000).

Individualistic Versus Collectivistic Orientations. The different sleeping experiences of children around the world reflect the relevance of early socialization experiences for understanding the development of cultural values. As noted in Chapter 2, a key dimension for understanding cultural variability around the world is individualism-collectivism. As this concept is so important to the ways that people think in different cultures, we would expect that cultural variation along this dimension would emerge early in life. Indeed, much research suggests that it does. For example, in one study young European-American and Chinese children (age range 3 to 8 years) were interviewed about themselves and their early memories (Wang, 2004). Compared with Chinese children, American children were more likely to describe themselves with individualistic statements about their own qualities and preferences (e.g., "I like hockey" or "I'm a very smart person") and were less likely to describe themselves with collectivistic statements (e.g., "I am from Albany" or "I am in the second grade"—we'll explore this point in more detail in Chapter 5, Self and Personality). American children were also less likely to refer to others when describing themselves, compared with the Chinese children. By an early age children in different cultures are socialized to differentially attend to individualistic versus collectivistic aspects of themselves.

These different orientations appear to emerge because of the ways children interact with their parents. If you look in a North American bookstore for advice on parenting, you'll typically find whole sections devoted to the topic (which itself raises an interesting question: If parenting is assumed to reflect universal and instinctive caregiving responses, why do people have to read so many books to learn how to do it properly?). For example, one strategy that is frequently emphasized in North American parenting books (e.g., the "Positive Discipline" series) is to acknowledge children's feelings or perspective in order to gain their compliance. A North American mother might say, "I know you want to put paint on the cat. That looks like a lot of fun. But I don't want you to do that." The mother is thus empathizing with the child's perspective and is taking his lead. Does this sound like familiar or good parenting to you? Indeed, parenting strategies such as this, and of letting the child take the lead while the mothers take a supporting role and elaborate on the child's ideas and preferences, are very common among upper socioeconomic status North Americans. In contrast, however, interactions between Chinese children and their mothers are quite different. Chinese mothers are more likely to lead the interactions and introduce the topics, while the children learn to follow their mother's lead (Haight, 1999; Wang, 2001; Wang, Leichtman, & Davies, 2000). How might these different parenting styles affect the ways children develop? It would seem that the North American children come to learn that they are independent agents to whom their mothers respond, whereas the Chinese children learn that they are relational beings who need to respond to their mothers. Other research finds that North American mothers are more likely to discuss their children's successes and their positive emotional experiences with them, thereby emphasizing what the children are able to accomplish. In contrast, Chinese mothers are more likely to call attention to their children's mistakes and transgressions, thereby elaborating on how they need to change to better fit in (Miller, Wiley, Fung, & Liang, 1997; Wang, 2001). How do you think these early experiences might shape the ways children tend to view themselves? Mothers play an important role in socializing their children to develop culturally appropriate ways of viewing themselves. And as we have seen, mothers go about socializing their children in different ways across cultures.

Attachment Styles. Much research on cultural differences in children's interactions with their mothers has explored the attachments that children form in their early years. Young infants go through a process of first being more attracted to people than to inanimate objects, then they begin to discriminate between familiar and unfamiliar people, and then, after a few months of age, they develop the capacity to form special relationships with certain specific individuals, usually the mother and other close relatives (Schaffer & Emerson, 1964). **Attachment theory** hypothesizes that infants and parents are biologically prepared to establish close attachments with each other (Bowlby, 1969), and research on this theory has investigated the different kinds of relationships that young children develop with their parents.

Researchers have proposed three styles of attachments that infants form with their caretakers (Ainsworth, Blehar, Waters, & Wall, 1978). These different attachment styles are investigated by identifying how children responds in the "strange situation," a setting in which their reactions to some standardized situations are observed in the presence or absence of their mother and a stranger. The first attachment style is called **secure attachment**; infants who display this occasionally seek their mother's presence when she is around, and intensify their desire to be close to her after being left alone in an unfamiliar situation. Securely attached infants are curious and explorative when in a novel environment with their mothers present. The second attachment style is **avoidant attachment**; these infants show little distress on their mother's absence, and avoid her on her return. The third attachment style is

anxious–ambivalent attachment. Children with this attachment style show frequent distress when the mother is either present or absent. These children will sometimes want to be near the mother, but often after being near her they will resist and push her away. These three attachment styles account for the divergent ways in which young infants form attachments with their parents.

As with most other topics in psychology, the majority of research on attachment has been conducted with Americans (for a critical review, see Rothbaum, Pott, Azuma, Miyake, & Weisz, 2000). This research reveals that the most common attachment style is secure attachment, which accounts for approximately 62% of mother–child relationships that were studied (Campos, Barrett, Lamb, Goldsmith, & Stenberg, 1983). Avoidant attachments accounted for about 23%, and anxious–ambivalent attachments were common in approximately 15% of mother–child pairs. Hence, among Americans, secure attachments are the most common. Moreover, as the literature describes it, secure attachments are viewed as the ideal, reflecting what are seen as healthy relationships, yet also allowing children to function independently within the context of their secure relationships. Avoidant attachments and anxious–ambivalent attachments are each perceived as being problematic, preventing children from developing a sense of trust or intimacy.

Attachments are not just an issue for the mother–child relationship. Subsequent research demonstrated that the attachment style children formed with their mothers can shape the kinds of romantic relationships that they develop (Hazan & Shaver, 1987). People who view themselves to be in secure romantic relationships (i.e., they find it easy to get close to others and to depend on them) tend to recall their interactions with their parents as similarly secure. Those in avoidant romantic relationships (i.e., they report feeling it difficult to be close to others or to trust them) recall their early relationships with their parents similarly. And those in anxious/ambivalent romantic relationships (i.e., they wish their partner would get closer, but often end up driving him or her away) recall similar childhood relationships with their parents. The proportions of Americans who report having these kinds of romantic relationship styles closely mirror the proportions who have the same styles of attachments with their parents. Again, secure romantic relationships are viewed as the ideal, with the other two styles viewed as problematic.

It wasn't long, however, until researchers started to investigate attachment styles in other cultures. The results suggested that there was nothing fundamental about the proportions that had emerged from the American studies.

For example, attachment styles among mothers and infants have been explored in north Germany (Grossman, Grossmann, Spangler, Suess, & Unzner, 1985). Contrary to what was found in the United States, the most common attachment style was the avoidant style, and this was viewed as the ideal. North German mothers associated avoidance with signs of early independence, a culturally valued trait. Secure attachments, and the kinds of motherly behaviors that fostered these (such as coddling a toddler rather than letting it walk on its own), in contrast, were viewed as signs that the child was spoiled. The ideal child, according to the German researchers, was one who was independent, not clinging or demanding, and would unquestioningly obey his or her parents' commands. I recall a common admonition that I used to hear from my own German-born grandparents: "Children should be seen but not heard."

Research on attachment styles in the Israeli kibbutz found yet another pattern (Sagi et al., 1985). Early in the 20th century Zionist pioneers set up a system of communal child care to free the adults to spend more time engaged in economically productive work. Children who were raised in the most traditional form of the kibbutz from the age of 3 months on spent their entire days and nights, with the exception of a 3-hour dinner break with their parents, in a communal environment with a caretaker and several other children of their own age. These children thus did not have as much time to develop exclusive attachments toward their own parents. The most common attachment style of kibbutz-reared Israeli infants was the anxious–ambivalent style. Secure and avoidant attachments were relatively low compared to the American norms (see Figure 4.4). How do you think the different attachment styles of these children might affect them as they grow older?

In sum, there is considerable variability in the kinds of relationships children develop with their caretakers, and children in different cultures have different experiences that lead to these attachment styles. The most common attachment style is not universally the secure attachment style, nor is this viewed everywhere as the best kind of parent-child relation. Nor are all three of these attachment styles found everywhere. For example, some researchers were unable to find *any* children in their various Japanese samples who were categorized as having avoidant relationships with their mothers (Miyake, 1993; Miyake, Cheng, & Campos, 1985). Such avoidant styles were also found to be absent among the Dogon in West Africa (True, Pisani, & Oumar,

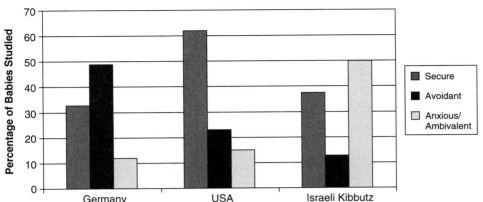

FIGURE 4.4

The prevalence of different attachment styles varies between cultures.

2001), where an infant is in constant proximity to the mother. Furthermore, some researchers have even questioned whether some of the theoretical assumptions that underlie attachment theory (e.g., notions of dependence and autonomy) make sense in the same way in non-Western cultural contexts (Rothbaum, Weisz et al., 2000). These researchers question whether the distinctions between secure, avoidant, and anxious-ambivalent attachments are relevant distinctions in cultures such as the Japanese. Taken together, the research reveals that there is considerable cultural variability in attachment styles. Children's earliest experiences, and the relations that they develop with their caretakers, are importantly influenced by the child-rearing practices that are most common in their cultural environments.

Noun Biases. Another window into the early experiences of childhood is through language learning. Young children, typically around the age of 18 months, enter a period of accelerated word learning when their vocabularies begin to increase dramatically. A great deal of research has indicated, however, that this increase in vocabulary is not distributed equally across all different forms of words; the first words that young children tend to learn are nouns (e.g., Gentner, 1982; Huttenlocher & Smiley, 1987). This preponderance of nouns relative to verbs and other relational words in young children's vocabularies is known as a **noun bias**. The existence of this noun bias is informative with respect to the experiences that young children have.

Researchers have argued that the noun bias indicates that nouns are more salient, refer to more concrete concepts, and are easier to isolate from the environment than other words, such as verbs, and this is why children learn them first (Gentner, 1982; Glietman, 1990). To the extent that this is true, we should see evidence of a noun bias everywhere and in every language. The majority of research on the noun bias has been conducted with North Americans, and there is a great deal of evidence that North American children tend to learn nouns much quicker than verbs. However, the noun bias is much more difficult to identify in some other cultural groups, particularly among East Asians. For example, in one study Chinese toddlers were found to use more verbs than nouns (Tardif, 1996), and in another, there was no evidence of a noun bias among Korean toddlers (Choi & Gopnik, 1995). The noun bias does not appear to be as universal as it was originally supposed. Another study found that when North American college students are asked to guess a word that they couldn't hear in a conversation between a mother and child, they tend to guess that it was a noun (Lavin, Hall, & Waxman, 2006; also see Gillette, Gleitman, Gleitman, & Lederer, 1999), revealing a noun bias; Chinese-speaking college students, however, did not show this bias.

One possible explanation for this cultural difference is not a cultural explanation but a linguistic one. Perhaps there is something about the nature of the languages that makes nouns or verbs more salient. Indeed, the structure of English is such that nouns tend to come in rather salient locations, such as at the end of the sentence, as in "He dented his new car." On the other hand, some East Asian languages (such as Japanese and Koreans) place verbs in salient positions at the end of sentences. For example, to say that someone ate a cookie in Japanese you would say the words in the order of "She cookie ate." Moreover, unlike in English, Chinese, Japanese, and Korean languages all allow for nouns (and pronouns) to be dropped when the context is clear, so that the verbs remain in salient positions in the sentences. For example, to say "I love you" in Japanese you can get away with just saying "Love," and it will be understood from the context who is loving whom. Indeed, if it's *not* clear from the context who is doing the loving and who is being loved, then you probably shouldn't be saying it! Perhaps, then, the cultural differences in noun biases simply reflect how various languages highlight nouns and verbs differently. This explanation may prove to be correct, although it still begs the question of why East Asian languages allow for noun or pronoun drops, whereas the English language (and many other Western languages) do not (Kashima & Kashima, 1998).

An alternative explanation is that young children learn to communicate about objects differently across cultures. How might a North American mother play with a 1-year-old with a toy, such as a truck? We might expect her to say something like "Look at this truck. It's a big, strong truck! Look, here's another truck. It's a yellow truck. It has black wheels. They can drive fast. Trucks, let's go to the garage." Such communications highlights how the truck is separate from its environment, and it describes the truck in terms of its characteristics. In contrast, an East Asian mother playing with her child and the same truck might say, "Here comes Daddy truck. He's saying hello to older brother truck. Daddy truck loves older brother truck. They're going to the beach together for a picnic." Such communication highlights relationships between the trucks. How might these kinds of conversations shape the way children attend to their worlds? One important line of research, which we'll return to in Chapter 9, Cognition and Perception, is that Westerners tend to perceive the world in a more analytic fashion, seeing objects as

American reading primers like the one on the left emphasize individualism, while Chinese readers like the one on the right tend to focus on relationships. The Chinese text above says, "Xiao Zhiang is a very nice boy. He is my best friend. We always study together and play together. We have a lot of fun together" (Gilovich, Keltner, & Nisbett, 2006)

discrete and separate, whereas East Asians are more likely to perceive the world in holistic terms, stressing the relations between objects (e.g., Nisbett, Peng, Choi, & Norenzayan, 2001). It is plausible that the cultural differences in the noun bias reflect this difference in thinking about the world.

Much research suggests that mothers' interactions with children do vary across cultures as in the example conversations above. American mothers are more likely to call attention to objects than are East Asian mothers (Bornstein et al., 1992; Morikawa, Shand, & Kosawa, 1988), and these differences are identifiable even among very young infants. Parents from all cultures will talk about children's toys with them; however, Western mothers tend to talk more about the toys, whereas East Asian mothers more often use those toys as part of a social routine (Tamis-LeMonda, Bornstein, & Cyphers, 1992). East Asian mothers more effectively communicate actions than North American mothers, whereas North American mothers more effectively communicate objects than East Asian mothers (Lavin, Hall, & Waxman, 2006; Lavin, Hall, & Leung, 2006). It appears that the early worlds of infants and toddlers vary in systematic ways. Western children are directed to attend to objects, whereas East Asian children are directed toward the relations among objects.

Difficult Developmental Transitions

The Terrible Twos. As a father of a 2-year-old, I have recently learned to add some strict routines to my life. I used to not pay much attention, for example, to whether I pushed the elevator button as we left our apartment or I let someone else do it. I have since learned that the success of the day hinges on being sure that I do not carelessly push the elevator button before my 2-year-old son has the chance to do so. Otherwise our day starts off with a half hour long tantrum of inconsolable ear-splitting screams as my son vents his anger and frustration at having been deprived of his favorite task. It really is quite a spectacle. Other parents tell me that this stage will end soon, and it's this belief that helps me get through the day. They say my son is in his terrible twos.

The idea that children pass through a difficult transition during their early toddler years is viewed as a hallmark of development, at least by North Americans (Wenar, 1982). Around the age of 2 there is an unmistakable increase in noncompliant and oppositional behavior. Many 2-year-olds, my son included, will say "No" to virtually anything that is asked of them by their exasperated parents. Although this obstinacy tends to be very draining on parents, many Western researchers describe it as an important developmental milestone when the young toddler begins to establish his or her individuality, and this is seen as the foundation for mature relationships (e.g., Sroufe, 1979). Indeed, some forms of noncompliance among American children have been shown to predict *fewer* behavioral problems later in life (Kuczynski & Kochanska, 1990). The tantrums of the terrible twos are seen to serve an important function in the young child's socialization to be a mature, verbally assertive individual.

What makes it all the harder to deal with the terrible twos as a parent is to discover that it doesn't have to be this bad. Two-year-olds in many other cultures are not as obstinate and difficult as North Americans. Particularly among various nomadic hunting societies, such as the Aka Pygmies of Africa, where children are held by a caretaker for much of the day, this developmental stage is not as evident (Hewlett, 1992). Among the Zinacantecans in Mexico, infants do not go through this transition of obstinacy. Rather than asserting control and striving for independence, Zincantecan 2-year-olds change their status from mother's baby to a member of the courtyard children's group (Edwards, 1994; Rogoff, 2003). Without the interactions with their parents that try to inculcate a sense of individualism and independence, these early and rather clumsy efforts to exert autonomy and control by young toddlers are rarely seen.

Similarly, Japanese toddlers have been shown to make fewer demands on their parents than their American counterparts and are less likely to assert their disobedience (Caudill & Schooler, 1973). Those occasions when Japanese toddlers do act unruly tend not to be viewed as signs of blossoming individuality but rather as indicators of their immaturity (Lebra, 1994). The developmental goal embraced by Japanese parents is much less a desire to see their children learn how to individuate and assert themselves than it is to learn how to accommodate to others and to become part of a harmonious social group (Rothbaum et al., 2000). Even by the very young age of 2, toddlers raised in North American environments seem to be embracing aspects of autonomy and individualism through their clumsy efforts to exert control over their worlds. When, in contrast, children are raised with cultural goals of interdependence, such signs of noncompliance often appear to be replaced by efforts to fit in and belong.

Adolescent Rebellion. On Tuesday, April 20, 1999, two teenage students, Eric Harris and Dylan Klebold, walked into Columbine High School in Jefferson County, Colorado, carrying heavy artillery with the express purpose of killing their classmates. At the end of their horrific rampage Harris and Klebold committed suicide, but not before killing 12 fellow students and a teacher, and wounding 24 others. It is one of the deadliest school shootings the world has ever witnessed. Although it is difficult to offer a complete explanation for such an unusually rare and appalling event, one account is clearly relevant. Harris and Klebold were adolescents. And one thing that characterizes adolescence is that more than any other developmental stage, it is often a period of great turmoil (although, thankfully, rarely as tumultuous as the lives of Harris and Klebold).

In the West, adolescence is typically described as a chaotic period of "storm and stress" when teens act out against authority figures, commit acts of delinquency and criminal behavior, suffer from a great deal of emotional stress, and are at risk for substance abuse and suicide. Hollywood has often portrayed the young adolescent as angry, distraught, confused, and intentionally disobedient, as in such classics as *Rebel without a Cause*. Evidence for adolescence as a troubled period can also be seen by looking at historical trends when there were large concentrations of adolescents, such as during the 1960s when all those baby-boomers born in the years after World War II were in their teens, and protests, demonstrations, and outright rebellion were near daily occurrences.

As in the lives of Harris and Klebold, adolescence has also been viewed as an especially violent phase of life. The association between adolescence and violence has been perceived as so reliable that sociologists make predictions about crime rates by tracking the percentage of the population who are between the especially violent ages of 14 and 21 (e.g., Fox, 1978). Male adolescents seem to be especially violent when there are relatively few females around (Vandello, 2004), arguably because they are competing with each other for access to mates. Violence seems to be associated with adolescence.

The traditional view of the turmoil of adolescence was that it arose from the hormonal changes associated with puberty (Hall, 1916). That is, it was considered a biological development as inevitable as changes in voice or the growth of breasts. However, there has since been a great deal of controversy surrounding the universality of adolescent rebellion. In 1928, Margaret Mead famously made the case that adolescents growing up in Western Samoa enjoyed a carefree and smooth transition to adulthood, somehow avoiding all the difficulties so common in the West. Over 50 years later, however, Mead's observations were challenged by Derek Freeman (1983), who argued that Samoan adolescence was at least as tumultuous as it was in the West, and he attributed Mead's allegedly mistaken observations to her informants, who teased her and made up stories. Despite the unresolved controversy in this one instance, there have been investigations from many other areas of the globe regarding the prevalence of adolescent rebellion.

One investigation reviewed the ethnographic database (specifically, the Human Relations Area Files, a record of all published ethnographies) to explore what the adolescent experience was like in 175 different pre-industrial societies (Schlegel & Barry, 1991). The researchers discovered evidence for both similarities and differences. On the one hand, all the cultures viewed adolescence as a distinct period of life, separate from childhood and adulthood, in which some restructuring and role-learning occurred. This suggests that adolescence itself is not a cultural invention and seems to be an existential universal. On the other hand, however, there were some pronounced cultural differences in the experiences of adolescents. Many cultures demonstrated tendencies for adolescents to act in the rebellious ways familiar to the West; however, this was by no means universal. Rather, expectations for such antisocial behaviors were present only in 44% of societies with respect to boys, and only 18% of societies for girls. The majority of the cultures studied did not expect adolescents to behave especially disobediently. Furthermore, the notion that adolescence is universally associated with violence received little support. Rather, only 13% of societies expected adolescent boys to occasionally act violent, and only 3% of societies had such expectations for girls. Adolescence as a developmental stage that is associated with rebellion and violence thus does not meet the criteria to be categorized as a functional universal. There is important cultural variation.

Whether adolescence is a tumultuous life stage does not seem to be determined randomly. A number of investigations have identified some variables that predict whether a given society will likely be associated with difficult adolescent times. For example, the adolescence experiences of people in Germany, Scotland, Japan, Bali, and Batak were compared, and the results indicated that both individualism and modernity seem to increase the difficulties in adolescence (Trommsdorff, 1995). In particular, there appears to be more conflict between children and their parents in individualistic societies,

"I'm sorry, but so far medical science hasn't come up with a cure for adolescence."

where children seem to view parental control as a constraint they must resist.

Some features of modern Western societies seem to be associated with increased adolescent distress. These include the sheer range of opportunities that confront children as societies industrialize and become more urbanized (Dasen, 2000). One task in adolescence is for youths to learn how to accept adult roles. This is much more straightforward when there are fewer role distinctions and when youths are more in contact with adults, as they are in more traditional, agricultural societies. For example, if your parents are farmers and there really aren't any options available for you other than farming, then you're probably not going to need to spend years racking your brain over what you're going to do with your life. The answer is straightforward: You're going to farm. In more complex modern societies, however, the range of roles available to children is quite staggering, and adolescents spend a longer period in school preparing for those roles while being kept largely separate from adults. This set of circumstances increases the stress and confusion of adolescents and appears to be largely responsible for the tumultuousness of adolescence in the West.

Socialization Through Education

Testimony to the argument that humans are dependent on their ability to acquire cultural information to succeed in life is the fact that you are reading this chapter right now. You're probably in your early twenties or older and are reading this chapter for a university or college course. Think about that for a moment. You've been around this planet for some time now. You passed the physical age some time ago that allows you to start reproducing and raising your own children, you're fully grown physically, your government recognizes you as an adult with full responsibilities, and yet you're still in school! Our cultural worlds are complex enough now that to succeed in them requires more than a decade of effort to acquire the necessary cultural information. We depend on this cultural information to excel, and it is no coincidence that as our cultural worlds become more complex, the average amount of education that people receive increases accordingly.

Given all the time we spend in school, we might question the kind of impact this long exposure to education has on our psychological experiences. How do you think formal schooling affects the ways people think? Obviously schooling provides us with some explicit kinds of knowledge, both in terms of techniques that we learn (e.g., how to multiply fractions, how to identify the predicate in a sentence) and content that we absorb (e.g., the elements in the periodic table, the date of the signing of the Magna Carta). This is the kind of information that is covered in textbooks, is discussed in class, and shows up on exams. However, we learn other kinds of knowledge through formal schooling that is not explicitly taught. Schooling leads people to think in ways that are different from the thought processes of people who do not experience formal schooling. For example, try to memorize the following list of words. Look at the words below for one minute, and then try to write down as many as you can on another sheet of paper.

elephant	zebra	lacrosse
hammer	basketball	wire cutter
football	screwdriver	giraffe
hacksaw	leopard	volleyball
hockey	wrench	hyena

How did you go about doing this task? It is fairly likely that you used a technique that no teacher ever explicitly taught you: clustering. When encountering such a list many people will cluster the words together by category. It is far more efficient to group these words into the categories of African mammals, sports, and tools than to try to memorize the words on their own. Clustering places fewer burdens on your memory as it imposes an organization that makes the task far simpler. However, this technique of clustering is not relied upon equally by everyone. People who have attended school are more likely to apply this—and many other kinds of learning strategies. For example, schooling improves perceptual skills for analyzing two-dimensional patterns (Rogoff, 1981) and leads people to reflect more on how information is organized (Goody, 1977). Much research has documented the ways schooling affects how people think (e.g., Cole, Gay, Glick, & Sharp, 1971; Luria, 1971; Rogoff, 2003; Scribner & Cole, 1973). Education doesn't just teach you facts but also shapes how you think about the world generally.

Much of our intellectual capability is sustained by knowledge that is built into the ways that problems are framed. For example, could you calculate the answer to the following arithmetic problem?

$$642$$
$$\times\ 439$$

With a little thought and effort, you could probably solve this question if you applied the strategies that you learned in math class. That is, you could likely solve it by doing something like this.

$$
\begin{array}{r}
642 \\
\times\ 439 \\
\hline
=\quad 5778 \\
1926 \\
\underline{2568} \\
=\ 281838
\end{array}
$$

However, imagine that I had presented the same problem to you like this: $642 \times 439 = ?$ Or I had asked you the same problem orally. The question is no longer so straightforward, is it? Being able to solve multiplication problems is greatly facilitated by placing the numbers in vertical arrays with columns. If the numbers are not properly aligned, the task is much more difficult. In an important way, then, the organization of the numbers into a vertical array accomplishes much of the thinking necessary to solve the problem. Without this cultural tool of vertically presented columns of numbers, we are hard-pressed to do multiplication. And we tend to be unaware of how dependent our thinking is on such cultural tools until we are in a situation when that tool is not available to us. This suggests that, in some ways, we do not solve multiplication problems by ourselves. We do so in conjunction with the capabilities of our cultural tools (Wertsch, 1998). And the process of formal education provides us with many such tools.

It can thus be quite problematic to attempt to assess the intelligence of people with no formal schooling when testing skills that are shaped by education. In 1912, in a time of increasing racism in the United States as the country was admitting vast numbers of immigrants, the U.S. Public Health Service hired the psychologist H. H. Goddard to help screen out immigrants with "inferior minds," perceived as a threat. As new immigrants stepped off the boat at Ellis Island they were peppered by Goddard's assistants with various questions to assess their intelligence. Many of the immigrants had no schooling whatsoever nor any exposure to the cultural context from which these questions were derived. The results of Goddard's testing: 83% of Jews, 80% of Hungarians, 79% of Italians, and 87% of Russians were classified as "morons"—the technical term that Goddard invented to indicate poor intellectual functioning (see Gould, 1981, for an in-depth description of this period of intelligence testing). Obviously, Goddard's test did not provide an accurate assessment of the immigrants' true potential, and it underscores the challenges of comparing people's capabilities across cultures. Do you think it's possible to develop a way to accurately measure people's cognitive abilities that is equally valid for individuals everywhere in the world, regardless of their experiences?

Schooling thus plays an important role in shaping people's thinking. How could we go about identifying how schooling affects people's thinking? Would it work if we just found people with differing levels of education within a particular culture, and then compared how they thought? Unfortunately, it is not straightforward to study the influences of formal education on thinking; a number of other variables might separate people who have received a great deal of formal schooling from those who have not. If we think about the difference in the use of clustering strategies between schooled and unschooled people, for example, it is possible that the difference between these two groups has nothing to do with schooling but with something that is related to schooling, such as intelligence. That is, clustering might be a strategy that requires a certain amount of intelligence, and the fact that people who have been to school use more clustering than those who have not might be because intelligent people are more likely to attend school in the first place. This is not an unreasonable challenge to comparisons of schooled and unschooled people, as there are likely many reasons that some people choose to, or are able to, receive an education that are relevant to how their minds work. The variable of whether a person has received formal schooling is confounded with the many other variables that might distinguish the kinds of people who receive education from those who do not.

One of the most ambitious attempts to explore the effects of schooling was conducted by Harold Stevenson (1982). He investigated neighborhoods in rural Peru where only 53% of children attend school and compared the family circumstances of children who attended school with those who did not. He found a number of differences between these two groups: For example, the parents of children who attended school generally had received more education, they were more likely to be literate, and they were more likely to possess items in their house that might stimulate cognitive development— for example, books, toys, or radios. Because of these differences between the children who received education and those who did not, it is not appropriate to simply compare the cognitive differences between the two groups. You also need to statistically control for any relations between cognitive abilities and the various family circumstances that differed across the groups. Stevenson collected an enormous amount of data and was able to discern how schooled and unschooled children differed in ways that were independent from their family circumstances. Put simply, he found that a few years of schooling led to some rather dramatic effects on the cognitive abilities of children. Controlling for all the other variables, Stevenson still demonstrated that schooling led to improved contextual memory, spatial memory, serial memory, and visual and sequential analysis. That is, the schooling led the children to process information in a more efficient manner. Formal schooling affects how people think.

Case Study: East Asians and Math Education. If education affects how we think, then we might expect that any differences in the ways cultures go about educating their children might lead to cultural differences in psychological processes. Educational experiences are not constant across cultures. Rather, how societies opt to educate their children reflects their implicit beliefs about what kinds of knowledge are most important, what kinds of learning styles should be encouraged, and what kinds of teaching styles are most effective. The educational strategies that a culture adopts will influence the ways its citizens think.

One way to investigate how schools affect the ways children think is to compare schools and students from different cultures in their performance in various subjects. Some subjects, such as reading and language arts, make for problematic comparisons across cultures because the languages, choice of reading materials, and writing styles often vary greatly across cultures. On the other hand, math is an especially appropriate subject for cross-cultural investigation as everywhere you go the answers are the same. Not surprisingly, much research has explored math performance in various cultures around the world. This research is very telling about how our schooling shapes the way we think.

One large-scale research program examined students' performance on math tests, focusing on students who grew up in East Asia and those who grew up in the United States (Stevenson & Stigler, 1992). The researchers administered the same math exam to different groups of students in schools in cities in China, Japan, Taiwan, and the United States; the tests were matched along a number of different demographic characteristics. Both first-grade and fifth-grade students were compared across the four cultures. Figure 4.5 shows the performance of the schools on the math tests. Each dot in the figure represents the average performance for each of the schools.

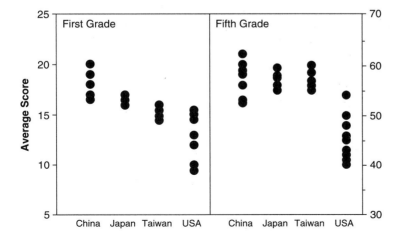

FIGURE 4.5

The dots represent the average math test scores for individual schools in different countries.

*"Big deal, an A in math. That would be a D
in any other country."*

The figure shows a number of quite remarkable trends. One is a far greater spread in the average math performance of each school among the American schools than among the schools of the other countries. That is, there are more similarities among schools in the East Asian countries, particularly in Japan and Taiwan, than among the U.S. schools. Second, on average, the students in the East Asian schools performed much better on the math test than did the American students. Third, the cultural differences become even more pronounced as the children continue to participate in their respective educational systems. By the fifth grade, the very best performing U.S. school in the study performs about the same as the very worst school in each of the other countries. These are quite enormous differences in performance. And they are differences on a real-life concrete task: math tests. So how can we make sense of these cross-national differences?

Some answers to this question have been identified and are rather surprising (Stevenson & Stigler, 1992). It is not that East Asian mothers prepare their children better for math education than do American mothers, before the children enter kindergarten. Rather, the opposite seems to be true. Whereas 90% of American mothers reported teaching numbers at home to their preschool-aged children, only 36% of Japanese mothers did. Japanese mothers do devote a great deal of time to their children's education; however, they do not usually start this until after the child enters kindergarten. The belief is that life stages are clearly divided, and young childhood is a time for play and not education, but once the child has reached school age, then education becomes the dominant goal. Stevenson and Stigler argue, in contrast, that American parents do not change their child-rearing strategies that much as their children age. The belief appears to be that because education is important, it should begin as early as possible and continue throughout the child's life.

There are some key differences in the way math is taught in the various schools. For example, East Asian children spend more days in school (240 days per year in Japan versus 180 days per year in the United States), a greater percentage of class time is devoted to math education in the Asian school day than in the American, Asian teachers spend a greater percentage of time in the classroom lecturing compared with their American counterparts (90% in Taiwan compared to 46% in the United States), and Asian math lessons are far more likely to use real-world examples than their American counterparts (approximately 80% of examples are real-world in Japan compared to about 10% of examples in American classes). Asian teachers also assign more homework to students. Fifth graders in the United States had less than half as much homework assigned to them as Taiwanese students. These teaching differences surely play an important role in how children learn math.

In addition to cultural differences in educational experiences, psychological differences in the ways children and parents conceptualize learning are also important to understanding these performance differences. First, Asian parents seem to view education as more central to their children's lives than do American parents. Look at how the house is structured. Even though American houses tend to be far larger than their East Asian counterparts, and Americans on average have more purchasing power than people in any Asian country, Asian parents are more likely to provide their children with a desk. One study revealed that 98% of Taiwanese fifth graders had a desk in their home compared with only 63% of Americans. The presence of a desk not only provides children with a place to work but also sends a signal from the parents that studying is an important and valued activity. There are also other cultural differences in education. For example, fifth graders were asked to imagine that there was a wizard who would grant them anything they wished for (Stevenson, 1992). About 70% of the wishes listed by Chinese had to do with education—they wished for success in school or to be able to go to college. In contrast, only about 10% of American children wished for things relevant to education. And, tellingly, the most common wish among those 10% was to have *less* school! There are pronounced differences in how education is valued across cultures.

The cultural differences in performance also seem to be related to the expectations of children and their mothers. On average, the East Asian children are doing so much better as a group on math tests than the American children that one might expect East Asian mothers to be especially satisfied with their children's performance. This does not seem to be the case; rather, the American mothers report being far more satisfied with their children's performance than the East Asian mothers—and this difference in standards seems to change with age. Compared with mothers of first-grade children, Chinese and Japanese mothers of fifth-grade children reported that a higher standard of achievement was necessary for them to be satisfied with their children's math performance. In stark contrast, the standards of American mothers were lower for their fifth-grade children than for their first-grade children. Over time, Chinese and Japanese mothers set higher and higher standards whereas American mothers set lower and lower standards. When mothers were asked to state the minimal standard that would lead them to be satisfied with their child's performance, American mothers gave a number that was considerably *below* the level at which they expected their child to perform. In contrast, East Asian mothers gave a number that was considerably *higher* than where they expected their child to perform. In sum, it appears to be far easier to meet the standards of American mothers than East Asian mothers. This would suggest that American children have less reason to work hard at their studies than East Asian children.

SUMMARY

People are not born with their cultures; they are born culture free (or are at least conceived culture free; in utero cultural experiences may possibly affect development); however, people begin attending to cultural information and being socialized by that information from very early in their lives. Becoming a cultural being is a developmental process, and as we age we are shaped more and more by the cultural practices and institutions in which we participate. This process is evident in that cultural differences in psychological processes tend to become more pronounced with age.

There is much evidence that a sensitive period for learning language exists, and other evidence suggests that this is so for learning cultural meaning systems as well. The existence of these sensitive periods suggests that people are biologically prepared to learn a language or culture in the initial years of life.

Various cultural practices differ across cultures, and these differences emerge at young ages. Parents choose sleeping arrangements differently across cultures, and these decisions reflect underlying cultural values. Whether children develop secure, avoidant, or anxious-ambivalent relations with their parents also varies importantly across cultures. Children learn to attend differently to nouns and verbs across cultures, and this is likely due to the ways that parents call their attention to features of objects or the relations among objects.

Cultures also differ in some key developmental transitions. The "terrible twos" is an infamous transition period that Western toddlers are likely to go through; however, it seems to be considerably less terrible in cultures where children are not as encouraged to be independent. Likewise, although adolescence is often viewed as a time of rebellion and adolescence in the West, most subsistence societies around the world do not experience it this way.

Much of human socialization occurs through the schools, and the process of being educated shapes our thinking in quite profound ways. Moreover, cultures differ in the ways that they educate their children, and these differences affect the ways that children perform in their classes.

5

Self and Personality

In the summer of 2000, at the Olympic Games in Sydney, two gold-medal winners spoke to the media. Misty Hyman had just won the gold medal for the United States in women's swimming, specifically in the 200-meter butterfly stroke. She explained her victory to the press as follows: "I think I just stayed focused. It was time to show the world what I could do. I am just glad I was able to do it. I knew I could beat Suzy O'Neil, deep down in my heart I believed it, and I know this whole week the doubts kept creeping in, they were with me on the blocks, but I just said 'No, this is my night.'" Around the same time, Naoko Takahashi had just won the gold medal for Japan in the women's marathon, and she explained her victory this way: "Here is the best coach in the world, the best manager in the world, and all of the people who support me—all of these things were getting together and became a gold medal. So I think I didn't get it alone, not only by myself" (from Markus, Uchida, Omoregie, Townsend, & Kitayama, 2006, p. 103). Although both athletes had received the same instructions from the International Olympic Organization about how to talk to the media, they offered quite different accounts of their victories. An analysis of the national media coverage of Japanese and American Olympic athletes of the 2000 and 2002 Olympics revealed that these two responses were not atypical; overall, Japanese and American athletes tended to explain their performance in ways that contrasted with each other (Markus et al., 2006). Americans focused more on how their performance reflected their own personal characteristics whereas the Japanese focused more on how their performance was guided by the expectations of others.

These contrasting media accounts are not indicative only of people's different theories for athletic success; they reflect something more fundamental. They highlight some profound cultural differences in the ways people come to understand themselves. The heart of who we think we are, our self-concepts, vary in important ways across cultures.

This chapter explores the role of culture in how we understand ourselves. We will investigate how culture shapes a number of key aspects of the self-concept. Furthermore, we will also consider the role that gender plays in how we view ourselves, and the similarities and differences of people's personalities around the world. This chapter looks at the tensions between culturally universal and variable aspects of our psychology. How similar to or different from people in other cultures around the world are we in our feelings of identity and our understanding of what makes us tick? This question has a number of profound implications as we explore the ways that cultural experiences shape our thinking.

Who Am I?

Sometimes, in the middle of the night, when we're all alone, we might ponder that most profound of questions: "Who am I?" This question is not only relevant to our existential musings but is also important in psychological research as it addresses the nature of our self-concepts and the foundation of our identities. The self-concept holds a privileged position in psychology, as we'll see later, because the nature of our selves strongly influences the ways we perceive and interact with our social worlds.

Please take the opportunity now to think about the ways you would answer the question of "Who am I?" In the box on the next page, write down 20 statements that begin with "I am _____." Complete the statements in the way that you feel best describes who you are. You'll get a lot more out of this chapter if you try to describe yourself in this way. This exercise is a well-used measure of the self-concept known, appropriately enough, as the Twenty-Statements Test (Kuhn & McPartland, 1954).

Twenty-Statements Test

I am _____.	I am _____.
I am _____.	I am _____.
I am _____.	I am _____.
I am _____.	I am _____.
I am _____.	I am _____.
I am _____.	I am _____.
I am _____.	I am _____.
I am _____.	I am _____.
I am _____.	I am _____.
I am _____.	I am _____.

What do you think your self-description tells people about your cultural background? This exercise reveals the extent of culture's influence on our identities in at least two ways: one rather superficial, and one much deeper. At the superficial level, your self-description might include some culturally shaped statements such as "I'm a Vancouver Canucks fan," or "I am a devotee of jazz." These statements are cultural products in that you can't be a fan of the Vancouver Canucks without having participated in a cultural meaning system that includes hockey as a spectator sport (or more specifically, one that includes the Canucks as a hockey team), nor can you view yourself as an aficionado of jazz if you haven't been exposed to the music and its surrounding culture. However, these kinds of self-statements might reveal only a superficial influence of culture, as the culture is merely providing the *content* about the ways we think of ourselves. That is, a consideration of culture's influences at this level does not say much about why we describe ourselves with these kinds of preferences. Indeed, if we imagine that we had instead been born and raised somewhere else, such as in Afghanistan, and described our identities in terms of our favorite sport of *Buzkashi* (the national sport, which involves passing a goat carcass among players on horseback) and our preferences for folk music played on the *rohab* (something like an Afghani

Buzkashi, the national sport of Afghanistan.

violin), our identities might not be all that different. We would still be defining ourselves in terms of sports and music, and the difference would be that we were exposed to different kinds of sports and music. It's possible, then, that we might appear highly similar across experiences in these two diverse cultural worlds and vary only in terms of the content of things that we would be thinking about.

There is a deeper and more penetrating influence of our cultures on our self-descriptions that is harder to detect. This influence isn't seen so much in the content of the statements as in their structure. What categories of statements do we consider when we think about ourselves? For example, one type of statement that you might have included in your self-description is "I am creative." What does this type of statement have to say about how culture shapes the self-concept? At first glance, it would hardly seem to be culturally influenced, as there are creative people in all cultures of the world. However, what is noteworthy about this kind of statement is that it reveals a specific kind of understanding about ourselves. That is, defining ourselves as creative individuals suggests that we think in terms of having enduring traits, such as creativity, that exist across situations. This kind of statement refers to an inner attribute about the self—creativity—that has a number of telling features: It is relatively abstract (it encapsulates different kinds of thoughts and behaviors across different situations); it is likely experienced as stable (we don't expect our creative aspect to dissipate during the summer vacation or after we get our degree); and it can exist by itself (we do not need others around to be creative). Hence, a simple statement about ourselves such as "I am creative" can suggest a variety of ways that we think about ourselves.

Contrast the above kind of statement about oneself with another kind that one could make—for example, "I am a younger brother." How does this statement reflect on a person's cultural background? At first glance this statement is not obviously culturally influenced, as there are younger brothers in all cultures of the world. However, in a self-description it is telling. First, it implicates a significant other in one's self-concept. One can't be a younger brother unless one has an older brother or sister. It defines a role in terms of whatever ideas one has regarding appropriate behaviors or responsibilities that are relegated to younger brothers. It also emphasizes a hierarchical relationship as it underscores that one is younger than one's other siblings. In sum, this kind of statement highlights an experience of self that is connected with others, and in ways that are specific to the role of being a younger brother.

People all over the world are able to think of themselves in terms of both abstract psychological attributes and concrete roles and relationships. However, it is quite possible that the degree to which they view themselves in these two separate ways varies importantly across cultures. Some cultures might encourage people to focus on their enduring inner attributes, such as personality traits, attitudes, or abilities, as a means to understand themselves. Other cultures, in contrast, might encourage people to focus on their connections with others by considering themselves in terms of concrete roles, relationships, and group memberships. Indeed, much research suggests that people from different cultures vary in precisely this way.

One study explored this question among Kenyans and Americans by asking people to describe themselves in the same way that you did in the exercise using the Twenty-Statements Test (Ma & Schoeneman, 1997). As Kenya is a developing society the authors divided their Kenyan sample into groups that should theoretically vary in terms of how much they were exposed to Western cultural ways. They reasoned that Kenyan university students in

Nairobi should be the most Westernized group in their Kenyan sample (as they participate in an education system that was shaped by the country's British colonial past), employed adults in Nairobi might be slightly less Westernized, and traditional indigenous Kenyan groups, in this case the Samburu and the Masai, would be the least Westernized. These Kenyan groups were contrasted with a sample of American undergraduates. How did people from these different groups describe themselves?

The results were striking (see Figure 5.1). The most popular kinds of self-descriptions for the Americans were personal characteristics, such as their traits, attitudes, and abilities, which accounted for 48% of their self-descriptions. In contrast, these kinds of statements comprised less than 2% of the Masai and Samburu self-descriptions. The statements made by the Masai and Samburu generally reflected their social identity, specifically, their roles and memberships, which accounted for over 60% of their self-descriptions. In stark contrast, such statements accounted for only 7% of American self-descriptions (people also used some categories other than personal characteristics or social identity, such as their possessions or interests). It appears that the Masai and Samburu think of themselves in vastly different ways from those reported by American undergrads. It is important to note that Americans do sometimes think of themselves in terms of roles, and Masai and Samburu sometimes consider their own personality traits. However, the degree to which people from these cultures consider these different aspects of themselves varies

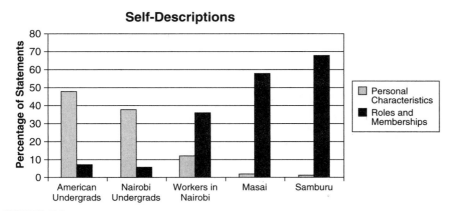

FIGURE 5.1

The proportion of self-descriptions that considered personal characteristics versus roles and memberships across cultural groups.

considerably. The other two Kenyan groups fell in between, with the university students being closer to the American pattern and the workers more closely resembling the Masai and Samburu patterns. These results suggest that the ways Kenyans and Americans think about themselves diverge profoundly.

This pattern of cultural differences is not unique to Kenyans and Americans. The Twenty-Statements Test is one of the most widely used cross-cultural psychological measures. The American pattern of emphasis on personal characteristics has emerged in many other Western cultures, such as those of Australia and Britain (Bochner, 1994), Sweden (Watkins, Yau, Dahlin, & Wondimu, 1997), and Canada (Leuers & Sonoda, 1999) whereas the Masai and Samburu pattern of a greater emphasis on roles and memberships appears in cultures from much of the rest of the world—for example, among Cook Islanders (Altrocchi & Altrocchi, 1995), Malaysians (Bochner, 1994), Chinese (Triandis, McCusker, & Hui, 1990), Native Americans (Fryberg & Markus, 2003), Puerto Ricans (Hart, Lucca-Irizarry, & Damon, 1986), Indians (Dhawan, Roseman, Naidu, & Rettek, 1995), Japanese (Bond & Cheung, 1983), and Koreans (Rhee, Uleman, Lee, & Roman, 1995). Furthermore, these cultural differences are already evident among kindergarten-age children (Wang, 2004). Please examine your own responses to the Twenty Statements Test to see how much your self-concept is based on personal characteristics or on roles and memberships.

This one difference in the way that people think about themselves has considerable importance in cultural psychology. Every human is ultimately a distinct individual, unique from everyone else; at the same time, we are also a highly social species. Our survival and fitness depend both on the things that we accomplish as individuals and on our abilities to interact successfully with others. It is perhaps not surprising, then, that this dimension underlying our proclivities to focus on how we are ultimately distinct from others or on how we are importantly connected with others is the most researched psychological dimension across cultures.

Independent Versus Interdependent Views of Self

The findings from the Ma and Schoeneman study suggest that there are at least two different ways people might see themselves. One way of viewing the self is reflected in many of the statements made by the American under-grads in that study. That is, the self can be thought to derive its identity from its inner attributes. These attributes are assumed to reflect an essence of the individual in that they are the basis of the individual's identity, they are viewed as stable across situations and across the lifespan, they are perceived to be unique (in the sense that no other individual possesses the same configura-tion of attributes), they are self-contained in that they are perceived to arise from the individual and not from interactions with others, they are viewed as significant for regulating behavior, and individuals feel an obligation to publicly advertise themselves in ways consistent with these attributes. Markus and Kitayama (1991) referred to this self-contained model of the self as the **independent view of self**.

Figure 5.2 represents a graphic view of this kind of self (the figure is derived from the writings of Markus and Kitayama and more recent research). A number of features from this illustration are key to understanding this kind of self-concept. First, note that the circle around the individual does not over-lap with any of the borders surrounding its significant relationships. This shows that independent individuals experience their identities as largely dis-tinct from their relationships. Second, the X's inside the circles reflect aspects of identity—the kinds of features that people consider when they think of themselves. The bold X's reflect the especially important, self-defining aspects of identity. For those with independent selves, these important aspects tend to lie within the individual. Some examples of these aspects would be a per-son's attitudes, personality traits, preferences, opinions, abilities, and individ-ual qualities. Third, the border around the individual is drawn with a solid line, to indicate that the self is bounded, and as such, its experience is rather stable and does not change much from situation to situation. The independ-ent view of self is experienced as self-contained and exists as a relatively coherent and inviolate entity. Fourth, the border around the ingroup that separates one's close relations from one's more distant relations is drawn with a dotted line to indicate that it is fluid. This shows that others can move between the boundary of ingroup and outgroup relatively easily. Individuals with independent identities still feel much closer to ingroup than outgroup members; however, they do not view them in fundamentally distinct ways. The key boundary is between self and non-self, and, for the most part, oth-ers are viewed, and interacted with, as though they were non-self. In sum,

Independent View of Self

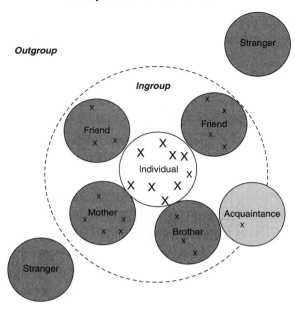

FIGURE 5.2

independent selves tend to be viewed as distinct, autonomous entities whose identities are grounded in a variety of internal component features, and who interact with other similarly independent entities.

Another way of considering the self is reflected in the kinds of statements commonly made by the Masai and Samburu. That is, the self can be viewed as a relational entity that is fundamentally connected to, and sustained by, a number of significant relationships. This is a profoundly different orientation of the individual. Rather than elaborating on how behavior and thoughts emanate from the individual's inner features, viewing oneself as part of an encompassing social relationship means that behavior is recognized as contingent upon perceptions of others' thoughts, feelings, and actions. When people are focused on how they are connected with others, it is important for them to consider how their behaviors will affect others, and likewise, they must organize their own psychological experiences in response to what others are apparently thinking and doing. With this view, individuals are not perceived as separate and distinct entities but as participants in a larger social unit. Their experience of identity is reflexive in that it is contingent on their position relative to others, and their relationships with those others.

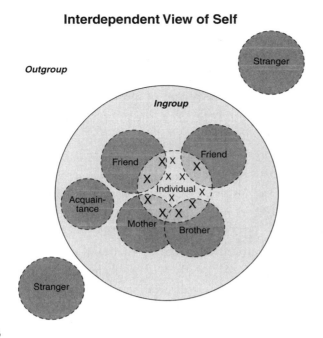

Interdependent View of Self

FIGURE 5.3

Markus and Kitayama labeled this second construal of self the **interdependent view of self**, which is represented graphically in Figure 5.3. Consider how the features in this figure contrast with those from the previous figure. First, contrary to the independent view of self, the border surrounding the interdependent self overlaps considerably with an individual's significant relationships. This shows that interdependent individuals' identities are importantly connected with others and are not experienced as distinct, unique entities. Second, the bold X's that indicate the key aspects of identity for interdependent individuals rest at the intersection between the individual and his or her significant relationships. This indicates that interdependent individuals' identities are importantly grounded in their relationships with others. Relationships come in a variety of forms, and they require people to take on particular roles (such as father, student, friend, lover, daughter) that govern how they feel and behave toward their relationship partners. Likewise, these relationships indicate the groups to which a person belongs, and his or her identity can be experienced on the basis of these different group memberships. Interdependent individuals also perceive aspects of identity that are based on internal characteristics, as shown in Figure 5.3; however, the small

X's show that these are relatively less central to their identity. A third feature of the interdependent self is indicated by the dotted line that encapsulates the individual. This shows that the identity of the interdependent person is experienced as somewhat fluid in different situations. Depending on the situation, and the role that the person occupies in that situation, the experience of self will vary accordingly. Last, the border that separates the ingroup from the outgroup is drawn with a solid line to indicate a relatively significant, and stable distinction. Relationships with one's ingroup members are self-defining for those with interdependent selves; therefore, the people with whom these relationships are established assume considerable importance. People do not easily become ingroup members, and nor do close relationships easily dissipate into outgroup relations. People with interdependent selves tend to view ingroup and outgroup members quite distinctly and may behave quite differently toward these individuals. In sum, interdependent selves consist largely of nodes within networks of individuals tied together by specific relationships, whose identities are grounded in those relationships, and who are contrasted against other networks of individuals.

Identifying cultural differences in the self-concept has had important implications for psychology because the self-concept shapes much about how people think—not just about themselves but about the world more generally. One metaphor that is often used to help make sense of how our minds work is the computer. Computers, like our minds, take in information, execute various programs or heuristics to process that information, and reach conclusions regarding the information considered. One important way that our minds differ from computers, however, is that we have self-concepts. Our self-concepts serve a number of key functions, and these functions represent some of the central themes of research in social psychology. Our self-concepts organize the information that we have about ourselves, they direct our attention to information that is viewed to be relevant, they shape the concerns that we have, they guide us in our choice of relationship partners and the kinds of relationships that we maintain, and they influence how we will appraise situations, which, in turn, influences the emotional experiences that we have about them. In sum, the ways that people view themselves are central to topics of human cognition, motivation, emotions, and relationships. Understanding that there are patterns of how self-concepts are constructed across cultures enables us to make predictions of how specific psychological phenomena will also differ across cultures.

Individualism and Collectivism

Self-concepts are shaped by the cultural practices that direct what individuals attend to, value, believe, and are able to attain. So what shapes cultural practices? In addition to the constraints and affordances of the physical environment, cultural practices are also shaped by the kinds of self-concepts a culture's members have. In this way, culture and self can be said to make up each other (Shweder, 1990).

The two different views of self described by Markus and Kitayama are not randomly distributed across our planet but emerge in places where there are cultural practices that sustain them. For example, what kind of self do you think would be more likely to develop in a culture where children are typically provided with their own bedrooms, where college students earn their own money from summer jobs to help pay for their entertainment and college tuition, where employees are paid on the basis of how much profit they help the company earn, or where the elderly take out their savings to pay the costs of moving into retirement homes? As you know from the previous chapters, such cultures are typically referred to as *individualistic* cultures. People participating in individualistic cultures are more likely to elaborate on independent aspects of themselves, and they come to feel distinct from others and emphasize the importance of being self-sufficient. Likewise, interdependent selves are more common in cultures where children typically co-sleep with their parents, where education is primarily a matter decided on by families, and where marriages are arranged by parents, and so on—*collectivistic* cultures. People participating in a collectivistic culture are more likely to attend to interdependent aspects of their self-concepts, such as their close relationships and group memberships.

Where do we find individualistic and collectivistic cultures? This question was first explored a few decades ago by Geert Hofstede, a Dutch psychologist. Hofstede was hired by IBM to explore the values and concerns of their workers around the world. He gave questionnaires to 117,000 employees in IBM offices in 40 different countries. In addition to the items that IBM was interested in for assessing workers' interests and opinions, Hofstede also included some items that explored values purportedly related to individualism. He was able to map out the world in terms of its individualism by calculating an individualism score for each of the 40 countries; this is presented in Figure 5.4. Hofstede's country scores show a clear and striking pattern.

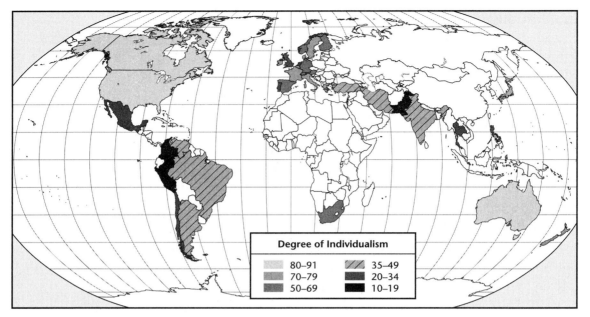

FIGURE 5.4

This map shows the degree of individualism and collectivism among IBM employees around the world. It shows a greater degree of individualism in Great Britain and in the United States, Canada, Australia, and New Zealand, which are former British colonies. Areas without shading were not surveyed in this study (based on data from Hofstede, 1980).

According to his data, the most individualistic country in the world is the United States, closely followed by other English-speaking countries and other Western European nations. On the other end of the distribution, countries that scored high in collectivism (or law in individualism) were various nations in Latin America and Asia. Other research has also found evidence of collectivism in countries in Asia, Africa, Southern Europe, and the South Pacific (e.g., Hofstede, 1983; Schwartz, 1994; Verkuyten & Masson, 1996). In sum, if we took a head count around the world we would surely find that most people participate in collectivistic cultures where interdependent selves are more common; these cultures likely encompass over 80% of the world's population. Although interdependent selves thus appear to be more common throughout the world, most research in psychology has emerged in cultures where independent selves predominate. This raises a serious question: How well do the psychological theories that have been generated in Western cultural contexts apply to other cultures of the world?

Furthermore, one does not have to look in especially exotic places to find evidence of collectivism. Indeed, there are pronounced pockets of collectivism even in the United States. In one study, people from the different states were surveyed to calculate a collectivism score for each state (Vandello & Cohen, 1999). The one with the highest collectivism score by far was Hawaii, probably because of that state's large population of people with Asian ancestry. The next most collectivistic states were Utah and the states of the Confederate South. In contrast, the least collectivistic states were in the Mountain West, the Great Plains, the Northeast, and the Midwest. The other regions fell in between. It is noteworthy that some of the highest concentrations of universities in the United States are in the Northeast and the Midwest. Not only has psychological research been largely concentrated in countries that are overall high in individualism, but within the United States at least, much of that research has been conducted in regions of the country that are especially individualistic. Similar within-country differences in individualism have been found in Japan as well (Kitayama, Ishii, Imada, Takemura, & Ramaswamy, 2006).

We have a long way to go before having a clear understanding of the different kinds of psychologies that exist around the world. Cultural psychologists have started to make some progress by studying people from collectivistic cultures. However, the majority of this research, as you'll see, has been conducted with people from East Asian cultures, such as China, Korea, and Japan, with results usually compared to findings from Western samples. Some recent research—and I suspect that a growing proportion of future research as well—is beginning to consider the nature of psychological processes from many other cultures around the world.

Beyond Individualism and Collectivism

Research on the dimension of individualism and collectivism, and on the associated dimension of independent and interdependent self-concepts, has served as the foundation for many key cultural psychological theories. Perhaps this dimension may ultimately prove to be the most important dimension for capturing cultural variation; however, it is not the only dimension that we can consider. A number of other cultural dimensions have also been investigated by researchers across cultures, such as power distance, uncertainty avoidance (Hofstede, 1980), vertical-horizontal social structure (Triandis, 1996), relationship structure (Fiske, 1992), intellectual autonomy (Schwartz, 1994), context-dependence (Hall, 1976), social cynicism, social complexity (Leung & Bond, 2004), and societal tightness (Triandis, 1989). Thus far, none of these other dimensions have revealed the breadth of explanatory power or empirical support that individualism-collectivism has marshaled. However, these new dimensions have not yet received a great deal of attention, and as we continue to explore these and other possible dimensions of cultures we will have a better system for understanding cultural variation. Hofstede (1980) launched an ambitious project in trying to map out the cultures of the world when he first conducted his massive study of cultural values of IBM workers. As our methods improve and our theories develop, we may one day be able to confidently realize his goals with a more extensive and sophisticated set of cultural dimensions.

A Note on Heterogeneity of Individuals and Cultures

It is much simpler to refer to people as though they had *either* an independent *or* an interdependent construal of self, as I've done in the preceding paragraphs. However, I use this dichotomy only as an explanatory device. In reality, people cannot be categorized so cleanly into these discrete categories; rather, the experience of self appears to track a continuum. I'm sure you can think of times in your own life when, for example, you felt very connected with others, and times when you've felt very distinct. Every individual surely has both interdependent and independent aspects of self; however, people do vary considerably in the degree to which they are closer to the independent or the interdependent exemplars described above. As such, everyone occasionally experiences the self as a separate self-contained unit or as an interconnected, relational unit, and how people differ can be seen as the proportion of the time that they think of themselves in each of these ways, or as their default way of viewing themselves. One important determinant of how often people are experiencing themselves as independent or interdependent is the situations they encounter on a daily basis. Situations that highlight independent aspects of the self will be more frequently encountered when participating in an individualistic culture in which cultural practices emphasize personal goals over collective ones. Likewise, situations that facilitate interdependent aspects of the self are more frequently encountered when individuals participate in collectivistic cultural contexts.

Not only are individuals more varied and complex than the schematics in Figures 5.2 and 5.3, but cultures too are highly variable and are resistant to simple categorization. As you've surely noted yourselves, there are many ways that you are different from the people around you, and you know some individuals who seem to be more independent and others who are more interdependent. We all know people from our cultures who do not come close to approximating the prototypical individuals represented in Figure 5.2. All cultures are highly heterogeneous and contain a great variety of people. When we speak of a culture as individualistic we mean that, on average, people in that culture are exposed to more cultural messages that encourage them to think in independent ways. Individuals will respond to those cultural messages in a variety of different ways, with some embracing them more than others. The culture has some coherence in that people in the culture are exposed to a similar set of messages through the media, the institutions they belong to, and the norms and practices that are common. It is important to remind yourself every now and then as you are reading that the cultural differences this book describes reflect general patterns of differences, and not all-or-none statements.

Gender and Culture

The constructs of independence and interdependence have been useful for understanding cultural variation in psychological processes. Could they also be useful for understanding differences between men and women? Indeed, a number of researchers have concluded that the features of interdependent identities seem more characteristic of women than men, and likewise, the features of independent identities seem more characteristic of men than women (e.g., Bakan, 1966; Gilligan, 1977). Do you believe men think in ways that are more prototypic of Western cultures and women think more in ways prototypic of non-Western cultures? Rather than saying that women are from Venus and men are from Mars, should we instead be saying that women are from Asia and men are from America?

One study directly explored this question (Kashima, Yamaguchi, Kim, Choi, Gelfand, & Yuki 1995). The researchers asked men and women in Western (the United States and Australia) and Eastern (Japan and Korea) cultures to complete a number of different measures of independence and interdependence. They combined all the measures, and using rather complicated statistical procedures, they extracted what were the underlying factors of these measures. That is, they simplified the large number of different items from the various scales into four underlying measures. These underlying factors were *collectivism* (Sample item: "I am prepared to do things for my group at any time, even though I have to sacrifice my own interest"), *agency* (Sample item: "I stick to my opinions even when others don't support me"), *assertiveness* (Sample item: "I assert my opposition when I disagree strongly with the members of my group"), and *relatedness* (Sample item: "I feel like doing something for people in trouble because I can almost feel their pains"). For all these factors there were significant cultural differences: namely, the Western cultures scored higher on agency and assertiveness whereas the Eastern cultures scored higher on collectivism and relatedness. The researchers also compared the genders on these measures. Significant gender differences emerged on only one factor: relatedness, in which women scored higher than men. There were no gender differences for collectivism, agency, or assertiveness. This suggests that it is not accurate to say that women are like Asians and men are like Americans. Women are apparently more interdependent than men only with respect to their attention to others' feelings and concerns. They do not appear to differ on the other factors associated with individualism/collectivism.

And what can we make of the gender differences found here? Are these too the result of particular cultural practices? Are women higher on relatedness than men because cultural norms dictate that women should be socialized to be more attentive to their relations than men? Or, alternatively, do these gender differences transcend cultural explanations?

The evidence for these questions is mixed. First, consider a very large-scale study that investigated people's perceptions of gender differences around the world (Williams & Best, 1990a). Men and women from 25 countries were asked how they felt men and women differed. Specifically, the respondents were given 300 trait adjectives, and they were asked whether each trait was more characteristic of men or women. The researchers established the criterion that if more than two-thirds of the respondents within a country agreed on whether the item characterized men or women, they would say there was a consensus within that country for the item. Likewise, they set the criterion that if more than three-fourths of the countries reached a consensus for any of the items they would conclude that there is a cross-cultural consensus for whether the item was viewed to be more characteristic of men or women. A large number of items revealed a consistent cross-cultural consensus regarding which traits better characterize men and which better char-

TABLE 5.1
Adjectives Consensually Associated with Each Sex

Associated with Men

Adventurous	Unemotional	Self-Confident
Dominant	Wise	Arrogant
Forceful	Ambitious	Assertive
Independent	Energetic	Opportunistic
Masculine	Inventive	Rational
Strong	Logical	Realistic
Aggressive	Clear-Thinking	Reckless
Autocratic	Coarse	Serious
Daring	Cruel	Stolid
Enterprising	Determined	Boastful
Robust	Disorderly	Confident
Stern	Egotistical	Humorous
Active	Hardheaded	Ingenious
Courageous	Hard-hearted	Obnoxious
Progressive	Having Initiative	Unkind
Rude	Lazy	
Severe	Loud	

Associated with Women

Sentimental	Emotional	Charming
Submissive	Fearful	Talkative
Superstitious	Softhearted	Anxious
Affectionate	Weak	Kind
Dreamy	Sexy	Meek
Feminine	Curious	Pleasant
Sensitive	Gentle	Shy
Attractive	Mild	
Dependent	Affected	

Items are presented in order of the strength of the cross-cultural consensus

acterize women (see Table 5.1). Note, importantly, that these are people's *perceptions* of what the genders are like rather than actual measures of how the different genders behave. These measures are thus most aptly viewed as consensual *stereotypes* about men and women.

Some underlying dimensions were identified from this list of traits, showing that respondents saw particular differences between men and women. One dimension that emerged was the overall positivity of views of men and women. Averaged across all cultures, there was a slight trend that the male stereotypical traits were viewed as more admirable than the female ones. However, within specific cultures, there was considerable variance. For example, in Japan, Nigeria, and South Africa, male stereotypes were viewed considerably more positively than female ones. In contrast, in Austria, Italy, and Peru, female stereotypes were viewed more positively than male ones. A second dimension was how active the two genders were perceived to be. Across all cultures, male stereotypes were perceived to be considerably more active than female ones. Although there was some cultural variability (male stereotypes were viewed as especially active in Scotland, New Zealand, and Bolivia, and female stereotypes were viewed as especially active in Japan, the United States, and Ireland), there was no country in which female stereotypes were viewed as more active than male ones. The third dimension was strength. In all cultures, male stereotypes were more associated with perceptions of strength than female ones. Again, although there was some cultural variability (male stereotypes were perceived strongest in Nigeria, Japan, and South Africa, and female stereotypes were strongest in Italy, the United States, and Germany), in no country were female stereotypes perceived as stronger than male ones. These data show that although there is some cultural variability in terms of how men and women are perceived, overall there are some striking similarities across cultures in gender stereotypes that seem to transcend cultural explanations.

On the other hand, there are clear cultural differences in the ways people view issues of gender equality. People in some cultures believe that women should be treated the same as men; in others, people believe that men should be granted more rights, privileges, and power than women. For example, women represent only about 3% of elected officials in Arab nations whereas they represent 45% of the Swedish Parliament. In Brazil, approximately the same percentage of men and women are literate; in

"You know, in some cultures the male does things."

TABLE 5.2
Mean Scores on the Sex Role Ideology Scale

	Males	Females
Netherlands	5.47	5.72
Finland	5.30	5.69
Germany	5.35	5.62
England	4.73	5.15
Italy	4.54	4.90
Venezuela	4.51	4.90
United States	4.05	4.66
Canada	4.09	4.54
Malaysia	4.05	4.01
Singapore	3.61	4.39
Japan	3.70	4.01
India	3.81	3.88
Pakistan	3.34	3.30
Nigeria	3.11	3.39

Higher numbers represent more egalitarian gender attitudes, whereas lower numbers represent more traditional gender attitudes.

Pakistan, twice as many men as women are literate. In sum, although there are some similarities in how men and women are perceived across the world, there are marked differences in the equality of the opportunities that men and women have.

One study used the Sex Role Ideology (SRI; Kalin & Tilby, 1978) scale in 14 countries to investigate people's attitudes toward how men and women should act (Williams & Best, 1990b). The SRI includes items that reflect "traditional" views on gender (Sample item: "For the good of the family, a wife should have sexual relations with her husband whether she wants to or not"), and more "modern" or "egalitarian" views (Sample item: "Marriage should not interfere with a woman's career any more than it does with a man's"). Men and women from each culture answered the items on a scale that ranged from 1 (Very traditional gender views) to 7 (Very egalitarian gender views). The means for the different countries are presented in Table 5.2.

Several findings from this study are noteworthy. First, there are some strikingly different views toward gender equality around the world. In the

Netherlands, Finland, and Germany, on average, people expressed views that men and women should be treated quite similarly. In contrast, in India, Pakistan, and Nigeria people tended to believe that the roles, obligations, and rights of men and women are clearly different (with men being perceived to have more rights than women). Second, regardless of where the data were collected, within a culture, men and women tended to share fairly similar views about gender equality. For example, women in India, Pakistan, and Nigeria are more likely to embrace traditional gender attitudes than are women from European nations. This suggests that attitudes toward gender equality are part of the cultural discourse and shape people's views in those cultures. Third, in every case except for two nonsignificant reversals (i.e., Malaysia and Pakistan), males had significantly more traditional gender views than females—probably because traditional gender views benefit men more than women.

A number of other variables were included in the study to explore what features of a culture predicted egalitarian gender views. One variable that seemed to have a large impact on gender views was the percentage of people in the country who embraced a particular religion. Countries in which a large percentage of the population practiced Christianity, in particular Protestantism, were more likely to have egalitarian gender views whereas countries with a large percentage of Muslims were associated with more traditional gender views. It is intriguing to note that the geographic location of the cultures was also associated with gender views, with more northern countries expressing more egalitarian views, and more southern countries expressing more traditional gender views (although the authors did not speculate on whether this was anything more than a coincidence). Also, the more urbanized the country, on average, the more likely people were to have egalitarian views. Last, the country's individualism score (obtained from Hofstede's data summarized in Figure 5.4) also correlated positively with egalitarian views. As these are correlational data, it is not clear whether these are causes of greater gender equality or consequences of it.

Another way to consider how culture influences people's perceptions of gender is to determine which gender identity is viewed to be more essentialized (i.e., to reflect an underlying unchangeable essence). Which gender do you think is more essentialized? That is, which gender do you think has less flexible ways of being expressed in socially approved ways? Take the case of American culture. Research suggests that Americans tend to view male gender identity to be more essentialized than female gender identity (e.g., Feinman, 1981). For example, most Americans do not seem to find it disturbing or unusual for women to present themselves like men (such as wearing pants, getting their hair cut short, or not wearing facial makeup) or to participate in stereotypically male behaviors (e.g., girls playing with trucks, or girls playing ice hockey). This suggests that Americans do not essentialize female gender identity to a great degree. In contrast, many Americans do find it disturbing or unusual for men to present themselves as women (such as wearing dresses, high-heeled shoes, or lipstick), or to participate in stereotypically female behaviors (e.g., boys playing with dolls, or boys taking ballet lessons). This suggests that Americans view male identity to be less changeable and thus more essentialized. In general, the gender that is associated with more power in a culture is the one that is more likely to be essentialized.

Mahalingam investigated the way Hindu Indians viewed gender identity. He noted that in Hindu myths, many more male gods change into female ones than female goddesses change into male gods (Mahalingam, 2003). Hindu religion involves goddess worship, and many of the most powerful gods are women (e.g., Shakti, Kali, Durga, Maya). According to Hindu religion, female identity is viewed as pure, strong, and powerful. This suggests that Indians should be more likely to essentialize female identity than male identity. Mahalingam conducted a number of studies to investigate this. In one study he asked Indian participants to imagine that Kumar (a male) had his brain switched with Mina (a female; Mahalingam & Rodriguez, 2003). How would we then expect Kumar's and Mina's bodies to act? On average, Indians felt that Kumar's body would act more like a woman if it had Mina's brain in it. In contrast, on average, they felt that Mina's body would continue to act like a woman, even with Kumar's brain in it. That is, they felt that the male gender identity was more mutable, and less essentialized, than the female gender identity (also see Mahalingam, 2003). In sum, perceptions of gender identity vary importantly across cultures. Although more cultures need to be investigated to reach firm conclusions, it appears that when females are viewed as more powerful, they also have more essentialized identities, whereas the reverse holds true where males are viewed as more powerful.

Some Other Ways That Cultures Differ in the Self-Concept

Although the field of cultural psychology dates back to the 19th century, it had little theoretical foundation to build on until Markus and Kitayama provided this distinction between independent and interdependent selves. Below we consider how cultural differences in independent and interdependent self-concepts lead to other differences in ways of thinking about the self.

Self-Consistency. One important way that the self-concept shapes our psychology is in how we think and behave across different situations. Some people seem to act pretty much the same across all different situations. Whether they're with their friends at a bar, or with their colleagues at work, or with their family at home they seem to be acting pretty much the same. These people would score very high on a measure of self-consistency. Regardless of the situation they are in, they behave largely in the same way. Other people seem to act quite differently depending on whom they are with. They might appear very quiet and respectful with their professors, outspoken and opinionated with their friends, and very caring and doting toward their grandparents. These people would score rather low on self-consistency. Different aspects of their identities are much more salient in some situations than in others.

Cultures vary considerably in the degree that individuals are motivated to be consistent across situations. For example, consider the results of the following study (Kanagawa, Cross, & Markus, 2001). The researchers wanted to investigate the effect of context on the ways people view themselves. They designed a simple but elegant study. College students from Japan and the United States were asked to complete the Twenty-Statements Test like the one you did at the beginning of this chapter. Straightforward enough. However, they manipulated a variable that is rarely considered by people who conduct questionnaire research—namely, the context the participants were in at the time of the study. The researchers specifically varied who was sitting near the students when they filled out the questionnaire. In one condition (an authority condition), students completed the questionnaire in a professor's office. In another condition (a peer condition), students sat next to a fellow student when they answered the items. In a third condition (a

TABLE 5.3
Ratio of Positive Statements to Negative Statements

	Authority	Peer	Group	Solitary
American	3.77	3.26	3.30	3.22
Japanese	.35	.69	.50	1.19

group condition), the students completed the questionnaire in a large group that consisted of about 20–50 people. Finally, in a fourth condition (a solitary condition), the students completed the questionnaire alone in a room.

A person's self-descriptions can be summarized in a variety of different ways. Let's focus here on how positively participants described themselves. The researchers coded each statement to see if it referred to a positive feature about the self or to a negative feature. They then calculated the ratio of positive to negative statements that students made about themselves. The findings are shown in Table 5.3.

First, looking at Table 5.3, we can see that the American responses, on average, were far more positive than the Japanese ones. We'll explore this puzzling finding more in Chapter 6, Motivation. Second, the American responses looked quite similar across the four conditions. Although their responses varied a little depending on what condition they had been assigned to, for the most part their responses appeared to be rather unaffected by the environment. They appeared quite similar regardless of situation. In contrast, the Japanese responses varied considerably across situation. They were much less self-critical when they were by themselves than when they were with others, especially when they were with a professor. The general positivity of Japanese individuals' attitudes toward themselves appears to vary depending on who is in the room with them.

This pattern of results challenges an implicit methodological assumption of studying people's personalities. In the past, there has been little concern about the context in which our personality measures were used. The measures were assumed to work well across time and situation, as they should, if people's self-concept exists separately from their contexts. Although this might be true for the measurement of independent selves, the results of the Japanese sample here call this into question. Depending on the context, the same question can yield quite different results (also see Cousins, 1989, and Oishi,

Diener, Scollon, & Biswas-Diener, 2004, for further evidence of the context specificity of the East Asian self). Furthermore, it's not at all clear *which* context provides the most accurate or self-defining results. Which could be called the true self: the one measured in the solitary context or the one measured with peers? How should we describe a Japanese individual's self-concept if it appears quite different depending on whom the person is sitting by at the time? Do we describe it as the average across the different situations? At present we don't have good answers to these questions, but they reveal just how much of a challenge it is to study the interdependent view of self. Given that the theories and methods used in psychology have largely emerged from the study of people with predominantly independent views of self, we need to be careful when we try to use these to study people with different views of self-concept.

How consistently people view themselves is thus important for both our methods and our theories. The motivation to be consistent has held a privileged place in social psychology. Leon Festinger, one of the most influential social psychologists of all time, saw this motivation to underlie what is, perhaps, social psychology's favorite theory: cognitive dissonance. Festinger proposed that we have a powerful motivation to be consistent and that cognitive dissonance is the distressing feeling we have when we observe ourselves acting inconsistently (Festinger, 1957). This distressing sense is disturbing enough that we feel a great need to rid ourselves of it. One way to do so would be to start acting more consistently. But often this can be very difficult to do. Another strategy would be to change our attitudes so that we no longer appear to be so inconsistent. This latter strategy is known as dissonance reduction. The premium that is placed on acting consistently is evident in the great lengths people will sometimes go to in convincing themselves that their actions are consistent.

For example, consider the plight of the cigarette smoker. We all know that smoking is dangerous—it says right on the cigarette package in big bold letters that smoking can kill you. Yet many people still smoke. This creates a lot of distressful dissonance because the individual's likely attitude—that he or she wants to live a long and healthy life—is clearly at odds with the smoking behaviors that are slowly and surely taking a toll on their bodies. What is a smoker to do? Well, one straightforward way to reduce the dissonance would be to quit smoking. This would quickly restore a sense of consistency. However, if you have ever tried to quit smoking, you'll know that it can be an extremely challenging and difficult endeavor. In general, changing our behaviors is a rather effortful and momentous undertaking. What is often easier than changing our behaviors is to change our attitudes. One way is to convince ourselves that smoking is so immensely pleasurable that it is worth the lung cancer that we quite likely will get. The dissonance is reduced because the smoker has found a new way of perceiving some consistency in her behaviors—the consistency between her deep passion for smoking and her willingness to make significant sacrifices in order to maintain this habit. Alternatively, a smoker might convince himself that although, in general, smoking might be dangerous, his own habit is conveniently less so. People might believe, like Bill Clinton, that they aren't really inhaling, or that they're only smoking so-called mild cigarettes, or that the harmful effects of smoking only occur to people who really abuse themselves by smoking extreme quantities. Evidence for this strategy appeared in one survey that found 60% of people who smoke between one and two packs a day called themselves moderate smokers (Tagliacozzo, 1979). To nonsmokers this seems like an awful lot of smoking; however, this kind of rationalization by the smokers preserves some consistency. They seem to be thinking "Although smoking lots is bad for your health, I'm not smoking all that much, so I'll be OK." Indeed, these kinds of rationalizations show that sometimes people are so motivated to be consistent that they can even end up killing themselves through their efforts.

One other way we can see our desire to avoid dissonance is when we make choices. Imagine that you've been accepted into two different schools and that you need to decide which one to attend. Let's say that you've been accepted into the University of British Columbia and Carleton College in Minnesota. They are both very good schools, so how would you make such a decision? One thing that you might try when making such important decisions is to make a list of pros and cons. For example, you might list some of the good points about choosing to attend UBC, such as the beautiful location, and the affordable tuition. On the downside, however, you might note that classes are very large and impersonal at UBC, and that British Columbia has a lot of rainy days in the winter. In contrast, when considering Carleton College you might note some good points such as the small classes and the opportunity students have to work closely with faculty. However, on the downside, you might decide that the location of the school is somewhat isolated and the tuition is quite high.

What should you decide? It's a tough call, as both schools have their strengths and weaknesses. But let's imagine that in the end you choose to attend UBC. You are now faced with some issues that are inconsistent with the choice that you've made: The cons about choosing UBC and the pros about attending Carleton are all inconsistent with your decision. What to do with all this inconsistent information? According to dissonance theory, here is where you would be motivated to rationalize your decision. You can do this by coming to see the points that are consistent with your decision as being especially important (you now start to think that being near the mountains and ocean, while saving money from the cheaper tuition, is really what matters), and you can come to see the points that are inconsistent with your decision as being relatively inconsequential (you now might ask yourself "who really cares about small classes and student-faculty interactions?"). Note that this rationalization work happens *after* you made your decision because this is when the potential inconsistencies emerge. If you had instead decided to attend Carleton you would be equally motivated to rationalize your decision in the opposite direction.

Do people from different cultures show similar kinds of dissonance reduction tendencies when they make decisions? It would seem that if individuals are motivated to be consistent with their roles rather than with their internal attributes (such as their attitudes), dissonance would be a different issue for those with interdependent self-concepts. An inconsistency between one's decisions and one's attitudes would not be as urgently in need of resolution.

We conducted a study to compare dissonance reducing tendencies between Japanese and Canadians when they make choices (Heine & Lehman, 1997). We advertised for Japanese and Canadians to participate in a study that was ostensibly about music preferences in return for receiving a music CD. The participants were given a list of 10 CDs that they had earlier rated as desirable. They were then asked a number of questions about those CDs including the first half of our dependent measure, "How much would you like to own this CD?" They answered by placing a mark on a 110-mm line that ranged from "Would not like this CD at all" to "Would like this CD very much." Then participants were presented with two of those CDs (namely, their 5th- and 6th-ranked choices) and were told that they could take one of those home with them as compensation for their participation. So the participants had to make a choice between two CDs that they had, on average, rated to be similarly desirable. After they had made their choice we investigated whether they had rationalized their decision. The participants were again asked to evaluate all 10 CDs by answering the same question about how much they would like to own each one. Participants' ratings of the CDs that they made *after* they had chosen their CD were compared with their ratings made *before* they had chosen their CD. If people are rationalizing their decision, they should prefer their chosen CD even more and like their rejected CD even less after they have made their decision. This change in ratings before and after a person's decision is known as the spreading of alternatives (Steele, Spencer, & Lynch, 1993). The bigger the change in their preferences, the more people are rationalizing their decisions.

Did people try to rationalize their decisions? The Canadians showed clear evidence that they were rationalizing their decisions. On average, the spread of alternatives was over 9 mm. This Canadian pattern replicates much past work on dissonance (Brehm, 1956; Steele et al., 1993), demonstrating how people (or North Americans, at least) engage in post-decision dissonance reduction. The Japanese results, however, were strikingly different. The Japanese participants showed no tendency to rationalize their decisions. They did not appear to have much motivation to ensure that their decisions were consistent (also see Kashima, Siegal, Tanaka, & Kashima, 1992).

But is it reasonable to claim that Japanese don't have motivations to be consistent? More recent work has identified some different kinds of motivations for consistency among East Asians. One study found that East Asians will rationalize decisions that they make for *others*, which suggests a motivation to have their behaviors be consistent with others' expectations (Hoshino-Browne et al., 2005). In that study, Japanese who ordered food from a restaurant for others to eat showed more rationalization than when they were just ordering food for themselves. The opposite pattern emerged for European-Canadians. Likewise, Japanese were found to rationalize their decisions when they consider the decisions they think others would make, which also suggests a motivation to be consistent with others' decisions (Kitayama, Snibbe, & Markus, 2004). These studies suggest that East Asians are not less consistent than North Americans but they are consistent in different ways. North Americans appear to aspire for consistency within themselves whereas East Asians are concerned with being consistent with others. Hence, there is a similarity across cultures in motivations to keep something consistent; however, what people try to keep consistent varies importantly across cultures.

These differences in the kinds of consistency that people pursue can have marked effects on their behaviors.

One way to see the effects of motivations for consistency on people's behaviors is to look at how these motivations affect people's responses to advertisers. Our desire to be consistent is something that advertisers or fund-raisers play on to encourage us to give them more of our money. For example, if you've ever agreed to contribute money to someone raising funds for a particular cause, you'll likely be reminded of your past contributions the next time the fund-raiser contacts you. By reminding you that "You've helped us out before," the fund-raiser is trying to push your "need for consistency" buttons. After all, if you're the kind of person who has given money to "Amnesty International" in the past and if your attitudes haven't changed much since then, you should be prepared to contribute money to the organization the next time they contact you as well. If you give on one occasion but not the other, you're not being very consistent. Fund-raisers exploit our desire for consistency all the time, and the value of consistency to us is obvious if we're often willing to pay money to preserve it (see Freedman & Fraser, 1966, for a striking demonstration of this motivation).

However, if people with interdependent self-concepts are less motivated for consistency within themselves, they should be less affected by fund-raisers who remind them of their past behaviors. On the other hand, as we have noted, such people tend to be especially attentive to others. This orientation toward others suggests that they might be motivated to act in ways consistent with how others similar to themselves have acted.

One study investigated this hypothesis among samples from Poland and the United States (Cialdini, Wosinka, Barrett, Butner, & Gornik-Durose, 1999). Although perhaps not as collectivistic as cultures in East Asia and Latin America, Poland is considerably more collectivistic than the United States (Reykowski, 1994). The authors hypothesized that this cultural difference should lead Poles to be more affected by trying to be consistent with how others have behaved, and Americans to be more affected by trying to be consistent with how they themselves have behaved in the past. Participants were asked to imagine how they would respond to a request by a marketing representative from Coca-Cola to take part in a survey about their beverage preferences. The kind and amount of consistency was varied across conditions. In a *self-consistency* condition, participants were asked to imagine that in the past they had always complied with similar requests. In a *peer-*

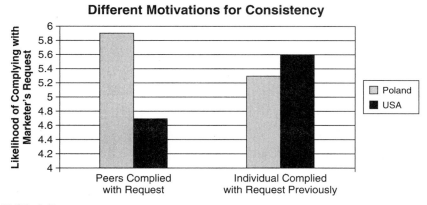

FIGURE 5.5

Whereas Poles are more likely to comply with a marketer's request if their peers had done so earlier, Americans are more likely to comply if they already complied with the marketer's previous request.

consistency condition, participants were asked to imagine that their classmates always complied with similar requests. The dependent measure of this study was how likely participants thought they themselves would be to comply with the marketing representative's request.

The pattern of results nicely captured the authors' hypotheses. Looking at Figure 5.5 we can see that the Americans were more influenced than the Poles by the information about their past performance. If Americans felt they had complied with these kinds of requests in the past, they assumed that they would be consistent and comply with them again. In contrast, the Poles were more influenced by the information about what their classmates had done. If their classmates had complied with these kinds of requests, Poles assumed that they would be consistent with their classmates' behaviors and comply as well. This suggests that marketers and fund-raisers in different cultures need to adopt different strategies to have maximal influence.

As much research has demonstrated, then, people with independent views of self are motivated to be consistent across situations. Why should people differ in their need to be consistent? Not all human behaviors are rational or necessarily functional within their cultures; however, when researchers are trying to understand why people behave in the ways they do, a good place to start is often to assume that their behaviors are functional. This reasoning would suggest that people with independent views of themselves must realize some benefits when they act consistently. What are the favorable outcomes associated with acting consistently, and are these outcomes distributed equally across cultures?

These questions were investigated in a cross-cultural study (Suh, 2002). Koreans and Americans were compared with regard to their self-consistency. This was accomplished by asking people to indicate how well a list of traits characterized them in a number of different situations—for example, when they were with their friends, with their families, with a professor or by themselves. A consistency coefficient was calculated for each individual, which revealed how similarly people viewed themselves across the different situations. Not surprisingly, given what we learned in the study that compared self-descriptions across the contexts in which they were written (Kanagawa et al., 2001), Koreans viewed themselves as far less similar across situations than did Americans. The participants were also asked to complete a measure of their subjective well-being, which indicates how satisfied people are with their lives. Moreover, two informants (one friend and one family member) of each participant were asked to evaluate the participant in two ways: First, they were asked how socially skilled they thought the participant was. Second, they were asked how likable they thought the participant was. The individual's consistency coefficients were then correlated with both their well-being scores and the evaluations of the informants. The results are shown in Table 5.4. For Americans, there were strong positive correlations between consistency and each of the other variables. Apparently, there are clear benefits in the United States for being consistent. People feel better about themselves if they see themselves as consistent, and other people view consistent individuals to be especially socially skilled and likable. Consistency has its rewards in the United States. Some of those rewards were evident in the 2004 U.S. presidential election campaign when John Kerry was negatively

TABLE 5.4
Cross-Cultural Comparison of Correlations with Self-Consistency

	USA	Korea
Correlation with Well-Being	.44	.19
Correlation with Social Skills	.37	.12
Correlations with Likability	.33	−.02

portrayed for failing to be consistent—a "flip-flopper," who couldn't be trusted—in contrast to the resolute steadfastness of President George W. Bush.

In contrast, in this study, Koreans realized few benefits for being consistent. The correlations between consistency and the other desirable qualities were much smaller for the Korean sample. Being consistent in Korea is not associated as strongly with feeling good about oneself (see Campbell et al., 1996, for similar findings with Japanese), or with being perceived as especially socially skilled or likable. Koreans are likely less consistent across situations than Americans because there are fewer benefits in Korea for viewing oneself consistently in this way. We would expect just such a pattern when we consider the importance of adhering to the requirements of one's roles in an interdependent cultural context.

Self-Awareness. The self is a unique entity as it can be considered from two very different vantage points. On the one hand, we can consider ourselves from the perspective of an object, the same way that we perceive the rest of the world. That is, the self can be experienced as the "me" that is observed and interacted with. On the other hand, in much of everyday experience we can consider ourselves from the perspective of the subject—the "I" that observes and interacts with the world. How do you think these two different perspectives of the self might impact the ways you behave and feel about yourself?

When individuals are considering themselves from the perspective of the subject they are said to be in a state of **subjective self-awareness**. In this state, people's concerns are with the world outside themselves, and they are largely unaware of themselves as individuals. Their attention is directed away from themselves. This is the state you are in as an audience member when your awareness is directed to the stage. People tend to experience this state as positive, a time when we are free of the nagging concerns that we often have about ourselves, especially regarding how we might not be living up to our ideal standards. It is a time when individuals are free to escape themselves.

When individuals consider how they appear to others, in contrast, they are experiencing themselves as an object, and are said to be in a state of **objective self-awareness**. In this state, their concerns are directed specifically at themselves. They are conscious of being evaluated and are likely to consider how they are faring by comparing themselves to a set of standards.

In the vast majority of cases, when people consider themselves as an object they become aware of ways they might be falling short of their standards. This is because we tend to be very critical when we are adopting the perspective of an audience, as we take on the role of the judge. And, as the judge, we tend to be fairly critical, as we're always able to conjure up standards with which to compare ourselves that are higher than our current levels of performance. As such, the experience of objective self-awareness tends to be aversive as we become aware of our shortcomings. It is not a pleasant state and people actively seek to avoid it, especially when they have recently not performed well (Gibbons & Wicklund, 1976).

The states of objective and subjective self-awareness are said to be mutually exclusive, so that at a given instant, we are either thinking about ourselves as objects or we are contemplating the world (including ourselves) as subjects. However, individuals can quickly oscillate between these two states when a stimulus encourages them either to think about themselves as an object or to attend elsewhere.

Much research in self-awareness theory has been conducted among North Americans. Typically, this research compares a control group with a group who are in the presence of stimuli that affect their state of self-awareness. For example, some stimuli increase the proportion of time people are in a state of objective self-awareness, such as seeing themselves in a mirror, knowing a camera is videotaping them, or hearing their own tape-recorded voice (Duval & Wicklund, 1972). These stimuli call attention to ourselves as objects—the way we appear to others. Other stimuli increase the proportion of time that a person is in a state of subjective self-awareness—for example, engaging in intense physical exercise (which makes people focus on their physical sensations; Duval & Wicklund, 1972) or watching television (which attracts people's attention away from themselves; Moskalenko & Heine, 2003). These stimuli call attention to thoughts other than ourselves as an object. As noted above, people are more likely to be aware of falling short of standards when they are in a state of objective self-awareness, and they become more self-critical.

Participants in one study were recorded while they read out loud an abstract philosophical passage as part of a study that was supposedly investigating the relation between linguistic factors and success (Ickes, Wicklund, & Ferris, 1973). Afterward participants were asked to complete a measure of actual-ideal self-discrepancies. That is, they were asked to evaluate themselves and to evaluate the kind of person they would ideally like to be. The magnitude of the discrepancy between these two self-evaluations indicates how self-critical individuals are feeling. However, participants were divided into two separate experimental conditions. Half of them were put in a state of objective self-awareness by listening to a tape recording of their own voices. The other half were not put in this state as they instead listened to a tape recording of someone else's voice. The participants were then compared to assess how self-critical they were. Consistent with the predictions of self-awareness theory, those who listened to their own voices had larger self-discrepancy scores than those who did not. The researchers interpreted this as indicating that those who heard their own voices spent a greater proportion of their time considering themselves as an object than did those who heard someone else's voice. Comparable findings also emerged when participants were put in front of a mirror rather than hearing their own voice (Ickes et al., 1973).

Conversely, in a study we conducted, American students were asked to complete the same kind of self-discrepancy measure either immediately after watching a few minutes of a television program (containing some nature scenes with no dialogue) or without having seen the program (Moskalenko & Heine, 2003). The results indicated that those who had just watched the television program showed more positive self-assessments (they viewed themselves as being more similar to their ideal standards) than those in the control condition. We interpreted this difference as indicating that those who had just watched television had spent a greater proportion of their time attending to things outside themselves and so were less aware of their potential shortcomings.

How might we expect culture to affect people's self-awareness? It would seem that individuals who have a more interdependent view of self would tend to focus more on monitoring their sense of belongingness and connection with others than those with more independent views of self. Indeed, if people are considering whether they are fitting in with others they must take the perspective of an object and think about how others are viewing them. "Did I just offend Ravinder?" "Andres seems to like my sense of humor," and so on. In other words, interdependent individuals should be more likely to be considering themselves from the point of view of an audience. Is this really the case?

Cross-cultural research on self-awareness is rather new and thus far it has focused only on comparisons between East Asians and North Americans of

European descent. Consider the following question: Remember a time when you were the center of attention. For example, think back to your high school graduation to when you received your diploma in front of the whole auditorium. Think carefully about the image that comes to your mind about this event. Now, I'd like you to evaluate the imagery in your memory. One way you might have conjured up this memory is from the perspective that you had as a subject at that time. That is, you could remember the images you saw as you walked up the stage, walked over to your principal, took the diploma that she handed to you, turned to the audience, and then walked off the other side of the stage. This kind of memory is called a "first-person" memory as it contains the imagery that you experienced firsthand. Another way you might recall your high school graduation is from the perspective of the audience. That is, you might recall seeing yourself walk up the stage and over to the principal, receive your diploma from her, and then walk off the other side. Of course, this imagery was never available to you firsthand. To the extent that you have this kind of memory it suggests that you were attending a lot to how you thought people in the audience were viewing you. Your thoughts of their perceptions would leak into your own memory, providing you with some "third-person" imagery. Is the imagery from your memories of your high school graduation more consistent with a first-person perspective or a third-person perspective?

In one study, Asian-Canadians and Euro-Canadians were contrasted on this kind of question (Cohen & Gunz, 2002). When controlling for the amount of imagery that people had for memories when they were *not* the center of attention (in which no one, interdependent or independent, should be taking on the perspective of the audience because the audience was not watching them), the Asian-Canadians revealed significantly more third-person imagery in their memories of being at the center of attention than did the Euro-Canadians across a variety of different situations (see Figure 5.6). These findings suggest that Asian-Canadians so habitually consider the perspective of significant others that they start to see themselves in their mind's eye in terms of how they think they appear to others!

Other research further supports this hypothesis. For example, have you ever tried to tap out a tune with your fingers on a table and have a friend try to guess what song it was? How did the friend do? Quite likely, he or she was unable to identify the song you tapped, as this is an extremely difficult task. However, from the point of view of the tapper it might seem that

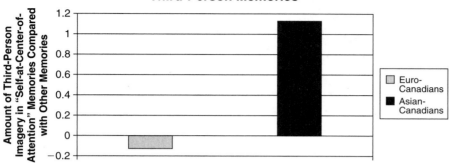

FIGURE 5.6

European-Canadians' memories of being the center of attention are just as likely to include third-person imagery as are their memories of times when they were not the focal point. In contrast, Asian-Canadians' memories of being the center of attention feature more third-person imagery than memories in which they were not the focus.

this shouldn't be so difficult. The tapper hears both the tapping with her fingers and in her head the complete song played by all the separate instruments. It seems quite obvious to the tapper what song she is tapping, as she can hear all the imagined music behind the taps. To the listener, however, all he hears is a monotone tapping on the table. If Westerners are less able to attend to the perspective of others, they should tend to be overconfident in their estimates of how likely a listener is to identify a song that they tap because they have a more difficult time ignoring their own perspective and taking on the perspective of a listener. East Asians, on the other hand, should be quite adept at imagining the perspective of a listener, thereby ignoring the background music that is in their heads, and they should be more accurate at estimating how well a listener can identify their tapped tunes. Indeed, one study demonstrated precisely this cultural difference (Cohen & Hoshino-Browne, 2005).

It would seem that if people with interdependent selves are chronically considering themselves from the perspective of an audience we could hypothesize that they should be spending a greater proportion of their time in the state of objective self-awareness. Compared with North Americans, then, East Asians should be more likely to take on the perspective of an object rather than the subject. One way this hypothesis can be tested is to see what happens when East Asians are confronted with stimuli that prime objective self-awareness, such as being placed in front of a mirror. If one tends to be in a state of objective self-awareness already, then seeing oneself in a mirror should have little impact on one's self-perceptions. In contrast, it would seem that if one is less frequently in a default state of objective self-awareness then seeing oneself in a mirror should have a considerable effect on one's self-perceptions.

We set out to test this hypothesis (Heine, Takemoto, Moskalenko, & Lasaleta, 2007). Japanese and American students were asked to evaluate themselves on a measure of actual-ideal self-discrepancies either in front of a mirror or not. Remember that larger actual-ideal discrepancies indicate that people are being more critical about themselves. The results (see Figure 5.7) showed that Americans became significantly more self-critical in front of a mirror than when no mirror was present. This finding replicates previous findings with Americans (Ickes et al., 1973). In contrast, Japanese were unaffected by the mirror. Regardless of whether they were viewing themselves in a mirror and seeing how they appear to the world or were just thinking about themselves the way they typically do, they evaluated themselves in the same way. Apparently, the habitual self-view of Japanese is very similar to the perspective they have in front of a mirror. It is perhaps also telling that Japanese and American self-discrepancies look quite similar when both participants are in front of a mirror. When Americans are considering themselves as an object, as when they are in front of a mirror, they appear to be thinking thoughts about themselves similar to those of Japanese with or without a mirror.

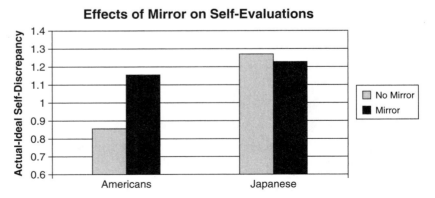

FIGURE 5.7

Whereas Americans are more self-critical when they are in front of a mirror than when they are not, Japanese self-evaluations are unaffected by the presence of a mirror.

Japanese (a, b) and American (c, d) participants in Leuers and Sonoda's study took these photographs to describe themselves.

Further evidence that East Asians have more habitual awareness of an audience can also be seen in a creative study about self-descriptions (Leuers & Sonoda, 1999). Rather than just ask participants to describe themselves using the Twenty-Statements Test, the researchers thought it would be interesting to ask participants to describe themselves through another medium: photographs. American and Japanese participants were given a disposable camera and were instructed to take pictures of things and people that captured their self-identity. The pictures were then developed, coded, and analyzed. The results indicated that Japanese presented themselves far more impeccably in these pictures than did Americans, who were more apt to show themselves, in the words of the authors, "warts and all." For example, Japanese were more likely to pose formally in the pictures, be dressed nicely, and arrange their belongings in neat piles. Americans, in contrast, were more likely to be caught in an active spontaneous scene; some were not even wearing clothes, and their belongings were often photographed unarranged and thrown into a haphazard pile. These results suggest that the Japanese present themselves as though to an evaluating audience, carefully polished and choreographed. In contrast, the Americans tended to present themselves from the perspective of the individual, with less concern for creating a favorable impression.

Implicit Theories Regarding the Nature of the Self

The nature of our self-concept is shaped by the implicit theories that we have about it. Implicit theories guide our interpretation of much of what happens in the world. For example, you might believe that it's dangerous to walk through a particular neighborhood by yourself late at night because of your belief that much violence occurs there, especially to solo pedestrians in the dark. Or you might believe that if you're on a date, you'll make a more favorable impression if you don't wear your rattiest pair of sneakers, as you believe that people on dates evaluate each other based on the clothes they are wearing. These theories are implicit in the sense that they represent a set of beliefs we take for granted, usually without engaging in much active hypothesis testing. Implicit theories are a great place to explore cultural influences on psychology as they reflect the beliefs that people have. In a number of significant domains in life the theories people have about the way things work can vary substantially across cultures (e.g., Chiu, Dweck, Tong, & Fu, 1997).

One kind of implicit theory we possess is about the nature of our selves. For example, we might believe that our self-concepts are largely in flux and respond to the efforts we make. The belief that we can easily change, and are expected to change, is referred to as an **incremental theory of self** (e.g., Dweck & Leggett, 1988). This theory of self represents the belief that a person's abilities and traits are malleable and can be improved. The attributes that one possesses (for example, one's soccer-playing skill, one's extraversion, or one's intelligence) are not seen to remain constant across one's life but are perceived as reflecting how hard one has worked on them.

In contrast to this view, one could instead embrace a theory that aspects of the self are largely resistant to change, which is known as an **entity theory of self**. People who endorse this set of beliefs tend to view their abilities and traits as largely fixed, innate features of the self. Individuals with this view see their attributes to be largely inborn. As they get older, their attributes are viewed to stay largely the same. Which of these two implicit theories of the self best captures your own views?

Whether individuals possess more incremental theories or more entity theories for a given domain in life can have a large impact on the efforts they make. If people hold an incremental theory about intelligence, they will tend to think that how intelligent they are is due to how much they study. Studying hard is believed to make one more intelligent. The implication of embracing such a theory of intelligence is that if they aren't satisfied with their intelligence, then they must not have made enough effort. People with incremental theories about intelligence should thus be strongly motivated to study hard, especially when their grades aren't as good as they want. There is always room for improvement if people hold incremental theories.

Entity theories, in contrast, suggest that aspects of the self reflect an essence of the individual—an essence that remains largely removed from the efforts a person makes. If people's attributes are stable over their lifetime and reflect self-defining characteristics, people should be less inclined to view their attributes as the products of their efforts. Indeed, to the extent that a person strongly embraces an entity theory of self, making continued efforts can suggest a problem. It might suggest that an individual's innate abilities are not adequate and that efforts are needed to compensate for them. People with entity theories of self should thus not make many efforts in the face of failure.

Much research has demonstrated that people holding an incremental theory of self respond to difficulties differently from those holding an entity theory of self. For example, when people embracing an entity theory of intelligence encounter a failure they are more likely to blame their static intellectual ability. People with more incremental theories, in contrast, respond to failures by focusing on their efforts and the strategies they utilized (Henderson & Dweck, 1990). Also, people who are having trouble in their classes are more likely to take remedial courses if they embrace incremental theories of self than if they tend to favor entity theories (Hong, Chiu, Dweck, Lin, & Wan, 1999). If your abilities are a function of your efforts, it makes sense to increase your efforts when you're not doing well enough.

People from different cultures do indeed appear different in the extent to which they embrace incremental views of self. North Americans are less likely to hold an incremental view than people from some Asian cultures (e.g., Norenzayan, Choi, & Nisbett, 2002). This makes sense when you consider the cultural differences in the consistency of the self that we discussed earlier. If your self varies from situation to situation, it seems unlikely that you would embrace an entity theory. These cultural differences are evident when you ask people what abilities are based on. For example, over 60% of Chinese high school students said that the key to success in math was to study hard. In contrast, less than 25% of American high school students felt this way (Stevenson & Stigler, 1992). In one study, we asked students in the United States and Japan to estimate how much of intelligence is due to what you're born with and how much is due to how hard you try (Heine et al., 2001). Americans responded that a majority of intelligence was inborn whereas Japanese stated that the majority of intelligence was due to your efforts.

Given this pattern of cultural differences between East Asia and North America, it might not be surprising to learn that different kinds of exams are given in the two cultures. To get into a good American university you typically need to get an acceptable score on the SAT. The SAT was originally designed to measure innate aptitudes and not efforts in one's classes. (It turns out that studying hard can increase one's SAT scores significantly. This has been a source of frustration for the test-makers, as the tests are no longer serving the function they were originally designed for, and this has sparked much policy debate about their utility.) Also, IQ tests are regularly given in public schools in the states, and the results of these influence decisions on whether students should attend gifted or remedial classes. In contrast, in Japan, to get into a good university you need to do well on a university entrance exam that tests your mastery of a large amount of material (a sample question might be "Who built the Suez Canal and when?"). Successful performance on these tests is viewed to be largely due to how hard one studies for them. It is not unusual for students to spend much of their time in high school, and one or more years after graduation, attending cram schools to help them master the material. Furthermore, IQ test results are not given out in public schools, and teachers are averse to discussing differences in abilities among students (Tobin, Wu, & Davidson, 1989). So the different university entrance exams that are given in Japan and the United States reflect and sustain the different kinds of implicit theories of intelligence that people in these countries have. The different ways that we educate people shape the theories that people hold about the nature of intelligence; likewise, the theories that we have shape the decisions that our schools make for educating people. This is one way that we can see the mutual influence of cultural practices (like entrance exams) and psychological processes (like implicit theories of intelligence).

Personality

It goes without saying that people are different. Here, I'm not referring to the systematic differences that exist across cultures—the focus of much of this chapter. Rather, I'm referring to the obvious fact that people in any given culture differ from their compatriots in many important ways. For example, even though George W. Bush and John Kerry are similar in growing up in wealthy families, attending Yale, and trying to be elected president of the United States, in many ways, as repeatedly emphasized in their respective presidential campaigns, they have strikingly different personalities. The ways that people are different from each other has been a primary concern of the field of personality psychology.

One key approach in personality psychology has been to describe people in terms of underlying personality traits. There is no shortage of terms that can be used to describe people like George W. Bush or John Kerry (and they might not always be nice ones!), or anyone else you know. Indeed, by one count, there are approximately 18,000 personality trait words in the English language (Allport & Odbert, 1936). Some of these terms are probably familiar to you (e.g., outgoing, conservative), whereas others are probably not (e.g., accrescent, vulnific). We thus have a very rich vocabulary for categorizing people according to personality.

It would seem to be a cultural universal that people everywhere try to categorize others based on personality traits. However, the earlier discussion in this chapter on the prevalence of those traits in people's self-descriptions, and the extent to which people believe themselves to be consistent across situations or malleable to experience, suggests that the utility or importance of personality traits might vary significantly across cultures (Markus & Kitayama, 1998). In support of this notion, a study was conducted with Americans in which they were asked how much their identity was grounded in their personality traits or in their group memberships (Oishi, Lun, & Sherman, 2006). For some Americans their group memberships were as important as their personalities to their identity; for other Americans their personalities were

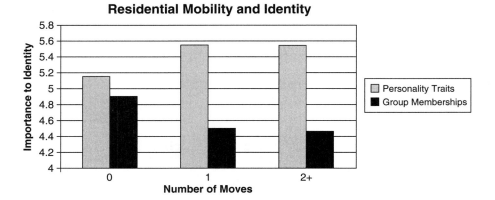

FIGURE 5.8

People who have moved to different neighborhoods value their personality traits more and their group memberships less, compared with those who have never moved.

much more important to their identity than their group memberships. The difference between these groups was based on how many times the participants had moved in their lives. Americans who had never moved prior to going to college, compared to those who had moved at least once, viewed their group memberships as more important; those Americans who had moved before going to college, compared to those who had never moved, viewed their personality traits to be a more significant part of their identities (see Figure 5.8). Likewise, Americans who had never moved preferred interactions with people who accurately perceived their collective identities, whereas those Americans who had moved preferred interactions with those who accurately perceived their individual personalities. And the more times people had moved, the more pronounced was this pattern. Apparently, if you're part of a stable network of relationships, your collective identity is especially important to you. In contrast, if you move around so that your network of relationships becomes less stable, your identity becomes more based on the traits that you carry with you. Furthermore, because Americans, on average, are an especially mobile population compared with many other countries in the world (Oishi et al., 2006; Schmitt, 2001), this can help explain why they develop independent self-concepts with identities that hinge on their personality traits. One can imagine that had the study of psychology emerged in more residentially stable populations, the topic of personality would be viewed as less central to identity, and psychologists might instead be studying group memberships.

Despite this variance in the centrality of personality traits to identity, there is ample evidence that people across a wide array of cultures can clearly recognize systematic temperament differences across individuals they know (e.g., McCrae et al., 2005). Everywhere around the world people can notice who is more talkative and who is more shy, or who is more dominant and who is more submissive. Many different personality typologies have been proposed around the world that serve to classify people into different types. For example, Hippocrates proposed that there were four basic types of human temperaments that depended on the balance of the four fluids, or humors, that were present in the body: blood, yellow bile, phlegm, and black bile. Ayurvedic medicine from India proposes that there are three metabolic body-types, thus maintaining that one's metabolism rate provides the foundation of individual temperaments. A question frequently asked by Japanese that often surprises Westerners is about their blood type, as the four blood types are perceived to underlie reliable differences in personality in Japan. In short, across cultures and history, people have come up with a remarkably diverse array of ways for explaining people's personalities.

The Five Factor Model of Personality. The approach most widely accepted by personality psychologists to view the different kinds of personality traits is the **Five Factor Model of Personality**, or "The Big Five" (although this model does have its critics; e.g., Block, 1995; McAdams, 1992). According to this model, there are five underlying personality traits, or "core traits." If you would attempt to measure people's personalities by use of any substantial list of personality traits (an extreme example would be the nearly 18,000 traits identified by Allport and Odbert), you would find a great deal of overlap between many of the traits, allowing the list to be reduced to a much smaller number of traits. One reason for the overlap is that many trait terms are synonyms (e.g., shy, introverted, quiet) and likely do not reflect independent traits. Also, we could simplify our list of personality traits much further by noting how many seemingly distinct-sounding personality traits tend to have substantial correlations with other traits. For example, people who are more authoritarian in their personalities also tend to be more religious, conventional, and dogmatic; they tend to have negative attitudes toward obesity and homosexuality; and they tend to be less gregarious and less open to aesthetics and ideas (Butler, 2000). Because these traits correlate with each other they cannot be said to represent independent traits.

Factor analysis is a technique that can identify groups of things that are alike or different. As an example, consider what kinds of athletic talents one needs to do well at a decathlon competition. The decathlon consists of 10 different events, so to do well, it would seem that one would need to have 10 skills that are unique to those 10 events. But are all those skills so unique? Could we instead reduce those 10 skills to a smaller number? For example, the decathlon includes the 100 meter sprint and the 110 meter hurdles. Both of these events require speed. Likewise, the decathlon includes both the discus throw and the shot put. Both of these events require upper body strength. If we did a similar analysis for all the sports in the decathlon we might be able to identify some underlying "factors," such as speed and upper body strength, that could predict how well one would do on all 10 events. Rather than needing to identify skills for all 10 events, then, we might be able to predict someone's performance on the decathlon by identifying only a few underlying skills. Factor analysis is the technique that allows one to do this. It can simplify a long list of items into a much shorter list of underlying factors by investigating the patterns of correlations among the various items.

In the case of personality testing, factor analysis has been used to reduce the great number of personality traits to a much more manageable number. Specifically, in the Five Factor Model, there are only five underlying personality traits: openness to experience, conscientiousness, extraversion, agreeableness, and neuroticism (which can be remembered by the acronym OCEAN). **Openness to experience** reflects a person's intelligence and curiosity about the world. **Conscientiousness** can be seen as indicating how responsible and dependable an individual is. **Extraversion** indicates how much an individual is active or dominant. **Agreeableness** is the extent to which a person tends to be warm and pleasant. Last, **neuroticism** is the degree to which an individual can be seen as emotionally unstable and unpredictable. These five are argued to be fundamental traits as they can't be reduced to a smaller number of traits (i.e., the five factors are largely uncorrelated with each other).

The Five Factor Model proposes that all personality traits largely reflect some combination of these different five core traits. That is, all personality traits should show significant correlations with at least one, if not more, of these core traits. To the extent that a personality trait consistently failed to correlate with any of the core traits would suggest that this trait itself was an additional core trait (if so, we would then have the Six Factor Model). However, this is not to say that there is nothing more to any specific personality trait than some combination of the Big Five core traits. For example, although a sense of humor correlates positively with extraversion and not with any of the other Big Five traits, there likely is something about a sense of humor that goes well beyond just extraversion (Saucier & Goldberg, 1998). Hence, these factors can be seen to reflect the basic structure of personality although there are some subtle, yet important, ways that individual traits can lie beyond this basic structure.

The idea that much of what entails personality can largely be understood by five factors is an important idea, and it is one that has led to much speculation about how well this model would generalize elsewhere. Do you think the five-factor structure is something basic about human nature, something that we should find in the personalities of people in all cultures that we examine? Can human personality be largely captured by these five specific traits? Alternatively, do you think the Five Factor Model reflects ideas about personhood that are limited to the West, where the bulk of this research has been conducted? A number of large and costly research projects have been launched to explore this fundamental question.

A questionnaire that measures the Big Five, the Revised Neuroticism, Extraversion, and Openness Personality Inventory (which goes by the catchy acronym of the NEO-PI-R; Costa & McCrae, 1992) has been distributed to thousands of people in dozens of cultures around the world. In one study, people from 50 different cultures used this scale to evaluate people that they know (McCrae et al., 2005). The scale was translated into the local languages of the respective cultures. In all 50 cultures, people's responses organized themselves along the five factors, just as they do among Americans, for whom the scale was originally developed. Likewise, a number of other investigations have used the NEO-PI-R to have people evaluate themselves in many different cultures (Allik & McCrae, 2004; Yik, Russell, Ahn, Fernandez-Dols, & Suzuki, 2002). These studies have tended to reveal the same pattern of results. Apparently, wherever one goes, people can think of themselves and others in terms of the same five basic personality traits. Human nature is such that personality traits organize themselves in certain, particular ways.

Actually, the claim made by personality psychologists is even broader than this. Researchers have recognized some of the Big Five traits in a number of animal species (Gosling & John, 1999). For example, behavioral patterns consistent with all of the Big Five traits have been identified in chimpanzees (King & Figueredo, 1997), and some traits—for example, neuroticism—have been identified in species as diverse as hyenas (Gosling, 1998), guppies

(Budaev, 1997), and octopuses (Mather & Anderson, 1993). It is possible that the Five Factor Model (or at least some of its dimensions) represent fundamental responses to biological challenges encountered by many, if not most, species. If this is true, it follows that the Five Factor Model should indeed be evident in humans of all cultures.

On the other hand, one could raise the question of whether the Five Factor Model provides sufficient coverage to capture all the personality variation in the world. The cross-cultural research discussed above has shown that personality as measured by the same scale, the NEO-PI-R, has the same basic five dimensions everywhere. However, the NEO-PI-R was developed through the exploration of English personality terms, largely with Americans. Would we expect the same pattern to emerge if, in contrast, questionnaires were developed from trait terms that were derived from different languages and from different cultures? Do the Big Five personality dimensions emerge regardless of what traits one considers, or do they arise from the kinds of personality traits that are discussed in English?

A number of investigations have explored this question. One study explored the kinds of personality dimensions that would emerge if the investigation considered indigenous Chinese personality traits rather than relying on English ones (Cheung et al., 1996). To launch this enterprise, the researchers first rigorously explored the kinds of personality traits common in Chinese. They looked in Chinese novels, Chinese proverbs, people's personality descriptions, and what had been discussed in the Chinese psychology literature. These efforts revealed 26 unique personality constructs (as well as another 12 clinical constructs). Some of these sound familiar to Western ears, such as trustworthiness, contentment, and thrift. Others are less familiar: for example, somatization, face, *ren qin* (loosely translated as relationship orientation, although that doesn't capture some important cultural nuances), harmony, modernization, and "Ah-Q mentality" (which reflects a set of personality shortcomings captured by a character in a satirical novel). These constructs were then put into a questionnaire (entitled, appropriately enough, the Chinese Personality Assessment Inventory; CPAI), and Chinese participants indicated how much each one applied to them. Following this, the same kind of factor analytic technique was used to reveal the underlying factors.

This procedure revealed a number of factors from the Chinese personality constructs. The factors were not the same as the Big Five; rather, four factors emerged that were captured by the following labels: Dependability (reflecting responsibility, optimism, and trustworthiness), Interpersonal Relatedness (reflecting harmony, thrift, relational orientation, and tradition), Social Potency (reflecting leadership, adventurousness, and extraversion), and Individualism (reflecting logical orientation, defensiveness, and self-orientation). Further analyses included the Chinese Personality Assessment Inventory and a measure of the Five Factor Model (Cheung, Cheung, Leung, Ward, & Leong, 2003). That analysis revealed that there was substantial overlap between three of the factors; namely, neuroticism correlated with dependability, extraversion correlated with social potency, and individualism correlated with agreeableness. Openness to experience did not correlate with any of the Chinese factors (this factor is the least reliably found of the five factors), and Interpersonal Relatedness was uncorrelated with any of the Big Five factors. This suggests that Interpersonal Relatedness might be a sixth personality factor that is especially salient in Chinese culture. Whether Interpersonal Relatedness is a reliable sixth factor in Western samples has yet to be demonstrated.

Similar approaches have been taken in other cultures. An indigenous list of Filipino personality traits was developed and the underlying factors were explored through factor analysis (Church, Reyes, Katigbak, & Grimm, 1997; Church, Katigbak, & Reyes, 1998). This analysis revealed five traits that were highly similar to the Big Five; however, it also revealed two additional factors: Temperamentalness, and a Negative Valence dimension, which did not correlate strongly with any of the Big Five. Likewise, an investigation of Spanish personality constructs revealed seven underlying personality factors, although these did not map as well to the Big Five (Benet-Martinez & Waller, 1995, 1997). In general, investigations such as these reveal that although the Five Factor Model does appear to be quite cross-culturally robust, it does not appear to provide an exhaustive list of personality traits in other cultures. When personality structures are explored with indigenous personality terms, some additional dimensions emerge.

Although the structure of the Five Factor Model identifies similar traits across all cultures that have been studied, the actual scores that people have for each of the Big Five traits varies considerably across cultures. One large-scale cross-cultural study contrasted people's scores on the Big Five traits in 36 different cultures around the world (McCrae, 2002), revealing a number of notable cross-cultural differences (see Table 5.5 for a summary). For

TABLE 5.5
Cross-Cultural Comparison of Scores on the Big Five Traits

Country/Group	Neuroticism	Extraversion	Openness	Agreeableness	Conscientiousness
			Factor		
Austria	52.9	48.4	59.1	48.2	46.7
Belgium	53	47.7	51.8	50	46.6
Canada	50.5	51.7	51.6	51.9	49.2
China	53.1	44.5	48.3	47.8	50.3
Croatia	52.8	45.1	49	47.5	53.2
Czechs	54.2	47.4	52.3	50.7	47.5
Denmark	46.5	52.8	46.5	52	47.5
Estonia	49.7	49.9	52.6	50.8	49.6
France	55.4	47.3	54.1	52.1	47.4
German Swiss	53.2	48.5	58.9	47	49.6
Germany	52.8	47.3	56.7	49.1	46.7
Hispanic Americans	49.5	47.5	51.2	47.1	51.6
Hong Kong	53.3	37.6	49.2	54.6	49.2
Hungary	53.8	47.1	53.7	47.9	50
Indonesia	48.6	43.3	49.9	51.9	50.3
Italy	55.6	46.6	52.6	48.9	50.4
Japan	55.3	41.7	51.7	47.7	42.6
Malaysians	54.2	42.5	46.6	58.5	54.2
Marathi Indians	49.1	40.7	51.4	56.7	55.7
Netherlands	48.6	43.9	55.7	54.6	48.6
Norway	47.4	53.6	51.5	49.9	45.7
Philippines	50.8	43.8	51.8	52.9	51.5
Peru	50.8	45.5	50	48.6	49
Portugal	55.5	46.3	49.2	51.2	50.3
Russia	53.6	45.2	49.1	46.7	46.5
South African Blacks	49.1	41.4	47.7	50.4	47.9
South African Whites	51.9	47.2	54.4	52.2	47.9
South Korea	53.6	40	51.4	52.3	48.8
Spain	57.1	48.3	48	49.4	48.3
Sweden	46.3	50.6	46	56.5	45.7
Taiwan	51.5	42	50.2	54.5	48.1
Telugu Indians	52.3	43.5	44	55.9	54
Turkey	50.9	50.3	50.8	48.5	50.4
United States	50	50	50	50	50
Yugoslavia	51.1	47.6	56	48.4	51.7
Zimbabwe	50.9	42.3	47	51	51.8

These are standardized scores with all means set relative to the U.S. mean, which is designated to be 50 for each trait.

example, the world champions of neuroticism are the Spaniards, the least extraverted people in the world are Hong Kong Chinese, the nationality that is most open to new experiences is Austrian, the most agreeable people in the world are Malaysian, and the world's least conscientious nation is Japan. Do the findings in this table fit with your own intuitions? It is important to note that all these data are based on cross-cultural comparisons of subjective means on self-report measures. As discussed in Chapter 3, there are various response biases associated with such comparisons, and it is possible that such biases have distorted the results shown in Table 5.5 (see Heine, Buchtel, & Norenzayan, 2007, for further discussion). It will be important for us to find convergent evidence from other methods to confidently draw conclusions about cross-cultural differences in people's personality traits.

SUMMARY

The self-concept is central to much of psychological research, and it varies in important and systematic ways across cultures. Individuals who participate in cultural practices and scripts common in individualistic cultures are likely to develop an independent view of self, in which they tend to highlight how they are separate from others, and how their identity is based on inner attributes that are relatively stable across time and situation. In contrast, individuals who participate in cultural practices and scripts more commonly found in collectivistic cultures are more likely to develop interdependent views of self, in which their connections with significant others are emphasized, and will tend to see their identity as largely arising from social roles, memberships, and relationships. Because people do not respond to information from the world directly, but only encounter it in terms of how it is organized by their self-concepts, cultural differences in self-concepts importantly implicate a wide variety of psychological processes. A few ways that we can see psychological consequences for these cultural differences in views of self are that people from individualistic cultures tend to strive for more consistency in their actions, they are more frequently in a state of subjective self-awareness, and they are more likely to conceive of many attributes as stable entities in contrast to the views of people from more collectivistic cultures. In later chapters we will see how these differences in the self-concept will be associated with a variety of other psychological experiences, such as emotions, motivations, cognitions, and relationships.

People everywhere can consider themselves and others in terms of personality traits. Research indicates that personality structure appears quite similar across diverse cultural contexts; the Five Factor Model of personality is supported in every culture where it has been explored. However, there is some evidence that the Five Factor Model is not sufficient to account for all the personality variability in some cultures, as inventories generated from indigenous terms in some cultures reveal additional factors. Also, the extent to which the five personality traits are common in particular cultures varies considerably around the world.

6

Motivation

Assuming that you're a student somewhere taking a course on culture and psychology, I'd like you to consider a question. "Why are you a student?" You might have many different answers for this question. Some of you are students because you want to enhance your status in society. Some of you are captivated by learning new things. Some of you want the bigger paychecks down the road. Some of you want to please your parents. Some of you are trying to delay finding a job. Some of you are doing it because it's what everyone else seems to be doing. Perhaps all of these reasons, and others, apply to your case.

Why you are a student might seem like a simple, or even banal, question to ask. However, your underlying reasons for this speak to your motivations, and these reflect a great deal about how you understand yourself and the world around you. As this chapter will show, the kinds of things that motivate us vary importantly across cultures. Coming to have a better understanding of ourselves and of people from other cultures is fostered by learning about what drives us and others. We need to consider what makes people tick.

Simply put, we are motivated to pursue the things we want and to avoid the things we don't want. To a certain extent, the things we want or don't want are very similar to what others around the world want also. We all desire things that improve the quality of our lives, such as getting access to nice material rewards, having stimulating relationships, and earning the respect of our peers (Kenrick, Li, & Butner, 2003). However, the ways we get access to those nice rewards, the kinds of relationships we might find stimulating, and the ways by which we secure the respect of our peers are influenced considerably by our cultural environments. Moreover, the decisions that we make in our lives involve trade-offs, such as the one you might have made in deciding to live a student's life for a few years rather than taking the money you would have earned if you had instead started a career fresh out of high school. The trade-offs we are willing to accept reflect how we value different outcomes, and our values, in turn, are shaped a great deal by culture (e.g., Schwartz & Bilsky, 1990). As you read this chapter, you may realize the reasons that you have for being a student, or for explaining any of the other behaviors you engage in, speak a great deal to the cultural experiences you have had growing up.

This chapter explores how some fundamental motivations vary across different cultural contexts. We will discuss how the concerns we have, and how we work toward addressing those concerns, are importantly shaped by our cultural experiences. We will consider questions such as these: "How universal are needs for self-esteem?" "How are people from different cultures motivated to seek control?" "Are people from different cultures equally likely to strive to fit in with others?" The notion that people's experiences shape their psychology is the primary theme that guides the discussion of this chapter.

Motivations for Self-Enhancement and Self-Esteem

Many research ideas are sparked by events witnessed in everyday life. Some of my own research has contrasted Japanese and North Americans in their motivations, and many of the ideas I studied stemmed from experiences I had living in Japan. Upon receiving my B.A., I spent two years in a small town in southwestern Japan teaching English at a junior high school there. In many ways it was an ideal place for a budding cultural psychologist as the town had been somewhat isolated from Western influences. Indeed, I was the very first Westerner to have ever lived in the town, and this set the stage for a two-year comedy/drama of mutual cross-cultural misunderstandings. Such misunderstandings can often lead to the discovery of interesting cross-cultural differences.

One occasion in particular sticks in my mind. It was the very last day of the school year, and a Japanese teacher and I were preparing a lesson we would co-teach to a class of graduating ninth-grade students. We thought it would be fun if I would give the class a graduation speech in English and the Japanese teacher would translate any of the words the class didn't understand. So I went in front of the class and started saying the kinds of things I'd heard at graduation speeches while I was growing up in Canada. For example, I told them how proud I was with how well they had learned their English. And I went on about how talented they were, how they each had such special individual strengths, and I wrapped things up by urging them to remember that they could accomplish anything they wanted as long as they believed in themselves.

Well, the bit about their learning their English well was something of an exaggeration as no one in the class seemed to understand a word of my speech. So the Japanese teacher, who had been taking notes throughout my speech, started to give an accurate word-by-word translation. And as I was looking out at the class during his translation I saw the class look progressively more and more confused and uncomfortable, until finally the students erupted into a bout of enormous laughter. But the Japanese teacher, who always was really good, seemed to sense the awkwardness of the moment, and he quickly changed gears. As I listened to his apparent "translation" of my speech, I noticed that he was now saying things that had never been in my original speech. He told them, for example, that if they thought English class in junior high school had been hard, that they would be rudely surprised because high school English was going to be far more difficult. And he reminded them that they were sorely lacking some basic English skills as none of them had been able to understand my very simple speech. He emphasized that they had an enormously difficult task ahead of them, and that they were going to have to put in very long hours and to keep persisting at their studies.

I remember at the time I was wondering what on earth the Japanese teacher was trying to do. That's not how you motivate people—telling them how difficult things are going to be and emphasizing how poor their skills are. But to my surprise, looking out at the class, the students started to stand up straight, they had a look of determination in their eyes, and they responded in unison with a powerful "*Hai!*"—a "Yes, sir!"—and they looked ready to take on the world. Of course, this is the effect I had been trying to achieve with my feel-good "You're all terrific" speech, but my words had failed miserably. This was not an isolated incident, and throughout my 2 years as a teacher I was chastised many times by the other teachers for praising the students too much. As they told me, "How can you expect them to keep trying if you're telling them that they're already good enough?" This seemed to suggest a key cultural difference in how people are motivated, and that was an idea that I followed up over the years with a number of studies.

My own tendency to put a positive spin on the students' strengths reflected a powerful motivation that has received much research attention: **Self-enhancement** is the motivation to view oneself positively. Research (that has primarily been conducted with North Americans) reveals that people apparently have a strong need to view themselves positively. This need is evident across a diverse array of methodologies. First, if you ask people to evaluate themselves you find that the vast majority of them have high self-esteem. For example, we found that 93% of one large sample of European-Canadians had self-esteem scores that were above the midpoint of the scale (Heine, Lehman, Markus, & Kitayama, 1999). That's a lot of high self-esteem folks walking around. You can measure your own self-esteem by completing the self-esteem scale below.

You can also see evidence for self-enhancement motivations in measures of self-serving biases. **Self-serving biases** are tendencies for people to exaggerate how good they think they are. One study that demonstrated self-serving biases asked American college professors to evaluate how good they were at being at a professor (Cross, 1977). Can you guess about what per-

The Rosenberg Self-Esteem Scale				
	Strongly Disagree			*Strongly Agree*
I feel that I'm a person of worth, at least on an equal basis with others.	1	2	3	4
I feel that I have a number of good qualities.	1	2	3	4
*All in all, I am inclined to feel that I am a failure.	1	2	3	4
I am able to do things as well as most other people.	1	2	3	4
*I feel I do not have much to be proud of.	1	2	3	4
I take a positive attitude toward myself.	1	2	3	4
On the whole, I am satisfied with myself.	1	2	3	4
*I wish I could have more respect for myself.	1	2	3	4
*I certainly feel useless at times.	1	2	3	4
*At times I think I'm no good at all.	1	2	3	4

Items with a * are reverse scored. For those items subtract your answer from 5 to get your score. Then add all of your individual scores up. The lowest possible score is 10 and the highest is 40, with the midpoint being 25.

Source: Rosenberg, 1965.

centage thought that they were better than the average American college professor? 94%! Now we say that this is a *bias* because 94% of people clearly cannot be better than average. That's not how average works. Approximately 50% of people are better than average in any given domain, and approximately 50% are worse than average. I imagine that you wouldn't have a hard time deciding which of your professors you think are above or below average, and your evaluations would likely be closer to the distributions governed by the laws of statistics. Obviously, these professors did not have a very accurate or objective perspective when they evaluated themselves. Much research has revealed that one important reason people have such biased views of themselves is because they are motivated to view themselves positively.

In case you're chuckling about how out of touch these professors are, it's informative to note that these self-serving biases are not confined to academics. They've been reliably observed among elementary school children, high school children, college students, and working adults (see Taylor & Brown, 1988, for a review). Take a minute to think about whether you would evaluate yourself as above or below average for each of the following characteristics: ability to get along well with others, creativity, considerateness, driving ability, loyalty, dependability. My bet is that most of you think that you're above average for *all* of these. Now it's possible that you might very well be better than average for all of these. Some people surely are. However, one thing that helps to sustain these unrealistically positive assessments of ourselves is that we rarely encounter concrete information in these domains. Without this information, there is nothing to prove that we are not above average. In other domains of life in which our relative standing compared to others is more clearly observable, such as our height, calculus ability, or free-throw shooting skills, we are much less likely to hold such unrealistic views of ourselves (Dunning, Meyerowitz, & Holzberg, 1989). We are quite accurate about our standing when we encounter incontrovertible evidence; however, in the absence of that we're likely to interpret the evidence in the most favorable way or just round upward when given half the chance (also see Kunda, 1990). This is evidence for people's motivations for self-enhancement.

Perhaps the most striking evidence of our motivations to view ourselves positively comes from studies that investigate what people sometimes do to secure a positive evaluation of themselves. Despite our motivations to view ourselves positively, often we encounter information about ourselves that doesn't look very favorable. Sometimes a prospective romantic partner rejects our advances, or sometimes we get poor grades in our classes. How do we go about keeping a positive self-view when our experiences aren't providing us with much to feel positive about?

Well, it turns out that people who are motivated to secure a positive self-view are often resourceful enough to figure out a way to get one. For example, if you get a bad grade in class you could try a lot of different strategies to make yourself feel good again. You might engage in **downward social comparison** by comparing your performance with the performance of someone who is doing even worse than you (Festinger, 1954). When we compare ourselves to someone worse off than ourselves we create a favorable comparison that casts our own performance in a positive light. So an easy way to feel better about the C you received on your paper is to hang out with the people who got D's. This is usually a good occasion to avoid the people who got the A's—when we compare our performance with someone who is doing better than we are this is known as an **upward social comparison**. In many kinds of situations upward social comparisons tend to be rather painful as the contrast can make your own performance look that much worse (although there are important exceptions to this pattern; Lockwood & Kunda, 1997). Another strategy you might try is **compensatory self-enhancement** (e.g., Baumeister & Jones, 1978), in which you acknowledge the poor grade you got in class, but you instead start to think about your excellent clarinet-playing skills. When engaging in this strategy you can focus on, and perhaps exaggerate, how good you are at something unrelated to your setback so that you can compensate for the pain of your setback, and can again self-enhance by recruiting some other kinds of positive thoughts about yourself. You might also try some **discounting** of your setback. Discounting is reducing the perceived importance of the domain in which you performed poorly (e.g., Simon, Greenberg, & Brehm, 1995). For example, to relieve yourself of the sting from your bad grade you might say something to yourself like "Who really cares about chemistry anyway? I'm not going to become a chemist." Alternatively, you might try to make an **external attribution** for your poor performance. External attributions means that we attribute the cause of our actions to something outside ourselves, in contrast to internal attributions when we locate the cause within ourselves, such as our abilities (e.g., Zuckerman, 1979). Hence, we can shift the blame for our poor grade elsewhere and think to ourselves "The professor was impossible to understand," or "I didn't have enough time to prepare for the exam because of my cousin's wedding." Or, you might try to **bask in the reflected glory** of a successful group to which you belong. We do such basking when we emphasize our connection to successfully performing others and feel better about ourselves by sharing in the warm glow of the other's success. For example, research reveals that people are more likely to refer to their university's football team with the pronoun "we" than "they" if the team has recently won a game and if the individual has just done poorly himself or herself on a test (Cialdini et al., 1976). People wish to rid themselves of the bad feelings of their poor performance by aligning themselves with their more successful football team. In sum, we have an impressive arsenal of tactics to protect and enhance our self-views. Given the range of strategies we have to choose from, it becomes less surprising that so many people do have such high self-esteem and such unrealistically positive views of themselves.

The evidence from this psychological research, then, quite clearly shows that motivations for positive self-views are powerful and pervasive. However, given that the vast majority of research conducted on this topic has involved highly individualistic North American participants, we might question whether this tendency is commonly found outside of the continent as well. This is a reasonable concern, as much research has identified a pronounced positive relationship between independent self-construals and self-esteem within a variety of different cultures (e.g., Oyserman, Coon, & Kemmelmeier, 2002; Singelis, Bond, Lai, & Sharkey, 1999). Would people from more collectivistic backgrounds show similarly strong motivations to enhance themselves?

One study investigated this question by comparing the positivity of self-views of Mexican-American and European-American preschool and elementary schoolchildren (Tropp & Wright, 2003). The children were shown the photographs of eight other children and a photograph of themselves. They were asked to choose the photographs of the children who possessed a number of positive characteristics, such as "Who is smart?" or "Who is nice?" Overall, the children from both cultural groups tended to view themselves quite positively as they usually included their own pictures. However, the European-Americans did so even more, choosing their picture for 92% of the positive characteristics whereas Mexican-Americans did so for 82% of theirs. Even at this young age there is evidence of cultural variation in positive self-views.

A similar question was explored by contrasting Native American and European-American university students (Fryberg & Markus, 2003). The students were asked to describe themselves in an open-ended questionnaire. Similar to the findings with Mexican-Americans, the self-views of the Native Americans were less positive than were those of the European-Americans. Indeed, the Native Americans listed less than half as many positive statements about themselves as did the European-Americans. Because Native Americans tend to have less independent self-concepts than European-Americans, these findings are again consistent with the argument that independence and self-enhancement are related. However, there do seem to be some exceptions to this rule, as a few relatively collectivistic cultures (e.g., the Maori in New Zealand [Harrington & Liu, 2002], African-Americans in the United States [Major, Spencer, Schmader, Wolfe, & Crocker, 1998], Israeli Druze [Kurman, 2001]) have shown levels of self-enhancement comparable to those found in more individualistic settings.

The cultural variation in self-enhancement is even more striking when we compare North Americans of European descent to people living in East Asia, particularly those from China, Japan, and Korea. Whereas 93% of European-Canadians have high self-esteem, only about 55% of Japanese do (Heine et al., 1999). Likewise, tendencies to show self-serving biases are far less common among East Asian samples than Western ones (e.g., Norasakkunkit & Kalick, 2002). These differences in positive self-views are sustained by the ways people attend to and interpret events in the world. Consider the following study: Japanese and American college students were asked to list as many success or failure experiences they could remember having had in their lives (Endo & Meijer, 2004). The American pattern suggested a self-enhancing tendency in that Americans listed more success memories than failure memories (62% vs. 38%) whereas Japanese listed slightly fewer success memories than failure ones (48% vs. 52%). Unless American life really does provide people with more winning experiences, and Japanese provides people with more losing ones, we can conclude that Americans find successes more memorable, probably because they think about them more, whereas Japanese tend to find failures more memorable, because they think about these more. Much other research is consistent with this conclusion (e.g., Kitayama, Markus, Matsumoto, & Norasakkunkit, 1997; Kurman, Yoshihara-Tanaka, & Elkoshi, 2003; Hamamura & Heine, 2007).

Indeed, research on self-enhancing tendencies among people of Asian descent shows a striking lack of enhancement motivations. For example, if we consider the tactics that people (or at least North Americans) have been shown to use to recruit positive self-views that we discussed above, we find pronounced cultural variations. For example, after experiencing a failure, Asian-Canadians were three times more likely to seek upward social comparison targets than downward ones, whereas European-Canadians sought about as many upward as downward comparison targets (White & Lehman, 2005). North Americans often compensate for their failures by inflating their self-assessments in other unrelated domains; however, Japanese show the reverse tendency (Heine, Kitayama, & Lehman, 2001a). Whereas after failing on a task North Americans tend to discount the importance of the task, Japanese view the task as even more important (Heine et al., 2001b). Much research reveals that North Americans tend to make more external attributions for their failures, but Japanese often make more external attributions for their successes (e.g., Endo & Meijer, 2004). And while Americans tend to bask in the reflected glory of their sports teams, Japanese sports fans are likely to be more critical of their own teams than of the opposition (Snibbe, Kitayama, Markus, & Suzuki, 2003). These cultural differences are pronounced, evident across a broad range of different methodologies (29 different methodologies, at last count; Heine & Hamamura, 2007), and the East Asian samples often show a tendency to exaggerate a negative self-view. Do East Asians really view themselves in more self-critical terms than North Americans? Can you think of any other alternative explanations for why East Asians appear to self-enhance less?

One alternative possibility is that East Asians really are just as motivated as Westerners to evaluate themselves positively; however, various Western biases in our research methodologies prevent us from seeing these motivations. For example, East Asians may be more motivated to enhance their group selves rather than their individual selves, and comparisons of people's individual self-enhancing tendencies don't capture group self-enhancing motivations. This hypothesis is intriguing; however, many studies find that Westerners show stronger motivations than East Asians to enhance their group selves as well (e.g., Heine & Lehman, 1997; Snibbe et al., 2003), which challenges this alternative explanation. Another possibility is that East Asians value a different set of traits from those that have been explored in research thus far, and if they were asked to evaluate themselves on especially important traits the cultural differences would be reduced. Although some evidence supports this alternative account using one methodology (e.g., Brown & Kobayashi, 2002; Sedikides, Gaertner, & Toguchi, 2003), other methodologies reveal the opposite pattern. A look at all the published studies on this topic stand in contradiction of this account (see Heine, Kitayama, & Hamamura, in press, for a review). Another possibility is that these studies are not measuring people's "true" feelings but are instead tapping into differences in cultural norms for describing oneself. That is, East Asians may be just feigning modesty in these studies (and perhaps Westerners are feigning their bravado; see Kurman, 2003). One source of evidence that is consistent with this is that East Asians appear to feel as good about themselves as do Westerners based on answers to a test that measures unconscious associations between the self and other positive and negative words (Heine & Hamamura, 2007; Kitayama & Uchida, 2003). This evidence suggests that East Asians *like* themselves as much as Westerners. However, when it comes to assessments of their *competence* East Asians appear to be more self-critical (also see Tafarodi & Swann, 1996). Even studies that investigate people in anonymous situations and employ hidden behavioral measures find clear evidence for this cultural difference in how they evaluate themselves (e.g., Takata, 2003; Heine et al., 2001b). Overall, the research provides converging evidence that East Asians do not have as strong a desire as Westerners to view themselves positively.

Now how might this cultural difference in self-views emerge? A short answer would be that people learn self-enhancement motivations from their families and schools. In one set of studies parents in Taiwan and the United States were interviewed regarding their attitudes toward child rearing (Miller, Wang, Sandel, & Cho, 2002; Miller, Wiley, Fung, & Liang, 1997). It was found that parents often used stories about the child's past behaviors to socialize them. Can you recall the kinds

"Why are you special?
Because I'm your mommy, and I'm special."

of stories your parents told you as a child? Interestingly, the stories that were more often told by European-American parents focused on a past success of the child. In stark contrast, the Taiwanese parents were more likely to tell stories about past transgressions of the child (Miller et al., 1997; also see similar findings by Wang, 2004). American stories thus focused children's attention on their strengths, whereas Taiwanese parents were more likely to focus children's attention on areas that needed correcting. Furthermore, when researchers explicitly asked parents what they thought about self-esteem they got highly divergent answers from the two groups (Miller et al., 2002). The European-American parents viewed self-esteem as central to child rearing and saw it as a positive quality that enhanced children's development and that should be cultivated by parents. The Taiwanese parents, in contrast, had little to say about the words that most closely approximated self-esteem (it's telling that there is no direct translation of self-esteem in many East Asian languages), and what they did have to say about it was often somewhat negative—for example, expressing the belief that too much self-esteem can lead to frustration when things aren't working out well for the children. Similarly, North American schools are more likely than their East Asian counterparts to make efforts to inculcate self-esteem in students (e.g., Lewis, 1995; Stevenson & Stigler, 1992). In sum, cultural environments in North America and East Asia provide different opportunities for learning ideas regarding whether positive self-views are desirable or not.

However, the above answer is not complete. If we learn our attitudes about self-esteem from our parents and schools, then where did our parents and schools get these views in the first place? One way to address this question is to look at the emergence of motivations for positive self-views over history. Unfortunately, for those of us who are interested in investigating this kind of question, the history of motivations hasn't provided us with a fossil record. We need to look for some rather indirect evidence to see changes in motivations over time. This question was explored by an analysis of some historical literature (Baumeister, 1987). First, this analysis revealed that the notion of individual selves didn't really emerge in Western literature until the 12th century, when the Christian concept of the last judgment changed from being an issue of the salvation of collectives to the salvation of individual souls. It was also around this time that literature began to use devices based on the idea that different characters had different perspectives of events (Hanning, 1977). Furthermore, not until the 16th century and the birth of the Protestant Reformation did something akin to self-enhancing motivations first became clearly evident. Many of the early Protestant sects maintained a belief in **predestination.** Predestination was the belief that before we were born, it was already determined whether we were one of the fortunate "elect" who would spend eternity in blessed heaven after our passing, or were one of the wretched many who were doomed to burn in hell forever. Which group a person was assigned to was a distinction that obviously mattered a great deal to members of these Protestant sects. Because no one had access to God's ledger to determine whether he or she was on the right list, people had to rely on cues to discern their fates. The primary cue that a person was part of the elect was that he or she possessed absolute certainty about this fact. Any doubt regarding whether an individual was of the elect was to be seen as proof that the person was not, so individuals became highly motivated to interpret events in their lives as signs that God was viewing them favorably. The distinction between spending eternity in heaven or in hell was a sufficient motivator to lead people to make great efforts to interpret their situation in a favorable light. With this, it was argued, our motivations for self-enhancement grew (also see Weintraub, 1978). We'll return to consider the key role of the belief in predestination for other motivations later in this chapter.

The Protestant Reformation may have been a helpful impetus in the growth of self-enhancing motivations; however, given that there is evidence of such motivations in many non-Protestant nations, this cannot be the whole story. There is a clear positive relation between independence/individualism and self-esteem (the correlation ranges from .33 to 51; Heine, 2003). Why might these two constructs tend to go hand in hand? One way to understand this is to consider what happens when the self-concept becomes more and more focused on the lone individual, as it does in individualism. When one's beliefs start to migrate to the idea "I'm all that I've got" there would seem to be a greater need to view oneself positively. If all that I've got is not very good, this would seem to be a real problem for the individual. Cultural messages common in individualistic cultures encourage people to be self-sufficient and not to rely on others (e.g., Markus & Kitayama, 1991). It would be extremely difficult to achieve these goals if one did not view oneself positively. This reasoning suggests that as cultures become more individualistic, rendering people more concerned with being able to take care of themselves and to carve their own paths, there should be a corresponding motivation to view oneself positively.

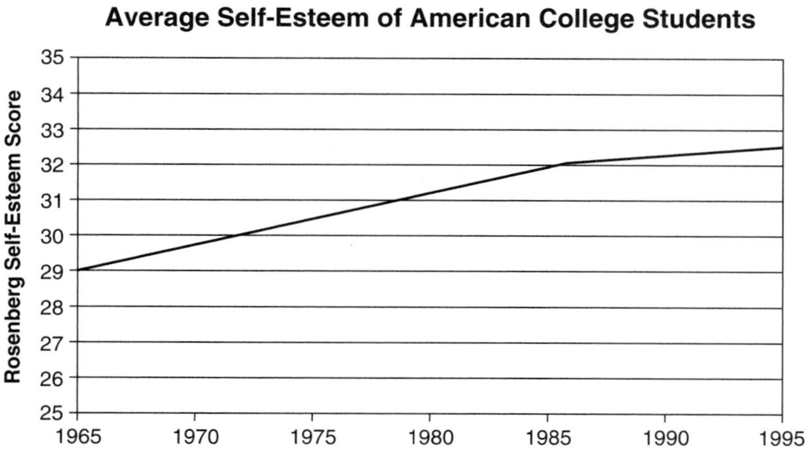

Average Self-Esteem of American College Students

FIGURE 6.1

The average self-esteem of American college students has increased over the last few decades.

We can see evidence for this relation between individualism and self-esteem by looking at the United States. As noted in Chapter 2, much evidence suggests that the United States has become more individualistic since the 1960s. For example, people are spending less time with their families, the divorce rate has increased, and people are less likely to get involved in community organizations (e.g., Putnam, 2000; Rosen, 1998). Evidence also suggests that self-esteem has been rising in the United States over the same period (Twenge & Campbell, 2001). Figure 6.1 shows this relation clearly. Americans who have recently graduated from college had considerably higher self-esteem when they were college students than their parents' generation did when they were in college. I would predict that self-esteem has similarly been increasing in other cultures where individualism has increased, although this has yet to be investigated. Cultural messages and institutions change and adapt over time, and it follows that psychological processes, such as motivations for self-esteem, will change as well.

Motivations for Face and Self-Improvement

Another way to address the question of why motivations for positive self-views vary across cultures is to consider the different kinds of positive views that a person might desire. One way of having a positive self-view is to have high self-esteem. That is, the individual views himself or herself positively. Another way is to have a good deal of "**face**." Face is an interesting concept that is of considerable importance in much of the world, although many Westerners don't have a great understanding of it. Indeed, the expression "to lose face" didn't enter the English language until the late 19th century as a direct translation from Chinese (Oxford English Dictionary, 1989). Face has been defined as the amount of social value others give you if you live up to the standards associated with your position (e.g., Ho, 1976). The higher your position, the greater is the amount of face that is available to you. Hence, the president of a company has a lot of face, whereas the person in the mailroom has very little. In hierarchical collectivist societies, such as the kinds found in East Asia, face takes on special importance. What matters is not how positively you think of yourself but whether significant others think you're doing well. If others grant you face, you'll enjoy all the perquisites that come with the enhanced status and power. In such a cultural context, people can become highly motivated to maintain and enhance their face. Can you think how people would be motivated differently if they are trying to maintain face or if they are trying to build self-esteem?

One important characteristic of face is that it's more easily lost than it is gained. Because the amount of face that you have access to is determined by your position, you can't readily increase your face unless you get a promotion. This renders face as something that is difficult to enhance. However, face is lost whenever individuals fail to live up to the standards of their roles (Ho, 1976). It is thus always vulnerable, and because others determine a person's face, people must count on the goodwill of others to be able to maintain their face. Given that face is so easily lost, a good strategy for people would be to adopt a very cautious approach and try to ensure that they are not acting in a way that might lead others to reject them (Hamamura & Heine, in press). If they can attend to any potential weaknesses and work toward correcting them by improving themselves, they should decrease the chance that others will view them as having lost face.

This kind of defensive, cautious approach to not losing something is known as a **prevention orientation**. This is in contrast with a concern with advancing oneself, and aspiring for gains, which is known as a **promotion orientation** (Higgins, 1996). These two orientations are fundamentally different, are evident across a wide range of species (e.g., Jones, Larkins, & Hughes, 1996), and are even associated with activation in different hemispheres of the brain (Tucker & Williamson, 1984). When we are engaged in a promotion focus we are trying to secure good things, and when we are engaged in a prevention focus we are trying to avoid bad things. A loss of face is one of those bad things that people are motivated to avoid.

If a concern with face leads to a prevention orientation, and East Asians are more concerned with face, then we should expect to see greater evidence of prevention orientations among them. Much research has confirmed this pattern (e.g., Elliot, Chirkov, Kim, & Sheldon, 2001; Lockwood, Marshall, & Sadler, 2005). For example, in one study Hong Kong Chinese and Americans were asked to rate how important some tennis games were (Lee, Aaker, & Gardner, 2000). The Chinese saw the games described as opportunities to avoid a loss as more important than those described as opportunities to win, and the Americans showed the opposite pattern. Of course, in tennis avoiding a loss and securing a win amount to the same thing; however, how the game is described in terms of prevention and promotion leads people to think about it in different ways.

How do you think a promotion focus or prevention focus might affect how people respond to the successes and failures they encounter in their lives? It would seem that if people have a promotion focus, they will strive for opportunities for advancement, and, as such, should focus their efforts on things they can do well because these will provide more opportunities for success. Things they do poorly, in contrast, should be avoided, because these are not likely to lead to success. In contrast, people with a prevention focus should focus their efforts on things they don't do well because correcting shortcomings will help them avoid a failure. This suggests that East Asians and Westerners should respond quite differently to successes and failures. Is this the case? We asked Japanese and Canadian participants to come into the laboratory where they received private feedback that they had done either very well or very poorly on a creativity test (Heine et al., 2001b). The participants were then left alone in a room with another set of creativity items and they were timed on how long they persisted on this task. The results are shown in Figure 6.2. The Canadians persisted significantly longer after success than failure, a finding that replicates much work that has been done on persistence research in the West (e.g., Feather, 1966; Pyszczynski & Greenberg, 1983). In stark contrast, the Japanese persisted significantly longer after failure than success. Apparently, the Canadians, maintaining a promotion focus, were more interested in working on things they did well, as these were more likely to provide them opportunities to view themselves positively. The Japanese, in contrast, maintaining a prevention focus, were more interested

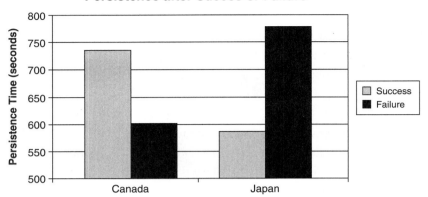

FIGURE 6.2

Canadians are more likely to persist on a task for which they think they are talented, while Japanese persist more on tasks for which they believe they are untalented.

in working on the things they did poorly, apparently so they could improve themselves and be less likely to fail in the future. This **self-improvement** motivation, a desire to seek out potential weaknesses and work on correcting them, is a strong motivation in East Asian contexts (e.g., Hoshino-Browne & Spencer, 2000; Kitayama et al., 1997). Interestingly, this cultural difference has even been shown to influence our choice of leisure activities. Oishi and Diener (2003) found that when given a choice to play either basketball or darts, European-Americans tend to choose the activity they do well whereas Asian-Americans do not.

Religion and Achievement Motivation

The studies discussed above demonstrate how motivations for achievement in the face of success and failure vary across cultures. What motivates people to achieve has been a question that has attracted much interest. And what is perhaps the most profound cultural psychological theory that was ever proposed targeted this question. In 1904–1905 Max Weber published a highly influential and controversial series of essays entitled *The Protestant Ethic and the Spirit of Capitalism*. Weber recognized a fundamental tenet of cultural psychology that in contrast to most events in the natural world, human behavior is necessarily interwoven with meaning. Events do not simply impinge themselves upon us; it is our interpretation of what those events mean that motivates us to respond accordingly. Weber's work has been enormously influential so we will look closely at it—and some of its implications for modern cultural psychology.

Weber was interested in how the radical doctrine of capitalism was able to emerge out of the traditional economies of the medieval era. Capitalism encapsulated a way of thinking that was dramatically different from anything that had existed before in the Western world. At the time Weber published his ideas, the dominant theory was Marxism, which proposed that capitalism emerged as the result of a surplus of capital that accumulated during the shift from an agricultural economy to an industrial one. In contrast to the economic determinism of Marxism, Weber viewed capitalism as the product of people's deriving meaning from a particular cultural context. He proposed that capitalism grew out of a belief system that was rooted in a number of cultural ideas that began emerging in the 16th and 17th centuries in Western Europe and in North America. The ideas that became the foundation for capitalism were ones that grew out of the Protestant Reformation.

Protestantism initially emerged as a reaction to perceived corruption in the medieval Catholic Church, but it contained ideas that shaped much more than the spiritual lives of its followers, and ultimately, of the societies that were built around it. One idea to emerge from Protestantism was that individuals were able to communicate with God directly and were not dependent upon the Church as an intermediary. This individualized relation between each person and God has been argued to be central to the blossoming of individualism that emerged during the Reformation, and continues to influence much of Western society today.

A related idea grew out of this individualized relation between God and each person. Martin Luther, the founder of Protestantism, proposed that each individual had a "**calling**," that is, each person had a unique God-given purpose to fulfill during his or her mortal existence. The idea was that we were all God's servants in the world, and that each of us was given a specific duty or job to do while we tended the planet. God gave each individual unique skills and capabilities to enable that person to fulfill his or her calling, and it was incumbent upon individuals to discover what their calling was. The highest moral duty that individuals were believed to have was to serve God well by working hard at their calling. By developing this notion of a calling, Luther was able to imbue daily labor with a spiritual significance that had traditionally been reserved for religious activities such as prayer and ritual. With the Protestant Reformation, work had become a moral obligation rather than something necessary for subsistence. As such, people's attitudes shifted from work as a means to survive to work as an inherently meaningful activity in itself (Weber, 1904/1992). Weber maintains that this shift in attitude had an enormous impact on society. Intriguingly, in 2006 Pope Benedict XVI offered some advice that seems to be consistent with Weber's distinction between Protestant and Catholic attitudes toward work: "We have to guard ourselves, as St. Bernard observed, against the dangers of excessive activity, regardless of the office one holds, because too many concerns can often lead to hardness of heart and suffering of the spirit." That is, the Pope claimed that too much work can be seen to interfere with one's spiritual development, in contrast to the Protestant view that spirituality is actualized through one's work.

As discussed earlier in this chapter, some early sects of Protestantism (in particular, some early Puritan sects that included Calvinism, Methodism, Pietism, and Baptism) proposed the radical idea of predestination, in which people believed that it was already determined by God, before they were even born, who was going to heaven and who was going to hell. Weber proposed that this belief of predestination played a key role in the development of capitalism. How might a belief in predestination affect one's attitude toward work? You might expect that if their fates were predetermined, people might respond by deciding to have a good time while on earth because there wasn't anything they could do to change their fates. They might as well just live it up while they could. However, this interpretation was rarely embraced. Rather, the notion of predestination brought with it "a feeling of unprecedented inner loneliness" (Weber, 1904/1992, p. 104), and individuals were highly motivated to escape it by convincing themselves that they were of the privileged elect. No one knew for sure whether he or she was among the elect, although a feeling of certainty of one's elect status was the best sign that one could come by. The evidence for this certainty was seen to lie in the products of one's efforts to fulfill one's calling. It was believed that God would not reward those who were doomed to burn in hell, so any sign of material success was perceived as evidence that one was of the elect. Furthermore, because one's time on earth was to be spent serving God through one's calling, rather than enjoying the fruits of one's labor (the fun times for Puritans were not perceived to begin until after they had died and

More recent evidence that Protestantism and capitalism are linked, as Max Weber argued.

gone to heaven), any accumulated wealth was to be reinvested to further one's efforts and to accumulate even more wealth and evidence of one's status among the elect. Modern capitalism, as Weber viewed it, was thus concerned with the accumulation of wealth for its own sake and not for the sake of the material pleasures that it brought. Weber proposed that it was in this fertile soil of ideas that capitalism took root and blossomed.

The notion that predestination was key to the Protestant sects that initially populated the United States might be surprising to many good Protestants out there today, as predestination is no longer a belief of contemporary Protestant sects. Firm beliefs in predestination did not last more than a couple of generations, probably because this is not the kind of idea that has much lasting appeal (Landes, 1999). However, Weber proposes that it lasted long enough to be converted into a more enduring secular code of behavior that included honesty, hard work, seriousness, and the thrifty use of money and time. These attitudes toward work can be seen in some influential Puritan writings in the early days of the United States: "Time is short, and work is long" advised the Puritan Richard Baxter, and Benjamin Franklin (who was raised in a Calvinist family) reminded people that "Early to bed, early to rise makes a man healthy, wealthy and wise," and that "God helps them that help themselves." John Wesley, the founder of the Methodists, explicitly exhorted "all Christians to gain all they can, and to save all they can; that is, in effect to grow rich" (Weber, 1904/1992, p. 175). Weber argued that the spread of these secular attitudes throughout Protestant communities laid the foundation for the development of capitalism.

What do you think of Weber's thesis? As you might imagine, his ideas were, and continue to be, controversial. Many different groups found much to disagree with in them. Weber's characterizations of Catholicism as having a retarding influence upon modern economic development ended up alienating many Catholics; his description of Puritan life as being bound up in an ecclesiastical straitjacket was not appreciated by many Protestants; people of other religious backgrounds felt ignored (there is clear evidence of a moralized work ethic among people of Confucian and Jewish backgrounds, for example, something Weber did investigate in some of his other works); and Weber's contention that religious ideas can transform economies really perturbed the Marxists and most economists (Giddens, 1992). Many people have made their academic careers out of critiquing Weber's ideas.

Nonetheless, there is much evidence that is consistent with Weber's thesis. Some evidence comes from economists and historians who note that power and wealth moved in Europe from places like Spain and northern Italy before the Protestant Reformation began in 1517, to Northern European Protestant centers in Germany, Scandinavia, the Netherlands, and England, until its most colossal bloom in the 20th-century United States, the most Protestant nation in the modern world (e.g., Landes, 1999). A consideration of per capita income among countries of the world found that nations that were largely Protestant earned more than those that were mixed Protestant and Catholic, and that these earned more than those nations that were predominantly Catholic (Furnham, 1990). Interestingly, now that many European nations are becoming less religious, the distinction between Catholic and Protestant nations is becoming less clear. In recent decades the average number of hours worked in the Protestant North in Europe has dropped precipitously alongside a steep drop in church attendance in these same nations. Ferguson (2003) maintains that as Northern Europeans are losing their Protestant faith they are also losing the sense of spiritual obligation to live an ascetic, hard-working lifestyle. He notes that during this same period Americans have not shown a drop in religiosity and have shown a striking *increase* in the length of the average workweek. A few decades ago, it was observed that Protestants in the United States were more likely to enter high-status nonmanual occupations than Catholics of the same occupational origin, controlling for a variety of other societal variables (Jackson, Fox, & Crockett, 1970). In the mid-20th century a study revealed that Protestant nations were far more industrialized than their Catholic counterparts (McClelland, 1961).

These examples reflect culture-level variables that differ between societies with predominantly Catholic or Protestant influences. There are also examples of differences in psychological variables between Catholics and Protestants. One variable to consider is the degree of individualism that exists in Protestant countries compared with elsewhere. The six most individualistic countries in the world according to Hofstede's measures (1980) are largely Protestant (see Figure 5.4 on page 188), whereas the least individualistic Western societies are largely Catholic (countries dominated by various Asian religions also tend to score low in individualism). Pronounced differences in the embracing of an intrinsic work ethic were observed between Western European Catholics and mainstream Protestants (interestingly, the relation was clear both by contrasting individuals of different religions *within* countries and by comparing countries) as evident in a measure of work values (Giorgi & Marsh, 1990). The Protestant ethic has been associated with negative attitudes toward laziness and being overweight (Quinn & Crocker, 1999). McClelland's (1961) classic cross-cultural comparison of Weber's thesis found that Protestant parents expected their children to become self-reliant at an earlier age than did Catholic parents. McClelland also investigated the stories written by young boys and found that those written by German Protestants had more evidence of strong achievement motivations than those written by German Catholics.

However, some cross-cultural research that compares the average scores from self-report measures of the Protestant work ethic has provided evidence that is not obviously consistent with Weber's thesis (e.g., Furnham, Bond, & Heaven, 1993). Given the methodological challenges of comparing means across cultures in self-report surveys described in Chapter 3, and the great diversity in measures that have been used to measure the Protestant work ethic (Furnham, 1990), it is hard to know what to make of this mixed pattern of results. Laboratory studies that manipulate independent variables in controlled settings would be especially useful to explore Weber's thesis.

One line of research that has examined different behaviors among American Protestants and Catholics in laboratory settings has been conducted by Sanchez-Burks and colleagues (Sanchez-Burks, 2002; Sanchez-Burks, Nisbett, & Ybarra, 2000). Sanchez-Burks (2002) was interested in exploring an aspect of Protestant ideology that was emphasized by Calvinism; that is, when Protestants are engaged in their morally sanctioned work, they should be entirely focused on their work and thus maintain a rather detached attitude toward potential distractions, such as other people (Bendix, 1977; Hampden-Turner & Trompenaars, 1993). So, Protestants should maintain a relational style toward others that is relatively detached while they are working; however, in contexts where there are no work obligations, they should switch back to a more attentive relational style (Weber, 1947). Working hard is good, and playing hard is good, but the idea is not to mix the two. To the extent that Weber is correct in arguing that cultural beliefs specific to Protestantism have come to shape contemporary people's attitudes, we should be able to see differences in Protestants' relational styles in work contexts compared with those of other cultural groups.

Sanchez-Burks (2002) sought to test this hypothesis by comparing Protestants and Catholics in two different settings. The participants in his experiment were all European-American students raised either as Protestants or as non-Protestants (Catholics, atheists, and other religious backgrounds). These participants were assigned to engage in a task in either a work environment or a casual nonwork setting. In the work context the experimenters created an atmosphere of serious business. The participants were invited to take part in a business interview and were greeted by a firm handshake from an experimenter dressed in a business suit. The participants were told to work together on solutions for a business case. In contrast, in the casual context participants were welcomed by an experimenter wearing jeans who placed a Hawaiian lei around their necks to emphasize a casual and relaxed atmosphere. The task for this condition was to create a top 10 list of vacation spots. This condition made it clear for participants that this was a task that they did not need to take too seriously. Participants in the two conditions worked together with a confederate of the experimenter who was kept blind to the participants' religious background. An experimenter left the two alone in a room and their interactions were videotaped with a hidden camera.

The goal of this study was to see whether people were differentially engaging in a detached relational style between the casual and work conditions.

How might one measure whether someone is in a detached relational style? Sanchez-Burks opted for a rather creative way of assessing this: He measured how much the participant was mimicking the confederate's behaviors. Past research reveals, rather remarkably, that when people are being attentive to another in a social interaction they start to mimic their partner. If the partner touches his face, the person will likely touch her face; if the partner shakes his foot, she will shake her foot (see Bargh, Chen, & Burrows, 1996; Chartrand & Bargh, 1999). The interesting thing about this mimicry is that people are usually completely unaware that they're doing it. Next time you're in a conversation with someone start shaking your foot and see if you can get your conversation partner to do the same. Sanchez-Burks used this same methodology, instructing his confederates to shake their feet the entire time they were talking with the participants. The dependent variable was how much the participants shook their own feet when they were with the confederate compared with another time when they were alone. The results were rather striking in two respects. First, female participants shook their feet quite a bit, and did so the same amount across conditions. Sanchez-Burks interpreted this pattern as suggesting that women might have a heightened relational sensitivity compared with men, something which has been the focus of much scholarly debate (e.g., Gabriel & Gardner, 1999; Kashima et al., 1995). Second, male participants revealed a pattern precisely in line with predictions derived from Weber's thesis (see Figure 6.3). That is, male non-Protestants were just as likely to mimic the confederate's foot-shaking in a casual setting as they were in a work setting. In stark contrast, the Protestant males showed very little evidence of mimicry in the work setting, but they showed considerable mimicry in the casual setting. It appears that when Protestant males are focused on a work task they are able to shut out relational concerns, something that neither Protestant women or non-Protestants seem to do. Other studies by Sanchez-Burks find related differences between Protestants and non-Protestants (see Study 1 in Sanchez-Burks, 2002; Sanchez-Burks et al., 2003; Sanchez-Burks et al., 2000). When Protestants are actually working they do not seem to have much interest in anything else.

In sum, to the extent that Max Weber was correct more than a century ago, we can understand some of our motivations toward work to come from religious ideas that people encounter in their cultures. Weber's thesis remains controversial; however, a great deal of evidence in support of it has been

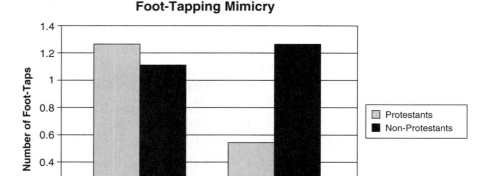

FIGURE 6.3

Male Protestants show less unconscious mimicry of others in work settings than in casual settings. Non-Protestants, on the other hand, are equally likely to show such mimicry across both settings.

marshaled from a variety of different disciplines. It is difficult to account for this evidence without accepting the basic tenets of his theory. Laboratory investigations of Protestant ideology are relatively new to psychology, and there will surely be further challenges and validations of Weber's thesis in the future.

Agency and Control

Perhaps the most fundamental way that culture can shape our motivations is through our perceptions of control. All organisms have their needs and desires. A critical challenge for organisms is to work within the constraints of their environments toward achieving those needs and desires. Given that humans, unlike other organisms, live in cultural environments, getting what we want requires us to make efforts that are constrained by what our cultures lead us to believe about how the world works. Imagine, for example, what you would do if you wanted to get a raise from your boss. You might believe that you will have more luck getting that raise if you ask your boss directly for it, if you compliment your boss on his new business plan, if you start working extra hard, if you secure a competing offer from another potential employer, or if you keep your mouth shut and don't rock the boat. Which strategy you pursue will reflect what theories you have about how you can exert control over your environments with respect to getting raises, and these theories will come from your beliefs about yourself and your environment.

One theory we possess that is relevant to our experiences of control is whether we perceive our identities to be easily malleable and changeable or stable and fixed. Recall from Chapter 5 that these two implicit theories are known as incremental and entity theories of self, respectively. In addition to the implicit theories we have about the malleability of the self, we also have implicit theories about the malleability of the world. For example, we can see the world as something that is fixed and beyond our control to change (an **entity theory of the world**), or we can think of the world as flexible and responsive to our efforts to change it (an **incremental theory of the world**). To the extent that different cultures perceive selves and their social worlds to be more or less fluid and malleable, they will possess different theories about how individuals can, should, and do act.

Su and colleagues (Su et al., 1999) offer a nice metaphor to capture the potential ways that our selves and social worlds can be malleable. Imagine that you want to build a stone wall. You might try a couple of different approaches. One is to emphasize the integrity of the wall at the expense of the individual stones. That is, you could have a clear plan of the shape of the wall that you want to erect. You could choose stones that were of approximately the correct size and you would carve them down so that they fit perfectly into the wall. The stones would change to accommodate the wall. An alternative way to build the wall would be to allow the wall to take on the shape of the individual stones. You could choose stones that were roughly of the right size and shape and you would assemble them into the wall. If a stone that you chose had a bumpy protuberance then the wall would likewise have that same bump. The wall would change in shape to reflect the nature of the individual stones. The enterprise of stone wall building will vary a great deal depending on whether you view the individual stones or the resultant wall as flexible, and capable of being changed.

In many ways life is like building a stone wall and people are the stones. On occasions there are clear social constraints that individuals must adjust themselves to; at other times social relationships and organizations will change to adjust themselves to the nature of their individual members. Although we sometimes see ourselves as more flexible than our social worlds, and sometimes see the social worlds as potentially more malleable than we are, the extent to which we hold these beliefs can vary importantly across cultures.

Primary and Secondary Control. Rothbaum, Weisz, and Snyder (1982) proposed that there are at least two ways we can gain control in our lives. The first way they labeled "**primary control**." People achieve a sense of primary control by striving to shape existing realities to fit their perceptions, goals, or wishes. Primary control is an enormously researched construct in psychology, and it also goes under the related names of an internal locus of control, influence, and agency. It's the kind of control you perceive when you decide you want a hamburger and you go down to a burger joint to get yourself one. The chain of events that was initiated to get that hamburger into your stomach was predicated on a belief that you have the efficacy to influence your social environment to get what you want.

Rothbaum and colleagues proposed another kind of control that has been less researched by psychologists, which they labeled "**secondary control**." People achieve a sense of secondary control when they attempt to align themselves with existing realities, leaving the realities unchanged, but exerting control over their psychological impact. It involves accepting one's circumstances (Morling & Evered, 2006). Secondary control is also known as adjustment, and is related to the construct of an external locus of control. It's the kind of control that you perceive when you're with a group of people going for lunch and the group decides to get a pizza, and you come to feel that a pizza is just what you'd like for lunch. Your desires and goals adjust themselves to what your environment is most likely to provide. Which kind of control do you think you experience more often?

Although everyone experiences primary and secondary control on occasion, cultures do differ in the extent to which people engage in these two strategies. In hierarchical collectivistic cultures, such as in East Asia, the social world remains somewhat impervious to efforts by a lone individual to change things (e.g., Chiu, Dweck, Tong, & Fu, 1997). Power and agency tend to be concentrated in groups or in leaders of groups, or it is mandated by the role that one occupies; therefore there are many domains in which the individual is unable to exert much influence. Likewise, as we discussed in Chapter 5, East Asians are more likely to have a flexible and incremental view of themselves. When the individual is perceived to be more mutable than the social world, we'd expect people to be quite willing to adjust themselves to fit in better with the demands of their social worlds.

In contrast, people from Western cultures tend to stress the malleability of the world relative to the individual (Su et al., 1999). For example, in the Bible God told Adam that he would have dominion over all the earth; the world was there for humans to change and use to their liking. This belief persists in the West and is manifest in the view that the individual has potential control of shaping the world to fit his or her own desires. When people view individuals to be the center of experience and action, they accordingly look to individuals as a source of control. Moreover, the independent self, as discussed in Chapter 5, is perceived as relatively immutable and consistent. This view of self as an immutable entity, working within the context of a mutable world, sustains a perception of primary control.

Weisz, Rothbaum, and Blackburn (1984) see many socializing experiences in Japan that lead Japanese to be more comfortable with engaging in secondary control strategies. For example, Japanese infants spend much more time in contact with their mothers and thus learn to adjust themselves to what their mothers are doing. Japanese workers change jobs far less frequently than their Western counterparts, and it was not uncommon for workers to be promised lifetime employment—a system ensuring that the employee learns to adjust himself or herself to whatever demands the company places on them. This can be contrasted with clear primary control attitudes expressed in such American ballads as "Take This Job and Shove It" or "I Did It My Way." Weisz and colleagues propose that these and other socialization experiences lead people to seek strategies of control that are most likely to lead to beneficial consequences within the constraints of their respective cultural environments.

One study that investigated whether control strategies differed between Japanese and Americans, in line with the hypotheses of Weisz and colleagues, was conducted by Morling (2000). Having attended several aerobics classes in both Japan and the United States, Morling noticed some differences in attitudes that seemed to speak to different control strategies. She created a questionnaire that addressed people's reasons for choosing their aerobics classes and what they tended to do when the instructor initiated a move that was too difficult for them; she passed this out to students in aerobics classes in Japan and the United States. Her results are very informative. For example, when asked why they chose the particular class they did, Americans were more likely than Japanese to say it was because the class was at a convenient time for them (i.e., they chose to exercise when they wanted), whereas Japanese were more likely than Americans to say it was because the class was of the appropriate level for them (i.e., they adjusted their schedules so that they would be a better fit with the class). Also, when asked what they did when the instructor initiated a move that was too difficult for them, Japanese were more likely than Americans to say that they would try hard to keep up (i.e., they adjusted their routine to the instructors' standards) whereas Americans were more likely than Japanese to say that they would do their own move instead (i.e., their preferences determined their routine). Both Japanese and Americans take aerobics classes for the same goal—to get into shape; however, we can still see the different control strategies that are pursued to realize these goals.

Further work has found parallel evidence for differences between Japanese and Americans in their control strategies (Morling, Kitayama, & Miyamoto, 2002). In one study, participants were asked to list occasions when they had either tried to influence their surrounding people or objects (i.e., primary control experiences) or tried to adjust themselves to the surrounding people or objects (i.e., secondary control experiences). As shown in Figure 6.4, Americans were better able to recall situations they had influenced than those in which they had adjusted; Japanese remembered more adjusting situations than influencing ones. The term "secondary control" might

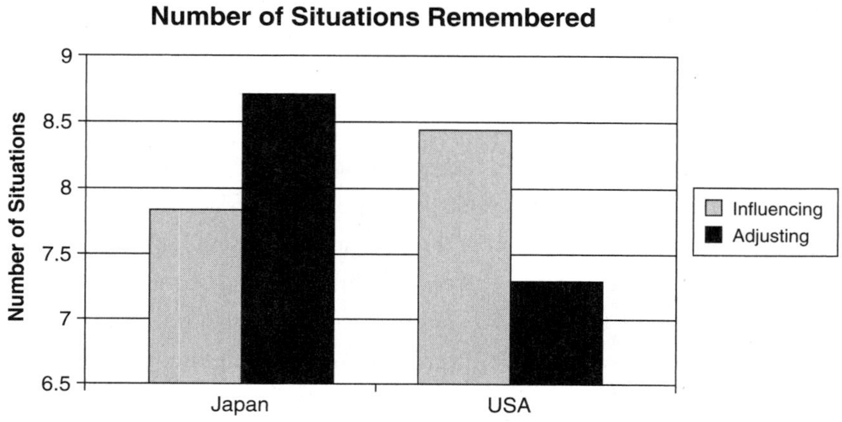

FIGURE 6.4

Japanese recall more adjusting situations than influencing ones, whereas Americans recall more influencing situations than adjusting ones.

thus be a misnomer in Japan as this type of control appears to be more common there than "primary control." However, both Japanese and Americans evaluated influencing situations to have felt more powerful than adjusting ones, suggesting that primary control might universally be experienced as powerful (primary control may thus be a good candidate for a functional universal). Despite the apparent universality of the perceived power in primary control situations, Japanese reported feeling more powerful about their adjusting situations than the Americans did. This cultural difference was evident in the way participants described their adjusting experiences. For example, Americans were more likely than Japanese to report feeling that they were compelled to adjust, as though it was against their will. They often described their experiences as something that they "had to do"—for example, "I had to adjust last school year when one of my roommates' boyfriend moved into our house." In contrast, the Japanese situations rarely indicated that the individual felt compelled to adjust or that the adjustment experience was negative. In sum, experiences of primary control seem to be more frequent among people from Western than Eastern cultural backgrounds, and a variety of other studies have reported comparable findings (e.g., Bond & Tornatzky, 1973; Chang, Chua, & Toh, 1997; Mahler, 1974; Seginer, Trommsdorff, & Essau, 1993). Likewise, the East Asian pattern of relatively weaker feelings of primary control has also been found in African samples (e.g., Smith, Trompenaars, & Dungan, 1995).

Being part of a group can mean that an individual must sometimes go along with others to get along well. Secondary control strategies are an effective means for managing one's successful functioning in group contexts. However, if we spend a great deal of our time thinking of ourselves as members of groups, and thinking of others in terms of the groups to which they belong, we might also think of control in a different way. That is, we might start to perceive groups as agents, as entities that can make decisions and exert control. The idea of groups as agents is rather unfamiliar to psychologists who tend to equate agency with individuals, and this might reflect the path of our field's development, growing largely out of Western, individualistic cultural contexts. Do people in collectivistic cultures see groups as agents in similar ways that people in individualistic cultures see individuals as agents?

One way this question has been investigated was to analyze how newspapers in different countries referred to the agents implicated in scandals involving rogue traders (Menon, Morris, Chiu, & Hong, 1999). For example, in

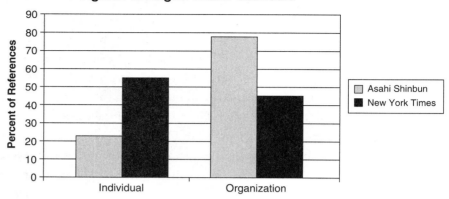

FIGURE 6.5

In explaining rogue trader scandals, Japanese newspapers tend to focus more on the organizations involved than the individuals, whereas American newspapers tend to focus more on the individuals than the organizations.

1995 the British stock trader Nick Leeson was convicted of fraud for his part in a scandal that resulted in the loss of over a billion dollars and the ultimate collapse of his employer, Baring's Bank. Menon and colleagues were interested in how newspapers in the United States and Japan (specifically, the *New York Times* and *Asahi Shinbun*) reported this and various other rogue trader scandals that were in the news. Did they see the problem as ultimately lying with the individual, such as Nick Leeson, or did they see the problem to be due to the management of the organization, such as Baring's Bank? Who ultimately had responsibility, and thus control, over the event? The researchers analyzed the articles about the scandals and checked the frequency with which the articles addressed the individuals involved or the organizations that employed them. As shown in Figure 6.5, the *New York Times* was more likely to explore the scandals in terms of the problems with the individual trader. In stark contrast, however, the *Asahi Shinbun* focused its reporting on the problems inherent in the organizations that could allow this scandal to occur. Note that these newspaper stories were about the identical scandals, and this pattern of results was obtained for scandals that occurred in both the West and Japan. Apparently, Japanese are more likely to see events in the world as occurring due to the behaviors and decisions of groups, whereas Americans tend to understand events in terms of the individuals involved (also see related work by Markus, Uchida, Omoregie, Townsend, & Kitayama, 2006; Yamaguchi, Gelfand, Ohashi, & Zemba, 2003). Furthermore, cultures appear to differ not only in their explanations of human behaviors but also in the animal world as well. One study found that Americans were more prone to explain a rancher's accident in terms of the behaviors of a rogue cow, whereas Chinese preferred to explain the same accident in terms of the unruly behaviors of the entire herd (Menon et al., 1999). The same event can be understood quite differently depending on one's view of agency.

Making Choices. One way that people can exercise control over their worlds is by making choices. By deciding where we live, what food we'll have for dinner, what time we'll wake up in the morning we're able to structure our lives so that they match our desires. We make countless choices every day and they are perhaps the most direct way we engage in primary control strategies.

Choice is something that is surely valued everywhere; however, the extent to which people value choice, and exercise it, is influenced by the contexts we are in. If we imagine situations in which individuals are quite separate from others, for example, such as an author who lives alone and works at home, we can see that she has a great deal of freedom in the kinds of choices to make every day. She might be free to sleep when she wants, eat what she wants, and work when she wants. Many of her goals would be personal, and there would be few interpersonal constraints on the daily choices she made. In contrast, imagine a situation in which many individuals are interdependent with others, such as players on a professional basketball team. Choices that individuals make regarding their basketball playing are clearly no longer free of interpersonal constraints. A player does not have the choice to go to practice when he feels like it, to get extremely drunk the night before a big game, or to shoot the ball himself if a teammate is in a better place to make the basket. His behaviors must adjust themselves to the constraints imposed on him by his interdependence with others. Indeed, because becoming part of a team renders a player's own goals to be largely consistent with those of his teammates (you all want to win the game, after all), it is likely that he would not feel that his choices had been stripped away when he is required to coordinate his behaviors with others. Because the player wants the team to do as well as possible he will want to ensure that he is behaving in a way that maximizes the likelihood that the team will win. In sum, more choices are available to individuals acting alone than to those who are part of an interdependent network; however, when individuals share the same goals as their group, the limits on their choices are likely not experienced as aversive.

Individualistic and collectivistic cultures also vary on this same continuum. In individualistic societies people are less dependent on the actions of others than they are in collectivistic ones. People in collectivistic societies should, on average, be more concerned with the goals of their groups and more willing to adjust their behaviors (and reduce their choices) to coordinate with the actions of the group toward those goals.

Perhaps the strongest evidence for cultural variation in the valuation of choice can be seen in the domains in which people exercise free choice. Most Westerners, for example, spend a good portion of their time obsessing about a few key choices that will have a big impact on their lives: "What kind of job should I get?" "Who should I marry?" "Where should we live?" "Should we have kids, and if so, how many and when?" These tend to be seen as personal decisions, or decisions between a husband and wife. Many people take years to decide these issues and often evaluate their lives with respect to the success of these decisions. Would you be willing to allow other people to make these decisions for you?

In many parts of the world, important decisions such as these are seen to reflect upon the entire extended family, and often they are not made by the individual but by his or her parents. "What kind of job should I get?" "You'll take over the family business." "Who should I marry?" "We've found someone for you from a good family on the other side of town." "Where should we live?" "You'll live with the husband's family." "Should we have kids?" "Yes, starting as soon as possible, and as many as possible."

The influence of our cultural socialization is readily apparent here as most Westerners have an extremely difficult time imagining not making these kinds of choices on their own. Given that many Westerners assume that the success of their lives and their happiness is contingent on these decisions, they assume that having these choices relegated to others—for example, to their parents—would result in a life of misery. I think this is a reasonable reaction to the extent that a person is solely focused on his or her personal goals. However, remember that in collectivistic societies (where parental decision making is more common) individuals tend to identify with their group's goals. If you also want what is best for your extended family, it very well might not feel like you are being stripped of your freedom to choose, but that you are engaging in action that was thoughtfully and wisely decided as furthering your family's goals. Indeed, there is little evidence from some collectivistic societies that people are any happier when they make these kinds of choices themselves or when they are made by their families (e.g., Gupta & Singh, 1982).

It is important to remember that we're not talking about individuals surrendering their choices to a random number generator or to their arch-rival; the ones who are making the decisions care a great deal about them and know a lot about their personal needs and the family's needs. We can likely suspect that choices made by random or by someone who doesn't care much for us would not serve our needs well, but choices made by a caring person who is considering our own personal and family interests may serve us just fine. This is a critical distinction for understanding why individuals in collectivistic cultures are willing to allow some choices to be made for them by others, and it is clearly evident in the remarkable study described below.

Iyengar and Lepper (1999) explored how children from different cultural backgrounds would respond to situations in which they made choices on their own or had the choices made by someone else. Fifth-grade students were recruited from two elementary schools in the San Francisco Bay area. The students whose results were analyzed were those who were of (non-Hispanic) European-American background and those who were of East Asian background (specifically, Japanese, Chinese, and Vietnamese). The Asian-American students all spoke an Asian language at home with their families. These students were invited to play a computerized math game called "Space Quest." Their task in the game was to ensure that their ship had enough fuel to reach Planet Ektar to save the world from imminent disaster. They received points along the way for answering arithmetic problems correctly, and if they reached 50 points before their computerized opponent did, they won the game.

The students were randomly assigned to one of three different conditions. In the "*personal choice*" condition the students were allowed to make a number of choices that were all irrelevant to their success in the game. For example, they could choose which of four icons would represent their spaceship, and which of four names they would give to their spaceship. Students in this condition had the freedom to choose for themselves. In the "*outgroup choice*" condition students saw the same four options for the spaceship icons and possible names; however, one of these four was highlighted and they were told "These are the spaceships that are available for you. We're giving you the one shown below because that was what most of the third graders at the last school wanted." Students in this condition did not have the freedom to make this choice, and instead, the choice was made for them by someone whose opinion they did not value very highly (the researchers conducted a pretest and discovered that fifth graders have very little respect for third graders from other schools). Last, students in the *"ingroup choice"* condition were shown the same options and were told that they were assigned to a particular space-ship because "that was what most of the students in your class wanted." That is, the students did not have the freedom to choose, but they could expect that their fellow classmates likely made pretty good decisions. The students then all had the opportunity to play the "Space Quest" game for 20 min-utes. The dependent variable was how many games they attempted during that time (a measure that should indicate how much intrinsic motivation the students had toward the game). The results were rather striking (see Figure 6.6).

The students of European background attempted the most games when they got to choose their own spaceships. They played significantly fewer games when either the third graders or their classmates made their choices

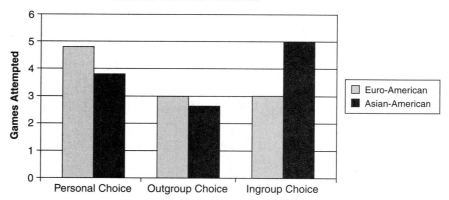

Motivation to Play a Game Depending on the Kind of Choice Allowed

FIGURE 6.6

European-Americans make more attempts to play a game in which they must make choices than a game in which others make the choices. In contrast, Asian-Americans make more attempts to play a game in which an ingroup member made choices for them than one in which either an outgroup member made the choices or they made the choices themselves.

for them. That is, the Euro-American students seemed to react rather negatively to the idea that others were making choices for them, regardless of who those others were.

In contrast, the Asian-American students attempted the most games when their classmates chose their spaceships for them. Indeed, they seemed to be more motivated to play the game in this condition than when they made their own choices. However, like the Euro-Americans, they were not very motivated when an undesirable other (the third graders from another school) made their choices for them. The Asian-Americans, thus, shared some similarities but some important differences with the Euro-Americans in regard to their attitudes toward choices. Like the Euro-Americans they seemed to be motivated when they made their own choices, and were not motivated when an undesirable other made their choices for them. However, in stark contrast with the Euro-Americans, Asian-American students seemed especially motivated when a trusted other made choices for them (a similar pattern was also found in another study when the children were told that their mothers had made the choices for them). Apparently, Asian-Americans viewed the situation of their ingroups making choices for them as opportunities to promote harmony and a sense of belongingness with their other group members. Euro-Americans seemed to view the same situation as something that stripped them of their freedom to choose.

In general, making individual choices seems to be especially valued in individualistic cultures, and this appears to be the most true in the United States—the world champion of individualism. One study contrasted people from the United States with those from France, Germany, Italy, Switzerland, and the UK. Participants were asked whether they would prefer a choice of 10 ice cream flavors or 50 ice cream flavors. The majority of people in each of the European cultures said they would prefer a choice among only 10 flavors, whereas in the United States, a majority of people said they would prefer a choice among 50 flavors (Rozin, Fischler, Shields, & Masson, 2006). Likewise, Americans (and Britons) prefer to have more choices on menus from upscale restaurants than do citizens of the other European countries (Rozin et al., 2006). The American results are especially interesting as research reveals that, even for Americans, too much choice is aversive. Although Americans will reliably tell you that they prefer having many choices, their behaviors indicate that they actually fare better when they have only a few choices to make (Iyengar & Lepper, 2000). Having too much choice can be quite debilitating at times, as making choices requires a great deal of cognitive resources (Schwartz, 2004).

Because people in collectivistic cultures tend to identify with group goals more than do people in individualistic cultures, they should be more content with exchanging some individual control for control by valued others. There are other ways, however, that we can see cultural differences in perceived control. In the 20th century many countries embarked on an enormous real-life experiment as various governments around the world became communist. There were many consequences of communism, both positive and negative; however, one consequence was that there was less relation between an individual's efforts and an individual's outcomes. For example, a communist farmer who wanted to increase his wealth could not simply devote more energies to tending his crops. This might increase the yield of his crops, but this increased yield would go to the country as a whole rather than to his own private livelihood. To the extent that individuals' efforts are not clearly linked to their outcomes they should experience relatively less feelings of primary control.

The Cold War was at its peak when the Soviets erected the Berlin Wall in 1961. Despite the great human suffering that this sad historical event caused, it also resulted in a unique opportunity to explore the psychological consequences of communism. Prior to the second world war, Berlin was a unified city that shared a common culture and history. After the city was divided into two, the lives of Berliners reached a fork in the road. The Western half returned to its democratic and capitalist prewar past, whereas the Eastern half became communist. As the two halves shared a common heritage we should expect that any psychological differences that exist between the two are likely due to the different experiences they encountered with their respective political and economic systems. Unfortunately, the governments had other things on their agenda than cross-cultural psychological research, and few researchers were granted access to the divided city.

One exception is the work of Oettingen and colleagues (Oettingen, Little, Lindenberger, & Baltes, 1994; Oettingen & Seligman, 1990). These researchers visited the two Germanys prior to unification and were able to conduct a number of interesting cross-cultural experiments. In one series of studies they passed out questionnaires to elementary school children in both East and West Berlin to investigate the students' perceptions of control and efficacy. For example, children were asked to respond to the question "If I want to do well in school, I can." To the extent that one has feelings of primary control and efficacy, one should endorse this item. It reflects people's beliefs in whether they can change their behavior to effect a positive outcome in their studies. They found that the West Berlin children endorsed this item significantly more than the children from East Berlin. Their findings across the items from the questionnaire and the different studies they conducted were consistent with this pattern: West German children felt that they had more control (at least in their school work) than East German children. Would you think that this difference is due to the specific policies that were enacted within their respective school systems, or from attitudes that the students learned from life outside of school?

It would seem that decreased feelings of control might be associated with some psychological costs. Much research with people (and animals) has revealed that when individuals are unable to avoid harmful situations they can experience something known as **learned helplessness**. In learned helplessness, an individual feels that he or she is unable to control or avoid unpleasant events, and the person will suffer from stress, and potentially depression (e.g., Abramson, Seligman, & Teasdale, 1978). If East Germans had less control over their life outcomes than West Germans, we might expect that they should show signs of learned helplessness. Oettingen and Seligman (1990) investigated whether people in East and West Berlin differed in signs of learned helplessness, notably depression. Although the researchers were not allowed to collect questionnaire data from adults in East Berlin, they were resourceful in trying to measure depression in another way. They visited bars in East and West Berlin and observed the customers there. They looked for any behavioral signs of depression, such as frowns and smiles, slumped body postures, or a lack of expressive gestures. Their results showed a clear pattern: East Berliners were far more likely to be showing overt signs of depression than West Berliners (see Figure 6.7). A reasonable interpretation of their data is that East Germans felt greater learned helplessness as they had less direct control over the outcomes in their lives.

Many different kinds of contexts afford or constrain a sense of control, with a democracy and a totalitarian government being two such examples. We can also see cultural variation in perceptions of control if we look within 21st-century democratic countries, such as the United States. As we noted in Chapter 1, the vast majority of psychological research is conducted with

FIGURE 6.7

Bar patrons in East Berlin showed more outward signs of depression than bar patrons in West Berlin.

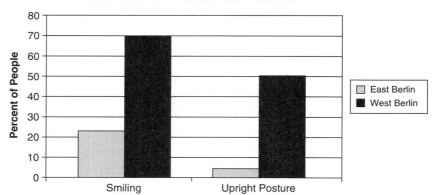

Behaviors of German Bar Patrons

a limited sample that is not only largely restricted to participants from Western cultural backgrounds but is also usually further limited to college students from those same cultural backgrounds. College students are not necessarily representative of humankind; one way they differ from the rest of the population is that they are more likely to be from upper-middle-class backgrounds and are more likely later to raise their own families in an upper-middle-class environment. Non-college-educated people, in contrast, are more likely to be from lower-middle-class or working-class backgrounds.

How might we expect people of upper-middle-class backgrounds to differ in their perceptions of control from those with working-class backgrounds? One obvious way is that working-class people earn less money and have fewer choices available because of that. If your income is not large enough, you can't consider some of the choices that wealthier people routinely make (e.g., whether to send their children to private schools, whether to pay for the best medical care, whether to move to a safe neighborhood, or whether to go on a resort vacation). With fewer financial resources, people must accept many situations in life rather than being able to choose from a range of alternatives. Working-class people and upper-middle-class people also have different kinds of relationships; the working-class individuals tend to have fewer friends, they live closer to them, they have more frequent contact with family, and they rely more on relatives for material assistance (Allan, 1979). In sum, working-class adults participate in a different cultural world from that of upper-middle-class adults; they are more likely to face hardships in their lives, and they have less control over these hardships compared to upper-middle-class people.

One study explored differences in control experiences by comparing working-class and upper-middle-class Americans (Snibbe & Markus, 2005). In one of their studies, Snibbe and Markus asked people at a shopping mall to complete a questionnaire for which they were offered a pen in compensation. Actually, the primary question the researchers were interested in was what people thought of the pen they received. In a "*free choice*" condition the experimenter let the participants choose any pen they wanted. In a "*usurped choice*" condition, the participant was allowed to choose a pen; however, after he or she made the choice the experimenter said "I'm sorry. You can't have that pen. It's the last one of its kind that I have. Here—take this one." The experimenter then replaced the chosen pen with the same kind of pen that the previous participant in the "free choice" condition had chosen (this was done to ensure that the identical pens were actually received between the two conditions). At the end of the questionnaire the participants were asked to evaluate the pen they had received. You can see the evaluations of the working-class and upper-middle-class participants in Figure 6.8. The working-class participants were almost as satisfied with the pen they received in the usurped choice condition as they were in the free choice

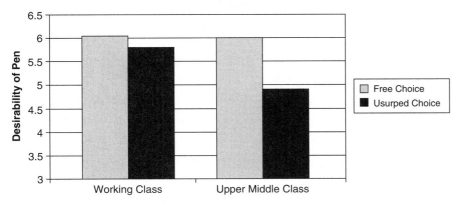

FIGURE 6.8

Whereas upper middle class people prefer pens that they chose themselves over those they did not choose, the preferences of working class people were not affected by who chose the pens.

condition. In contrast, however, the upper-middle-class participants were significantly less satisfied when their choice had been taken away from them. The researchers argue that upper-middle-class Americans are raised to favor choices and to express themselves through their choices. As such, they learn to respond quite negatively when they believe that they do not have any choice in a situation. In contrast, working-class Americans grow up learning that much of what you encounter in life is beyond your control, and that a good way to maintain your independence is to emphasize your integrity and resilience during tough times. This orientation leads them to accept and cope with occasions when they don't end up with what they wanted. Several other studies further support this result (see Snibbe & Markus, 2005). Even within a country, we can see clear differences in people's perceptions of choice and control. Do you think there are other phenomena discussed in this book that might appear quite different if the samples were working-class people instead of college students?

Motivations to Fit In or to Stick Out

On many occasions when we're deciding how to behave in a group, we can decide to go either of two ways. First, we can strive to act in a way that fits in well with others, thereby increasing group harmony at the expense of our own individual distinctiveness. Alternatively, we can decide to act in such a way that we stick out from others, highlighting our uniqueness at the potential risk of not getting along so well with others. We are often in the position to make such a decision, and the way we reach our decisions is influenced by our cultures.

Perhaps the most dramatic exploration of how people decide whether they should fit in or stick out was conducted by the eminent social psychologist Solomon Asch (Asch, 1956). Asch was interested in when people would conform, that is, when they would go along with the crowd. Conformity is a particularly interesting topic in a Western context as conformity tends to be viewed rather negatively in most Western societies; however, as Asch's and others' research reveals, Westerners conform all the time. Take a look at the clothes that you're wearing right now. Surely you feel that you chose what clothes you would wear today; however, you might notice that the choice that you reached is quite similar to that made by your closest friends. For example, you're probably *not* presently wearing a zoot-suit, a corset, or a grungy flannel shirt. The point here is that these clothes are not fashionable now, or at least not when and where I wrote this paragraph. Often when we feel that we're making a unique choice we're really making choices that allow us to fit in to consensually agreed upon norms for how good, interesting, and responsible people behave. We are often conforming, even when we're not aware of it.

Asch wanted to explore a stronger example of conformity. He wanted to see when people would conform and clearly be aware that they were doing so. His experiment proceeded like this.

"My mom says that in twenty years we'll look back on our mode of dress and be amused by these clearly excellent choices. I think not."

A participant would arrive in the lab to take part in a study that was supposedly about visual perception. Sitting beside this person in the lab were a number of other students who appeared to be participants as well. The experimenter gave the group an extremely straightforward task. They were shown three lines of clearly different lengths and were asked which one of those three was the same length as the target line (Figure 6.9). The correct answer to this question was obvious to everyone. Asch found out that hardly

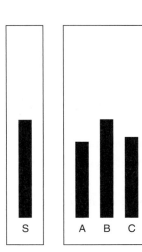

FIGURE 6.9

The kinds of stimuli used in Solomon Asch's study of conformity. Participants were presented with the sample line (S) and asked which of the other three lines' length matched the sample.

anyone got the answer wrong when tested individually. However, before the individual had the chance to offer his or her own answer, a number of the other "participants" (who were actually confederates of the experimenter) answered and with apparent certainty, indicated a line that was clearly different from the target line. When it was the participant's turn he or she had a choice to make. Does he or she offer the answer that appears obviously correct, even though it contradicts what everyone else was saying? Or does the person go along with the group and offer what appeared to be a patently wrong answer? Remarkably, 75% of Asch's American subjects conformed on at least one of the 12 trials of the experiment. Conformity is common indeed.

So what was motivating people in Asch's study to conform? An answer to this can be seen in a variant of the study that Asch conducted (Asch, 1962). Rather than have a subject give his answer after hearing several confederates give what was an obviously incorrect answer, Asch reversed the situation. He had one confederate give what was clearly an incorrect answer after having several real subjects offer the correct answer before him. When the confederate did this, the rest of the participants turned around and laughed at him! Apparently, deciding to stand up against a crowd can be so ludicrous that people find it quite funny. It seemed so ridiculous that even the experimenter couldn't help laughing! One potential cost of not conforming is that people might laugh at you.

There are other social costs to not conforming. People tend to take an active dislike to those who won't conform. An early study instructed a confederate to offer a dissenting opinion to a group (Schacter, 1951). Later the group was required to reduce their size by choosing one person to leave. Not surprising to anyone who has watched episodes of the TV series *Survivor*, it was the dissenter who was quickly voted out of the group. People would rather not associate with those who won't agree with others. If you won't go along, you likely won't get along. It's rather ironic that those people who we hold in high esteem for standing out from the crowd and forging their own paths, like Galileo, Luther King, Darwin, Gandhi, and Van Gogh, were often widely hated during their own lifetimes for expressing such counter-normative ideas. There are pronounced social costs to not conforming.

Given these social costs to not conforming, we would expect that people from cultures that are more socially cohesive would be more willing to conform. The social costs to dissenting must be considerably greater in collectivistic societies in which people feel more obligation to their ingroup members and have a stronger motivation to achieve a sense of belongingness. The Asch study has been a popular one, and it's been replicated well over 100 times all around the globe. A meta-analysis of these studies revealed one clear trend: Although Americans show a great deal of conformity in the Asch paradigm, people from more collectivistic cultures conform even more, especially when they are conforming to their ingroups (Bond & Smith, 1996). Motivations to fit in are more powerful in cultural contexts that encourage people to maintain strong relationships with others.

In contrast to a motivation to conform, we can also consider people's motivations to stick out and to be unique. Why might people be motivated to think of themselves as different from others? How would you think this motivation might be related to independent and interdependent views of self? As you've already learned, people with independent views of self see their identity as ultimately grounded in their individual qualities. Their identity is not shared with others and thus is perceived to be fundamentally unique. Maintaining a view of oneself that is consistent with cultural values of independence, then, should be aided by striving to view oneself as a unique and special individual. In contrast, a motivation to be different should not be so pronounced among those who value interdependence, where concerns with fitting in are more important.

Is there evidence in support of this hypothesis? Consider the following clever experiment (Kim & Markus, 1999): People who were in the departure lounge at the San Francisco airport were approached while waiting for their flights. Participants of Asian descent who were waiting for a flight to East Asia and people of European descent who were waiting for a flight to a non-Asian destination were approached. Participants were asked to fill out a brief questionnaire and, in return for their time, they were offered a pen. The experimenter had a bag full of red and green pens; she would pull out a handful of five of them, and ask each person to choose a pen. By doing this the experimenter ensured that all passengers had to make a choice between pens of two different colors, and that they also had to choose between pens that were either of a majority color (three or four pens of the same color) of those of a minority color (one or two pens of the same color). About half the time the majority color was red, and about half the time the majority color was green. The findings were quite striking, as seen in Figure 6.10. The European-Americans were much more likely to choose the pen of the

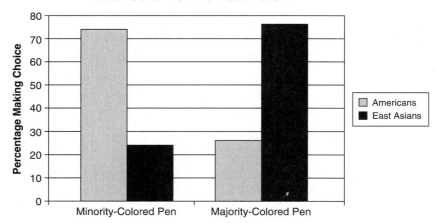

FIGURE 6.10

When given the choice, Americans tend to prefer minority colored pens whereas East Asians prefer majority colored pens.

minority color, regardless of what that color was. Somehow, it seemed that European-Americans viewed pens of a relatively unique color—in terms of its minority number—as more desirable. In stark contrast, the East Asians were more likely to choose the pen of the majority color, considering the less unusual pen more desirable. Apparently, the European-Americans desire to express their uniqueness by making what they think are unique choices, whereas East Asians desire to express their belongingness by making what they think are common choices. Other analyses and studies corroborated that the participants made these divergent choices because of distinct self-expressive motives, and not, for example, because the East Asians were trying to avoid taking the experimenter's last red pen (Kim & Markus, 1999; also see Kim & Drolet, 2003).

Motivations for uniqueness are thus quite different between these two cultural groups. An important question to consider is how these particular motivations, and cultural ideas more generally, come to be so widespread within cultures, yet so different between cultures. Obviously, these ideas must somehow be communicated to individuals within these cultures. How might we go about exploring the ways different ideas are communicated differently across cultures?

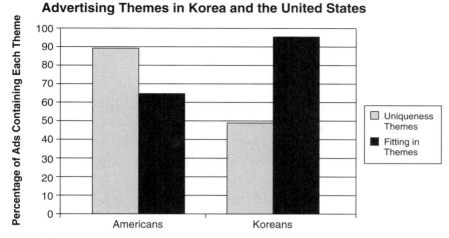

FIGURE 6.11

American magazine ads contain more themes valuing uniqueness than fitting in, whereas the opposite is true of Korean ads. Some ads included more than one theme.

One strategy would be to look at messages in advertisements. Advertisers are very savvy folks, and their job is to persuade people. The kind of message that would be most persuasive is one that reflects ideas that are widely shared within a culture. One study investigated themes in magazine advertisements in Korea and the United States, evaluating them as expressing either uniqueness or conformity (Kim & Markus, 1999). Several categories of magazines (e.g., business magazines, women's magazines) from each country were examined. Each ad was coded as containing a theme for conformity (e.g., "Seven out of 10 people are using this product," or "Trend forecast for spring: Pastel colors!") or a theme for uniqueness (e.g., "Ditch the Joneses," or "The Internet isn't for everybody. But then again, you are not everybody"). The researchers then compared how frequently the themes appeared in each ad. As you might expect, uniqueness themes were more common in American ads than in Korean ones, and conformity themes were more common in Korean ads than in American ones (Figure 6.11). This finding suggests that the kinds of cultural messages people encounter on a day-to-day basis help to reinforce the different views of self prevalent in the two cultures. The next time you look at magazine ads, consider how much they are tapping into readers' motivations to be unique or to fit in.

SUMMARY

Why we act in the ways we do is a question that reveals our underlying motivations. These motivations are influenced in a variety of ways through our cultural backgrounds. For example, the motivation to view oneself positively is shaped by culture. North Americans of European descent are especially concerned about their self-esteem, and they engage in a variety of tactics to boost the positivity of their own self-view. East Asians, in contrast, tend to be more concerned about face, and they employ a preventive, self-improving tactic to ensure that they maintain this.

Motivations to work hard are moralized in cultures with predominant Protestant populations, apparently because of ideas stemming from early Protestant sects that such hard work on one's calling (and the material rewards that were thus accumulated) were evidence that God viewed one favorably.

Striking evidence of culture's influence on our motivations can be seen in studies of control and choice. In collectivistic cultures individuals are often in situations when they must yield their own preferences to others. In such situations they can excise control better by altering their personal expectations and preferences than by trying to change the outcome. This kind of control, known as "secondary control," is more evident among people from East Asian than Western backgrounds. Other situations prevent individuals from being able to exercise much control, such as being a citizen in a totalitarian society or being in the working class in the United States. People from these backgrounds are less likely to pursue their own choices or are more willing to accept what they have received.

Cultures also shape our motivations to fit in or to stick out in a group. People from collectivistic backgrounds are more motivated to maintain harmonious relationships, and this can be facilitated by acting in ways consistent with the behavior of others. Individualists, in contrast, are more motivated to stick out and to perceive themselves as unique.

Morality, Religion, and Justice

The first few months of 2006 were extremely volatile, and the world witnessed a widespread series of enraged demonstrations. Throughout the Muslim world in the Middle East, Africa, Asia, and among Muslim groups in North America, the South Pacific, and Europe, people were furiously, and sometimes violently, expressing their rage. The demonstrations left dozens of people killed and a number of embassies were burned to the ground. Flags were torched on a daily basis, and there were repeated calls for the violent deaths of the offenders. What was the source of all this widespread outrage? Cartoons. A few months earlier, a Danish newspaper had published cartoons that depicted the Muslim prophet Muhammad. This publication violated a deeply held belief among Muslims that the prophet should never be portrayed. All the worse, many of the cartoons showed the prophet in deliberately offensive ways, such as with a bomb in his turban. Later, citing the importance of freedom of expression, newspapers from many countries around the world reprinted the cartoons, which resulted in even more anger and further fanned the flames of outrage.

The issue of whether it was inappropriate to publish caricatures of Muhammad deeply polarized the world. People on each side of the conflict were furious and rather mystified at the reactions of those on the other side. Many Westerners were puzzled over why the cartoons sparked such outrage. Many understood that the cartoons could be seen as offensive to some, but, as many Western commentators argued, such kinds of offense are the price that people pay to live in a society that treasures the value of freedom of expression. The editor of the Danish newspaper justified his decision to publish the cartoons by noting that Christian images are satirized quite frequently—for example, a recent and much publicized Danish painting showed Jesus with an erection. So why not Muhammad?

On the other hand, many Muslims view the issue of caricaturizing Muhammad in largely sacred terms. They say that some behaviors are viewed be so deeply offensive that they should never be tolerated, even if they might limit one's freedom of expression. Many Muslims do not believe that freedom trumps all other values. Indeed, the sign of one Muslim protestor captured the angry feelings shared by many with the message "Freedom go to Hell!" The publication of the cartoons was viewed by many Muslims to be an attack on the Muslim faith and a gesture to further aggravate already strained relations between the cultures. Later in this chapter we'll make sense of why some Muslims and some Christians saw the publication of the Muhammad cartoons in such different terms.

The cartoon controversy, and the growing tensions between some people of Christian and Muslim faiths over recent years, underscores the central role of culture in world affairs. The conflict reflects what Samuel Huntington had in mind in 1993 when he wrote *The Clash of Civilizations* and argued that the fundamental source of conflict in the new world would not be primarily ideological or economic, but that the largest conflicts will be those that divide the world in cultural and religious terms.

Huntington's thesis has been controversial, in part because a common perception of many people, particularly academics, is that the world is quickly becoming secularized. That is, as the world develops and progresses, and science continues to make one discovery after another, religious explanations of phenomena are becoming supplanted by rational and scientific explanations. This view, known as **secularization theory**, holds that religion is on the decline, and that people around the world are discovering new secular and rational ways to make sense of their lives. The 19th-century German philosopher Friedrich Nietzche was an early proponent of this view when he famously claimed "God is dead" as we entered the century of science.

There is no doubt that science has made enormous progress since Nietzche's time, and that many prefer scientific explanations over religious accounts. However, this trend of exploding scientific discoveries, together with a move toward a more educated populace across the world, is not living up to Nietzche's predictions. God is not dead, at least not in the minds of the majority of the world. In the United States, despite having the world's largest economy and being home of the greatest number of scientific advances over the past century, religion has not been on the wane. Approximately 94% of Americans report believing in God (Greeley, 1991), and there are many signs that religiosity has been increasing over the past decades in the United States (e.g., Greeley & Hout, 1999). Many of the religions of the world, especially Islam and Christianity, are growing at breakneck speed (Jenkins, 2002). If anything, religion is growing in importance across the planet (Berger, 1999).

Herein lies a problem in which cultural psychology is caught right in the middle. Religiosity appears to be on the upswing around the world, and people from different cultures and religions are coming into contact with each other more than ever before. However, there has been growing hostility between the different faiths. September 11, 2001, forced everyone to confront the pronounced and important cross-cultural variation that exists in what is perceived to be a good way of living one's life. Osama bin Laden and many other Islamic extremists view countries with industrialized Christian cultures, particularly the United States, as lands of depraved infidels, where people have lost their way. Likewise, many fundamentalist Christians view much in Islam as inherently immoral. The Reverend Franklin Graham, for example, called Islam a "very evil and wicked religion." How can people from different cultural and religious backgrounds view what is right and wrong in such different ways? The consequences of cultural differences in perceptions of morality underlie many of the past and, surely, future conflicts around the world.

This chapter explores how moral reasoning and perceptions of justice are both similar and different across cultures. Whereas some moral violations are quite universally recognized as problematic, the perception of others varies considerably, addressing a central theme of this book regarding the tension between universal and culturally variable aspects of mental processes. Understanding another culture's basis for deciding what is right and wrong is an inherently challenging task. Perhaps in no other domain of psychological research are the challenges of conceptualizing cultural differences more daunting. How do we evaluate what is right and wrong in other cultures if our moral standards were acquired through socialization in our own culture? Are our moral standards limited to our own cultural context, or do moral principles transcend culture? Given the inherent difficulties in addressing these questions, I think

"You picked the wrong religion, period. I'm not going to argue about it."

this is a good occasion to take a step back and think about how we can learn to understand cultural variation more generally. Below I contrast three different perspectives for making sense of cultural variation. These perspectives can help guide our interpretation of the cultural differences we encounter on the topic of morality.

Universalism, Evolutionism, and Relativism

Anthropologists offer three interpretive models for making sense of cultural diversity: universalism, relativism, and evolutionism (see Shweder & Bourne, 1984). Each of these three models represents a distinct way of looking at other cultures and each has its respective adherents.

Universalism is the perspective that sees people from different cultures as largely the same, and that any observed cultural variability exists only at a superficial level. Whereas exotic idea systems may appear at first blush to be quite foreign, a universalist perspective maintains that a more careful analysis will reveal common underlying processes. A universalist would argue that although you say tomato and I say tomahto, we're still talking about the same red fruit in our salads. Universalists assume that people are the same wherever you go and the differences that we see across cultures are largely differences in terms of conventions and are of little significance. Universalists urge us not to get hung up on cultural peculiarities as these contribute little to our understanding of what drives humans to act in the ways they do (for an extended discussion of this perspective see Tooby & Cosmides, 1992).

For example, consider the case of language. Variability in languages is immediately apparent—we simply cannot understand people who speak in languages that we haven't learned. As Steve Martin said, "Boy, those French have a different word for *everything!*" However, a closer examination of languages reveals that they do have much in common. Noam Chomsky (1965) proposed the notion of a universal grammar that is evident in all languages of the world. Across diverse language groups there are many universal features of word orders and morphemes (Greenberg, 1963). Some evidence for universal grammar also derives from observations that people who grow up without hearing correct grammar (such as those who grow up hearing their parents speak a "pidgin language"—a language created out of a mixture of different languages as a means of communicating among people who don't share a common language) end up creating and speaking grammatically complex languages themselves (called "creole languages"—languages learned by people whose parents speak a pidgin language). Unlike the pidgin languages they descended from, creole languages have a fixed morphology and syntax and complicated grammatical rules. For creole languages to share grammatical features with other languages of the world, despite their origin in spontaneous pidgin languages, is further testimony that there is a universal grammar (see Pinker, 1994, for a review). A universalist perspective on language, then, looks past the diverse appearances of languages of the world to identify what they share in common.

One way, then, to make sense of cultural variability is to claim that it exists only at a superficial level (e.g., Buss, 1989; Poortinga & Van Hemert, 2001), and that it largely vanishes on closer inspection. Many cultural psychologists have some sympathy for this perspective, as they see the value of considering a common underlying foundation to people's mental processes. However, many of these same cultural psychologists would quickly balk at the assumption that phenomena observed among Westerners are universal unless cross-cultural data could be shown to support such a claim.

The second way of making sense of cultural diversity is **relativism**. In contrast to universalism, the relativist perspective maintains that cultural diversity in ways of thinking is not superficial but reflects genuinely different psychological processes. The relativistic perspective maintains that culture and thought are mutually constituted. Cultural practices are viewed to lead to certain habitual ways of thinking, and because cultural practices vary considerably across cultures, relativists also expect ways of thinking to vary. For example, as we learned in Chapter 6, people in many East Asian cultures are much more concerned with face than are people in Western individualistic societies; the reverse is true for self-esteem (Heine, 2005). Because relativists believe that psychological phenomena emerge from specific cultural contexts, they typically place less emphasis on whether one culture's psychological tendencies are described as better or worse than those of any other culture; the default assumption is that cultural practices reflect a solution to the challenges faced by that culture. This isn't to say that different cultures are never evaluated; indeed, there are many cultural practices of other cultures (and your own culture) that could be viewed as harmful or problematic. However, relativists would typically urge people to be slow to pass judgment on other cultures (e.g., Shweder, 2000) and first consider why the various cultural practices exist as they do. For the most part, cultural psychologists tend to emphasize a relativistic perspective, and on most occasions, cultural variation in this textbook is described from this perspective.

A third perspective on cultural variation is **evolutionism**. Similar to relativism, the evolutionist perspective maintains that cultural variability reflects genuine differences in psychological processes. Also similar to universalism, this perspective maintains that there really is only one way that the mind has evolved to think. The evolutionist perspective interprets cultural differences in ways of thinking as reflecting increasing stages of development. This perspective maintains that some ways of thinking are more mature or advanced than others, and people of different cultures would all think in the same ways once they reached the same point of development or participated in a cultural context that allowed for the full expression of the mind's capabilities. The evolutionist approach for investigating cultural variability is first to identify a particular psychological process as a standard of mature or advanced thinking, and then to evaluate other cultures by how closely they match this standard.

For example, look at the drawings in Figure 7.1. You probably think the line on the left looks longer than the line on the right, even though if you measure the two you'll see that they're the same length. This is known

FIGURE 7.1

Because of the Müller-Lyer illusion, the line on the left looks longer; the angles at the corners suggest that it is farther away than the line on the right. People who are raised in cultures where there are not carpentered corners are not susceptible to this illusion.

as the Müller-Lyer illusion. However, research by Segall, Campbell, and Herskiovits (1963) found that the Kalahari Bushmen from southern Africa (and various other hunting and gathering groups) were far less susceptible to this illusion than were adults living in the United States and Europe. The reason for this cultural difference, they proposed, is that if you grow up in a carpentered world and encounter a lot of objects with corners, you learn that the angles of how those corners appear to you can be informative for judging the size of things. For example, in Figure 7.1, the line on the right looks shorter than the one on the left because the corners suggest to us that the line on the right is closer to us than the one on the left, so we infer the left line must be longer. If you aren't exposed much to corners (especially when you are children; McCauley & Henrich, 2006), which is the case for people in many hunting and gathering societies, then you don't learn that corners provide cues to depth and you wouldn't be susceptible to the Müller-Lyer illusion. If we maintain that there is a universal predisposition to the Müller-Lyer illusion, but it is only evident if people have had experiences of a carpentered world that allows for its expression, then we are offering an evolutionist argument to interpret the cultural variability. People in hunting-gathering societies who have not encountered many corners have not developed their potential to be susceptible to the illusion.

Ethnocentrism and Interpreting Cultural Variability

The evolutionist perspective tends to be met with the most resistance by cultural psychologists. And they resist it because of concerns about whether one can objectively identify a standard for evaluating a psychological phenomenon. For example, they would question an evolutionist account of the Müller-Lyer illusion as it seems dubious to assume that humans' perceptual systems evolved to function in a carpentered world when the existence of carpentered worlds didn't appear until so recently in human history. Being raised in carpentered worlds would thus seem to be a poor standard by which to rank the perceptual capabilities of people across the world. Rather, they would typically take a relativistic perspective in which the perceptual system is shaped by experiences, so that being raised in a forested world leads one to not perceive the Müller-Lyer illusion whereas being raised in a carpentered world leads one to rely on corners to perceive depth.

As discussed in Chapter 1, ethnocentrism is a difficult barrier to overcome in trying to understand the ways of other cultures. Typically, ethnocentrism leads people to assume that their own culture's way of life is in some ways better or more natural than that of others. To avoid adopting an ethnocentric perspective is extremely difficult because we are socialized precisely to think in ways consistent with our cultural values and to evaluate practices in terms of how well they fit with what our culture views to be good or bad. Because of our ethnocentrism bias, it is an enormous challenge to consider standards for psychological phenomena that would be universally valid, rather than ones that are favored within one's own culture.

As a demonstration of just how hard it is to step outside our own cultural framework when evaluating cultural practices, consider how we would investigate the highly controversial question, "Which cultures provide the highest quality of life?" You could use many different quality of life standards to rank cultures, and these different standards would yield vastly different rank orderings of nations. For example, you could operationalize the quality of life as meaning the average level of positive emotional experiences among cultural members, as this would indicate people's subjective satisfaction with how their lives are going. A rank ordering of cultures on this variable would yield Puerto Rico and Mexico to be the world's developmental standard of positive emotions (Inglehart, 2004). Alternatively, you could consider longevity as a quality of life standard, as this would provide an objective index of the physical health of different cultural groups. This operationalization of quality of life would reveal that Singapore and Japan are the developmental standard (Central Intelligence Agency, 2006b). Or, a case could be made that per capita income is the best indicator of quality of life, and then Norway and the United States would represent the developmental standard (Central Intelligence Agency, 2006a). Another possibility is to measure quality of life in terms of how well countries minimize inequality among their citizens, and then Denmark and Japan would represent the standard (Human Development Reports, 2005). Or you might opt for the lowest suicide rates as an indicator of a good life, and then Egypt and Peru would be seen as providing the highest quality of life for their citizens (Schmidtke et al., 1998). Evolutionary biologists discuss success in terms of an organism's "fitness," which reflects its number of surviving offspring. By that standard of quality of life, the Palestinian Territory and the Democratic Republic of Congo would score the highest in the world (Population Reference Bureau, 2006). You might consider many other variables to reflect quality of life (spiritual satisfaction, education, lowest crime rates, cleanliness of environment, stability of family relations, number of Nobel Prizes), and for each one you would get a different ranking of the world's cultures and thus a different developmental progression. It is possible to rank cultures on any given variable; however, the problem is in choosing the variable that makes sense. People from different cultures won't agree on the yardstick for measuring cultures because they do not agree on what each culture values most (e.g.; Schwartz & Sagiv, 1995). This problem is inherent in all efforts to evaluate phenomena across cultures; however, given the tight overlap between values and morality, it is most salient when we consider how cultures differ in their ideas of what is right or wrong.

Kohlberg's Stages of Moral Development

The most influential model of moral reasoning in psychology is one derived from the evolutionist perspective. Lawrence Kohlberg (1971) provided a developmental framework for understanding people's abilities to reason morally. He maintained that moral reasoning implicated cognitive abilities, and that these abilities would progress as individuals developed, matured, and were educated. The ways we conceive of what is right and what is wrong hinge on the stage of moral development we have reached

Kohlberg proposed a three-level model that could capture the developmental progression of moral reasoning in all cultures of the world (his model further distinguished between more fine-tuned stages, which I don't discuss here). Kohlberg's model has been enormously influential in the study of moral reasoning and has sparked an immense amount of research, both supporting it and challenging it. The levels are briefly summarized below.

Level 1: The Preconventional Level

At this level individuals understand the cultural rules and labels of what is good and bad but interpret these labels in terms of either the physical or hedonistic consequences of their actions. Preconventional moral reasoning suggests that people interpret morality based on a calculation of how much better or worse off they would be for acting in a certain way. What determines whether an action is good or bad is whether it satisfies one's own needs, and occasionally the needs of others. Morality at this level is about trying to behave in a way that provides the best overall return.

Level 2: The Conventional Level

At this level, people are able to identify themselves with a particular group and social order, and they show loyalty toward this group. The social order of the group is actively maintained, supported, and justified by individuals' efforts to live up to the group's standards. Conventional moral reasoning is about viewing actions as moral to the extent that they help maintain and facilitate the social order. Actions are seen as morally wrong if they involve violating any rules or laws that the social order has maintained, regardless of what those rules or laws are about. This level dictates that morality is about following the rules, and individuals should not question where those rules come from.

Level 3: The Postconventional Level

At the postconventional level, moral values and principles are seen to exist separately from the authority of the social groups that hold them. Moral reasoning is based on the consideration of abstract ethical principles of what is right and wrong, and moral decisions are reached based on the logical extensions of those principles. Whether others agree with you or whether there are rules that contradict you are independent of whether the action is viewed to be moral. Good behavior is seen as that which is consistent with a set of universal ethical principles that emphasize justice and individual rights.

Researchers use Kohlberg's model to determine the levels at which people or cultures make decisions to solve moral dilemmas. Participants are presented with moral dilemmas, and they are asked what the right solution to that dilemma is. Researchers are more interested in the reasons participants give to justify their answers than the answers themselves. Here is an example of the kind of moral dilemma that is presented to participants.

> In Europe, a woman was near death from a special kind of cancer.
> There was one drug that the doctors thought might save her. It was
> a form of radium that a druggist in the same town had recently dis-

covered. The drug was expensive to make, but the druggist was charging 10 times what the drug cost him to make. He paid $200 for the radium and charged $2,000 for a small dose of the drug. The sick woman's husband, Heinz, went to everyone he knew to borrow the money, but he could only get together about $1,000, which is half of what it cost. He told the druggist that his wife was dying, and asked him to sell it cheaper or let him pay later. But the druggist said, "No, I discovered the drug and I'm going to make money from it." So Heinz got desperate and broke into the man's store to steal the drug for his wife. Should Heinz have done that? Why or why not?

Kohlberg maintains that the three levels in his model represent a *universal* pattern of moral development the world over. His own words best summarize this claim: "almost all individuals in all cultures use the same . . . moral categories, concepts, or principles, and all individuals in all cultures go through the same order or sequence of gross stage development, thought they vary in rate and terminal point of development" (1971, p. 176). The model is proposed to be universal as the levels are always seen to follow sequentially. People do not reason at a conventional level before they have reasoned at a preconventional level, and this is argued to be as true of Americans as it is of Zambians. The different levels of the model reflect different abilities and motivations to attend to and conceptualize moral concerns. One aspect of the model that is *not* proposed to be universal is in the levels that different cultures reach. Kohlberg makes no claim that Americans and Zambians are equally likely to reason at the same level. Likewise, Kohlberg never claims that the full range of moral levels should be evident in all cultures. That is, the model presupposes cultural variation in the extent of people's moral reasoning capacities.

Kohlberg's model is an example of an evolutionist perspective of cultural variation. A developmental standard has been identified: moral reasoning that emphasizes abstract ethical principles based on justice and individual rights (a standard, incidentally, which is inherent in the moral reasoning of the U.S. Constitution). Furthermore, we are able to measure how far individuals or cultures fall short of this standard, outlining a developmental sequence. Kohlberg's model has been enormously influential in the study of moral psychology, but how well does this evolutionist perspective explain moral reasoning across cultures?

Cross-Cultural Evidence for Kohlberg's Model. Much cross-cultural research has explored the applicability of Kohlberg's model. One review explored the 45 studies that had been conducted up until that point, which had investigated the different levels of moral reasoning in 27 different cultural areas from around the world (Snarey, 1985). The results indicated some universality in moral reasoning. In all cultural groups there were adults who reasoned at the conventional levels, and in no cultural groups did the average adult reason at the preconventional level, although many samples of children revealed evidence of preconventional reasoning. This review suggests that Kohlberg's model might be universally applicable in explaining preconventional and conventional moral reasoning around the world. However, evidence of postconventional reasoning—reasoning based on justice and individual rights—was not universally found. Although every urban Western sample contained at least some individuals who showed reasoning based on justice and individual rights, not a single person from the traditional tribal and village folk populations that were studied showed such reasoning. An evolutionist interpretation of this pronounced cultural difference is that the traditional societies do not provide the educational experiences necessary for their members to reason about justice and individual rights in postconventional terms. A relativist interpretation, in contrast, would emphasize that urban Western environments are one kind of environment and tribal environments are another kind of environment, and that people develop a moral framework that best fits their environment. The lack of reasoning about justice and individual rights among tribal and folk populations suggests to the relativist that there might be different categories of moral reasoning that are missing from Kohlberg's framework.

Kohlberg claimed that his model of moral reasoning was equally applicable around the world; however, the cross-cultural evidence raises some questions about this claim. The data indicate that Kohlberg's developmental trajectory of reasoning about justice and individual rights is especially good at capturing the moral reasoning of Westerners, but it does not describe well the moral reasoning of much of the non-Western world. Although it is possible that Westerners do show more sophisticated stages of moral reasoning than most of the world, there is the risk of an ethnocentric bias in defining the developmental standard on the basis of the kind of reasoning observed in Western cultures. Another possibility is that Kohlberg's model is a good description of Western moral reasoning that fails to generalize well to other cultural contexts because it is bound up in Western understandings about moral value. How might we test which of these two possibilities is most compelling? Some researchers have addressed this question by exploring whether there are other ethical principles aside from justice and individual rights on which people in other cultures base their moral reasoning.

Ethics of Autonomy, Community, and Divinity

Shweder and colleagues (Shweder, Much, Mahapatra, & Park, 1997) argue that Kohlberg's model of moral reasoning represents just one of three different codes of ethics that guide people's moral judgments around the world. They refer to the code of ethics inherent in Kohlberg's model as an **ethic of autonomy**. This ethic views morality in terms of individual freedom and rights violations. There is an emphasis on personal choice, the right to engage in free contracts, and individual liberty. An act is seen as immoral under the ethic of autonomy when it directly hurts another person or infringes on another's rights and freedoms as an individual. For example, an immoral action would be to steal someone's lunch money, as that causes harm to that person. The ethic of autonomy appears to be of critical importance in all cultures, and indeed it's hard to imagine how any culture could function if its members did not view harming each other to be problematic.

A second code of ethics that Shweder proposes is an **ethic of community**, which emphasizes that individuals have duties that conform with their roles in a community or social hierarchy. According to this code there is an ethical principle to uphold one's interpersonal duties and obligations toward others. Actions are seen as wrong when individuals fail to perform their duties. For example, an immoral action would be a son's failure to attend his parents' wedding anniversary celebration because he doesn't feel like it. Immoral behaviors are perceived as those that involve a failure to live up to the duties and obligations associated with one's roles.

A third code of ethics that Shweder proposed is an **ethic of divinity**, which is concerned about sanctity and the perceived "natural order" of things. This code contains the ethical principle that one is obligated to preserve the standards mandated by a transcendent authority. It involves a belief that God (or Gods, depending on one's religion) has created a sacred world, and everyone's obligation is to respect and preserve the sanctity of this world. In this

"Why is it we never focus on the things that unite us, like falafel?"

ethic, actions are seen as immoral if they cause impurity or degradation to oneself or others, or if one shows any disrespect for God or God's creations. For example, caricaturizing the prophet Muhammad is a blatant violation of this ethic for many Muslims. Immoral behavior in this ethic is framed in terms of sinning against the sacredness of God.

These three different codes of ethics would be seen as moral codes to the extent that they reflect an understanding of right and wrong that is not based on either one's own subjective preferences (which would indicate that the belief is viewed as a personal choice) or a community's view of what is right and wrong (which would indicate that the belief is seen to be a matter of convention). Although Westerners have a tendency to view the ultimate principles of proper behavior as those that protect individual rights, in much of the world, the ethics of community and divinity serve as important moral principles. Because these three ethics are not equally elaborated across all cultural contexts (as we'll see below), they lie at the root of some important cross-cultural grievances. For example, in the case of the cartoon controversy introduced at the beginning of this chapter, it appears that the Muslim protestors are viewing the controversy more from the perspective of the ethic of divinity, and publishing cartoons that deface Muhammad are unacceptable according to this ethic. In contrast, the reasoning of the Western newspaper editors appears to be based on the ethic of autonomy, and censoring free speech is intolerable according to this ethic. It is difficult for these two conflicting groups to see eye to eye on this issue, then, because their understanding of what is right and wrong is grounded in different moral frameworks.

Ethic of Community

Much research has been conducted on the important role of the ethic of community in guiding moral reasoning. Carol Gilligan has made the case that interpersonal obligations represent a kind of morality that is distinct from an emphasis on individual rights, and that women are more likely to reason this way than are men (e.g., Gilligan, 1977). Although there has been much controversy over whether these gender differences in moral reasoning really exist (e.g., Gilligan & Attanucci, 1988; Walker, 1984), there has been much development of Gilligan's claim that an interpersonal foundation of moral reasoning exists, and that it is more prominent in some non-Western cultures.

Gemeinschaft and Gesellschaft Relations. The debate between whether interpersonal obligations and justice obligations vary in different cultures can be traced back to work by the 19th-century German sociologist Ferdinand Tonnies (1887/1957). Tonnies argued that there are two means by which individuals can relate to each other in a group. Some groups are characterized as **Gemeinschaft**, which loosely translates from German as "community." Gemeinschaft groups are characteristic of smaller folk organizations, and within these groups, interpersonal relationships play an especially important role. Gemeinschaft relationships bind people together with the social glue of concord, that is, relationships are viewed as real, organic, and ends in themselves. People feel connected to others because they feel a unity of spirit, and these relationships tend not to be thought of in instrumental terms, nor are they often evaluated or negotiated. The relationships are core to an individual's identity and they reflect an understanding of the self that is consistent with an interdependent self. The integral role of interpersonal relations in Gemeinschaft groups suggests that obligations associated with one's relationships would take on the weight of full moral obligations (Snarey & Keljo, 1991).

In contrast, Tonnies argued that another kind of group can be characterized as **Gesellschaft**, which literally means association or society. Gesellschaft groups, which are more characteristic of modern Western societies, treat relationships as imaginary, instrumental, and means to ends. The primary focus within these groups is on autonomous individuals who are bound to one another through social convention. That is, groups come up with their own sets of rules, norms, and laws by which individuals need to behave, and these rules arise out of public consensus. Relations in Gesellschaft groups tend to be perceived as relatively impersonal and somewhat contractual, which leads to the necessity of justice obligations to govern over disputes between individuals. In Gesellschaft groups, individuals can't be expected always to behave in prosocial ways toward others as they don't have strong obligations toward them, so formalized rules are necessary to keep people in line. When inter-personal relations are reduced to serving utilitarian means among autonomous individuals, as they largely are in Gesellschaft groups, then a morality of justice should take precedence.

In Gemeinschaft groups, the interpersonal obligations that bind individuals together are not objective or impartial enough to be governed by a system of justice and contracts (Snarey & Keljo, 1991). A good example of a Gemeinschaft group is the nuclear family. For the most part, it seems very unfamily-like for families to create contractual agreements regarding who will do the dishes, to govern disputes by appealing to abstract principles of justice, or to give each family member (including young children) equal rights and power over all family decisions. I realize that among some North American families there has been a growing trend in this direction (take the example of children suing their parents, or parents paying children piecemeal rates for completing various chores), which is evidence that North America has become such a prototype of Gesellschaft relations that even the nuclear family has been affected. Throughout most of the world, these kinds of family arrangements would be viewed as incomprehensible, as many other cultures are more firmly entrenched in a Gemeinschaft tradition.

Ethic of Community in India. People the world over have obligations toward others; however, an important question is whether they interpret these as *moral* obligations. When I say "moral" here I means something specific, and something that might differ from people's typical understanding of the word. Moral obligations are different from other responsibilities in a couple of important ways. First, moral obligations are viewed as *objective obligations*. That is, people believe that they have an obligation to act in a certain way, even if there is no official rule or law that requires them to do so. If the obligation exists only when a law is present, then the obligation is perceived as a matter of convention.

Second, moral obligations are perceived as *legitimately regulated*. That is, people should be prevented from engaging in a moral violation, or they should be punished if they act in such a way. If people feel that someone should not be prevented from engaging in the act, then they are viewing the act as a matter of personal choice and not a moral obligation. Most Westerners, for example, would view pickpocketing as a violation of a moral obligation because stealing from another is perceived as wrong, regardless of what rules or laws exist, and that pickpockets should be prevented from stealing. In contrast, most Westerners would view failing to attend a friend's graduation ceremony as a matter of personal choice rather than as a violation of a moral obligation. Westerners might expect people to attend their friend's ceremonies, but they generally don't think they should be punished for not attending. As another example, most Westerners would view a 17-year-old who bought a beer from a bar as committing a conventional violation, not a moral one, as they could imagine that in some cultural contexts this action would not be breaking a law. Violations are considered to be moral ones only if they are objective obligations that can be legitimately regulated.

One study contrasted the moral reasoning of Indians and Americans by comparing how they viewed a number of different episodes in which people were acting unkindly toward someone in need (Miller, Bersoff, & Harwood, 1990). The unkind behavior in these scenarios can be seen as violations of a social responsibility. The question the researchers considered was whether these violations were manipulated in moral terms. Two independent variables were varied in those scenarios. One, the extremity of the person's need varied, ranging from something that was a minor inconvenience to something that was potentially life-threatening. Second, the relationship between the actor and the recipient varied—whether the person in need was a young child of the target, a best friend of the target, or a stranger to the target. Here is an example of a low need situation with a best friend target:

> A 30-year-old woman wants directions to an art store. Her best friend
> is busy reading an exciting book and so she refuses to give the woman
> directions to the store.

Participants are then asked a number of questions regarding whether it would be acceptable in some contexts or cultures for the target not to help the friend (i.e., is it an objective obligation?), or whether the target should be made to help her friend (i.e., is it a legitimately regulated obligation?).

Figure 7.2 shows the percentage of participants that viewed the targets' behavior in moral terms (i.e., they saw it as an objective obligation that could be legitimately regulated). A few notable patterns emerged here. First, Indians and Americans are quite similar in their perceptions of moral obligations for people in extreme need situations. Almost everyone in both cultures felt that people had a moral obligation to help someone if that person was in a

FIGURE 7.2

Compared to
Americans, Indians
view a broader class
of ethical breaches
in moral terms.

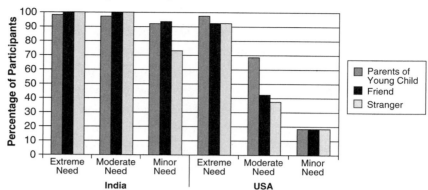

Percentage Viewing Breaches in Moral Terms

life-threatening situation. The preservation of life might be viewed as a universal moral obligation.

The cultures differed considerably more in their perceptions of the moderate and low need situations. Virtually all Indians viewed situations in which someone was in moderate need to be a moral obligation, regardless of their relation to that person. It seems that Indians viewed situations in which anyone who had a reasonable claim of need (some of the examples of episodes of unkind behavior were not comforting someone who was about to have knee surgery, or not providing a ride to someone who needed to go to a ceremony to give a speech) as ones in which they had a moral obligation to help. If someone decided that he or she wasn't going to comfort someone who was about to have knee surgery, Indians felt that the person should be punished, and that punishment would be deserved in all possible contexts. Although Americans were quite likely to think that parents had moral obligations toward their children in these situations, they saw very little moral obligation toward their friends or strangers here. Rather, the Americans tended to perceive the situations as matters of personal choice rather than something that a person could be forced to do. Note that this does *not* mean that Americans wouldn't help friends and strangers in these situations, but that they felt that they shouldn't be forced to help. Indians didn't see these as matters of choice, but felt that people could be forced to offer help if they didn't want to. Even in minor need situations (such as whether you offer someone directions or lend them money to see a movie) Indians were likely to perceive these in full moral terms, whereas Americans very rarely did.

Indians indicated that they felt people could be punished for not offering directions to a friend. Social responsibilities can take on full moral force among Indians in ways that they do not for most Americans.

The moral force of interpersonal obligations was more dramatically demonstrated in another study (Miller & Bersoff, 1992). It is one thing to say that you have a moral obligation, and it is quite another to decide to give up something important to fulfill that obligation. We can often gauge the strength of people's motivations by examining the kinds of things they would give up to preserve them. Imagine, if you will, what you would do if you were in Ben's situation below.

> Ben was in Los Angeles on business. When his meetings were over, he went to the train station. Ben planned to travel to San Francisco in order to attend the wedding of his best friend. He needed to catch the very next train if he was to be on time for the ceremony, as he had to deliver the wedding rings.
>
> However, Ben's wallet was stolen in the train station. He lost all of his money as well as his ticket to San Francisco.
>
> Ben approached several officials as well as passengers at the train station and asked them to loan him money to buy a new ticket. But, because he was a stranger, no one was willing to lend him the money he needed. While Ben was sitting on a bench trying to decide what to do next, a well-dressed man sitting next to him walked away for a minute. Looking over at where the men had been sitting, Ben noticed that the man had left his coat unattended. Sticking out of the man's coat pocket was a train ticket to San Francisco. Ben knew that he could take the ticket and use it to travel to San Francisco on the next train. He also saw that the man had more than enough money in his coat pocket to buy another train ticket.

What should Ben do? Should he steal the ticket so he can deliver the wedding rings to his best friend in time for the wedding, or should he not take the ticket and miss the wedding? Importantly, we have to imagine that these are the only two possible solutions—there would be no other way for Ben to get to the wedding in time.

This is a tough call, as obviously neither of these solutions is very satisfying. The first solution would require Ben to commit a justice violation, as he would be causing harm to the other innocent passenger. On the other hand, the second solution would require Ben to violate an interpersonal obligation, as his friend was counting on him to deliver the rings on time. Without the rings, the wedding would be ruined. Either way Ben is committing a violation. We would expect, however, that his decision will indicate which violation he perceives to be more serious. Think about what you would do if you were in Ben's shoes.

Participants were presented with a number of scenarios that pitted interpersonal and justice obligations against each other. Similar to the previous study, the extremity of the situation was varied; in this case, they varied in terms of how serious the justice violations were. In the example above, for Ben to steal the train tickets was seen as a moderate justice violation. Hindu Indian and American college students were asked to decide what the target in the scenarios should do: Should he protect the interpersonal obligation or should he protect the justice obligation? The results are shown in Figure 7.3.

One thing to note about these results is that aside from the Indians in the minor justice breach scenarios, there was a great deal of variability within cultures. Within each culture, many people would choose the justice obligation and many would choose the interpersonal obligation. There is not a widely shared understanding of what is the best way to resolve these kinds of conflicts. Despite this variation within cultures, there is a clear difference across cultures. Indians are more likely to resolve the conflict by fulfilling

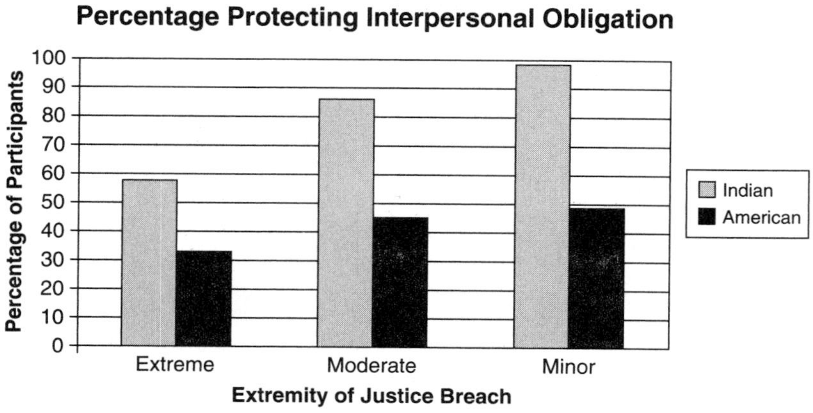

Percentage Protecting Interpersonal Obligation

FIGURE 7.3

When interpersonal and justice obligations conflict, Indians tend to prefer protecting interpersonal obligations, whereas Americans tend to prefer protecting justice obligations.

their interpersonal obligations than are Americans. Furthermore, other questions in the study revealed that whereas both Indians and Americans viewed the justice breaches in moral terms, Indians were far more likely to view the interpersonal breaches in moral terms (that is, objective obligations that could be legitimately regulated) than were Americans. This demonstrates just how seriously interpersonal obligations are taken by Indians—they were perceived as more serious than justice ones.

Ethic of Divinity

The third ethic that Shweder proposed was the ethic of divinity. The abstract ethical principle that Shweder argued to be inherent in this moral code was that one is obligated to respect or preserve the sanctity of the natural order of things, as dictated by a transcendent moral authority (such as God). Immoral actions according to this ethic are those that are perceived to violate the natural order of things. What does it mean to violate the natural order of things? To get an idea, consider the following scenario used in a study of violations of the ethic of divinity (Haidt, Koller, & Dias, 1993):

> A man goes to the supermarket once a week and buys a dead chicken. But before cooking the chicken, he has sexual intercourse with it. Then he cooks and eats it.

All right, perhaps I should have warned you that that was coming. I chose that example from the study because it's very effective at making the point. Now that you've read this, I'm guessing that you're most likely thinking this man's behavior is repulsive, bad, and disgusting; and that you might even be upset that I asked you to read it. If those are your feelings, you're probably sensing that the natural order of things has been breached. You're experiencing a violation of the ethic of divinity.

However, moral reasoning is not just about having a gut level reaction that some kinds of behaviors are bad. There are many kinds of actions that we perceive as bad, but not necessarily immoral. Remember that for something to be considered immoral we need to view it as universally wrong and as something that should be prevented. In this particular example, let's assume that the man's behavior was part of a regular ritual in another culture. Would his behavior be wrong then? If you say "no," then you are making the case that this behavior can be understood as a social convention and thus not in full moral terms. Do you think this man should be prevented from doing this again, or punished in any way? Should we make laws against having sex with chickens, or forbid grocers from selling the man any more chickens? If you think "no," then you are interpreting his behavior as a matter of personal choice—a rather unsavory choice, to be sure—but a choice nonetheless.

When this scenario was posed to students at the University of Pennsylvania (who, on average, can be considered to be of high socioeconomic status), only 23% said that the man's behavior would be wrong even if this practice was part of a custom in another culture, and only 27% said that the man should be punished or prevented from doing this again. That is, the majority of Penn students did not view the man's behavior as immoral, although the vast majority perceived it to be quite disgusting.

The same question was also posed to high- and low-socioeconomic-status people in two cities in Brazil as well as to low-socioeconomic-status people in Philadelphia. People responded rather differently. Among the Brazilians, about 50% of the high-status participants viewed the practice to be universally wrong, and about 56% of them felt that the man should be punished. That is, roughly half of the high-status Brazilian participants viewed the behavior in moral terms. For the low-status Brazilians, in contrast, about 87% viewed the behavior as universally wrong, and about 83% felt that the man should be punished. The low-status Americans responded very similarly to the low-status Brazilians, with 87% universalizing their judgments and 80% believing that the man needs to be punished. That is, the majority of the low-status people, regardless of whether they were from Brazil or the United States, viewed the man's behavior as immoral.

Why do we find the same behavior viewed as largely not immoral by one group of participants and largely immoral by the other? Other questions the participants were asked shed some light on this question. They were also asked whether the man's behavior was causing harm to anyone or whether they would feel bothered if they saw his behavior. In general, most people did not see the man's behavior as causing anyone much harm, but most people said they would feel bothered if they witnessed this event, and these responses did not differ across the different samples. However, these questions did reveal an important cultural difference in terms of how people were concluding whether the behavior was immoral. For the high-status samples, particularly the students from Penn, participants were more likely to view the man's behavior as immoral if they felt that someone was being harmed than if they said they would feel bothered by the event. That is, whether they viewed the man's behavior as immoral hinged largely on whether these participants felt that the behavior caused anyone (usually the man himself, in this instance) any harm. They appeared to operate under the ethic of autonomy principle that moral violations stem from causing harm. In contrast, the low-status participants were more likely to view the man's behavior as immoral if they said they were bothered by the event than if they felt that anyone was being harmed. That is, a moral judgment was largely precipitated on whether these participants found the event to be bothersome or disgusting. The low-status participants were not relying much on an ethic of autonomy, and instead seemed affected by their emotional reaction to seeing a violation of the perceived natural order.

In sum, when we consider other ethical principles that can guide moral reasoning, it appears that the ethic of autonomy is not the only game in town. Furthermore, the tendency of the low-status participants in the Haidt study to base their moral decisions on how bothered they were suggests that the task of reaching moral judgments might not always occur in cold, cognitive terms, in the way that Kohlberg describes. Rather, people often come up with moral justifications to rationalize the strong emotions they have when witnessing undesirable behaviors (Haidt, 2001).

Culture Wars

One interesting point about the American participants in the Haidt study is that the data for the high- and low-status participants were collected just three blocks apart. The college student data were collected on the University of Pennsylvania campus, and the data from the low-socioeconomic-status people were collected from a street corner in an inner city neighborhood that bordered the campus. Three blocks was all that separated a world of difference in reasoning about what is immoral. This difference underscores something important: There are pronounced differences of opinion on moral issues even within a country, something that has been described as a "culture war" ongoing within the United States (Hunter, 1991).

Currently, there is a highly polarized public debate regarding a number of hot-button political issues in the United States. Some of the key topics of controversy are abortion, sexuality, and euthanasia. These debates are often marked by angry protests, and repeated arguments that go largely unheeded by the opposing groups. Why don't people come to accept the arguments from the other side and reach a peaceful consensus on these topics? Historically, it was believed that many of the differences of opinion on political issues within the United States were drawn along the lines separating religious denominations, such as Catholics, Jews, and Protestants. While religious denomination is one important way that cultural worldviews differ within the country, it is probably not the most relevant difference for making sense of the opposing political alliances that divide the nation today. Hunter proposed that a culture war exists in the United States and that the battle lines are drawn between those who have an "impulse toward orthodoxy" versus those who have an "impulse toward progressivism" (Hunter, 1991, p. 43), regardless of their religious denomination.

Religious adherents who are **orthodox** are committed to the idea of a transcendent authority. This authority is viewed to have existed long before humans and as operating independently of people. Furthermore, this authority is perceived to be more knowledgeable and more powerful than all of human experience. In the orthodox view this transcendent authority originated a moral code and revealed it to human beings in the sacred texts of the respective religion. This moral code is perceived to stand across all times and circumstances and should not be altered to accommodate any societal changes or individual differences. Rather, individuals and society are expected to adapt themselves to this ordained moral code (Jensen, 1997).

On the other hand, adherents of **progressive** religions emphasize the importance of human agency in understanding and formulating a moral code. Progressivists reject the view that a transcendent authority reveals itself and its will to humans; they believe that humans play an integral role in the formulation of a moral code. Progressivists believe that because social circumstances change, our moral code must change along with them. In this important way, progressivists differ from the orthodox. Note, however, that this is a broad distinction, and an individual's religious impulses and political values do not always fall so neatly into these two types.

Which of Shweder's three moral ethics are typically used by orthodox and progressivists when they reason about moral issues? Jensen (1997) reasoned that the ethic of divinity seems to bear a close affinity with orthodox conceptions of morality. Orthodox individuals seek to follow sacred guidelines granted by a transcendent authority as they attempt to come closer to moral and spiritual purity. This emphasis appears to be very much in accordance with the emphasis on striving for purity and avoidance of degradation that characterizes the ethic of divinity. Likewise, the ethic of autonomy has many similarities with progressivists' conceptions of morality. The ethic of autonomy allows individuals to choose what is right and wrong provided they do not encroach on the rights of others or cause harm. Hence, there are some theoretical parallels in the distinction between progressivists and the orthodox and the ethics of autonomy and divinity. The ethic of community, on the other hand, which defines moral agents in terms of their social groups and views moral obligations as stemming from the individual's memberships in those groups, seems to characterize all religious orientations, regardless of whether one is more orthodox or progressivist. In sum, we might expect that the two camps of the "culture war" that Hunter refers to can be characterized by the ethics they use to make sense of what is right and wrong.

Jensen (1997) tested this hypothesis by contrasting American Baptists who belonged to either fundamentalist (orthodox) sects or mainline (progressivist) sects. The participants were asked to explain their moral judgments on a variety of politically charged issues, such as suicide or divorce. Jensen examined their responses to see how similar their justifications were to each of the three ethics. For example, participants were asked whether they felt that abortion was wrong, and to explain their answer. Of the orthodox participants, 100% gave at least one reason that was consistent with the ethic of divinity—that is, they spoke of God's exclusive authority to end human life or they referred to the biblical injunction against taking another person's life. Here is an example reply from an orthodox Baptist to the question of abortion.

> In the Ten Commandments, [God] said that we should not commit murder. . . . I believe in general when a person disobeys God that it has negative repercussions. I think that's why God tells us the things that He does. He knows what's good for us, and if we'd listen to Him, we'd save [ourselves] a lot of trouble.

This participant's responses indicate that we have an obligation to respect God's commands, and that we would be better off if we did just that. There is no questioning of what God might have meant about murder, nor whether this commandment might be interpreted differently in the context of abortion in modern, Western societies. In contrast, when the progressivists reasoned about abortion, 90% of them offered at least one reason that was consistent with the ethic of autonomy; that is, they tended to emphasize that individuals had to interpret the scriptures and reach a conclusion for themselves that avoided harming others. Here's an example reply from a progressivist Baptist:

> There really has to be some sense of rightness and wrongness that has to transcend what God would think, or what the priest would think, or what my mother would think. It's not up to them, it's up to you. . . . I ultimately believe that every individual has to do what they have to do.

Overall, there were pronounced differences in the kinds of reasons that members of the different Baptist sects gave for justifying whether a practice could be seen as morally right or wrong. Figure 7.4 shows the average number of reasons given by midlife adult participants that were consistent with the three different ethics across all the different political issues (Jensen, 1997). Progressivists made moral decisions based primarily on the ethic of autonomy (stressing individual rights) and the ethic of community (stressing obligations toward others); the orthodox were more likely to make their

FIGURE 7.4

The justifications of orthodox Baptists tended to reflect the ethic of divinity, whereas the justifications of progressivist Baptists tended to reflect the ethics of autonomy and community.

judgments based on the ethic of divinity. The most pronounced differences were with respect to the ethic of divinity and the ethic of autonomy. Although the differences between sects were large, people from each sect occasionally offered justifications from each of the three different ethics. We all have the potential to reason in these three different ways, although we tend to favor one ethic over the others. There is a striking moral divide in the ways that people consider political issues, even within the same religion. Subsequent research by Jensen identified this same difference in the use of the three codes of ethics among progressive and orthodox Hindu Indians (Jensen, 1998), which demonstrates that this distinction within cultures is widespread—and is possibly universal. People make judgments of what is right and what is wrong in importantly different ways. What we aren't able to say from these data, however, is whether people learn these different reasoning styles from the churches they attend, or whether people with different reasoning styles choose to go to churches that are consistent with their dominant moral ethic. Regardless of the source of these moral reasoning differences, people do have markedly distinct ways of considering political issues.

Emotions and Moral Violations

How do we identify a moral violation? One argument is that we notice moral violations the same way we notice other events in the world that have relevance to us (Haidt, 2001): We have a feeling that we attend to. In Chapter 8 we'll discuss how emotions appear to have evolved to serve as cues to get us to act in ways that aid our survival. As an example, the feeling of fear serves as a useful signal that we should get out of harm's way. However, as humans are a social species, it follows that we would also benefit by having some emotions that help us to act in ways that facilitate our success in the social world. For instance, we feel angry when we believe that we've been cheated, and this emotion will guide our behavior in wanting to punish those who cheated us and discourage them from doing it again. Perhaps evolution has shaped our emotions to aid us in acting in moral ways, as moral behaviors facilitate our survival as a social species.

Is our morality built on a foundation of emotions? This view has been controversial and was rejected for some time, as earlier perspectives on moral reasoning focused on rational approaches that viewed reason and reflection to be the basis of moral judgments (e.g., Kohlberg, 1971; Turiel, Killen, & Helwig, 1987). Recent theorizing and research, however, is consistent with the idea that when we encounter moral violations we intuitively sense that something is wrong, and we attend to whatever our feelings are signaling (Haidt, 2001). Once we are aware that something appears to be wrong, we can come up with reasons to justify why the thing that sparked our negative emotional reaction must be a moral violation (Haidt & Joseph, 2004). That is, the reasoning follows the emotional experience.

Here is a dramatic demonstration of the primary role of emotions in moral reasoning (Wheatley & Haidt, 2005): In one study, highly hypnotizable participants were given a post-hypnotic suggestion to feel a flash of disgust whenever they encountered the word "often." Then participants read a number of vignettes, including one that described what was a completely innocuous behavior. That vignette read "Dan is a student council representative at his school. This semester he is in charge of scheduling discussions about academic issues. He *often* picks topics that appeal to both professors and students in order to stimulate discussion." Participants were then asked how much they approved of Dan's behavior. Those participants who had been hypnotized to feel disgust on reading the word "often" disapproved of Dan's behavior more than those who had been hypnotized to respond to a different word that was absent in the vignette. When asked to justify their decisions, those people who had felt disgust offered some rather bizarre reasons to disapprove of Dan's behavior. One participant said, "It just seems like he's up to something," while another referred to Dan as a "popularity-seeking snob." Apparently, the participants came up with rationalizations to make sense of why they inexplicably felt bad feelings on reading about Dan's behavior.

If emotions guide our morality, what specific emotions are involved? First, our emotional experiences will likely guide our *own* behavior in deciding what is right or wrong. The powerful emotions of guilt and shame can be effective in keeping us in line by having us conduct ourselves in ways consistent with an internalized view of the social order (Freud, 1900/1976; Rozin, Lowery, Imada, & Haidt, 1999). Knowing that acting in an immoral fashion is likely to make us feel really bad is one key reason we don't go about committing crimes or hurting others very often. At least this is true for most of us. Research on that small but highly visible and problematic group of people diagnosed as psychopaths reveals that one distinguishing feature of psychopaths is that they do not experience many feelings of guilt or shame (Hare, 1999). Not surprisingly, without these emotional ties to harness them in, psychopaths are far more likely than the rest of the population to engage in criminal behavior.

Humans appear to have also evolved emotions that are sensitive to moral violations in *others*. As research on Shweder's three codes of ethics has revealed, there are different kinds of moral violations that concern us. Rozin and colleagues (1999) propose that we don't attend to moral violations in general, but that we attend to the *specific* kind of moral violation we have perceived. They propose that we do this by having a different emotional reaction to violations of each of the three different codes of ethics.

Violations of the ethic of autonomy involve actions that directly hurt others because they infringe on their rights and freedoms as individuals. Rozin and colleagues maintain that when people feel that harm has been caused or rights have been taken away, they tend to respond with *anger*. That is, anger signals autonomy violations.

Violations of the ethic of community involve actions in which a person fails to carry out his or her duties within a community or within a hierarchical group. People who witness others who do not live up to their duties toward a group or who are not doing their share are predicted to have feelings of *contempt*: That is, they will tend not to like those who shun their duties. Contempt should signal community violations.

Violations of the ethic of divinity involve actions in which people disrespect the sacredness of God or causes impurities or degradations to themselves or to others. People who observe someone who violates the sacred natural order of things are predicted to have feelings of *disgust* about those behaviors. Disgust signals divinity violations.

A good way of remembering the model proposed by Rozin and colleagues is to look at the first letters of the ethics codes and corresponding emotions. They all match up nicely (Autonomy—Anger, Community—Contempt, Divinity—Disgust). You have to figure that any theory that has matching letters like this must be correct!

Rozin and colleagues tested their hypothesis by providing participants with a number of vignettes describing violations of the codes of autonomy, community, or divinity. The participants were asked to indicate what emotion best captured the feeling that the person in the vignette was likely to be having at the time. Table 7.1 shows a few examples of the ethics violations that they used.

TABLE 7.1
Examples of Ethics Violations

Autonomy Violation	Someone is edging ahead of a person in a long line.
Community Violation	A person is hearing about someone who doesn't go to his or her mother's funeral.
Divinity Violation	A person is hearing about a 70-year-old male who has sex with a 17-year-old female.

In accordance with the predictions of Rozin and colleagues, the most common emotional reaction people had to autonomy violations was anger; the most common emotional reaction to community violations was contempt; and the most common emotional response to violations of divinity was disgust. This pattern of reactions was significantly greater than what would be expected by chance. Moreover, this pattern was observed among both American and Japanese participants, suggesting that the model generalizes across cultures and might even be universal. However, many participants in the studies reported having other emotional reactions that were not predicted by the model. This might suggest that the relations between moral violations and emotion are not quite so clear-cut as their model suggests (recall how the hypnotized participants who felt disgust came to disapprove of Dan's student organizing behaviors, although there would seem to be little in the way of a divinity violation there). Alternatively, people's choosing emotions other than the ones predicted by this model might indicate that the specific vignettes described behaviors that violated more than one ethic. For example, it's possible that the vignette in Table 7.1 that described the divinity violation also incorporates an autonomy violation (the 17-year-old female's rights were violated), and a community violation (older men have duties to behave properly toward young women). This demonstrates that there may be considerable overlap among the different codes of ethics and that some actions can be offensive in multiple ways at once.

The Morality of Thoughts

In 1976, while running for the U.S. presidency, Jimmy Carter made a public apology. He confessed that he was guilty of having looked at women with lustful thoughts and of having committed adultery in his heart many times. Carter's confession raises an interesting moral question. Are we morally responsible for the thoughts we entertain? This question addresses the boundaries of our moral worlds—the domains in which we feel it is appropriate to make judgments about what is right and wrong versus the domains in which we feel that such judgments are not relevant. How do our cultural experiences shape where we draw this boundary?

We can contrast Carter's guilty feelings about his lustful fantasies with the apparently unrepentant feelings that Sigmund Freud had about all of the rather nasty thoughts that he entertained. Although there is no evidence that Freud engaged in much of the way of immoral behaviors (he was a highly respected citizen in Victorian era Austria), he certainly considered some provocative thoughts. A view of the rather sordid and wanton ideas that jostled about in Freud's mind is provided by exploring his vast and highly influential writings. Many of Freud's most memorable notions were generated, in part, as he explored his own dreams and introspections. These ideas included his views of the unconscious mind as a cauldron of seething urges, in which boys secretly desire to kill their fathers and have sex with their mothers, girls are distraught in their envy for not having a penis, and the whole of humanity struggles to corral their degenerate motivations to destroy life. If having bad thoughts was a moral issue, then Freud was guilty indeed. However, it is hard to imagine that Freud could have devoted so much thought and effort to exploring his introspections on these unsavory topics if he had felt much guilt for broaching them. Indeed, there is no evidence from his writings that such thoughts bothered him; yet, by all respects, he was an upstanding citizen. Apparently, Freud did not share Carter's view that one's thoughts fall into the domain of moral governance.

Carter and Freud differ from one another in many ways, and one that is relevant to their different moral reasoning is their religious backgrounds. Jimmy Carter was raised as a Southern Baptist, one of the most fundamentalist sects in Protestantism (although he abandoned the sect at the age of 76, interestingly, over a disagreement in moral worldviews). Freud was raised Jewish. Can we see differences in people's views on the morality of thoughts between these two cultural traditions?

Jewish and Christian dogma differ in terms of their holy scriptures. Jewish doctrine is based on the Hebrew Bible and the debates on this doctrine that are included in the Talmud. In contrast, Christian doctrine is based in part on the Hebrew Bible (known to Christians as the Old Testament) but is primarily oriented toward the New Testament, which includes the teachings of Jesus. Exploring these texts reveals some differences relevant to the morality of thoughts. The first place in the Christian Bible that we see clear evidence that thoughts were to be moralized is in the New Testament. It is there that Jesus made the point later echoed by Jimmy Carter, "you have heard that it was said 'you shall not commit adultery': but I say to you, that everyone who looks on a woman to lust for her has committed adultery with her already in his heart" (Matthew 5: 27–28: New American Standard version).

In contrast, the Old Testament contains the foundation of the Judeo-Christian moral code in the Ten Commandments. It is interesting that 8 of the 10 commandments specifically refer to behaviors (e.g., killing is wrong, stealing is wrong), and only two refer to thoughts (e.g., it is wrong to not honor one's parents, it is wrong to covet anything of your neighbor). Even with these last two, however, there is debate as to whether they refer to thoughts or behaviors. Cohen and Rozin (2001) showed that whereas Protestants were more likely to view the commandment to honor one's parents in terms of having respectful thoughts toward one's parents, Jews were more likely to view it in terms of one's behaviors (e.g., honoring your parents by taking care of them when they're old). In sum, there is evidence of a transition from a general emphasis on being a good person by behaving in moral ways that characterized the Jewish half of the Bible (the Old Testament) to an emphasis on being a good person by thinking in moral ways, as stressed in the Christian half of the Bible (the New Testament).

There is also a greater emphasis on faith in Christianity (especially Protestantism) than in Judaism. For example, membership in Judaism is defined by descent; traditionally, one becomes Jewish by being born to a Jewish biological mother. In contrast, membership in Protestant sects is primarily defined by beliefs. For example, one does not become a member of the Baptist church until one publicly accepts the Christian faith and is baptized. The New Testament states "that whosoever believeth in him [Jesus, that is] should not perish, but have eternal life" (John 3:15). In contrast to this emphasis on beliefs in Christianity, much of traditional Judaism emphasizes particular practices, such as keeping kosher by avoiding certain foods, like pork. Jewish faith does not state that it is wrong to *desire* nonkosher foods; what is important is that one doesn't eat them. In contrast, compared with Judaism, Christianity has fewer practices and instead places more emphasis on one's private communications with God. Reflecting this differential emphasis in practices and beliefs, a survey asked Jewish and Protestant participants how important practices and beliefs were for being religious; the results revealed that Jewish participants rated practices as more important than beliefs for being religious, whereas Protestants put greater emphasis on beliefs than practices (Cohen, Siegel, & Rozin, 2003).

Would Christians and Jews differ in their views on whether it was wrong for people to have bad thoughts, even if they never acted upon them? In one study, participants read some vignettes that described people who were thinking about immoral behaviors (Cohen & Rozin, 2001). Here is a sample vignette from the study.

> Mr. B. is a 1992 graduate of the University. Since graduation, Mr. B. has worked at an entry-level job in a marketing firm. Mr. B. married his University sweetheart six months after they both had their graduation from University. Mr. B. and his wife do not have any children. One of Mr. B.'s colleagues at work is a very attractive woman. This woman sometimes flirts with Mr. B. and they both know that she would be willing to have a sexual affair with him. For an average of about 20 minutes a day, Mr. B. consciously entertains thoughts about having a sexual affair with his colleague by thinking about where they would have an affair and what it would be like to have an affair with her.

After reading the vignette, participants were asked some questions about Mr. B. One question they were asked was what they thought of Mr. B. The Protestant participants reported viewing Mr. B. in significantly more negative terms than the Jewish participants did. Having adulterous thoughts is viewed as more immoral by Protestants than Jews. A second question asked how bad it would be if Mr. B. actually had the sexual affair. Importantly, Jewish participants viewed sexual affairs in at least as negative terms as the Protestant participants did. There was no difference between the religions in how they viewed immoral *behaviors*. Even though there were no religious differences in terms of the perceived immorality of the behaviors, there was a pronounced religious difference in people's reactions to someone thinking about engaging in such behaviors. Apparently, Protestants view one's thoughts to be governed by moral concerns, whereas Jews do not. The moral domain for Jews is focused on what people do, and not what they think about doing.

This religious difference suggests that Protestants and Jews might have different theories about how the mind works. If you can be held morally responsible for your thoughts it would seem that you must believe these thoughts to be somewhat under your control. It hardly makes sense to morally condemn something that is beyond an individual's control. Not surprisingly, research reveals that Protestants believe people have more control of their thoughts than Jews do (Cohen & Rozin, 2001). Furthermore, one reason to be concerned about someone engaging in immoral thoughts is the possibility that these thoughts might increase the likelihood that the person will engage in the immoral behavior. Indeed, Protestants, more than Jews, have been shown to believe that thoughts lead to behaviors (Cohen & Rozin, 2001). Protestants tend to see thoughts as greasing the path toward behaviors. Not only do the religions differ in their beliefs in the morality of thoughts; they differ importantly in their beliefs about what thoughts do and whether we can control them.

Culture and Distributive Justice

Another way to consider what people view as right and wrong is by attending to the ways that they distribute resources. We can go about assigning rewards (or punishments) to individuals in a number of different ways, and these ways speak to our beliefs about what is fair. For example, your instructor can give out a limited number of good grades to the class. What is the most fair way for your instructor to distribute them? One way would be to distribute them by the **principle of need.** The principle of need dictates that resources are directed toward those who need them the most. If your instructor operated on the principle of need, he or she would give the best grades to those students who were in most need of them. A student, say, who was planning to go to law school as a means to earn the money to support his sick mother would receive a higher grade than a student who was going to become a professional athlete. A second way that grades could be distributed is by the **principle of equality.** This principle dictates that resources should be shared equally among the members of a group. Your instructor, in this case, could assign everyone in the class the exact same grade, regardless of what each one did in the course. Or your instructor could distribute grades based on the **principle of equity.** This principle states that resources are distributed based on an individual's contributions. The more an individual produces, the more resources he or she receives. The ratio between individuals' inputs (their efforts and abilities in the course) and their outputs (the grades they receive) are held constant. Instructors following this principle would distribute grades based on how many questions the students answered correctly on the exam.

Grades are an unusual resource as they serve the function of indicating how much one has learned, rather than of being a reward in their own right. Because of this, it is likely that instructors everywhere operate exclusively on the principle of equity. However, in the distribution of other kinds of resources, such as salary, the principle of equity is not so universal. The principle of equity does appear to be the dominant form of resource distribution in the West. Most companies in the West compensate their employees by basing their salary largely on what the individual achieves. A pure example of the principle of equity can be seen in companies where salespeople are paid exclusively by commission. The more one sells, the more one earns, and the ratio between one's inputs and outputs is held constant. A social system that rewards individuals on the basis of the equity principle is known as a **meritocracy**, and meritocracies tend to be more common in individualistic societies. Meritocracies have their benefits and costs. They can lead workers to be highly motivated to work hard, as their earnings depend on their efforts, and this tends to increase productivity. However, because there usually is only a finite amount of resources that can be distributed among employees, when one worker does especially well, this means that the others are doing relatively worse, and will be paid less. Meritocratic systems tend to breed competition among workers, thereby potentially disrupting harmonious relations among them.

In much of the rest of the world (and in industries in the West that have a more collectivistic base through the power of labor unions), the principle of equality is adhered to more. In practical terms, the principle of equality is rarely applied in its strongest form, which would be that every individual receives the exact same level of compensation. Rather, equality tends to be preserved within a certain range of constraints, such as one's age, or official credentials. So, for example, all individuals might get the same size of raise each year; however, those who have been at the company longer have

"O.K., if you can't see your way to giving me a pay raise, how about giving Parkerson a pay cut?"

received more raises and hence are being compensated more. This latter system is known as a **seniority system**, in which time with the company or age are being rewarded. Seniority systems reflect the principle of equality as there is no competition among individuals for compensation. It is determined by the same calculus for everyone. Seniority systems weaken the link between one's inputs and one's outputs so that individuals might not be motivated to work as hard, although they do promote harmonious relations by decreasing intragroup competition. Interestingly, although it is often assumed that merit-based pay is the way to ensure the greatest amount of effort from one's employees, Japanese workers have traditionally been among the hardest working in the world (e.g., there is a great deal of voluntary overtime and many never take their vacations), and Japanese companies tend to have more seniority-based pay than American organizations (e.g., Ouchi & Jaeger, 1978). The relation between efforts and the principle of equity or equality appears to depend considerably on the cultural context.

The principle of need is institutionalized in most modern industrialized societies through institutions such as universal health insurance where the sick get more benefits than the healthy, or a welfare system, in which those who are needy receive more benefits than those who are not. However, the principle of need also governs people's beliefs in distributing resources in many less formal situations, such as contributing to charities, or giving money to beggars.

Which of these three principles of distributing resources do you think is the most fair? Your answer to this reflects your underlying values—values that have likely been shaped by the norms that you have been exposed to in your culture.

Consider the following study that explored how these different principles of resource distribution were embraced across cultures (Murphy-Berman, Berman, Singh, Pachauri, & Kuman, 1984). The researchers presented Indian

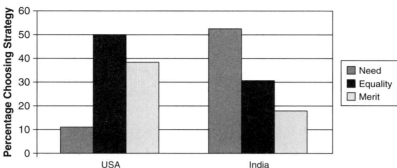

FIGURE 7.5

When allocating resources, Americans are more likely to emphasize equality and merit, whereas Indians are more likely to emphasize need.

and American participants with a scenario describing a company that had to make a decision about distributing a bonus between two employees. One of the employees was described as having excellent work performance and had an adequate economic situation. The other employee had only average work performance, but was in a poor financial situation with an illness in the family. The participants needed to decide how to divide up the bonus money. They could choose to give most of the money to the excellent worker, most of the money to the needy worker, or they could split it evenly down the middle. Figure 7.5 shows the results. The most popular solution for the Americans was to split the money down the middle (the equality principle) with a decision to favor the excellent employee (the equity principle) being a close second. Americans viewed the decision to favor the needy employee (the need principle) to be the least desirable. In stark contrast, the favorite solution of Indians was to give the majority of the money to the needy employee, and the least favorite solution was to reward the excellent employee.

A similar study that contrasted Japanese and Australian workers found that Australians preferred an equitable distribution of rewards more positively than did Japanese (Kashima, Siegal, Tanaka, & Isaka, 1988). What is perceived as fair and just, then, can vary importantly around the world. Westerners are more likely than those from other cultures to view the equity principle to be the most fair. Indians are most impressed by allocations that take into account the need of the parties involved.

SUMMARY

People do not share the same foundation for their morals around the world, and this is at the root of many disagreements both between and within cultures. There are at least three separate codes of ethics by which people can reason morally, and these vary in their distribution around the world. High-socioeconomic Westerners who belong to progressive sects are likely to base their moral judgments on the ethic of autonomy. With this ethic, they base their judgments of right and wrong on whether individual rights have been protected and justice has been delivered. A violation of this ethic is signaled by the experience of anger. In India, and likely other cultures in which inter-dependent concerns are more salient, people are likely to make moral judgments based on the ethic of community. This ethic maintains that people have interpersonal duties toward others that they are morally obligated to uphold. People feel contempt toward those who do not fulfill their duties. Among lower-socioeconomic Westerners and adherents of orthodox religions, people are more likely to subscribe to the ethic of divinity. Actions that violate the perceived natural order of things and sully God's creations are viewed in moral terms. Disgust is the emotional signal that the ethic of divinity has been violated.

There is variation in the domains under which people consider whether moral violations have occurred. Protestants appear to view thoughts in moral terms, as they believe that thoughts are relatively controllable and lead to future behaviors. In contrast, Jews tend not to view thoughts in moral terms, as they believe that they are less controllable and are less likely to lead to future behaviors.

The ways that people distribute resources are indicative of their perceptions of what is fair and just. The principle of equity, in which resources are tied to an individual's contributions, is more favored in the West than it is in India or Japan. In contrast, the principle of need, in which resources go to the needy, is respected more in India.

Emotions

Liget is a key emotion in the life of the Ilongot—an indigenous hunting and gathering tribe that lives in the Northern Philippines. One cannot really understand many of the customs of the Ilongot unless one understands *liget*. But understanding *liget* is somewhat of a challenge for English speakers as the concept does not map neatly on to any English emotion terms. The closest approximation is a combination of the English words anger, passion, and energy. The anthropologist Michelle Rosaldo (1980) provides a detailed account of *liget* among the Ilongot, with whom she lived for a number of years. *Liget* is experienced when one is insulted, disappointed, irritated, but especially when one is envious of another. It can be aroused by all-night songfests, pride of accomplishments, or the death of a loved one. *Liget* is seen as a wellspring of energy. When an individual's *liget* gets worked up it can allow the person to work in the fields all day or to climb high in the trees. As one of Rosaldo's informants said, "If it were not for *liget*, we'd have no life, we'd never work." *Liget* is something that derives from interactions among people, particularly when they compete against each other and become envious of others' accomplishments. It is also sometimes cultivated through various magic rituals. *Liget* is believed to exist in concentrated form in semen, and thus it is assumed to be more common among men than among women (although women can, at times, feel much *liget* as well). But primarily, *liget* is possessed by striving youths, energetic hunters, and violent men.

The most dramatic demonstration of *liget* occurs in the Ilongot's head-hunting rituals. Until the 1970s, the Ilongot frequently engaged in head-hunting raids on neighboring tribes. When asked why they killed others in these raids, the men would answer that they kill because of *liget*. Head-hunting is a demonstration of the strong feelings of *liget* that are believed to make men great. On these raids, men would play reed flutes and pound their heads to heighten their *liget* as they headed off on a trek to a distant village.

Two Ilongot youth engaged in a ritual duel.

Once their *liget* had reached a crescendo, further fueled by chewing on the narcotic leaves of the betel nut, they would rush in and attack their victim. The attack would end when the victor would toss the severed head of his victim high into the air. After the raid had ended, the victors would sing a celebratory song, put flowery reeds in their hair, and return to their villages empowered, glorified, and full of *liget*.

A question to consider here is how universal is the emotion *liget*? Do you think you have ever felt *liget*? Not its display in a head-hunting ritual, of course, but the emotion itself—a frothy feeling of anger, passion, and energy that can lead either to extreme concentration and productivity or to chaos. Likewise, do you think the Ilongot might ever feel the same kinds of emotions that you do? For example, think of a situation that has made you embarrassed, and how you felt at that time. Now imagine how you think Ilongots would feel in that same situation. Do you think they would feel the same as you did, or would their motions be different? If you think their feelings would be different, do you think they could ever have the same kinds of feelings that you experienced in your situation?

I imagine that it's difficult for you to answer these questions. It's hard enough to imagine how someone else from our own culture would feel, let alone someone from a culture as distant as the Ilongot. Yet these are precisely the kinds of questions that emotions researchers have been wrestling with. And I think "wrestling" is an apt metaphor in this case, as the question of whether emotional experiences are similar or different across cultures is one of the most contentious in cultural psychology.

The controversy regarding the role of culture and emotion focuses on a fundamental question that has guided our investigation in the other chapters in this book: to what extent are our psychological experiences universal and to what extent are they shaped by our cultural experiences? In the case of emotion, as you will see, there have been strong arguments made for both cases—that emotions are experienced identically around the world and that cultural experiences determine the kinds of emotions one has. Scholarly debates are very important to a field, as they force researchers to sharpen their arguments and lead people to conduct clever studies that provide evidence to shed light on the disagreements. The study of culture and emotions is a classic example of such a debate, and this chapter will consider the evidence regarding whether people's emotional experiences are similar or different across cultures. Let's take a stroll down the front lines of this controversy.

What Is an Emotion?

Before we can begin a fruitful investigation into a topic it's necessary to have a good understanding of what we are studying. But herein lies the rub. Emotions turn out to be remarkably difficult to define. For the most part, we feel that we can recognize our emotions easily enough. We feel quite sure that we know when we feel happy or afraid—these are highly salient and important experiences in our lives. In many ways, emotions are a central and focal part of our subjective worlds. Although emotions are perceived as very central to the human experience, describing what they are is not at all straightforward. The controversy that exists regarding the similarities and differences of people's emotional experience around the world is surely based on the disagreement about how we can define emotions in the first place. Let's consider two different theoretical perspectives regarding the nature of emotions that have guided the debate regarding the universality or relativity of emotional experience.

The James-Lange Theory of Emotions. As with so many other key ideas in American psychology, the study of emotions begins with William James

(James, 1950/1890). James proposed a thought experiment in which we imagine that someone out for a hike has stumbled upon a bear. The hiker's heart starts pounding and he runs away experiencing that highly salient emotion of fear. James's question was, "What is the fear that the hiker experienced in this situation?" Where precisely is the emotion here? His answer was that it was the hiker's pounding heart. That is, James proposed that our emotions are the physiological responses or "bodily reverberations" to stimuli in our worlds. A contemporary of James, Carl Lange, proposed that these physiological responses were products of our autonomic nervous system, such as changes in our heart rate, breathing, pupil dilation, tear secretion, blood flow to our skin, and stomach contractions, and the theory became known as the **James–Lange theory of emotions**.

The James-Lange theory maintains that our bodies respond to stimuli in the world by preparing us to react in a survival-facilitating way (such as running away from the bear), and our emotions are our bodily changes that signal how we should behave. As James reasoned, what would be left of our feelings of joy, rage, love, or any emotion if we removed the heart palpitations, queasiness in the stomach, or muscle tension? We'd be left with a pure, cold, intellectual state like that of Spock on *Star Trek*. According to James, emotions are precisely those physical sensations that make us feel human.

We of course have a wide variety of different emotions, and this suggests that we must also have an accordingly wide variety of bodily responses. James felt that each emotion word that we have is the description of a different bodily state. Embarrassment is the sensation of our blood rushing to our faces, love is the feeling of our stomach turning end over end, and fear is the sensation of our pounding hearts. Emotions, according to this view, are all about our physiological experiences. And some research has revealed support for the James-Lange theory in identifying distinctive physiological patterns that correspond to certain emotions (e.g., Ekman, Levenson, & Friesen, 1983; Levenson, 1992), although other surveys of the literature call into question the specificity of the physiological patterns associated with emotion (Barret, 2006; Cacioppo, Berntson, Larsen, Poehlmann, & Ito, 2000; Murphy, Nimmo-Smith, & Lawrence, 2003; Phan, Wager, Taylor, & Liberzon, 2002).

Since he first proposed it, James's theory of emotions has since been expanded in many ways, so that emotions are no longer seen to be just the physiological experience, but also include appraisals, nonverbal expressions, neural patterns, and subjective feelings (e.g., Barrett & Russell, 1999;

Ellsworth, 1992; Mesquita & Frijda, 1992). However, its focus on the physiological experience has been central to a number of key theories on emotional experience (Ekman, 1972; LeDoux, 1996; Panksepp, 1998).

The Two-Factor Theory of Emotions. Not everyone saw things the same way as James. Another contemporary of James, Walter Cannon, quickly criticized the James-Lang theory because the autonomic nervous system seemed to be too clumsy and slow to be differentiated into all the emotional states we experience. In some ways, it seemed at the time that the key components of the autonomic nervous system, the sympathetic and parsympathetic nervous systems, were either just turned on or off. Cannon thought that such a simple and ponderous system could not provide the complexity to cover the wide array of emotions we feel. Those researchers who conceptualized the autonomic nervous system as too diffuse and ungainly offered a different take on what emotions are (for a review, see Barrett, 2006). Rather than viewing emotions as primarily consisting of our physiological responses, this competing school of thought maintained that emotions were primarily our *interpretations* of those bodily responses. This view, the **two-factor theory of emotion** (named for the factors of the physiological signals and the interpretation of those signals), redirected the focus of emotions away from the physical body and into the mind.

Stanley Schacter and Jerome Singer were the most famous proponents of the two-factor theory. They contended that emotion researchers had neglected to study people's interpretations of their physiological sensations because the earlier studies and thought experiments had never separated people's interpretations from their actual physiological sensations. Their reasoning suggests that the hiker in James's thought experiment experienced fear at sensing his pounding heart because there was no other reasonable way to interpret his bodily sensations in that situation. One could imagine other situations in which the hiker's heart would be pounding—for example, being on a steamy date with an attractive partner—when the hiker would interpret his physiological sensations as indicating that he was in love. Schacter and Singer reasoned that you could identify the separate roles of the interpretation and the physiological sensation only if you disentangled them. Their way of doing so was to conduct an elaborate experiment that controlled for the source of participants' physiological arousal and their interpretation of that arousal.

To separate their participants' interpretations from the source of their arousal Schacter and Singer (1962) needed to do two things. First, they needed to provide the participants with situational cues to guide their interpretation. They did this by having participants assigned to a situation that was to lead them to interpret their feelings as euphoria or to one that would lead them to interpret their feelings as anger. Those assigned to the "euphoria" condition were asked to complete a questionnaire in a lab stocked with props and a confederate, whose job it was to get the participant in a giddy, playful mood. The confederate did this by playing with the props, such as shooting wads of paper at the participant with a slingshot, making paper airplanes, and playing with a hula hoop that was lying around. The researchers reasoned that participants in this condition should interpret any arousal they were feeling as due to their feeling giddy—or, in the experimenter's terminology, euphoric. In contrast, participants assigned to the "anger" condition completed a questionnaire alongside the same confederate, whose job here was to get the participant to join him in expressing his frustration and outrage at the rudeness of the items in the questionnaire. The questionnaire helped the confederate with this task as it included a list of rather insulting items such as "Which member of your immediate family does not bathe or wash regularly?" and "With how many men (other than your father) has your mother had extramarital relationships?" If that last question was not enough, the lowest answer that the participant could select as a response to it was "4 and under"! Participants in this condition should interpret any physiological arousal that they were feeling as due to their anger at being subjected to such an insulting situation.

The second factor that Schacter and Singer manipulated was the amount of physiological arousal the participants would be experiencing. Under the guise that the experiment was investigating how a new vitamin called Suproxin affected vision, participants were given an injection under one of four different conditions. In a Placebo condition, participants were given an injection of saline and were truthfully told that the injection would not have any side effects on their state of arousal. In an Epinephrine-Informed condition participants were given an injection of epinephrine, and were truthfully told that the injection would cause their arousal to increase. Epinephrine is the synthetic equivalent of adrenaline, a neurotransmitter that heightens arousal in the sympathetic nervous system. In an Epinephrine-Uninformed condition, participants were given an injection of epinephrine, but they were falsely told that it *would not have any side effects* of increased arousal. Last, in an Epinephrine-Misinformed condition (which was run only with participants in the Euphoria situation), participants were given the shot of epinephrine, but they were falsely told that it would have the side effect of *decreasing their arousal*. These last two conditions were key. Participants in them should have felt a great deal of physiological arousal from the injection, but they wouldn't know where the arousal came from. Schacter and Singer reasoned that they would look to the situation to interpret their feelings (especially for those in the Epinephrine-Misinformed condition), and they would conclude that their arousal was due to their experiences in the situation: that is, either due to their giddy feelings from goofing around with the confederate in the Euphoria condition or to their annoyance from being insulted in the Anger condition. In contrast, the researchers predicted that participants in the Placebo condition would experience little arousal and thus would experience little emotion. Likewise, those in the Epinephrine-Informed condition would experience little emotion because, although they experienced much physiological arousal, they would attribute it to the side effects of the injection they had received. Emotion in the study was measured both by having participants indicate their feelings on a questionnaire and by having hidden observers note the facial expressions the participants were making.

Although the results of the study were somewhat complicated, in general they supported Schacter and Singer's predictions (for a simplified summary see Table 8.1). The strongest emotions were experienced by those in the Epinephrine-Misinformed and Epinephrine-Uniformed conditions. Participants in these conditions were feeling a great deal of arousal but they had no good explanation for it. So they came to interpret their arousal by looking to the situation they were in. Those who were in the Euphoria situation

---

TABLE 8.1
Schacter and Singer's Findings: Evidence Supporting the Two-Factor Theory of Emotion

	Euphoria Condition	*Anger Condition*
Placebo condition	Relatively little euphoria	Relatively little anger
Epinephrine-Informed condition	Relatively little euphoria	Relatively little anger
Epinephrine-Uninformed condition	Much euphoria	Much anger
Epinephrine-Misinformed condition	Most euphoria	(Condition wasn't run)

explained their arousal as a result of their feeling euphoric while those in the anger situation attributed it to their feeling angry. The emotional experience came from participants interpreting their arousal in light of their beliefs of the situations that they were in. If the same physiological information can be interpreted as either euphoria or anger, two very distinct emotional experiences, then this suggests that despite the different physiological patterns that different emotional states might have (e.g., Ekman et al., 1983; Levenson, 1992), we don't have an especially fine-tuned awareness of our bodily sensations. Much subsequent research, using a variety of manipulations of arousal and several measures of emotions (e.g., Dutton & Aron, 1974; Zillman, 1978), have converged to show that people look to cues from their environment to help them label their physical sensations.

The James-Lange theory and the two-factor theory suggest two very different origins for our emotions, and these theories make different predictions regarding whether emotional experience is universal or culturally variable. If the various extensions of the James-Lange theory are correct—that emotions are largely based on the particular and specific physiological reactions that people have to various events—this suggests an evolutionary origin to human emotions. That is, if our emotions are specific biological signals that alert us to events in our worlds, it would follow that this biological machinery must have been assembled through evolution. For example, the physiological signals of fear that we experience upon encountering the bear in the woods serves us well in aiding us to get our bodies out of harm's way. In the past, individuals who did not experience those physiological signals of fear were more likely to have been caught by the bear and thus wouldn't have had the chance to pass their genes down to the next generation. Over millions of generations these affective signals would have been adaptive for our ancestors, and they thus became part of our genetic code. And because we share the same genetic code, and we all share the same ancestors up until very recently (it was not until about 60,000 years ago that some Homo sapiens left Africa), we have all inherited these adaptive physiological signals. The James-Lange theory thus suggests that people in all cultures should have the same emotional experiences. In support of this, research reveals that there are distinctive physiological patterns of emotions that are similar among people from diverse cultural backgrounds (e.g., Levenson, Ekman, Heider, & Freisen, 1992; Tsai, Chentsova-Dutton, & Freire-Bebeau, 2002; but see Barrett, 2006, for a contrary view). The James-Lange theory, and other theories that focus on the centrality of physiology in emotions, makes the case for universality in emotional experience.

On the other hand, if the two-factor theory of emotions is correct—that emotions are our interpretations of our physiological signals—this suggests that in addition to a physiological basis, our emotions are grounded in the belief systems that shape our interpretations. Because our belief systems are influenced a great deal by culture (e.g., Markus & Kitayama, 1991; Schwartz, 1994), the two-factor theory suggests that people might interpret their physiological signals in different ways across cultures. And research reveals important cultural differences in the experience of emotions (e.g., Kitayama, Mesquita, & Karasawa, 2006; Mesquita, 2001; Tsai, Knutson, & Fung, 2006). The two-factor theory, and other theories that focus on the centrality of interpretation in emotions, thus makes the case for cultural variability in emotional experience.

The Role of Appraisals in Emotions. One feature that is common to theories derived from both the above perspectives is their recognition that we have physiological responses to events that we witness in our environments. One key point, however, is that the emotional response is not determined directly by the event itself. Rather, it is our **appraisal** of what the event means that leads to the response. Appraisals are the way we evaluate events in terms of their relevance to our well-being. For example, in James's famous thought experiment, the hiker stumbling upon the bear had a fear response. However, bears are not necessarily frightening—for example, think of how cute they look in zoos. It is not the perception of the bear per se that leads to our physiological response, but it is our appraisal of the bear as being potentially threatening to us that sparks the emotion. Bears in zoos aren't a threat to us, so we don't feel scared when we see them.

Because humans are all of the same species, we have a number of common concerns that should lead to similar appraisals. Our environments share a number of common features, and everywhere people confront situations that, for example, provide them with opportunities for gain, cause them to lose something precious, are novel, place them in competition with others, are potentially hazardous to their health, and provide them with access to mates. Given the overall similarity of humans' environments and basic needs that humans share, there should be a good deal of similarity in the ways people appraise events across cultures. And universally similar appraisals should lead to universally similar emotional responses. We would expect that people everywhere, for example, would feel fear when their life is threatened, disgust when smelling rotten meat, and sadness when their child dies because these are experiences that are universally encountered, and they also should have similar meanings around the world. Much research has explored how some emotional appraisals are arguably universal (e.g., Boucher & Brandt, 1981), and thus importantly shed light on how the particular emotions evolved to serve as signals to guide people's behaviors (Rozin, Lowery, Imada, & Haidt, 1999; Tracy & Robins, 2006a).

On the other hand, there are also many differences in how people view events across cultures. Cultures differ in the ways people in them conceive of hazards, novelty, opportunities, and loss (Ellsworth, 1992). People from different cultures differ in their beliefs about how the world works (e.g., Chiu, Dweck, Tong, & Fu, 1997) and in what they view to be of value (e.g., Schwartz, 1994). How we appraise a situation is going to depend a great deal on how we understand what that situation means and its significance to us. Cultural differences in beliefs and values are going to shape the appraisals that people draw from events they encounter.

For example, consider the emotional response people will have upon discovering that they are sick. Illness is a universal problem for all humans, and thus you would expect many similarities in people's emotional responses around the world. However, there are good reasons to expect differences because cultures vary in their theories about what those illnesses mean. First, there is a great deal of cultural variability in terms of people's beliefs of the causes of illnesses. An American businessman who gets sick might see his illness as due to the guy on the subway who didn't cover his mouth when he sneezed. A Chinese mother might view that same illness in terms of an imbalance in her body caused by the stress that she was feeling because of a disagreement between her two uncles. An Azande tribesman might view the same illness as due to a witch in his community (perhaps posing as his best friend) casting a spell on him. A devout Catholic teacher might see the same illness as evidence that God is angry with her. A Ukrainian farmer might see an illness as coming from his failure to spit three times when he praised a neighbor's baby. Different explanations of the causes of events are going to lead to different appraisals of them. Furthermore, cultures will differ in their perceptions of the consequence and significance of getting sick. Having an illness might lead one to be shunned by the community, get the day off from work, worry about passing the illness on to one's old and frail neighbor who might not survive it, fall behind in one's assignments, be suspected of witchcraft, or suspect that it's the first sign of something more serious, such as AIDS. Cultures will vary both in terms of the likelihood that certain outcomes will occur and how people will view the significance of these outcomes. Hence, individuals in different cultures can have distinct appraisals of the same stimulus, the illness, because they are explaining the illness in different ways; and because the illness is going to have different consequences for them, these different appraisals should lead to different emotional responses. In sum, commonalities in people's appraisals across cultures will lead to similar emotional experiences, whereas cross-cultural divergences in people's appraisals will lead to different emotional experiences.

So how we appraise situations determines the emotional response that we have to them. The relation between appraisals and emotions, however, is a little tricky. For example, consider how you might appraise the situation of what it is like to throw stones at ptarmigans (which are small birds that live in the Arctic). How would that situation make you feel? Many Utku Eskimos describe this situation as one that makes them feel especially happy (Briggs, 1970). Throwing stones at ptarmigans can thus be a basis of happiness. In contrast, a study exploring the antecedents of happiness among Belgians found no one who described throwing stones at ptarmigans (Scherer, Wallbott, & Summerfield, 1986). So does this mean that there's a cultural difference in the experience of happiness between Utku and Belgians?

We can make sense of this question in two ways. One way is to think that both Utku and Belgians feel happy during enjoyable events, and it's just that they differ in terms of what events they find enjoyable. Stoning ptarmigans is appraised as an enjoyable event among the Utku, whereas Belgians appraise other kinds of events as enjoyable, such as a weekend trip to the countryside. If Belgians and Utku are in situations that lead them to reach the same appraisal (an event that is enjoyable), they will have the same emotion (happiness). This is an argument for similar emotional experiences across cultures. However, there is something circular about this kind of argument. If happiness is what people feel when they appraise an event as enjoyable, then, by definition, if an event is appraised as enjoyable, there must be happiness. By this reasoning it is not possible to conceive of any kind of cultural variation in emotional experience because we cannot separate the appraisal from the emotion.

However, we can conceive of cultural differences in emotions if we reason about this differently. If we define emotion as *the affective response to an appraisal*, then there is no point in investigating the link between appraisals and emotions (Shweder, 1994). This definition maintains that emotions and appraisals are inseparable. If we subscribe to this definition of emotions, then explorations of cultural variation in emotions would just require us to investigate whether there are cultural differences in *appraisals*. And there is little doubt that there is a great deal of variation across cultures in appraisals (e.g., Ellsworth, 1992; Mesquita & Frijda, 1992). You probably wouldn't feel quite the same emotion as an Utku if you threw stones at a ptarmigan. Why is that? Well, ptarmigans are not a regular part of your existence, you probably have grown up within a cultural meaning system that includes the directive of being nice to birds, and unlike the Utku, ptarmigans are not part of your diet so you would have no good reason to want stoned ptarmigans to begin with. Your emotional response to the identical behavior, throwing a stone at a ptarmigan, would likely differ considerably from that of an Utku because the action does not carry the same cultural meaning for you. And because it does not carry the same meaning for you, you would appraise it differently. Of course, you would feel the identical way that an Utku did upon stoning a ptarmigan if you had made all the same appraisals that he had, but the point is that you wouldn't draw this same pattern of appraisals unless you were immersed in the same cultural world. When we conceive of emotions as inseparable from appraisals, we expect to find great variation across cultures in their daily emotional experience.

In sum, the literature on culture and emotions has been controversial because of the different ways that people have considered emotions. Researchers who emphasize the physiological basis of emotions and who focus on the kinds of emotions people experience following different appraisals are more likely to view emotional experiences as largely universal. In contrast, those who focus on the interpretive aspect of emotions and conceive of emotions as inseparable from appraisals are more likely to view emotions as culturally variable.

Does Emotional Experience Vary Across Cultures?

As the preceding section suggests, the question of whether emotions vary across cultures hinges on how you conceive of emotions. Two aspects of emotions have received the most study: an objectively visible aspect, facial expressions; and a subjectively experienced aspect, people's descriptions of their emotional experiences. Let's consider each of these in turn.

Emotions and Facial Expressions. When you're happy you tend to orchestrate the various muscles in your face to construct a beaming smile. Why is that? Did you learn by interacting with others that this was the appropriate way to express happiness in your culture? Or was the linkage between your happiness and your smiling hard-wired into your brain from birth? On the one hand, facial expressions are a means to communicate with others, and many of our other ways of communicating are heavily dependent on what we learn in our cultures. As an extreme example, consider what words you use to express happiness. In English, people say happiness, in Portugese people say *felicidade*, and in Japanese people say *shiawase*. Around the world there seems to be a rather arbitrary pairing of phonemes with the experience of happiness. Might there not be a similarly arbitrary pairing of facial muscle movements with the experience of happiness as well? Perhaps in some cultures people frown when they're happy.

On the other hand, unlike our languages, our facial expressions often appear to be rather reflexive. The same facial expressions that adults make are made by very young infants (Izard, 1994), including those who were born blind and thus have never seen the expressions before (reviewed in Ekman, 1973). This suggests that facial expressions are part of our biological makeup, and since humans share the same biology everywhere, facial expressions should be the same worldwide.

Evidence for Cultural Universals in Facial Expressions. Charles Darwin was one of the first scientists to seriously consider whether emotional facial expressions were common across all people of the world (Darwin, 1872/1965). Darwin reasoned that humans and other primates likely shared a common ancestor, and thus one place to look for evidence of universals in facial expressions would be to look at other primates, especially at our closest genetic relatives, chimpanzees. If chimpanzees made facial expressions that resembled those of Darwin's fellow compatriots in Victorian England, then this would be highly suggestive of human universals. It becomes much harder to argue that universals do not exist within a species if you find commonalities *across* species. Indeed, Darwin noticed some striking parallels in the expressions that various primates made with those that humans made, at least for some of our emotional expressions. This is suggestive that our capacity to express some

Some examples, noted by Charles Darwin, that other primates make emotional expressions similar to those of humans. The one on the left was said to be in a placid state, the middle one was said to be happy about being caressed, and the one on the right was said to be disappointed and sulky (Darwin, 1872/1965).

particular emotions through our faces has been around for some time, at least since the time that chimpanzees and humans shared a common ancestor. If we've had the same tendencies to make facial expressions at least since humans and chimpanzees had a common ancestor, it would seem that humans from all over the world, who all share that same distant ancestor, should also express their emotions in similar ways. Is this the case?

The researchers who have contributed most in answering Darwin's query have been Paul Ekman and his colleagues. Ekman and Friesen (1971) took thousands of photos of people posing six different emotional expressions (anger, disgust, fear, happiness, sadness, and surprise). They reduced their set of photos to those that were most easily recognized by Americans and then showed this set to individuals in Argentina, Brazil, Chile, Japan, and the United States. The participants were asked to select which of a set of six emotion terms best matched the feeling that a person was showing in a photo. If people had no idea which emotions were expressed in the pictures they would have identified about 1 out of 6 (16.7%) correctly by guessing (see Table 8.2). However, the participants tended to identify the emotion correctly in between 80% and 90% of the photos. That is, people in these five different cultures showed a great deal of agreement about what feelings the different facial poses were expressing. They paired smiles with happiness, scowls with anger, frowns with sadness, gapes with surprise, grimaces with disgust, and startles with fear. These findings are supportive of a claim for universals in emotional expression.

TABLE 8.2
Percentage Correct in Recognition of Facial Expressions Across Cultures

	Happiness	Disgust	Surprise	Sadness	Anger	Fear
U. S.	97	82	91	73	69	88
Brazil	97	86	82	82	82	77
Chile	90	85	88	90	76	78
Argentina	94	79	93	85	72	68
Japan	87	82	87	74	63	71

Source: Ekman & Friesen, 1971.

However, demonstrating that a psychological process is universal is not such a straightforward task. It is possible, for example, that Ekman and Friesen obtained such similar responses among these different cultures because the cultures weren't all that different to begin with. The five cultures they had explored were all industrialized, literate cultures, and people from them had all been exposed to a lot of the same media images. For example, around the time that Ekman and Friesen were collecting their cross-cultural data, the Hollywood movie *Butch Cassidy and the Sundance Kid* had been playing in theaters in all five countries. Perhaps participants in those countries outside the United States learned that people expressed happiness by smiling by watching Paul Newman's electric grin up on the silver screen. That is, even though Ekman and Friesen collected data from different cultures, it is possible that people from those cultures all *learned* to express emotions with their faces in the ways they did. To be more confident that emotional expressions are universal you would need to explore people who hadn't had much experience with other cultures. Only then could you ensure that people had not learned how to interpret other cultures' typical emotional expressions but that the various cultures really did perceive emotional expressions in the same way.

Ekman's solution to addressing this shortcoming was to try to find a culture that had the least possible exposure to Western ways. He chose the Fore of the inner highlands of New Guinea. The Fore had not seen any movies or magazines, they didn't speak any English or any other language influenced by a Western tongue, and they had never worked for Westerners. The Fore were from a culture that was one of the least exposed to Western ways on

The expressions of Fore men when they were asked to show how their faces would appear if they experienced the following: a. "Your friend has come and you are happy." b. "Your child has died and you are sad." c. "You are angry and about to fight." d. "You see a dead pig that has been lying there for a long time."

the planet. If the Fore made the same facial expressions that Westerners did, even though they had had virtually no contact with Westerners, then the case for universality would be greatly strengthened. Ekman went to investigate whether the Fore would smile or frown when they were happy. What did he find?

It turns out the Fore smiled. And they frowned when they were sad, and scowled when they were angry, and so on. Ekman demonstrated this by creating some stories appropriate for each of the six emotions. For example, he asked the Fore participants to imagine how they would feel, and to make a corresponding facial expression, in the following situations: (a) "Your friend has come, and you are happy," (b) "Your child has died," (c) "You are angry

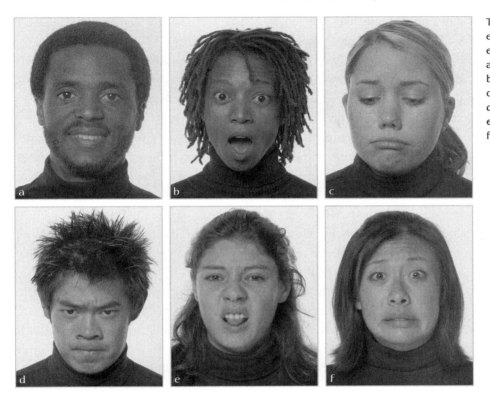

The six basic emotional expressions:
a. happiness,
b. surprise,
c. sadness,
d. anger,
e. disgust, and
f. fear.

and about to fight," and (d) "You see a dead pig that has been lying there for a long time." Above you can see the kinds of facial expressions the Fore made in response to each of these situations (Ekman, Sorenson, & Friesen, 1969). The odds that by chance people would tend to make facial expressions so similar to the ones that you and I make, even though they have had no contact with our cultures, are extremely remote. This is strong evidence that some facial expressions are universally similar around the world (although see Russell's 1994 critique of the inconsistency of the findings).

Ekman and colleagues proposed that there is a set of basic emotions that are universally recognized around the world. This basic set is argued to include at least six emotions: anger, fear, happiness, sadness, surprise, and disgust. There is also debate over whether other emotions—in particular, contempt, shame, embarrassment, pride, and interest—are universally recognized enough to justify being added to this set (e.g., Keltner, 1995; Tracy & Robins, 2006b). Given Ekman's findings you surely already know what each of the basic expressions looks like, but just to make sure, you can see examples of them on the previous page.

Evidence for Cultural Variability in Facial Expressions. The above evidence, coupled with the findings from dozens of other studies on the topic gathered by Ekman and others, demonstrates that our emotional expressions are not just something that we learn growing up. Although there may be a different word to express "happiness" in almost every language of the world, everywhere around the world people communicate their happiness by orchestrating their facial muscles in a fairly similar way. This is clear evidence for a universal, biological substrate to our emotional expressions. Given that movements of the facial muscles can be seen as part of the physiological component of emotions, it follows that in this domain of facial expression we would see much evidence for universality. However, even here there is also some evidence for cultural variability.

Although Ekman and others' research clearly reveals that in every culture that has been studied people are able to recognize the facial expressions of the basic emotions, there are some intriguing cultural differences. For example, when shown pictures of posed facial expressions from one culture (for example, Americans of European descent), some cultures perform a little better than others. The success rates for identifying American-posed faces was better among English speakers than among other Indo-European language speakers (e.g., Swedish, Greek, Spanish), and these samples performed better than those who spoke non-Indo-European languages (e.g., Japanese, Turkish, Malaysian), and all of these groups performed better than those from preliterate societies (e.g., the Fore and Dani from New Guinea; Russell, 1994). All groups performed significantly better than chance; however, Americans performed best of all at identifying the emotions posed by American actors.

Building on this observation, researchers made a meta-analysis of all the past research on cross-cultural recognition of facial expressions and noted that, on average, people were about 9% more accurate in judging the facial expressions of people from their own culture than those of another culture (with, on average, people showing about 58% accuracy overall; Elfenbein & Ambady, 2002). Moreover, the more people had been exposed to another culture, the more accurate they were at decoding facial expressions from that culture. Likewise, urban dwellers have been found to be more accurate at identifying facial expressions than rural people, apparently because they have had contact with a more diverse array of people (e.g., Ducci, Arcuri, Georgis, & Sineshaw, 1982). If you recall the different levels of universality that we discussed in Chapter 1, what can we conclude from these findings about the level of universality for recognizing facial expressions?

First, the notion that the facial expressions people make in different cultures are arbitrary and completely learned, which would indicate a nonuniversal, is obviously incorrect. Furthermore, the above meta-analysis revealed that, across cultures, people are 58% accurate overall in recognizing facial expressions, a number that far exceeds chance performance; this result demonstrates that regardless of culture, people make the same kinds of emotional expressions for the same kinds of situations. This evidence thus transcends the standards for existential universals and provides support that the facial expressions for the basic emotions are at least functional universals. That is, the particular facial expressions for the basic emotions are used in the same kinds of contexts across cultures—they serve the same function. However, there is cross-cultural variability (about 9%) in recognizing facial expressions posed by people from other cultures, and this demonstrates that recognizing facial expressions does not meet the standards of an accessibility universal. In sum, such recognition is best described as a functional universal.

A separate issue regarding cultural variation in the recognition of facial expressions has to do with the distinction between "basic" and "nonbasic" emotions. By definition, the basic emotions are those that have a distinct facial expression that is recognized across cultures, whereas the nonbasic emotions either do not have a clear and reliable facial expression or are not recognized across cultures. However, there does not appear to be a clear-cut boundary separating those that are basic from those that are not. For example, Figure 8.1 shows how well Indians and Americans recognized the emotions associated with 14 different facial expressions (Haidt & Keltner, 1999). Recognition was high for a few of the basic emotions, such as anger, disgust, and happiness, but gradually trailed off from there. The graph does not indicate a clear place where the basic emotions end and the nonbasic ones begin. It is not clear whether the decreasing performance toward the right side of the figure indicates emotions that do not have a clearly distinct facial expression or whether there is greater cultural variability in the experience of those emotions. Either way, this figure calls into question the utility of the distinction between universal basic emotions and culturally variable nonbasic ones. We'll return to the issue of basic and nonbasic emotions later.

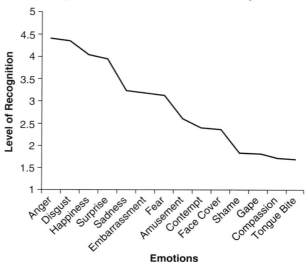

FIGURE 8.1

There is a gradient of recognition for various facial expressions of emotions, with no clear point that separates so-called "basic" from "non-basic" emotions.

Displaying Emotions Versus Experiencing Them. Ekman's theory of emotions maintains that when encountering the same situation, people will have the same emotional response, which will be linked to the corresponding facial muscles. However, even those researchers who most strongly argue for a universalist position on emotional facial expressions acknowledge that people have much conscious control over their facial muscles (although there is some debate over how much control they have; see Parkinson, 2005, for a review). On many occasions, people may choose to not express all the emotions they are experiencing. There would seem to be good evolutionary advantages to being able to conceal one's true feelings. For example, you would certainly be less successful at chasing off a threatening opponent if your face advertised your feelings of fear than if you were able to hide your fear by showing a menacing anger expression. Likewise, playing poker would be a rather futile exercise if people revealed their emotions in their faces when looking at their cards. Emotional facial expressions would seem to serve the important function of communicating our feelings, and we would benefit greatly from being able to control what information our faces were communicating in any given instance.

Much research confirms that the facial expressions we display are those we choose to display rather than ones that simply reflexively appear when we have the emotion. For example, consider the following experiment conducted in the rather exotic culture of the American bowling alley. The experiment was designed to test a straightforward question: "When do people smile while they are bowling?" The researchers set up a hidden camera at the end of the bowling alley above the pins that was pointed at the bowler (Kraut & Johnston, 1979). This recorded the facial expressions of the bowlers while they faced the pins. They set up a second camera behind the bowler. This camera recorded the facial expressions of the bowlers when they turned to look at their teammates. When people throw a good ball and get a strike, they often smile. But when does that smile occur? Do they smile on seeing the good news—that is, as they watch the pins go down and learn that they got a strike? Or do they smile when they turn to their teammates to communicate their happy feelings about having gotten the strike?

It turns out that the bowlers didn't usually smile until they turned to look at their teammates. Although the bowlers were surely happy about having knocked all the pins down, they didn't express that happiness in their faces until they had an opportunity to communicate with others. Furthermore, the smiles that are expressed by bowlers appear to be genuine smiles (known as Duchenne smiles) and not contrived ones (see Ruiz-Belda, Fernandez-Dols, Carrera, & Barchard, 2003). Likewise, athletes who have just won Olympic medals and are surely experiencing some of the happiest times of their lives, do not smile all that much until they are looking out at an audience, as when it is their turn to stand on a podium (Fernandez-Dols & Ruiz-Belda, 1995; however, for contrary arguments see Matsumoto & Willingham, 2006). These studies, and much other research (e.g., Carroll & Russell, 1997; Fridlund, 1991; Reisenzein, Bordgen, Holtbernd, & Matz, 2006), demonstrates that we have a great deal of control over our facial expressions: They do not just arise reflexively, and we are able to moderate those expressions to express the feelings we would like to communicate to others (for a review see Parkinson, 2005). Our facial expressions are very much under our control, and we exert control over them to help us create desired impressions in others.

Cultural Display Rules. Ekman and colleagues argue that the capacity to produce and recognize particular facial expressions is identical across cultures. What varies, they argue, are the **display rules** that cultures maintain for emotional expression (Ekman & Friesen, 1969). Display rules are the culturally specific rules that govern which facial expressions are appropriate in a given situation and how intensely they should be exhibited. Some cultures encourage people to display their emotions in clear, if not exaggerated, form. For example, among certain Arab populations it is dishonorable if a man does not respond to an insult with a great demonstration of anger (Abu-Lughod, 1986). Other cultures encourage people to express their emotions in muted form or to conceal them altogether. For example, among the Utku Eskimos, public expressions of anger are strongly condemned (Briggs, 1970). This notion of display rules suggests that even though people in different cultures vary considerably in how strongly they express certain emotions, it is possible that they are all experiencing the same underlying feelings.

Evidence to support this line of reasoning can be seen in one study (Ekman, 1972; Friesen, 1972). Americans and Japanese participants were asked to view some highly stressful films, such as a disturbing clip of a circumcision ritual, while unbeknown to them, a camera recorded their facial expressions. In one condition, the participants watched the films while alone in the room. In this condition, the Americans and Japanese made similar facial expressions—for example, they showed clear expressions of disgust. In a second condition, the participants watched the film with an older experimenter sitting beside them observing them. In this condition, the Americans showed facial expressions that were quite similar to those that they made when they were by themselves. In contrast, the Japanese tended to smile or hide their feelings of disgust with their hands throughout much of the films in this condition. These results suggest that there are different display rules operating for Americans and Japanese. When in the presence of a superior, Japanese appear motivated to present a polite, smiling face, thereby masking their true emotional experience. This suggests that Japanese culture encourages a more restrained expression of emotions than does American culture.

Evidence of cultural variability in display rules of emotion can also be found in hospitals. I am told that in a number of emergency rooms in North America some of the medical staff privately joke among themselves by referring to some patients as having symptoms of AMS: Acute Mediterranean Syndrome. This syndrome refers to the observations by some ER personnel that people from many Mediterranean cultures communicate their discomfort and pain at several decibels louder than those from many other cultures. The medical staff identify some patients as having AMS to warn each other

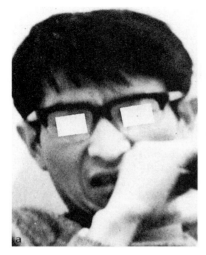

When watching an unpleasant film in private, Japanese (a.) and American (b.) participants both spontaneously reacted with a similar expression of disgust. When watching in the presence of an authority figure, however, Japanese participants tended to conceal their expression, either by muting it or attempting to cover it with a hand. The facial expressions of American participants were similar in both conditions.

that they are likely to get an earful. The staff in these emergency rooms do not appear to have identified an illusory correlation. Much research corroborates their observations and finds that there are clear cultural differences in the ways pain is expressed. For example, one comparison of Italian and Irish clinical admissions to a hospital found that 57% of the Italians reported being in pain in contrast to only 33% of the Irish (Zola, 1966). Another study found that patients of Italian and Jewish backgrounds communicated their pain much more openly than those of Irish and Anglo backgrounds (Zborowski, 1969; also see Bates, Edwards, & Anderson, 1993), although some kinds of self-report measures of pain do not reveal consistent cultural differences (Zatzick & Dimsdale, 1990). Cultural differences in pain expression appear to be more pronounced among older patients than among younger patients (e.g., Koopman, Eisenthal, & Stoeckle, 1984), highlighting how emotional expression is shaped by cultural experiences over time. Whether the greater cries of pain of more emotionally expressive people lead to greater *experience* of pain is an interesting but very difficult question to address.

In addition to governing the intensity with which emotions are expressed, display rules also shape the kinds of facial expressions that people might display. For example, when Americans are embarrassed they tend to make a

FIGURE 8.2

Americans and Indians both recognize the photo on the left as a prototypical embarrassment display. However, only people in India recognize the photo on the right as a ritualized display of embarrassment.

facial expression along the lines of that shown in the left side of Figure 8.2. They turn their head away, look down and to the side, smile with pressed lips, and touch their face. However, Indians often express their embarrassment by biting their tongues, as shown in the right side of Figure 8.2. The expression shown in the left side of the figure is recognized as embarrassment quite accurately by both Americans and Indians; however, the tongue bite is recognized as embarrassment by Indians but not Americans. This suggests that the tongue bite represents an expression that is voluntarily produced rather than reflexively generated (Haidt & Keltner, 1999). Voluntarily produced emotional expressions such as the tongue bite suggest the existence of cultural display rules that lead people to express idiosyncratic facial expressions, known as **ritualized displays**, that differ from the ostensibly universal facial expressions identified by Ekman and colleagues. Of course this adds a layer of complexity to the challenging task of interpreting emotional expressions across cultures. When we see someone's facial expression it is not always clear whether we are looking at a universal facial expression or one governed by cultural display rules.

Facial Feedback Hypothesis. An important point about display rules is that they presuppose that emotional experiences are unaffected by facial expressions. The theory maintains that the experience of the basic emotions is more or less constant across cultures, although cultures vary in how they choose to display those facial emotions. However, are emotional experiences and expressions completely unrelated? One view, known as the **facial feedback hypothesis**, suggests that they are not. The facial feedback hypothesis proposes that one source of information we utilize when inferring our feelings is our facial expressions. So if we are trying to figure out if we feel happy, one clue that we might consider is whether we are smiling. After all, our faces are more likely to be smiling when we have happy feelings than when we have feelings of sadness or disgust. This correlation between our facial expressions and feelings might thus be relied on in interpreting our feelings.

One study investigated whether people's emotions were influenced by the expressions their faces were making (Strack, Martin, & Stepper, 1988). The researchers reasoned that you couldn't just ask people to make certain facial expressions before inquiring about their emotional experiences, as they might come to suspect the purpose of the study (e.g., why did the experimenter ask me to smile before he asked me to rate my happiness?), and this would affect the findings. Because of this, the experimenters sought to manipulate people's facial muscles into a smile or frown without their participants being aware that they were actually smiling or frowning. Their unique solution was to ask participants to hold a pen in their mouth. One group was instructed to hold a pen between their teeth without having it touch their lips. A second group was instructed to hold a pen between their lips without having it touch their teeth. As Figure 8.3 shows, when you do this the muscles around your mouth are in similar positions as when you are smiling and frowning, respectively. Then participants were asked to rate how amused they were with a number of cartoons. Quite remarkably, the pen in teeth group found the cartoons to be more amusing than the pen in lips group! Apparently, participants were inferring how amused they were by the cartoons by considering what their facial muscles were doing, although none of them appeared to be aware that they were doing so. There thus appears to be some wisdom to the advice to put on a happy face!

The facial feedback hypothesis suggests that culturally divergent display rules might affect more than just people's expressions of their emotions. If your culture encourages you to express your emotions clearly in your faces you may infer that you're feeling strong emotions, whereas if your culture encourages you to deamplify or mask your emotions you might conclude that you're not feeling much emotion. American culture is one in which

 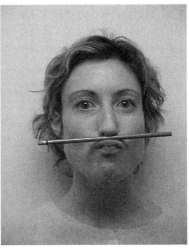

FIGURE 8.3

Facial muscle movements can affect the experience of emotion. People holding a pen between their teeth tend to find cartoons more amusing than people holding a pen above their lips.

people are encouraged to express their emotions whereas Japanese culture is one in which people are encouraged to exert considerable control over their emotional expressions. How do the cultures compare in their emotional experiences?

Cultural Variation in Intensity of Emotional Experience. A number of studies have compared the emotional experience of Japanese and Americans using a variety of different techniques. For example, Japanese and American participants were asked to report on occasions when they had experienced certain emotions (Matsumoto, Kudoh, Scherer, & Wallbott, 1988). The Americans reported feeling those emotions longer and more intensely than the Japanese did. Similarly, in another study Japanese and American students completed a questionnaire a number of times per day over a week to indicate the emotions that they had been experiencing (Mesquita & Karasawa, 2002). The Japanese were about three times as likely as Americans to report that they had *not* been feeling any emotions (also see Kitayama, Markus, & Kurokawa, 2000; Wang, 2004, for similar findings). These studies suggest that the cultural display rules governing the deamplifying and masking of emotions in Japan might be leading the Japanese to experience fewer and less intense emotions than Americans.

In some cultural contexts the expression of intense emotions may make it problematic for fitting in well with others, particularly for the expression of such interpersonally disruptive emotions as anger. It can be difficult for an interdependent group to function well if members are angry with each other, particularly if someone lower in the hierarchy feels anger toward someone of higher status. The individual would appear to fare better by not expressing that anger. However, much research with Westerners has revealed that people with hostile tendencies are at increased risk for cardiovascular disease (e.g., Diamond, 1982; Mann, 1977). Furthermore, some have maintained that the reason hostility leads to cardiovascular disease is that hostile people have more occasions when they need to inhibit their anger. That is, some researchers maintain that it is the *suppression* of an anger response that results in less cardiac regulation of heart rate, and thus a slower recovery of the heart rate following an initial angering event (e.g., Brosschot & Thayer, 1998). If the inhibition of anger leads to cardiovascular stress for people from all cultures, then it would seem that people from cultures in which inhibition of anger is more common would suffer from more heart disease, as they would more often be trying to bottle up their angry feelings. Alternatively, perhaps in cultures where the expression of anger is problematic people tend to *experience* anger less intensely.

This hypothesis was investigated in a couple of studies that compared Chinese-Canadians and European-Canadians in their anger responses (Anderson & Linden, 2006). In a first study, people were provided with some scenarios that typically provoke feelings of anger. For example, one scenario read "You go with your family to a restaurant where the food is superb and prices are low, but the service is terrible. There are many people in the restaurant; you wait a quarter of an hour and the waiter has not yet come to your table to take your order." Participants were asked how angry they would be, and which of four strategies they would take. One strategy is to express the anger (e.g., to complain to the manager); a second strategy is to suppress outward signs of anger (e.g., to wait quietly, while getting angrier inside); a third strategy is to distract oneself from the anger source (e.g., change the topic of conversation); and a last strategy is to generate a less angry appraisal of the event (e.g., convince yourself that the staff are very busy). The results indicated two things: first, Chinese-Canadians, on average, found the scenarios to be less anger-provoking than did the European-Canadians. They imagined feeling less anger if they had been in those situations. Second, the most common response to the anger-provoking event for European-Canadians was for them to openly express their anger. In contrast, for the Chinese-Canadians, their most common response was to reappraise the situation in a less angry way or to make efforts to distract themselves from the anger-provoking event. That is, whereas the European-Canadians felt much anger and tended to express it openly, the Chinese-Canadians adopted strategies to minimize their anger response, and accordingly, felt less angry.

In a second study, participants were examined to see how they physiologically responded to an anger-provoking incident (Anderson & Linden, 2006). Chinese-Canadians and European-Canadians were brought into a lab where they were exposed to a rather rude and unprofessional experimenter. Throughout the course of the experiment, their blood pressure was measured. People from both cultural groups initially responded with similar degrees of anger to the obnoxious experimenter, which was measured both by a self-report questionnaire and by their blood pressure. Both groups of participants showed an initial jump in their systolic blood pressure, which indicates an anger response. After that angry response, participants' blood pressure slowly dropped back down to baseline levels. Of interest here is that the blood pressure of the Chinese-Canadians recovered to baseline levels significantly more quickly than the blood pressure of European-Canadians (see Figure 8.4). None of the participants openly expressed their anger to the experimenter (although some were given the opportunity to complete a written evaluation of the experimenter, which did not significantly influence the results), and thus participants were in a situation where they needed to inhibit the expression of their anger. Apparently, inhibiting their anger led to a slower recovery of blood pressure for European-Canadians than it did for Chinese-Canadians. This suggests that the Chinese-Canadians experienced their anger less intensely than European-Canadians and were more comfortable with strategies that served to reduce their experience of anger, whereas the European-Canadians suffered from physiological consequences if they did not openly express their anger.

Likewise, other cultures also vary in the intensity with which people experience their emotions. For example, the Kaluli of New Guinea tend to show their emotions particularly intensely and dramatically (Schieffelin, 1979). Similarly, people from various Arab cultures also tend to prefer strong and passionate emotional displays (Abu-Lughod, 1986). Some cultures fall on the other extreme. The Balinese have a preference for emotional "smoothness" where the emphasis is on avoiding strong emotional feelings, for both posi-

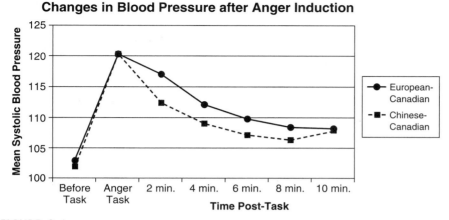

FIGURE 8.4

After being angered, Chinese-Canadians' blood pressure returns to its baseline level more quickly than European-Canadians' blood pressure does.

tive and negative emotions (Geertz, 1983). The goal is to stay on an even keel, even when one is encountering extreme events in one's life.

Cultural display rules thus importantly alter the ways that people express their emotions, and this, in turn, can potentially alter their emotional experiences. To the extent that expressions of emotions are inextricably linked to the experience of emotions, this adds a further layer of complexity in evaluating the evidence for the universality or cultural variability of emotional experience.

Emotion and Language

As described above, much research supports the existence of a set of basic emotions that are experienced comparably around the world. The Polish psychologist Anna Wierzabicka (1986), however, calls our attention to the fact that all the basic emotions have a clear English label. The problem with this, she argues, is that many other languages do not have labels that correspond to some of these so-called basic emotions. She suggests that if a universal theory of emotions was posited by, say, a Pole, they likely would have not included the term disgust because there is no term that closely corresponds to this in the Polish language. It would seem to be a problem if our universal theory of basic emotions, which has arisen largely from American researchers, maps so much better in English emotion terminology than in that of other languages.

Consider the Natyashastra, which is an Indian treatise of emotion that was written in the second century A.D. (see Shweder & Haidt, 2000). The Natyashastra identifies a list of eight basic emotions. That list overlaps somewhat with the list derived from Ekman and colleagues' research (there are emotions that correspond to the English terms of anger, fear, sadness, and disgust); however, it did not include words that corresponded to the other basic emotions of happiness or surprise. Nor did it overlap with other contenders for the status of "basic emotions," such as pride, embarrassment, shame, interest, or contempt. Furthermore, the Natyashastra included four emotions that are not typically seen as "basic" emotions (love, amusement, enthusiasm, and wonder; Masson & Patwardhan, 1970). There thus appears to be some disagreement across cultures as to what the "basic" emotions are.

Indeed, when it comes to exploring how different cultures describe their emotional experiences we see tremendous cultural variation (Russell, 1991). On one extreme is the English language, which has over 2,000 different emotion words. English speakers are particularly well equipped to describe the most subtle of variations in their emotional experience. On the other extreme are the Chewong of Malaysia, who have only eight emotion words (only three of which—anger, fear, and shame—map on to Ekman's basic emotions). Given this difference in the lexicons, it certainly is not surprising that so much interest in research on the emotions has emerged from English speakers and not from the Chewong.

The degree of cultural variation in emotional description is not just in terms of the number of emotion words that different groups have. People categorize their emotions in very different ways as well (Russell, 1991). For example, the Buganda of Uganda (who speak Luganda) do not make a distinction between sorrow and anger. The Gidjingali aborigines of Australia use one word (*gurakadj*) to express both shame and fear. Samoans use one word, *alofa*, to express both love and pity. The Utku Eskimos do not distinguish between feelings of kindness and gratitude. The Ifaluk in Micronesia do not even have a word for "emotion" but instead lump all internal states together (Lutz, 1988). The emotional lexicon is carved up in remarkably different ways across cultures.

Furthermore, despite the enormous number of emotion words in the English language, there are many emotion words in other languages that have no equivalent in English. Some of these reflect feelings that English speakers are probably familiar with, even though the language doesn't contain a single term to express them. The best-known example is *schadenfreude*, which is the German term to express the feelings of pleasure that one gets when witnessing the hard times that befall another. Some other cases of novel emotion terms seem to express feelings that are not especially familiar to most English speakers, such as *liget*. Other less familiar emotion words include the Javanese term *iklas*, which refers to somewhat pleasant feelings of frustration (Geertz, 1959), and the Japanese word *amae*. *Amae* captures the relatively pleasant feelings that one experiences when one is allowed to emphasize his or her dependence on another. It often involves tendencies to behave inappropriately toward a close other, as a gesture to demonstrate how secure the relationship is (Doi, 1971).

Personally, I have had a great deal of experience in Japan, and my occupation as a cultural psychologist demands a certain openness to culturally divergent ways of thinking. Despite this, my own experiences with *amae*-situations are often frustrating and completely bewildering to me. I am quite certain that although I have a decent intellectual understanding of *amae*, I do not experience the emotion in the same way that most Japanese do. I think this is so because the kinds of inappropriate behaviors that demonstrate one's dependence on another carry different meanings and appraisals for me given my own Canadian cultural upbringing. I would argue that the cultural diversity in emotion terms arises from the different clusters of appraisals that are frequently encountered in different cultures. For example, if inappropriate behaviors toward a loved one are consistently met with responses that indicate that your relationship is strong, this will lead to the pleasant cluster of feelings that constitutes *amae*. If the same behaviors are met with frustration or distancing from your loved one, you would appraise the situation differently and feel a different emotion.

Much cross-cultural research thus reveals that there are many exotic specimens in the emotion zoo. However, one important question to consider when looking at the dizzying array of emotion words around the world is how much do the emotion words matter? Could it be that the labels are irrelevant to the experiences of emotion? Some researchers argue that the diversity in emotion terms is relatively meaningless as our language use does not affect our underlying psychological experience (e.g., Pinker, 1994). Other researchers view the diversity in emotion terms to be highly telling of cultural diversity in emotional experience (e.g., Russell, 1991). This disagreement gets to the heart of a controversial debate on **linguistic relativity**—that is, the extent to which the ways people think are influenced by the words they use. We'll return to this important debate in Chapter 9, Cognition and Perception. At present, we can say that there is tremendous diversity in emotional experience across cultures in terms of how it is described in words. Whether this diversity is captured in people's own thoughts and internal states remains debatable; however, recent research on linguistic relativity in other domains (see Levinson, 1997; Roberson, Davies, & Davidoff, 2000) suggests that people's emotional experiences might differ depending on the words they have available to express their feelings.

Cultural Variation in Kinds of Emotional Experiences

In addition to research that has contrasted facial expressions and emotion terms across cultures, other research has attempted to investigate people's emotional experiences. How similar or different are people's daily emotional lives across cultures?

If you recall the differences we discussed between those with interdependent and independent selves in Chapter 5, we have a nice theoretical framework from which to draw hypotheses about how we might expect emotional experience to vary across cultures. Those with interdependent selves are more concerned with maintaining a sense of interpersonal harmony and thus should be more aware of how events in the world impact others close to them as well as themselves. Those with independent selves, in contrast, should focus more intently on how events impact themselves, or how events might serve to distinguish themselves from others. This suggests that people with independent selves and interdependent selves will *appraise* situations differently—either looking at situations as providing opportunities to distinguish themselves from others or to affect their relations with others. This hypothesis was tested by comparing those from a more collectivistic culture (Surinamese and Turkish immigrants to Holland) with those from a more individualistic culture (mainstream Dutch citizens of Holland; Mesquita, 2001). In accordance with these very predictions, the Surinamese and Turks expressed more relational concerns and attended more closely to how situations affected others, compared with the Dutch. Moreover, the Surinamese and Turks were more likely than Dutch to ensure that others attended to the same events, thereby sharing the experience with the participants. This suggests that the emotional experiences of those who are more interdependent are more interpersonally engaged than these experiences among more independent individuals.

Along a similar line, descriptions of daily emotional experiences were compared among Japanese and Americans (Kitayama et al., 2000). People were provided with a number of emotions that varied on two dimensions and asked how often they experienced them. One dimension was whether the emotion was positive or negative (e.g., happy vs. guilty). A second dimension was whether the emotion was interpersonally engaged or disengaged, that is, whether the experience involved connecting with others or distinguishing oneself from others. These two dimensions were combined to form four separate categories of emotions. Some examples of these different categories are shown in Table 8.3.

The researchers were interested in assessing how good these various emotions felt. Toward this end, they correlated how often participants reported experiencing the positive interpersonally engaged and disengaged emotions with how often they reported feeling some general positive emotions, such as feeling happy, calm, or elated. The pattern of correlations was quite striking,

---

TABLE 8.3
Emotion Categories Used in Kitayama et al.'s Study of Emotions Associated with Happiness

Positive Interpersonally Engaged Emotions	Negative Interpersonally Engaged Emotions
Respect	Anger
Shitashimi (friendly feelings)	Futekusare (sulky feelings)
Positive Interpersonally Disengaged Emotions	**Negative Interpersonally Disengaged Emotions**
Proud	Ashamed
Yuetsukan (superior)	Oime (indebted)

TABLE 8.4
Correlations Between Different Types of Positive Emotions

	Positive interpersonally engaged emotions and *general positive emotions*	*Positive interpersonally* disengaged emotions and *general positive emotions*
Japanese	.58	.20
Americans	.30	.54

as shown in Table 8.4. Those Japanese who reported feeling a great deal of positive interpersonally engaged emotions reported a lot more positive feelings in general. In contrast, Americans who reported feeling a great deal of positive interpersonally disengaged emotions reported much more positive feelings in general. In contrast, the positive interpersonally disengaged emotions for Japanese and the positive interpersonally engaged emotions for Americans were not closely tied to general positive feelings. This suggests that Japanese feel especially good when they're focusing on how their emotional experiences lead them to connect with others, whereas Americans feel especially good when they're dwelling on those emotional experiences that distinguish them from others. What makes us feel good appears to vary importantly across cultures (also see Kitayama et al., 2006, for similar findings).

Cultural Variation in Subjective Well-Being and Happiness

Is happiness necessary for a good life? This is a rather heavy existential question, and it becomes much more challenging when you consider it from a cross-cultural perspective. Happiness is indeed a universal emotion, and people everywhere often pursue activities that make them happy. Happiness feels very good, and it signals to the individual that all is well. Furthermore, much research demonstrates that there are tangible benefits to being happy. For example, happiness is associated with increased longevity and career success, at least in North America where this research has been largely conducted (Lyubomirsky, King, & Diener, 2005). Given that happiness is so pleasurable, and that it apparently has such beneficial consequences, shouldn't all cultures strive to maximize their degree of happiness?

Coming up with an answer to this question depends on how one views happiness. Happiness does seem to be a central value among many people from Western cultures. Indeed, the pursuit of happiness has been central enough to American culture that it was described as an "unalienable right" in the Declaration of Independence. This pursuit is alive and well in North America, and much of the West, as evidenced by the findings from many surveys that approximately 89% of Americans and 85% of Canadians report being quite happy, and these numbers have remained constant over the past 60 years (Veenhoven, 1993).

However, happiness has not always had such a central role in Westerners' lives. In 1843, the British historian Thomas Carlyle noted that "'happiness our being's end and aim' (a famous quote on happiness from the English poet, Alexander Pope) is at bottom, if we will count well, not yet two centuries old in the world." Carlyle is referring to changes during the Enlightenment when the world began to be seen as a more rational and predictable place, and that happiness was believed to be achievable through efforts to pursue a good life. Prior to this shift, people's concerns were less about how they could become happy and more about how they could be saved.

What does the cross-cultural literature have to say about happiness around the world? One piece of evidence comes from the study described above that compared Japanese and American daily emotional experiences (Kitayama et al., 2000). When comparing the frequency with how often participants reported feeling the different kinds of emotions, the two cultures showed an intriguing pattern. Japanese participants reported that they felt about the same amount of positive and negative emotions. Their emotional experience was rather even-handed with respect to the valence of the emotion. In contrast, American participants reported that they experienced far more positive emotions than they did negative emotions. Moreover, Americans and Japanese reported experiencing about the same number of negative emotions, but Americans reported experiencing far more positive emotions than Japanese did. Apparently, American emotional experiences are dominated by positive emotions, but Japanese emotions are as likely to be positive as negative. Are Japanese less happy than Americans?

Before addressing this, it's important to note that this cultural difference in emotional experience is not at all specific to Americans and Japanese. A great deal of research has explored how positive emotional experiences are distributed around the world. Much of this research has investigated cultural differences in **subjective well-being**. Subjective well-being is the feeling of how satisfied one is with one's life. Research consistently reveals that there are pronounced cultural differences in subjective well-being. In general, the nations that score highest on this measure are Scandinavian and Nordic countries, much of Latin America, various English-speaking countries, and Western Europe. On the low end are the former Soviet republics and some impoverished countries in Africa and South Asia (Diener & Diener, 1995; Diener, Diener, & Diener, 1995; Inglehart & Klingemann, 2000). Around the world people are not equally satisfied with their lives.

Well-being does not just vary across cultures but across regions within cultures. In one investigation, various measures of subjective well-being were contrasted across five regions of the United States: New England, the Mountain region, West South Central, West North Central, and East South Central (the researchers were unable to collect data from other regions; Plaut, Markus, & Lachman, 2002). Participants from each region evaluated their well-being in terms of their health, their sense of autonomy, their satisfaction with their identities, their emotions, their relations with others, and with their sense of social responsibility. The researchers standardized their results so that people in each region could be compared with people from other regions on their well-being on these dimensions (i.e., positive z-scores indicate that a region had scores that were on average higher than the national average). As can be seen from Figure 8.5, there was much variation in the well-being profiles across the country. People in New England and the Mountain states, on average, were faring better on most domains of well-being than were other regions in the country. Well-being thus varies both across countries and across regions within countries. Why would rates of well-being differ across cultures?

Many factors contribute to influence the overall satisfaction that people have with their lives. A not surprising one is wealth. On average, people who live in countries in which they have access to enough wealth to easily meet the basic needs of life tend to be considerably more satisfied than those who do not. Indeed, some of the least satisfied folks in the international comparisons come from countries such as Bangladesh and Cameroon where many people don't have adequate food and clean water to survive easily. However, the relation between money and happiness is not universally strong. Money and happiness seem to be most closely connected at very low levels of wealth, where a few extra dollars can make the difference between surviving or not.

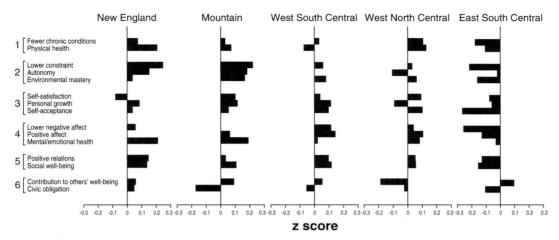

FIGURE 8.5

These are the well-being profiles for various regions of the United States. Bars pointing to the left indicate low scores and less well-being, whereas bars that point to the right indicate high scores and greater well-being.

For example, a strong correlation of .45 was found between income and life satisfaction among respondents in the slums of Calcutta (Biswas-Diener & Diener, 2002). The relation between income and subjective well-being is much smaller in developed nations, although it is still positive (Diener & Biswas-Diener, 2002). On average, once a country has an average GDP of at least 40% of that of the United States, there is no longer any pronounced relation between money and subjective well-being (Diener et al., 1995). In sum, money can buy a lot of happiness if you're struggling to survive; however, it has much less impact if your basic needs have been met.

Another factor that predicts the subjective well-being of nations is human rights. On average, those countries that promote human rights the most tend to have the happiest citizens. Conversely, those countries

"Right. Money isn't everything—what's the other thing again?"

in which people live under the constant threat of being thrown in jail for suspicions of plotting against the government, on average, are not very happy. The overall equality among people in a country also is associated with greater subjective well-being (Diener et al., 1995). The Scandinavian and Nordic nations, which have various social policies to minimize differences in opportunities among its citizens, tend to have some of the happiest people around. It seems that people feel good when their rights are not threatened and they have opportunities that are comparable to those of their neighbors.

These are the factors that have emerged consistently across studies. However, they do not seem to be the only factors that matter, as many nations have average subjective well-being scores that depart considerably from what would be predicted from these factors alone. In particular, many countries in Latin America show average subjective well-being scores that are much higher than would be predicted by the variables of wealth, human rights, and equality (Diener, 2001) whereas countries in East Asia show much lower subjective well-being scores than would be predicted by these factors (Diener, Suh, Smith, & Shao, 1995). There must be other factors that influence well-being that have yet to be reliably identified.

The above research shows that a variety of factors predict subjective well-being in *similar* ways across nations. However, there also appear to be some factors that predict life-satisfaction *differently* across cultures. Consider the question of whether the "good life" can be attained mostly by doing what a person would like to do or by doing what a person thinks he or she should do. In what kinds of cultural contexts might we expect people to base their life satisfaction on whether they are doing the kinds of things they would like to do? It would seem that if people have a more independent view of self, satisfaction with their lives should be based on whether they feel they are acting in ways consistent with their inner desires. If you recall, people with independent selves tend to view their identity as being grounded in inner attributes, such as their personality traits, attitudes, and opinions. If someone acts in ways consistent with those inner attributes it should feel good, as this would represent a culturally appropriate way of being—that is, a good life, independent style. This question was investigated by exploring whether feelings of life satisfaction are more highly correlated with overall positive affect in individualistic cultures than in collectivist cultures (Suh, Diener, Oishi, & Triandis, 1998). Indeed, there was clear evidence to support this: People in individualistic societies were far more likely than those in collectivist societies to base their life satisfaction on how many positive emotions they were experiencing. Positive emotions appear to be seen as the basis of a good life in individualistic cultures.

So what is life satisfaction based on for people with more interdependent selves? Suh and colleagues reasoned that people with interdependent selves would feel good about their lives if they were living up to others' standards for being a good person. That is, if they felt they were highly respected by others, they might feel very good about their lives. Indeed, people in collectivistic cultures showed a higher correlation between their life-satisfaction scores and being respected by others for living up to cultural norms, compared with people from individualistic cultures. Living up to cultural norms seems to be viewed as the basis of a good life in collectivistic cultures.

Another key factor that influences people's judgments of life satisfaction is the theory they embrace regarding how happy they think they should feel. Some people think life should be full of happy experiences, whereas others believe life should consist of both the happy and sad times. The theory that you endorse is going to influence how you make sense of your satisfaction, regardless of what your actual daily experiences are. Consider the following study (Oishi, 2002). American participants were asked to complete a brief questionnaire at the end of every day to indicate how satisfied they had been that day. After doing this for 7 days, participants were also asked to think back over the past week in which they had been completing the questionnaire and to indicate how satisfied they had been with that week. The participants were divided into two samples: those of European descent and those of Asian descent. Participants from other cultural backgrounds were not included in the study.

The findings were quite revealing, as can be seen in Figure 8.6. When people looked back retrospectively at their weeks, the European-Americans remembered having a much better week than the Asian-Americans had. At first glance, this difference would seem to suggest that the European-Americans encountered more satisfying events in their weeks than the Asian-Americans. However, if you look at the right side of the graph you see how positively the participants rated their satisfaction each day of the week. There was no cultural difference here. That is, it seems that European-Americans and Asian-Americans are having comparable weeks in terms of the satisfying events that

FIGURE 8.6

European-Americans and Asian-Americans give similar overall satisfaction ratings about their experiences. However, when both groups look back on their experiences, European-Americans recall them as more satisfying than do Asian-Americans.

they experience, but the European-Americans are remembering their weeks as having been better than they really were whereas the Asian-Americans seem to be remembering their weeks as having been about as good as they had experienced them. What can we make of this finding?

It seems that when people reflect on their day, they recall the events that happened and rate their satisfaction accordingly. However, when they consider a longer time period, their estimates are more likely to reflect the theories they hold about what life should be like (e.g., Robinson & Clore, 2002). European-Americans appear to be operating under an implicit theory that they should be happy whereas Asian-Americans seem to operate under the theory that emotional experience, like other aspects of life, should be balanced and consist of both positive and negative experiences (Rodgers, Peng, Wang, & Hou, 2004). We'll return to make sense of the East Asian desire for balance in Chapter 9, Cognition and Perception. These findings indicate that when people think back over their lives they are likely to interpret their feelings with respect to these culturally divergent theories, but when they consider their feelings at a given time those theories do not come much into play. It is quite possible that many of the observed cultural differences in subjective well-being are based on the different theories that people from different cultures have about how they should be feelings about their lives.

Furthermore, the question of cultural variation in happiness is further complicated in that the *kinds* of positive emotions people desire also seem to vary considerably across cultures. Not all positive emotions are created equal. Some positive emotions, such as excitement and elation, involve a great deal of arousal. Other positive emotions, however, such as feeling calm or at peace, involve a low degree of arousal. Some work by Jeanne Tsai and colleagues (Tsai, Knutson, & Fung, 2006) reveals that these two kinds of positive emotions are sought after differently by Americans and East Asians. Specifically, Americans are more likely to seek out positive emotions that are high in arousal compared with those that are low in arousal, whereas East Asians prefer low arousal emotions over high arousal ones. There is much evidence for this cultural difference across a wide array of life activities between the two cultural groups. For example, a comparison of facial expressions that were shown in characters in American and Taiwanese children's storybooks revealed that the American faces more often showed feelings of excitement and had significantly bigger smiles than the Taiwanese faces. The authors of these books seem to be aware of what their audiences want, as subsequent analyses revealed that European-American preschool children preferred the pictures of excited faces more than the Taiwanese preschoolers did, and they also felt more similar to the characters who were engaged in high arousal activities; the Taiwanese children felt more similar to the characters engaged in low arousal activities (Tsai, Louie, Chen, & Uchida, in press). Further evidence for this cultural difference can be seen in Christian and Buddhist teachings and practices. A content analysis of classic Christian and Buddhist texts (e.g., the Gospels of the Bible and the Lotus Sutra) as well as contemporary Christian and Buddhist self-help books revealed that high arousal states were encouraged more in the Christian texts whereas the low arousal states were more encouraged in the Buddhist texts. Furthermore, some Christian sects include enthusiastic religious practices such as jumping, shouting, and applause; Buddhist religious practices emphasize meditation and the calming of one's mind (Tsai, Miao, & Seppala, 2007). In addition, there are various activities that encourage high or low arousal states, and cultures differ in the frequency they practice those. For example, European-Americans are more likely to engage in active-individual activities such as jogging or rollerblading whereas Asian-Americans are more likely to engage in passive activities such as sightseeing and picnicking (Gobster & Delgado, 1992). In sum, European-Americans are more likely to engage in activities that lead to high arousal positive states whereas those from East Asian backgrounds aspire for more low arousal positive states. The pursuit of happiness across cultures, then, also appears to depend importantly on the kinds of positive emotions people desire.

What can we conclude about cultural variation in the pursuit of happiness? First, it appears that cultures do differ in the average degree of well-being they experience, and that these differences hinge, in part, on some universal relations between well-being and such variables as wealth (at low ends of the wealth spectrum), human rights, and equality. However, the question is also complicated as people in different cultures view happiness and positive emotions in quite different terms. Among Westerners, interpersonally disengaging acts feel especially good, subjective well-being is associated with positive feelings, people operate under the implicit theory that more positive feelings are better, and high arousal positive emotions are preferred. Among East Asians, in contrast, interpersonally engaging acts feel especially good, subjective well-being is associated with appropriate role behaviors, people operate under the implicit theory that it is good to experience both positive and negative feelings, and low arousal positive emotions are more sought after. Cultures vary in their happiness, in part, because they have quite different ideas about what happiness is and is derived from.

Conclusions Regarding Cultural Variation in Emotions

The field of culture and emotions has experienced considerable debate regarding the role of culture in shaping the emotions. Much of this debate grows out of researchers' different conceptions of emotions and of the aspects of emotions they study. What can we conclude about cultural variation in emotional experience?

If we focus on facial expressions, there is good evidence for universality in emotions around the world. For the most part, people are universally adept at producing and recognizing facial expressions associated with the basic emotions. There is not evidence for accessibility universals here, however, as people perform worse when evaluating the facial expressions of those from other cultures than from their own. Furthermore, the extent of universality in the expression of other nonbasic emotions is less promising.

Looking at emotional experience, there is more evidence for cultural diversity. People from different cultures vary in the intensity with which they experience emotions, the kinds of things that they feel best about, and the degree to which they experience positive versus negative feelings. Emotional experience varies more across cultures than do people's facial expressions for the basic emotions.

Last, considering the emotional lexicon, there is tremendous variability in the kinds of words that people use to describe their experiences. Cultures vary not only in the number of emotion words that they have but also in the ways they carve up the emotional space, with many English emotion words not existing in other languages, and many non-English emotion words not existing in English. The question of how much people's emotional experiences are shaped by the words they choose to describe them is a difficult and controversial one. Some argue that emotion words are largely irrelevant to the experience; others maintain that it is telling that people in different cultures label their experiences in such different ways. We'll return to this question when we discuss linguistic relativity in the next chapter.

SUMMARY

There is considerable debate about the best way to conceive of emotions. Some theories have focused more on the physiological markers of emotions; others focus more on the interpretive aspects of emotions. In general, theories that focus on the physiological aspects of emotions predict less cultural variability, and theories that focus on interpretive aspects of emotions expect much cultural variability. Both theories recognize that appraisals are a key part of emotions.

Research on facial expressions reveals much consistency around the world in the ways that people recognize the basic emotions of fear, anger, happiness, sadness, surprise, and disgust. These expressions are not the product of cultural learning but reflect universal physiological reactions. However, some aspects of the ways people express their emotions are shaped by cultural learning, and people are less accurate at recognizing facial expressions of people from different cultures than of people from their own culture.

Facial expressions serve an important communicative function, and people do not show on their faces all the emotions they are experiencing. In general, people's faces convey far more expressions when they are communicating with others.

Cultures vary in the display rules that shape how emotions are expressed. Display rules guide both the intensity through which emotions are expressed and the ways they are expressed. Some cultures communicate their emotions more directly whereas others express them in more moderated form.

Cultures vary tremendously in their vocabulary for emotions. Some cultures have many more emotion words than others, and there is often little overlap between these emotion words. For example, terms for the basic emotions are not represented in all languages, and many emotion words from other languages do not exist in English.

People with interdependent selves are more likely to appraise situations with regard to relational concerns than are people with independent selves. Also, people with interdependent selves are more likely to feel happy when they have interpersonally engaged positive emotions whereas people with independent selves are more likely to feel happy when they experience interpersonally disengaged positive emotions.

Cultures around the world vary considerably in their degrees of subjective well-being. Subjective well-being is affected by such variables as wealth, protection of human rights, and income equality. People's report of their subjective well-being is also affected by whether they believe that life should be consistently good or that life is inherently composed of both good and bad events. Furthermore, some kinds of positive feelings, such as high arousal states, are more desired in Western cultures whereas low arousal positive feelings are more desired among East Asian populations.

Cognition and Perception

Imagine that you are walking through a museum and you come across some art from different cultures. You may find terra cotta figurines from Nigeria, totem poles from the Pacific Northwest, Chulucanas pottery from Peru, marble statues from Greece, or bronze Buddhas from Thailand. Indeed, if there is one thing that varies tremendously across cultures, and across historical time, it is artistic traditions. But what can we make of the different traditions we see? Are they just a matter of convention, where, for some reason, a certain style became popular at a particular time and place and subsequent artists respond to that style, either by emulating it or challenging it? Or could these differences tell us something about the underlying psychology of people from those cultures?

This is a question that Taka Masuda and colleagues (Masuda, Gonzalez, Kwan, & Nisbett, 2005) have considered. As he visited art galleries in Europe and East Asia, Masuda noticed some striking differences in the paintings produced in those countries. One thing he observed (and later documented empirically) is that the horizons in landscape scenes were painted considerably higher (about 15% higher on average) in East Asian pictures than in Western ones. Second, he noted that figures in portraits were much larger in Western pictures than they were in East Asian ones (on average the Western faces were three times as large). These cultural differences emerged consistently across a variety of different themes and styles.

So what might these differences in artistic convention between the two cultures be telling us? Perhaps they simply reflect the vagaries of fashion, and for some reason high horizons and small portrait figures came into vogue in East Asia in ways that they didn't in Europe. Many would view this as the only acceptable account of cultural differences in artistic traditions. However, Masuda, his supervisor Richard Nisbett, and their colleagues have offered a much bolder interpretation: East Asian art looks different from Western art

The painting by the Flemish artist Berckheyde (top) and the one by the Japanese artist Hokusai (bottom) are both landscape river scenes. However, Berckheyde paints the horizon at a lower level than does Hokusai. On the next page, the portrait on the left is by French painter Blanche, and the portrait on the right is by a Chinese painter of the Qing dynasty. The subject of the French portrait occupies a larger portion of the painting than do the subjects of the Chinese portrait. These differences in style are commonly found between Western and Eastern artists.

because people from these cultures are literally *seeing* the world differently. They argue that these different artistic styles reflect some fundamental differences in basic cognitive and perceptual processes that exist between these two cultures (Masuda, Gonzalez et al., 2007; Nisbett, 2003).

Now an argument for cultural variation in basic cognitive and perceptual processes is a bold one indeed. If there is a hierarchy of the different fields within psychology, then the study of cognition and perception is seen by many to be the field that occupies the throne. Research on cognition and perception is esteemed so much because it purports to be informing us about the most elementary and essential psychological processes. Researchers in this field question how our minds work—how they are able to process the streams of information that individuals encounter as they go about their daily lives. Such researchers are striving to isolate the building blocks of our psychological experiences, the images that our eyes perceive, the ways we encode and retrieve our memories, how we categorize information, and the ways we understand the objects and events that we encounter. Given the fundamental questions that occupy researchers of cognition and perception, it is quite remarkable that it is in this domain that some of the clearest evidence for cross-cultural variability appears. This recently found and quickly growing body of evidence for cultural variability in cognition and perception is calling into question some very basic assumptions that psychologists have held about how the mind operates.

This chapter explores the ways basic cognitive and perceptual processes vary across cultures. Some questions that we'll investigate are, "Do people from different cultures think and see the world differently?" "Do people attend to different kinds of information when they communicate with others?" "Does our language affect the ways we think?" The exploration of cultural variation in cognition and perception is guided by the two themes of this book. First, there are cognitive tools that are universally available to people; however, as you'll see, in some of these studies it appears that these tools are not always used with the same frequency or for the same purpose. Second, the cultural differences that do appear in these basic cognitive and perceptual processes arise because of the different experiences that people have growing up in their respective cultures.

Analytic and Holistic Thinking

To understand the differences in the painting styles between East Asia and the West we need to take a step back. First, consider the following question: Which of these three is least like the other two? A dog, a carrot, and a rabbit. When answering this question, people typically give one of two kinds of answers (Chiu, 1972; Ji, Zhang, & Nisbett, 2004). One common answer is the carrot. Both the dog and the rabbit are animals, so they share common attributes, which differ from the attributes of the carrot, which is a vegetable. This kind of answer reflects a taxonomic categorization strategy in that the stimuli are grouped according to the perceived similarity of their attributes. Taxonomic categorization answers are especially common among Westerners in these kinds of studies. The second common answer is the dog. Rabbits and carrots go together because rabbits eat carrots. Rabbits and carrots have a relationship, which dogs don't share. This kind of answer reflects a thematic categorization strategy in that the stimuli are grouped together on the basis of causal, temporal, or spatial relationships among them. Thematic categorization is especially common among East Asians. This difference in categorization strategies reflects an underlying difference in the ways that people attend to their worlds. Nisbett and colleagues (Nisbett, 2003; Nisbett, Peng, Choi, & Norenzayan, 2001) refer to these ways of attending to the world as analytic and holistic thinking.

Analytic thinking is characterized by a focus on objects and their attributes. Objects are perceived as existing independently from their contexts, and they are understood in terms of their component parts. The attributes that make up objects are used as a basis for categorizing them, and a set of fixed abstract rules is used to predict and explain the behavior of these objects. As we'll soon see, analytic thinking, in general, is more common in Western cultures than it is elsewhere, particularly in East Asia (i.e., China, Japan, and Korea).

In contrast, **holistic thinking** is characterized by an orientation to the context as a whole. It represents an associative way of thinking, where there is attention to the relations among objects and among the objects and the surrounding context. Objects are understood in terms of how they relate to the rest of the context, and their behavior is predicted and explained on the basis of those relationships. Holistic thinking also emphasizes knowledge gained through experience rather than the application of fixed abstract rules. Holistic thinking is more common in East Asian and other cultures than in Western cultures.

The origins of analytic and holistic thinking are argued to arise from the different social experiences people have within individualistic and collectivistic societies. As we discussed in Chapter 4, Development and Socialization, people in collectivistic societies tend to be socialized in relational contexts and to have their attention directed at relational concerns (e.g., Lavin, Hall, & Waxman, 2006; Tamis-Lemonda, Bornstein, & Cyphers, 1992; Wang & Conway, 2004). People in individualistic societies, in contrast, are more likely to be socialized to be independent and to have their attention focused on objects (e.g., Bornstein et al., 1992; Wang & Conway, 2004). These kinds of cultural experiences lead people to have either primarily independent or interdependent self-concepts

If you recall from Chapter 5, Self and Personality, people with independent self-concepts come to understand people by focusing on their inner attributes and attending less to relationships. People with interdependent self-concepts, in contrast, tend to conceive of people in terms of their relationships with others. Nisbett and colleagues argue that these cultural differences in ways of understanding *people* also shape the kinds of information people attend to in their physical environments (also see Kühnen, Hannover, & Schubert, 2001; Kühnen & Oyserman, 2002).

Nisbett and colleagues further suggest that these cultural differences in analytic versus holistic thinking between Westerners and East Asians were also present between Greeks and Chinese 2,500 years ago. Analytic thinking is evident in the Platonic perspective that the world is a collection of discrete, unchanging objects that can be categorized by reference to a set of universal properties. Such thinking can be seen in Aristotle's view that a stone falls through the air because the stone possesses the property of "gravity" and that a log floats on water because the log possesses the property of "levity." Analytic thinking is further evident in the Greek development of an elaborate formal logic system that searched for the truth according to abstract rules and syllogisms that existed independently of observations.

In contrast, holistic thinking was evident among the ancient Chinese in that their intellectual traditions of Confucianism, Taoism, and Buddhism emphasized harmony, interconnectedness, and change. Although the Greek preference for discrete concepts and abstract principles led to the invention of science, the Chinese tendency to view the world as consisting of continuously interacting substances led them to discover action at a distance two thousand years before Galileo did. The Chinese had knowledge of magnetism, acoustic resonance, and the moon's role in the tides long before Westerners did, even though they lacked a scientific tradition at the time (Nisbett, 2003). Holistic thinking is further evident among the Chinese medical traditions and in the culture's emphasis on harmony among people and nature. According to Nisbett and colleagues, cultural differences in ways of thinking between Westerners and East Asians persist to this day because ancient Greece and Confucian China provided the intellectual groundwork from which modern Western and East Asian societies have evolved.

How analytic and holistic thinking styles took root in ancient Greece and Confucian China is not well understood (although, see Nisbett, 2003, for some informed conjectures). Some research suggests that holistic thinking is quite widespread throughout the world and that analytic thinking is the relatively unusual thinking style, in that it is largely restricted to people who have had much contact with Western society or education systems. For example, one study found that Arabs showed at least as much evidence of holistic thinking as did Chinese (Norenzayan, 2005). Knight, Varnum, and Nisbett (2005) found that Eastern Europeans were more holistic in their thinking than Western Europeans, and that those from southern Italy (which is more interdependent) gave more holistic responses than those from northern Italy (which is more independent).

My colleague, Joe Henrich, relayed a story to me about visiting the Mapuche in Chile, a local indigenous population of subsistence farmers, to investigate holistic and analytic thinking there. He asked people to make a decision about the task described above—namely, of a dog, a carrot, and a rabbit, which does not belong? Almost everyone that he spoke with gave the holistic response and said that the dog didn't belong because the carrot had a relationship to the rabbit. After many holistic answers he finally found someone who gave him what seemed to be an analytic answer as he said that the carrot didn't belong. Henrich, relieved at finding some evidence for analytic thinking at last, then asked the man why the carrot didn't belong. The man answered that it was because the dog took care of the rabbit (which apparently it did in his household)! In sum, there is evidence that holistic thinking characterizes the thinking of people from much of the globe. Interestingly, the same places where holistic thinking are found are also the places where there has traditionally been little psychological research. We may well have overestimated the pervasiveness of analytic thinking.

This hypothesized cultural difference in analytic and holistic thinking styles manifests in a number of rather profound ways. Below I provide a fairly long section describing the many ways this cultural difference has been shown to emerge in some very basic psychological processes. Much of this work has been conducted by Richard Nisbett and his students who have primarily focused on comparisons of North Americans and East Asians, although many of the findings from East Asians are seen in other non-Western cultures as well.

Attention

One of the most fundamental psychological process is attention—that is, at a given time, where is our cognitive activity directed? It follows that analytic thinkers, who tend to perceive the world as consisting of discrete objects, would be more likely to focus their attention on separate parts of a scene—those parts that represent discrete objects of interest. In contrast, holistic thinkers, who tend to perceive the world as consisting of an interrelated whole, should direct their attention more broadly, across an entire scene.

An early finding from the psychoanalytic tradition lent support to the idea that East Asians and Westerners showed different attention to stimuli. In 1949 some European Americans and Chinese Americans were asked to describe what they saw in some Rorschach ink blots (Abel & Hsu, 1949). The Rorschach is a projective test in which people report what they see in an ambiguous stimulus. The results revealed that these two groups of Americans apparently saw things quite differently. The European-Americans were more likely to describe what they saw based on a single aspect of the card, say a little blotch on the bottom that looked like a Ferrari. In contrast, the Chinese-Americans were more likely to give "whole-card" responses, describing what they saw based on the entire image on the card.

This finding was largely ignored by the field for about 50 years, as no one had any way of making sense of this cultural difference. Perhaps it was a fluke. However, many other studies have recently built on this intriguing finding and have extended it in important ways.

For example, to the extent that East Asians habitually perceive the world in holistic terms they should be especially good at certain kinds of tasks; the attention that holistic thinkers direct to the entire scene should mean that they would be especially good at detecting relations among different events. This hypothesis was investigated by showing American and Chinese students pairs of pictures on the computer (Ji, Peng, & Nisbett, 2000). The pairings were set so that when one picture was shown (e.g., a light bulb), the other picture (e.g., a coin) was shown either 0% of the time, 40% of the time, 60% of the time, or 100% of the time. Later the participants were shown just one of the pictures (e.g., the light bulb) and asked the likelihood that the other picture (e.g., the coin) would appear beside it. To succeed on this task you have to be especially good at attending to the relations between these different pictures, something that holistic thinkers should do well. The results indicated that the Chinese estimates of the likelihood that the correct picture would appear were more accurate than the estimates of the Americans. Apparently, Americans focused more on the individual objects than they did on the relations between the objects.

There are other kinds of tasks that holistic thinkers should perform especially *badly*. Their tendency to focus on entire scenes should mean they would do poorly on tasks that require you to separate a scene into its component parts. An example is the Rod and Frame task. The goal is to say whether the rod is pointing straight up. What makes this task challenging, however, is that the frame around the rod is rotated independently and thus it provides misleading information. To be able to do the Rod and Frame task properly you have to be able to ignore the misleading information of the frame and focus solely on the rod. Analytic thinkers, with their tendency to perceive the world as separate objects, should fare well on this task. Analytic thinkers tend to show **field independence**—that is, they can separate objects from their background fields. Holistic thinkers, in contrast, tend to show **field dependence** in that they tend to view objects as bound to their backgrounds. Research shows that people's ability to judge the rod's angle while ignoring the frame relates to their general social orientation. People who attend a lot to others develop more of an orientation toward the field. Those who are more outgoing are more field dependent than people who are more introverted (Witkin, 1969). Similarly, farmers who live in societies where they must coordinate their actions with others are more field dependent than people who hunt and gather or herd animals (Witkin & Berry, 1975). People in industrialized societies also tend to be quite field independent, except for people living in highly industrialized East Asia, where clear evidence for field dependence is found. That is, in general, East Asians do relatively poorly on tasks such as the Rod and Frame (Ji et al., 2000; Kitayama, Duffy, Kawamura, & Larsen, 2003).

This field dependence identified among East Asians has been further investigated in a number of other studies. Consider what people see when they look at a scene. In one study, American and Japanese participants were shown some animated computer images of an underwater scene, complete with swimming fish, waving seaweed, and floating bubbles (Masuda & Nisbett, 2001). The participants were asked to describe what they saw. The Japanese participants made about 60% more references to background objects than did the Americans, who tended to talk more about the fish at the center of the scene. After the participants had described a number of these scenes they were then shown some additional scenes that included the same focal fish they had seen before. However, some of those fish were presented with the same background they had appeared in earlier, whereas other fish were shown with a novel background. The participants were asked whether they had seen the fish in the picture before. As shown in Figure 9.1, when the fish was shown with its original background the Japanese were more likely to recognize the fish than were the Americans. In contrast, when the fish was shown with a novel background the Americans were more likely to recognize the fish than were the Japanese. This indicates that the Americans tended to perceive the fish separately from their background—indeed, their recall was not influenced by whether the fish was presented with the original or a novel background. The Japanese participants, in contrast, seem to have seen the fish and the background scenery as bound together. When the background

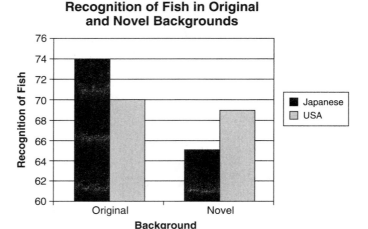

FIGURE 9.1

Although American participants recall fish that they have seen regardless of the background against which they are presented, Japanese recall fish shown with their original background significantly better than those shown with a novel background.

is changed, the fish no longer look quite the same. And because the researchers were concerned that the results could have been influenced because the Japanese participants had greater familiarity with fish, they replicated the study with photos of American animals and American scenery. They found the same pattern of findings as with the fish. When looking at the identical scenes, Americans and Japanese appear to be perceiving them differently.

Now these findings raise a big question. Are people from different cultures really seeing things differently or are they retrieving different information from their memories? Our memories are not veridical snapshots; we recall some information better because we find it distinctive and interesting, and we recall other information better because it fits with our expectations and is understood. It is thus possible that the cultural differences we see in the above studies occur solely at the retrieval end of the process, whereby the perceptual experiences are identical across cultures.

The best way to provide an answer to this important question is to use an eye-tracker, a device with which researchers can determine precisely where someone is looking at any given instant. What would happen if the eye movements of East Asians and Westerners were contrasted? In one study Japanese and American participants looked at some animated scenes on a computer (Masuda, Ellsworth et al., 2007). In the scene they saw a target person in the foreground surrounded by other people in the background. Each of the people was showing an emotional facial expression. Sometimes the background faces showed expressions inconsistent with the target person (e.g., the target person was smiling but the background people were frowning), and sometimes they showed expressions consistent with the target person. The task for the participants was to identify the emotion the target person was experiencing. The results showed, first, that Japanese judgments of the target person's emotional expression were influenced by the expressions of the people in the background. In contrast, the expressions of the background people had no impact on the judgments of the faces for the Americans. This again provides evidence that East Asians attend more to the background context than Westerners do.

In this study, the participants viewed the scenes while they were connected to an eye-tracker, so every movement of their eye was monitored. The test question was whether people from the two cultures were looking at the same things. Figure 9.2 shows the percentage of time participants were looking at the central figure compared to the background. In the first 1,000 milliseconds there is little cultural difference (although this difference is significant). That is, both Americans and Japanese are spending more than 90% of the time looking at the target figure, with the American percentage a little higher than

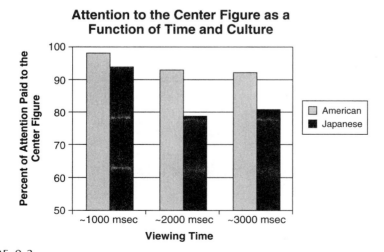

FIGURE 9.2

When looking at a picture, Americans focus more on the center figure than do Japanese, especially after the first second has passed.

the Japanese. In the next two 1,000 millisecond intervals people in both cultures start to look a little more at the background. But this is especially so for Japanese. Whereas the Americans are still devoting over 90% of their attention to the central figure, the Japanese are devoting somewhere between 70% and 80%. Furthermore, this pattern does not seem to be limited to scenes in which the background is composed of other people, which arguably might be more interesting for those with more interdependent selves. Similar cultural differences have been found when Chinese and American students looked at inanimate scenes (Chua, Boland, & Nisbett, 2005). Again the Americans were more likely to attend to the foreground objects than were the Chinese, who looked more at the background. Furthermore, the Chinese participants made more **saccades** than did the Americans. Saccades are the extremely quick eye movements that shift people's gaze from one fixation point to another. Compared to the Americans the Chinese were more systematically scanning the entire scene.

These studies suggest, quite remarkably, that people from different cultures are not seeing the same things, even when they are looking at identical scenes. The stimuli perceived by our brains are different across cultures. Our eye movements occur largely outside of our voluntary control, suggesting just how deeply these cultural differences in attention lie. East Asians have been socialized from such a young age to attend to relationships that they do so unconsciously by continually scanning scenes. Westerners, in contrast, have been socialized to attend to focal objects and they thus habitually tend to direct their attention at such objects.

This brings us back to the paintings that we saw at the beginning of this chapter. If you recall, Masuda and colleagues found that horizons tend to be painted significantly higher in East Asian paintings than in Western ones. A higher horizon calls attention to the depth of the setting and allows for all the different objects and places within a scene to be seen in relation to each other, whereas a lower horizon reduces the range of the scene that is visible. The East Asian paintings thus naturally direct an audience's eyes to the relations among the different objects and places within a scene whereas Western paintings tend to direct an audience's attention to particular focal objects. The same kinds of physical landscape scenes are represented quite differently by artists depending on their cultural background.

Likewise, Western portraits tended to show larger figures than East Asian ones. The larger figures, in particular the larger faces, serve to focus one's attention on the portrayed individual. The figure comes to dominate the scene and stands apart from the background. In contrast, in the East Asian portrait the individual remains firmly ensconced within the surrounding context. Comparing the two portraits here, it is not difficult to tell which culture has cultivated more of a sense that individuals are distinct and autonomous centers of agency.

It is possible, however, that the differences in the paintings reflect old artistic conventions rather than the aesthetic preferences that people presently have. To investigate whether cultural differences in perception affect the art people produce today, Masuda and colleagues asked participants to draw some pictures on their own (Masuda, Gonzalez et al., 2005). Specifically, American and Japanese college students were asked to draw a landscape scene within 5 minutes that contained at least a house, a tree, a river, a person, and a horizon. They were told they could draw any additional objects that they wanted. A couple of representative examples are shown below. Two characteristics of the drawings were analyzed. First, as in the paintings, the height of the horizon in the picture was measured. Replicating the findings from the paintings in the art museums, Japanese drew a horizon that was significantly higher in the picture than it was for the Americans. Also, the Japanese tended to provide a more complex background in their drawings in that they included 75% more contextual objects than did the Americans. Overall, Japanese were

The house on the left is a representative landscape drawing by an American participant in Masuda and colleagues' study and the one on the right is a representative drawing by a Japanese participant. The American drawings had lower horizons and fewer objects to contextualize the scene (Masuda, Gonzalez, et al., 2005).

more likely than Americans to situate their objects in context. In sum, aesthetic preferences appear to be influenced by culturally influenced tendencies to attend to foreground objects or background scenes.

In Chapter 4, Development and Socialization, we discussed how child-rearing styles could lead people from different cultures to develop more analytic or more holistic ways of thinking. However, this might not be the whole story behind these cultural differences. Cultures differ in many ways, and this documented difference between East Asian and Western thinking styles might stem from other cultural factors in addition to child rearing. For example, consider whether it's reasonable to assume that the landscapes one habitually sees will influence whether one is likely to attend more to focal objects or to backgrounds. Some landscapes are so populated with different objects and contours that they naturally draw your attention out to the various features in the background. To investigate this possibility, Japanese and American landscape scenes were contrasted (Miyamoto & Nisbett, 2006). From each country one large city (Tokyo and New York), one medium-sized city (Ann Arbor, Michigan, and Hikone, Shiga Prefecture), and one small city (Chelsea, Michigan, and Torahime, Shiga Prefecture) were selected. These cities were chosen as each city in a pair was matched along several dimensions. Then the researchers went out with cameras to take pictures of a number of places in those cities; specifically, pictures of hotels and elementary schools. The pictures were taken from identical perspectives and distances. Some pictures of these are shown on the next page.

The pictures were then subjected to a "particle analysis" in which a computer program outlined the boundary of each object and counted the number of objects in each scene. The results indicated that there were significantly more objects in the Japanese pictures than in the corresponding American ones. This demonstrates that the scenes that Japanese and Americans see on a day-to-day basis vary in their complexity.

These findings suggest that the relatively busier scenes of day-to-day life in Japan would lead Japanese to be more likely to attend to the background than Americans, although the results are not conclusive. To show that the busy scenes in Japan have an impact on people's attention to backgrounds, it is necessary to demonstrate that holistic perception (i.e., attending to the background) increases when people view busy scenes. To test this, the pictures of the cities that were obtained from the first study were used in a sec-

Small   Medium   Large

City Size

This grid of photos compares similar types of locations in small, medium, and large cities in Japan and the United States. In general, the Japanese scenes have more distinct objects than the American scenes.

ond study to "prime" both Americans and Japanese by showing them either Japanese or American scenes. Then, to assess their participants' attentional styles, researchers showed them another picture on the computer of a scene of an airport. What was special about this airport scene was that the scene kept changing. Some of the changes were in objects in the foreground (e.g., a plane would change colors), and some of the changes were in the background (e.g., the control tower would appear in different places). Other research has found, quite remarkably, that people will not notice such changes, even substantial changes, unless they are directly attending to the location that is changing. This inability to detect change in a scene is known as "change blindness" (Rensink, O'Regan, & Clark, 1997). If people are showing a holistic attentional style, attending to the background, they should notice more of the changes in the background than people who are showing an analytic attentional style, and are attending to focal objects in the foreground. Two things of interest emerged. First, overall, Japanese noticed more of the changes to the background than did Americans, which reflects their greater holistic attentional tendencies (also see Masuda & Nisbett, 2006, for similar results). Second, both Americans and Japanese were more likely to identify the changes in the background when they had been primed with pictures of Japanese scenes than when they had been primed with pictures of American scenes. In sum, the busy scenes of Japanese day-to-day life appear to make both Japanese and Americans more holistic in their attentional styles.

Understanding Other People's Behaviors

Whether a person is attending in a holistic manner or an analytic manner has a number of important consequences. For example, consider how an individual would go about understanding another person's behaviors. Imagine you see an acquaintance, Dan, in a store arguing angrily with a shop clerk. You very well might wonder why Dan is behaving like this. One way to explain Dan's behavior would be to consider his internal characteristics. For example, perhaps he has a short temper, and his arguing is evidence of his sometimes disagreeable personality. A second way would be to consider characteristics of the situation he is in. Perhaps Dan is angry because he purchased some defective merchandise and the store clerk is not allowing him to exchange it. These are two very different ways of explaining the same behavior.

Trying to understand people's behavior by considering their inner characteristics is an extension of an analytic way of thinking. Analytic thinking involves understanding objects by identifying their underlying attributes, and this is akin to trying to understand people and their behavior by considering their inner qualities—such as their personality traits. In contrast, explaining people's behavior by considering how the situation is influencing them is an extension of a holistic way of thinking. It requires considering the individual's relations with his or her context. Given what we know about cultural differences in analytic and holistic ways of thinking, we would expect Westerners to be more likely to explain people's behaviors in terms of their underlying dispositions (i.e., they will make **dispositional attributions**) and East Asians—and perhaps people from other cultural backgrounds as well—to be more likely to explain people's behaviors in terms of contextual variables (i.e., they will make **situational attributions**).

The Fundamental Attribution Error. Imagine you experienced the following: You read an essay written in the 1960s by a person who was asked to write about Fidel Castro, who at the time was widely perceived as the United States' number one enemy. The essay makes a number of arguments that are clearly pro-Castro. What do you think the essay writer's true attitudes are toward Castro? Well, you would have no reason to doubt the writer's motives so you would surely assume that he or she has favorable attitudes toward Castro. And you would likely assume that the writer had negative attitudes toward Castro if the essay included many arguments that are anti-Castro. It is perfectly reasonable to assume that the essay writer has written about his or her true attitudes. Now, however, imagine that before reading the essay you are told that the writer had been instructed to write with a perspective that was to be used in a debate—that is, those who wrote pro-Castro essays had been told to write an essay defending Castro whereas those who wrote anti-Castro essays had been told to write an essay criticizing Castro. Your task remains the same: identifying the essay writer's true attitudes toward Castro. What do you think? Well, it's not so straightforward now, as we shouldn't assume that the writer has expressed his or her true attitude because of instructions to take a particular position. Really, the essay tells us virtually nothing about the writer's true attitudes. However, as Jones and Harris (1967) found in a classic social psychological study, people still assume that the person who was instructed to write a pro-Castro essay had positive attitudes toward Castro and that the person who was instructed to write an anti-Castro essay had negative attitudes toward Castro. That is, they attributed the behavior of writing the essay to reflecting the essay writer's underlying personality even though it was clear to them that the writers had no choice in what they wrote. This tendency to ignore situational information (such as the conditions under which the writers wrote their essays) while focusing on dispositional information (the essay writers' assumed attitudes) is known as the **fundamental attribution error**. It is termed fundamental as it is viewed to be deeply ingrained in us. When we see people acting, we assume they are doing so because of their underlying dispositions, and we tend to ignore the situational constraints that might be driving their behavior.

However, as with so many other psychological phenomena, this research had been conducted almost exclusively with North American participants. A natural question emerged: How fundamental is the fundamental attribution error? Is it a universal tendency to explain other people's behaviors primarily in terms of their personality while ignoring other situational influences?

The anthropologist Clifford Geertz suggests that it is not. He asserts that people in some other cultures—for example, the Balinese—do not tend to conceive of people's behaviors in terms of underlying dispositions, but instead see them as emerging out of the roles the people have (Geertz, 1975). This idea was developed further by Shweder and Bourne (1982), who contrasted Indians and Americans in terms of the ways they described others. Indians, from the state of Orissa, tended to describe others by saying things like "She brings cakes to my family on festival days." In contrast, Americans were more likely to say things like "She is friendly." That is, Americans were more likely to conceive of people in terms of abstract personality traits than were the Indians, who attended to others in terms of the concrete behaviors they engaged in. Comparable cultural differences in tendencies to focus on traits is also evident in a number of other experimental paradigms (e.g., Argyle, Shimoda, & Little, 1978; Maass, Karasawa, Politi, & Suga, 2005; Zarate, Uleman, & Voils, 2001).

This question was further explored with the same national groups (Miller, 1984). In an attempt to learn the age at which these different ways of understanding people's behaviors emerged across cultures, children (8, 11, and 15 years of age) and university students were recruited from India and the United States. The participants were asked to describe a situation when someone had behaved in either a prosocial manner or a deviant manner, and then to explain why the person had behaved that way. For example, this is an example of a deviant behavior described by an Indian participant:

> This concerns a motorcycle accident. The back wheel burst on the motorcycle. The passenger sitting in the rear jumped. The moment the passenger fell, he struck his head on the pavement. The driver of

the motorcycle—who is an attorney—as he was on his way to court for some work, just took the passenger to a local hospital and went on and attended to his court work. I personally feel the motorcycle driver did a wrong thing. The driver left the passenger there without consulting the doctor concerning the seriousness of the injury—the gravity of the situation—whether the passenger should be shifted immediately—and he went on to court. So ultimately the passenger died.

The reasons people gave for the actor's behaviors were examined, noting, in particular, whether they made explanations that referred to the actor's general disposition or to the context. Other reasons for the actor's behavior are not included here. Figure 9.3 reveals that the 8-year-olds gave quite similar responses between the two cultures. However, as the American sample got older, they were more likely to make dispositional attributions whereas their situational attributions remained largely unchanged. In contrast, as the Indian sample got older, they made more situational attributions whereas their dispositional attributions did not change significantly. By the time they were

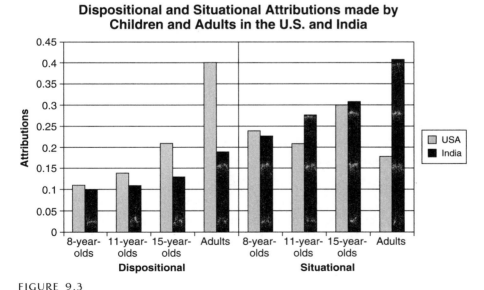

FIGURE 9.3

Although Indian and American children show similar attribution patterns, as Americans get older they tend to make more dispositional attributions, and as Indians get older they tend to make more situational attributions.

adults, the Americans showed clear evidence for the fundamental attribution error by explaining people's behaviors as largely due to their personalities. In contrast, the Indian adults did not show any evidence for the fundamental attribution error; rather, they showed evidence for a *reverse* fundamental attribution error as they tended to focus more on the situation than on the disposition. The fundamental attribution error does not look so fundamental any more.

This cultural difference in the way people explain the behavior of others has some important consequences (e.g., Lee, Hallahan, & Herzog, 1996). For example, how do we make sense of a person's behavior when it is against the law or causes great harm to others? This question was investigated by exploring the way newspaper articles described instances of behaviors that were undeniably antisocial—namely, mass murder (Morris & Peng, 1994). One instance was of a Chinese graduate student living in the United States who, on losing an award and failing to get a job, returned to school to kill his supervisor and several others. A second instance was of an American postal worker who, on losing his job, returned to work and, well, "went postal" and killed his supervisor and several others. Both of these stories were covered in the *New York Times* and the *World Journal*, the leading English and Chinese language newspapers. The newspaper articles about the stories were analyzed and each occasion was noted when the reporters offered details about the disposition of the accused (e.g., having a "very bad temper," being "mentally unstable") or about the situation that were relevant to the killings (e.g., had a "rivalry with a slain student," "had been recently fired"). Regardless of the particular story, the American stories overall made more references to the disposition of the accused than to the situation. In stark contrast, the Chinese stories made more references to the situations that had provoked the accused than to the person's disposition. Even the causes of extreme behaviors are interpreted differently across cultures. Indeed, these results suggest that courts in different cultures will likely view responsibility for crimes in quite different ways (for a striking contrast of how criminal responsibility is viewed in the Japanese and American legal systems see Hamilton & Sanders, 1992). These findings suggest that personality information is not seen as equally important for explaining the behavior of others in all cultural contexts, although the cultural differences are most pronounced when the situational information is made highly salient (e.g., Choi & Nisbett, 1998). Even though the structure of personality appears to be largely similar across cultures (see Chapter 5, Self and Personality), Westerners tend to use this information more for understanding others (and themselves) than do East Asians (also see Cousins, 1989; Suh, 2002).

Reasoning Styles

Another indication that an analytic or holistic orientation affects people's thinking is in the ways they reason. For example, if analytic thinkers tend to view the world as operating according to a set of universal abstract rules and laws, they will apply such rules and laws when they try to make sense of a situation. In contrast, holistic thinkers should be more likely to make sense of a situation by considering the relationships among objects or events. They should look for evidence of similarity among events or of temporal contiguity of events. This suggests that analytic and holistic thinkers might go about solving problems in quite different ways.

Look at Figure 9.4. There are two groups of flowers and there are two target objects. The task for you is to decide which target flower, A or B, is more similar to those in Group 1 and which is more similar to those in Group 2. What do you think?

This example is tricky as it pits two different reasoning styles against each other. If you are to make the decision based on the application of an abstract

FIGURE 9.4

To which group do the two target flowers belong? This stimulus pits associative reasoning against rule-based reasoning.

rule, then you would conclude that Flower A goes with Group 2 and Flower B goes with Group 1. The reason is that the only characteristic that consistently distinguishes the flowers in Groups 1 and 2 is the shape of the stems. All the flowers in Group 1 have a curved stem whereas all of the flowers in Group 2 have a straight stem. Applying this rule would lead you to conclude that Flower A belongs to Group 2 and Flower B to Group 1. This way of thinking would be an example of formal logical reasoning, which is argued to be more common among analytic thinkers.

In contrast, if you were to base your decision on the similarity of the target flowers to the groups you would have reached a different conclusion. Flower A is more similar to most of the flowers in Group 1 because most of the flowers in that group have round petals, have one leaf, and have only one circle. Likewise, Flower B is more similar overall to the flowers in Group 2. However, none of those features characterize all the flowers in the group so these similarities do not become rules. Therefore, in this picture the application of a rule leads to a different solution than would be reached with similarity-based judgments.

American and East Asian participants were presented with a set of pictures like this, each of which involved a conflict between the application of a rule and similarity-based judgments (Norenzayan, Smith, Kim, & Nisbett, 2002). When presented with such stimuli, European-Americans were more likely to base their decisions on the application of the rule whereas East Asians were more likely to base their decision on the perceived similarities of the stimuli. As would be expected, Asian-Americans fell in between the other two groups (see Figure 9.5).

Note, however, that this study shows that East Asians are more likely to use holistic reasoning in a situation when there is a *conflict* between an analytic and a holistic solution. In situations when there is no conflict Westerners should be able to engage in holistic reasoning and East Asians should be able to rely on analytic reasoning strategies. One domain in which we see problems that require purely analytic reasoning strategies is in most math and science problems. Because these problems typically do not have the kind of conflict between holistic and analytic strategies that we saw in the studies by Norenzayan and colleagues, East Asians should have no difficulty solving them, even though they involve analytic thinking. As we saw in Chapter 4, Development and Socialization, if anything, East Asians tend to excel on purely analytical problems.

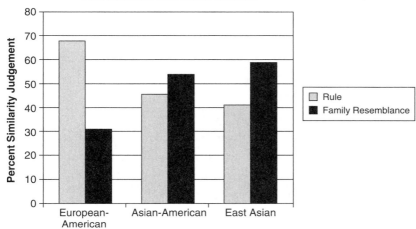

Differences in Similarity Judgments between Americans and East Asians

FIGURE 9.5

When deciding whether two stimuli are similar, European-Americans rely more on rule-based reasoning whereas East Asians base their reasoning more on family resemblances.

Another way that holistic or analytic thinking influences reasoning styles is in the kinds of information people perceive to be relevant to a task. A truly holistic thinker is aware of the countless ways that things in the world are related to each other. For example, putting pressure on a point on one's heel could be seen to help relieve a headache. A drop in the stock market could be seen to influence the birth rate. Holistic thinkers tend to see actions as having distal, and sometimes unexpected, consequences. In contrast, analytic thinkers should focus their attention on the relations between a relatively small number of discrete objects or events. For example, one billiard ball is seen to move when another collides with it. Cutting taxes is seen to increase the amount of disposable income consumers have. Analytic thinkers should be more concerned with *direct* relations between objects or events.

Imagine, as participants in a study were asked, how you would go about solving a murder mystery (Choi, Dalal, Kim-Prieto, & Park, 2003). All you know is that a graduate student is suspected of killing his advisor. You have 97 different items of information that you can consider to help you crack the case. Some of these seem to be directly relevant to solving the murder—for example, what the graduate student was supposedly doing on the night in question, or whether the graduate student had a history of violence. In contrast, the direct relevance of some of the items is not so clear—for example, the graduate student's favorite color or the way the professor was dressed. What information would you use to solve the murder?

The answer to this question appears to differ between Koreans and Americans. When given the opportunity to exclude any information they found to be irrelevant to the case, Americans discarded more information than did Koreans. For more analytical Americans, the murder mystery could best be solved by focusing only on those items that were most relevant to the case. In contrast, the more holistic Koreans felt that a greater number of the items had possible relations with the murder. For holistic thinkers the world consists of many overlapping and related events. Some details that might seem trivial at first glance could ultimately prove to be relevant.

Toleration of Contradiction

In addition to the holistic view that everything is fundamentally interconnected, East Asians seem also to share a corresponding view that reality is continually in flux. This sense of the ultimate fluidity of reality is captured in the Tai Chi, the symbol that encompasses the Yin and the Yang. The Yin and the Yang represent opposites (literally, they mean the moon and the sun), and they indicate that the universe is constantly in flux, moving from one opposite pole to the other and back again. The darkness of the night will yield to the brightness of the day, which will lead to the darkness again, and the cycle will continue to repeat. This belief in a fluid and cyclical reality is perhaps most clearly evident in the writings of Lao Tzu, the legendary founder of Taoism. In the *Tao Te Ching*, he said, "To shrink something, you need to expand it first. To weaken something, you need to strengthen it first. To abolish something, you need to flourish it first. To take something, you need to give it first" (Lao Tzu, 2000 version). This view not only highlights that reality is in flux but it also indicates that opposing truths can be simultaneously accepted.

Around the time of Lao Tzu, a few thousand miles away, Aristotle was offering a very different scheme for making sense of the world around us. He proposed the law of contradiction, in which he submitted that no statement could be both true and false, and thus "A" could not equal "not A." This law is at the heart of much of logical reasoning. In stark contrast to this Aristotelian law, ancient Chinese thought, as captured in the *I Ching* (*The Book of Changes,* 1991), includes a principle of contradiction. Because everything is perceived to be fundamentally connected with everything else and constantly in flux, real contradiction ceases to exist. If "A" is connected with "not A," and if "A" is always changing into "not A," then "A" is no longer in contradiction with "not A." With this orientation toward the world, contradiction is not something to be rejected, but should be accepted. This acceptance of contradiction has been termed **naïve dialecticism** (Peng & Nisbett, 1999). It reflects a profoundly different way of making sense of the world compared with Western logical reasoning.

Consider the following two arguments:

A: A sociologist who surveyed college students from 100 universities claimed that there is a high correlation among college female students between smoking and being skinny.

B: A biologist who studied nicotine addiction asserted that heavy doses of nicotine often lead to becoming overweight.

Can you see the apparent contradiction in these two arguments? One argument is that smoking leads to weight loss whereas the other is that smoking leads to weight gain. They are not strictly contradictory, as it is possible for both of them to be true, even from a logical perspective. However, the general thrust of the arguments are in opposition to each other. Take a moment to think about how compelling you view these two arguments to be.

Chinese and American students were given these arguments as well as a number of other contradictory pairs (Peng & Nisbett, 1999). Half the participants received only one argument (either Argument A or Argument B), with which they indicated how compelling they found it to be. As shown in the left halves of the two figures in Figure 9.6, both Americans and Chinese who received only Argument A tended to view it as more compelling than those who received only Argument B. Because these participants saw only one argument they did not witness any potential contradiction. The other half of the participants were asked to evaluate both the contradictory

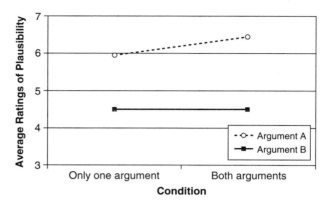

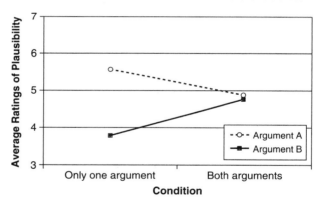

FIGURE 9.6

When Americans encounter two contradictory arguments, they come to view the better argument as even more compelling than when they encounter this same argument by itself. In contrast, when Chinese encounter two contradictory arguments, they come to view the weaker argument as more compelling than when it is presented by itself.

arguments. These participants saw a potential contradiction. How did seeing the contradiction affect their evaluations of the arguments?

First, let's look at the right half of the American figure. These participants read both of the contradictory arguments. The top line in the graph indicates that Americans who encountered the contradictory Argument B were even more convinced that Argument A was compelling than those who had read only Argument A. This is a puzzling response, although it is consistent with some past research with Westerners (Lord, Ross, & Lepper, 1979). It would seem that if participants did not find Argument B to be compelling, a normative strategy would be to ignore it, or perhaps to hedge their bets by being a little less confident in Argument A. But the Americans who saw Argument B instead responded by being even more confident in Argument A. The Americans are thus responding to the contradiction by denying that it exists—they are confident that Argument A is the better argument, and thus they are denying that there is a problematic contradiction.

Next, look at the right half of the Chinese figure. The top line indicates that the Chinese became less convinced in the plausibility of Argument A when they encountered an apparently contradictory argument, even though that argument tended to be viewed as less plausible. They appear to have adjusted their evaluations in the light of the evidence, which would seem to be a sensible strategy for reaching sound conclusions. The bottom line of the figure, however, indicates a puzzling pattern. When the Chinese participants encountered Argument B by itself they did not find it to be very plausible. However, when they saw this rather unconvincing argument paired with the more compelling Argument A that makes the opposite case, they were then *more* convinced by the rather implausible Argument B. The idea that smoking was associated with weight gain was compelling to them only if they had also read an argument that smoking was associated with weight loss! My helplessly undialectical mind cannot make heads or tails of this kind of reasoning. Apparently, the Chinese are reacting to the arguments in that they have noticed the contradiction, and this reminds them that the world is often contradictory, making it difficult to say which side is right and which is wrong. The contradiction is accepted as it is, and they do not seem motivated to get rid of it.

This greater tolerance for contradiction found among East Asians is not just evident in how they reason about the external world. We can also see it in the ways that people think of themselves. For example, in one study Chinese and American participants were asked to describe themselves in an open-ended questionnaire (Spencer-Rodgers, Peng, Wang, & Hou, 2004). The Chinese were significantly more likely than Americans to provide statements that were in apparent contradiction with each other (e.g., Chinese individuals would provide answers that suggested they had both high self-esteem and low self-esteem; also see Bagozzi, Wong, & Yi, 1999). Likewise, other research has found that Koreans would endorse items that suggested they were introverted *and* that they were extraverted (Choi & Choi, 2002), and Japanese were more likely than Canadians to hold contradictory views of their personalities (Hamamura, Heine, & Paulhus, 2007). In sum, East Asians appear to hold views about themselves that are more contradictory than those that are held by North Americans. Even within themselves, East Asians can tolerate apparent contradictions.

Because East Asians more than Westerners perceive life as fluid and changing, other interesting cultural differences emerge in the ways people think. Westerners also understand that the world changes; however, it appears that their views on change are slightly different from those of East Asians. Relative to East Asians, Westerners appear to view change as occurring in more linear ways. For example, if a stock has risen over the past year, it will likely rise again next year. The earth has grown warmer over the past few decades indicating that it will continue to grow warmer over the next few as well. The birth rate has dropped over the past generation so it will probably continue to drop over the next generation. Change appears to occur in rather static and predictable ways.

In contrast, East Asians appear to believe that change itself happens in rather fluid and unpredictable ways. Consider the following story which is known to almost every Chinese:

> One day an old farmer's horse ran away from him. His neighbors came by to comfort him, but he said "How can you know it isn't a good thing?" And a few days later, his horse came back, bringing a wild horse with it. His neighbors came to congratulate the old man, who said, "How can you know it isn't a bad thing?" A few weeks later, the old man's son was trying to ride the horse and he fell off, breaking his leg. When the neighbors came over to express condolences, the old man said "How can you know it isn't a good thing?" The next month a war broke out, and all the able-bodied young men were recruited to fight it. The old man's son did not have to go because of his broken leg, and he survived with his father. (cited in Ji, 2005)

This story shows that change can happen at any time and often in precisely opposite ways of what one is anticipating. To the extent that this story captures widely shared beliefs among East Asians, we would expect differences in the ways people predict how the future will unfold. One study investigated this question by providing Chinese and American students with a number of graphs indicating the past performance of a number of trends, such as the global economy growth rates or the worldwide death rate for cancer (Ji, Nisbett, & Su, 2001). Participants were asked to estimate what they thought would happen over the next few years. The Chinese were almost twice as likely as Americans to predict that the trend would reverse direction in the future whereas Americans were more likely than Chinese to assume that the trend would continue on in the same direction as in the past. This suggests that attitudes toward the future vary considerably across cultures, and that East Asians, in general, are more likely than Westerners to expect that the future will unfold in unexpected ways.

Talking and Thinking

One characteristic that makes us human is that we talk. Having a spoken language is one key way that humans differ from other species, and this has been argued to be, in part, responsible for humans' impressive cultural achievements. However, there is more to the story than just that humans talk. We also need to consider why we talk and the consequences of talking. Interestingly, this very basic task of talking has some dramatically different implications for the ways we think across cultures.

Consider this excerpt from a newspaper article reported in the *San Jose Mercury News* (cited in Kim, 2002).

> A professor . . . encourages his Asian students to speak up in class by making it part of the class grade. He makes speaking in front of the class mandatory for some assignments. "Once they understand this is the norm you expect, they'll get used to it," he says. "But you have to make it clear." (Lubman, 1998, p. A12)

This reporter is focusing on an issue that is commonly discussed in colleges and universities with a large population of students of Asian descent. Often students of Asian background speak up less in class than people of other cultural backgrounds (Tweed & Lehman, 2002). This relative silence is often viewed as a cause for concern and tends to be perceived by professors and other students as shyness or even a lack of interest in the class. Drawing these kinds of inferences reveals an assumption that talking reflects thinking and engagement in class. Heejung Kim (2002), however, argues that this assumption about talking is very much grounded in Western cultural practices, and that talking can affect people from different cultures in quite different ways.

Talking and language have held a privileged position in much of Western intellectual history. Kim notes that among the ancient Greeks, Homer concluded that there was no greater skill than to be a good debater, and Socrates thought that knowledge existed within people and could be revealed only through verbal reasoning. In Judeo-Christian beliefs the "Word" was viewed as sacred because of its divine power to create. Within the United States the freedom to speak one's mind is a birthright, protected by the First Amendment to the Constitution. Speaking is valued in the West because it is viewed as an act of self-expression and as inextricably bound to thought.

In contrast, however, in many East Asian cultural traditions there has been considerably less emphasis on talking, if not outright suspicion of the spoken word. Lao Tzu wrote, "He who knows does not speak. He who speaks does not know." Practitioners of many Eastern religions pursue truth through silent meditation rather than through spoken prayer. And as a Korean proverb states, "An empty cart makes more noise." In many ways, Eastern cultural traditions have not cultivated a belief that thought and speech are closely related.

There are rather pronounced cultural differences in speech among young children. Japanese mothers have been shown to speak less to their young children than their American counterparts (Caudill & Weinstein, 1969), and Chinese infants as young as 7 months of age have been shown to vocalize less in response to laboratory events than Euro-American infants (Kagan, Kearsley, & Zelazo, 1977). Comparable differences have also been found among older children (Minami, 1994). It is important to understand that less speech does not necessarily mean less communication. Indeed, the closer the relationship, the more people are likely to rely on nonverbal communication rather than the spoken word (Azuma, 1986; Clancy, 1986), a point to which we'll soon return. Nonetheless, the data on the development of speech among East Asian compared to Western children is suggestive that talking might have different implications across cultures.

Kim (2002) reasoned that if talking really does have a different relation with thinking for East Asians and Westerners, then you should see variations in performance on cognitive tasks depending on whether participants are asked to speak. Namely, expressing one's thoughts out loud should interfere with the performance of East Asians on cognitive tasks whereas it should have little impact on the performance of Westerners. To investigate this question, participants were asked to complete a version of Raven's Progressive Matrices, the nonverbal IQ test we discussed in Chapter 2. The participants were all born in the United States and had English as their native language. Half of them were of European descent, and half of them were of East Asian descent (their parents were all born in an East Asian country). The 20-item test was separated into two halves of 10 items each. For the first 10 items of the test the participants were asked to sit alone in a room and to work through the test without speaking at all. For the second 10 items the participants remained by themselves in a room yet they received one of two sets of instructions. Participants who were assigned to a "Thinking Aloud" condition were asked to talk aloud into a computer microphone as they worked through the second half of the test. The participants were simply vocalizing their thoughts as they solved the items. In contrast, participants who were assigned to an "Articulatory Suppression" condition were instructed to repeat the alphabet out loud into a computer microphone as they worked on the items. (I'll explain the rationale for the Articulatory Suppression condition later.) The key variable was the number of items in the second half of the study that participants answered correctly in the allotted time period compared to the number they had answered correctly in the first half.

First, look at the left half of Figure 9.7. These scores reveal the impact that talking aloud had on the performance of participants compared to answering the items in silence. The European-Americans performed about the same on the test when they were speaking as when they were silent (the difference between the two conditions is not significant). This suggests that talking and thinking are very much related for European-Americans. In stark contrast, however, Asian-Americans performed significantly worse on the test when they were talking aloud. Expressing their thoughts out loud interfered with their thinking. This suggests that, at least for the kinds of items in Raven's Progressive Matrices, Asian-Americans will perform better if they are able to think quietly to themselves. Rather than indicating a lack of engagement among Asian-Americans, silence in the classroom often might indicate some good thinking.

So why would there be this cultural difference? As we learned earlier, people of Asian descent are more likely to engage in holistic thinking whereas

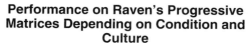

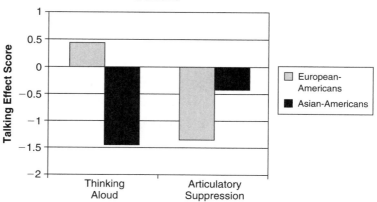

FIGURE 9.7

Thinking aloud impairs the performance of Asian-Americans on IQ test items, although saying the alphabet aloud while thinking has little impact on their scores. In contrast, thinking aloud has little impact on the performance of European-Americans, whereas reciting the alphabet impairs their performance.

Westerners are more likely to engage in analytic thinking. Holistic thinking involves an attention to the whole and the perception of how various parts are interrelated. The nature of holistic thinking makes it very difficult to express in words because speech is ultimately a sequential task. When you speak, one idea follows another. You can't easily describe multiple relations at once. In contrast, analytic thinking, with the emphasis on focusing on separate parts, lends itself very well to the spoken word. Each part can be described separately and sequentially. As such, speech is likely to interfere with performance on holistic tasks.

Some evidence of the interference between speech and holistic thinking can be seen when people are asked to describe faces. People's faces consist of various parts; however, people, including Westerners, tend to see them more as interrelated wholes. For example, one study showed people a number of pictures of faces and they were asked to describe each face they saw (Schooler & Engstler-Schooler, 1990). In describing the picture of Tom Cruise, people might say something like "He has thickish eyebrows, a big smile, dark hair, and is very attractive." However, those few observations hardly do justice to Tom Cruise's face. You've surely met hundreds of people who would fit this description, but they do not look like Tom Cruise.

There is much more to his face, and to anyone's, than the few statements people can offer in describing them. After describing the faces they saw, participants looked at another set of faces and were asked to indicate which ones they had seen before. Interestingly, the results indicated that people were better able to recognize the faces they had previously seen if they had *not* tried to describe them before. Apparently, their verbal descriptions interfered with their ability to process the face as a whole, causing them to have poorer recall.

Kim reasoned that if Asian-Americans were indeed thinking holistically as they tried to solve the items in the Raven's test, then they should be relatively unaffected by a verbal task that was unrelated to the test. This was the purpose of including the Articulatory Suppression condition in her study. Participants in that condition recited the alphabet while trying to solve the Raven's items. She reasoned that in this condition, the Asian-Americans should be free to think about the items in the test in the way that was most natural to them (i.e., considering the relations among the different parts of the items holistically), and they could then engage in the separate, and not very demanding, task of reciting the alphabet. Because these two tasks are so different they should cause very little interference with each other and performance should be largely unaffected. In contrast, however, if talking and thinking are fundamentally connected for European-Americans, then being asked to recite the alphabet while thinking about something else should be challenging. European-Americans in the Articulatory Suppression condition are having to engage in two verbal tasks at once: their verbal thoughts about how to solve the Raven's items, and their verbal thoughts associated with the alphabet. The results, as indicated in the right half of Figure 9.7 support this reasoning. European-Americans did very poorly on the IQ task when they were reciting the alphabet, indicating that their thoughts while solving that task apparently were verbal and were interfered with by their verbal recitation of the alphabet. In contrast, reciting the alphabet had no significant effect on the performance of the Asian-Americans. This suggests that the thoughts in the Asian-American participants' heads while solving the Raven's items were largely nonverbal thoughts. There thus seem to be some profound cultural differences in the ways people think, verbally or nonverbally, at least for the kinds of items in the Raven's test.

This cultural difference in the relation between talking and thinking has other implications as well. If what you say is viewed to be consistent with what is in your head, then speech can serve an important role for self-expression. To the extent that talking and thinking are viewed as intertwined, it is reasonable for others to infer things about you based on what you say. People can reveal themselves to the world by the things they say. In contrast, if talking is not so intimately connected with thinking, then people will see less of a connection between what one says and who one is.

Are there cultural differences in the relation of speech and self-expression? To investigate this question, European-Americans and Asian-Americans were asked to complete a questionnaire and they were then given four pens to choose from as compensation (Kim & Sherman, 2007). In one condition, participants were asked to write down which pen they would like; in the other, they never expressed their choice verbally. Then, they were allowed to take a pen. However, after they had taken their pen the experimenter asked for it back, saying that it was the last one she had, and she gave the participant an obviously inferior pen to replace it. Next, the participants completed another survey which included some questions about their satisfaction with the pen that they received. Not surprisingly, people, in general, were not especially happy with the inferior pen they had received after the experimenter took away their chosen pen. However, what was noteworthy was that the European-American evaluations of the pen hinged on whether they had earlier been asked to express their pen choice verbally (see Figure 9.8).

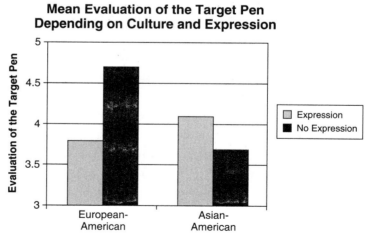

FIGURE 9.8

European-Americans who express their pen preferences evaluate a pen that was forced upon them more negatively than do those who did not express a pen preference earlier. Asian-Americans' pen evaluations were unaffected by whether they had expressed their preferences.

Those who had expressed their choice verbally for the pen that was taken from them were less satisfied with the inferior pen than those who did not express their choice. In contrast, the evaluations of the Asian–Americans were not significantly affected by expressing their choice. It seems that for the European–Americans, stating their choice was an act of self-expression and resulted in a greater feeling of commitment toward the soon-to-be usurped pen. In contrast, expressing their choices had no impact for the Asian–Americans and suggests that verbal self-expression is less of a concern for them.

Explicit Versus Implicit Communication

There is more to communicating with others than just expressing in words what you want to say. Much of what is communicated in the course of a conversation goes beyond the actual words that are used and is expressed in nonverbal gestures, facial expressions, and voice tone. You may have discovered, for example, how easy it can be to inadvertently upset someone in an e-mail or text message exchange. When the person cannot see your smile and wink, or hear the jovial tone of your voice, it is not always clear from what you have written whether you are making a joke or are saying something rude. All the nonverbal cues that are so important for effective communication are absent. Hence, people often resort to adding emoticons or abbreviations such as ;-) or LOL to their e-mail or text messages to add the nonverbal contextual cues that are lacking in these exchanges.

Although nonverbal communication is a big part of communication in all cultures, there are some rather pronounced cultural differences in the degree to which communication relies on explicit verbal information versus more implicit nonverbal cues. In explaining these cultural differences, Edward Hall (1976) made a distinction between high context and low context cultures. In a **high context culture,** people are deeply involved with each other, and this involvement leads them to have much shared information that guides behavior. There are clear and appropriate ways of behaving in each situation, and this information is widely shared and understood so it does not need to be explicitly communicated. Much of what is to be communicated can be inferred because people have a great deal of information in common that they can rely on, and thus they can be less explicit in what they say. In contrast, in a **low context culture** there is relatively less involvement among individuals, and there is less shared information to guide behavior. Because of relatively less shared information among individuals, it is necessary for people to communicate in more explicit detail, as others are less able to fill in the gaps of what is not said.

East Asian cultures are good examples of high context cultures whereas North American, and English-speaking cultures more generally, are good examples of low context ones. Typically, what is conveyed in some East Asian languages is considerably less explicit than what is communicated in English. As an English speaker who has struggled with learning Japanese I can testify that the difference in the explicitness of the language can be extremely challenging. A question in Japan such as "Is it OK if I park my car here?" might very well be answered with a pause, a strained look on the face, and only the words "Well, a little." It has taken years of effort for my helplessly explicit mind to learn that the words that are said in many situations are sometimes less important than the way they are said. A pause and a strained look on one's face sends the signal that is very clear to any native Japanese speaker, yet still remains rather opaque to me, that the person has information to communicate to me that he thinks I will find dissatisfying—namely, that it's not OK for me to park my car there. The key information is conveyed nonverbally, with the content of the words sometimes being rather empty.

One real-life situation in which nonverbal information is not communicated is when people leave messages on answering machines. Such messages do not allow speakers to receive any nonverbal cues about how their conversation partner is responding to their message. Rather, the speaker is left to deliver his entire message without any feedback. Given this, it is not surprising that people tend not to like speaking to answering machines. However, speaking to answering machines should be especially challenging for Japanese given their reliance on nonverbal communication. Indeed, research reveals that Japanese tend to actively avoid leaving messages on answering machines and are less than half as likely as Americans to do so. Furthermore, the reasons that Japanese offer for not liking answering machines are different from the ones offered by Americans. Americans say they don't like answering machines because they are worried that the target person might not check their messages, whereas Japanese don't like answering machines because they say that it's hard to speak without getting feedback (Miyamoto & Schwarz, 2006). Furthermore, Japanese seem to struggle much more than Americans when actually trying to leave a message on a machine. In one study, Japanese and American participants left a message on an answering machine while engaging in a demanding cognitive task. Although the two cultures did not differ in their performance on the cognitive task prior to leaving a message, while they were speaking into the answering machine the Japanese performance on the cognitive task fell significantly below that of Americans (Miyamoto & Schwarz, 2006). Apparently, it is far more cognitively demanding for Japanese to leave a message because they are trying hard to imagine how their target person will react to it.

Some clever lab experiments have further demonstrated a cultural difference in people's reliance on nonverbal communications (Ishii, Reyes, & Kitayama, 2003; Kitayama & Ishii, 2002). Japanese and American participants were presented aurally with words that were either pleasant (e.g., grateful, refreshment) or unpleasant (e.g., bitter, complaint), and these words were presented with either a pleasant sounding tone or with an unpleasant sounding tone. For some of the words the explicit meaning matched the tone, and for some the meaning of the words was opposite to the tone in which it was delivered. The participants were instructed either to ignore the tone of the word and answer whether the meaning of the word was pleasant or unpleasant or to ignore the meaning of the word and comment on whether the tone sounded pleasant or unpleasant. The key variable of interest was how long it took participants to respond when the tone and the meaning of the words were in conflict. The Americans showed more interference in their judgments when they made judgments about the vocal tone (while ignoring the meaning of the words) than they did when making judgments about the meaning of the words (while ignoring the vocal tone). This suggests that they chronically attend to the meaning of what is said more than they do to the tone in which it is spoken. In contrast, the Japanese participants showed the opposite pattern of results. Japanese showed more interference when they needed to attend to the meaning of the word and ignore the tone than they did when attending to the tone while ignoring the meaning. This suggests that Japanese are habitually attending to the tone in which things are said more than they are to the precise content of what is being said.

One alternative explanation to account for these results is that there is something about the Japanese language that requires people to attend to tone more than English. If this was the case, then the cultural differences would simply reflect the linguistic skills required by the languages rather than a cultural difference. To test for this alternative account the researchers replicated the study with another high context culture that used two languages. Specifically, Filipinos are collectivist, and many people are fluent in both the languages of Tagalog and English. If Filipinos have more difficulty ignoring vocal tones than the meaning regardless of the language they are speaking, this would suggest that the findings reflect cultural differences in attention to context rather than features of the language. Indeed, this is precisely what the researchers found (see Ishii et al., 2003).

Linguistic Relativity

The results of the Ishii et al. study demonstrate that specific features of the Tagalog and English languages do not explain why Filipinos attend to vocal tones more than Americans. However, the question raised here is an interesting one to explore more generally. How much does the language we speak affect how we think? This question was first formally proposed by Edward Sapir and his student Benjamin Whorf, and has become known as the Sapir-Whorf, or more commonly, the Whorfian (or linguistic relativity) hypothesis (Whorf, 1956). The strongest version of this hypothesis is that language determines how we think—that is, we are unable to do much thinking on a topic if we don't have the relevant words available to us. This strong version of the hypothesis has been almost universally rejected; much thought clearly occurs outside of language; for example, prelinguistic infants and toddlers show evidence for quite complex thinking in the absence of language. A weaker version of this hypothesis is that the language we speak affects how we think. It is mostly with respect to the weaker version that there has been much debate, controversy, and research.

The Whorfian hypothesis has a certain amount of intuitive appeal, and it has independently been proposed by a number of eminent thinkers (see Hunt & Agnoli, 1991, for a review). For example, Herodotus claimed that the Greeks and Egyptians thought differently because the Greeks wrote from left to right whereas the Egyptians wrote from right to left (Fishman, 1980). A couple thousand years later Einstein (1954) wrote, "Thus we may conclude that the mental development of the individual, and his way of forming concepts, depends to a high degree upon language. This makes us realize to what extent the same language means the same mentality. In this sense, thinking and language are linked together" (p. 336). George Orwell also realized the power of language on thought in his dark futuristic novel *1984,* in which the secret police developed a new language, "Newspeak," as a way of controlling the thoughts of the people. And today we can still see evidence that the Whorfian hypothesis is taken seriously in the movement for people to speak in terms that are "politically correct," or to use words that are deemed to be consistent with desired outcomes. The reasoning is that if people use words such as "physically challenged" rather than "handicapped" to describe people confined to wheelchairs, they will be more likely to think of these people as being capable and competent, which should serve to empower them. In many ways, the words that we speak are assumed to affect the ways that we think.

However, despite the intuitive appeal of the Whorfian hypothesis, it has been subject to some of the most intense debate and controversy in the field of psycholinguistics (e.g., Pinker, 1994; Roberson, Davies, & Davidoff, 2000). What kind of hard evidence is there for the Whorfian hypothesis? You can imagine how useful cross-cultural research could be for testing this hypothesis. One obvious way that many cultures differ from each other is in the languages that their people speak. And it is not just that different languages have different words for the same objects—the English horse is called a *cheval* in French and a *hevonen* in Finnish. Rather numerous words and concepts simply do not exist in many languages of the world. The question is thus whether people who speak different languages think in some different ways as well.

We briefly visited this hypothesis in Chapter 8, Emotions, in discussing that many emotion words are not shared across different languages. For example, the English language does not have an equivalent for the German word *schadenfreude.* Does this mean that English speakers experience this emotion more weakly than or differently from German speakers? The challenge with this question is that we really have no good way of testing it. Someone might think that he can experience *schadenfreude* the same as a typical German, but how could we really know that this is true? There are no clear physiological indicators of such emotions, and we have no way of knowing how our own internal emotional experiences compare with those of others. So the Whorfian hypothesis in the context of emotional experiences across cultures has remained largely untested.

Tests of the Whorfian hypothesis have emerged in other contexts as well. Much of the debate has occurred in the context of color perception and memory. Color is an especially appropriate domain for investigating the Whorfian hypothesis because, perceptually, color is a continuous variable that extends gradually through all the hues of the rainbow; yet linguistically it is a discrete variable, as we have particular color terms for certain ranges of light wavelengths within the color spectrum. More important, different languages parse the spectrum of colors in dramatically divergent ways.

An analysis of the different color lexicons known for all the subsistence societies around the world that have been investigated has revealed some intriguing patterns (Berlin & Kay, 1969). There is tremendous diversity in the ways people label colors, and this diversity emerges in systematic ways. All known languages have a minimum of two color terms. The one identified language (Dani) that has only two terms had words that were glossed as "black" (which included all dark-hued colors) and "white" (which included all lighter hues). Next in line are languages that had precisely three color terms. All of the languages with three color terms had words that were glossed as black, white, and red (which included some oranges, yellows, browns, pinks, and purples, with red being the focus of the category). Languages that have precisely four color terms had words that approximated the colors of black, white, red, and either green or yellow. Languages with five color terms have the same words including words for *both* green and yellow. Languages with six color terms add blue to the list, and languages with seven terms include a word for brown. And languages with eight color terms add either purple, pink, gray, or orange to the list. Furthermore, the focal point of each of these color categories (e.g., the most prototypical green in an array of different shades of green) is largely similar across language groups. In sum, people who speak different languages carve up the color spectrum in some rather divergent ways; however, these differences do not emerge arbitrarily, and there are some strikingly consistent patterns across languages.

Does the fact that people from different cultures have carved up the color spectrum differently affect how people perceive colors? Take the example of the English color term "blue." English speakers use this word to refer to the color of the sky, blueberries, and the South Pacific Ocean. The Japanese word for blue is *ao*, and this word is also used to refer to the color of the sky, blueberries, and the South Pacific Ocean, but the same term is used to refer to the color of a lawn, a freshly shaven scalp, and what English speakers would call a green traffic signal. A Whorfian question automatically arises:

When Japanese and English speakers look at the same patch of lawn, are they actually perceiving the same color?

The strongest test of this kind of question has been conducted by contrasting people who speak languages that differ the most in terms of their color lexicons (Japanese color terms, for the most part, map quite clearly onto their English counterparts, making for a weaker comparison). Rosch Heider (Rosch Heider, 1972; Rosch Heider & Olivier, 1972) conducted a seminal series of studies investigating this question. She visited the Dugum Dani, a stone-age agricultural population living in Irian Jaya that purportedly had only two color terms. Rosch Heider contrasted the performance of this group on a variety of color perception tasks with that of English-speaking Americans. The results of her studies indicated that the Dani remembered colors in similar ways to Americans, despite having such divergent color categories. Furthermore, the Dani could learn and recall new words that were associated with colors that corresponded with the foci of the eight basic chromatic categories of English more easily than they could learn words for colors that occupied intermediate points along the color spectrum. In sum, the evidence suggested that color perception and memory were largely independent from the color words that were in a language. The results of these studies were enormously influential and were interpreted as providing convincing evidence that language does not affect color perception; also, the results more generally were interpreted to suggest that the Whorfian hypothesis was untenable in other domains as well.

Rosch Heider's studies were largely perceived as having the final say on the Whorfian debate over the next 30 years, despite the fact that various researchers called attention to a number of potentially serious flaws in the experimental design and interpretation of these studies (e.g., Lucy & Shweder, 1979; Ratner, 1989; Saunders & Van Brakel, 1997) and that several calls for the need to replicate these findings went unheeded (e.g., Davies, 1997; Gellantly, 1995). More recently, research by Roberson and colleagues (Roberson et al., 2000; Roberson, Davidoff, Davies, & Shapiro, 2005) have attempted to address some of the criticisms of Rosch Heider's earlier studies.

Roberson and colleagues (2000) studied monolingual Berinmo speakers from isolated villages in Papua, New Guinea, whose language contains five basic color terms; these correspond, roughly, to black (*kel*), white (*wap*), red (*mehi*), yellow (*wor*), and green (*nol*). In addition, Roberson and colleagues

(2005) investigated monolingual Himba speakers, who are semi-nomadic cattle herders from Namibia. The Himba language also contains five basic color terms, which, likewise, correspond roughly to black (*zoozu*), white (*vapa*), red (*serandu*), yellow (*dumbu*), and green (*burou*), although the boundaries of these colors differ somewhat from those of the Berinmo. Although there is much overlap between the color boundaries and exemplars for the three languages, there are some clear differences.

Roberson and colleagues (2000, 2005) replicated the same basic methodology of Rosch Heider and contrasted the performance of the Berinmo and Himba with English-speaking Britons. First, their replications of Rosch Heider's work called into question the evidence for universal color perception on a number of rather technical grounds. Simply put, they found considerable evidence for cultural variation in the ways that people in the different cultures learned and remembered colors. Second, they included some studies that went beyond some perceived shortcomings in the original methodology of Rosch Heider. The Roberson studies were based on the idea that different color categories should affect people's **categorical perception** of colors. Much research has shown that we tend to perceive stimuli in categorical terms—that is, we tend to perceive stimuli as belonging to separate and discrete categories, even though the stimuli may gradually differ from each other along a continuum. For example, there is a continuum of sounds that exists between the phonemes of "ba" and "pa," however, any sound that exists along that continuum is perceived by English speakers as either "ba" or "pa," and not as something in between (MacMillan, 1987).

Roberson and colleagues reasoned that a good test of whether color labels influence our perception would be whether people given different color labels are similarly affected by the boundaries that exist between color categories. Participants were shown three different colored chips and were asked which of two chips, Chip 1 or Chip 2, was more similar to the target chip. The chips were chosen so that the target chip was equally distant from Chips 1 and 2 in terms of hue; however, Chips 1 and 2 fall into two different perceptual categories. For example, Chip 1 is typically labeled green whereas Chip 2 is typically labeled blue. Furthermore, the target chip is usually labeled green. Most English speakers show some evidence for categorical perception, as they are more likely to say that the target chip is more similar to Chip 1 than it is to Chip 2, because the target chip and Chip 1 share the same category, whereas the target chip and Chip 2 do not.

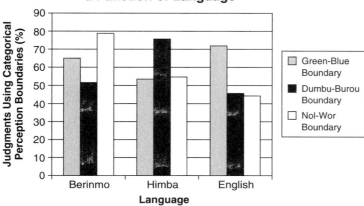

FIGURE 9.9

People make more judgments consistent with categorical perception for stimuli that cross the boundary between two color labels in their own language, compared with stimuli that cross a color-label boundary in other languages.

Likewise, Roberson et al. also included triads of color chips that were based on the color categories of the Berinmo and of the Himba. English speakers, Berinmo speakers, and Himba speakers were shown a number of such triads and asked to indicate which chip was more similar in color to the target chip. As can be seen in Figure 9.9, there was some evidence that people from the different cultures made different choices. Namely, the English speakers were most likely to make judgments in line with categorical perception for stimuli that crossed the Blue-Green boundary. In contrast, the Berinmo speakers were most likely to show evidence for categorical perception when they discriminated between two stimuli that crossed the *Nol-Wor* boundary. Likewise, the Himba speakers were most likely to discriminate between colors that crossed the *Dumbu-Burou* boundaries. In sum, people show evidence that their perception of the different colors is influenced by the color categories used in their respective languages. Language can affect color perception.

Linguistic relativity can also be considered in terms of people's spatial descriptions. Every language has the capability of describing how objects are distributed in space, yet there are some rather fundamental ways that languages differ in how they do this. English speakers often identify locations based on their position relative to the speaker, using terms such as left, right,

*"O.K., there's the sun, so that
direction is 'up.' "*

front, and back. For example, you may guide shoppers through a supermarket freezer by letting them know that the frozen peas are located in front of the Brussels sprouts and to the left of the pyrogies. These directions would no longer be applicable if the person approached the freezer from the other side; they would be reversed—reflecting their relativistic basis. The directions are accurate only from the perspective of the speaker. In contrast, the same kinds of directions as given by speakers of Guugu Yimithirr, an aboriginal group in Australia, would not include any of these relative terms. Rather, the person would be guided by saying that the peas are located east of the Brussels sprouts and south of the pyrogies, a set of directions that are not influenced by the location of the speaker. That is, speakers of Guugu Yimithirr identify space in absolute terms, as described by the cardinal points on a compass. The Whorfian question that arises from the linguistic differences between speakers of English and Guugu Yimithirr is whether people who speak these languages differ in their thinking as well.

Because Guugu Ymithirr lacks relativistic direction terms, it would seem that its speakers would need to be constantly attending to cardinal directions when interacting with their world. Otherwise, they would have no way of describing spatial locations if they were subsequently asked about what they had seen. In contrast, English speakers would not need to attend to cardinal directions as they can conceive of space, and communicate it to others, using terms relative to the location of their bodies.

How might people who speak different languages recall scenes they encounter? One study sought to test a Whorfian question of whether Guugu Ymithirr speakers and Dutch speakers (Dutch is like English in having relative direction terms) would remember scenes differently (Levinson, 1997). For example, in one study, participants were shown a row of figures of a cow, a pig, and a person on a table in one room (see Figure 9.10). In that room, the table was against the north wall so participants were facing north. Then, they were asked to go to a different room which had a similar table containing the same figures except now the table was against the south wall so participants were facing south. The participants were asked to re-create the same scene they had witnessed in the other room. Most of the Dutch respon-

Dutch and Guugu Ymthirr Perceptions of the Spatial Arrangement of Objects

Original stimulus shown (Participant facing North).

Most common Dutch solution (Participants facing South).

Most common Guugu Ymithirr solution (Participants facing South).

FIGURE 9.10

After viewing a group of stimuli, Dutch and Guugu Ymithirr participants were brought into another room facing a different direction. When asked to arrange the same stimuli to match their earlier order, Dutch participants arranged them from right to left, and Guugu Ymithirr participants arranged them from East to West.

dents tended to re-create the scenes based on their own position relative to the animals. Because the cow was left of the pig which was left of the person in the original room, they maintained these relative positions in the new room. In stark contrast, most of the Guugu Ymithirr speakers re-created the scenes in absolute terms. That is, because the cow had been west of the pig which had been west of the person when they had been in the first room facing north, when they were in the second room facing south, they preserved the positioning of these animals relative to the cardinal directions. This meant that the cow was now placed to the right of the pig which was to the right of the person—the exact opposite arrangement that the Dutch speakers had produced!

Apparently, even when entering different rooms in a building the Guugu Ymithirr speakers are constantly attending to which direction is which. The Whorfian explanation is that because their spatial language is solely in terms of the cardinal directions, they conceive of the arrangement of their world only with respect to these directions. Dutch speakers, in contrast, elaborate more on directions relative to their physical selves, so it is less useful to attend to the cardinal directions in most situations. The Guugu Ymithirr tendency of conceiving of directions in ways that are not relative to their bodily location appears to be more common among subsistence populations throughout the world and is also more similar to the ways that chimpanzees understand directions (Haun, Rapold, Call, Janzen, & Levinson, 2006). It appears that the tendency to attend to directions relative to one's own egocentric position is a relatively recent development, and one that is peculiar to some industrialized cultures.

Following up on this work, some preliminary research by Lera Boroditsky and Alice Gaby has explored whether languages with different spatial referencing would also influence the ways that people represent the passage of time. Building on earlier research demonstrating that people's understanding of time is grounded in their understanding of space (Boroditsky, 2000), Boroditsky and Gaby (2006) reasoned that English speakers tend to see time as passing from the left to the right. So, for example, if English speakers were to arrange the pictures in Figure 9.11 (which are pictures of Lera Boroditsky's grandfather at various ages) in the correct temporal sequence, they would arrange them from left to right, and they would do this regardless of what direction they were facing. The idea that left is perceived as the origin of time in English is somewhat arbitrary and is likely determined by the fact that English is written from the left to the right. In contrast, Arabic is written from the right to the left, and Arabic speakers likewise see time passing from the right to the left. The important point is that for English speakers time passes from one relative spatial marker (the left side of one's body) to another (the right side), and this does not change depending on the direction one is facing. Boroditsky and Gaby investigated Australian aborigines from the village of Pormpuraaw, who, like the Guugu Ymithirr, tend to use only absolute spatial markers when referring to directions. Among those in

FIGURE 9.11

English speakers think of time as passing from left to right, whereas as Australian aborigines think of time as passing from East to West. Hence, an aborigine would chronologically arrange the pictures differently depending on the direction he or she is facing.

Pormpuraaw, time is seen to pass from the East to the West, tracking the sun's movement across the sky. The preliminary analyses suggest that when they were asked to arrange the pictures in Figure 9.11 in temporal sequence they tended to arrange the pictures from East to West. This means that when they sat in a room facing South, they usually arranged the pictures in the same way as the English speakers, as East is on their left side. However, when they sat in a room facing North, they often arranged the pictures in the exact opposite order from the English speakers, with the pictures going from right (East) to left (West)! This further demonstrates how spatial perception, and time perception, are grounded in the linguistic markers available in one's language.

The above studies regarding color and spatial perception are consistent with a weak version of the Whorfian hypothesis. That is, the results support the notion that the language differences between the cultural groups influenced the way the participants thought about the tasks. Language can influence thought.

Is there *any* support for a stronger version of the Whorfian hypothesis, namely, the notion that we are unable to think about something unless we have the corresponding language available to us? As I noted earlier, the strong version of the Whorfian hypothesis has been almost universally rejected. Indeed, many of the challenges to Whorfian arguments have been those that reject the strong version of the hypothesis. For example, Berlin and Kay's (1969) findings regarding the patterns of color categories across cultures, as well as the similarities in the focal colors of those categories, are evidence that color categories are not arbitrary nor solely dependent on the language that one speaks. Likewise, the argument that English speakers can recognize the emotion *schadenfreude* even though they do not have a word for this emotion is evidence against the strong version of the Whorfian hypothesis (e.g., Pinker, 1994; although note, that the rejection of the strong version of the Whorfian hypothesis has no bearing on whether the weaker version is supported). In sum, there have been many demonstrations that the strong version of the Whorfian hypothesis is not tenable.

The kind of evidence that would be necessary to support the strong version of the Whorfian hypothesis is evidence demonstrating that people cannot entertain some concepts in the absence of the appropriate words. Despite the many studies that provide evidence against the strong Whorfian argument, there is one line of research that provides support for it.

In many ways it would seem that mathematics is one domain that is independent from culture. After all, mathematicians and physicians have proved the existence of various mathematical principles that occur outside of our cultural worlds, such as Einstein's famous equation, $E = mc^2$. This equation is as true in America as it is in the Amazon or in the constellation of Andromeda. Mathematical principles exist outside of culture, regardless of our ability to understand them.

However, mathematics is also a domain in which we can see pronounced cultural variation in people's understanding. You most likely learned a base-10 number system at school; however, this is a system that itself is a cultural invention and that has not always been around. The Mayans and Aztecs had a base-20 number system and the ancient Babylonians had a base-60 number system. The ancient Romans, despite all their technological achievements, did not have an understanding of the concept of zero, which was invented by Hindus in India in around the third century. Likewise, there was no real conception of probability in the West before Pascal invented one in the 17th century. People in many cultures today learn to do calculations on an abacus, and those who do tend to conceive of numbers in a different way from those who do not, as is evident in the kinds of errors they make. Our ability to reason with numbers very much reflects the experiences we have had in our cultures, and most modern industrial cultures have developed to the point that they require their citizens to spend years learning how to think in mathematical terms.

The most compelling evidence that much of our competence with mathematics and numbers is learned through cultural experiences, rather than being innate, comes from looking at the numerical systems of various subsistence societies. A number of cultures have relatively impoverished number systems.

For example, the Piraha, a tribe from the Lowland Amazon region of Brazil, has a number system that contains only the numbers 1, 2, and many. They have no terms for any specific numbers greater than 2. The strong test of the Whorfian hypothesis that begs to be asked here is whether people who do not have number terms in their language can understand the concepts of those numbers.

The Piraha have been studied to investigate the kinds of mathematical computations they are able to do. In one of the studies the researcher placed a number of nuts in a can (Gordon, 2004). The participants were then shown the nuts in the can and were allowed to inspect them for some time. The experimenter then removed the can from view of the participants and would remove one nut at a time. After each nut was removed, the participants were asked whether there were any nuts remaining in the can. The participants did well on this task when there were initially up to two nuts in the can; however, their performance steadily dropped in trials that contained increasing numbers of nuts. Those participants who were shown a can containing six nuts rarely were able to correctly determine when the last nut was removed. They did not seem to be able to perform this task well with numbers larger than 2.

In another task participants were shown an array of objects—for example, five batteries. They were then given some nuts and asked to place out the same number of nuts as there were batteries. Similar to the nuts in the can task, participants could do this task well with small numbers; however, their performance deteriorated considerably as the numbers got larger (for similar findings with another culture, the Mundrukuku of the Amazon, see Pica, Lerner, Izard, & Dehaene, 2004). However, in all the tasks conducted, the magnitude of the errors that the Piraha made increased with the magnitude of the numbers they were asked to estimate. This suggests that although the Piraha do not have concepts for specific numbers greater than 2, they do seem able to have rough quantity estimation skills. They know, for example, that 12 batteries is a larger quantity than 8 batteries, even if they are unable to count out to numbers of this magnitude. This suggests that quantity estimation skills might be innate whereas numerical skills beyond 2 are acquired through cultural experiences. Parallel findings for the development of numerical competence in children is also consistent with this notion (Dehaene, 1997). In sum, in the absence of linguistic terms for specific numbers, people from some cultural groups do not seem able to understand the associated numerical concepts. This is some evidence for the strongest version of the Whorfian hypothesis (but for a dissenting view see Gelman & Gallistel, 2004).

In sum, the literature on linguistic relativity has been controversial since the Whorfian hypothesis was first proposed. For decades Rosch Heider's early results had been viewed as evidence that color perception occurred independently of language, and conclusions from those findings had been generalized to challenge all Whorfian questions. However, recent studies have called into question those initial findings, and compelling evidence for Whorfian effects has now emerged across a number of domains. The debate is by no means over, however, and with the Whorfian door propped open again we might see researchers attempt to explore linguistic relativity in a wider array of domains than those considered before. To the extent that Whorf was correct, it follows that there should be much variation in psychological processes across cultures because languages diverge so much from each other. The Whorfian hypothesis provides a useful tool with which to make predictions for the kinds of cultural differences that are likely to emerge.

How We Understand Humans' Place in the World

One key question that humans, curious creatures that we are, strive to figure out is our place in the natural world. How are we similar to or different from other animals around us? Carey (1985, 1995) argued that children come into this world with an understanding of living things that is fundamentally **anthropocentric**—that is, young children project qualities of people onto animals. Up until the age of 10 or so, children tend to see animals as reflections of humans, having the same kinds of characteristics and experiences as people. For example, in one study young children were told that humans have a green thing inside them called an "omentum." Then they were asked whether they thought that dogs have an omentum inside them. Most of the children said yes. However, if the children were instead told that dogs have an omentum inside them, and were then asked whether humans had an omentum, most of them said no. The children thus projected properties of humans onto other animals more than they projected properties of animals onto humans. Another indication that children are anthropocentric resulted in these findings: Young children assumed that bees were more likely to have human features than they were to think that bees had features from other bugs (Carey, 1995). This suggests that young children, up until the age of 10 or so, have a fundamentally human-centered view of the animal kingdom. They learn to understand animals by generalizing from what they know about people.

However, these studies were all conducted with American participants. How much would these findings generalize to the understanding of the world held by people from other cultures? Indeed, in many ways, American children have rather impoverished experiences with animals. Most city-raised American children do not encounter many animals in the wild. Furthermore, much of what they learn about animals comes from what they see on television or read in books, and this often does not portray animals accurately. For example, children watching television will see that Donald Duck not only knows how to speak English (albeit, not very clearly), but he can also read, fly an airplane, and dance the samba. Perhaps the anthropocentrism that these children have demonstrated reflects their somewhat limited exposure to animals rather than a universal developmental characteristic. Because they know so little about what animals are really like they naturally project what they know about other living beings—namely, people. In contrast to the kinds of experiences that American children have, people in many other cultures live and interact closely with a wide range of different kinds of animals. Perhaps children who are raised in environments where they coexist with many species of animals will not show the typical pattern of anthropocentrism.

To investigate this possibility, some studies contrasted rural and urban European-American children with Menominee children (a Native American tribe living in Wisconsin), and Yukatek Maya children and adults (an indigenous tribe living in the Yucatan peninsula of Mexico) (Atran et al., 2001; Ross, Medin, Coley, & Atran, 2003). The participants in these studies were given the same kinds of questions that Carey had originally posed to her Euro-American participants. The results showed that the European-American children, especially the urban ones, tended to demonstrate the same kind of anthropocentric ways of thinking that Carey had identified. In contrast, however, the Menominee and the Yukatek Maya children did not show evidence for anthropocentrism. They were just as likely to project features from animals to humans as they were to project humans to animals. Humans thus do not appear to be innately anthropocentric. The ways that people understand and classify other animals appears to be influenced by their experiences with animals.

SUMMARY

The field of cognition and perception is concerned with some of the most basic and fundamental operations of the mind. Yet it is within this field that some of the clearest evidence for cultural variation has emerged.

The most researched cultural distinction regarding cognition has been the contrast of East Asians and Westerners in their thinking styles. Westerners tend to reason in analytic ways; they view objects as static and separate from each other, and understand those objects on the basis of their internal properties and how they correspond to abstract rules and principles. In contrast, East Asians (and people from many other cultural traditions) tend to reason in holistic ways, understanding objects and events as being fundamentally connected with each other, bound to a background context, continually changing, and governed by harmonious relations.

Much evidence has been amassed to support this distinction between Westerners reasoning analytically and East Asians reasoning holistically. East Asians perform relatively better on tasks that involve detecting relations among events, whereas Westerners perform relatively better on tasks requiring separation of an object from its background. East Asians tend to see foreground objects as bound to their background context whereas Westerners focus on foreground objects and relatively ignore the background. This cultural difference appears to be driven by where people are looking, as East Asians are more likely to scan an entire scene whereas Westerners devote more of their visual attention to focal objects. These cultural differences in perceptual habits are also identifiable in aesthetic preferences. East Asian art tends to emphasize the context by consisting of relatively small figures and scenes with relatively high horizons in contrast to Western pictures, where figures are relatively large and horizons are low.

These differences in analytic and holistic thinking affect how people from different cultures understand others. Westerners are more likely than East Asians to explain the behavior of others as arising from their dispositions, whereas East Asians are more likely to view behavior as being a function of situational constraints.

Westerners are more likely than East Asians to rely on abstract rules for reasoning. When abstract rules conflict with information about similarity, East Asians tend to prefer the similarity information whereas Westerners prefer the abstract rules.

The tendency for analytic thinkers to view objects as separate and internally consistent means that contradiction cannot be tolerated. In contrast, the tendency for holistic thinkers to view the world as consisting of fluid and interrelated parts leads to a belief that contradiction is natural. East Asians thus seem less troubled by Westerners of contradiction in the world and in themselves. Furthermore, East Asians tend to see even change as changing, and they are less likely to view the future as unfolding linearly compared with Westerners.

Speaking is an inherently analytic act, as ideas are expressed sequentially, one after the other. Hence, it should not be especially difficult for Westerners to speak while they are thinking, because both speaking and thinking involve analytic thought. In contrast, holistic thoughts are difficult to express verbally. Hence, East Asians show some interference between thinking and speaking, at least for some kinds of problems. East Asians tend to perform worse at a simultaneous task when they are speaking out loud, whereas speaking has no impact on the performance of Westerners.

People in high context cultures should attend more to nonverbal cues and rely less on explicit language, whereas those in low context cultures need to attend carefully to explicit communication. East Asians have an easier time ignoring the explicit content of what is communicated whereas Westerners find it easier to ignore the tone with which something is said.

The Whorfian hypothesis suggests that the language people use affects their thoughts. Although this hypothesis was rejected for a few decades, recent research has found much evidence in support of it. People perceive color differently depending on the color terms that are available in their language; language affects how people perceive spatial arrangements of things; and people in languages without terms for some numbers do not seem to be able to understand the associated numerical concepts.

The ways that people categorize the world, and their place within it, varies with their experiences. Whereas Western children tend to project human qualities onto animals this tendency is less evident among children who have interacted more with animals.

10

Mental and Physical Health

At the age of 14, Keisuke appeared to be a normal, mentally healthy teenage Japanese boy. Then one day he went into the family kitchen, closed the door behind him, and did something rather unusual. He refused to leave. Three years later he had still not left the kitchen, nor during that time had he allowed anyone else in. His mother left meals for him at the door three times a day, and he made use of the toilet that was adjacent to the kitchen. The kitchen was filled with garbage as Keisuke hadn't taken any out since he first moved in there. At first his family cooked on a makeshift stove and ordered a lot of take-out food, but on realizing that their son was not going to be leaving, they ended up building another kitchen in the house. It is possible that Keisuke is still living alone in the kitchen today.

As unusual as Keisuke's lifestyle may seem, perhaps the most remarkable fact about his story is how common it is. Keisuke suffers from a condition known as *hikikomori*, which translates loosely as social withdrawal. It typically first appears among Japanese students at junior high and high schools when they decide that they no longer want to go to school (sometimes in response to a bullying incident) or to have much social interaction with anyone. The typical response is to shut oneself off from the outside world and spend one's days reading books, playing video games, or watching television. It is about three times more common in boys than girls, and it is especially common among the oldest sons in families. Although the condition was virtually unheard of in earlier decades, today approximately 1.2 million Japanese in their teens and twenties suffer from it. Some estimate that as many as 1 man in 10 in his late teens or early twenties is living as a recluse—many have not left their houses or said a word to anyone for years. It has become a social epidemic with tragic consequences for the families involved.

There is a growing cottage industry of explanations for the causes of *hikiko-mori*. Some say it is a reaction to the extreme pressure from parents to do well in school; others attribute the phenomenon to the relative homogeneity of Japanese society, so that people who do not fit in can only feel comfortable in the isolation of their homes; others argue that the recent epidemic may be a result of the extremely low birthrate in Japan, which means that many children grow up without much socializing influence from siblings; and some maintain that it is the product of a particular kind of parenting style—a reaction to the pressures of being the oldest son in a family with a demanding father and an over-indulging mother. Perhaps it is a function of all of these, although at present there is no consensual explanation.

We can think of *hikikomori* in a number of ways as being particular to Japanese culture in the late 20th and early 21st centuries. First, the hypothesized causes of the disorder, summarized above, are less likely to be present elsewhere. Also, the reactions of parents to *hikikomori* sufferers might emerge differently across cultures. For example, one American psychologist who has researched *hikikomori* argues that if his child behaved like Keisuke, the first thing he would do would be to break down the kitchen door and deal with the child directly (Rees, 2002). Most Japanese parents would not think to take such a direct approach, and the most renowned Japanese expert on *hikikomori*, Tamaki Saito, maintains that doing so would only make matters worse, perhaps driving the sufferers into violence or suicide. Cultures vary in the ways that parents deal with their children, and in particular, how they deal with a child who is behaving inappropriately. Furthermore, the kinds of symptoms that go along with *hikikomori* do not match any other set of symptoms that is published in the *DSM-IV* (the diagnostic manual of the American Psychiatric Association that is used in much of the Western world). Indeed, those with *hikikomori*, when considered by the criteria in the *DSM-IV*, do not fit into a single category and are diagnosed with a wide range of different conditions including social phobia, obsessive-compulsive disorder, depression, and schizophrenia (Sakai, Ishikawa, Takizawa, Sato, & Sakano, 2004). And while an occasional person outside Japan might meet the description of a typical *hikikomori* sufferer, in no other culture is the prevalence nearly as high as it is in Japan. *Hikikomori*, for all intents and purposes, appears to be a uniquely Japanese form of psychopathology in its presentation and its prevalence.

This raises an important question: What does it mean to say that a psychological disorder is far more present in one culture than in another? At the very least, cultural differences in such disorders demonstrate that we cannot simply conceive of those disorders as automatically and uniformly unfolding from a set of innate biological causes. Human biology is largely the same everywhere, yet psychological disorders present themselves in a variety of strikingly different ways around the world. These cultural differences tell us that in some ways, culture is implicated in the expression and experience of psychopathology.

This should perhaps not be too surprising, given what you have read in the earlier chapters. In many ways, the minds of people from different cultures do appear to operate in some distinct ways. And if normal psychological functioning differs across cultures in the various ways that we have discussed, then it follows that departures from what is normal would likely also differ across cultures as well. This suggests that the criteria for what constitutes mental health and what constitutes problematic abnormalities will importantly vary across cultures (for reviews see Kleinman, 1988; Lopez & Guarnaccia, 2000).

This chapter explores how culture shapes both people's mental and physical health. With regard to mental health we will explore how culture shapes clinical and psychiatric conditions. Reflecting a central theme of this text, we will see whether mental disorders are particular to certain cultures or are universally prevalent. The second half of this chapter examines how culture shapes our physical health. Addressing the second guiding theme of this book, we will investigate the ways people's cultural experiences shape the biological mechanisms that provide the foundation for their physical health. First, we will consider the role of culture in mental health.

Mental Health

What Is a Psychological Disorder? The question of what constitutes a psychological disorder has always challenged psychiatrists and clinical psychologists. Disorders are usually defined with respect to behaviors that are rare and cause some kind of impairment to the individual, although there are many exceptions to this general pattern. Alcohol abuse, for example, is considered a disorder, but it would not seem that rare if you attended a frat party.

On the other hand, 20th-century pianist Glenn Gould's musical talents were indeed rare, and his obsession with music greatly interfered with his social life but at the same time made him one of the most famous pianists of his time. It's not clear whether his musical talents and obsessions should be described as a disorder. Although identifying the conditions that could be labeled disorders is often challenging, the question becomes even more difficult when behaviors are problematic in one culture but not in another.

For example, consider *dhat* syndrome, a disorder frequently observed in a number of South Asian cultures (see Obeyesekere, 1985). *Dhat* syndrome is characterized by a belief among young men that they are leaking semen, which causes them to be morbidly anxious, as semen is largely viewed by them to be a source of vitality. The religious scriptures of the Hindus state, "Forty meals produce one drop of blood, 40 drops of blood give rise to one drop of bone marrow, and 40 drops of marrow form one drop of semen" (Akhtar, 1988). According to this view, semen is a very precious commodity, and an excessive loss of it is feared to result in serious illness. *Dhat* syndrome is often associated with crippling feelings of guilt and anxiety among its victims about having indulged in certain disapproved sexual acts (such as masturbation) that have apparently caused them to spring a more enduring leak.

Now imagine that a team of American psychiatrists wished to study the prevalence of *dhat* syndrome in North America. To do so they would take all the appropriate methodological steps for conducting sound cross-cultural comparisons. They would consult the original diagnostic manual for *dhat* syndrome that is published in Hindi, and they would translate it into English, taking all the necessary precautions to produce an accurate translation. Then the psychiatrists could apply these diagnostic criteria to North Americans, making careful attempts to ensure that there was consistency among the different psychiatrists involved in the study. All these efforts would then allow the psychiatrists to determine the prevalence of *dhat* syndrome in North America.

What might be some problems in studying *dhat* syndrome in North America? Well, because North Americans tend not to view semen as a precious resource, a key source of vitality, or as a bulwark against disease, they likely wouldn't be all that anxious about losing it. Furthermore, because norms regarding appropriate sexual behavior differ between South Asia and North America, most North American males would likely not feel much guilt at the thought of engaging in acts that caused them to lose semen. Without the culturally shared beliefs regarding semen, sexual activity, and health that are prevalent among South Asians, the entire category of *dhat* syndrome would likely be rather meaningless to most North Americans and to North American psychiatrists. To be diagnosed with the disorder of *dhat* syndrome one must have a particular set of beliefs regarding the relations of semen, sexual activity, morality, and health that would cause one to be concerned about losing semen in the first place. And such beliefs are derived from participating in particular cultural contexts, such as those found in South Asia. Without the necessary cultural participation, it is highly unlikely that one could experience *dhat* syndrome as a disorder in the way that many South Asians do (see Kleinman, 1988, for further discussion).

Although it may be evident that applying an unfamiliar South Asian diagnostic category in North America would be a rather fruitless endeavor, what may be less obvious is that much cross-cultural psychiatry has often been conducted in the reverse of this situation (Kleinman, 1988). Because the field of psychiatry was largely developed in the West, the disorders that are observed in the West, such as depression, social anxiety, and schizophrenia, are often viewed as the basic categories of diagnosis. When psychiatry is exported to other cultures, there is a tendency to evaluate the psychopathologies found in those cultures in terms of how well they fit into the basic categories developed in the West. It is possible that in some cases the Western categories of diagnosis do indeed reflect universal categories of mental illnesses, just as there are many universal categories of physical illness, such as diabetes, cancer, or influenza. However, it is also possible that in some cases the disorders reflect culturally specific ways of thinking that are really not meaningful in other cultures. This distinction between universal categories of mental illness and culture-bound syndromes is not always straightforward, as the symptoms of some disorders might also vary across cultures, even though the underlying causes of the problems might be the same.

Below, let's consider how various psychopathologies differ or are similar across cultures. We'll begin first by exploring some conditions that appear to be culture bound, and then we'll consider some that appear to be more universal.

Culture-Bound Syndromes

Culture-bound syndromes are those that appear to be greatly influenced by cultural factors, and hence occur far less frequently, or are manifested in highly divergent ways, in other cultures. The cases of *hikikomori* and *dhat* syndrome are examples of culture-bound syndromes, in that in many other cultures the symptoms that characterize *hikikomori* and *dhat* are largely absent or do not cluster together, they do not occur in the same kinds of circumstances, or do not appear at anywhere near the frequency that they do in the places where they have been primarily identified. As such, to gain a good understanding of *hikikomori* or *dhat* it is important to consider the cultural values and understandings that go along with them. Many culture-bound syndromes have been identified, a few of which are discussed below.

Eating Disorders. Eating disorders are some of the more common psychological disorders present among North American college student populations, particularly among women. Take the case of bulimia nervosa, a disorder often characterized by binge eating and induced vomiting. Estimations for prevalence rates among female students have reached as high as 19% at American universities (Halmi, Falk, & Schwartz, 1981), although studies using more stringent criteria put this estimate closer to 5% to 7% (Heatherton, Nichols, Mahamedi, & Keel, 1995). Episodes of binge eating not associated with bulimia are even more common, with approximately one-quarter of female college students reporting past or current occasions of repeated binge eating (Heatherton et al., 1995). The reported rates had been so high that some media had claimed that eating disorders had reached epidemic proportions (e.g., Brody, 1982), although more recent research suggests those fears were largely overblown (Bushnell, Wells, Hornblow, Oakley-Browne, & Joyce, 1990).

How common are eating disorders across cultures? The two most common clinical manifestations of eating disorders are **anorexia nervosa** and **bulimia nervosa**. The symptoms of these two conditions are relatively homogenous, both within and across cultures. To be diagnosed with anorexia nervosa one must refuse to maintain a normal body weight, be intensely fearful of gaining weight, deny the seriousness of one's low body weight, and, for postmenarcheal females, miss three consecutive menstrual cycles. To be diagnosed with bulimia nervosa one must experience recurrent episodes of binge eating (when one eats an unusually large amount within a 2-hour period while feeling a lack of control over this eating) along with recurrent inappropriate behaviors to prevent weight gain (e.g., self-induced vomiting, misuse of laxatives, excessive exercise), which happens at least twice a week for 3 months, have one's self-evaluation be unduly influenced by one's body weight, and not to be concurrently diagnosed with anorexia nervosa.

One commonly held view is that both anorexia and especially bulimia are culture-bound syndromes (e.g., Gordon, 1990). Some evidence for this is that the rates of both these disorders have been increasing quite dramatically over the past 50 years (Keel & Klump, 2003). For example, in Denmark the incidence of anorexia nervosa and bulimia nervosa each increased by more than a factor of four from the 1970s to the late 1980s (Pagsberg & Wang, 1994). The ages at which people develop eating disorders has gotten significantly lower over recent years; it is not uncommon to find 9-year-olds who refuse to eat (Rosen, 2003). Although researchers have yet to specify precisely what is causing such dramatic increases across time, it seems likely that changing cultural norms are at least partly responsible. For example, contestants in the Miss America pageant and *Playboy* centerfolds have become thinner over the past several decades (Garner, Garfinkel, Schwartz, & Thompson, 1980), and there has been an increase in the number of articles published in women's magazines on methods for weight loss (Wiseman, Gray, Mosimann, & Ahrens, 1992). Hence, a likely factor in the increase in eating disorders is that women are receiving more and more cultural messages that attractive bodies are thin.

Furthermore, there is evidence that bulimia and anorexia (for which the evidence is more mixed) are more prevalent in some societies, particularly those with Western cultural influences, than in others. First, for bulimia, there is a striking absence of documented cases in much of the world, particularly in Africa and in the Indian subcontinent, and the few documented cases in other regions of the world, such as in the Middle East and in Southeast and East Asia, appear to be in places where there is more Western influence. In particular, in places where starvation is a real threat to people's lives it does seem hard to imagine how people could seek to binge and purge. Furthermore, analyses of the historical literature reveal little evidence in past times of the kinds of behaviors that are symptomatic of bulimia (Keel & Klump, 2003). By all accounts, it appears that bulimia is a culture-bound syndrome that is largely confined to modern cultures with Western influence.

The picture for anorexia is somewhat more complex. As noted earlier, rates of anorexia have been increasing over past decades, but a number of studies have failed to find cases of anorexia in some cultures. For example, Mumford, Whitehouse, and Choudry (1992) found no evidence of anorexia in one large sample of Pakistani school girls. Zhang and colleagues (1992) also found no evidence of anorexia in a large sample of Chinese university students. However, other studies have found clear evidence of anorexia in diverse cultural contexts with relatively little Western influence, such as in the Caribbean island of Curacao (Hock, van Harten, van Hoeken, & Susser, 1998), Nigeria (Nwaefuna, 1981), Iran (Nobakht & Dezhkam, 2000), and Korea (Lee et al., 1987).

Keel and Klump (2003) reviewed the historical literature regarding self-starvation and found many instances of people voluntarily starving themselves while in the presence of food. For example, in the Italian peninsula since the 12th century, 261 saints have been canonized. For those about whom there is adequate information, about half of the saints refused food and became greatly emaciated because of a belief that this reflected divine intervention—a condition termed "holy anorexia" (Bell, 1985). Similar observations of religiously motivated self-starvation were also evident in the 17th and 18th centuries among teenage girls throughout Europe who modeled themselves after ascetic medieval saints (Bemporad, 1996). Although the motivations behind such acts of self-starvation do not seem to be about weight concerns as they largely are today, it is conceivable that people with temperaments that predispose them toward anorexic symptoms were especially attracted to ascetic lifestyles. That is, the same kind of inherited predisposition toward self-starvation might manifest itself in motivations for religious asceticism in some contexts and avoidance of weight gain in others.

Hence, on the one hand, we see rates of anorexia increasing around the world, and there is less reliable evidence for anorexia in some cultures than in the West, suggesting that there are clear cultural influences on the disorder. On the other hand, there are clear instances of anorexia around the world and there are many historical examples of people starving themselves. Unlike bulimia nervosa, which has all the hallmarks of a culture-bound syndrome, anorexia seems to have many symptoms that are universal, although they are still influenced a great deal by culture. In particular, excessive concerns about one's weight may be especially susceptible to cultural influences. This suggests that anorexia may well be an existential universal in that it is present everywhere, although the frequency varies considerably across cultures. Anorexia does not meet the standards for a functional universal, however, as in some contexts a similar motivation (i.e., self-starvation) is associated with different ends (avoiding becoming overweight vs. being spiritually ascetic).

Koro. One clinical syndrome that has been identified in a variety of countries in South and East Asia, particularly in Southern China, is termed *koro*, which, in the Malay language, literally means the head of a turtle. This aptly

A Chinese man suffering from a koro attack and trying to prevent his penis from shrinking into his body.

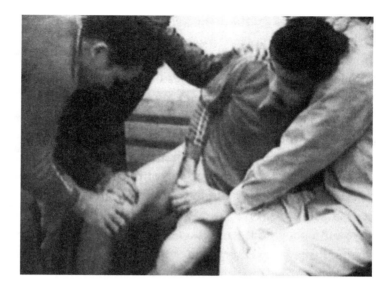

named syndrome is most common among men where it manifests as a morbid fear that one's penis is shrinking into one's body. This event is believed to have harmful consequences, including death, and causes tremendous anxiety and terror among those afflicted. It is far less common among women where it tends to manifest as a similar fear that one's nipples are shrinking into one's body. There have been epidemics of *koro*. For example, in 1967 in Singapore there was an epidemic of swine flu, which led to the widespread inoculation of pigs. Later, rumors spread that one would develop *koro* after eating inoculated pig meat, and soon hospitals were inundated with hundreds of people presenting *koro* symptoms (Ngui, 1969). *Koro* meets all the criteria for a culture-bound syndrome as its symptomology is nearly absent in other cultures (Tseng, 2001), although the cultural factors that affect its prevalence are less clear. However, some American men who have had bad experiences while high on marijuana have reported *koro*-like symptoms (3 men out of a survey of 70 who reported having negative marijuana-induced experiences), when they too had the fear of their penis shrinking into their bodies. The experiences were so frightening to them that all those men reported cutting back on their marijuana usage after the incident (Earleywine, 2001). This and a number of other rare incidents reported around the world suggest that there may be some components of *koro* that are universally accessible; however, they only seem to manifest as a clinical syndrome only within certain cultures.

Amok. *Amok* is a phenomenon identified in a number of Southeast Asian cultures that has been defined as "an acute outburst of unrestrained violence, associated with (indiscriminate) homicidal attacks, preceded by a period of brooding and ending with exhaustion and amnesia" (Yap, 1951). Running *amok* occurs primarily among males, and is thought to be instigated by stress, a lack of sleep, and alcohol consumption. One theory of the relation between *amok* behavior and Malay culture, where it is most commonly found, is that there are cultural traditions, especially in traditional rural parts of Malay, for people to be passive and nonconfrontational (Carr, 1978). The suggestion is that some who are unable to find culturally sanctioned means to express their frustration ultimately explode in an uncontrolled fit of anger and unresolved tensions. Running *amok* still occurs in several Southeast Asian countries, and the rate has been increasing in the latter half of the 20th century (Teoh, 1972). It has been common enough in Malaysia that police stations there all had a special two-pronged weapon, depicted in the rightmost part of the drawing below, which allowed police to capture an *amok* runner by pinning him against a wall. Most people who run *amok* end up being killed in the act, and the few survivors who have been caught have had a divergent set

This picture shows a Malaysian man running amok while a group chases him in an effort to subdue him. The fork-like object at the far right is a special weapon that used to be kept in Malaysian police stations to catch people who ran amok.

of symptoms that have been diagnosed with a variety of other mental disorders, including schizophrenia, endogenous depression, and epilepsy (Schmidt, Hill, & Guthrie, 1977).

Although much of the symptomology and cultural meaning associated with *amok* appears to be specific to certain Southeast Asian cultures, there are similar phenomena—such as the mass killings that occasionally occur at schools, offices, and neighborhoods—in the United States and other Western cultures. It is unclear whether these similar behaviors are indicative of a common underlying disorder.

A whole menagerie of rather bizarre clinical syndromes have been identified in specific cultures but are largely absent in the Western world (for a thorough review, see Tseng, 2001). For example, **frigophobia** (primarily identified in China) is a morbid fear of catching a cold, which leads people to dress themselves in heavy coats and scarves even in summer (Chang, Rin, & Chen, 1975). *Susto* is a condition peculiar to Latin America in which people feel that a frightening experience has caused their souls to be dislodged from their bodies, leading to a wide range of physical and psychological symptoms (Rubell, O'Nell, & Collado, 1985). **Voodoo death**, largely found in Africa, is a condition in which people are convinced that a curse has been put on them or that they have broken a taboo, which results in a severe fear reaction that sometimes leads to their own deaths (Hughes, 1996). *Latah*, identified primarily among people of various Southeast Asian cultures but also in Siberia and among the Ainu in Japan, is a condition in which people fall into a transient dissociated state after some kind of startling event, such as being tickled or thinking they have seen a snake. The person usually exhibits some kind of unusual behavior, such as barking like a dog, shouting sexually charged statements, or acting in culturally inappropriate ways, but retaining no memory of the outburst (Suwanlert, 1988). *Malgri* is a syndrome of territorial anxiety that has been identified among various Australian aboriginal groups. When people enter the sea or a new territory without engaging in the appropriate ceremonial procedures, they are thought to be invaded by a totemic spirit, and they grow physically sick, tired, and drowsy (Cawte, 1976). *Agonias* is an anxiety disorder identified among Portuguese and Azoreans when people report a wide array of symptoms, including a burning sensation, a loss of breath, hysterical blindness, sleeping, and eating disorders (James, 2002). **Brain fag syndrome**, observed primarily among students in West Africa and China, is associated with complaints of intellectual and visual impairment, and a burning sensation in the head and neck.

Patients complain of developing the syndrome after excessive mental work, such as studying for an exam. In essence, they complain that their brains are exhausted and can no longer function (Prince, 1960; Wen, 1995). **Ataques de nervios** is a condition most identified with Puerto Ricans, in which emotionally charged incidents, such as funerals or family conflicts, bring on such symptoms as palpitations, numbness, and a sense of heat rising to the head (Guarniccia, Canino, Rubio-Stipec, & Bravo, 1993). **Arctic hysteria** is a hysterical attack peculiar to Inuit populations, in which patients experience a sudden loss or disturbance of consciousness, leading them to tear off their clothes, roll around in the snow, and speak unknown languages (Gussow, 1985). These various disorders, which do not map clearly onto any syndromes commonly identified in the West, along with other less studied ones from various small-scale societies (for a review, see Littlewood & Lipsedge, 1987), further attest to the diverse ways that cultural context shape psychological experiences, both normal and abnormal.

Universal Syndromes

Whereas culture-bound syndromes indicate that culturally derived meanings play a fundamental role in the development of psychopathologies, universal syndromes highlight the biological foundation of mental illness. However, even though the following syndromes are universally observed, you'll see that the manifestation of these syndromes also can vary quite dramatically across cultures.

Depression. Depression is one of the most commonly identified psychological disorders in the West. It is also perhaps the most familiar disorder, as everyone has experienced some of the symptoms of depression, such as sadness, a sense of futility, and a loss of energy. For most people, these occurrences are relatively fleeting and are typically confined to the aftermath of a tragedy or personal disappointment. For others, however, these feelings can last for long periods of time and can become extremely debilitating. If they are severe enough, the person might be diagnosed as having a major depressive disorder (MDD).

The most widely accepted definition of an MDD is the one provided by the *DSM-IV*. To receive such a diagnosis a person must show evidence of at least five of the following nine symptoms, including at least one of the first two, for two weeks or more: (a) depressed mood; (b) an inability to feel pleasure; (c) change in weight or appetite; (d) sleep problems; (e) psychomotor change; (f) fatigue or loss of energy; (g) feelings of worthlessness or guilt; (h) poor concentration or indecisiveness; (i) suicidality; he or she must also meet a number of additional criteria. The prevalence of MDD varies depending on the specific criteria applied in making the diagnosis, and recent surveys have found lifetime prevalence rates in the United States (meaning that a person has been diagnosed with an MDD at least once) range from about 4.9% to 17.1% of the population (Kessler et al., 1994; Robins & Regier, 1991). Using less stringent criteria, researchers have found that as many as 44% of Americans are depressed at any given point in time (Flaherty, Gavira, & Val, 1982). In sum, the prevalence of depression varies depending on how the diagnostic criteria are applied; however, it appears to be a very common psychopathology.

In contrast, depression is less commonly diagnosed in some other cultures, in particular, in China. For example, epidemiological surveys have found that the rates of depression in China are approximately one-fifth of those found in the United States (Kessler et al., 1994). In 1993, one survey of psychopathology cases in seven regions of China showed that out of 19,223 people surveyed, only 16 fulfilled the criteria for a lifetime depressive disorder (Zhang, Shen, & Li, 1998, cited in Parker, Gladstone, & Chee, 2001)—a rate hundreds of times lower than that found in North America. Furthermore, throughout Chinese medical history there has been far less acknowledgment of any disorders that resemble depression than there has been in the West (for a review, see Ryder, 2004). As common as depression is in North America, it has been, and continues to be, far more rare in China.

China is not the only country where depression rates are relatively lower than they are in the West, but some cultures evince rates that are considerably higher (e.g., in one survey Nigeria had a rate four times that of the United States; Ingram, Scott, & Siegle, 1999). However, international studies of depression have found cases that fit the *DSM-IV*-based definition of MDD in every culture that has been explored. This evidence provides support for the universality of MDD as a diagnostic category. Even so, given the striking variability in the prevalence of depression across cultures, there has been much debate about what we can infer from international applications of the diagnostic criteria of the *DSM-IV* (see Kleinman, 1988).

The question of the universality of depression is also complicated by another important set of issues. Not all depressed individuals show the same symptoms. Some of the key symptoms for depression are psychological (e.g., depressed mood and feelings of guilt) whereas some are primarily physiological (e.g., fatigue, sleep problems). Interestingly, there appear to be reliable cultural differences in whether people emphasize psychological or physiological symptoms of depression. In general, people are said to be experiencing **somatization** when they feel symptoms primarily in their bodies. In contrast, when their symptoms are primarily in their minds, people are said to experience **psychologization** (a word rarely used by Western psychiatrists, perhaps reflecting what is normative in the West; Ryder, 2004).

The anthropologist and psychiatrist Arthur Kleinman conducted a landmark study in a psychiatric hospital in Hunan province in China. There he assessed 100 patients who had been diagnosed as having **neurasthenia**. A psychiatric condition first described by American neurologist George Miller Beard, neurasthenia is a nervous syndrome of more than 50 symptoms (Beard, 1869). It was described as "an exhaustion of the nervous system," with symptoms of poor appetite, headaches, insomnia, weakness in the back, hysteria, and an inability to concentrate. It was so commonly diagnosed among Americans in the 19th century and up through World War I that it was known as "the American disease." The diagnosis faded out over the 20th century as the symptoms of neurasthenia (e.g., exhaustion, headaches, insomnia) began to be seen as less important than the underlying psychopathology, and neurasthenia was completely dropped from the *DSM* over a quarter of a century ago. It is no longer recognized by North American psychiatrists or clinicians as a coherent diagnostic category.

After extensive interviews with each of the neurasthenia patients, Kleinman (1982) concluded that 87% of them could be described as suffering from some form of clinical depression. The chief complaints of these patients were primarily somatic: headaches (90%), insomnia (78%), dizziness (73%), and various physical pains (49%). In only 9% of the patients was depressed mood offered as a chief complaint. Furthermore, studies have shown that Chinese who fit the diagnostic criteria of neurasthenia but not those for depression still respond well to antidepressant medications (e.g., Zhang, 1989).

Other studies have confirmed that somatization is more common among Chinese presentations of depression than it is among Westerners (e.g., Chang, 1985; Parker, Cheah, & Roy, 2001). For example, one study compared psychiatric outpatients in China and Canada, and employed three different assessment procedures: unstructured clinical interviews (which allowed patients to choose what to report), structured clinical interviews (in which patients were asked specifically whether they did or didn't have certain symptoms), and questionnaires (which allowed patients a greater sense of privacy and anonymity in responding to structured questions; Ryder et al., 2007). The findings indicated that Chinese patients experienced more somatic symptoms and fewer psychological ones than the Canadian patients in all of these methods. These studies suggest that among Westerners diagnosed with depression the key symptoms that patients identify and clinicians attend to are psychological; among Chinese diagnosed with the same condition, however, the key symptoms that patients often identify and clinicians attend to are physical. The same condition, depression, appears to manifest itself more in mood-related concerns among Westerners and more in headache and sleep-related concerns among Chinese.

What causes these cultural differences in the presentation of depression? One possibility is differences in the social stigma associated with having a mental illness. For the Chinese, acknowledging a psychological disorder rather than a physiological one might have greater social costs than would occur in Western contexts. Much evidence suggests that there is such a cultural difference in the stigma associated with mental illness (Lin & Lin, 1981; Ryder, Bean, & Dion, 2000). The experience of depression might indeed be identical across cultures, but because of the social stigma, the Chinese may be less willing than Westerners to *discuss* their psychological difficulties. Cultural differences in stigma are surely relevant to the cultural differences in somatization of depression. However, the cultural differences in somatization are as pronounced in patients' private responses to specific probes in questionnaires regarding their condition as they are in patients' public, spontaneous descriptions of their condition, suggesting that there is more to the cultural difference in somatization than merely stigma (Ryder et al., 2007).

A second possibility for the cultural differences in symptom presentation is that the symptoms experienced by people across different cultures may be the same, but people from some cultures tend to focus on, and hence *notice*, certain symptoms more than people from other cultures. For example, Westerners might attend more to their psychological symptoms as these are somehow more meaningful to them than they are to the Chinese, even though the symptoms might be identical. Some findings that Westerners appear to be more sensitive than East Asians to their own emotional experiences are consistent with this reasoning (e.g., Matsumoto, Kudoh, Scherer, & Wallbott, 1988; Mesquita & Karasawa, 2002). Furthermore, studies with Chinese psychiatric patients reveal that they attend less to their emotional states than do Westerners, findings that are also consistent with this account (Ryder et al., 2007).

A third possible explanation of the cultural differences in symptom presentation is that the symptoms are *experienced* differently across cultures. That is, the same underlying difficulty emerges relatively more in terms of somatic symptoms among Chinese whereas it emerges more in terms of psychological symptoms among Westerners. Since at least the time of Descartes, Western thought has drawn a clear distinction between the mind and body as separate domains. In contrast, such a distinction is less emphasized in Chinese thought. For example, in contrast to the tendency of Western medicine to distinguish between physical and mental illness, Chinese medicine tends to view mind and body as integrated. Tendencies to psychologize distress suggest that mind and body are distinct, and it is possible that depression is experienced differently across cultures because people's commitment to the notion of the duality of mind and body varies across cultures (Cousins, 1990). Unfortunately, no direct research has investigated this question.

The different symptoms that depressed Chinese and Western patients report call our attention to a real challenge in psychiatric and clinical diagnoses. What can be said about the nature of a disorder, like depression, if it can apparently manifest itself in different ways? If the reported experiences are different across cultures, how do we know that people are suffering from the same disease? One strategy is to identify a core set of symptoms of depression that are present in all cultures and exclude the symptoms that are not universally present. However, if we focus only on what is universal we may miss some culturally specific symptoms that carry a great deal of meaning in some cultures but not in others. For example, depressed mood does not appear to be a core symptom of depression among Chinese, yet for Westerners, depression is largely about depressed mood. Applying a universal template for depression does reveal incidents of depression in all cultures, but it raises a difficult question of what the experiences are of those people who do not fit such a template. Because fewer people match the template in some cultures than in others, the template itself may contain some culturally specific information and might reflect the cultural biases of the researchers (Kleinman, 1988). The universal features of depression are informative; however, the culturally specific features tell us much as well.

Social Anxiety Disorder. One of the most common anxiety disorders is **social anxiety disorder** (previously known as social phobia): specifically, the fear that one is in danger of acting in an inept and unacceptable manner, and that such poor performance will result in disastrous social consequences (Clark & Wells, 1995). We all suffer some social fears on occasions, as we find ourselves in situations where we realize, often quite rationally, that we may look foolish and perhaps lose the favor of others. Social anxiety is well documented around the world, reflecting the universal concerns that people share as a social species. Not fitting in with others can be problematic, so it is natural for people to have anxieties centered around the key challenges in their lives.

It would seem that social anxiety concerns should be especially prevalent in cultural contexts where there is more emphasis on the value of fitting in with others. For example, many East Asian cultures put a premium on saving face and maintaining social harmony. If social concerns are of greater importance in East Asian cultures than they are in North America, we might expect East Asians to evince more concerns and anxieties about the possibility of committing an embarrassing faux pas.

There is much evidence that social anxiety concerns are more pronounced among East Asians than they are among North Americans. A number of studies have found that Americans of East Asian descent are more likely to endorse social anxiety symptoms on questionnaires than are European-Americans (Okazaki, 1997; Okazaki, Liu, Longworth, & Minn, 2002). Similarly, interdependence has been found to be associated with heightened social anxiety and independence with lower social anxiety among both East Asians and Westerners, highlighting the association with concerns for social harmony and the experience of social anxiety (Norasakkunkit & Kalick, 2002). The associations between these variables are so tight that in one investigation a measure of interdependence was statistically identical to a measure of social anxiety—the two scales overlapped so much in that study that it was impossible to separate them statistically (Hong, 2005). In many ways, being interdependent appears to be highly similar to being socially anxious.

The similarity of interdependence and social anxiety raises the possibility that people should view social anxiety disorder as less of a problem in Asia than they do in the West. That is, if it's so common to be concerned about interpersonal relations, people might be less likely to view their anxieties as being especially impairing (for discussion, see Hsu, 2004). Indeed, although East Asians tend to score higher than Westerners on measures of social anxiety, epidemiological surveys find far less evidence of people who meet clinical criteria of social anxiety disorder in East Asia than in the West. For

example, epidemiological studies conducted in East Asia find lifetime prevalence rates of social anxiety disorder of approximately 0.5% (Hwu, Yeh, &
Chang, 1989; Lee et al., 1987), which contrasts with estimates of at least 7%
in North America and Europe (Wittchen & Fehm, 2003). The causes behind
the relatively lower rates of diagnosed cases of social anxiety disorder among
East Asians still remains largely unknown (Hsu, 2004).

At the same time, when people's social anxieties do become problematic,
there is evidence that they are presented differently across cultures. In the
early 20th century—about 50 years before social phobia was labeled a disorder in the West—a Japanese psychiatrist identified a disorder that he called
taijin kyoufushou (TKS) (Morita, 1917). This term translates loosely as a phobia of confronting others. It is similar to social anxiety disorder in that it is
a fear specifically elicited by social situations. However, the symptoms of TKS
are quite distinct from those of social anxiety disorder. People with social
anxiety disorder tend to be preoccupied with anxieties that they will make
fools of themselves in social situations and that everyone will publicly discover their faults. In contrast, TKS involves a number of physical symptoms,
many of which are imaginary; these include extensive blushing, body odor,
sweating, and a penetrating gaze (for a thorough review of TKS, see Cousins,
1990). The typical criteria for a diagnosis of "severe TKS" (which is a diagnostic category) are that the individual is not only preoccupied with these
symptoms but is also certain that they will create a great deal of unease in
others. In fact, the major preoccupation of people with severe TKS is how
uncomfortable and tense *others* will feel around them because of the imagined repulsiveness of their physical faults. People with severe TKS avoid social
situations primarily for the fear of disturbing others (Miyamoto & Onizawa,
1985). This focus on the discomfort of others has led TKS to be labeled as
the "altruistic phobia" (Kasahara, 1986).

TKS differs from social anxiety disorder in the West in a number of other
ways. First, it is a more prevalent disorder in Japan than social anxiety disorder is in the West. TKS is the most common phobia in Japan, and it is
also the most common anxiety disorder there, with about the same prevalence rate as obsessive-compulsive disorder (Mori, Kitanishi, & Fujimoto,
1989). The various categories of TKS are classified by the particular bodily
aspect that is feared (e.g., eyes, excessive sweat) in contrast to social anxiety
disorder, which is classified largely by the kind of social situation that is most
feared (Lee, 1987). Furthermore, whereas social anxiety disorder is more

common in the West among women than men, TKS is more common in Japan among men than women (Yamashita, 1977/1993). Interestingly, the situations that lead to the most severe cases of TKS anxiety are those in which one is with acquaintances. Many people with TKS are perfectly fine among close friends or family, as well as around strangers; however, they are most distressed when they are among those with whom they have relationships of an intermediate degree of closeness (Kasahara, 1986). TKS is distinct enough from social anxiety disorder, and rare enough outside of East Asia (it has more recently been identified in Korea and mainland China; Tseng, 2001), that it is often considered a "culture-bound" syndrome, similar to *dhat*, *koro*, and *amok*.

In sum, social anxiety disorder represents a universal syndrome that is identified everywhere around the world. However, in East Asian contexts many of the symptoms of social anxiety are more common than they are in the West, common enough, perhaps, that social anxiety could be thought of there as a somewhat normal rather than an abnormal condition. The manifestation of clinically problematic concerns about one's social functioning does appear to vary across cultures, with Western social anxiety disorder having a set of symptoms very different from those of Japanese TKS.

Suicide. Suicides are one of the most tragic consequences of mental illnesses, yet they perhaps represent the category of mental illness most easily compared across cultures because the outcome of the behavior is well-defined, and official data are regularly kept around the world. Unlike depression or anorexia, for example, where there is some dispute about the cross-cultural utility of the diagnostic criteria, there is much consensus around the world about what suicide is, although the behavior may be motivated by a wide range of different conditions.

Although suicide is recognized quite similarly around the world, its frequency varies enormously. For example, in Lithuania, in 1994 the suicide rate was 81.9 men and 13.4 women per 100,000 people. This rate is several hundred times higher than that of Egypt, where in the same year the rate was only 0.1 men and 0.0 women per 100,000 people (Schmidtke et al., 1998). This degree of variation is far greater than observed in most other mental disorders. Suicide is a more significant part of some cultures than others and is virtually absent in Egypt and in some other Muslim cultures, where the religion is especially prohibitive toward suicide. Furthermore, people in different cultures tend to commit suicide at different points in their lives. Fig-

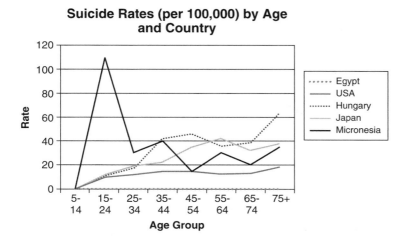

Suicide Rates (per 100,000) by Age and Country

Legend:
- Egypt
- USA
- Hungary
- Japan
- Micronesia

FIGURE 10.1

Suicide rates vary considerably in different countries.

ure 10.1 shows the suicide rates for different age groups for a few different cultures. In all the cultures, with the possible exception of Egypt, there was an increase in the suicide rates among the elderly. Aside from Egypt and Micronesia, the suicide rates were also quite similar across cultures for adolescents, after which the rates diverge considerably (WHO, 2004).

Figure 10.1 reveals that Micronesia is a striking outlier here, and it warrants some discussion. Micronesia did not always have a high suicide rate; in the 1960s, for example, it was less than half that of the United States (Rubinstein, 1992). However, in the 1970s the island nation documented a dramatic increase in suicides. The pattern of the suicides was strikingly similar across most cases. The vast majority occurred among adolescent males living at home, and typically, these males had no outward signs of any psychological disorder or of substance abuse. The suicides tended to be sparked by arguments among their peers or families, often about seemingly trivial matters. For example, suicide notes have indicated that an adolescent boy killed himself because his parents refused to give him extra money for some beer, and another killed himself because an older brother chastised him for making too much noise (Gladwell, 2000). The method of suicide is also almost always the same: the person asphyxiates himself. He attaches a noose to a tree or door, puts the noose around his neck, and then bends forward until the noose tightens, cutting off his air supply. The highest rates of suicides appear to be limited to certain islands and suburban regions of those islands. The striking similarity in this unique pattern of suicides and in their restricted geography suggests that these ritual behaviors have become part of the local cultural environment. It is still not clear what has caused this cultural change; among the theories offered are changes in the culture's dominant family structure from a lineage-based to a nuclear household (Hezel, 1987); a loss of employment opportunities (Macpherson & Macpherson, 1987); or a loss of traditional roles for young men as the society has Westernized (Rubinstein, 1983). Also, the epidemic may be a tragic series of copy-cat suicides (Gladwell, 2000).

Micronesia is not the only place where suicide rates have risen as traditional cultures have Westernized. Suicide rates also tend to be high in many colonized indigenous populations around the world. For example, in Canada the suicide rate for First Nations adolescents is five times higher than for mainstream adolescents. This tragedy raises the important question of what it is about First Nations youth that makes them particularly susceptible to suicide.

One suggested factor is that some of First Nations communities are no longer able to provide a compelling cultural narrative to which adolescents could feel connected (Chandler, Lalonde, Sokol, & Hallett, 2003). That is, many First Nations youth can no longer identify with their traditional culture, which has largely been eradicated, and they are also unable to identify with mainstream Canadian culture. Perhaps the absence of a compelling cultural identity is behind the heightened suicide rate among First Nations people in Canada. To test this hypothesis, researchers evaluated the degree to which each First Nations community's current cultural environment was connected to that same culture's past and future. This revealed the cultural facets of the community with which young people could identify. Controlling for other relevant variables such as socioeconomic status, population density, and geographic location, a clear relation emerged between the community's suicide rate and various indicators of its connection to the traditional cultural past (e.g., whether the community had its own political bodies, cultural facilities, self-governed education system, traditional community law enforcement, and was negotiating a claim to traditional lands). Specifically, the more connections a community had with its traditional culture, the lower was the community's suicide rate. Indeed, the suicide rates in communities with the most links to the traditional past were no higher than those of mainstream Canadians.

The higher suicide rates among First Nations communities with few ties to their cultural heritage and the unique case of suicides among Micronesian adolescents demonstrates that people's motivations for suicide can vary considerably across cultures. In the West, suicide is most often seen as stemming from depression, substance abuse, health problems, economic misfortune, and other tragic life events. Although suicides around the world often also share such motivating circumstances, in some cultures, there appear to be other motivations for suicide that are less familiar to the West. Japan is an example of a culture where suicide plays an unusually significant role. The most famous single incident of suicide in Japan is documented in the true legend of the *Chuushingura*, better known in the West as the "Forty-Seven *Ronin*." In 1701, on being humiliated by a high official of the emperor, a feudal lord named Takumi no Kami committed a form of ritual suicide known as *seppuku*: He killed himself by thrusting a sword into his own belly. His 47 retainers then decided to avenge his death by arranging an elaborate plot two years later to assassinate the high official who was responsible for his humiliation. Following the assassination, all 47 retainers then committed *seppuku* to preserve the honor of their families.

This idea of committing suicide to accept responsibility and preserve one's honor can still be observed in modern Japan. In 1998, Katsutoshi Miwata, the baseball scout for the Orix Blue Wave, and the one credited with discovering Ichiro Suzuki of the Seattle Mariners, was trying to persuade a top high school pitcher, Nagisa Arakaki, to join the Blue Wave. When Arakaki refused because he wanted to play for another team, Miwata responded by committing suicide, apparently to take responsibility for his failure to recruit the young player. Another famous instance involved Juzo Itami; at the time of his suicide in 1997 he was Japan's most internationally renowned movie director and had directed the cult classic *Tampopo*. A tabloid had informed him that they were going to report that he was having an affair with his assistant. Itami responded to the report by killing himself, which, according to his suicide note, was the only way he could "prove his innocence." Again, these are instances of motivations for suicide that are less familiar among Westerners, and they reflect the different cultural meanings that suicide has in Japan.

In sum, suicidal tendencies are universal in that they are observed everywhere. However, cultural influences on suicide are clearly evident as suicide prevalence rates vary tremendously, and the motivations behind suicide also differ across cultures.

Schizophrenia. One of the most debilitating and prevalent mental disorders is schizophrenia. To receive a diagnosis of schizophrenia one must have two or more of the following symptoms, each present for a significant period of time during a 1-month period: delusions, hallucinations, disorganized speech, grossly disorganized or catatonic behavior, or negative symptoms (e.g., flattening of mood or a loss of speech; APA, 1994). Schizophrenia has been a primary concern for psychiatrists throughout history, and an enormous amount of research has explored it. Despite all this research, our understanding of the causes of schizophrenia are still incomplete. We do know that there are clear genetic factors that greatly affect one's likelihood of developing schizophrenia. Although only about 1% of the population develops schizophrenia, for those with a cousin with the disorder (with whom they share approximately 12.5% of their genes), their likelihood increases to 2%. Those with a schizophrenic sibling (who shares 50% of their genes) have a 9% chance of developing it, and those with a schizophrenic identical twin (who shares 100% of their genes) have a 48% probability of developing schizophrenia themselves (Gottesman, 1991). Furthermore, there is evidence that certain experiences in the womb can affect the likelihood that those with genetic predispositions will develop schizophrenia (e.g., Cannon, 1998), and clear neuroanatomical differences can be identified between schizophrenic and normal people (e.g., Cannon et al., 1998). Yet, at the same time, despite the clearly identified relevant genes and prenatal experiences, much is still not known about the causes of schizophrenia. After all, even though identical twins share the same genes, the same mother's womb, and similar family experiences, a person with an identical twin with schizophrenia still has a greater than 50% chance of not developing the disorder.

Given the clear biological foundation of schizophrenia, it should not be surprising to learn that schizophrenia emerges quite regularly across cultures. Two large multinational epidemiological studies of schizophrenia across a dozen study centers around the world revealed that the annual incidence rates of schizophrenia ranged from 1.5 to 4.2 per 10,000 when a broad definition of schizophrenia was used, and a range of incidence of 0.7 to 1.4 per 10,000 when a strict definition was applied (Jablensky et al., 1991; WHO, 1973). All the centers had high scores of specific symptoms such as a lack of insight, predelusional signs, flatness of affect, and auditory hallucinations. Furthermore, longitudinal studies have found that although neurotic disorders appear to be on the increase in some cultures, rates of schizophrenia have remained constant over time (Lin, Rin, Yeh, Hsu, & Chu, 1969). The uniformity of the symptoms and the narrowness of the range of prevalence speaks to the cultural similarity of the manifestations of this disorder.

However, even within a condition with such an obvious biological foundation as schizophrenia, there is striking evidence for cultural variability. First, it is important to note that the set of universal diagnostic criteria for schizophrenia that was developed for the study excluded the majority of psychotic patients at each of the centers studied. In a way, then, the similarity of the symptoms of those diagnosed with schizophrenia around the world is, in part, an artifact of the method that was applied: Anyone who experienced different symptoms was simply not included in the study (Kleinman, 1988). Second, there was considerable variation in the subtypes of schizophrenia that were identified across cultures. Paranoid schizophrenia (characterized by delusional visions) was the most commonly observed subtype in most locations, although the proportions varied considerably across locations. For example, 75% of schizophrenics in the United Kingdom received a diagnosis of paranoid schizophrenia compared with only 15% of those in India (WHO, 1973). Although catatonic schizophrenia (characterized by a near absence of motor activity and an insensitivity to external stimuli) was rarely observed in the West (only 1–3% of cases in the United States and the UK), it accounted for over 20% of the cases of schizophrenia in India. Catatonic schizophrenia and paranoid schizophrenia are dramatically different manifestations of the disease, yet the proportions of these subtypes varied widely across the cultures studied.

Furthermore, the most striking finding regarding cultural variation that emerged from these studies was that the course of schizophrenia was *better* for patients in the less-developed societies than in the more industrially advanced ones (Leff, Sartorius, Jablensky, Korten, & Ernberg, 1992). This finding is all the more remarkable given that schizophrenia rates are higher in lower social classes than they are in higher ones (e.g., Hollingshead & Redlich, 1958) and that health outcomes tend to be worse for lower classes for diseases more generally. One argument for this is that developed societies have more positions with wage labor, which result in people's jobs becoming vulnerable during recessions. The uncertainty that one may no longer have a job has been argued to serve as a trigger for the emergence of schizophrenia (Warner, 1985). Other explanations have focused on cultural differences in family dynamics across these cultures that can ameliorate an individual's condition (e.g., Vaughn & Leff, 1976). Thus far, explanations for cultural differences in the course of schizophrenia largely remain speculative.

In sum, there is much cross-cultural consistency of schizophrenia around the world—in many ways, schizophrenia emerges as one of the most universally similar psychopathologies across cultures, which fits with the biological bases of the disease that have been identified thus far. However, it is telling that even in the case of a disease with such a clear biological foundation as schizophrenia it can present itself in such different ways across cultures, and that the course of the disease also varies importantly. This cultural variation in a universal psychopathology underscores the critical role that culture plays in mental health.

Physical Health

The findings of cross-cultural variation in the presentation of schizophrenia points to a larger question. To what extent is our physical health impacted by our cultural experiences? Traditionally, physical health was viewed as largely a biological issue, and many would assume that it largely lay outside the realm of cultural influences. However, the burgeoning field of health psychology has made it clear that psychological variables are inextricably linked with our physical health, and as we have seen, culture influences a wide range of psychological variables. Furthermore, a rapidly expanding number of research programs have been documenting many aspects of human health and biology that are indeed influenced by cultural experiences, and some of these in rather profound ways.

Biological Variability of Humans

To the extent that human biology varies across cultures there are largely two distinct categories of explanation of this variation. One is that humans in different parts of the world were subject to different selection pressures over many generations, and this resulted in the human genome diverging across different populations. In other words there are *innate* biological differences across cultures. The second category of explanation is that people living in different cultures have experiences within their own lifetimes that have an impact on their biology. That is, they are *acquired* biological differences. Let's consider both of these in turn.

Genetic Variation Across Populations. The most salient example of genetic variability of humans across different populations is skin color. There are

Human skin color evolved to allow the ideal amount of ultraviolet radiation to penetrate the skin in different climates.

striking differences in the darkness of people's skin around the world. It ranges from dark brown among people with ancestry from equatorial Africa, aboriginal Australians, and Melanesians, to a very light-hued yellowish pink among some northern Europeans. Why this variation? After all, it has only been approximately 60,000 years since some modern humans first left Africa, so any changes in skin color occurred after this date. The most compelling explanation for the causes of skin color variation lies in the body's ability to synthesize Vitamin D. Vitamin D is necessary for the intestines to absorb calcium and phosphorus from food for bone growth and repair. Vitamin D is not synthesized in the body unless shortwave ultraviolet radiation (UVR) penetrates the skin layer and catalyzes its production. So the skin must allow enough UVR to pass through to synthesize the Vitamin D. On the other hand, too much UVR can cause the breakdown of folic acid, which can cause anemia or birth defects, or it can cause skin cancer. Hence, humans evolved in Africa, where there was much UVR, to have enough melanin in their skin that sufficient UVR could penetrate to synthesize Vitamin D, but not enough to break down folic acid. However, when humans moved to places where there was less UVR, and such places tend to be roughly correlated with latitude, they needed to absorb relatively more UVR, and thus those with less melanin in their skin had a survival advantage over their darker skinned relatives.

Analyses of the amount of UVR that reaches the earth's surface in different parts of the globe correlate strongly with skin color, with variation in UVR predicting 77% of skin reflectance in the Northern Hemisphere and 70% in the Southern Hemisphere (Jablonski & Chaplin, 2000). There are a number of exceptions, where people's skin color diverges from what would be predicted by the amount of UVR that is present; however, these exceptions tend to support the link between UVR and Vitamin D synthesis. For example, the Inuit of Greenland have far darker skins than would be predicted by the small amount of UVR that reaches the earth there. However, the Inuit eat a diet that is especially rich in fish and sea mammal blubber and these are high in Vitamin D; therefore, they do not require as much catalysis from the sun. Conversely, some people in the Philippines, Vietnam, and Cambodia have lighter skins than would be predicted, and in these cases the populations had migrated from higher latitudes only in recent millennia and apparently had not yet evolved appropriately darker skins (Diamond, 2005).

Skin color is a case where geographical factors (i.e., levels of UVR) have affected the genotype. There are also instances of cultural factors shaping the genotype. For example, most adults in the world who drink milk develop the symptoms of lactose intolerance because they do not have the lactase enzyme in their intestines. This state, known as lactase nonpersistence because lactase does not persist from childhood through adulthood, was present in the ancestral population of humans before they left Africa. Later, some populations, particularly those in northern Europe, developed a mutation for lactase persistence (Hollox, 2005). Recent genetic analyses reveal that lactase persistence has developed in areas precisely where cows have been domesticated for the longest periods of time, as evidenced by the highest genetic diversity among the cattle populations (Beja-Pereira et al., 2003). Dairy farming has been shown to predate the selection of lactase persistence (Holden & Mace, 1997), and thus this genetic change has occurred sometime in the last 10,000 years since people began to domesticate cattle. In sum, the cultural practice of dairy farming, which brought with it various advantages, led to the selection of lactase persistence among those populations. This is an example of culture shaping genetics.

The notion that human populations vary in their genomes is, of course, enormously controversial. However, the genetic variance that has been identified thus far appears to be largely limited to domains where there would be strong selection pressures that endured over many generations, such as resulting from geographic differences that affected the thermal regulation of bodies (affecting things like skin color and body shape; Cavalli-Sforza & Cavalli-Sforza, 1995), resistance to pathogens that are endemic to certain geographic regions (e.g., genetic malarial resistance; Allison, 1954), and dietary practices that endured across generations, such as milk drinking in northern Europe and fish eating among the Inuit in Greenland. In general, cultural factors are unlikely to play much role in shaping the genome because cultures are quite fluid and change over generations. Genetic evolution occurs at a slow pace across many, many generations, so aside from some large-scale cultural changes (such as the change from hunting and gathering to agriculture), it is unlikely that cultural factors have played a strong selective role in human evolution. Furthermore, thus far there is no compelling evidence of any genetic variation underlying psychological processes, and I suspect that any that might ever be found would also be strongly tied to the selection pressures of geographic factors that persisted across hundreds of generations.

Acquired Physical Variation Across Cultures. There is also evidence of striking physical variation of people across the world that exists independently of genetics. Take the example of the Moken, a tribe of sea nomads in Southeast Asia, who spend 7 to 8 months a year living on small boats in the archipelagos off of Burma, Thailand, and Malaysia. They depend on diving to spear fish, and to retrieve clams, sea cucumbers, lobsters, and other food from the ocean floor. The challenge in this endeavor is that, as any swimmer knows, underwater vision tends to be blurry. Being able to focus underwater would greatly increase one's chances of bringing home a tasty meal. Remarkably, Moken children have more than twice the underwater visual acuity of European children (Gislen et al., 2003). And they accomplish this visual acuity through controlled accommodation that is followed by maximal pupil constriction—a process very similar to what enables seals to see clearly underwater (Gislen & Gislen, 2004). This ability is likely not a genetic adaptation. Research shows that it is acquired through practice, and that European children can also be trained to develop the same kind of underwater visual acuity as Moken (Gislen, Warrant, & Kroger, 2005). The difference is that the Moken develop this ability without explicit training and by participating in cultural practices of frequent diving for food.

Obesity and Diet. One striking way that people from various cultures differ from each other is in their weight. If we compare cultures in obesity rates using the standard definition of obesity as having a body mass index (BMI) score of at least 30, we can see tremendous variability in obesity rates around the world, ranging from approximately 1.5% of Chinese women to 55% of Samoan women (see Figure 10.2; WHO, 2005). Although there is good evidence that genetic factors are predictors for body weight, and it is possible that certain weight-relevant genes are more common in one culture than in another, culture clearly plays an important role in cross-national differences

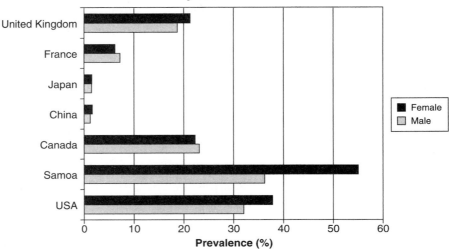

FIGURE 10.2

Obesity rates vary dramatically across cultures. The data shown here are based on BMI measurements calculated by the following formula: $BMI = 703 \times (\text{weight [lbs.]}/\text{height}^2 \text{[in.]})$. A BMI of less than 18.5 is considered underweight, more than 25 is considered overweight, and over 30 is considered obese.

in body weight. Obesity rates have risen dramatically across the world over the past few decades, particularly in the United States and the UK (see Figure 10.3; OECD, 2004). This fact cannot be explained by genetic accounts—there has not been an influx into these countries of people carrying genes for obesity. Rather, it is more likely that there have been cultural changes over that time that have given rise to this increase. Some key candidates for the obesity epidemic that are often discussed are a greater reliance on high-calorie foods, such as fast food and soda; a less active lifestyle as people engage in more sedentary activities, such as surfing the Web and playing computer games; and a more suburban lifestyle, which involves more driving and less exercise.

Even within the West, there are large discrepancies between nations in obesity rates. For example, the rate of obesity in the United States is about five times what it is in France. This fact is perhaps all the more surprising if you consider the kinds of food in the typical French diet. Compared with American cuisine, French cuisine characteristically is rich in delicious yet fat- and sugar-heavy products such as cream, butter, cheese, foie gras, rich pastries, and chocolate. Reflecting the high amounts of fat in their diets, French

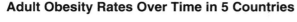

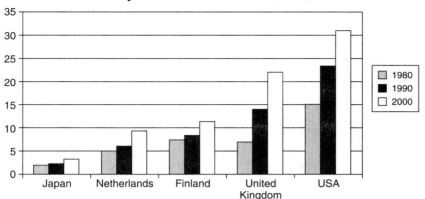

FIGURE 10.3

Over the past few decades, people in many parts of the world have been getting heavier.

tend to have higher blood cholesterol levels than Americans (Renaud & de Lorgeril, 1992). However, despite the greater prevalence of fat in much of French cuisine, the French have a longer lifespan, are thinner, and have lower heart disease rates than do Americans (Richard, 1987). This combination of a diet rich in fats yet lower rates of heart disease has puzzled researchers for decades and has been termed the "French Paradox."

One possibility that has emerged as the favorite explanation of the French paradox is that French drink more wine than Americans, which serves to inhibit platelet reactivity and thereby reduces the risk of coronary heart disease (Renaud & de Lorgeril, 1992). However true this might be, Paul Rozin and colleagues suggest an alternative account (Rozin, Kabnick, Pete, Fischler, & Shields, 2003): The French eat significantly fewer calories per day than Americans, and they do so because they live in different cultural environments, which affects the sizes of their portions and their attitudes toward food. Rozin and colleagues reasoned that the amount people eat is largely determined by what is put in front of them, or the size of individual portions of food that are sold at stores. So, for example, if the question is how much yogurt a person will eat, the answer is likely determined by the size of the yogurt container. People do not tend to eat one and a half individual-serving containers of yogurt; rather, they eat however much yogurt is in a single container. Rozin and colleagues explored this question by going to supermarkets in France and the United States and measuring the sizes of portions. Yogurt containers in the United States are about 80% bigger than they are in France, and a variety of other foods sold in individual servings—such as chocolate bars, soft drinks, and lasagna—are also larger. Even the fruit is

THE SECRET SHAME OF PARIS

PREDAWN ROUNDUP OF FAT FRENCHWOMEN

larger in the United States than it is in France! Also, food that is served in international chain restaurants varies in size. If you ask for a medium order of french fries at McDonald's in France and in the United States, you'll get about 70% more fries in the States. Chicken McNuggets are the same size in both countries, suggesting that these products are shipped internationally; however, a grilled chicken sandwich is bigger in the United States than it is in France. Rozin and colleagues suggest that this is because the grilled chicken is made from a distinct part of the chicken, and that chickens are also bigger in the United States than they are in France! Furthermore, Rozin and colleagues found that the quantities specified in cookbooks are also larger in the United States than in France. Americans consume more calories than French precisely because the cultural norms for the sizes of portions are larger for Americans. Rozin and colleagues argue that this excess caloric consumption explains a good part of the reason that obesity rates and coronary heart disease rates are so much higher in the United States than in France.

Rozin and colleagues also address the French Paradox by drawing attention to a number of important ways that French and American attitudes differ toward food. One key difference is that the French view eating as a more leisurely and enjoyable activity than do Americans (Rozin, Fischler, Imada, Sarubin, & Wrzesniewski, 1999). The French tend to spend more time eating their food than Americans do. When they are at McDonald's, French spend approximately 50% longer than Americans do eating their food (Rozin, Kabnick, et al., 2003), and this is despite the fact that they're consuming fewer fries, drinking smaller soft drinks, and eating smaller grilled chicken sandwiches. Food is expected to be savored in France. One way this is evident is in people's reaction to the following question: "If you were vacationing and had to choose between the following hotels including meals, which one would you pick? A luxury hotel with average food or an average hotel with excellent food?" Approximately 80% of French chose the hotel with the better food, compared with only 40% of Americans (Rozin et al., 1999).

Americans seem to have conflicted attitudes toward food, especially among women. Rozin and colleagues (1999) show that Americans make more effort to consume products that appear to have been altered to make them healthier—for example, being made with less salt, fat, or sugar—than the French do. Whereas about 80% of American females report eating products in which fat has been removed from them (such as low-fat yogurt) a few times a week, only about 20% of French males do. Despite these efforts to eat food that is apparently healthier, however, only about 35% of Americans claim to be healthy eaters in contrast to about 75% of French. When asked to list whatever words come to mind when one thinks of the word "food," one of the top responses among American females was "fattening," which did not appear on the French lists of frequent responses (Rozin, Kurzer, & Cohen, 2002). For Americans, the prototypical free association to the word chocolate was "fattening," with 27% of people listing it, whereas only 4% of French (and 0% of Indians) listed this (Rozin, personal communication). Relatedly, and tellingly, a survey of American college students from various regions across the country revealed that 14% of American women reported feeling too *embarrassed* to ever buy a chocolate bar (Rozin, Bauer, & Catanese, 2003). In a comprehensive survey of attitudes toward food among French, Americans, Japanese, and Belgians, Rozin and colleagues found that women have more negative attitudes toward food than do men, and that American women have the most negative attitudes of all (Rozin et al., 1999). The average responses of the participants in each culture and sex are expressed in Figure 10.4 using something known as Chernoff figures (Chernoff, 1973). In

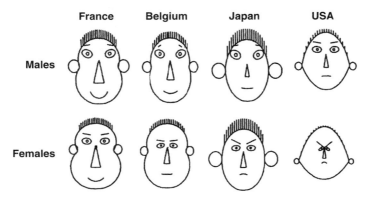

FIGURE 10.4

In this diagram, larger features represent more positive attitudes towards food. American women have strikingly negative attitudes toward food.

these figures, each element of the face (i.e., the curve of the mouth, the slant of the eyebrows, the distance between the eyes, the shape of the head) is tied to the response of a particular question about food. The more the average participant's response to that item reflects a negative attitude, the more the facial feature reveals a small and unhappy face. To summarize the results, males in all cultures have fairly positive attitudes toward food, especially the French and Belgians. The females have much less positive attitudes toward food, with American women being especially negative.

Culture and Height. It is likely not too surprising to have read that culturally shared dietary habits can influence the average weight of people in a culture. However, what is less obvious is that culturally shared dietary habits can have a striking impact on the average height of people in a culture. If you travel to the Netherlands today one fact of the people there will likely strike you. They're tall. On average, Dutch are the tallest people on the planet. They are so tall that ambulances sometimes have to keep their back doors open to allow for patients' legs (Bilger, 2004).

Typically, people tend to think of genetic factors as responsible for height, and genes are usually the best way of explaining why people on the school basketball team are taller on average than people on the debating team—basketball players tend to have taller parents than debaters. Genes play a key role in explaining individual differences in height within a particular culture. However, genes are less useful for explaining height differences between cultures and across historical periods (Malcolm, 1974). For example, although Dutch men today have an average height of 6'1", slightly more than three inches taller than the average American man who stands just under 5'10", in 1865, American men averaged 5'8", which was approximately three inches taller than the average Dutch man at the time, who then stood at 5'5" (the data for men are far more available, as most of these data come from military records, although similar patterns are evident for women; Floud, 1994; Shay, 1994). These rather dramatic changes in the average height of people in a country make it more difficult to look to genes for an answer. Rather, dietary factors are more likely responsible.

In the late 19th century, Americans were on average among the tallest in the world, reflecting their relative advantage in income (their GNP per capita was third highest in the world). At that time, American men stood approximately the same height as Australians, one inch taller than Britons, two inches taller than Norwegians, three inches taller than the French, four inches taller than Italians, and over seven inches taller than Japanese (Floud, 1994; Floud & Harris, 1997; Steckel, 1994; Whitwell, de Souza, & Nicholas, 1997). At the same time, the Netherlands was going through something of an economic slump. The Dutch economy did not start to recover until the second half of the 19th century, and then the average height of Dutch people increased accordingly as their average incomes increased, and continued to increase until this day (Drukker & Tassenaar, 1997).

The reasoning for this link between wealth and height is that wealth brings a healthier diet, especially around the ages when people go through growth spurts, such as in infancy and in adolescence (Steckel, 1983). During periods of greater wealth, people are able to get more vitamins and nutrients at those critical growth periods. Furthermore, specific aspects of diets in cultures appear to impact height. For example, the average height of Japanese has increased by approximately four inches since the end of World War II, and this period has coincided with a national campaign to provide milk in the schools (Lim, n.d.). However, average heights of people in various countries have not steadily grown across time but have fluctuated, coinciding with broad-scale societal changes that impacted diet. The average height of Europeans tended to shrink during the Industrial Revolution as people began to move into the cities, populations swelled, and average caloric intake dropped in many places (Komlos, 1998). In sum, height is closely tied to diet, especially at the ages of key growth spurts in the lifespan.

What remains a puzzle, however, is that on average Americans have largely stopped growing taller whereas people in much of the rest of the world have continued growing as their incomes have improved. In most other industrialized countries today, but not in the United States, people tend to be taller than their parents. One theory is that American teenage habits of eating fast food are depriving these young people of crucial growth-related nutrients and has resulted in the American growth spurt shifting from its vertical axis to a horizontal one. Another explanation is that income inequality is greater in the United States than in the Netherlands and other northern European countries where people are taller, and this disparity in incomes results in inadequate diets for many poorer Americans, thereby pulling down the national height average (see Bilger, 2004). Another explanation that appears compelling on the surface does not seem to be responsible. That is, America receives more immigrants from places where people have historically been shorter (such as Mexico and East Asia). However, this cannot be the key factor in the findings discussed above, as most of the contemporary American data are based on residents who are native-born and speak English at home, and the ethnic backgrounds of the samples are examined separately. The lack of a vertical growth spurt among Americans remains largely a puzzle.

In sum, physical characteristics of people around the world, such as their ability to focus their eyes underwater, their weight, and their height vary importantly, and they do so largely because of their participation in different cultural worlds. These examples provide striking evidence that culture is not something that simply lies outside of people. In many ways, cultural participation manifests itself physically inside people as well.

Culture and Health

One of the most important influences of culture is its effect on our health. In recent years there has been a growing realization among medical researchers that people's cultural backgrounds have important and often not well understood implications for their health.

Socioeconomic Status and Health. If you picked a person at random in any industrialized country in the world and you wanted to predict how long he or she would live, the one question you could ask that would give you more predictive power than almost any other is "What is your household income?" Socioeconomic status (SES), on average, plays an enormous role in people's health—a role that until a few decades ago was all but invisible to health researchers. Through a variety of different paths, many of which are still not clearly understood, SES impacts health in dramatic and often surprising ways.

Consider a classic study that examined the mortality of civil servants in England across a 10-year period (Marmot, Shipley, & Rose, 1984). The civil servants each belonged to one of four hierarchically ranked employment categories. The researchers found that compared to the top administrators, members of the executive class were 60% more likely to die over that 10-year period, the clerical staff were 120% more likely to die, and the unskilled laborers were 170% more likely to die. There was a clear relation between employment category and mortality, and those with the highest SES tended to live the longest. These are very large differences (indeed, they are larger than the difference between smokers and nonsmokers; Marmot, 2004), and

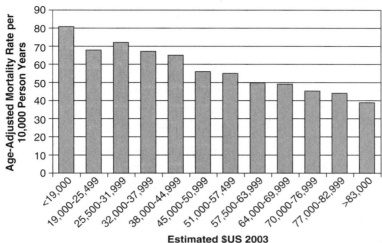

Relation Between Mortality and Income in the U.S.

Y-axis: Age-Adjusted Mortality Rate per 10,000 Person Years (0 to 90)

X-axis (Estimated $US 2003): <19,000 | 19,000-25,499 | 25,500-31,999 | 32,000-37,999 | 38,000-44,999 | 45,000-50,999 | 51,000-57,499 | 57,500-63,999 | 64,000-69,999 | 70,000-76,999 | 77,000-82,999 | >83,000

FIGURE 10.5

On average, in the United States, the larger one's income, the longer one will live.

they have been replicated in many different industrialized nations, such as Denmark and Norway (Lynge, 1984), Finland (Koskenvuo, Kaprio, Kesaniemi, & Sarna, 1978), France (Leclerc, Lert, & Goldberg, 1984), Japan (Kagamimori, Iibuchi, & Fox, 1983), and New Zealand (Pearce, Davis, Smith, & Foster, 1985).

Take the case of the United States. Figure 10.5 shows the age-adjusted mortality rate for Americans of varying income levels (Wilkinson, 1994). This graph shows that with almost every increase in income, mortality rates are lower, and these differences emerge even among those whose incomes are at the highest levels. These kinds of findings were initially met with much resistance and were originally suspected to be the result of various kinds of statistical artifacts—which have since largely been ruled out. Decades of research have now consistently revealed that SES has a very strong relation with health outcomes. If there ever was a good argument to get a university degree and pursue a high-paying career, it's that you'll likely live longer.

Status differences in health are not limited to industrialized societies. Consider the health of three West African ethnic groups that co-reside in northeast Burkina Faso: the Fulani, Mossi, and Rimaibe. This region is endemic with malaria, and it is a major cause of death there. The Mossi and Rimaibe have been living in this region for thousands of years and have developed much genetic resistance to malaria over this time. The Fulani, in contrast, moved to this region in the early 19th century as part of the Islamic invasion of sub-Saharan Africa. Unlike the Mossi and Rimaibe, they have not developed much genetic resistance to malaria (Modiano et al., 2001). However, despite being more genetically vulnerable to developing malaria, the Fulani are far *less* likely than the Mossi and Rimaibe to actually develop malaria (Modiano et al., 1996). An apparent reason for this is that the Fulani are the dominant ethnic group in this area. When they first arrived, they conquered, enslaved, and decultured the other ethnic groups, including the Mossi and Rimaibe (see Gordon, 2000). The higher status that they have as conquerors appears to provide them with enough health benefits to more than make up for their greater genetic vulnerability to malaria (Wallace & Wallace, 2002).

Why SES is related to health has proved to be a complex problem, with no obvious single answer. One part of the relation is quite direct. Your health may be seriously compromised if you don't have enough money to pay for adequate health care. However, this explanation goes only so far in explaining the findings. Indeed, in the British civil servant study, described above, all the workers had the same access to state-provided health care, yet there were still pronounced differences. Furthermore, if the SES differences were a result of differential access to medical treatment, it would follow that the differences should be more pronounced for diseases that are amenable to treatment than for those that were not. However, such a pattern does not emerge—rather, if anything, the social classes differ more for those diseases that are the *least* amenable to treatment (Bunker & Gomby, 1989). If the key variable were access to medical services, you would expect the class differences to disappear when you examined the differences between income levels at the highest end of the distribution, as there should be little variation among these groups in terms of the kinds of medical services people can afford. However, the differences in health tend to be just as large among adjacent SES groups who are at the high end of the income spectrum. Access to health services, although surely relevant, is not the main reason for the differential health outcomes across the SES spectrum.

So what might be behind these striking class differences? One possibility could be that people lower in SES are more likely to have jobs that placed them in hazardous situations, such as having to deal with poisonous toxins or being vulnerable to workplace accidents. However, this explanation could not explain findings such as those from the British civil servant study; all those people had office jobs, yet status still predicted their health outcomes. Another explanation is that poorer people are more likely to participate in cultural contexts that encourage unhealthy habits, such as smoking, eating fast food, or living a rather sedentary lifestyle. These behaviors are surely relevant to health, and there is clear evidence that people in lower SES groups are more likely to smoke, eat a poorer diet, and exercise less (e.g., Crespo et al., 1999; Kaplan & Keil, 1993). However, even when the different levels of these behaviors among the SES groups are controlled for, there still remains a clear relation between SES and health (e.g., Kaplan, 1985; Marmot et al., 1984; Siegrist & Marmot, 2004).

The strong relation between SES and health is an enormous puzzle that is presently occupying researchers from many different fields around the globe. There is surely a range of different kinds of variables that are behind this relation. More recently a growing body of evidence has pointed to psychosocial variables that underlie the relation between status and health (e.g., Chen, 2004; Marmot, 2004). For example, research has revealed that personality characteristics such as hostility and pessimism are associated with increased risk for illnesses. The experiences of growing up in a lower-SES neighborhood, where school achievement tends to be relatively worse than in higher-SES neighborhoods (thereby precluding future employment opportunities) and people are more likely to witness delinquent and criminally dangerous behaviors (e.g., Chase-Lansdale & Gordon, 1996; Leventhal & Brooks-Gunn, 2000; Sampson & Groves, 1989), would seem to predispose people toward having an overall sense of mistrust and cynicism; this could lead lower-SES individuals to be more hostile and less optimistic about their futures compared with higher-SES individuals. This explanation can address some of the heightened health risks among the poorer classes; however, it is less able to account for the health differences that are observed among the wealthiest groups.

A key variable that has been proposed for mediating the role between status and health outcomes is stress (Marmot, 2004; Sapolsky, 2005). When people are facing severe chronic stressors in their lives, their risk for medical illness often increases. There appear to be two primary mechanisms that are responsible for this: Chronically stressed people are more likely to engage in health-compromising behaviors such as smoking and drinking in order to cope with the difficulties in their lives, and stress directly weakens the immune system's ability to fight off infections and manage other threats (Miller & Cohen, 2005; Segerstrom & Miller, 2004). In general, people who experience less stress are healthier. And in many ways stress often derives from psychological interpretations of events. For example, you would likely feel far less stressed discussing your university experiences with a friend than with someone who was interviewing you for a job that you desperately want, even though you might be talking about the identical topics.

Certain cultural environments can also produce feelings of stress. For example, New York City is an extremely busy, congested, noisy, competitive, and stimulating environment. Might the experience of living in this kind of environment lead to stress and negative health outcomes? One study investigated the prevalence of deaths due to ischemic heart disease, a condition that has been linked to acute and chronic stress (e.g., Leor, Poole, & Kloner, 1996; Mittleman, Malone, Maclure, Sherwood, & Muller, 1998). Residents of New York were 55% more likely to die from this condition than the population at large (Christenfeld, Glynn, Phillips, & Shrira, 1999). It is possible that this finding is related to the kinds of people who move to New York, such as the Type A personality types who are attracted to a stressful lifestyle. However, the study also found that visitors to New York were 38% more likely to die from ischemic heart disease while they were visiting than if they had stayed at home. Apparently, there is enough stress from a visit from New York that it can increase one's vulnerability to a heart attack. Moreover, long-term residents of New York who move out of the city were shown to be 20% *less* likely to die from ischemic heart disease than expected; this statistic suggests that they had likely habituated somewhat to the stress levels of New York, so when they were in an environment characterized by a more "normal" range of stress, it was less stressful to them, and their health benefited accordingly.

Stress can be experienced for a variety of different reasons; however, it is especially likely to be present when a person is feeling a lack of control (e.g., Bugental & Cortez, 1988). Low feelings of control have been shown to be related to a number of negative health outcomes: People who feel that they do not have much control in their jobs tend to have a higher risk of heart disease (e.g., Marmot, Bosma, Hem-

ingway, Brunner, & Stansfeld, 1997), and low levels of control more generally are associated with poor physical functioning and an increased likelihood of illness (e.g., Feldman & Steptoe, 2004; Seeman & Seeman, 1983). One dramatic demonstration of the link between control and health can be seen in a classic study by Langer and Rodin (Langer & Rodin, 1976; Rodin & Langer, 1977). Residents of a nurisng home were divided into two conditions; in one condition they were allowed to have control over a number of minor life events (e.g., deciding when a plant should be watered, or deciding when visitors would come). Those in the other condition did not receive any such control intervention. As the months went by, those who had been provided with the opportunities for control required fewer medications, were rated as being in better health, and on average, lived longer than those in the no intervention group.

Control is relevant for making sense of the link between SES and health because people in higher social positions report feeling more in control than those in lower positions (Marmot, Kogevinas, & Elston, 1987), and these differences are related to health outcomes (Berkman & Breslow, 1983). For example, one study found that although, in general, lower-SES people had worse health outcomes, those who felt that they had much control in their lives had levels of health and well-being comparable with people in higher income groups (Lachman & Weaver, 1998). Chen (in press) found that providing low-SES adolescents with some sense of control in a stressful situation led them to show less physiological reactivity (an indication of vulnerability to illness) than teenagers who were not provided with feelings of control. In contrast, high-SES adolescents were unaffected by the manipulation that gave them feelings of control, suggesting that they already experienced sufficient control over their lives. Perhaps the best-supported explanation for why low-SES people tend to have worse health outcomes than high-SES ones is that they feel less control in more aspects of their lives.

Stress and feelings of a lack of control tend to be more pronounced among those who occupy a subordinate position and are subject to the demands of people who are able to make decisions for them. This is true not just of humans. Research with various primate populations has revealed that those who are subordinate in a hierarchy experience greater stress hormone levels when they belong to a social system where hierarchy is maintained through intimidation rather than through direct physical attacks, when the hierarchy is stable, when subordinate individuals are unable to easily avoid dominant individuals, and when they have low availability of social support (for a review, see Sapolsky, 2005). The societal features that produce the greatest stress among subordinates in various primate populations are remarkably similar to those experienced by many low-SES people in modernized industrialized societies.

It is not only objective SES that is so critical to people's experiences; subjective SES is at least as predictive of health outcomes (Adler, Epel, Castellazzo, & Ickovics, 2000). That is, *feeling* poor can matter as much as actually *being* poor. This suggests that the experience of relative deprivation, of knowing that others are doing better than you, might lead to stress and its associated negative health consequences. In support of this, that there is little relation between absolute level of income and health across cultures above a minimum threshold of income. For example, if you look at life expectancy at birth in various countries along with the GDP per capita of those countries, you can see a striking curvilinear relation (see Figure 10.6). Below a GDP per capita figure of approximately $10,000 per year, there is a clear relation between the absolute wealth of a nation and the average life expectancy of its citizens. Apparently, different amounts of average income of a nation at lower levels can make a dramatic difference in people's health outcomes, and this is most likely a result of whether countries can provide basic medical

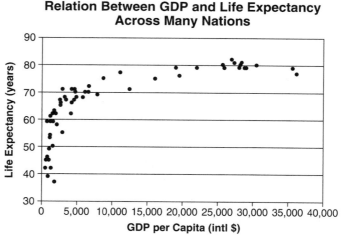

FIGURE 10.6

Each dot represents a country. There is a clear relation between GDP and life expectancy, until the average GDP per capita reaches $10,000. Beyond that point, there is virtually no relation.

services. Above $10,000, however, the curve largely flattens out, suggesting very little relation between absolute wealth and life expectancy. Many of the countries in the flat part of that curve have average incomes that are lower than those of the lower-SES Americans shown in Figure 10.5, yet people of those countries do not appear to be much worse off in health outcomes than those from wealthier countries. In contrast, poorer Americans are doing far worse than wealthier Americans. The relation between income and health, above this cutoff point around $10,000, is thus largely a relation between health and one's income *relative* to those around one. Cross-national comparisons reveal some striking evidence for the health problems associated with relative deprivation. For example, Indians living in the poor province of Kerala have far lower absolute incomes than poor African-Americans in the United States. However, people in Kerala outlive African-Americans by a substantial degree (Sen, 1999). The Keralians are poor in absolute terms; however, they likely feel less poor because nearly everyone around them is poor. In contrast, poor Americans often earn an income that is not that low by international standards, but they are poor compared to their fellow Americans, and their health suffers accordingly.

In support of the role of relative deprivation in negative health outcomes, in countries where there is relatively less income inequality, life expectancy tends to be longer. Among industrialized nations, the correlation between a country's Gini coefficient (which reveals the extent of income inequality in the country) and the average life expectancy of its citizens at birth is $-.81$, a remarkably strong negative relation (Wilkinson, 1994). Japan has the longest average life expectancy in the world, and it also has the most egalitarian income distributions of any major industrialized nation (Marmot & Davey Smith, 1989). Further evidence for the role of income inequality is that the relation between health and social class is weaker in countries with more equal income distributions such as Sweden and Norway than in countries with a wider spread, such as the United States or the UK (Lundberg, 1991; Vagero & Lundberg, 1989). The reasoning is that pronounced differences in status across individuals create feelings of relative deprivation that are much greater—and probably lead to more stress and illness—than if the differences in status are smaller.

One dramatic demonstration of the relation between relative status and health is a study that compared the mortality of actors and actresses who won Oscars with those who were nominated for Oscars but did not win

(Redelmeier & Singh, 2001). These two populations are similar in many respects and are all among the highest end of the socioeconomic spectrum. However, those who won Oscars lived, on average, 3.6 years longer than those who were nominated but did not win. Furthermore, those who won multiple Oscars lived 2.7 years longer than those who had won only once. Oscar nominees and winners cannot be said to suffer from any kind of absolute deprivation; however, there is apparently enough benefit associated with the satisfaction of being recognized as the best in his or her field to provide Oscar-winning actors and actresses with quite pronounced health benefits. Although it may be lonely at the top, evidently it can be pretty healthy.

Ethnicity and Health. Socioeconomic status is implicated in people's health outcomes in another way. Disadvantaged minorities around the world also tend to be of lower SES, and they often experience worse health outcomes than do majority members. In particular, in the United States, African-Americans suffer from relatively worse health outcomes. An examination of the 15 leading causes of death in the United States, African-Americans had higher death rates than European-Americans for 12 of them (see right side of Table 10.1). On average, African-Americans tend to be of much lower SES than European-Americans, so many of the reasons for their higher mortality can likely be explained by the SES difference.

However, other factors than SES seem to be involved in the poor health outcomes of many African-Americans. When African-Americans and European-Americans of the same SES are compared, some categories of health problems are still more pronounced for African-Americans. In particular, their infant mortality rates are about double those of European-Americans (NCHS, 1993), and these differences also hold for those who are highly educated (e.g., Pamuk, Makuc, Heck, & Reuben, 1998). Likewise, hypertension is particularly high among African-American men, and unlike other health outcomes, hypertension rates are slightly higher for African-American men with college degrees than they are for African-American men with less education (although the opposite pattern holds for African-American women and for European-American men and women; Diez-Roux et al., 1999; Hypertension Detection and Follow-Up Program Cooperative Group, 1977; Pamuk et al., 1998). What can explain these differential outcomes if not SES?

Health differences between African-Americans and European-Americans have been noted for some time, and historically there was a tendency to

TABLE 10.1
Relative Prevalence of Causes of Death Among Three U.S. Ethnic Groups

Causes of Death	African-Americans vs. European-Americans	Hispanics vs. European-Americans
1. Heart Disease	African-Americans Higher	European-Americans Higher
2. Cancer	African-Americans Higher	European-Americans Higher
3. Stroke	African-Americans Higher	European-Americans Higher
4. Respiratory Diseases	European-Americans Higher	European-Americans Higher
5. Accidents	African-Americans Higher	European-Americans Higher
6. Diabetes	African-Americans Higher	Hispanics Higher
7. Flu and Pneumonia	African-Americans Higher	European-Americans Higher
8. Alzheimer's Disease	European-Americans Higher	European-Americans Higher
9. Kidney Diseases	African-Americans Higher	No difference
10. Septicemia	African-Americans Higher	European-Americans Higher
11. Suicide	European-Americans Higher	European-Americans Higher
12. Cirrhosis of the Liver	African-Americans Higher	Hispanics Higher
13. Homicide	African-Americans Higher	Hispanics Higher
14. Hypertension	African-Americans Higher	Hispanics Higher
15. Pneumonitis	African-Americans Higher	European-Americans Higher

NCHS, 2003; Williams, 2005.

assume that the differences were due to genetic differences between the races (Wise, 1993). However, beyond the very prominent difference of skin color, there is little evidence of systematic genetic differences between African-Americans and European-Americans (Cornell & Hartmann, 1998; Lewontin, 1972). Rather, the greatest degree of genetic variability in human populations occurs within Africans themselves, as humans have lived in Africa far longer than anywhere else, leading to much diversity between different African populations (Cavalli-Sforza, Menozzi, & Piazza, 1994). Even so, the assumption that any differences between African-Americans and European-Americans are based in genetics is commonly made, with unfortunate consequences.

Consider the ethnic difference in hypertension rates mentioned earlier. This high rate has led some to search for African "hypertension genes." However, a comparison of hypertension rates of Americans and West Africans in Africa (from whom most African-Americans are descended) reveals that West

Africans have hypertension rates about the same as those of European-Americans, and only African-Americans score especially high compared with these other groups (Akinkugbe, 1985; Rotimi et al., 1996). Furthermore, the relevant genetic markers of hypertension do not vary between Africans and African-Americans, greatly weakening the notion of a genetic cause for the high hypertension rates among African-Americans (Rotimi et al., 1996). As hypertension is clearly linked to stress, a more parsimonious explanation would be that something about being African-American in the United States, with the resultant discrimination and experienced racism, leads to the stress causing hypertension (Williams, 2003). Perceptions of discrimination and education are positively correlated among African-Americans (Forman, Williams, & Jackson, 1997), which might help to explain why hypertension rates are higher among higher-SES African-American males than they are among lower-SES African-American males. Research further reveals that African-Americans who most strongly aspire to achieve in the face of discrimination are most at risk for hypertension (James, 1994). Similar arguments about the role of experienced racism in health outcomes have been made to account for the ethnic differences in infant mortality (e.g., David & Collins, 1991; Samuels, 1986) and negative health outcomes among African-Americans more generally (Williams, Yu, Jackson, & Anderson, 1997). In sum, being the target of racism and discrimination appears to be directly related to the average poorer health outcomes of African-Americans.

On the other hand, not all disadvantaged minorities suffer adverse health outcomes. Latinos in the United States do not tend to suffer much from adverse health outcomes. For the most part, their health outcomes on a variety of measures are quite similar to those of European-Americans, and in a number of cases their health outcomes are unexpectedly positive. As shown in the right half of Table 10.1, compared to European-Americans, Latinos tend to have *lower* mortality rates for 10 of the 15 leading causes of death (NCHS, 2003; Williams, 2005; also see Markides & Coreil, 1986). This ethnic difference is all the more puzzling because Latinos are of lower SES than European-Americans and hence should be expected to suffer worse health outcomes. The surprisingly healthy outcomes of Latinos across a variety of conditions has been labeled the "epidemiological paradox" (Karno & Edgerton, 1969).

This paradox is not easily explained. A number of artifactual accounts to explain this paradox have largely been discounted. For example, one theory known as the "healthy migrant hypothesis" proposes that only the healthiest Latinos were able to endure and survive the often taxing and potentially dangerous move to the United States (e.g., Sorlie, Backlund, Johnson, & Rogot, 1993). Hence, the mortality rates in this country capture only the healthiest subset of Latinos. An alternative account, known as the "salmon bias," proposes that many Latino immigrants return to their home countries when they are old or ill and thus their deaths are not included in the U.S. data (e.g., Pablos-Mendez, 1994). However, neither of these hypotheses is well supported by the evidence (e.g., Abraido-Lanza, Dohrenwend, Ng-Mak, & Turner, 1999). Moreover, the epidemiological paradox does not apply equally to all groups of Latinos. Puerto Ricans, for example, do not show some of the same unexplained health benefits as Mexicans (e.g., Fuentes-Afflick, & Lurie, 1997), and there are no clear explanations for this.

Why do some groups of Latinos have such unexpected health benefits? One explanation is that Latinos engage in more healthful behaviors than non-Latinos. For example, Latinos are less likely to drink and smoke than non-Latinos (although they also tend to exercise less; Perez-Stable, Marin, & Marin, 1994). However, the longer they live in the United States, the more likely Latinos are to engage in unhealthy behaviors, as they come to drink more, smoke more, and are more likely to become obese (Abraido-Lanza, Chao, & Florez, 2005). On the other hand, some cultural factors that are more pronounced among Latinos, such as the high value placed on child bearing (Poma, 1983) and the emotional support provided by the community (Anderson et al., 1981), appear to provide an important health buffer. Perhaps Latinos also derive health benefits from their unusually high levels of positive affect (e.g., Diener, 2001), which other studies have shown to yield significant health benefits (Ostir, Ottenbacher, & Markides, 2004). These variables may explain part of the reason Latinos have such healthy outcomes, but much of the paradox still remains unresolved and will continue to occupy researchers for some time.

Medicine and Culture

I still recall the first time I caught a cold in Japan when I was living there with a host family. It was an especially vicious cold, and I was feeling absolutely miserable laid up in bed. My host grandmother, *obaachan*, ever attentive to my well-being, seemed especially concerned about the bad shape that I was in. So she showed up at my room with some food to make me feel better—a plate of boiled octopus. She insisted that when you were sick you really need to get as many nutrients as possible, and that boiled octopus was an especially rich source of the nutrients that my sick body so clearly lacked. At the time I had zero appetite, I was feeling nauseous, and I was in a pretty lousy mood. In fact, at that point, there were few things in life less appealing to me than a plate of boiled octopus. Just looking at it was difficult. *Obaachan* could not seem to understand how I could be so ignorant about taking care of my own health. Who would refuse a plate of boiled octopus when he was sick? At the same time, I've always clung to the belief—one that is equally culture bound—that when I'm sick what will make me feel better is a bowl of chicken soup.

Truth be told, neither *obaachan* nor I really knew all that much about treating illnesses. Neither of us had any training in medicine, and our understanding about illnesses and their treatments, for the most part, was derived from folk theories passed down by our own parents and grandparents. This book has focused on the ways culture shapes the psychological experiences of people around the world, and our respective cultures have shaped how *obaachan* and I understood illnesses and their treatments. However, culture also shapes the psychological experiences of doctors around the world, and, importantly, it shapes how doctors think about your health. Although there is a great deal of agreement among doctors globally regarding the causes of various illnesses, their symptoms, and their recommended treatments, there is also a surprising degree of cultural variation. If you visit a doctor in another country you may realize just how much medicine does vary across cultures. In some extreme cases, standard procedures in one culture would be seen as medical malpractice in another (for a review, see Payer, 1996).

The medical profession is one of the oldest in the world, and virtually all cultures have individuals who specialize in treating people's health. Traditionally, medical practices have derived from local practices—in particular, religious beliefs—as well as from procedures developed by trial and error, and various shamans and healers developed techniques, rituals, and medicines from their own experiences and from knowledge that was passed down across generations (see Clements, 1932; Murdock, 1980). Traditional views of medicine depart greatly from those of modern medical science. An analysis of the theories of the cause of illness across 186 traditional non-Western societies around the world revealed a great degree of variability (Murdock, 1980). Whereas modern medicine views many illnesses as emerging from the deterioration of organ systems, stress, or infections, none of the 186 societies viewed organ deterioration as an important cause of illness—only 3 of the 186 (Ingalik, Javanese, and Siamese) viewed stress as an important cause of illness, and only 1 (Japanese) viewed infection as a major cause of illness. In contrast, in traditional non-Western societies, beliefs in supernatural causes of illness are quite widespread. These range from theories that aggressive spirits such as ghosts cause disease (which is the most widespread theory of disease around the world), to accounts of witchcraft, sorcery, mystical retributions, and sinful violations of taboos.

Among the Azande of West Africa, the primary cause of illness is believed to be witchcraft (Evans-Pritchard, 1976). Some Zande are believed to be witches, and the source of their witchcraft is believed to be a small organ in their bodies, which can be inherited from their parents. They do not perform any rites, use any potions, or cast any spells—rather, witches conduct their witchcraft entirely through their minds. When a Zande develops a slowly progressing illness, it is believed to be caused by a witch who is consuming the soul of its victim's organs, a little bit at a time. In contrast, when a Zande develops a sudden and acute illness, the cause is thought to be a spell cast on him or her by a sorcerer. The Azande belief system is not unusual in traditional cultures around the world, and although the specific theories underlying illness vary considerably across societies, in traditional societies the vast majority of theories are supernatural in nature.

In modern times, medicine has come to rely on the scientific method, in which controlled experiments between different procedures and medicines are conducted, and the results of these are shared across the international medical community. Supernatural beliefs play a far less significant role with most practitioners of modern medicine; however, it is still not uncommon for laypeople to view illnesses as developing from supernatural causes, primarily on religious grounds or on the belief that taboos have been broken or that spirits are threatening the patient. In general, though, modern medicine is grounded in scientific procedures.

The central role of science in modern medicine would suggest that a great deal of universality would exist in doctors' understanding of disease throughout the world. However, doctors tend to be trained within the cultures that produced them and their patients. Hence, a lot of medical training does occur within the context of particular cultural meaning systems, even when the training involves internationally recognized practices (see Angel & Thoits, 1987).

One way that cultures differ is in the metaphors they embrace to indicate a healthy body. In traditional Chinese medicine, for example, a healthy body is one in which the dialectical forces of yin and yang are in balance. Any imbalances in them is believed to ultimately lead to illness. For example, a person who has a condition known as "liver fire" will have symptoms such as headaches, flushed face, and anger, and this is believed to be caused by having too much yang and not enough yin. Such an imbalance could be corrected by acupuncture, herbal remedies, exercise, diet, and lifestyle. The metaphor of balancing opposing forces and energies is what guides traditional Chinese medical thought.

Perhaps it is not too surprising that traditional Chinese medicine differs as much as it does from modern Western medicine, given all the discussion in this book about differences in psychological experiences (such as holistic thinking styles) between people from Eastern and Western cultures. However, there are considerable variations even among doctors of Western cultures in their understanding of medicine.

For example, there are rather striking differences between medical practices of French and American doctors, as described by the medical journalist Lynn Payer (1996). In France, the metaphor of the body that guides doctors is the *terrain*, a word that doesn't translate well into English but is perhaps best captured by words such as "constitution" or "resistance." Somewhat similar to Chinese medicine, this view emphasizes that a sense of balance is key to health, as balance stimulates the immune system. This emphasis on balance shifts drug consumption away from antibiotics to various tonics and vitamins believed to strengthen the immune system. Long rests and spa visits are also important parts of a lifestyle that rejuvenates the *terrain*. Similarly, hospital stays are relatively long in France (about double the time in the United States for the same procedures) to provide ample opportunity for recuperation.

The French are more likely than Americans to see encounters with dirt and germs as not threatening but as possibly having beneficial effects—something that can strengthen the *terrain* and guard one against developing future illnesses. Accordingly, French practices with regard to germs differ from American ones—for example, with respect to how frequently one should bathe. A 1976 article in *Le Monde* stated that the French hospital patient had a right to a *monthly* bath, and to weekly foot-washings (Leulliette, 1976). French dermatologists recommend that people, even those with oily hair, should wash their hair no more than once a week because this allows a greater amount of oil to be secreted (Aron-Brunetiere, 1974). Because of the French attitudes toward bathing, per capita consumption of soap in France is about half of that of England (Payer, 1996). As a striking example from history, Louis XIV is reported to have bathed only twice in his life, and both times were prescribed by his doctors. Napoleon, getting ready to return from a long battle, is reported to have written a romantic letter to his wife Josephine telling her "Don't bathe, I'm coming home," reflecting the view that the body in its natural state, rather than scrubbed clean and coated with deodorants, is more attractive.

In contrast, Payer argues that American doctors see the body as a machine that needs to be tended regularly to ensure that it is running well. When there are problems with the body, it is often treated in ways that you might expect with a machine. American medicine is the most aggressive in the world—surgical procedures are used far more than in other countries (e.g., cesarean sections, coronary bypass surgery, mastectomies, hysterectomies) where malfunctioning parts are either removed, replaced, or physically altered (see Vayda, Mindell, & Rutkow, 1982). American doctors are more likely than doctors from other European countries to use surgery rather than drugs, and when drugs are prescribed in the United States, they are prescribed at higher dosages than in virtually any other country. In contrast, it is relatively rare for American doctors to prescribe rest and relaxation as curative agents.

When American doctors seek a cause for why the machine has started to malfunction, they are more likely than those from European countries to search for an external cause, such as bacteria or viruses. They prescribe more antibiotics than doctors from elsewhere, and Americans tend to be more concerned about cleanliness and avoiding contact with germs (e.g., not sitting directly on public toilet seats, not kissing family members with colds) than people from European countries. The belief is that the body is healthy in its default state unless it runs afoul of an offending germ or external threat.

A recent study by Rozin and colleagues (Rozin, Leeman, Fischler, & Shields, 2006) demonstrates the influence of cultural

"Don't forget to take a handful of our complimentary antibiotics on your way out."

experiences on physicians' understanding of medicine. In this study, laypeople and physicians were interviewed in five countries: France, Germany, Italy, the United Kingdom, and the United States. They were asked 20 questions concerning the relation between diet and health; for example, they were asked how much they agreed with statements about the value of vitamins, food-related hygiene, eating in moderation, and the healthfulness of certain products, such as fish, meats, and grains. The answers to all 20 questions were compared on the basis of the respondents' occupations (doctor vs. layperson) and country of origin. For 15 of the 20 items there were significant cultural differences—that is, the views of doctors and laypeople from some countries were different from those in other countries. In contrast, for only 1 of the 20 items was there a significant difference between doctors and laypeople. For the vast majority of items, doctors and laypeople within the same cultured tended to have similar answers to the questions. Furthermore, when the overall pattern of responses between doctors and laypeople in the five countries were compared using a multidimensional scaling analysis, a striking pattern emerged. Figure 10.7 shows the similarities between 10 different

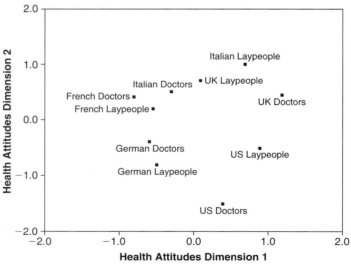

Similarity of Health Attitudes Among Doctors and Laypeople from Various Countries

FIGURE 10.7

In the five countries surveyed, doctors' attitudes towards diet and health tended to resemble the attitudes of lay people from their own cultures more closely than attitudes of doctors from other cultures.

groups of participants in terms of their overall pattern of responses to the 20 items as grouped along two underlying dimensions of health attitudes; groups that are closest to each other have the most similar views. The pattern of beliefs and attitudes of doctors in four of five countries more closely resembled those of laypeople from their own countries than they resembled the views of doctors of other countries. That is, at least for these particular questions, where people were raised had a bigger impact on how they viewed the relations between various aspects of diet and health than whether they had received formal medical training.

SUMMARY

Just as normal psychological processes vary across cultures, so do abnormal ones. The extent of cultural shaping of psychological disorders is most evident in culture-bound disorders, which are disorders that are largely limited to certain cultures. Many of these disorders, such as *koro*, *dhat*, or *amok*, appear quite foreign to Westerners, and they do not fit in to any of the more familiar diagnostic categories used by Western psychiatrists.

Some universally identifiable psychopathologies, such as depression, social anxiety, suicide, and schizophrenia, also are presented in culturally variable ways. Most noteworthy are the findings that symptoms of depression are likely to be somatized within some cultures (e.g., China) and psychologized in others (e.g., North America). Social anxiety is also universally present; however, it is very common in East Asia—so common that it is viewed as more normative there than in the West. When serious anxiety disorders present in Japan, they are more likely to do so with the symptoms of *taijinkyofushou*, which includes a very different set of symptoms from those of social anxiety disorder. Suicides vary a great deal in their frequency across cultures and in the motivations leading to them. Schizophrenia perhaps is the most cross-culturally similar disorder; however, even here there is cultural variation in the subtypes of schizophrenia that are most common and in the course of the disease.

Physical health is also affected by culture. First, there are some instances of genetic variation across human populations that have health consequences: fair-skinned people are more at risk for skin cancer in low latitudes, and people whose ancestors were cattle farmers for many generations are more likely to have lactase persistence. Second, people's biology can also vary across cultures with respect to acquired characteristics. For example, the Moken learn how to focus their eyes underwater, and body weight and height are related to certain dietary habits.

Health outcomes vary quite dramatically across socioeconomic status (SES) with people of lower SES being more vulnerable to a wide array of ailments and diseases than people of higher SES. These differences appear to affect people's feelings of psychological control over their lives. There are cultural features that interact with SES that affect health outcomes. African-Americans tend to have worse health outcomes for a variety of diseases, and some of these appear to be due to experiences with discrimination. Conversely, Latino-Americans tend to have better health outcomes than would be expected, although the reasons for this are not clear.

Doctors are also products of their cultures, and understandings of medicine vary greatly across cultures. Even between highly industrialized societies such as France and the United States there are differences in the theories that doctors have about the causes of diseases, and this leads to differences in the ways they treat them.

11

Interpersonal Attraction, Close Relationships, and Groups

Here's an observation of mine: Brad Pitt and Angelina Jolie are two very attractive people. You might agree. Readers of People.com voted the two of them the most beautiful man and woman in 2005. So there seems to be some consensus among us that as physical attractiveness goes, Brad Pitt and Angelina Jolie are about as good as it gets. But most of the readers of People.com and myself share a common cultural context. Most of us live in North America, watch movies that are by and large made in Hollywood, and see the same magazine covers in the checkout lines. So all of this raises an important question. Do people share the same standards of physical attractiveness around the world? Would Brad Pitt and Angelina Jolie cause heads to turn in other parts of the world as well?

This chapter explores how culture shapes the ways people relate to others. It considers this question from a few different perspectives: how people are attracted to others, how they form close relationships with others, and how they understand the nature of groups, and, likewise, how being a member of a group influences people. We will consider such questions as these: How universal are our standards of interpersonal attraction? Does the nature of friendships and romantic relationships vary across cultures? Do people perform better when they're evaluated as individuals or as members of groups? Our investigations of these and other questions are guided by a consideration of how people's experiences in their cultures shape their thinking, and we will also focus squarely on the contrast of universal versus culturally relative psychologies.

Angelina Jolie and Brad Pitt are certainly considered attractive in the United States. Would they be seen as attractive everywhere?

Interpersonal Attraction

Returning to the example of Brad Pitt and Angelina Jolie, are there universal standards of attractiveness around the world? In answering that question we need to contrast the similarities and differences in the ways people go about trying to make themselves more attractive. A glance at some bodily decoration strategies around the world reveals a good deal of cultural variation in what is viewed as attractive. Consider the different ways people alter their faces to make themselves beautiful. Among the Paduang in Thailand, women elongate their necks by several inches by inserting an increasing number of brass rings around them as they grow up. Among the Mursi in Ethiopia, women stretch their lower lips by inserting progressively larger ceramic disks in a hole that has been cut through the lip. Among the Ainu of northern Japan, women often tattoo their faces in what looks like a moustache around their lips. Among Westerners, women darken their eyelashes with mascara, paint their lips with lipstick, and shave the hair from their legs. Indeed, it would seem that if anything is influenced by cultural norms and context, fashion would have to be near the top of the list.

These photos show (a) a Paduang woman from Thailand, (b) a Mursi woman from Ethiopia, (c) an Ainu woman from Hokkaido, Japan, and (d) a Texan woman (Jessica Simpson). Each uses different strategies to make herself more attractive.

Charles Darwin (1871) too was struck by the cultural diversity in standards for what is considered an attractive face. Yet he also noticed some similarities across cultures, as he stated in one of his books: "Mr. Winwood Reade . . . who has had ample opportunities for observation, not only with the Negroes of the west coast of Africa, but those of the interior who have never associated with Europeans is convinced that their ideas of beauty are, on the whole, the same as ours." Much research has supported Darwin's friend's observations, that despite the stunning array of fickle strategies humans adopt to make themselves more physically appealing, there are numerous commonalities across cultures in what is perceived as attractive.

First, what kinds of faces are thought of as attractive? One variable that matters is complexion. Around the world there appears to be striking agreement here. Skin that looks free of blemishes, blotches, sores, and rashes is viewed as more attractive than skin that does not (Ford & Beach, 1951; Montagu, 1986). Indeed, a sizable portion of the multibillion dollar cosmetics industry is directed at selling products that conceal anything that makes one's skin appear less than pristine. Why would people be so concerned with their complexions? According to evolutionary reasoning, people should be especially attracted to healthy mates who would likely produce healthy offspring that would survive. We do not know for sure how healthy people are by looking at them; however, blemishes and sores on their skin could be useful indicators regarding the presence of parasites or diseases. Responding to the apparent health of the skin could thus have been a useful heuristic for sizing up the health of one's potential mate in the ancestral environment. Our ancestors who preferred blemish-free skin would have been more likely to have healthy mates and have surviving offspring than those who preferred imperfect skin. As such, over time, preferences for perfect skin would have become more common in the human gene pool.

A second characteristic that appears to be universally viewed as attractive is bilateral symmetry. Simply put, we are most attracted to people whose left sides of their faces and bodies look identical to their right sides. The reason for this, according to evolutionary biologists (e.g., Gangestad, Thornhill, & Yeo, 1994), is that bilateral symmetry is an indicator of developmental stability. Given ideal growing conditions, an organism's right and left sides will develop identically. However, genetic mutations, pollution, pathogens, and stresses encountered in the womb can lead organisms to develop in slightly asymmetrical ways. The more asymmetrical someone is, the more likely he or she is to have various genetic mutations or to have developed in less than ideal circumstances, and the less likely the person is to be in prime health. We all have certain degrees of asymmetry and, in general, the less symmetrical we appear, the less attractive we are perceived to be. An attraction to symmetry appears to be so fundamental that it is not limited to humans. Even more symmetrical scorpion flies are perceived as more attractive by other flies (i.e., they get more mates) than less symmetrical ones (Thornhill, 1992).

A third characteristic of attractive faces is that they tend to be average. Not average in the sense that we are especially attracted to people who are average in their attractiveness. Instead, this means that facial features that are close to the average in size and in configuration are perceived as most attractive. With a few notable exceptions (e.g., men tend to prefer some youthful features in women, whereas women prefer some masculine features in men; Cunningham, 1986; Cunningham, Barkee, & Pike, 1990), average-size noses, average-size eyes, average-size smiles, and average-size distances between the eyes, and so on, are perceived as most attractive. At least two mechanisms seem to be at work here. First, people with average-size features are less likely to have genetic abnormalities than people with deviant features, thus reflecting genetic health (Rhodes et al., 2001). A second reason people prefer average features is because we can process quickly something that resembles a prototype, and quick processing is associated with good feelings and feelings of attraction (Winkielman & Cacioppo, 2001). Average faces can be thought of as prototypes of faces. Interestingly, the attractiveness of average faces appears to hold across cultures too. In one study, the faces of a number of Euro-Australians and a number of Japanese were averaged together, both within and across cultures (Rhodes et al., 2005). Participants in both cultures viewed the average faces to be most attractive, regardless of the faces' culture of origin. The researchers also averaged the Australian and Japanese faces together. They found that the biracial averaged face was the most attractive face of all, particularly as judged by members of the opposite sex. It is not certain why biracial faces are perceived as most attractive, but one reasonable explanation is that they represent the best average of all the faces the participants have encountered in their lives. Extending from this we would expect that a face that was the average of faces from all cultures in the world would be seen as the most attractive of all, especially in multicultural societies where people are exposed to faces from many different cultures.

The attractiveness of average features, however, does not seem to generalize well to our perception of bodies. In general, it does not seem to be true that we are most attracted to people of average weight, average height, with average-size muscles, breasts, hips, and so on. Rather, the kinds of bodies that tend to be seem as most attractive are often those that depart considerably from average.

One aspect of people's bodies that varies considerably in its perceived attractiveness across cultures (in particular for the perceived attractiveness of women) is weight. If you were to look at the covers of women's magazines

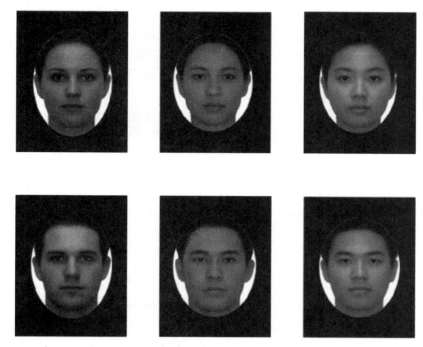

Average faces tend to be especially attractive. These photos were all created by averaging several other photos together. The photos on the left are averaged faces of Caucasian Australians, the photos on the right are averaged faces of Japanese, and the photos in the center are averaged faces of Eurasians. Most people find the averaged Eurasian faces to be the most attractive of the set of photos (Rhodes et al., 2005).

in the West today you likely would conclude that the kind of female body viewed as attractive is remarkably thin. If you opened those magazines and read some of the articles you would also find a great deal of attention placed on losing weight, new diets, exercise regimes, and the occasional story about the high prevalence of eating disorders. Given how ubiquitous the images are for thin female models in Western culture you might be tempted to conclude that preferences for thin female bodies are universal. Such a conclusion, however, would be grossly incorrect. Consider the conclusion about attractive bodies reached by Ford and Beach, an anthropologist and psychologist who wrote a highly influential book entitled *Patterns of Sexual Behavior*. They looked at the standards of beauty in the United States at the time they wrote their book in 1951 in conjunction with the standards of beauty they saw in the rest of the world's cultures; they concluded that it was a human universal that *heavier* women are viewed as the most attractive. The female models that currently grace the covers of the fashion magazines prove that Ford and Beach's conclusion is obviously incorrect—at least in Western culture today, thin is in. The changes in the standards of what constitutes an especially beautiful female body as it was seen in the United States in 1951 and today are quite dramatic. The shift is even more dramatic when you look at the kinds of bodies that were glorified in the days of Rubens or Renoir. What was prized as the ideal female form then is not the same as what appears to be prized now. The cultural differences in standards of beauty for female bodies differ not just across historical context but across current cultural ones as well. Much research has found that in some cultures people view the ideal female body to be far heavier than what is typically preferred among Westerners. The ideal body weight preferred by many cultures within Africa are for heavier body weights for both men and women compared with the norms in the West (Cogan, Bhalla, Sefa-Dedeh, & Rothblum, 1996). Indeed, in Western Africa, the term "fat" is often viewed as complimentary, indicating strength and beauty (Cassidy, 1991). Within the United States as well, African-Americans have heavier ideal body weights than European-Americans and feel less social pressure toward thinness (Kumanyika, Wilson,

The norms for an attractive female body have changed over time. From left to right: Peter Paul Rubens's "The Three Graces" (1639), Auguste Renoir's "Nude Woman Seated" (1876), and supermodel Kate Moss (2003).

& Guilford-Davenport, 1993; Neff, Sargent, McKeown, & Jackson, 1997). In sum, there is much variation in the kinds of bodies that are viewed as most attractive.

Hence, research suggests that although there is tremendous cultural variation in ways that people make themselves fashionable, there is also much that humans agree on with respect to who is beautiful. Brad Pitt and Angelina Jolie, in all likelihood, would be viewed as attractive anywhere they go, given their symmetry, clear complexion, and average-size features. However, they likely wouldn't be seen as the most beautiful people in some other contexts because there are specific cultural norms for attractiveness that they wouldn't meet. For example, Angelina Jolie could perhaps boost her perceived attractiveness among Africans if she gained several pounds, and she could attract the attention of more Paduang if she stretched her neck a few inches. There are both universal and culturally specific features of physical attractiveness.

Other Bases of Interpersonal Attraction. Aside from physical characteristics, other processes are involved that influence whether we're attracted to someone either as a friend or a romantic partner. I'm going to go out on a limb and guess that none of the readers of this book are best friends with Rugi Ngoma from the village of Chitimba, Malawi. Am I correct? Well, then, please consider who your best friend is. Now think for a minute how you ended up becoming so close to your best friend but not with Rugi. Well, one difference between your best friend and Rugi is that you've surely met your best friend, and I'm guessing that you probably haven't met Rugi. This rather obvious point underscores an important aspect of how we form interpersonal relationships, known as the **propinquity effect** (Festinger, Schacter, & Back, 1950). People are more likely to become friends with people with whom they frequently interact. Pretty straightforward stuff. Recently, the Internet has allowed for many relationships to develop in cyberspace, but these still are based on interactions, virtual as they may be. Of relevance for cultural psychology, it is difficult to imagine a culture in which the propinquity effect would not hold true. It would seem to be a good candidate for an accessibility universal.

I imagine that the propinquity effect does not strike you as especially profound. It might even seem kind of silly to think that people have spent time and resources to research something as obvious as this. But a couple of features of the propinquity effect are not as obvious as they seem. First, it is surprising to learn how powerful it is. People generally realize that they are more likely to develop relationships with people they see more frequently, although they probably don't realize just how much this affects their choice of friendships. Consider the friendships that were developed at the Maryland Police Academy in the early 1970s (Segal, 1974). At this academy, the new recruits were lined up in the alphabetic order of their last names, and this order influenced where they sat in class and where their dorm rooms were located. One study investigated the friendships that developed among the new police recruits. People were asked to nominate their closest friend at the academy. Their nominations are presented in Figure 11.1. The numbers along the X and Y axes represent the names of the recruits in alphabetic order. If people had based their choices of friends on something other than the alphabetic order of their names the dots would be scattered randomly

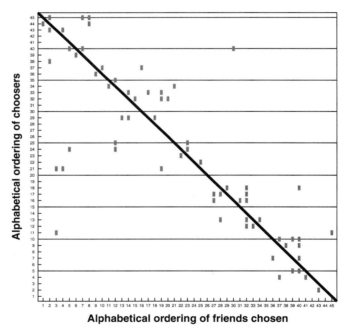

FIGURE 11.1

Trainees at the Maryland State Police Training Academy indicated who among their fellow trainees they had befriended. The numbers along the bottom indicate the alphabetical order of friends chosen, whereas the numbers on the left indicate the alphabetical order of the choosers (Segal, 1974).

across the figure. In reality, as you can see, the choices of friends cluster closely toward the diagonal of the figure, meaning that the alphabetic ordering of the recruits' last names played a large role in determining who they chose as friends. In fact, 45% of all the friendships were among those whose last name was adjacent to the chooser's name in alphabetical order, and the majority of the other friendships were with people whose last names were within a few letters of the chooser's last name. The simple fact of who stood next to whom was more important in influencing these police recruits' selection of friends than were their personalities, backgrounds, or religious beliefs. This study demonstrates how, in many ways, our friendships are not so much chosen by us but are chosen by the situational forces that bring us together.

A second nonobvious fact of the propinquity effect is in how it operates. One important basis of why propinquity is attractive is known as the **mere exposure effect**. That is, the more we are exposed to a stimulus the more we are attracted to it. This has been shown to be true for our attraction to other people, foreign words, music, and a variety of inanimate stimuli. Our attraction to frequently encountered stimuli appears to be due to the pleasant associations that we develop through classical conditioning when we learn that a stimulus is not threatening to us (Zajonc, 2005) and to the pleasant affect associated with easy-to-process stimuli (Winkielman & Cacioppo, 2001). Importantly, the mere exposure effect appears to be a cultural universal. For example, Japanese and Americans appear to be equally likely to come to like those people with whom they interact most frequently (Heine & Renshaw, 2002). This cross-cultural similarity in the mere exposure effect is not a surprise. Indeed, Zajonc and colleagues (Zajonc, Wilson, & Rajecki, 1975) found that even chickens are more attracted to those chickens they had been exposed to the most. If chickens and American participants are showing evidence of the same psychological processes then we shouldn't be surprised to learn that people from different cultures exhibit evidence of the same processes as well.

Similarity-Attraction Effect. Another powerful predictor of attraction is the **similarity-attraction effect.** People tend to be attracted to those who are most like themselves. Much research has shown that people are more likely to view someone as attractive either as a potential friend or a romantic partner if both are similar in their attitudes, economic background, personality, religion, social background, and activities (e.g., Byrne, 1961; Lydon, Jamieson, & Zanna, 1988; Newcomb, 1961). The similarity-attraction effect is one of the most powerful and reliably found predictors of when people will become friends or romantic partners.

How universal is the similarity-attraction effect? In the study with the chickens described above, Zajonc and colleagues also investigated whether chickens were attracted to similar others. The chickens in that study were dyed either green or red while still in their eggs to make them look either similar to or different from each other. It turned out that the chickens showed no hint whatsoever of a similarity-attraction effect. They were not any more attracted to the similarly colored chickens than to the differently colored ones. This raises the possibility that the similarity-attraction effect is not as fundamental a psychological process as the mere exposure effect since it is not found as broadly across species.

Does the similarity-attraction effect operate similarly in different cultures? Like many other psychological phenomena, the similarity-attraction effect has been studied almost exclusively in Western cultural contexts, where the evidence for its existence is quite unassailable. What might we find if we look in a non-Western context? We explored this question by contrasting the similarity-attraction effect between Japanese and North Americans (Heine, Foster, & Spina, 2007). For example, in one study we had Japanese and Canadian participants come into a lab where they briefly met a stranger of the same sex and nationality. They then went into separate rooms and completed either a personality measure or a measure of their social background. Next they were shown what was apparently the personality or social background measure of the stranger. However, the profile of the stranger the participants saw had actually been filled out by the experimenter, who had made these "responses" highly similar to those of the participant (a high similarity condition), or quite dissimilar (a low similarity condition). Participants were then asked to indicate how much they felt they would like the stranger. As shown in Figure 11.2, the Canadians showed evidence of the similarity-attraction effect, replicating much past research. They liked the highly similar person more than the dissimilar one. For the Japanese, in contrast, their liking for the stranger was unaffected by their apparent similarity. The pattern of results was identical regardless of whether participants found out about the stranger's personality or social background. Other studies also find that the similarity-attraction effect is consistently stronger among North Americans than Japa-

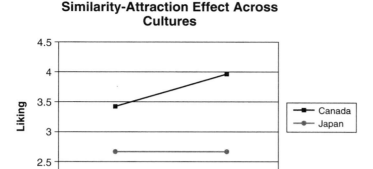

FIGURE II.2

Whereas Canadians better liked a stranger they considered very similar to themselves, Japanese attitudes toward strangers were unaffected by perceived similarity.

nese (Heine et al., 2007; Heine & Renshaw, 2002); however, in some studies, Japanese show a clear similarity-attraction effect as well.

Identifying cultural differences in psychological processes can also help us learn more about those processes within a Western cultural context. Knowing that Japanese and North Americans differed in whether they exhibited a similarity-attraction effect led us to investigate what other psychological variables might be behind the cultural difference—that is, we tried to "unpackage" the cultural difference. We reasoned that self-esteem might be a good variable to study to help us understand the cultural difference. As we discussed in Chapter 6, much other research had shown that Japanese have significantly lower self-esteem than Westerners (e.g., Heine et al., 1999). Furthermore, there seemed to be something quite egotistic in feeling that the people we find most interesting and desirable are those who are just like us. Indeed, we found that the similarity-attraction effect was highly related to self-esteem, and that when we statistically controlled for the cultural difference in self-esteem, the cultural difference in the similarity-attraction effect became significantly smaller (Heine et al., 2007). This suggests that the similarity-attraction effect may be a functional universal (the relation between self-esteem and liking similar partners is the same across cultures); however, the cultural variation in the magnitude of the effect demonstrates that it is not an accessibility universal.

Close Relationships

Humans are nothing if not social. In all cultures, most people live with others, eat with others, socialize with others, work with others, study with others, hang out with others, and sleep with others. We are born and raised in families and most of us go on to create families of our own. Most of our work activities take place with others, and there are relatively few times in the day when most people are all alone. Most events in our lives unfold in the context of the relationships we have with others.

Furthermore, relationships do not just occupy much of our time, but they also represent some of our most significant concerns. Researchers who have systematically eavesdropped on people's conversations find that the most common topic of conversation is gossip about other people (Dunbar, Marriott, & Duncan, 1997). Studies that track people's happiness over time find that our happiest times are when we are with others (Csikszentmihalyi & Hunter, 2003). People's most emotionally wrenching experiences involve the breakup of relationships and the deaths of loved ones (Holmes & Rahe, 1967). In sum, our relationships with others are concerns that dominate our lives, and it would be impossible to have a good understanding of human nature unless we also considered how people relate to others. This social foundation of human nature is universal in that there are no cultures in which people live as lone individuals. Despite this universality, however, the ways that people go about relating to others varies in some predictable and important ways.

Friends and Enemies. Few things in life are more special than friendships. Friends make good times more enjoyable and bad times less painful. They help us out when we're in need, they make us laugh, and they make us feel wanted and important. Friendships are important enough that they have been argued to be the key to success (Carnegie, 1936), and research has revealed that the quality of one's friendships is one of the best predictors of happiness (e.g., Csikszentmihalyi & Hunter, 2003). Most dramatic, perhaps, are the findings from research that having close friends increases the length of one's life (House, Landis, & Umberson, 1988). Given the obvious pleasures and benefits associated with friendships, the following poem (Kyei & Schreckenbach, 1975, p. 59) is a puzzle:

Beware of friends.
Some are snakes under grass;
Some are lions in sheep's clothing;
Some are jealousies behind their faáades of praises;
Some are just no good;
Beware of friends.

Why would we need to be wary of friends rather than trusting of them? Even more puzzling, this quote comes from a poem written by a Ghanaian and reflects a sentiment that is expressed quite commonly in West African worlds (Adams & Plaut, 2003)—a collectivistic cultural context. Why, in a cultural context that emphasizes people's fundamental conneciton with close others, can those others often be viewed with such suspicion?

Before we make sense of this puzzle, consider another question: Do you have any enemies? Let's define enemies as those who are wishing for your downfall or are trying to sabotage your progress. According to this definition, do you have enemies, and, if so, who are they?

If you're like the majority of Americans who have participated in the research by Glenn Adams and colleagues, you probably can't think of any enemies you have. Only 26% of Americans in one study reported that they had any enemies (Adams, 2005). In contrast, 71% of Ghanaians claimed that they were the target of enemies. While only a minority of Americans think that others are plotting against them, a substantial majority of Ghanaians do. Furthermore, among those Americans who do feel that they have enemies, they were more likely than the Ghanaians to view those enemies as coming from outside their group, such as those who held ethnic prejudices against their group. In contrast, Ghanaians were more likely to view their enemies as coming from within their ingroups, people such as neighbors, friends, or

Some examples of bumper stickers frequently seen in Ghana.

relatives (Adams, Anderson, & Adonu, 2004). The worlds of Ghanaian and American relationships appear to be very distant indeed.

At first glance, these cultural differences would seem to be at odds with what we would expect from the idea that people who are independent are more common in the United States and people who are interdependent are more common in Ghana. You might expect that the lone individual with few close ties or self-defining relationships would be the one who was most vulnerable to enemies and most suspicious of friends. After all, if people who are independent choose to view themselves as autonomous and distinct from others, this might suggest that they don't trust others very much. On the other hand, people who are interdependent and who allow others to become so close as to be key self-defining aspects of their identity should be especially trusting of those others. But the data suggest the exact opposite. How can we resolve this paradox?

Adams makes the case that these cultural differences in enemyships reveal the fundamental assumptions that people have regarding the nature of relationships. He proposes that people who are independent and interdependent perceive relationships in importantly different ways. Those with a more independent view of self perceive themselves as being fundamentally disconnected from others, and the only reasons such people would form connections is because they would choose to do so. The default state of the relations between two independent individuals can be seen as a null relationship. Relations develop only when the people involved in them decide that forming a relationship is to their advantage. Otherwise, no relationship would develop. Consider how one of Adams's (2005) American participants responded to the question of whether he had an enemy: "For me, it's really nonproductive. . . . I won't entertain or I won't stay engaged with that type of person. I mean, they may try, but one of my strengths is that I am pretty good at that, weaving my way out of that maze." For this participant, enemies are not a problem because he chooses not to engage with them. He appears to simply avoid those people with whom relations might not be productive, and thus no relationship, and no enemyship, would ever develop.

In contrast, for those who are more interdependent, the self is defined primarily on the basis of close relationships. Relationships are not so much chosen among individuals as they are perceived to exist by default. One is born into a family within a network of relatives, and these relationships are not up for negotiation. They simply exist, whether one likes them or not. Furthermore, one is born into a neighborhood, goes to a school, starts an occupation, and the people with whom one shares these contexts are also people with whom one has relationships. If people do not choose whom they will have relationships with but instead enter relationships that are perceived to exist naturally without negotiation, the default state between two such individuals is that they have a relationship. And those relationships are not always positive. Some people really do not get along with each other, but if deciding that they will not engage with each other is not an option, they will continue to have a relationship, albeit one that is frequently characterized by negative feelings. Perhaps the situation that comes closest to this for many Western people is with some in-laws. You might not like all your in-laws, but you still have to maintain relationships with them. In some instances relationships such as these, in which people have unavoidable relationships with people with whom they do not get along, might develop into full-blown enemyships. Such a view seems to be expressed by one of Adams's (2005) Ghanaian participants: "The world is such that everybody is bound to have enemies."

This view proposes that people from different cultures form relationships for different reasons. Relationships among those who are independent are entered into and maintained on a mutually voluntary basis. One can choose to make efforts to start a relationship or to dissolve a relationship. The existence of a relationship is rather tenuous and requires that the people involved agree that the relationship is beneficial and worth efforts to maintain it; otherwise it returns to the default status of a null relationship. This view of relationships seems to be emphasized by Western social psychologists, as the majority of research on relationships has targeted attraction and the formation of new relationships, especially romantic relationships, and also the dissolution of those relationships. There is almost no mention of less voluntary kinds of relationships, such as kin relations, within Western social psychological research (Adams et al., 2004). It seems that the theoretical model guiding this research is that relationships are conditional and voluntary, and will return to their null state if people decide they are unproductive.

In contrast, relationships among those who are interdependent appear to be viewed in less conditional terms. One is born into a relatively fixed interpersonal network—for example, one might be the second daughter of the Ackah family, a family of peanut farmers who live in a village just south of the town of Navrongo. The relationships one has with one's kin are not voluntary; the default state of relationships in this context is that there are relationships, whether they are always rewarding or not, and these enduring relationships come with a certain set of obligations. Judging from the studies by Adams and others, this model of unconditional kinship relations appears to shape the relations of people who are more interdependent, and thus relationships with friends, neighbors, and enemies tend to be perceived in unconditional, enduring terms. An important distinction is that interdependent people do not necessarily *value* or *desire* close relationships more than those who are independent. Rather, they view close relationships in natural, noncontingent terms, unlike the emphasis on voluntary relationships more characteristic of people who are independent.

One way this difference in views of relationships can be detected is by exploring the ways people think about friends. Friendships are universal relationships—we see them in all cultures; however, the nature of these relationships can vary. Adams and Plaut (2003) contrasted Ghanaian and American feelings about friendship. They noted a few interesting differences. First, Americans report having a larger number of friends than do Ghanaians. Furthermore, the thought of someone having many friends was also viewed differently across cultures. Many Ghanaians (but rarely Americans) reported viewing someone who had a large number of friends as rather foolish. One possible reason Ghanaians might not have as many friends, or think of someone having a lot of friends as foolish, is reflected in how people described friendships. The majority of Ghanaians emphasized that friends were people who would provide practical support; only a minority of Americans spontaneously listed this feature in their definition of friendship. For example, in one Ghanaian's description, "A friend is someone who is ready to help you, whether it is financially or socially, where there is a need. That's what I think is most important about a friend." This suggests that friendships among Ghanaians are perceived to involve more obligations than they do for Americans. Maintaining friendships in Ghana is less focused on sharing good times and more concerned with meeting the obligations of those friendships. These relationships are not just about deriving positive benefits but also about incurring some substantial costs when obligations need to be fulfilled. A person with many friends, then, is a person who also has many obligations, and this would seem to underlie the relatively smaller friendship networks among Ghanaians.

Love. Let's talk about love—that ineffable, indomitable, and invaluable commodity that likely occupies a substantial amount of your thoughts. Love has been written about, recited about, or sung about more than most any other topic, and psychologists too, perhaps foolhardily, have jumped into the fray. Let's start this one from the very beginning. Why do we have love?

It would seem that anything as powerful as love must serve an important function. Considering love from an evolutionary perspective we can see some good reasons for its origins. First, if we consider why people feel a sense of parental love, the answer seems quite obvious. Strong feelings of parental love goad people into committing the quite sizable amounts of time and resources needed to take care of their children. Humans have an especially long and dependent period of infancy, and if we did not feel very powerful feelings of love toward our children it would be very difficult for them to receive the enormous amount of care they need to survive. This can be contrasted with some other species—for example, sea turtles—whose offspring are born self-sufficient and for which we see no evidence of loving parental behaviors. Other species—for example, bears—do show a good deal of protective care from the mother; however, the father is nowhere to be seen. This suggests that young bears require care that can be provided by only the mother, and father bears are quite irrelevant for anything other than fertilizing the eggs. Humans, in contrast, require such an extended period of costly protective care and socialization that they fare best when they have two folks devoted to providing resources and socializing them. In the ancestral environment, it was likely that parents who did not feel especially strong love for their children were less likely to have their children survive the tenuous circumstances of a subsistence lifestyle; hence, those parents did not pass on as many surviving genes as did those who felt strong feelings of love for their children.

The reasoning for romantic love is similar. Evolutionary psychologists contend that the originating impetus for romantic love is the long vulnerable period of human childhood (e.g., Fisher, 2004). Because children in the ancestral environment would have been more likely to survive if there were two parents around to provide resources and socialization, some strong incentives were needed to keep the parents together so they would both stick around to support the children. According to this reasoning, romantic love was selected as the glue that keeps couples together. Those people who did not develop feelings of love for their partners would have been less likely to stay with them and would have ended up having fewer surviving offspring than those who felt strong feelings of love. Again, according to this line of reasoning, it's all about the kids. This is an evolutionary account for how love came to be.

Because we are all part of the same species, to the extent that this evolutionary account is correct, people from all cultures should be capable of feeling romantic love. And this does appear to be the case. One review of ethnographies of 166 cultures found clear evidence of romantic love in 89% of them (Jankowiak & Fischer, 1992). There was not clear evidence for romantic love in the remaining 11% of cultures; however, in all but one of these cases the ethnographies note that sexual affairs occur, but the researchers did not explore the motives behind why the people enter into them. The authors of the review concluded that the lack of evidence for romantic love in those 11% of societies was likely due to ethnographic oversight rather than a genuine absence of love. To the extent that they are correct, romantic love would qualify as a human universal—at least a functional universal, if not an accessibility universal. Furthermore, much research across cultures shows a number of striking similarities in people's feelings of love toward their partners (e.g., Kim & Hatfield, 2004; Neto, Mullet, & Deschamps, 2000; Philbrick & Opolot, 1980). However, there are some notable cultural differences too (e.g., Desai, McCormick, & Gaeddert, 1989; Murstein, Merighi, & Vyse, 1991).

Perhaps the most obvious example that culture shapes how people think about romantic love is the existence of arranged versus love marriages. The majority of marriages around the world have been arranged by families (Skolnick, 1987) rather than the couples themselves (although the percentage of arranged marriages has recently been dropping in many cultures around the world, such as in China, India, Japan, Turkey, and among orthodox Jews; Hortacsu, 1999; Sprecher & Chandak, 1992; Xu & Whyte, 1990). Even today within North America, there are many young people in their 20s, particularly those of Indian and Pakistani descent, who are participating in arranged marriages. There are different kinds of arranged and love marriages around the world. In Table 11.1, Broude and Green summarize the results of their survey of the mate selection tactics of 186 pre-industrial societies. The strategy that individuals can choose their own partners without needing to seek approval, which perhaps is the most normative strategy among Westerners

TABLE 11.1
Mate Selection Practices Among Pre-industrial Societies

	Men	Women
Parents choose partner; individual cannot object	13%	21%
Parents choose partner; individual can object	17%	23%
Individual choice and arranged marriages are both acceptable alternatives	18%	17%
Individuals, parents, kin, and others must reach agreement on an appropriate match	3%	3%
Individual selects partner autonomously; parental, kin, and/or community approval necessary or highly desirable	19%	29%
Individual selects partner autonomously; approval by others unnecessary	31%	8%

Based on Broude & Green (1983), pp. 273-274.

today, was evident in only 31% of pre-industrial societies for men, and only 8% for women. College students in a number of countries were asked the following question: "If a man (woman) had all the other qualities you desired, would you marry this person if you were not in love with him (her)" (Levine, Sato, Hashimoto, & Verma, 1995). Whereas approximately half of students from India and Pakistan said that they would marry this person (and another one quarter said that they were undecided), the vast majority (over 80%) of Americans, Britons, Australians, and Latin Americans said they would not, and only a small percentage (less than 5%) of people from these countries said they would. Apparently love is viewed as a necessary feature for a marriage to begin in some cultures, but not others. Interestingly, this identical question was posed to some American college students a little more than a generation ago, in a 1967 survey (the year that the Beatles recorded their hit single "*All you need is love*"). In that sample, 65% of the men, and only 24% of the women, said they would not marry someone they did not love (Kephart, 1967). Not only are there pronounced cultural differences in attitudes toward love, but current attitudes in the United States, particularly among women, are very different from what they were a few decades ago. Marrying someone because you have fallen in love with that person is a relatively new idea and is likely somewhat uncommon in the context of all the marriages that have occurred throughout human history.

The likelihood that a culture favors arranged over love marriages is not determined randomly. Rather, it appears to relate to the dominant kind of family structure in the culture. Goode (1959) proposed that romantic love would become more important in cultures as the strength of extended family ties became weaker. Powerful feelings of romantic love could be somewhat irrelevant, or even problematic, for marriage in cultures with strong extended family ties. The Western ideal of romantic love, characterized by intense feelings and mutual absorption, could be disruptive in cultures with large kin networks because such feelings can interfere with people's abilities to respect the wishes of their family members (Dion & Dion, 1993). Furthermore, the existence of strong kin relations provides considerable social pressures for a couple to stay together. In the absence of those social pressures, another kind of glue would be necessary to keep the couple together. Romantic love has been proposed to be that critical glue when other kin are not around (Inkeles, 1953). An analysis of data from 117 nonindustrialized societies found clear support for Goode's thesis (Lee & Stone, 1980). Marriages based on love were more likely in cultures with nuclear family structures than they were in cultures with extended family systems. The larger the number of important family relationships there are that one needs to consider, the more problematic it becomes to ignore their concerns and follow the passions of one's heart.

Relatedly, individualism, more generally, appears to be related to the likelihood that one emphasizes romantic love in marriages. Some research on romantic love has emphasized the critical role that idealization of one's partner has in the experience of romantic love. The Irish playwright George Bernard Shaw once cynically commented, "Love is a gross exaggeration of the difference between one person and everybody else." At one level, there seems to be some truth in Shaw's remark. For example, one study investigated dating and married couples' perceptions of their partners (Murray, Holmes, & Griffin, 1996). The study found that those people who idealized their partner the most (i.e., they viewed the individual in the most unrealistically positive terms compared with how they viewed other people, and with how their partners viewed themselves) also loved their partners the most and were more likely still to be together in their relationship several months later. The researchers' reasoning for why idealization seems to foster successful relationships is that positively distorted views of our partners should protect us from having to entertain thoughts about their unlovable characteristics. If a person sees her partner behave badly, such as when he gets angry and kicks the dog, leaves dirty laundry on the floor, or grows overweight, and considers these behaviors objectively, she might have a difficult time integrating the cognitions "I love my partner" and "My partner has many unlovable qualities." This dissonance can be avoided quite simply by distorting her views of her partner, so that undesirable behaviors are instead seen to indicate more positive qualities, such as that the partner is "emotional," "carefree," and "knows how to enjoy the good things in life." When partners are viewed in these ways, the relationship can be buffered against any ugly truths that might threaten it, and romantic love can thrive.

However, such idealization would seem to be less emphasized in more collectivistic cultures where individualized personal agency is not especially elaborated (Averill, 1985). If people's behaviors are perceived as less reflective of their dispositions, as they seem to be in collectivistic cultures (see Chapter 9), there should be less motivation to ensure that one's partner's personality is viewed in such rosy terms. Some research supports this hypothesis. In one study Japanese and Canadian college students were asked to evaluate the quality of their romantic relationship compared with what they thought most other people's romantic relationships were like (Endo, Heine, & Lehman, 2000). As shown in Figure 11.3, people in both countries showed some evidence for idealization in that they viewed their own romantic relationships

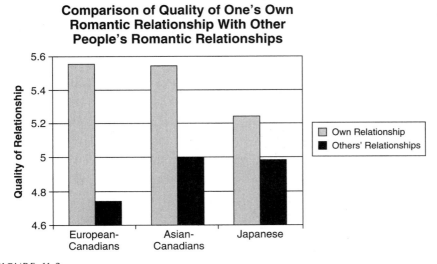

FIGURE 11.3

European-Canadians perceive the quality of their own romantic relationships to be far superior to those of other people. A similar bias holds for Asian-Canadians and Japanese, but it is much smaller.

as significantly more positive than how they viewed most other people's romantic relationships. However, the magnitude of this idealization (i.e., the gap between their evaluations of their own romantic relationship and their evaluation of most other people's romantic relationship) was significantly greater among European-Canadians than it was among Japanese, whereas Asian–Canadians fell in between. Hence, idealizations of one's romantic relationships appears to be more pronounced among people from more individualistic cultures. It is possible (although it has not yet been explored) that idealization does not predict relationship longevity among people from collectivistic cultures as well as it does among people from individualistic cultures.

I have found in my lectures on cultural psychology that the issue of arranged marriages is the topic my students seem to view as the most surprising to them. Indeed, many of my students are devoting a huge amount of their energy and time trying to find love, precisely because they hold the widely shared belief that love provides the foundation of a marriage. Trying to imagine, in contrast, that one could instead just marry whomever their parents suggested seems to strike many of my students (particularly those of Western descent) as outright unfathomable. They often ask, "How could you have a marriage without love?"

This question reveals a number of assumptions that many Westerners have about love. First is the belief that you will only love someone you have chosen for yourself. However, even though many arranged marriages start out with no feelings of love between the couple, typically the husband and wife come to feel strong feelings of love toward each other. An Indian colleague of mine who had been in a successful arranged marriage for some time explained it to my perplexed Western mind thus: Getting a husband is not all that different from getting a new puppy. When you first receive a new puppy, you have not yet developed feelings of love for it. However, you expect that you will come to love that puppy, and invariably, with time, you do. Likewise, someone in an arranged marriage does not warily approach the new partner as though he or she were a suspicious stranger in a dark alley. Rather the individual approaches that person as his or her new spouse with the expectation of eventually falling in love. And, with time, they usually do.

A second assumption about love is that it is ultimately an individualistic choice. Being a unique person, I could only come to love someone that I could connect with in a unique and special way. With this view, it seems essential that individuals choose their partner, as only they know their own idiosyncrasies well enough to identify a person they will love. In cultures where arranged marriages are common, however, there is more the view that marriages are the intersection of two families. With this view of marriage, it follows that the families would be in a better position to evaluate the likely success of a marriage rather than the lone individuals involved. People who enter arranged marriages thus usually trust their families to make the right decision for them, taking into account all the parties involved and making a choice based on what seems to be best for everyone in the long term. Often, then, people do not view their families as preventing them from making the best decision about whom they should marry—rather, they often trust that their families are the only ones who are positioned to make the best decision.

A third assumption commonly made about love is that a marriage that does not have love at the foundation is bound to be miserable. This does not seem unreasonable given that so many Western marriages do go through times of misery and often end up in divorce, and that those times of misery seem to coincide with declines in feelings of love. However, a look at cultures with arranged marriages does not seem to support this. First, in some cultures, people view arranged marriages as being more likely to succeed than love marriages. For example, a survey among adults living in various urban centers in India found that 74% of men and women believed that arranged marriages were more likely to succeed than love marriages (Kishwar, 1994). Furthermore, there appears to be a striking positive correlation between the amount that a culture emphasizes love as the basis of marriage and its divorce rate—an ironic fact that suggests the more we insist on maintaining love in a marriage the less successful we seem to be at doing it (Dion & Dion, 1993). Much evidence also suggests that those in arranged marriages are at least as satisfied with their marriages as those in love marriages. For example, Turkish couples (Hortacsu, 1999) and Israeli couples (Shachar, 1991) in arranged marriages have been found to be as much in love with their partners as those in love marriages. Members of the Unification Church, known colloquially as the "Moonies," undergo an unusual form of arranged marriage in that the Reverend Sung Myung Moon chooses the partners each member marries at a large mass ceremony of over 1,000 couples at a time. A study that followed these couples in the United States 3 years after they were married found no differences in the marital satisfaction or the marital dissolution of the Moonie marriages compared with rates for the general public (Galanter, 1986). Men in Japanese arranged marriages were found to be more satisfied than those in

*"I'm sure 'till death do you part' was only
an estimate."*

love marriages, and men in Chinese arranged marriages were as satisfied as those in love marriages. However, women in Japanese and Chinese arranged marriages were found to be less satisfied in arranged than love marriages (Blood, 1967; Xu & Whyte, 1990), suggesting that the costs of arranged marriages are borne largely by women in those cultures.

One extensive study compared marital satisfaction and the time spent in the marriage between Indian couples who were in either arranged or love marriages (Gupta & Singh, 1982). As shown in Figure 11.4, although in the initial years of marriage those in love marriages professed more love than those in arranged marriages, over time, it was those in arranged marriages who reported having the most love. This pattern held true for both men and women (for similar findings see Yelsma & Athappilly, 1988). Ironically, it was the marriages that started off with less love that ended up with more love. Perhaps some words from a Japanese colleague of mine, who has been in a successful arranged marriage for more than 30 years, can help make sense of the seemingly paradoxical findings of Gupta and Singh. As he described to me, when he first married his wife they had no love for each other—they were strangers at the time. Now, however, they have some love for each other. "Some love" seems like quite a bit in comparison with "no love." In contrast, he pointed out that those who have love marriages typically start out their relationships having a lot of love for each other. However, years later, it is not surprising if many of them report having less love than they had during their steamy courtship period. "Some love" doesn't seem so great compared to the "lot of love" that they had for each other earlier. As such, feelings of love might sometimes grow for those in arranged marriages and decline for those in love marriages because people have different standards of comparison. Of course, it is important to remember in all of this that individuals have vastly different experiences, and the fact that some arranged marriages work out well does not mean that those same benefits would be experienced by everyone across all contexts.

FIGURE 11.4

In India, people in love marriages report more love than those in arranged marriages in the first few years of marriage. In later years, however, those in arranged marriages profess more love than those in love marriages.

In sum, arranged marriages have traditionally been very common in the world, although they are currently declining in popularity. That they are declining does suggest that they are not currently perceived by people in cultures where they occur to be as desirable as they used to be, although in many cultures the evidence of their success rate is quite good.

Groups

The social nature of humans is not only evident in that relationships are always a pressing concern for people everywhere, but it is also evident in that people exist as members of various groups. People belong to nuclear families, extended families, neighborhoods, tribes, schools, clubs, teams, social cliques, offices, committees, and so on. A good portion of people's lives are experienced within the context of groups. This fact has not been lost on social psychologists, and the study of groups has been an important focus of research since the very beginning of that field.

Relations With Ingroups and Outgroups. People in all cultures belong to groups; however, there are ways that this belongingness differs. Consider what was discussed about the nature of independent and interdependent selves in Chapter 5. In Figure 5.2 on page 184, people with independent selves were depicted as showing that individuals had a number of close relationships with members of their ingroup; however, those relationships were less self-defining than were the corresponding relationships of those with more interdependent selves (see Figure 5.3 on page 185). Furthermore, people with independent selves were shown to have a rather permeable boundary between their ingroups and outgroups, whereas people with interdependent selves tended to have a more clear-cut boundary distinguishing these groups. Why would we expect to see people with independent and interdependent selves having different views toward ingroups and outgroups?

Although ingroup relationships are surely essential in all cultures, they take on special significance among those with more interdependent views of self. Because ingroup relations are so critical for self-definition for people in more interdependent cultures and they serve to direct appropriate behaviors in those contexts, it would be especially necessary to identify those with whom such significant relationships exist. Obligations to others are an important part of ingroup relations among interdependent people, so it is of vital importance for them to distinguish those toward whom they have obligations from those they do not. Becoming a member of an interdependent individual's ingroup is thus a rather substantial accomplishment, and these relationships should be entered more cautiously. It is not easy for outgroup members to become part of the valued ingroup, and it is rare for a member of the ingroup to lose his or her privileged status and fall into the outgroup category. This would suggest that the boundary distinguishing ingroups from outgroups would be particularly salient for members of interdependent cultures.

In contrast, a more independent person is likely to perceive himself or herself as existing and functioning separately from the social environment; therefore, the people in that environment are relatively more tangential to the independent individual's identity. New relationships can be formed and old relationships can be dissolved without having a large impact on an independent person's perception of his or her identity. Hence, people with independent selves should be more willing to form new relationships, maintain larger networks of relationships, and be less distressed should any of those relationships fade away over time. The boundary distinguishing ingroups from outgroups is less consequential to self-construction for those with independent selves, and it should hence be experienced as rather fluid and permeable.

There is convergent evidence from a variety of sources of the heightened distinction between ingroups and outgroups among those who are more interdependent. Ethnographic research on the relationships among some collectivistic cultures, such as the Japanese, richly describes this pronounced difference in behavior between contexts involving ingroups (*uchi*) and those involving outgroups (*soto*; e.g., Bachnik, 1992). Language, customs, and obligations vary considerably depending on whether the other is an ingroup or outgroup member. Empirical evidence from several different paradigms highlights the cultural difference in the nature of the boundary between ingroups and outgroups. For example, a number of studies were conducted that contrasted ingroups and outgroups between East Asians and North Americans (Iyengar, Lepper, & Ross, 1999).

One study investigated whether people showed an **actor–observer bias** in their evaluations of themselves and others. The actor-observer bias is the tendency to see one's own behavior as best explained by situational factors (e.g., I'm grumpy because I didn't get enough sleep last night) whereas the behavior of others is better explained by dispositional factors (e.g., He's grumpy because he's a jerk). The standard pattern of an actor-observer bias emerged among Euro-Americans who reported that personality traits were less descriptive of themselves than they were of others. That is, the Euro-American participants felt that their own personalities couldn't be summarized so succinctly, claiming that they sometimes acted because of situational pressures; conversely, the participants felt that others could be aptly described by a handful of personality traits. Of relevance here is that the participants felt the personality traits were equally useful for describing others regardless of whether they were ingroup (e.g., a friend) or outgroup members (e.g., an enemy; see Figure 11.5). In stark contrast, the Japanese participants viewed the personality traits to be descriptive of their outgroup members but not very applicable to either themselves or their ingroup members. Hence, the Japanese seemed to have lumped ingroup members with themselves, as contrasted against their outgroup members. The Euro-Americans contrasted themselves against others, regardless of whether those others were ingroup or outgroup members.

Furthermore, if you recall from Chapter 6, a study investigated how Euro-American and Asian-American children responded when they were able to make choices in a game they were playing compared with when those choices were made for them by ingroup members or outgroup members (Iyengar & Lepper, 1999). The Euro-American children reacted negatively when someone else made choices for them, regardless of whether the choicemaker was

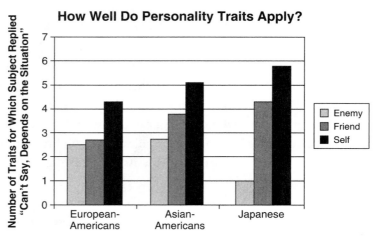

FIGURE 11.5

European-Americans view traits as equally descriptive for friends and enemies, but less descriptive for themselves. In contrast, Japanese consider traits similarly descriptive for themselves and friends, but more descriptive for enemies.

an ingroup member or an outgroup member. What was important for the Euro-American children was that they got to make the choices themselves. In contrast, the Asian-American children reacted negatively only when the choicemaker was an outgroup member. They were equally motivated to play the game when they made their own choices or when an ingroup member had made their choices for them.

Yamagishi and colleagues (e.g., Yamagishi, Cook, & Watabe, 1998; Yamagishi & Yamagishi, 1994) developed a model to explain trust and commitment among individuals in individualistic and collectivistic societies. They maintain that in a society characterized by strong group ties, feelings of trust are confined to that group. The stronger the bonds are among members within a group, the weaker are the ties between groups. One cannot have strong loyalties that conflict with each other. Hence, in collectivist societies such as Japan where commitment to ingroup members is strong there should be less of a willingness to cooperate with outgroup members. Collectivists should focus their trust on people with whom they share some kind of relationship. Yamagishi and colleagues' research finds that Americans tend to have higher levels of general trust toward strangers than do Japanese (Yamagishi & Yamagishi, 1994).

Evidence for larger distinctions between ingroups and outgroups is also available from studies that have explored conformity pressures. An extensive review of studies using Asch's conformity paradigm (see Chapter 6) reveals that the conformity of collectivists appears to be more contingent on the nature of the majority group than it is for people in individualistic societies (Bond & Smith, 1996). When in a situation with strangers, collectivists conform much as individualists do, or even show some evidence of anti-conformity (e.g., Frager, 1970). However, in a situation with their peers, collectivists show evidence of heightened conformity; indeed, out of the 133 studies in which the Asch conformity paradigm has been tested (Bond & Smith, 1996), the two studies that revealed the largest amount of conformity involved Fijian Indians and Japanese (both from collectivistic cultures) participants conforming to groups that included their peers (Chandra, 1973; Williams & Sogon, 1984). In contrast, the degree of conformity for Westerners did not appear to be contingent on the relationships between the subjects and those of the majority group.

In general, there is converging evidence that people from collectivist cultures view ingroup members as an extension of themselves while maintaining distance from outgroup members. People from individualistic cultures, in contrast, show a tendency to view themselves as distinct from all others, regardless of their relationships to the others. This finding highlights a problem in conducting research with groups across cultures. Many social psychological studies involve assessing how people behave in groups of strangers (e.g., Larson, Foster-Fishman, & Keys, 1994; Tajfel, 1970). More interdependent people may feel especially distant from those strangers and their behavior would likely be different from the behavior typically found in studies that have focused on more independent Western samples.

Bases of Group Identification. The above review of cultural differences in discriminations between ingroups and outgroups is lacking one important qualification: Do different cultures conceive of ingroups in the same ways? Are the relations with ingroup members stronger among collectivists than among individualists, as one might reasonably infer from the above discussion, or do collectivists have qualitatively *different kinds* of relations with ingroup members? Some recent research that contrasts Japanese and American ingroup relations suggests that the latter possibility might be true.

Much research on groups that has been conducted in Western contexts has conceived of groups as being entities (Yuki, 2003). That is, members of a group have a common identity, and people's connection with fellow group-members is based on that shared identity (e.g., we're both Stanford Univer-

Two Models of Ingroup Identity

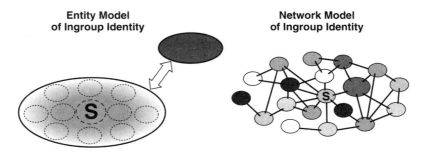

FIGURE 11.6

The entity model of ingroup identity is proposed to be more common among Americans, whereas the network model of ingroup identity is proposed to be more common among Japanese.

sity students). In contrast, East Asian groups can be perceived as networks of relationships. Individuals have specific connections with each other, and these connections establish roles and obligations. Within this network model, the connections between individuals serve as the basis of the ingroup. By this reasoning, two students at the same university don't have a common identity between them so much as they likely share some common friends (e.g., we're both friends of someone who is a friend of Maho Tanaka). The two kinds of group relations are shown graphically in Figure 11.6. In sum, ingroups among Americans are based on feelings of common identity, and as long as a basis of common identity can be recognized, Americans should come to view a person as an ingroup member. In contrast, ingroups among Japanese are based on common connections within their interpersonal networks. An individual is viewed as an outgroup member unless a common relationship is identified with that person. Earlier, we noted that there is considerable fluidity among group boundaries for individualists; it would appear that they are often able to recognize a common basis of shared identity with a stranger and thus establish an ingroup relationship with that person. Conversely, collectivists are much less likely to find a common relationship with a stranger.

It follows that these two different bases of group identification would lead Japanese and Americans to trust ingroup and outgroup relations differently, a premise that was investigated in a study by Yuki and colleagues (2005). The above model predicts that both Japanese and Americans should show trust with ingroup members because for Americans, ingroup members are people with whom they share a common identity, and for Japanese, ingroup members are people with whom they share either direct connections (e.g., we're friends) or indirect connections (e.g., we're friends of a friend of a friend). In this study, ingroup members were students from the same university as the Japanese and American participants. Outgroup members should not be trusted much by people of either culture because for Americans, outgroup members are people with whom there is no common identity, and for Japanese, outgroup members are people with whom there are neither direct nor indirect connections. In this study, outgroup members were students from another university at which the participant had no acquaintances. So far, the same predictions are being made for both cultures, albeit for different reasons.

However, the model makes the unique prediction that the two cultures will look different when people are considering whether to trust a person who is from another group but with whom one shares a potential indirect relationship. In this study, the researchers assessed how much participants trusted a student from another university at which they had an acquaintance. That is, universities at which participants had an acquaintance were contrasted with those universities at which participants did not have any acquaintances. If Americans are largely concerned about whether they share a common identity, then a student from a different university should be an outgroup member, regardless of whether the Americans have an acquaintance from that university. People from different universities do not share a common university identity. In contrast, if Japanese relationships are based on a network model, then a student who is from a different university can be perceived to be an ingroup member as long as there is a potential indirect connection between the student and the participant. Because the participants have acquaintances at the target student's university they may have an indirect connection to the target via their acquaintances.

In this study, American and Japanese participants were playing a computer game and had to decide whether to trust their opponent to give them a fair share of money. The opponent was either from their own university, from a university at which they didn't have an acquaintance, or from a university at which they did have an acquaintance. Figure 11.7 shows how much trust people from the two cultures had toward the three targets. As was predicted by the model, people from both cultures did not differ in how much they trusted the ingroup member or the outgroup member. However, the Japanese participants were more likely to trust the student from the other university when they knew someone from that student's university. Apparently,

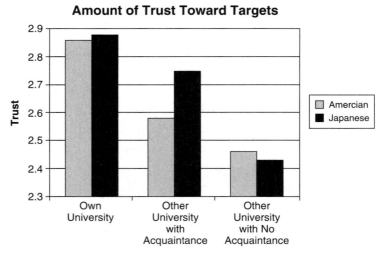

FIGURE 11.7

Although Japanese and Americans show similar levels of trust to someone from their own university and someone from a different university for which people have no acquaintance, Japanese trust those from another university where they have an acquaintance more than do Americans. The Japanese pattern is consistent with a network model of ingroup identity.

Japanese viewed this person to be similar to an ingroup member because they could conceive of a chain of indirect connections to that person. The findings from this study, along with those from some others (Yuki, 2003; Yuki et al., 2005), provide support that the bases of ingroup relations differ across cultures.

The Four Elementary Forms of Relationships. We have seen that cultures can vary in the structure of close relationships with others. How broad might this cultural variation be? Could people in some cultures have kinds of relationships that are completely unfamiliar to those in another culture?

Fiske (1991, 1992) would argue that the answer to this question is a resounding "No." Although we do see tremendous variation across cultures with respect to relationships, Fiske claims that there is some underlying structure that is common to all forms of relationships in the world. Specifically, he argues that all relationships are based on one or more of the four basic elements of sociality.

The first basic structure of relationship is known as **communal sharing**. With this view of relationships, the members of a group view themselves by emphasizing their common identity rather than by considering their idiosyncrasies. In communal sharing every person is treated the same—they have the identical rights and privileges as every other member of that group. One domain where communal sharing is especially operative is within the family. People in a family typically do not keep explicit track of what is taken and what is contributed by each member. All typically take what they need and contribute what they can, without any record-keeping. Usually, we would not expect that an older sister would deserve a larger piece of pie than a younger brother, or that the older sister would get more of a say on where the family should have their summer vacation than the younger brother. Rather, the ideal in communal sharing is that there is equality among all the members of the group. The resources tend to be pooled as belonging to the larger whole that transcends each of the individual members.

Of course, even within a family there is not complete equality. For example, the mother's opinion of what kinds of television programs a child should be able to watch might trump the child's own opinions. This reflects **authority ranking**, the second-relational structure. Within authority ranking relationships people are linearly ordered along a hierarchical social dimension. People with higher ranking have prestige and privileges that those with lower ranking do not; however, subordinates are often entitled to receive protection and care from those above. A prototypical example of authority ranking in action is in the military, where rank determines benefits, power, duties, prestige, and obligations. The lower-ranked members will earn less money, be allowed fewer privileges, and be obligated to follow the orders of those above them. Asymmetry underlies all authority ranking relationships.

A third basic relational structure is **equality matching**. This is based on the idea of balance and reciprocity. People keep track of what is exchanged and they are motivated to pay back what has been exchanged in equivalent turns. Although equality matching is perhaps the least familiar of the four relational structures to Westerners, it is quite common in many cultures around the world. Some examples of Western situations in which it operates are the exchange of Christmas cards, turn-taking, exchanging dinner invitations, and car-pooling—people keep track of what they have received and the system is out of balance until they have paid back the original benefits in kind. A non-Western example that is common in many societies throughout Africa, Asia, and the Caribbean is a rotating credit association (e.g., Fessler, 2002). On a fixed occasion, every family in a tribe makes an equivalent contribution of money to a pool and one family gets to take the entire amount. Each family gets a turn at this, so every handful of years each one enjoys a short period of wealth. People ensure that their contributions are equal and their chances of taking home the entire pot of money are also equal. Within equality matching relationships the relative position of individuals does not matter; each gets his or her own turn regardless of their rank.

Market pricing is the last kind of relational structure. It is distinctive in that it is concerned with proportionality and ratios. All the features of benefits that are exchanged can be reduced to a single underlying dimension, usually money. Similar to equality matching, people expect to ultimately receive something equivalent to what they have given; however, in market pricing, both sides of the exchange usually occur at once, and different kinds of goods can be exchanged. So, for example, I can purchase your pound of coffee with a sack of flour and six seashells because we have calculated that both sides of the transaction are equal in value. Or I can get your assistance in repairing my leaky roof in exchange for $500 as we came to an agreement that this is what your time and skills are worth. With market pricing, members of a party calculate the ratios of the goods that are exchanged so that the transaction will be equivalent in value for both parties. The relative status of individuals in the transaction is irrelevant. The CEO of the company is charged the same amount for a quart of milk as the new recruit in the mailroom. Furthermore, the parties in the exchange do not have to have any kind of formalized relationship with each other. For example, two strangers can use eBay to complete a transaction by calculating an agreed-upon value of the exchange. Market pricing relationships are highly ubiquitous in Western society, and modern theories of economics view all transactions in these terms.

Fiske maintains that all kinds of human relationships are constructed out of one or more of these four basic elements. It is possible that people might have relationships with the same people that are governed by all four elements. For example, within a family at dinner each person is allowed to eat until he or she is satisfied (communal sharing), the father might occupy the seat at the head of the table (authority ranking), for dessert each person can claim an equal-size cupcake (equality matching), and a child might be paid $1.00 for each time that she loads the dishwasher (market pricing). These four relational elements are said to be operational in relationships in all cultures. However, despite their hypothesized universal presence, there is also much cultural variation in the extent to which each operates. For example, market pricing is characteristic of a broader class of relationships within American culture today than it is among the Fore of New Guinea. Indeed, because market pricing can operate without any close relations between two individuals it is especially common within more individualistic societies. Equality matching is emphasized more in many traditional subsistence societies around the world where there often are elaborate rituals involving the reciprocal exchange of equally valued goods. For example, among the Trobriand islanders, men take long and dangerous open-ocean journeys to exchange shell-necklaces which have no "practical" value. Later on, the person who received the necklace is obligated to go on a similarly dangerous journey to exchange a similarly valued, and not especially practical, gift (Malinowski, 1922/1965). Authority ranking characterizes a greater degree of behavior in hierarchical class-based societies than it does in more egalitarian ones. And communal sharing, which is most evident in the context of families in the West, often generalizes to the tribal level in many smaller societies, characterizing a significant proportion of relational exchanges there. Hence, although these relational structures serve the same function around the world, some cultures rely on particular structures more than others.

Working With Others. If you are taking this course for credit at a college or university somewhere, then you are involved in a kind of task that will likely be somewhat rare in your career. That is, in most university courses students are evaluated solely in terms of what they accomplish as individuals in that course—the grades that you earn on various papers, assignments, and exams. In contrast, in the vast majority of careers, people are evaluated in terms of what they accomplish as part of a group. Doctors work together with other doctors, specialists, nurses, technicians, and various other kinds of hospital staff; businesspeople work as members of teams and deal with customers and clients; and scientists work with collaborators, students, and technicians; and so on. Most jobs involve working on tasks that are complex enough to extend beyond what a lone individual can accomplish. Much of the work we do is in the context of groups.

Social Facilitation. How is our performance affected when we are working with others? Do we accomplish more as members of a group than we do as individuals? The answer to these questions is, "It depends." It depends on a number of things. First, merely being surrounded by other people affects our performance. The presence of others creates physiological arousal, and this arousal affects how well we can work on a task. Arousal facilitates dominant response tendencies and inhibits secondary response tendencies. If a skill is well-rehearsed and practiced, individuals will perform it better when they are aroused. In contrast, if a skill is not well rehearsed, arousal will increase competing response tendencies and will interfere with the task. Because the presence of others increases arousal, people will perform well-learned tasks better, and poorly learned tasks worse when they are in the presence of others. This is known as **social facilitation**.

Social facilitation is a fundamental psychological process that is found across many different contexts. Research has shown that it is evident in many different animal species, including centipedes and cockroaches (Hosey, Wood, & Thompson, 1985; Zajonc, Heingartner, & Herman, 1969). If social facilitation is something that makes species as different as humans and cockroaches look similar, then we should not expect variation in social facilitation across cultures. Social facilitation appears to be a process that is operating at a fundamental biological level. It is not surprising to learn, then, that there are no published studies finding any kinds of differences across cultures in how people perform on tasks in the presence of others. Social facilitation appears to be an accessibility universal.

Social Loafing. A second way that our behavior is affected in groups hinges on how our performance is evaluated. Sometimes when we are in a group our individual performance is evaluated. A team of salespeople might be paid on commission depending on how many units they each sold as individuals. In some other group situations, however, our performance is evaluated on the basis of what the group accomplishes. For example, the team with the best proposal will win a contract, regardless of whether some individual team members contributed more than others. How does being evaluated as a group or as an individual make a difference?

In one classic study that investigated this, American participants were brought into a lab and were asked to pull on a rope that was attached to a measuring device (Ingham, Levinger, Graves, & Peckham, 1974). They were instructed to pull the rope as hard as they could. Those who pulled by themselves showed an impressive demonstration of their strength. On average, they pulled 130 pounds. Other participants pulled the rope in pairs; however, one member of the pair was actually a confederate of the experimenter.

The confederate was placed behind the participant, and although the confederate grabbed the rope and made every effort to appear to be pulling hard, he in fact contributed nothing. On average, participants in this condition pulled 118 pounds. Other conditions were run, all with the participant pulling at the front of the rope and with a number of confederates lined up behind, all putting on a great show that they were pretending to pull as hard as they could when in fact they contributed nothing. When there were three participants they averaged 107 pounds, and when there were six participants they averaged 101 pounds. In all conditions, the participants were instructed to pull the rope as hard as they could; yet as the number of confederates increased—people the participants thought were pulling the rope along with them—the less hard the participants tried. This is a dramatic effect. Pulling a rope is an example of a task in which it is impossible to tell for sure how much each individual member is contributing to the group's task. When it is not clear how much any individual is contributing, people often don't work as hard. This effect is known as **social loafing**.

Subsequent research revealed that there are some limiting conditions to social loafing. One is that people loaf more on simple tasks than on difficult ones. Apparently, if a task is challenging, it is intrinsically rewarding enough that people are less motivated to catch a free ride when they have the chance (Jackson & Williams, 1985). People have also been shown to socially loaf less with groups of friends than among groups of strangers, and groups that consist of all women loaf less than groups that consist of all men (Karau & Williams, 1993). These last two findings suggest one other key limiting condition of social loafing. If people care about their relations with their groups (as people do with their friends, and women apparently do so more than men), they are less motivated to catch a free ride at the group's expense.

Given that loafing is less common when people belong to groups in which they especially care about their relations within those groups, it follows that there might be less social loafing in interdependent cultures. One study contrasted Chinese children in Taiwan with American children in Florida (Gabrenya, Wang, & Latane, 1985). The children were given a task in which they had to attend to a number of tones that were presented in either their left or right ears. In some conditions the children were test by themselves; in another they were tested together with a classmate. Furthermore, half of the children were in the sixth grade and half were in the ninth grade. There were no cultural differences among the sixth graders. These children did not show any signs of social loafing. In contrast, a cultural difference emerged for the ninth graders. The American children showed significant social loafing as they performed 11.7% worse when they were in a pair versus when they were evaluated alone. In contrast, the Chinese children performed 8.7% *better* when they were in a pair compared with when they were alone. That is, the Chinese showed some evidence for the opposite of social loafing, what is sometimes referred to as **social striving**—working better when they are evaluated as a group than as individuals.

The effects of working in a group also seem to hinge on the nature of that group, for collectivists at least. Chinese and Israelis were found to perform better when they were working with members of an ingroup than when they worked alone, showing evidence for social striving (see Figure 11.8; Earley, 1993). In contrast, they performed slightly worse when they worked with outgroup members than when they worked alone. On the other hand, Americans performed better as individuals than they did when working either with ingroup or outgroup members, showing clear evidence for social loafing. In sum, whether people from collectivistic cultures show evidence for social striving or social loafing depends a great deal on who the others are in their group. In contrast, whether group members are ingroup or outgroup members has considerably less impact for Americans.

Competing Versus Cooperating. Another way that being in the presence of others can affect how one performs is when one is engaging in a task with an opponent. There are two kinds of such tasks. One is a zero–sum game in

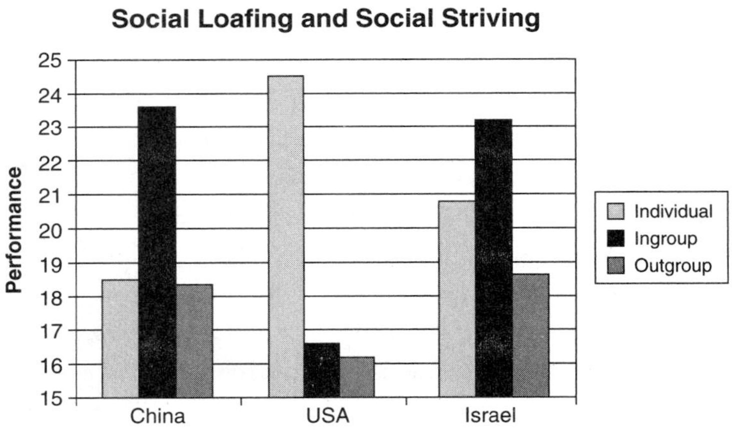

Social Loafing and Social Striving

FIGURE 11.8

Chinese and Israelis work hardest when they are working with an ingroup. In contrast, Americans work hardest when they are working as individuals.

which one individual's gains are entirely at the expense of the opponent. Chess is a good example of this. The outcome of chess is either a win for one person and a loss for the other, or a stalemate when neither wins nor loses. In chess the better one's own outcome is, the worse is that of one's opponent. Zero-sum games provide a basis for competition among individuals. The other kind of task is a non-zero-sum game, in which an individual's gains do not necessarily come at the expense of his or her opponent. Non-zero-sum games can have outcomes in which both parties win. An example of a non-zero-sum exchange is through trade. Imagine that Bill needs some extra money so he decides to sell his mint-condition 1968 "Barney Rubble" Pez dispenser on eBay. Melissa has been desperately searching for such a Pez dispenser to complete her Classic Flintstones Pez collection. Bill agrees to sell the Pez dispenser to Melissa for an agreed-upon price. Bill has gained from the deal, as he now has some extra money, and Melissa has also gained from the deal, as she now has completed her collection. Both are better off from the exchange. Non-zero-sum games provide a basis for profitable cooperation among individuals.

Would people from all cultures be equally likely to approach an exchange situation as an opportunity for profitable cooperation, where both can do well, or as an opportunity for competition, where one might be able to win big at the expense of his or her partner? One study explored this question by contrasting children in small towns from Mexico and California. A game was devised that was rewarding for people who played cooperatively but was punishing for those who played competitively (Madsen, 1971). A drawing of the apparatus in the game is shown in Figure 11.9. Two children sat oppo-

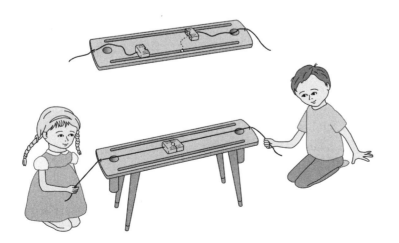

FIGURE 11.9

The apparatus for the cooperation game used by Madsen.

site each other and a marble was placed inside the marble holder in the middle. If the child pulled the marble holder over his or her cup, the marble would be released and the child would win that marble. However, if both children pulled at the same time, the magnets holding the marble holder together would come apart, and the marble would roll into the side gutters, leaving both children empty-handed. The way to win marbles in this game is to take turns with your partner. You win a marble each time your partner lets you have a turn, and your partner wins a marble each time you let him or her have a turn. The game consists of 10 turns total, so there are 10 possible marbles that can be won. What do you think happens when you let Mexican and American children play this game?

In one study, children of three different age groups played this game. First, 4- and 5-year-old American children played the game (the study didn't include a Mexican sample at this age). In the first 10 trials, the American children averaged 5.3 marbles per game, meaning that they successfully cooperated on about half the trials (see Figure 11.10). After the first 10 trials the experimenter explained to them how they could increase their winnings. They were shown how taking turns leads both kids to end up with a lot of marbles and that failing to take turns results in no one winning any marbles. The children then were allowed to play again after learning about this winning strategy. The American 4- and 5-year-olds now won, on average, 7.9 marbles, which means that they learned how to cooperate on about 80% of the trials. The children were largely able to realize the benefits of cooperation.

FIGURE 11.10

Mexican children tend to perform better than American children on a cooperation task.

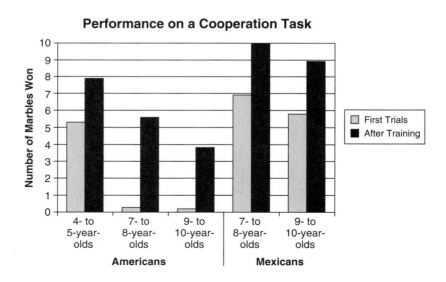

However, the benefits of cooperation were not as apparent to many of the older American children. When 7- and 8-year-old American children played they averaged only 0.3 marbles in the first 10 trials, and the 9- and 10-year-olds averaged only 0.2 marbles. The remaining 9.8 marbles ended up in the gutter. In the next 10 trials, following the explicit instructions about how to cooperate in order to win marbles, the children did a little bit better, but their performance was really not impressive. After the instructions the 7- and 8-year-olds averaged 5.6 marbles whereas the 10- and 11-year-olds averaged 3.8 marbles. Even when the strategy for winning marbles was made clear to these children, they often still seemed unable to resist their competitive urges to try to win more marbles than their opponents. Apparently, their competitive instincts were considerably stronger than their motives for profitable cooperation, and the relative strength of their competitive drive increased with age.

In stark contrast, the Mexicans seemed to have an easier time in learning the strategies for profitable cooperation. In the first 10 trials, the 7- and 8-year-olds earned 6.9 marbles and the 10- and 11-year-olds earned 5.8 marbles. After receiving the strategic tips from the experimenter the 7- and 8-year-olds scored a perfect average of 10.0 marbles, while the 10- and 11-year-olds were close behind with an average score of 8.9. Among the Mexican children, then, it seems that their motives for profitable cooperation trumped their competitive instincts.

Rural Mexico is a collectivistic culture, and it is likely that cultural differences in collectivism influenced how the children played the game. One important goal implicated in collectivism is a concern for maintaining harmony among one's relations. Rather than being solely concerned with one's outcomes as an individual, collectivists are more likely than individualists to also be concerned about the outcomes of others, preferring solutions that benefit both sides. In the marble example, although cooperating required individuals to wait on a given turn and allow their opponent to win a marble that they instead could have possibly won, this cooperation served to benefit both themselves and their opponents.

One real-life situation that is parallel to this marble game is when two opposing parties are negotiating with each other. Typically, in a negotiation, both parties are trying to improve the outcome for their side, which often comes at the expense of the other. When an acceptable position cannot be reached, both parties typically end up suffering, as the outcome achieved through cooperation is typically better than the outcome that results from failed negotiations. In the above example, the outcome for the American children who failed to negotiate was that they lost all the marbles. In real life, a not uncommon outcome of failed negotiations between two countries is war.

Given the results of the marble study, we might expect people from collectivistic backgrounds to be more willing to approach negotiations so that solutions could be reached that promoted harmonious relations, rather than those that exclusively benefited their own side. After all, it is likely that the groups will continue to have relations even after the negotiation ends.

There are two strategies one can pursue in negotiations. The first is confrontational or adversarial in nature—ignore the other side's position and only press for one's own cause. Some adversarial tactics include making threats or accusing the other side of making unreasonable demands. Adversarial strategies typically involve making the strongest possible case for one's own side while largely ignoring the claims made by the other side. A prototypic example is two lawyers presenting their opposing cases in the courtroom. They typically focus on polarizing their sides rather than seeking a compromise. Adversarial strategies often escalate the conflict until a victor is claimed, in which one side wins at the other's expense.

A second strategy is to seek compromises. For example, propose solutions that would hopefully increase the likelihood that the other party is satisfied with the deal, comply with what the other side asks, or seek assistance from a third party who does not have a vested interest in the disagreement to serve as a mediator. Compromising strategies typically work toward reducing conflict; a typical outcome is that neither party gets exactly what he or she want, but neither party loses out to the other.

A number of studies have investigated whether people from different cultures approach negotiations differently. In one set of studies the negotiating behavior of people from individualistic cultures (specifically Canada and the Netherlands) was contrasted with behavior of people from collectivistic cultures (specifically Japan and Spain; Leung, Au, Fernandez-Dols, & Iwawaki, 1992; Leung, Bond, Carment, Krishnan, & Liebrand, 1990). People from the two collectivistic cultures were more likely to comply with the other party's requests and to seek compromise than were people from the two individualistic cultures. In contrast, those from the two individualistic cultures were more likely than people from the collectivistic cultures to use strategies that involved threatening, accusations, and ignoring the other party's positions.

As in the marble study, people from collectivistic cultures seem to strive for more cooperative outcomes in their negotiations whereas those from individualistic cultures approach negotiations in a more competitive way.

The differences in negotiating strategies of people from different cultures suggest that cross-cultural negotiations might not always run smoothly. If one negotiator is accustomed to a willingness to compromise from the other side but finds the other side is seeking a victory, it will not be surprising if the negotiation is unsuccessful. Indeed, there is much anecdotal evidence that many cross-cultural negotiations end up badly as both parties are unable to figure out what the other side is trying to accomplish.

SUMMARY

Many physical features that people find attractive in others are common across a number of cultures. People in all cultures seem to be attracted to clear complexions, bilateral symmetry, and average features. However, there is considerable cultural variation in what is perceived to be an attractive body, particularly, an attractive female body. The current Western ideal of thinness was not prevalent in the West even a generation ago, and in many cultures, heavier bodies are preferred.

It is likely that people universally are attracted to those with whom they interact a lot. However, the well-researched finding that people are attracted to others who are similar to themselves does not generalize to the same degree in all cultures.

As people are a social species, relationships tend to be very important to them, regardless of what culture they come from. Despite the universal importance of relationships, however, there is a great deal of cultural variability in the ways people relate to others.

There are important cultural differences in how people conceive of friends and enemies. In West African cultural contexts, people view relationships as existing naturally, often without any effort by the individuals involved to pursue that relationship, and even when the basis of the relationship is not positive. In contrast, members of Western cultures appear to view some kinds of relationships as not existing unless people decide to make the effort to pursue them. These efforts seem to hinge on whether people think the relationship will be rewarding in some way. As evidence of this reasoning, West Africans view friendships as entailing costs as obligations are an important part of friendships; because of the heavy demands friendship can place on them, they are more cautious toward friends in general than are people from Western cultures. Moreover, West Africans are more likely than Westerners to view enemies as a natural part of their relationships.

The experience of romantic love appears to be found in all cultures, yet it plays a different role in marriages across cultures. In many current and historical cultures, marriages are arranged, and the relationship begins without much in the way of romantic love. In contrast, the norm in many other cultures is that members of a couple should love each other before they consider getting married. Cultures that have extended family systems are more likely to rely on arranged marriage systems than cultures with more nuclear family structures.

Much of human life occurs in the context of groups and there are some important cultural differences in how life in groups varies. For example, people from interdependent cultures make a clearer distinction between ingroup members and outgroup members. Also, the basis of ingroup identification varies as well. Japanese are more likely to view ingroups in terms of a network model whereas Americans generally base ingroup relations on a shared identity.

Although cultures vary in many ways with respect to their relationships, there appear to be four universal basic elements by which relationships can be understood. All relationships appear to consist of one or more of the following elements: communal sharing, authority ranking, equality matching, and market pricing. These basic elements can be combined to form the universe of possible human relations. However, even though these four basic elements are common everywhere, different cultures emphasize some more than others.

The presence of other people appears to lead universally to social facilitation, in which people perform well-learned tasks better and poorly learned tasks worse when in the presence of others than when they are alone. The phenomenon of social loafing—people engaged in a group task do not try as hard when their individual contributions are not monitored—varies considerably across cultures. In more collectivistic cultures there is less evidence of social loafing and sometimes evidence that people work harder in a group than when they are alone (social striving).

Cultures vary in the extent to which people are motivated to cooperate or compete with others. In many situations, people from collectivistic cultures are more likely to seek a cooperative solution than are people from more individualistic cultures. This cultural difference generalizes to the strategies that people pursue in negotiations.

12

Living in Multicultural Worlds

Michaelle Jean was born in Port-au-Prince, Haiti, a country that was discovered in 1492 by the Italian sailor Christopher Columbus. When Columbus arrived in Haiti and planted the flag of Spain there, the country was populated almost exclusively by the Arawak people. Early in the 17th century, British, Dutch, and French pirates established bases on the island, and ultimately the French claimed control of the country in 1664. For almost three centuries, the Spanish and French colonists imported slaves to Haiti from Ghana, Nigeria, Togo, Benin, and the Ivory Coast to develop Haiti's sugarcane and coffee industries. Many of Jean's ancestors were slaves who had intermarried with the Arawak as well as with Spanish and French colonists. At the age of 11, Jean's family left Haiti and moved to a town in rural Quebec. She attended university in Montreal and in Italy, and married a filmmaker from France. Jean is fluent in French, English, Spanish, Italian, and Haitian Kreyol. Her critics maintain that in past decades Jean was actively involved in the Quebec separatist movement. In 2005 Jean was appointed by Queen Elizabeth II to be the governor general of Canada—that is, she is the Canadian representative of the monarch of England.

So here's a question. Considering the historical and cultural context of Jean's ancestry and the experiences that she has had in her own life, what is Michaelle Jean's culture?

Obviously, no simple statement can meaningfully encapsulate Jean's cultural background. Haiti has been populated by people from many different parts of the globe, and Jean herself has lived in a number of different countries and has been exposed to a diverse array of cultural messages. Her biography highlights a real challenge for studying cultures. In many ways, they don't really exist. That is, cultures are not homogenous entities with clear-cut boundaries like many other things that people study, such as species. Today there are no societies anywhere that include only people from one

People with multicultural backgrounds, such as Michaelle Jean, highlight how heterogeneous cultures often are.

cultural background. Even the most homogeneous societies contain individuals with different cultural heritages, traditions, religions, and languages. Moreover, those parts of the world where most psychological research is conducted (North America, Western Europe, and Australia) have witnessed some of the greatest and most diverse influxes of immigration. These exchanges of people are occurring not just between neighboring countries with fairly similar cultural backgrounds, such as between Canada and the United States, but include the migrations of people across the furthest extents of the globe. For example, the city of Toronto contains more immigrants than it does nonimmigrants, and in the past decade the vast majority of these immigrants have come from non-Western nations. This cultural diversity makes it rather futile to make any specific statements about the culture of Toronto that would apply to all its citizens.

Currently worldwide, an estimated 130 million people are living in countries they were not born in—approximately the population of Japan. In the United States, about 10% of the population has moved there from another country (Suarez-Orozco & Suzrez-Orozco, 2001). For some immigrant groups within the United States the numbers are more striking: 59% of Latino-American children and 90% of Asian-American children were either born outside the United States or are second-generation residents (Zhou, 1997). With such large numbers of people crossing borders, encountering people from different cultures has become a very common experience for most people. In contrast, just a few centuries ago, in much of the world the only people who regularly encountered individuals from distant cultures were

What culture is
represented here?

explorers, diplomats, marauding warriors, and merchants. I often fantasize
about how much easier it would have been to be a cultural psychologist back
then, when cultures were relatively distinct and homogenous, and comparisons between cultures would have been more clear-cut. Alas, with such little contact between people of divergent cultural backgrounds, the world had
little use for us back then.

Although the ever-increasing contact between cultures has complicated
comparisons of their psychological processes, it has paved the way for investigating a different series of fascinating psychological questions. What happens to people's psychology when they move to a culture that is different
from the one where they were raised? Do some people fare better in this
experience than others? How are people's minds different if they have lived
in two distinct cultures throughout their lives? And what are some of the
psychological costs of being a member of a culture that is actively discriminated against by others? As the world continues to globalize and experiences
with other cultures become the norm rather than the exception, these questions take on fundamental importance. I think they represent the most pressing issues that cultural psychologists will face over the years to come.

This chapter will explore how people's psychology is affected when they
move to a new culture. Research that tracks migrating people across time
demonstrates, perhaps more clearly than other topics in this book, how an
individual's experiences shape his or her psychological processes.

Difficulties in Studying Acculturation

Acculturation is the process by which people migrate to and learn a culture that is different from their original (or heritage) culture. The study of acculturation is beset by certain difficulties and challenges that are unique to this topic. Although there have been literally thousands of studies relevant to acculturation, extracting a set of generalizable findings or any cumulative theories from them is difficult (Furnham & Bochner, 1986; Rudmin, 2003; Ward, 1996). Despite its great importance, the literature on acculturation remains more diverse, more contradictory, less coherent, and less empirically grounded than any other topic in this book.

Reaching consistent conclusions on acculturation is difficult for researchers because acculturating individuals have such widely varying experiences. How do you think these experiences might differ? People move to a new country for many reasons: Some are moving to be closer to family members; some move to seek fame and fortune; some move because they are refugees and have no choice but to leave their countries; some leave to study abroad with the intention of returning to their home country upon graduating; and some move as young children because their parents decide that it is in the family's best interest. Also, acculturating individuals move to dramatically different kinds of environments. Some move to cultural ghettos in which they can speak their original language and keep their old cultural traditions without having to interact much with members of their new host culture; some move to a rather homogenous neighborhood where they are the only ones who appear different; some move to an environment that actively discriminates against people from their cultural background; and some move to expatriate neighborhoods that consist largely of people who have recently migrated from places all over the globe. Furthermore, people move to cultures that vary in their similarity to their heritage culture. Some move from a rural community in their home country to an urban center in their new culture; some move to a place where the dominant language, religion, and cultural practices are very similar to those of their heritage culture; and some move to a cultural environment that is different from their own in almost every respect. Complicating matters even more, different individuals have very different personalities, goals, and expectations that affect their acculturation experiences. In sum, few commonalities occur for all acculturating individuals and this makes it challenging to identify common patterns. In this chapter I will discuss some key findings that have emerged from research on acculturation, but I remind you that these findings will probably not generalize well to all people's experiences.

What Happens When People Move to a New Culture?

One clear issue of agreement can be reliably extracted from the diverse literature on acculturation: Moving to a new culture involves psychological adjustment. This adjustment occurs over a wide variety of domains—acquiring a new language, learning new interpersonal and social behaviors, becoming accustomed to new values, often becoming a member of a minority group, and adjusting one's self-concept (e.g., Berry & Kim, 1988; Church, 1982; Furnham & Bochner, 1986; LaFromboise, Coleman, & Gerton, 1993). Given the influence that culture has on psychology, the adjustment that individuals go through when they move to a new culture can be enormous. How do people experience this adjustment?

Changes in Attitudes Toward the Host Culture. A number of studies have explored how **migrants'** psychological adjustment to new cultures unfolds across time. Migrants are defined as those who move from a **heritage culture** (their original culture) to a **host culture** (their new culture) and include those who intend to stay only temporarily (known as **sojourners**) and those who intend to move permanently (known as **immigrants**). A classic investigation was conducted on the adjustment experiences of Norwegian Fulbright scholars in the United States (Lysgaard, 1955). In that study an adjustment pattern was identified that was shared by many of the grantees. The experiences of these participants tracked what is described as a U-shaped curve, shown in Figure 12.1. The Y axis indicates how positive the migrants feel toward their host country. First, in the initial few months of their experiences the migrants were having an especially positive time in their visit. They were enjoying the new experiences, meeting new people, trying new foods, communicating with people in a foreign language, and feeling the excitement of participating in a novel and exotic environment. This stage has been labeled, appropriately, the "Honeymoon Stage" (Oberg, 1960). It is the existence of the Honeymoon Stage that keeps the tourism industry in business. Most travelers do not stick around in a new culture long enough

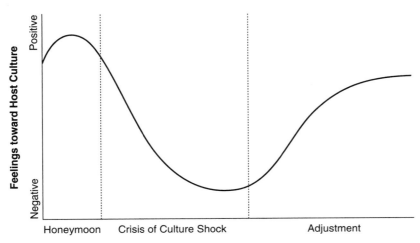

FIGURE 12.1

A common pattern of adjustment to acculturation. In the first few months people have very positive feelings towards the host culture, but over time this gives way to the negative feelings associated with culture shock. Over time, people often develop positive feelings towards the host culture.

to move past this stage, and they thus tend to view their experiences in new cultures to be, for the most part, pleasant and exciting.

Unfortunately, like other honeymoons, at some point the fun and excitement usually comes to an end. Following this Honeymoon Stage most visitors turn a corner and begin to have increasingly negative views toward their host culture. In fact, in the next months—specifically, in Lysgaard's data, between 6 and 18 months—participants typically experienced the most negative feelings of their sojourn in a stage that has been labeled the "Crisis" or "Culture Shock" stage (Oberg, 1960). In this stage, the earlier thrill of having novel and exotic experiences wears off and these experiences become tiring and difficult. At this stage recent migrants often realize that their language skills are not yet good enough for them to fully function in the new environment. They realize that they do not have a rich enough understanding of how the system works to thrive. The people they initially met who were interested in them because they were exotic and different are no longer so interested in those differences. Others have already heard their stories about what the weather is like in their hometown, what kinds of sports are popular, or which seemingly bizarre foods they eat during their holiday festivals.

Now others are interested in talking about things and events that are of concern to locals in the host culture, and recent migrants just don't have enough knowledge or understanding to fully participate in the conversations. At this point, recent migrants may also be discovering that the television programs just aren't as interesting as the ones they used to see in their home country, and they start to miss their favorite foods. This is the time that homesickness can become quite strong, as people miss all their close friends and family; they begin to long for the little things they used to never think much about—their daily discussion with the bus driver or their favorite snack that they can no longer get. These are the symptoms of **culture shock**. Culture shock is the feeling of being anxious, helpless, irritable, and in general, homesick that one experiences on moving to a new culture (Church, 1982). Culture shock can be so problematic that some people decide to quit their sojourn; some can end up having very negative memories of their experiences.

After wallowing for several months in this crisis stage, most of Lysgaard's sojourners started to adjust and began to enjoy their experiences more. Their language abilities improved, enabling them to function better in their daily lives. They became better able to make enduring friendships with the locals, and they adapted to things in the new culture, such as the television programming and the food, so that these no longer felt so strange. They had started to think more and more like the locals around them. This stage, labeled the "Adjustment" phase, tends to extend over a number of years, and with time, people become more and more proficient at functioning in their new culture.

Furthermore, some research finds that this U-shaped adjustment curve is not limited to being in a foreign country (Gullahorn & Gullahorn, 1963). Sojourners can go through the same adjustment stages *after* they return to their home country. Initially, on returning, people are elated to see their families and friends again and being able to eat their favorite foods. However, it is not uncommon for people soon to experience "reverse culture shock" and find themselves puzzling over why they do not quite feel at home any more and why they feel somewhat alienated from those around them. Their home culture often does not seem quite the same as they remembered it, and they are no longer an especially good fit. This unsettling sense too gives way to an adjustment period as they gradually acclimate themselves to the familiar life they once knew.

The U-shaped pattern of adjustment to new cultures seems to characterize the experiences of many migrants, and a number of other researchers have found evidence that tends to be consistent with this, although the timing of the stages varies considerably (e.g., Oberg, 1960; Richardson, 1974; Zheng & Berry, 1991). However, as you might imagine, the range of experiences that people have when moving to a new culture varies tremendously, and this U-shaped curve does not characterize the adjustment pattern of everyone's experiences (Church, 1982). In particular, some research has found that the initial Honeymoon Stage is not evident for many sojourners (Guthrie & Zektick, 1967; Ward & Kennedy, 1995). For many people, the first few weeks at the beginning of an extended stay are characterized by a lot of anxiety that prevents them from feeling much excitement about their new experience.

One societal feature of a host culture that seems to influence the acculturating individuals' adjustment is the ease with which migrants can be accommodated by the host culture. Lysgaard's original study of sojourners' adjustment investigated Norwegians moving to the United States. The U.S. is a country of immigrants and is one of the most ethnically diverse nations in the world. People from a wide variety of different backgrounds have come to view the United States as their home and have adjusted accordingly. In contrast, Japan is a country that is relatively ethnically homogenous: indeed, just under 99% of people living in Japan are Japanese. Trying to adjust as a migrant to a homogenous society would seem to be inherently more challenging. Regardless of how well people learn the customs or master the language, they will always stand out as different from the other 99% who are ethnically Japanese. One study tracked the acculturation experiences of a few hundred migrants to Japan and did not replicate the U-shaped curve that Lysgaard had found (Hsiao-Ying, 1995). Instead, a rather pessimistic L-shaped curve was identified, which shared the Honeymoon and Crisis stages found in Lysgaard's work; however, the researcher did not find any evidence for the Adjustment stage. Sadly, those who had lived in Japan for over 5 years were just as negative toward Japan as those who had been there for just over 1 year and who appeared to be in the depths of the Crisis stage. It is possible that in homogenous societies the adjustment phase just takes longer; had the researcher studied more individuals who had been there much longer (i.e., more than 10 years), she might have found evidence for the Adjustment stage. Nonetheless, the success of people's acculturation experiences seems to be importantly influenced by the homogeneity of the society to which they are trying to acculturate.

Who Adjusts Better? Of all the experiences that people adjust to, few impact more aspects of their lives than moving to a new culture. It would not be surprising to learn that people tend to respond differently to the myriad challenges posed by acculturation, depending both on the situation that they are in and their temperament. Acculturation experiences are diverse enough that we cannot predict how well a given person has adjusted to his or her new culture just on the basis of how many years the individual has spent there (Rhee, Uleman, Lee, & Roman, 1995). What are some features that influence how people will adjust to their acculturation experiences?

Cultural Distance. In acculturation, people have to learn the lifestyles of a new culture. How successful they will be in acquiring the necessary information to thrive in a new culture seems to be influenced by how much learning they need to do. Imagine someone was moving to a new cultural context in which absolutely everything was different. Such a situation would require a tremendous amount of learning, and most people would find this very difficult. In contrast, if someone moved to a new culture that was highly similar to the person's heritage culture there would be less learning to do and fewer difficulties. So one factor that should predict a person's success in adjusting to a new culture is the amount of **cultural distance** between the heritage culture and the host culture. Cultural distance is the difference between two cultures in their overall ways of life. We can hypothesize that the more cultural distance someone needs to travel, the more difficulty that person will have acculturating.

One way to test this hypothesis is to compare performance on various measures of acculturation across countries. An indirect measure of acculturation is language performance. Many studies show that one of the best predictors of acculturative success is language ability (e.g., Gullahorn & Gullahorn, 1963; Ying & Liese, 1991), and people's confidence in their mastery over the host culture's language greatly affects how they identify with that culture (Noels, Pon, & Clement, 1996). There are many similarities between language and culture, and a very good proxy for how familiar a person is with a culture is his or her skill with its language. Hence, the easier it is for migrants to learn the language of their host culture, the better they should fare in the acculturation process. One source of data for assessing how

TABLE 12.1

Average Scores on the Test of English as a Foreign Language (TOEFL)

Mother Tongue	Average TOEFL score
Dutch	261
German	251
French	228
Spanish	228
Afrikaans	221
Turkish	218
Farsi (Persian)	217
Indonesian	210
Korean	205
Japanese	186

easily people learn the language of the host culture is average country scores on the Test of English as a Foreign Language (TOEFL). International students who wish to study at a school in an English-speaking country typically need to take the TOEFL to gain admittance. Although average country scores on the TOEFL are influenced by many factors—such as the country's GNP, and the percentage of students in the country who take the exam—these scores also vary considerably based on participants' own mother language (see Table 12.1). Those who grew up speaking languages that are highly similar to English (e.g., Teutonic languages such as Dutch or German) perform better than those who grew up speaking other European languages that are a little more distant (e.g., Romance languages, such as French and Spanish). Moreover, speakers of Indo-European languages tend to perform better on the TOEFL than those who grew up speaking languages from highly distant language groups, such as Indonesian or Japanese (Educational Testing Service, 2003). The ease with which people will learn English is influenced by how distant their mother tongue is from English, and how much new learning will thus be involved.

There are other skills that need be mastered in addition to learning a new language when one moves to a new culture. For example, people also have to learn how to accomplish everyday tasks such as making friends and figuring out how to find a doctor, where to go to get a driver's license, or how to cook the strange-looking foods that are sold at the supermarket. Cultural distance encapsulates more than just language. A number of studies have investigated how well people acculturate depending on how much overall cultural distance migrants must cover. Ward and Kennedy (1995) compared the adjustment of Malaysian university students in New Zealand (a culture that is quite different from their own) and another group of Malaysian students in Singapore (a culture that is fairly similar to their own). The students completed a measure of sociocultural adjustment that assessed their daily problems in navigating through the new culture. After spending almost 3 years, on average, in the two countries, the Malaysian students who were studying in Singapore reported having fewer difficulties than those who were studying in New Zealand. Apparently, Malaysians, on average, seem to fit in better in culturally close Singapore than they do in more culturally distant New Zealand, and they consequently had an easier time getting by in Singapore. Other studies have found that sojourners from more distant cultures suffer from more distress, require more medical consultations (Babiker, Cox, & Miller, 1980), and have more social difficulties in general (Furnham & Bochner, 1982) than those who traverse less cultural distance. In particular, cultural distance seems to make it difficult to establish and maintain interpersonal relationships with members of the host culture.

People do not have to actually leave their country to be confronted with the need to acculturate to a new set of values. Various indigenous groups have found themselves, through no choice of their own, having to adjust to a culture imposed on them by a colonial force. For example, many distinct indigenous native populations throughout Canada have had to deal with the onslaught of cultural traditions that were forced on them by mainstream Canadian settlers. These various indigenous cultures provide an excellent test case for investigating the impact of cultural distance on acculturation; although none of them had to do any traveling to encounter mainstream Canadian culture, each of these cultures vary considerably from each other in terms of their own traditions. Some indigenous Canadian tribes such as the Tsimshian of the Northwest Pacific Coast region engaged in subsistence practices (primarily fishing for salmon and shellfish) that allowed them to accumulate large quantities of food and establish permanent, highly stratified settlements long before they had any contact with Europeans. In contrast, other tribes such as the Eastern Cree, who live just below the tree line in Northern Quebec, engage in subsistence practices (primarily winter hunting and summer fishing) that do not allow them to accumulate much food, so some of the bands are migratory and have low sociocultural stratification. Other tribes, such as the Carrier, who live on the Rocky Mountain Plateau of northern British Columbia, also engage in hunting and fishing like the Eastern Cree. However, because they have the possibility of accumulating large numbers of salmon at the headwaters of some rivers, and because their culture was influenced by the geographically close Tsimshian, the Carrier represent a culture with a moderate degree of food accumulation and social stratification. Berry and Annis (1974) reasoned that the complex social stratification of the permanent settlements of the Tsimshian was more similar to mainstream Canadian culture than were the less socially stratified, somewhat migratory patterns among the Eastern Cree, and the moderate stratification of the Carrier should be in between. Hence, they predicted that there should be a greater degree of acculturative stress among the Eastern Cree than among the Carrier, who, in turn, would experience more acculturative stress than the Tsimshian. Indeed, this is exactly what they found for a variety of measures of acculturative stress: The Tsimshian acculturated to mainstream Canadian culture with the fewest difficulties, the Eastern Cree had the most signs of stress, and the Carrier were intermediate. Again, we can see that cultural distance reliably predicts how difficult one's acculturation experiences will be.

Cultural distance is thus a useful variable for helping us predict who will fare the best in acculturating. However, people vary a great deal within cultures. They come in all sorts of psychological shapes and sizes, and it would seem that some people would fare better in the acculturation experience than others, regardless of what culture they are from. What kinds of individuals would have the easiest time acculturating?

Cultural Fit. One way this question has been explored is to see whether acculturation occurs more smoothly for those who are a better **cultural fit** with their host culture. Cultural fit is the degree to which an individual's personality is more similar to the dominant cultural values in the host culture. It would seem that the greater the cultural fit of a person with the host culture, the more easily he or she should acculturate to it. This hypothesis has been explored in a number of ways.

First, consider the personality trait of "extraversion," which reflects a general orientation toward seeking active stimulation from the environment and of being rather outgoing. Some have proposed that because extraversion should facilitate communication everywhere, extraverts should always fare better in the acculturation experience compared with introverts (Gardner, 1962). However, some research has found that the relation between extraversion and acculturative success is considerably more complicated than it first appears. One study found that Malaysians and Singaporeans who scored high on extraversion demonstrated more signs of psychological well-being while living in New Zealand than those who scored low (Searle & Ward, 1990). In contrast, however, another study found that English-speaking expatriates living in Singapore who scored high on extraversion reported feeling more boredom, frustration, depression, and health problems than those who scored low. Extraversion thus does not always facilitate acculturation (Armes & Ward, 1989). Rather, it appears that an extraverted personality makes a better cultural fit in New Zealand than it does in Singapore, and extraverts will fare better in the acculturation experience only where they fit in well with the culture (but note that this finding is not always replicated, e.g., Ward, Leong, & Low, 2004).

Another key individual difference variable to consider is the self-concept. It would seem that people with more independent self-concepts would be a better cultural fit in individualistic societies, such as that of the United States, compared with people with more interdependent self-concepts, and they would thus have more acculturative success. This hypothesis was investigated by exploring how well students from Korea, Japan, and China fared in their acculturation to the United States (Cross, 1995). Among the East Asian students, there was a positive relation between the independence of one's self-concept and the likelihood that one engaged in direct coping strategies. Those East Asians who were particularly independent were more likely to report that they came up with active strategies to cope with distress—for example, saying that they make a plan of action and try to get rid of a problem—compared with those who were more interdependent. Such direct coping skills would seem to be useful strategies for adjusting to the difficulties encountered in the acculturation experience. Moreover, among the East Asians, there was a positive relation between interdependence and perceived stress. The more interdependent were their self-concepts, the more stress they reported experiencing. However, this study also included a sample of American college students who were not acculturating. Among the American sample there were no significant relations between independence, interdependence, and stress or coping. Hence, interdependence is not always associated with stress and independence is not always associated with direct coping. Even so, among those who are acculturating to an individualistic cultural environment, an independent self-concept seems to facilitate adjustment, whereas interdependent self-concepts appear to interfere with it. Again, what seems to matter the most is having a personality that fits well with your new cultural environment.

Acculturation Strategies. Much psychological research has focused on people's acculturation strategies. Specifically, John Berry and colleagues (e.g., Berry & Sam, 1997) have proposed that two issues are critical to the outcome of one's acculturation. First, is whether people attempt to participate in the larger society of their host culture. Do people have positive attitudes toward their host culture, and are they actively seeking to fit in it? The second issue is whether people are striving to maintain their own heritage culture and identity as members of that culture. Do people have positive attitudes toward their heritage culture, and are they actively seeking ways to preserve the traditions of their heritage culture? These two issues lead to distinct strategies that are proposed to influence the likelihood that one will experience psychological stress in the acculturation process. Furthermore, these two issues are proposed to be independent, such that it is possible for someone to possess positive attitudes toward both their heritage and host cultures, negative attitudes toward both cultures, or positive attitudes toward one and negative attitudes toward the other. A person's acculturation strategies are measured by a questionnaire, an example of which follows. The four different acculturation strategies that people might have are shown graphically in Figure 12.2.

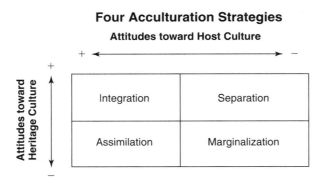

Four Acculturation Strategies

FIGURE 12.2

Positive or negative attitudes towards one's host or heritage cultures yield four different acculturation strategies.

Sample Items from the Vancouver Index of Acculturation

1. I often participate in my heritage cultural traditions.
2. I often participate in mainstream North American cultural traditions.
3. I am interested in having friends from my heritage culture.
4. I am interesting in having North American friends.
5. I believe in the values of my heritage culture.
6. I believe in mainstream North American values.
7. I enjoy the humor and jokes of my heritage culture.
8. I enjoy typical North American jokes and humor.
9. I would be willing to marry a North American person.
10. I would be willing to marry a person from my heritage culture.

From Ryder, Alden, & Paulhus, 2000.

The strategy that involves attempts to fit in and fully participate in the host culture while at the same time striving to maintain the traditions of one's heritage culture is known as the **integration strategy**. People using this strategy have positive views toward both their heritage and their host culture—they are seeking the best of both worlds. Conversely, the strategy that involves little or no effort to participate in the host culture or to maintain the traditions of the heritage culture is known as the **marginalization strategy**. People using this strategy have negative views toward both their heritage and their host cultures. This strategy is relatively rare and is theoretically puzzling (who do people identify with if not either their heritage or host cultures?), and some have proposed that it should not be considered a genuine "strategy" (e.g., Rudmin, 2003); it may, indeed, reflect little more than neuroticism.

On the opposite diagonal of the figure are two mixed strategies. The **assimilation strategy** involves an attempt to fit in and fully participate in the host culture while making little or no effort to maintain the traditions of one's heritage culture. It involves possessing positive attitudes toward the host culture and negative attitudes toward the heritage culture. It reflects a desire to leave behind the ancestral past so as to fit in with the host culture. Last, the **separation strategy** involves efforts to maintain the traditions of the heritage culture while making little or no effort to participate in the host culture. This strategy is composed of positive attitudes toward the heritage culture and negative attitudes toward the host culture. People pursuing separation strategies do not wish to acculturate to the host culture. They would prefer to continue to exist in the cultural world of their heritage culture.

In general, the most common strategy people are likely to pursue is the integration strategy. The least common strategy, in contrast, is the marginalization strategy, whereas assimilation and separation strategies fall in between, with neither being clearly more common than the other. A variety of factors influence which strategy a migrant will be likely to pursue. In general, a person will not strive to fit into the host culture if that culture shows a good deal of prejudice toward the individual's own cultural group. Furthermore, people who have physical features that distinguish them from the majority of those in their host culture will likely experience more prejudice than people who have physical features that allow them to blend in with their host culture, and thus more physically distinct ethnic groups are more likely to maintain negative attitudes toward the host culture and pursue separation or marginalization strategies (Berry, Kim, Power, Young, & Bujaki, 1989). Physically distinct ethnic groups are also more likely to actively support collective efforts to benefit their group's social position (Lalonde & Cameron, 1993). Likewise, people who are of lower socioeconomic status or who are members of indigenous cultural groups are more likely to pursue separation or marginalization strategies as the host culture does not typically offer them much that they desire. Conversely, people will be more likely to try to fit into the host culture if it values cultural diversity. A societal acceptance for diversity and multiculturalism leads migrants to adopt more positive attitudes toward the host culture and increases the likelihood that they will pursue integration or assimilation strategies.

The strategy people will pursue is also affected by a particular person-by-situation interaction. One personality variable, a **need for cognitive closure (NCC)**, appears to be relevant in influencing the acculturation strategy one will pursue. An NCC is a desire to have a definite answer to a question. For people who are high in NCC it does not matter so much *what* answer people receive, just so long as they have an answer; any firm answer is preferred to uncertainty. It has been proposed that people who are high in NCC will adopt an acculturation strategy that is affected by their early experiences in the host culture (Kosic, Kruglanski, Pierro, & Mannetti, 2004).

The reasoning is that the early days of an acculturation experience are always fraught with confusion and uncertainty. Everything is new, and migrants feel anything but certain about how they should behave. People who are high in NCC should thus want to combat this feeling of uncertainty by seeking others with whom they can connect. Connecting with others provides them with a sense of shared experiences, and this should result in increased feelings of certainty. One source of other people that migrants might be able to connect with are compatriots—others who are from their heritage culture who are also living in their new country. However, one does not always arrive in a place where one can find some compatriots. If migrants arrive in a place where they are isolated from their compatriots their only opportunity for social support will be to connect with the local population. Because people high in NCC desire certainty, their initial experiences, either connecting with their compatriots or connecting with the local population, will largely determine their acculturation strategy. That is, those who are high in NCC who connect with their compatriots at the beginning of their sojourn will probably adopt a separation strategy. In contrast, those who are high in NCC who initially connect with the local population will probably adopt an assimilation strategy. People low in NCC, in contrast, will not be so affected by their initial experiences in the new culture and thus will not be as influenced by the social network they first encounter.

To test this hypothesis, the experiences of Croatian immigrants to Italy were explored (Kosic et al., 2004). People who had moved to Italy on average 4 years earlier were contacted. The immigrants were asked to complete a questionnaire that included several measures: (1) an NCC scale, (2) a question about whom they had social relationships with in their first 3 months in Italy (i.e., whether they spent most of their time with other Croatians or with Italians), and (3) a sociocultural adaptation measure that assessed how well they had mastered daily life in Italy. These three measures yielded an interesting pattern shown in Figure 12.3. For participants who scored low in NCC, whether they initially had interacted with Croatians or Italians had no impact on how they adapted to Italian life. This makes sense because those low in NCC would probably not be attempting to get rid of their initial uncertainty by seeking shared experiences with others. In contrast, those high in NCC were greatly affected by the people they initially connected with. Those who socialized with Croatians in their first 3 months had an especially difficult time learning how to adapt to an Italian lifestyle (suggesting a sepa-

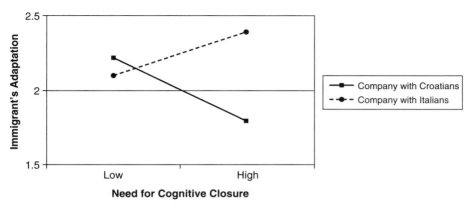

FIGURE 12.3

Croatians who scored high in a need for cognitive closure adapted better to Italian life if their initial interactions were with Italians rather than with their fellow Croatians. In contrast, initial interactions had little impact on Croatians low in a need for cognitive closure.

ration strategy), whereas those who socialized with Italians in their first 3 months fared quite well in adapting to Italian life (suggesting an assimilation strategy). For people high in NCC, their acculturation strategy was largely determined by the group of people around them when they first experienced the uncertainty and confusion of moving to a new place.

The four different acculturation strategies are hypothesized to yield different outcomes in the acculturation process. Specifically, the strategy that is hypothesized to result in the lowest degree of acculturative stress is the integration strategy. One possibility for the success of integration is that this strategy incorporates some protective features, such as a lack of prejudice and discrimination, involvement in two cultural communities and having access to two support groups, and having a flexible personality that allows for this (Berry, 1997). The least successful strategy is marginalization, which involves rejection of the dominant society, a loss of one's original culture, and weakened social support. Assimilation and separation strategies are proposed to be intermediate in terms of their mental health outcomes. A potential cost of assimilation is the loss of one's heritage culture and accompanying social support networks, and a sense of disconnection with the past. Separation strategies bear the cost of rejecting the host culture and all the protective features that it encapsulates, which often is accompanied by the individuals themselves being rejected by the host culture.

A number of studies provide evidence consistent with this hypothesized pattern of acculturation outcomes (e.g., Berry et al., 1989; Rivera-Sinclair, 1997; Yamada & Singelis, 1999); however, one meta-analysis revealed that many studies have failed to find this pattern (Rudmin, 2003). Furthermore, a sophisticated test of the different strategies found that whether a migrant tried to preserve his own cultural traditions had no impact on his acculturative adjustment (Ryder, Alden, & Paulhus, 2000). Rather, the only variable that mattered in this study was the person's attitude toward the host culture, and people with positive attitudes fared better than people with negative attitudes. If this is correct, it would suggest that the four-strategy model could predict adjustment just as effectively if it were reduced to a dimension underlying the assimilation versus separation spectrum. In sum, there has been much theoretical development of the four-strategy model; however, the empirical evidence of its utility remains mixed.

Some Pitfalls of Acculturation. The above discussion assumes that the adjustment migrants undergo when moving to a new culture is largely a good thing. That is, people acquire a set of skills, habits, and ways of thinking that work effectively in the new culture. However, it is quite possible that not all cultural habits picked up along the way are inherently desirable. For example, American culture is an outlier among the world's industrialized cultures on a great many dimensions (see Lipset, 1996, for a review), and as we saw in Chapter 10, one of these is weight. On average, Americans are among some of the heaviest people on the planet, and there are considerable health costs to the weight gains American cultural habits have produced. Immigrants who move to the United States are not immune to the consequences of American eating habits. One study found that among immigrants who had lived in the United States for less than a year, only 8% were obese. In contrast, among those who had lived in the country for 15 years, 19% were obese. This number approaches the obesity rate of 22% for American-born residents (Goel, McCarthy, Phillips, & Wee, 2004). Acculturating to the American way of life not only allows one to function more effectively in the United States, but it also causes one to function more heavily as well.

Parallel findings also emerge for Latinos who move to the United States. However, Latinos who lived in this country not only got heavier the longer they were here; they also became more likely to engage in less healthy behaviors, such as smoking and drinking (but in contrast, they also became more likely to exercise). These changes in lifestyle that came with acculturation are associated with a variety of adverse health outcomes for acculturated Latino-Americans compared with their less acculturated peers (Abraido-Lanza, Chao, & Florez, 2005).

A similar pattern can be seen among Japanese immigrants to the United States. The Japanese have the longest average expected lifespan of any major nation in the world, and they have remarkably low rates of coronary heart disease. However, Japanese who emigrate to the United States are more likely to get coronary heart disease than those who stay in Japan, but this increased risk for heart disease is evident only among those Japanese immigrants who have acculturated to an American lifestyle (Marmot & Syme, 1976). In contrast, Japanese immigrants who continue to embrace Japanese cultural traditions do not show any increased risk for heart disease. The difference in risk for heart disease was quite enormous—the more acculturated immigrants were three to five times more likely to have heart problems. It is still not clear from this study precisely what aspects of Japanese culture protect one from risk factors for heart disease (one of my Japanese friends is quite sure it's the miso soup).

There are other ways in which acculturating individuals can fare worse over time. One study found that among Vietnamese immigrants in New Orleans, the better they achieved in school, the more upwardly mobile they were, and the fewer delinquent acts they committed, the *less* they were integrated into the broader community (Zhou & Bankston, 1998). Because many immigrant groups are disadvantaged and discriminated against, they often live in poorer neighborhoods where the surrounding community is more likely to be struggling and is often caught up with problems of crime and dropping out of school. Somewhat ironically, those immigrants that assimilate into the surrounding community can end up having more difficulties than the ones who resist the cultural values of the community. Another study found that because European-American adolescents are more likely to disrespect authority figures than Latino adolescents, the more Latino immigrants acculturated to the mainstream culture surrounding them, the less seriously they took their studies and the worse they performed in school (Suarez-Orozco & Suarez-Orozco, 1995). Suffice it to say that not all cultural habits lead to positive outcomes, and immigrants who pick up these less desirable habits will also suffer their consequences.

Multicultural People

Thus far, we have discussed how people fare in the acculturation process. A separate question to consider is how people who have been exposed to multiple cultural worldviews organize their different experiences. Do their experiences get all mixed up and averaged together? For example, does a Peruvian who has moved to the United States end up feeling emotions that are roughly halfway between those common in Peru and those common in the States? The tendency for bicultural people to evince psychological tendencies in between those of their two cultures is termed **blending**. Alternatively, do multicultural people end up with multiple selves—feeling and thinking like a Peruvian in Peruvian contexts, and feeling and thinking like an American in an American context? The tendency for bicultural people to switch between different cultural selves is termed **frame-switching**. Which of these two possibilities, the blending model or the frame-switching model, best captures the ways multicultural people deal with their experiences in multiple worlds? There is evidence for both of these possibilities, which I discuss in turn.

Evidence for Blending. If multicultural people respond to their experiences in different cultures by blending and averaging them, we would expect them to show responses on psychological measures that are intermediate to responses of monocultural people from the different cultures. Asian-Americans, for example, would be expected to think not quite like either mainstream Americans or Asians but in some way that lies between the two. Many cross-cultural studies do include a bicultural sample in addition to two monocultural samples. The most common pattern of findings is evidence for blending—that is, the bicultural sample shows a pattern somewhere between the two monocultural samples (e.g., Heine & Hamamura, 2007; Iyengar, Lepper, & Ross, 1999; Kitayama, Markus, Matsumoto, & Norasakkunkit, 1997; Norenzayan, Choi, & Nisbett, 2002; Tsai, Simeonova, & Watanabe, 2004).

We explored the acculturation of self-esteem among people of East Asian descent who moved to Canada. If you recall from Chapter 6, North Americans are much more likely to elaborate on positive aspects about themselves and to have higher self-esteem than East Asians. To investigate what hap-

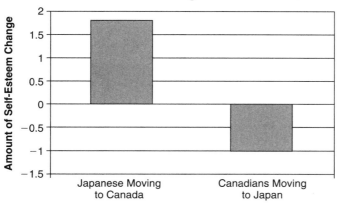

FIGURE 12.4

After 7 months living in Canada, Japanese show a significant increase in self-esteem, while after 7 months living in Japan, Canadians show a significant self-esteem decrease.

pens to self-esteem when one moves from a culture that tends to have lower rates of self-esteem to a culture that tends to have higher rates, we measured the self-esteem of Japanese exchange students living in Canada at two points in time: a few days after they had arrived in Canada, and then 7 months later (Heine & Lehman, 2004). As you can see in Figure 12.4, the Japanese students' self-esteem scores were significantly higher after they had been in Canada for a while than when they had just arrived. One possibility is that the Japanese students were exposed to Canadian cultural messages that encourage people to focus on their strengths, and this led them to have higher self-esteem. An alternative explanation is that the acculturation experience might lead to higher feelings of self-esteem for everyone, perhaps because people can derive a sense of pride and accomplishment for being able to get by in another culture. To investigate which of these two hypotheses is more compelling we also measured the self-esteem of Canadian English teachers who were moving to Japan at two points in time: a couple of weeks before they left Canada and then after they had been in Japan for 7 months. The teachers' self-esteem scores were significantly lower after having spent some time in Japan. This suggests that acculturation is not necessarily accompanied by self-esteem increases. Rather, a more parsimonious explanation is that people are exposed to novel cultural information when they move to a new culture. The information that people are exposed to in Canada appears to encourage them to focus on their strengths, whereas the information that people are exposed to in Japan appears to encourage them to focus on their weaknesses. Moreover, this exposure to new cultural information seems to affect the self-concept rather quickly—we found evidence of significant changes after only 7 months.

This study suggests that acculturative change in the self-concept can occur relatively quickly—after 7 months of living in another culture people do indeed change. A related question is how long does it take for people to completely acculturate to the norms of a host culture? Is 7 months of living in Canada enough to make a Japanese exchange student psychologically Canadian? In another study we investigated this question by comparing the self-esteem of several thousand students in Japan and Canada (Heine & Lehman, 2004). This large group of students was divided into subsamples that tracked a continuum with respect to their exposure to North American culture. In order of increasing exposure to North American culture, these categories were (1) Japanese who had never been outside Japan, (2) Japanese who had spent time in a Western country, (3) recent East Asian immigrants to Canada (who had been in Canada less than 7 years), (4) East Asians who immigrated to Canada more than 7 years ago, (5) second-generation Asian-descent Canadians, (6) third-generation Asian-descent Canadians, and finally, (7) European-descent Canadians. The self-esteem scores of these different subsamples were contrasted. As you can see in Figure 12.5, this classification resulted in a clear relation between exposure to North American culture and self-esteem. The longer those of Asian descent had spent participating in North American culture, the higher were their self-esteem scores. Moreover, it wasn't until those of Asian descent had been in Canada for three generations (that is, their grandparents had immigrated to Canada) that their self-esteem scores reached the level of European-Canadians. Apparently, at least with respect to self-esteem, acculturative changes in the self-concept extend across a long period of time. For self-esteem, it appears to take three generations to become fully acculturated. It remains to be seen, however, whether acculturative changes are as slow for people from all cultural backgrounds. It is possible that East Asians take longer to acculturate to North America than would immigrants from Europe because East Asians have a greater cultural distance to traverse. Moreover, it is not at all clear whether different psychological processes acculturate at the same rate. There has been scant research mapping out how psychological processes change with acculturation, and it is not at all clear how

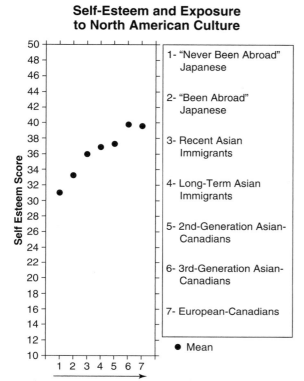

Self-Esteem and Exposure to North American Culture

Self Esteem Score (y-axis: 10 to 50)

Exposure to North American Culture (x-axis: 1 2 3 4 5 6 7)

1- "Never Been Abroad" Japanese

2- "Been Abroad" Japanese

3- Recent Asian Immigrants

4- Long-Term Asian Immigrants

5- 2nd-Generation Asian-Canadians

6- 3rd-Generation Asian-Canadians

7- European-Canadians

● Mean

FIGURE 12.5

On average, the more exposure one has to North American culture, the higher one's self-esteem is.

well the findings shown in Figure 12.5 would generalize to other psychological phenomena or to people acculturating from different cultural backgrounds (also see McCrae, Yik, Trapnell, Bond, & Paulhus, 1998).

Frame-Switching. The previous two studies provide evidence that is consistent with a blending view of acculturation. Over time spent in North America, the average person of East Asian descent comes to more closely resemble European-Americans and to less closely resemble East Asians living in East Asia. However, another interpretation is still possible to explain these findings. Perhaps in the above two studies people were either thinking like North Americans *or* they were thinking like East Asians. It is possible that after 7 months of life in Canada, only a small percentage of East Asians were thinking like North Americans. After 7 years in Canada, in contrast, a larger percentage of East Asians might have been thinking like North Americans, and after three generations, virtually 100% of Asian-Canadians were thinking like

European-Canadians. That is, rather than each person's self-concept being blended a little over time as new Western cultural experiences were slowly poured in, it is possible instead that the percentage of people thinking in Western ways increased with exposure to North American culture.

This alternative account of multicultural experience presupposes that multicultural people can develop multiple selves, each equipped to deal with a specific cultural environment. According to this view, multicultural people do not develop a blended self-concept that is an admixture of the different cultures they are exposed to, nor do they lose their heritage culture self once they have mastered their host culture self. Rather, the frame-switching view maintains that multicultural people develop mastery over both cultural worlds and develop divergent selves that can be selectively activated by different cultural contexts.

If we again use language as a proxy for culture, it becomes clear that the frame-switching hypothesis makes more sense than a blending hypothesis. For example, native Indonesian speakers who move to a predominantly English-speaking country do not end up speaking a blended language of "Englonesian." Rather, they speak Indonesian in Indonesian contexts and English in English contexts. Bilinguals learn to switch between languages depending on the context they are in. Although some people who emigrate may never learn the new language of their host culture completely fluently, and some migrants might largely forget the language of their heritage culture, there does not seem to be much blending of languages. To the extent that navigating multiple cultures is similar to navigating multiple languages, we would expect that people can also frame-shift between different cultures.

Indeed, from the subjective perspective of the multicultural person, there is much discussion about frame-switching between cultural contexts. For example, over a century ago the sociologist W. E. B. Du Bois (1903/1989) claimed that African-Americans experienced continual switching between "two souls, two thoughts, two unreconciled strivings, two warring ideals" (p. 5). The cultures of mainstream America and that of African-Americans (in particular, that of inner-city African-Americans) continue to be different enough that people need to learn how to behave differently depending on which context they are in. The sociologist Elijah Anderson (1999) describes in great detail how inner-city African-American children quickly learn to discriminate between the norms and unwritten rules that govern their schools and mainstream society and those that govern the streets. "Code-switching," as this particular kind of cultural frame-switching is referred to, is an essential skill for inner-city children to learn if they are to survive and succeed in these two divergent cultural contexts. Anderson argues that such children must learn to switch between the "code of the decent" and the "code of the street" as they deal with people in their school culture and their street culture. The code of the street permeates many aspects of life—in particular, the development of a reputation that one is tough and is not to be messed with. The only way an inner-city child can succeed, Anderson argues, is to be able to switch effectively between these two codes.

This code-switching has been discussed largely among sociologists in terms of the ways people need to *act and present themselves to others* in their respective cultures. When on the street, people must follow the code of the street, but when among "the decents," they need to act in ways that are congruent with mainstream American society. However, it is possible that this tendency to oscillate between two different cultural worlds is not isolated to the ways people act and present themselves to others—it might possibly affect the ways people are thinking at a basic psychological level as well.

Hong and colleagues (2000) proposed that multiculturals do engage in frame-switching, and that this frame-switching should be evident in how their minds operate at the most fundamental level. Borrowing from information science, Hong and colleagues propose that culture is represented in the brain as a network of specific information. For example, people exposed to American culture would have a set of ideas in their heads that cluster together, such as independence, confidence, freedom, individual rights, the Statue of Liberty, and capitalism. These ideas are networked together in the sense that they usually come in clusters. That is, people who are thinking about independence should be more likely to think of confidence and individual rights than those who are thinking about interdependence, because confidence and individual rights are more commonly associated with independence than interdependence. The mind forms links between those constructs that tend to get activated together, and thus, activating one construct that is part of a network should activate the other constructs of the network. Because information is dispersed in people's minds through networks, people who are "primed" or exposed to one part of an information network should be more likely to think in other ways that are part of that same network.

Consider this dramatic demonstration of priming: College students participated in a task requiring them to unscramble some sentences (Bargh, Chen, & Burrows, 1996). One-half of the students unscrambled sentences that contained some words related to the elderly—wrinkle, old, knits, and bingo. The other half unscrambled sentences that contained neutral words. At the end of the study, participants left by walking down a hallway. Unknown to them, an observer timed how long it took them to walk down that hallway. Remarkably, participants who had been exposed to words related to the elderly walked significantly slower than those who had been exposed to the neutral words. The reason is that people have a number of ideas associated with the elderly that form an information network, one of which is that elderly people tend to move quite slowly. Activating part of the information network (having people think of words like bingo and wrinkle) leads to related ideas and behaviors (such as walking slowly) to become activated as well.

Hong and colleagues applied this same kind of reasoning in their investigations of how the minds of multicultural people operate. They reasoned that people who were exposed to multiple cultural worlds would have multiple information networks in their heads. For example, a Chinese-American would have an information network regarding Chinese ideas and one regarding American ideas. Hong and colleagues reasoned that if people exposed to both Chinese and American cultures were primed with things that reminded them of the different cultures, they could be led to think in ways that are more consistent with the primed culture.

In one study they conducted, attributions were investigated among Westernized Chinese students in Hong Kong (Hong et al., 2000). They reasoned that having been educated in a former British colony, and in English, these students had had exposure to both Western and Chinese ways. If you recall from Chapter 9, Chinese are more likely to explain people's behaviors in terms of external attributions (e.g., situational factors) whereas Americans are more likely to explain people's behaviors in terms of internal attributions (e.g., personality factors; Morris & Peng, 1994). Quite remarkably, this pattern of results not only holds for how people explain the behaviors of people but also for how they explain the behaviors of fish. That is, Chinese are more likely to make external attributions to explain why a single fish is swimming ahead of a group (e.g., the fish is being chased by others), whereas Americans are more likely to explain the fish's behavior in terms of internal attributions (e.g., the fish is leading the others). Hong and colleagues were interested in how Hong Kong Chinese would explain the fish's behavior. They reasoned that the answer to this question is "it depends"—it depends

Hong and colleagues used stimuli like this as primes to document frame-switching taking place.

on which cultural knowledge network has been activated. If Hong Kong Chinese are thinking Chinese thoughts, they should explain the fish's behavior in terms of the pressures from the group it is in. In contrast, if they are thinking American thoughts, they should explain the fish's behavior in terms of its individual desires. They manipulated the kinds of thoughts the Hong Kong Chinese were having by showing them a number of cultural icons. Those in the "Chinese prime" condition were shown such pictures as a Chinese dragon, the Chinese Emperor's Summer Palace, a rice farmer, the Great Wall, and a mythical Chinese dancer. They were then asked to write several sentences about Chinese culture. In contrast, those in the "American prime" condition were shown pictures of Mickey Mouse, the U.S. Capitol building, a cowboy, Mt. Rushmore, and the Statue of Liberty, and were asked to write some sentences about American culture. They also had a "neutral prime" condition, in which participants viewed pictures of environmental scenes. Then, the participants saw computer images of fish swimming across the screen and were asked to explain their behavior.

Their results are quite striking and are shown in Figure 12.6. Students who saw the American primes explained the fish's behavior less in terms of the group's influence than those in a neutral prime condition. Likewise, those who saw the Chinese primes explained the fish's behavior more in terms of the group influencing it than those in the neutral prime condition. The Hong Kong Chinese were capable of explaining the fish's behavior in either the typically American or the typically Chinese way. They switched cultural frames depending on which cultural information network was activated.

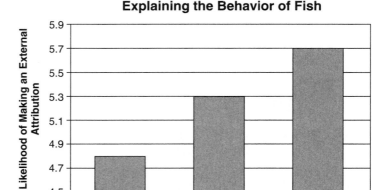

Explaining the Behavior of Fish

FIGURE 12.6

Hong Kong Chinese who are primed with American icons are less likely to make external attributions to explain the behavior of a single fish, whereas those primed with Chinese icons are more likely to make external attributions.

This is a profound finding and extends our understanding of frame-switching in dramatic ways. It is likely that the kind of code-switching people have discussed regarding African-Americans shifting between the "code of the street" and the "code of the decents" is a largely conscious process. That is, people are likely aware that they are adjusting their behaviors to fit in better with whichever group they are among. The findings of the study by Hong and colleagues, in contrast, surely do not represent conscious responses. People do not have an explicit idea in their head that Americans explain a fish's behaviors by making internal attributions whereas Chinese explain a fish's behavior by making external attributions. You probably did not know this fact about how people explain the behavior of fish before reading this book. Yet despite being unaware of these specific kinds of cultural information, the participants still ended up thinking in ways that were consistent with the primes they saw. Apparently, when thinking "American" thoughts people are more likely to think of a broad array of thoughts, many of which they are not aware of but that include the implicit notion that focusing on individuals is the way to explain behavior. These thoughts are associated with other thoughts, such as pictures of Mickey Mouse, not because of any causal relation between Mickey Mouse and internal attributions but because these thoughts tend to occur together. When thinking about Mickey Mouse, people are thinking about "American ideas" more generally, and this increases the likelihood that they will explain the behaviors of fish by focusing on the individuals. Bicultural people can shift between cultural frames with as small a prompt as thinking about a handful of pictures (also see Wong & Hong, 2005).

Not all biculturals should necessarily frame-switch to the same degree. Some biculturals, for example, tend to see their two cultural identities as quite compatible with each other. These people integrate aspects of both cultures into their everyday lives. They could be described as being high in bicultural identity integration (Benet-Martinez, Leu, Lee, & Morris, 2002). In contrast, other biculturals tend to see their two cultural identities as oppositional. That is, they feel that they can identify either with, say, their Chinese identity or with their American identity, but they cannot identify with both of them simultaneously. They may feel that they have to choose between their identities, depending on the situation. These people are low in bicultural identity integration. One hypothesis is that the greatest frame-switching should occur among those who are high in bicultural identity integration (Benet-Martinez et al., 2002). This is because these people can fluidly react to external cues in culturally consistent ways. For example, Chinese cues elicit their Chinese thoughts whereas American cues elicit their American thoughts. People who are low in bicultural identity integration, in contrast, tend to see their cultural identities in opposition with each other. Because of this, for example, when these people are in American contexts they feel especially Chinese, and when they are in Chinese contexts they feel especially American. The two identities feel largely opposed. Consequently, being primed with their culture should not lead them to react in culturally consistent ways. There is good evidence to support this hypothesis. In one study, the only biculturals who showed the kind of frame-switching identified by Hong and colleagues were those who scored high on a bicultural identity integration measure (Benet-Martinez et al., 2002).

Other kinds of primes that can lead people to frame-switch have also been explored. Because language and culture are so intimately connected, it is probably not surprising to hear that language can activate a cultural frame. Indeed, it seems that bilingual people tend to frame-switch when they shift between their languages. For example, students who had been born in China but had moved to Canada were asked to describe themselves in an open-ended questionnaire (Ross, Xun, & Wilson, 2002). One-half of those participants were asked to complete the questionnaire in Chinese whereas the other half were asked to complete it in English. The number of statements people made that were positive or negative about themselves were calculated. Those participants who completed the materials in English listed approximately three times as many positive statements as negative ones, reflecting a clear tendency to view themselves in positive terms. In stark contrast, those who completed the materials in Chinese listed about the same number of positive as negative statements about themselves. This pattern nicely replicates the cultural differences between East Asians and Westerners in self-enhancing motivations that were discussed in Chapter 6. The language that people speak seems to activate an associated cultural network, and this influences how they think. When bilinguals switch between languages they are not just bringing different vocabularies and grammars to mind—they seem to be bringing different selves to mind as well.

Although findings such as these provide clear evidence that Chinese-Americans and Hong Kong Chinese can be primed to think in culturally distinct ways, a question to consider is whether this effect is limited to biculturals. Indeed, it is debatable about just how bicultural Hong Kong Chinese are in the first place. One could argue that rather than the individual Hong Kong Chinese participants being exposed to two different cultural worlds, it might be more accurate to say that the participants are all exposed to a single, multifaceted culture. Hong Kong surely is not unique in being a country that is influenced by multiple cultural influences. That would seem to characterize virtually any large city today. Would we expect to find, then, that people who are traditionally thought of as monocultural might also have access to multiple cultural frames?

Recall the study discussed in Chapter 6 in which Chinese and Americans were compared in how they viewed the importance of a tennis game that was framed either as trying to secure a win (indicating a promotion orientation) or as trying to secure a loss (indicating a prevention orientation; Lee, Aaker, & Gardner, 2000). The Americans viewed the situation in which the player was trying to secure a win as more important than one in which he was trying to avoid a loss. Apparently, then, Americans tend to maintain promotion orientations. In contrast, the Chinese viewed the situation of trying to avoid a loss as more important than the one in which the player was trying to secure a win. Chinese appear to maintain prevention orientations. The researchers were interested in whether this cultural difference had anything to do with the fact that Chinese tend to be more interdependent than Americans. Perhaps, interdependence is associated with a prevention orientation. One way they tested this was to see whether Americans would also become more prevention oriented if they were led to think about their interdependence. They had Americans again consider which kind of tennis game was more important; however, the researchers manipulated whether the Americans were considering an individual's performance or a team's performance in a tennis tournament. The authors reasoned that an individual competition highlights one's independence, whereas a team performance highlights one's interdependence. Interestingly, they found a pattern of results that paralleled the cultural differences. That is, Americans who considered an *individual's* tennis game adopted a promotion orientation in that they viewed efforts to secure a win more important than efforts to avoid a loss. In contrast, Americans who considered a *team's* tennis game adopted a prevention orientation in that they viewed efforts to avoid a loss more important than efforts to secure a win. In sum, Americans could be led to think like Chinese with the priming of information that was related to interdependence—a key aspect of Chinese self-concepts. This priming was possible even though it's probably fair to assume that the American participants had very little knowledge of or exposure to Chinese culture. Yet they could think like Chinese when they considered the situation from an interdependent perspective.

The results of this study, as well as those from many other similar ones (e.g., Heine et al., 2001; Kuhnen, Hannover, & Schubert, 2001; Mandel, 2003; Trafimow, Triandis, & Goto, 1991), highlight that bicultural people are not the only ones who have access to multiple knowledge structures. But how could this be? How could Americans be primed to think in a way that is more characteristic of people in another culture that they don't know much about? The results of these studies suggest that although some ideas (such as independence or promotion orientations) might be more common among Americans than other ideas (such as interdependence or prevention orientations), these less common ideas are still present within American culture—that is, they are at least existential universals. Americans too sometimes think of themselves as interdependent and are concerned with a prevention orientation. Because of this, they too develop a knowledge network of ideas that are associated with interdependence and prevention orientations. Once a knowledge network exists, when any part of that network is activated through priming, the other parts of the network should also be activated. Hence, even monocultural people can probably be primed to think in ways that are more similar to other cultures to the extent that those ways of thinking are sometimes present in their own minds. Biculturals are not the only ones who can frame-switch.

However, we might wonder whether biculturals would be more adept than monoculturals at frame-switching because they might have more clearly demarcated information networks. Because biculturals often live in two distinct cultural worlds, it is likely that there would be a clearer division between their two views of self. For example, we might expect that a Chinese-American can feel and act very Chinese when with her extended family, yet feel very American when with her friends at school. If her experiences as Chinese or American are so clearly distinct from each other, it follows that the information networks regarding "Chinese" ways of thinking and "American" ways of thinking would be relatively nonoverlapping networks, with very strong linkages within each cultural mind-set. In contrast, monoculturals might have relatively looser knowledge networks around concepts such as independence and interdependence, and thereby would react relatively less consistently to primes they might encounter.

This question was investigated in a study that compared biculturals (Asian-Americans) and monoculturals (European-Americans—they are considered monocultural because mainstream American culture has been more influenced by people of European descent) with respect to how easily they could be primed (Gardner, Gabriel, & Dean, 2004). The participants were primed with either independent or interdependent aspects of themselves. The priming was accomplished by having participants read one of two versions of a paragraph that described a trip to the city. The independent prime version of the paragraph included only singular pronouns, such as *I*, *me*, and *mine*, whereas the interdependent prime version of the paragraph was identical to this except that it included plural pronouns, such as *we*, *us*, and *our*. Then participants were asked to rate the importance of certain values. Some of the values represented individualistic concerns, such as freedom, independence, and choosing one's own goals. Other values reflected collectivistic goals, such as belongingness, friendship, and respect for elderly. The values that Asian-Americans and European-Americans rated were compared across priming conditions. The results are shown in Figure 12.7.

A number of trends are indicated by this figure. First, people who were primed with independence, compared to those primed with interdepend-

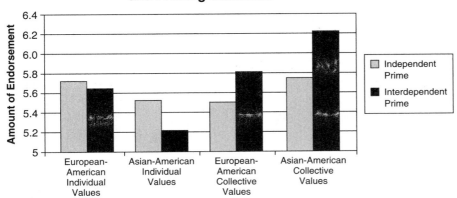

Value Endorsement by Culture and Priming Condition

FIGURE 12.7

The values of Asian-Americans are more affected by independence and interdependence primes than are the values of European-Americans.

ence, rated the individualistic values as more important and the collectivist values as less important. This shows that everyone is capable of frame-shifting. Second, regardless of the prime they received, European-Americans rated the individualistic values as more important than did Asian-Americans, whereas Asian-Americans rated the collectivistic values as more important than did European-Americans. This shows that the overall cultural difference in values emerged as expected. Third, this figure also shows that the primes had a weaker effect for European-Americans (i.e., the gap between the independent and interdependent primes are significantly smaller) than they did for Asian-Americans. That is, Asian-Americans showed more pronounced frame-switching than did the European-Americans. This provides nice evidence that although everyone can frame-shift, biculturals do so more strongly, and this is likely because they have more distinct and clear-cut knowledge networks consistent with their two cultural selves. Further research suggests that this frame-switching is especially prevalent among biculturals who were born in North America, compared to those who immigrated (Cameron & Lalonde, 1994; Tsai, Ying, & Lee, 2000). This may be because North American–born biculturals have a lifetime of bicultural experiences and have thus developed especially efficient frame-switching strategies, compared with immigrants who lived monocultural existences for much of their lives.

Different but Often Unequal

One might conclude from my rather Panglossian description of the accultur-ation experience that immigration is like getting used to a new pair of shoes. Although in the beginning there are some times of discomfort, over time, people happily grow into a comfortable and accepting new environment. For some people, the acculturation experience may indeed be a relatively pain-less, gradual process of adjustment that continues to improve over time as they become fully integrated into a multicultural community. However, one of the saddest facts of human existence remains that people from different cultures are not all treated with equal respect. Prejudice and discrimination have always been rampant, particularly within countries where people of dif-ferent ethnic backgrounds interact. For many people in the world, the expe-rience of moving to a new culture is fraught with active discrimination, systematic disenfranchisement, unjust treatment, mocking and humiliation, violence, and perhaps even threats to their lives. Moreover, the experience of prejudice against minorities is not limited to those who move to a new culture but also extends to those who have ancestors who are from a differ-ent cultural background. What are the consequences of living in a multicul-tural world in which some of the cultures are actively discriminated against?

Some of the most powerful and unsettling research on the experience of being disenfranchised has been conducted by Claude Steele and colleagues. Focusing on African-Americans, Steele highlighted a disturbing finding. African-Americans tend to drop out of school at far greater rates than do European-Americans. Moreover, they do so at all levels of schooling, from high school through graduate school. This sad and puzzling fact is not eas-ily explained. Critics of affirmative action might say that this is the result of placing African-Americans in overly demanding programs for which they are not fully prepared. The racist might argue that this shows that African-Americans are not as intelligent as European-Americans. However, what flies in the face of these accounts is that *regardless of their level of preparation* African-Americans, on average, are more likely to do worse in their classes and to ultimately drop out. That is, the same level of performance on entrance exam-inations such as the American College Testing Program (ACT) or the Scholas-tic Aptitude Test (SAT) results in worse performance at the university for African-American students than for European-American ones (Steele, 1992). Something must be happening that causes those African-American students—

who are equally prepared in terms of their test scores with European-Americans—to do worse in their studies.

Steele proposes that the primary cause in this case, and in many other cases where disenfranchised minority members fare worse, is due to something known as **stereotype threat**. Stereotype threat is the fear that one might do something that will inadvertently confirm a negative stereotype about one's group. Stereotypes represent cultural beliefs—that is, they are shared beliefs among members of a culture. It is not necessary that you believe the stereotypes to be aware of them; belief and knowledge about stereotypes are separate. Part of growing up in American culture is being exposed to the stereotypes that are sometimes discussed there, whether one believes them or not. A relevant example is the stereotype that African-Americans fare worse on intellectual tasks (this has been the stereotype that has been researched the most in stereotype threat studies). People experience stereotype threat when they realize that they are at risk for confirming a negative stereotype, and in so doing, they end up proving the stereotype. For example, if you are an African-American engaged in a very difficult intellectual task, it is likely that this negative stereotype about African-Americans will come to mind. The stereotype dictates that African-Americans have difficulty with challenging intellectual tasks and there you are, an African-American having difficulty with a challenging intellectual task. You are at risk for proving the stereotype. Steele and colleagues have shown through a number of elegant experiments that a variety of things happen to people when they are in a state of stereotype threat. First, they get quite stressed as they realize the parallels between their own performance and the stereotype. Some studies have found that blood pressure increases (Blascovich, Spencer, Quinn, & Steele, 2001), and people start showing evidence that they are thinking about the stereotype because they are more likely to be thinking of words like "dumb," "loser," and "black" (Steele & Aronson, 1995).

Most problematic, however, is that people who are under stereotype threat while taking a test start to do worse on the test. In one study, African-American and European-American Stanford students took a test that consisted of some verbal items from the Graduate Record Examination (Steele & Aronson, 1995). As any of you who have taken this exam will realize, these items are of enormous difficulty. In one condition, students simply took the test that was framed to them as a psychological task. In a second condition, prior to taking the test, the students were asked to check a box that

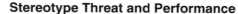

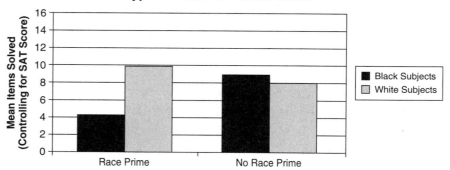

FIGURE 12.8

When asked to indicate their race prior to taking a difficult verbal test, African-Americans perform worse on the test than African-Americans who are not asked to indicate their race. In contrast, indicating one's race has no impact on European-Americans' test performance.

identified their race. The dependent measure was how many items people were able to answer correctly. As shown in Figure 12.8 there was clear evidence of stereotype threat happening. In the "no race-prime" condition, the African-American and European-American students did equally well. In this condition, no stereotype was activated and thus no one's performance was affected. In the "race-prime" condition, the performance of the European-Americans was unaffected—there is no widely shared stereotype regarding the performance of European-Americans on verbal tests, so there was no impact on performance. However, in the "race-prime" condition, African-Americans performed significantly worse than they had in the "no race-prime" condition. The stereotype that African-Americans do worse on intellectual tasks was activated and this dramatically interfered with their performance. Merely indicating their race caused them to do worse. This study demonstrated that when people experience stereotype threat they often end up acting in ways that are precisely consistent with the stereotype, and their behavior ends up proving it. And because ethnic minorities so often receive the brunt of negative stereotypes around the world, they are at risk for stereotype threat and proving the stereotypes. Although much of this research has targeted the experiences of African-Americans, this effect generalizes broadly to virtually all stereotyped groups. Comparable findings have shown that women will perform worse on math tests when reminded of their gender (Shih, Pittinsky, & Ambady, 1999), European-American students will perform worse on an athletic task when reminded of their race (Stone, Lynch, & Sjomeling, 1999), and elderly will perform worse on memory tasks when reminded of their age (Hess, Auman, & Colcombe, 2003).

The existence of stereotype threat can make the acculturation process of disadvantaged minorities difficult indeed. Knowing that others expect you to fare poorly and then encountering occasions when you succumb to stereotype threat can have long-term negative consequences. People may begin to cope with the stress of stereotype threat by disidentifying with the stereotyped domain (e.g., performing well in school) and adopting strategies to avoid reminders of the stereotype (e.g., dropping out of school), thus perpetuating the stereotype. However, now that researchers have identified this striking obstacle that thwarts the integration efforts of disadvantaged minorities, they are developing solutions to combat stereotype threat (e.g., Cohen, Garcia, Apfel, & Master, 2006; Dar-Nimrod & Heine, 2006; Good, Aronson, & Inzlicht, 2003). There are many reasons to remain optimistic that the deleterious consequences of stereotype threat will someday be reduced.

SUMMARY

Acculturation is an extremely important topic in this age of globalization and multiculturalism; however, it remains an especially difficult topic to study. People's acculturation experiences vary dramatically, and many studies on acculturation reveal contradictory findings. Research has indicated that the migrant often experiences a predictable sequence of attitudes toward the host culture, moving from a "Honeymoon Stage," when all is fun and exciting, to a sharp drop into the turbulent pool of the "Crisis" or "Culture Shock" stage, followed by a gradual period of "Adjustment," as he or she acculturates to the new environment.

Not everyone fares well in the acculturation process, and those who tend to have the easiest time come from cultures that are not too dissimilar from their host culture and have personalities that fit in well with the host culture. Having positive attitudes toward the host culture also facilitates acculturation, with integrators (and perhaps assimilators) suffering less stress than those with negative attitudes.

Migrants come to think in ways similar to those of their host culture. The initial signs of their change in thinking appear fairly quickly; however, it seems to take much time, perhaps generations, for migrants to think completely like natives of their host cultures.

Biculturals appear to hold multiple cultural information systems in their minds. When they are primed with one particular culture, they think in ways that are consistent with that culture. Monoculturals show evidence for this priming too; however, biculturals are especially adept at frame-shifting between their different cultural selves.

Last, the acculturation experiences of many migrants are fraught with discrimination, which can often result in the deleterious consequences of stereotype threat. This threat can serve to perpetuate negative stereotypes and stands as a great impediment to the acculturation process.

Glossary

accessibility universal The first and highest level of universality, which states that a given cognitive tool exists across cultures, is used to solve the same problem across cultures, and is accessible to the same degree across cultures.

acculturation The process by which people migrate to and learn a culture that is different from their original (or heritage) culture.

acquiescence bias A tendency to agree with most statements one encounters.

actor–observer bias A tendency to see one's own behavior as best explained by situational factors and the behavior of others as best explained by dispositional factors.

agreeableness A personality trait that indicates how warm or pleasant an individual is; part of the *Five Factor Model of Personality*.

agonias An anxiety disorder that can include a wide array of symptoms such as a burning sensation, a loss of breath, hysterical blindness, sleeping disorders, and eating disorders.

analytic thinking A type of thinking characterized by a focus on objects and their attributes.

anorexia nervosa An eating disorder characterized by a refusal to maintain a normal (high enough) body weight; an intense fear of gaining weight; denial of the seriousness of one's low body weight; and, for postmenarcheal females, missing three consecutive menstrual cycles.

anthropocentrism The tendency to project properties of humans, such as characteristics and experiences, onto other animals.

appraisals The way one evaluates an event in terms of its relevance to one's well-being.

anxious–ambivalent attachment An attachment style in which an infant shows frequent distress, both when his or her mother is present and when she is absent.

arctic hysteria A hysterical attack in which the patient experiences a sudden loss or disturbance of consciousness, leading him or her to tear off clothing, roll around in the snow, and speak unknown languages.

assimilation strategy An acculturation strategy that involves an attempt to fit in and fully participate in the *host culture* while making little or no effort to maintain the traditions of one's *heritage culture*.

ataques de nervios A condition in which emotionally charged incidents bring on symptoms such as palpitations, numbness, and a sense of heat rising to the head.

attachment theory A theory that posits that infants and parents are biologically prepared to establish close attachments with each other.

authority ranking A type of relational structure in which people are linearly ordered along a hierarchical social dimension in which higher ranking people have prestige and privileges while those ranking lower do not.

autokinetic effect An effect caused by the involuntary *saccades* of the eyes, which, in the dark, create the illusion of movement.

autonomy ideal A moral principle that young children should sleep alone so they can learn to be self-reliant and able to take care of themselves.

avoidant attachment An attachment style in which an infant shows little distress in response to his or her mother's absence and avoids her when she returns.

back-translation A method of translating research materials from one language to another whereby a translator translates materials from Language A to Language B and then a different translator translates the materials back from Language B to Language A. The original and twice-translated versions in Language A are then compared so that any discrepancies between them can be resolved.

bask in the reflected glory Emphasizing one's connection to successful others in order to feel better about oneself.

between-groups A type of experimental manipulation in which different groups of participants receive different levels of the independent variable(s).

blending The tendency for bicultural people to manifest psychological tendencies in between those of their two cultures.

brain fag syndrome A syndrome associated with complaints of intellectual and visual impairment and a burning sensation in the head and neck, usually occurring after excessive mental work.

bulimia nervosa An eating disorder characterized by recurrent episodes of binge eating along with recurrent inappropriate behaviors to prevent weight gain (e.g. induced vomiting), which happen at least twice a week for 3 months; a self-evaluation unduly influenced by one's body weight; and no concurrent diagnosis of *anorexia nervosa*.

calling In religious belief, the God-given purpose an individual is meant to fulfill during his or her life.

categorical perception Perceiving stimuli as belonging to separate and discrete categories, even though the stimuli may gradually differ from each other along a continuum.

collectivistic A term for cultures with many practices, institutions, and customs encouraging individuals to place relatively more emphasis on collective goals than individual ones.

communal sharing A type of relational structure in which the members of a group emphasize their common identity, and each have the same rights and privileges.

compensatory self-enhancement The means of compensating for doing poorly on a particular activity by focusing on how good one is at something unrelated to that activity.

conscientiousness A personality trait that indicates how responsible and dependable an individual is; part of the *Five Factor Model of Personality*.

contemporary legends Fictional stories told in modern societies as though they are true.

cultural distance The difference between two cultures in their overall ways of life.

cultural fit The degree to which an individual's personality is compatible with the dominant cultural values of his or her *host culture*.

culture-bound syndromes Groups of symptoms that appear to be greatly influenced by cultural factors, and hence occur far less frequently in some cultures than others, or manifest in highly divergent ways across cultures.

culture of honor A culture in which people (especially men) strive to protect their reputation through aggression

culture shock The feeling of being anxious, helpless, irritable, and generally homesick due to a move to a new culture.

dependent variable In an experiment, the variable or measure affected by manipulation of the *independent variable*.

deprivation effect A tendency for people to value something more when it is lacking in their culture.

discounting Reducing the perceived importance of the domain in which one has performed poorly.

display rules The culturally specific rules that govern which facial expressions are appropriate in a given situation and how intensely they should be exhibited.

dispositional attributions Explaining people's behavior in terms of their inner qualities, such as personality traits.

distal causes Initial differences that lead to effects over long periods of time and often through indirect relations.

downward social comparison An individual's comparison of his or her performance with the performance of someone who is doing worse.

dynamic social impact theory A theory suggesting that individuals influence each other through their interactions, which gives rise to clusters of like-minded people separated by geography.

emulative learning A type of social learning focused on the environmental events involved with a model's behavior, such as how the use of one object could potentially affect changes in the state of the environment.

encephalization quotient The ratio of an animal's brain weight to the brain weight predicted for a comparable animal of the same body size.

entity theory of self A view of the self in which a person's abilities and traits are largely innate features that the individual cannot change.

entity theory of the world A view of the world as something that is fixed and beyond an individual's control to change.

epidemiology of ideas A perspective on cultural evolution that contends there is no direct replication of ideas, but that each individual creates his or her own representation of a learned idea.

equality matching A type of relational structure based on the idea of balance and reciprocity in which people keep track of what is exchanged, and they are motivated to pay back what has been exchanged in equivalent turns.

ethic of autonomy A system of values that views morality in terms of individual freedoms and rights violations with an emphasis on personal choice, the right to engage in free contracts, and individual liberty.

ethic of community A system of values that emphasizes that individuals have duties pertaining to their roles in a community or social hierarchy.

ethic of divinity A system of values that emphasizes sanctity and the perceived "natural order" of things.

ethnocentrism The tendency to judge people from other cultures by comparing them to the standards of one's own culture.

evoked culture The notion that all people, regardless of where they are from, have certain biologically encoded behavioral repertoires that are potentially accessible to them, and that these repertoires are engaged when the appropriate situational conditions arise.

evolutionism A perspective that maintains that cultural differences in ways of thinking reflect advancing stages of development.

existential universal The third level of universality, which states that a given cognitive tool exists across cultures, although the tool is not necessarily used to solve the same problems across cultures, nor is it equally accessible across cultures.

external attribution Interpreting the cause of an action as something outside of oneself.

extraversion A personality trait that indicates how active or dominant an individual is; part of the *Five Factor Model of Personality*.

extremity bias When answering questions that require choosing a response from a scale (e.g. from 1 [Strongly Disagree] to 7 [Strongly Agree]), the tendency to choose a response near the endpoints of the scale.

face The amount of social value others give an individual if they live up to the standards associated with their position.

facial feedback hypothesis The notion that facial expressions influence emotional experience.

fecundity The ability to produce many copies of themselves that is an important feature of successful replicators (e.g., genes or *memes*).

fidelity The high level of accuracy in self-replicating or reproducing that is an important feature of successful replicators (e.g., genes or *memes*).

field dependence The tendency to view objects as bound to their backgrounds.

field independence The tendency to separate objects from their backgrounds.

frame-switching The tendency for bicultural people to switch between different cultural selves.

frigophobia A morbid fear of catching a cold, which leads people to dress themselves in heavy coats and scarves even in summer.

functional universal The second level of universality, which states that a given cognitive tool exists across cultures and is used to solve the same problem across cultures, but is more accessible to people from some cultures than others.

fundamental attribution error A tendency to ignore situational information while focusing on dispositional information when making judgments about people's behaviors.

Gemeinschaft A type of group that emphasizes interpersonal relationships as core parts of individuals' identities and views such relationships as ends in themselves.

generalizability The degree to which research findings about the particular samples studied can be applied to larger or broader populations.

Gesellschaft A type of group that emphasizes individual members' autonomy and views relationships as instrumental and as means to other ends.

heritage culture A culture identified as a person's culture of origin.

high context culture Cultures in which there is much consensual information shared among individuals, so that much can be understood without it needing to be explicitly stated.

holistic thinking A type of thinking characterized by an orientation to the context as a whole.

host culture A culture identified as the new culture when people move from one culture to another.

imitative learning A type of social learning in which the learner internalizes aspects of the model's goals and behavioral strategies.

immigrants People who move to a new culture and intend to stay permanently.

incest avoidance A moral principle that post-pubescent family members of the opposite sex should not sleep in the same room together.

incremental theory of self A view of the self in which a person's abilities and traits are malleable and can be improved.

incremental theory of the world A view of the world as flexible and responsive to an individual's efforts to change it.

independent variable In an experiment, the variable or condition that the experimenter manipulates in order to examine its effect on the *dependent variable*.

independent view of self A model of the self in which identity is thought to come from inner attributes that reflect a unique essence of the individual and that remain stable across situations and across the lifespan.

individualistic A term for cultures with many practices and customs encouraging individuals to prioritize their own personal goals ahead of collective goals and to emphasize the ways in which they are distinct from others.

ingroup Those individuals with whom one has particularly close and significant relationships.

integration strategy An acculturation strategy that involves attempts to fit in and fully participate in the *host culture* while at the same time striving to maintain the traditions of one's *heritage culture*.

interdependent view of self A model of the self in which individuals are perceived not as separate and distinct entities but as participants in a larger social unit where identity is contingent upon key relationships with *ingroup* members.

James-Lange theory of emotions A theory that maintains that emotions are primarily perceptions of physiological responses to stimuli.

latah A condition in which an individual falls into a transient dissociated state in which he or she exhibits unusual behavior after some kind of startling event.

learned helplessness The feeling of being unable to control or avoid unpleasant events, which causes stress and potentially depression.

linguistic relativity The extent to which the ways people think are influenced by the words they use.

longevity The relative stability and long duration that is an important feature of successful replicators (e.g., genes or *memes*).

low context culture Cultures in which there is relatively less consensual information shared among individuals, so that people need to rely heavily on explicit communication.

malgri A syndrome of territorial anxiety in which an individual grows physically sick, tired, and drowsy when entering the sea or a new territory without engaging in the appropriate ceremonial procedures.

marginalization strategy An acculturation strategy that involves little or no effort to participate in the *host culture* or to maintain the traditions of the *heritage culture*.

market price A type of relational structure concerned with proportionality and ratios; members of a party calculate the ratios of the goods that are exchanged so that the transaction will be equivalent in value for both parties

memes The smallest unites of cultural information that can be faithfully transmitted.

mere exposure effect An effect which states that the more people are exposed to a stimulus the more they are attracted to it.

meritocracy A social system that rewards individuals based on their own contributions, according to the *principle of equity*.

methodological equivalence In cross-cultural research, the concern with makings sure participants from different cultures understand the research questions or situations in equivalent ways.

migrants People who move from a *heritage culture* (their original culture) to a *host culture* (their new culture) including those who intend to stay temporarily and those who intend to move permanently.

minimally counterintuitive ideas Ideas that violate our expectations enough to be considered surprising and unusual but not too outlandish.

moderacy bias When answering questions that require choosing a response from a scale (e.g. from 1 [Strongly Disagree] to 7 [Strongly Agree]), the tendency to choose a response near the midpoint of the scale.

naïve dialecticism A perspective in which events and objects in the world are perceived as interconnected and fluid. Such a view leads to the acceptance of contradictions between two opposing beliefs.

natural selection The evolutionary process that occurs when 3 particular conditions are present: (1) individual members of a species vary on certain traits; (2) those varying traits are associated with different survival rates; and (3) those traits have a hereditary basis.

need for cognitive closure (NCC) A desire to have a definite answer to a question.

neocortex ratio The ratio of the volume of the neocortex to the volume of the rest of the brain, which is used as a proxy measure of intelligence.

neurasthenia A psychiatric condition characterized as a nervous syndrome consisting of over 50 symptoms including poor appetite, headaches, insomnia, weakness in the back, hysteria, and an inability to concentrate.

neuroticism A personality trait that indicates how emotionally unstable and unpredictable individual is; part of the *Five Factor Model of Personality*.

nonuniversal The fourth, and lowest, level of universality, which states that a given cognitive tool does not exist in all cultures and can be considered a cultural invention.

noun bias The tendency in young children to have a vocabulary with more nouns relative to the number of verbs and other relational words.

objective self-awareness A state of mind in which individuals consider how they appear to others and are conscious of being evaluated.

Occam's razor The principle that any theory should make as few assumptions as possible; maintains that, all else held equal, the simpler theory is more likely to be correct.

openness to experience A personality trait that reflects a person's intelligence and curiosity about the world; part of the *Five Factor Model of Personality*.

orthodox A term describing religious adherents committed to the idea of a transcendent authority that operates independently of people and is more knowledgeable and powerful than all of human experience.

outgroup Those individuals with whom one has only a weak relationship or no relationship.

pluralistic ignorance The tendency for people to collectively misinterpret the thoughts that underlie other people's behaviors.

power The capability of a study to accurately detect an effect (e.g. a cross-cultural difference) to the extent that one exists; a reflection of how well-designed a study is.

predestination A belief about the afterlife holding that prior to birth, it has already been determined whether one is among the "elect," who will spend eternity in heaven, or among those who will burn in hell forever.

prevention orientation A concern with corecting one's weaknesses and avoiding others' negative judgments.

primary control The control experienced when people strive to shape existing realities to fit their perceptions.

principle of equality The principle that resources should be shared equally among the members of a group.

principle of equity The principle that resources should be distributed based on an individual's contributions.

principle of need The principle that resources should be directed toward those who need them the most.

progressive A term describing religious adherents who emphasize the importance of human agency in understanding and formulating a moral code.

promotion orientation A concern with advancing oneself and aspiring for gains.

propinquity effect An effect which states that people are more likely to befriend people they interact with frequently.

protection of the vulnerable A moral principle that young children who are needy and vulnerable should not be left alone at night.

proximal causes Causes that have direct and immediate relations with their effects.

psychologization When symptoms of an illness are primarily experienced psychologically rather than physically.

ratchet effect The process by which cultural information becomes more complex and often more useful over time because an initial idea can be learned from others and then modified and improved by the learners.

reference-group effect A tendency for people to evaluate themselves by comparing themselves with others from their own culture.

relativism A perspective that maintains that cultural diversity in ways of thinking reflects genuinely different psychological processes and that culture and thought are mutually constituted.

respect for hierarchy A moral principle that post-pubescent boys are conferred social status by allowing them to not have to sleep with parents or young children.

ritualized displays Facial expressions that are expressed in some cultures but not in others as a function of cultural display rules.

Russian cultural-historical school A school of thought which argued that people interact with their environment through the "tools" or human-made ideas that have been passed down to them through history.

saccades Type of eye movement in which the gaze shifts quickly from one fixation point to another.

sacred couple A moral principle that married couples should be given their own sleeping space for emotional intimacy and sexual privacy.

secondary control The control experienced when people attempt to align themselves with existing realities, leaving their circumstances unchanged but exerting control over the circumstances' psychological impact.

secularization theory A view that religion is on the decline, and that people around the world are turning to secular and rational ways of understanding their lives.

secure attachment An attachment style in which an infant seeks his or her mother's presence when she is around, and the infant's desire to be close to her intensifies after being left alone in an unfamiliar situation.

self-enhancement The motivation to view oneself positively.

self-improvement The process of seeking out one's potential weaknesses and working on correcting them.

self-serving bias A tendency for people to view themselves in unrealistically positive terms.

seniority system A system that rewards individuals based on older age or a longer time spent with a company.

sensitive period A period of time in an organism's development that allows for the relatively easy acquisition of a particular set of skills.

separation strategy An acculturation strategy that involves efforts to maintain the traditions of the heritage culture while making little or no effort to participate in the host culture.

sexual selection The evolutionary process whereby individuals best suited to attract the healthiest mate will be the most likely to have surviving offspring.

similarity-attraction effect An effect which states that people tend to be attracted to those who are most like themselves.

situational attributions Explaining people's behavior in terms of contextual variables

social anxiety disorder A fear that one is in danger of acting in an inept and unacceptable manner, and that such behavior will bring disastrous social consequences.

social brain hypothesis The theory that cognitive demands inherent in social living led to the evolution of large primate brains.

social facilitation A tendency to perform a well-rehearsed and practiced skill better in the presence of others and to perform poorly learned tasks worse; both performance changes are attributed to the increased physiological arousal caused by the observers.

social loafing A tendency for members of a group to work less hard on a collective task when it is unclear how much each individual is contributing to the outcome.

social striving A tendency for people who especially care about their relations within the particular group to work better when they are being evaluated as a group rather than as individuals.

sojourners People who move to a new culture and intend to stay there only temporarily.

somatization When symptoms of an illness are primarily experienced physically rather than psychologically

stereotype threat The fear that one might act in a way that will inadvertently confirm a negative stereotype about one's group.

subjective self-awareness A state of mind in which individuals consider themselves from the perspective of the subject and demonstrate little awareness of themselves as individuals.

subjective well-being The feeling of how satisfied one is with one's life.

susto A condition in which an individual feels that a frightening experience has dislodged the soul from his or her body, leading to a wide range of physical and psychological symptoms.

taijin kyoufushou (TKS) A disorder similar to *social anxiety disorder* in that it involves fear elicited by social situations, but it is also characterized by physical symptoms including extensive blushing, body odor, sweating, and a penetrating gaze.

theory of mind A human ability to understand that others have minds that are different from one's own, and thus that other people have their own distinct perspectives and intentions.

transmitted culture The notion that people learn about particular cultural practices through social learning or by modeling the behavior of others who live near them.

two-factor theory of emotions A theory that maintains that emotions are primarily our interpretations of physiological responses to stimuli.

universalism A perspective that views people from different cultures as largely the same and maintains that any observed cultural variability exists only at a superficial level.

unpackaging Identifying the underlying variables that give rise to different cultural differences.

upward social comparison An individual's comparison of his or her performance with someone who is doing better.

voodoo death A condition in which an individual is convinced that he or she has been cursed or has broken a taboo, which results severe fear that sometimes leads to death.

within-groups A type of experimental manipulation in which each participant receives more than one level of the independent variable(s).

References

Abel, T. M., & Hsu, F. I. (1949). Some aspects of personality of Chinese as revealed by the Rorschach Test. *Journal of Projective Techniques, 13*, 285–301.

Abramson, L. Y., Seligman, M. E. P., & Teasdale, J. D. (1978). Learned helplessness in humans: Critique and reformulation. *Journal of Abnormal Psychology, 87*, 49–74.

Abraido-Lanza, A. F. Chao, M. T., & Florez, K. R. (2005). Do healthy behaviors decline with greater acculturation? Implications for the Latino mortality paradox. *Social Science and Medicine, 61*, 1243–1255.

Abraido-Lanza, A. F., Dohrenwend, B. P., Ng-Mak, D. S., & Turner, J. B. (1999). The Latino mortality paradox: A test of the "salmon bias" and healthy migrant hypotheses. *American Journal of Public Health, 89*, 1543–1548.

Abu-Lughod, L. (1986). *Veiled sentiments*. Berkeley, CA: University of California Press.

Adams, G. (2005). The cultural grounding of personal relationship: Enemyship in West African worlds. *Journal of Personality and Social Psychology, 88*, 948–968.

Adams, G., Anderson, S. L., & Adonu, J. K. (2004). The cultural grounding of closeness and intimacy. In D. Mashek & A. Aron (Eds.), *The handbook of closeness and intimacy* (pp. 321–339). Mahwah, NJ: Lawrence Erlbaum.

Adams, G., & Plaut, V. C. (2003). The cultural grounding of personal relationship: Friendship in North American and West African worlds. *Personal Relationships, 10*, 333–348.

Adler, N. E., Epel, E. S., Castellazzo, G., & Ickovics, J. R. (2000). Relationship of subjective and objective social status with psychological and physiological functioning: Preliminary data in healthy, White women. *Health Psychology, 19*, 586–592.

Agiobu-Kemmer, I. (1984). Cognitive aspects of infant development. In H. V. Curran (Ed.), *Nigerian children: Developmental perspectives* (pp. 74–117). London: Routledge Kegan Paul.

Aiello, L. C., & Wheeler, P. (1995). The expensive-tissue hypothesis: The brain and the digestive system in human and primate evolution. *Current Anthropology, 36*, 199–221.

Ainsworth, M. D. S., Blehar, M. C., Waters, E., & Wall, S. (1978). *Patterns of attachment: A psychological study of the strange situation*. Hillsdale, NJ: Erlbaum.

Akhtar, S. (1988). Four culture-bound psychiatric syndromes in India. *International Journal of Social Psychiatry, 34*, 70–74.

Akinkugbe, O. O. (1985). World epidemiology of hypertension in blacks. In W. Hall, E. Saunders, & N. Shulman (Eds.), *Hypertension in blacks: Epidemiology, pathophysiology, and treatment* (pp. 3–15). Chicago: Year Book.

Allan, G. A. (1979). *A sociology of friendship and kinship*. London: Allen & Unwin.

Allik, J., & McCrae, R. R. (2004). Toward a geography of personality traits: Patterns of profiles across 36 cultures. *Journal of Cross-Cultural Psychology, 35*, 13–28.

Allison, A. C. (1954). The distribution of the sickle-cell trait in East Africa and elsewhere, and its apparent relationship to the incidence of subtertian malaria. *Transactions of the Royal Society of Tropical Medicine and Hygiene, 48*, 312–318.

Allport, G. W., & Odbert, H. S. (1936). Trait-names: A psycho-lexical study. *Psychological Monographs: General and Applied, 47*, 171–220. (1, Whole No. 211).

Allport, G. W., & Postman, L. J. (1947). *The psychology of rumor*. New York: Holt, Rinehart & Winston.

Altrocchi, J., & Altrocchi, L. (1995). Polyfaceted psychological acculturation in Cook Islanders, *Journal of Cross-Cultural Psychology, 26,* 426–440.

American Psychiatric Association (APA). (1994). *Diagnostic and statistical manual of mental disorders (4th ed.).* Author.

Anderson, C. A. (1989). Temperature and aggression: Ubiquitous effects of heat on occurrence of human violence. *Psychological Bulletin, 106,* 74–96.

Anderson, E. (1999). *Code of the street: Decency, violence, and the moral life of the inner city.* New York: W. W. Norton.

Anderson, J. C., & Linden, W. (2006, April). *The influence of culture on cardiovascular response to anger.* Citation poster session presented at the annual meeting of the American Psychosomatic Society, Denver, CO.

Anderson, R., Lewis, S. Z., Giachello, A. L., Aday, L. A., & Chiu, G. (1981). Access to medical care among the Hispanic population of the Southwestern United States, *Journal of Health and Social Behavior, 22,* 78–89.

Angel, R., & Thoits, P. (1987). The impact of culture on the cognitive structure of illness. *Culture, Medicine, and Psychiatry, 11,* 465–494.

Arendt, H. (1964). *Eichmann in Jerusalem.* New York: Penguin Books.

Argyle, M., Shimoda, K., & Little, B. (1978). Variance due to persons and situations in England and Japan. *British Journal of Social and Clinical Psychology, 17,* 335–337.

Armes, K., & Ward, C. (1989). Cross-cultural transitions and sojourner adjustment in Singapore. *Journal of Social Psychology, 12,* 273–275.

Aron-Brunetiere, R. (1974). *La Beaute et la medecine.* Paris: Stock.

Asch, S. (1956). Studies of independence and conformity: A minority of one against a unanimous majority. *Psychological Monographs, 70,* (Whole No. 416).

Asch, S. (1962). *Social psychology.* New York: Prentice-Hall.

Asch, S. E. (1959). A perspective on social psychology. In S. Koch (Ed.), *Psychology: A study of a science. Vol. 3.* New York: McGraw-Hill.

Atran, S., Medin, C., Lynch, E., Vapnarsky, V., Ucan Ek', E., & Sousa, P. (2001). Folkbiology doesn't come from folkpsychology: Evidence from Yukatek Maya in cross-cultural perspective. *Journal of Cognition and Culture, 1,* 1–40.

Atran, S., & Norenzayan, A. (2004). Religion's evolutionary landscape: Counterintuition, commitment, compassion, communion. *Behavioral and Brain Sciences, 27,* 713–770.

Averill, J. R. (1985). The social construction of emotion: With special reference to love. In K. J. Gergen & K. E. Davis (Eds.), *The social construction of the person* (pp. 89–109). New York: Springer-Verlag.

Avis, J., & Harris, P. L. (1991). Belief-desire reasoning among Baka children: Evidence for a universal conception of mind. *Child Development, 62,* 460–467.

Azuma, H. (1986). Why study child development in Japan? In H. Stevenson, H. Azuma, & K. Hakuta (Eds.), *Child development and education in Japan* (pp. 3–12). New York: Freeman.

Babiker, I. E., Cox, J. L., & Miller, P. M. C. (1980). The measurement of culture distance and its relationship to medical consultation, symptomatology and examination performance of overseas students at Edinburgh University, *Social Psychiatry, 15,* 109–116.

Bachman, J. G., & O'Malley, P. M. (1984). Black-White differences in self-esteem: Are they affected by response styles? *American Journal of Sociology, 90,* 624–639.

Bachnik, J. M. (1992). The two "faces" of self and society in Japan. *Ethos, 20,* 3–32.

Bagozzi, R., Wong, N., & Yi, Y. (1999). The role of culture and gender in the relationship between positive and negative affect. *Cognition and Emotion, 13,* 641–672.

Baillargeon, R., & DeVos, J. (1991). Object permanence in young infants: Further evidence. *Child Development, 62,* 1227–1246.

Bakan, D. (1966). *The duality of human existence.* Chicago: Rand McNally.

Baltzell, E. D. (1979). *Puritan Boston and Quaker Philadelphia.* New York: Free Press.

Barber, B. R. (1995). *Jihad vs. McWorld: Terrorism's challenge to democracy.* New York: Ballantine Books.

Bargh, J. A., Chen, M., & Burrows, L. (1996). Automaticity of social behavior: Direct effects of trait construct and stereotype activation on action. *Journal of Personality and Social Psychology, 71,* 230–244.

Barrett, L. F. (2006). Solving the emotion paradox: Categorization and the experience of emotion. *Personality and Social Psychology Review, 10,* 20–46.

Barrett, J. L., & Nyhof, M. A. (2001). Spreading non-natural concepts: The role of intuitive conceptual structures in memory and transmission of cultural materials. *Journal of Cognition and Culture, 1,* 69–100.

Barrett, L. F., & Russell, J. A. (1999). Structure of current affect. *Current Directions in Psychological Science, 8,* 10–14.

Bates, M. S., Edwards, W. T., & Anderson, K. O. (1993). Ethnocultural influences on variation in chronic pain perception. *Pain, 52,* 101–112.

Baumeister, R. F. (1987). How the self became a problem: A psychological review of historical research. *Journal of Personality and Social Psychology, 52,* 163–176.

Baumeister, R. F., & Jones, E. E. (1978). When self-presentation is constrained by the target's knowledge: Consistency and compensation. *Journal of Personality and Social Psychology, 36,* 608–618.

Beard, G. M. (1869). *American Nervousness.* New York: Putnam's.

Beja-Pereira, A., et al. (2003). Gene-culture coevolution between cattle milk protein genes and human lactase genes. *Nature Genetics, 35,* 311–313.

Bell, R. M. (1985). *Holy anorexia.* Chicago: University of Chicago Press.

Bemporad, J. R. (1996). Self-starvation through the ages: Reflections on the pre-history of anorexia nervosa. *International Journal of Eating Disorders, 19,* 217–237.

Bendix, R. (1977). *Max Weber: An intellectual portrait.* Berkeley, CA: University of California Press.

Benedict, R. (1934). *Patterns of culture.* New York: Houghton Mifflin.

Benet-Martinez, V., Leu, J., Lee, F., & Morris, M. W. (2002). Negotiating biculturalism: Cultural frame switching in biculturals with oppositional versus compatible cultural identities. *Journal of Cross-Cultural Psychology, 33,* 492–516.

Benet-Martinez, V., & Waller, N. G. (1995). The Big Seven factor model of personality description: Evidence for its cross-cultural generality in a Spanish sample. *Journal of Personality and Social Psychology, 69,* 701–718.

Benet-Martinez, V., & Waller, N. G. (1997). Further evidence for the cross-cultural generality of the Big Seven factor model: Indigenous and Imported Spanish personality constructs. *Journal of Personality, 65,* 567–598.

Berger, P. L. (1999). *The desecularization of the world: Resurgent religion and world politics.* Grand Rapids MI: Eerdmans Berry, J., & Dasen, P. (1974). *Culture and cognition.* London: Methuen.

Berkman, L. F., & Breslow, L. (1983). *Health and ways of living.* Oxford, UK: Oxford University Press.

Berlin, B., & Kay, P. (1969). *Basic color terms: Their universality and evolution.* Berkeley, CA: University of California Press.

Berry, J. W. (1997). Immigration, acculturation, and adaptation. *Applied psychology: An international review, 46,* 5–68.

Berry, J. W., & Annis, R. C. (1974). Acculturation stress: The role of ecology, culture, and differentiation. *Journal of Cross-Cultural Psychology, 5,* 382–406.

Berry, J. W., & Kim, U. (1988). Acculturation and mental health. In P. Dasen, J. W. Berry, & N. Sartorius (Eds.), *Cross-cultural psychology and health: Towards applications* (pp. 207–236). London: Sage.

Berry, J. W., Kim, U., Power, S., Young, M., & Bujaki, M. (1989). Acculturation attitudes in plural societies. *Applied psychology: An international review, 38,* 185–206.

Berry, J. W., & Sam, D. (1997). Acculturation and adaptation. In J. W. Berry, M. H. Segall, & C. Kagitcibasi (Eds.), *Handbook of cross-cultural psychology* (Vol. 3, pp. 291–326). Boston: Allyn & Bacon.

Best, J., & Horiuchi, G. T. (1985). The razor blade in the apple: The social construction of urban legends. *Social Problems, 32,* 488–499.

Biernat, M., & Manis, M. (1994). Shifting standards and stereotype-based judgments. *Journal of Personality and Social Psychology, 66,* 5–20.

Bilger, B. (2004, April 5). The height gap: Why Europeans are getting taller and taller—and Americans aren't. *New Yorker,* pp. 38–45.

Biswas-Diener, R., & Diener, E. (2002). Making the best of a bad situation: Satisfaction in the slums of Calcutta. *Social Indicators Research, 55,* 329–352.

Blackmore, S. (1999). *The meme machine.* Oxford: Oxford University Press.

Blascovich, J., Spencer, S. J., Quinn, D., & Steele, C. M. (2001). African Americans and high blood pressure: The role of stereotype threat. *Psychological Science, 12,* 225–229.

Block, J. (1995). A contrarian view of the five-factor approach to personality description. *Psychological Bulletin, 117,* 187–215.

Blood, R. O. (1967). *Love match and arranged marriage.* New York: Free Press.

Bochner, S. (1994). Cross-cultural differences in the self-concept: A test of Hofstede's Individualism/Collectivism distinction. *Journal of Cross-Cultural Psychology, 25*, 273–283.

Bond, M. H. (1983). How language variation affects inter-cultural differentiation of values by Hong Kong bilinguals. *Journal of Language and Social Psychology, 2*, 57–76.

Bond, M. H. (1988). Finding universal dimensions of individual variation in multicultural studies of values: The Rokeach and Chinese value surveys. *Journal of Personality and Social Psychology, 55*, 1009–1015.

Bond, M. H., & Cheung, T. (1983). College students' spontaneous self-concept. *Journal of Cross-Cultural Psychology, 14*, 153–171.

Bond, M. H., & Tornatzky, L. G. (1973). Locus of control in students from Japan and the United States: Dimensions and levels of response. *Psychologia, 16*, 209–213.

Bond, R., & Smith, P. B. (1996). Culture and conformity: A meta-analysis of studies using Asch's (1952b, 1956) line judgment task. *Psychological Bulletin, 119*, 111–137.

Bornstein, M. H., & Korda, N. O. (1984). Discrimination and matching within and between hues measured by reaction times: Some implications for categorical perception and levels of information processing. *Psychological Research, 46*, 207–222.

Bornstein, M. H., Tamis-Lemonda, C., Tal, J., Ludemann, P., Toda, S., Rahn, C., Pecheux, M., Azuma, H., & Tamis-Lamonda, C. (1992). Functional analysis of the contents of maternal speech to infants of 5 and 13 months in four cultures: Argentina, France, Japan and the United States. *Developmental Psychology, 28*, 593–603.

Boroditsky, L. (2000). Metaphoric structuring: Understanding time through spatial metaphors. *Cognition, 75*, 1–28.

Boroditsky, L. & Gaby, A. (2006) East of Tuesday: Consequences of spatial orientation for thinking about time. In R. Sun (Ed.), *Proceedings of the 28th annual meeting of the cognitive science society*, p. 2657. Hillsdale, NJ: Lawrence Erlbaum.

Boucher, J. D., & Brandt, M. E. (1981). Judgment of emotion: American and Malay antecedents. *Journal of Cross-Cultural Psychology, 12*, 272–283.

Bowlby, J. (1969). *Attachment and loss: Vol. 1. Attachment.* New York: Basic Books.

Boyer, P., & Ramble, C. (2001). Cognitive templates for religious concepts: Cross-cultural evidence for recall of counter-intuitive representations. *Cognitive Science, 25*, 535–564.

Brehm, J. (1956). Postdecision changes in the desirability of alternatives. *Journal of Abnormal and Social Psychology, 52*, 384–389.

Briggs, J. L. (1970). *Never in anger: Portrait of an Eskimo family.* Cambridge, MA: Harvard University Press.

Brislin, R. W. (1970). Back-translation for cross-cultural research. *Journal of Cross-Cultural Psychology, 1*, 185–216.

Brody, J. (1982, July 14). Personal health. *New York Times.*

Brosschot, J. F., & Thayer, J. F. (1998). Anger inhibition, cardiovascular recovery, and vagal function: A model of the link between hostility and cardiovascular disease. *Annals of Behavior Medicine, 20*, 326–332.

Broude, G. J., & Green, S. J. (1983). Cross-cultural codes on husband-wife relationships. *Ethology, 22*, 273–274.

Brown, D. E. (1991) *Human Universals.* Philadelphia: Temple University Press.

Brown, J. D., & Kobayashi, C. (2002). Self-enhancement in Japan and America. *Asian Journal of Social Psychology, 5*, 145–168.

Bruner, J. (1990). *Acts of meaning.* Cambridge, MA: Harvard University Press.

Budaev, S. V. (1997). "Personality" in the guppy (Poecilia reticulata): A correlational study of exploratory behavior and social tendency. *Journal of Comparative Psychology, 111*, 399–411.

Bugental, D. B., & Cortez, V. L. (1988). Physiological reactivity to responsive and unresponsive children as moderated by perceived control. *Child Development, 59*, 686–693.

Bunker, J. P., & Gomby, D. S. (1989). Preface: Socioeconomic status and health: An examination of underlying processes. In J. P. Bunker, D. S. Gomby, & B. H. Kerner (Eds.), *Pathways to health.* Menlo Park, CA: The Henry J. Kaiser Family Foundation.

Burton, R., & Whiting, J. (1961). The absent father and cross-sex identity. *Merrill-Palmer Quarterly, 7*, 85–95.

Bushnell, J. A., Wells, J. E., Hornblow, A. R., Oakley-Browne, M. A., & Joyce, P. (1990). Prevalence of three bulimia syndromes in the general population. *Psychological Medicine, 20*, 671–680.

Buss, D. M. (1989). Sex differences in human mate preferences: Evolutionary hypotheses tested in 37 cultures. *Behavioral and Brain Sciences, 12*, 1–49.

Butler, J. C. (2000). Personality and emotional correlates of right-wing authoritarianism. *Social Behavior and Personality, 28,* 1–14.

Byrne, D. (1961). Interpersonal attraction and attitude similarity. *Journal of Abnormal and Social Psychology, 62,* 713–715.

Byrne, D., Clore, G. L., & Worchel, P. (1966). Effect of economic similarity-dissimilarity on interpersonal attraction. *Journal of Personality and Social Psychology, 4,* 220–224.

Cacioppo, J. T., Berntson, G. G., Larsen, H. T., Poehlmann, K. M., & Ito, T. A. (2000). The psychophysiology of emotion. In R. Lewis & J. M. Haviland-Jones (Eds.), *The handbook of emotion* (2nd ed., pp. 173–191). New York: Guilford.

Callaghan, T., Rochat, P., Lillard, A., Claux, M. L., Odden, H., Itakura, S., Tapanya, S., & Singh, S. (2005). Synchrony in the onset of mental-state reasoning: Evidence from five cultures. *Psychological Science, 16,* 378–384.

Cameron, J. E., & Lalonde, R. N. (1994). Self, ethnicity, and social group memberships in two generations of Italian Canadians. *Personality and Social Psychology Bulletin, 20,* 514–520.

Campbell, J. D., Trapnell, P., Heine, S. J., Katz, I. M., Lavallee, L. F., & Lehman, D. R. (1996). Self-concept clarity: Measurement, personality correlates, and cultural boundaries. *Journal of Personality and Social Psychology, 70,* 141–156.

Campos, J. J., Barrett, K. C., Lamb, M. E., Goldsmith, H. H., & Stenberg, C. (1983). Socioemotional development. In M. M. Haith & J. J. Campos (Eds.), *Handbook of child psychology: Vol. 2. Infancy and psychobiology* (pp. 783–915). New York: Wiley.

Cannon, T. D. (1998). Genetic and perinatal influences in the etiology of schizophrenia: A neurodevelop-mental model. In M. F. Lenzenweger & R. H. Dworkin (Eds.), *Origins and development of schizophrenia: Advances in experimental psychopathology,* pp. 67–92. Washington, DC: American Psychological Association.

Cannon, T. D., van Erp, T. G. M., Huttunen, M., Lönnqvist, J., Salonen, O., Valanne, L., Poutanen, V., Standertskjöld-Nordenstam, C., Gur, R. E., & Yan, M. (1998). Regional grey matter, white matter, and cerebrospinal fluid distributions in schizophrenic patients, their siblings, and controls. *Archives of General Psychiatry, 55,* 1084–1091.

Carey, S. (1985). *Conceptual change in childhood.* Cambridge, MA: Bradford Books.

Carey, S. (1995). On the origin of causal understanding. In D. Sperber, D. Premack, & A. Premack (Eds.), *Causal cognition.* Oxford: Clarendon Press.

Carey, S. (2004, Winter). Bootstrapping and the origins of concepts. *Daedalus.*

Carlyle, T. (1843). *Past and present.*

Carnegie, D. (1936). *How to win friends and influence people.* New York: Simon & Schuster.

Carr, J. E. (1978). Ethno-behaviorism and the culture-bound syndromes: The case of amok. *Culture, Medicine, and Psychiatry, 2,* 269–293.

Carroll, J. M., & Russell, J. A. (1997). Facial expressions in Hollywood's protrayal of emotion. *Journal of Personality and Social Psychology, 72,* 164–176.

Cassidy, C. M. (1991). The good body: When big is better. *Medical Anthropology, 13,* 181–213.

Cavalli-Sforza, L. L., & Cavalli-Sforza, F. (1995). *The great human diasporas: The history of diversity and evolution.* Reading, MA: Perseus Books.

Cavalli-Sforza, L. L., & Feldman, M. W. (1981). *Cultural transmission and evolution.* Princeton, NJ: Princeton University Press.

Cavalli-Sforza, L. L., Menozzi, P., & Piazza, A. (1994). *The history and geography of human genes.* Princeton, NJ: Princeton University Press.

Caudill, W., & Weinstein, H. (1969). Maternal care and infant behavior in Japan and America. *Psychiatry, 32,* 12–43.

Caudill, W. A., & Schooler, C. (1973). Child behavior and child rearing in Japan and the United States: An interim report. *Journal of Nervous and Mental Disease, 157,* 323–338.

Cawte, J. E. (1976). Malgri: A culture-bound syndrome. In W. P. Lebra (Ed.), *Culture-bound syndromes, ethnopsychiatry, and alternate therapies* (pp. 22–31). Honolulu: University Press of Hawaii.

Central Intelligence Agency. (2006, October 5a). *CIA world factbook rank order—GDP per capita.* Retrieved October 10, 2006, from https://www.cia.gov/cia/publications/factbook/rankorder/2004rank.html

Central Intelligence Agency. (2006, October 5b). *CIA world factbook rank order—life expectancy at birth.* Retrieved October 10, 2006, from https://www.cia.gov/cia/publications/factbook/rankorder/2102rank.html

Chandler, M., Lalonde, C., Sokol, B., & Hallett, D. (2003). Personal persistence, identity development and suicide. *Monographs of the Society for Research in Child Development, 68,* 1–129.

Chandra, S. (1973). The effects of group pressure in perception: A cross-cultural conformity study. *International Journal of Psychology, 8,* 37–39.

Chang, W. C. (1985). A cross-cultural study of depressive symptomatology. *Culture, Medicine, and Psychiatry, 9,* 295–317.

Chang, W. C., Chua, W. L., & Toh, Y. (1997). The concept of psychological control in the Asian context. In K. Leung, U. Kim, S. Yamaguchi, & Y. Kashima (Eds.), *Progress in Asian social psychology* (pp. 95–117). Singapore: Wiley.

Chang, Y. H., Rin, H., & Chen, C. C. (1975). Frigophobia: A report of five cases. *Bulletin of the Chinese Society of Neurology and Psychiatry, 1*(2), 9–13. (in Chinese).

Chartrand, T. L., & Bargh, J. A. (1999). The chameleon effect: The perception-behavior link and social interaction. *Journal of Personality and Social Psychology, 76,* 893–910.

Chase-Lansale, L. P., & Gordon, R. A. (1996). Economic hardship and the development of five- and six-year-olds: Neighborhood and regional perspectives. *Child Development, 67,* 338–367.

Chee, M. W., Caplan, D., Soon, C. S., Sriram, N., Tan, E. W. L., Tiel, T., & Weekes, B. (1999). Processing of visually presented sequences in Mandarin and English studies with fMRI. *Neuron, 23,* 127–137.

Chen, C., Lee, S.-Y., & Stevenson, H. W. (1995). Response style and cross-cultural comparisons of rating scales among East Asian and North American students. *Psychological Science, 6,* 170–175.

Chen, E. (2004). Why socioeconomic status affects the health of children: A psychosocial perspective. *Current Directions in Psychological Science, 13,* 112–115.

Chen, E. (in press). The impact of socioeconomic status on physiological health: An experimental manipulation of psychosocial factors. *Psychosomatic Medicine.*

Cheney, D. L., & Seyfarth, R. M. (1990). *How monkeys see the world.* Chicago, University of Chicago Press.

Chernoff, H. (1973). Using faces to represent points in k-dimensional space graphically. *Journal of the American Statistical Association, 68,* 361–368.

Cheung, F. M., Cheung, S. F., Leung, K., Ward, C., & Leong, F. (2003). The English version of the Chinese Personality Assessment Inventory. *Journal of Cross-Cultural Psychology, 34,* 433–452.

Cheung, F. M., Leung, K., Fan, R. M., Song, W., Zhang, J., & Zhang, J. (1996). Development of the Chinese Personality Assessment Inventory. *Journal of Cross-Cultural Psychology, 27,* 181–199.

Chiu, C., Dweck, C. S., Tong, J. U., & Fu, J. H. (1997). Implicit theories and conceptions of morality. *Journal of Personality and Social Psychology, 73,* 923–940.

Chiu, L. H. (1972). A cross-cultural comparison of cognitive styles in Chinese and American children. *International Journal of Psychology, 7,* 235–242.

Choi, D., Norenzayan, A., Hansen, I., Chen, J., & Hengl, S. (2002). *Overcoming the reference-group effect in measuring cultural values: Testing revisions of the Singelis (1994) Self-Construal Scale.* Poster presented at the 10th Ontario Symposium on Culture and Social Behavior. London, ON. June, 2002.

Choi, I., & Choi, Y. (2002). Culture and self-concept flexibility. *Personality and Social Psychology Bulletin, 28,* 1508–1517.

Choi, I., Dalal, R., Kim-Prieto, C., & Park. H. (2003). Culture and judgement of causal relevance. *Journal of Personality and Social Psychology, 84,* 46–59.

Choi, I., & Nisbett, R. E. (1998). Situational salience and cultural differences in the correspondence bias and in the actor-observer bias. *Personality and Social Psychology Bulletin, 24,* 949–960.

Choi, S., & Gopnik, A. (1995). Early acquisition of verbs in Korean: A cross-linguistic study. *Journal of Child Language, 22,* 497–529.

Chomsky, N. (1965). *Aspects of the theory of syntax.* Cambridge, MA: MIT Press.

Christenfeld, N., Glynn, L. M., Phillips, D. P., & Shrira, I. (1999). Exposure to New York City as a risk factor for heart attack mortality. *Psychosomatic Medicine, 61,* 740–743.

Chua, H. F., Boland, J. E., & Nisbett, R. E. (2005). Cultural variation in eye movements during scene perception. *Proceedings of the National Academy of Science, 102,* 12629–12633.

Church, A. T. (1982). Sojourner adjustment. *Psychological Bulletin, 91,* 540–572.

Church, A. T., Katigbak, M. S., & Reyes, J. A. S. (1998). Further exploration of Filipino personality structure using the lexical approach: Do the Big-Five or Big-Seven dimensions emerge? *European Journal of Personality, 12,* 249–269.

Church, A. T., Reyes, J. A. S., Katigbak, M. S., & Grimm, S. D. (1997). Filipino personality structure and the Big Five Model: A lexical approach. *Journal of Personality, 65,* 477–528.

Cialdini, R. B., Borden, R. J., Thorne, A., Walker, M. R., Freeman, S., & Sloan, L. R. (1976). Basking in reflected glory: Three (football) field studies. *Journal of Personality and Social Psychology, 34,* 366–375.

Cialdini, R. B., Wosinka, W., Barrett, D. W., Butner, J., & Gornik-Durose, M. (1999). Compliance with a request in two cultures. The differential influence of social proof and commitment/consistency on collectivists and individualists. *Personality and Social Psychology Bulletin, 25,* 1242–1253.

Clancy, P. M. (1986). The acquisition of communicative styles in Japanese. In B. B. Schieffelin & E. Ochs (Eds.), *Language socialization across cultures* (pp. 213–230). Cambridge, UK: Cambridge University Press.

Clark, D. M., & Wells, A. (1995). A cognitive model of social phobia. In R. G. Heimberg, M. Liebowitz, D. A. Hope, & F. Schneier (Eds.), *Social phobia: Diagnosis, assessment, and treatment* (pp. 69–93). New York: Guilford.

Clements, F. E. (1932). Primitive concepts of disease. *University of California Publications in American Archaeology and Ethnology, 32,* 185–253.

Clutton-Brock, T. H., & Harvey, P. H. (1980). Primates, brains and ecology. *Journal of Zoology (London), 190,* 309–323.

Cogan, J. C., Bhalla, S. K., Sefa-Dedeh, A., & Rothblum, E. D. (1996). A comparison study of United States and African students on perceptions of obesity and thinness. *Journal of Cross-Cultural Psychology, 27,* 98–113.

Cohen, A. B., & Rozin, P. (2001). Religion and the morality of mentality. *Journal of Personality and Social Psychology, 81,* 697–710.

Cohen, A. B., Siegel, J. I., & Rozin, P. (2003). Faith versus practice: Different bases for religiosity judgments by Jews and Protestants. *European Journal of Social Psychology, 33,* 287–295.

Cohen, D. (1996). Law, social policy, and violence: The impact of regional cultures. *Journal of Personality and Social Psychology, 70,* 961–978.

Cohen, D. (2001). Cultural variation: Considerations and implications. *Psychological Bulletin, 127,* 451–471.

Cohen, D. (in press). Four questions from a relatively young field. In S. Kitayama & D. Cohen (Eds.), *Handbook of Cultural Psychology.* New York: Guilford.

Cohen, D., & Gunz, A. (2002). As seen by the other. . . . The self from the "outside in" and the "inside out" in the memories and emotional perceptions of Easterners and Westerners. *Psychological Science, 13,* 55–59.

Cohen, D., & Hoshino-Browne, E. (2005). Insider and outsider perspectives on the self and social world. In R. M. Sorrentino, D. Cohen, J. M. Olson, and M. P. Zanna (Eds.), *Culture and Social Behavior: The Tenth Ontario Symposium.* (pp. 49–76). Hillsdale, NJ: Lawrence Erlbaum.

Cohen, D., & Nisbett, R. E. (1994). Self-protection and the culture of honor: Explaining southern homicide. *Personality and Social Psychology Bulletin, 20,* 551–567.

Cohen, D., & Nisbett, R. E. (1997). Field experiments examining the culture of honor: The role of institutions in perpetuating norms about violence. *Personality and Social Psychology Bulletin, 23,* 1188–1199.

Cohen, D., Nisbett, R. E., Bowdle, B. F., & Schwarz, N. (1996). Insult, aggression, and the Southern culture of honor: An "Experimental ethnography." *Journal of Personality and Social Psychology, 70,* 945–960.

Cohen, D., Vandello, J., Puente, S., & Rantilla, A. (1999). "When you call me that, smile!": How norms for politeness, interaction styles, and aggression work together in southern culture. *Social Psychology Quarterly, 62,* 257–275.

Cohen, G. L., Garcia, J., Apfel, N., & Master, A. (2006). Reducing the racial achievement gap: A social-psychological intervention. *Science, 313,* 1307–1310.

Cole, M. (1996). *Cultural psychology: A once and future discipline.* Cambridge: Belknap Press.

Cole, M., Gay, J., Glick, J. A., & Sharp, D. W. (1971). *The cultural context of learning and thinking.* New York: Basic Books.

Cole, M., & Scribner, M. (1974). *Culture and thought.* New York: Wiley.

Collard, M., Shennan, S., & Tehrani, J. J. (2005). Branching versus blending in macroscale cultural evolution: A comparative study. In C. P. Lipo, M. J. O'Brien, S. Shennan & M. Collard (Eds.), *Mapping our ancestors: Phylogenetic methods in anthropology and prehistory.* Hawthorne, NY: Aldine de Gruyter.

Cornell, S., & Hartmann, D. (1998). *Ethnicity and race: Making identities in a changing world.* Thousand Oaks, CA: Pine Forge Press.

Costa, P. T., Jr., & McCrae, R. R. (1992). *Revised NEO Personality Inventory (NEO-PI-R) and NEO*

Five-Factor Inventory (NEO-FFI) professional manual. Odessa, FL: Psychological Assessment Resources.

Cousins, S. D. (1989). Culture and selfhood in Japan and the U.S. *Journal of Personality and Social Psychology, 56,* 124–131.

Cousins, S. D. (1990). *Culture and social phobia in Japan and the United States.* Unpublished doctoral dissertation, University of Michigan.

Crespo, C. J., Ainsworth, B. E., Keteyian, S. J., Heath, G. W., & Smit, E. (1999). Prevalence of physical inactivity and its relation to social class in U.S. adults: Results from the Third National Health and Nutrition Examination Survey, 1988–1994. *Medicine and Science in Sports and Exercise. 31,* 1821.

Cross, P. (1977). Not can but will college teaching be improved. *New Directions for Higher Education, 17,* 1–15.

Cross, S. E. (1995). Self-construals, coping, and stress in cross-cultural adaptation. *Journal of Cross-Cultural Psychology, 26,* 673–697.

Csikszentmihalyi, M., & Hunter, J. (2003). Happiness in everyday life: The uses of experience sampling. *Journal of Happiness Studies, 4,* 185–199.

Cullum, J. G., & Harton, H. C. (in press). Cultural evolution: Importance and the development of shared attitudes in college residence halls. *Personality and Social Psychology Bulletin.*

Cunningham, M. R. (1986). Measuring the physical in physical attractiveness: Quasi-experiments on the sociobiology of female facial beauty. *Journal of Personality and Social Psychology, 50,* 925–935.

Cunningham, M. R., Barbee, A. P., & Pike, C. L. (1990). What do women want? Facialmetric assessment of multiple motives in the perception of male facial physical attractiveness. *Journal of Personality and Social Psychology, 59,* 61–72.

Custance, D., Whiten, A., & Fredman, T. (1999). Social learning of an artificial fruit task in capuchin monkeys (Cebus apella). *Journal of Comparative Psychology, 113,* 13–23.

Dar Nimrod, I., & Heine, S. J. (2006). Exposure to scientific theories affects women's math performance. *Science, 314,* 435.

Darwin, C. (1871). *The descent of man, and selection in relation to sex.* London: John Murray.

Darwin, C. (1872/1965). *The expression of emotions in man and animals.* Chicago: University of Chicago Press.

Dasen, P. R. (2000). Rapid social change and the turmoil of adolescence: A cross-cultural perspective. *International Journal of Group Tensions, 29,* 17–49.

David, R., & Collins, J. (1991). Bad outcomes in Black babies: Race or racism? *Ethnicity and Disease, 1,* 216–244.

Davies, I. R. L. (1997). Colour cognition is more universal than colour language. *Behavioral and Brain Sciences, 20,* 186–187.

Dawkins, R. (1976). *The selfish gene.* Oxford: Oxford University Press.

Deacon, T. W. (1997). *The symbolic species: The co-evolution of language and the brain.* New York: W. W. Norton.

Dehaene, S. (1997). *The number sense: How the mind creates mathematics.* Oxford, UK: Oxford University Press.

Desai, S. R., McCormick, N. B., & Gaeddert, W. P. (1989). Malay and American undergraduates' beliefs about love. *Journal of Psychology and Human Sexuality, 2,* 93–116.

Dhawan, N., Roseman, I. J., Naidu, R. K., & Rettek, S. I. (1995). Self-concepts across two cultures: India and the United States. *Journal of Cross-Cultural Psychology, 26,* 606–621.

Diamond, J. (1997). *Guns, germs and steel: The fates of human societies.* New York: Norton.

Diamond, J. (2005). Geography and skin colour. *Nature, 435,* 283–284.

Diamond, E. L. (1982). The role of anger and hostility in essential hypertension and coronary heart disease. *Psychological Bulletin, 92,* 410–433.

Diener, E. (2001, June 14–17). *Culture and subjective well-being—Why some nations and ethnic groups are happier than others.* Invited address presented at Thirteenth Annual Convention of the American Psychological Society, Toronto.

Diener, E., & Biswas-Diener, R. (2002). Will money increase subjective well-being? A literature review and guide to needed research. *Social Indicators Research, 57,* 119–169.

Diener, E., & Diener, M. (1995). Cross-cultural correlates of life satisfaction and self-esteem. *Journal of Personality and Social Psychology, 68,* 653–663.

Diener, E., Diener, M., & Diener, C. (1995). Factors predicting the subjective well-being of nations. *Journal of Personality and Social Psychology, 69,* 851–864.

Diener, E., Suh, E. M., Smith, H., & Shao, L. (1995). National differences in reported subjective well-being: Why do they occur? *Social Indicators Research, 34,* 7–32.

Diez-Roux, A. V., Northridge, M. E., Morabia, A., Bassett, M. T., & Shea, S. (1999). Prevalence and social correlates of cardiovascular disease risk factors in Harlem. *American Journal of Public Health, 89*, 302–307.

Dion, K. K., & Dion, K. L. (1993). Individualistic and collectivistic perspectives on gender and the cultural context of love and intimacy. *Journal of Social Issues, 49*, 53–69.

Doi, T. (1971). *The anatomy of dependence.* Tokyo: Kodansha.

Douglas-Hamilton, I., & Douglas-Hamilton, O. (1975). *Among the elephants.* New York: Viking Press.

Doyle, K. O., & Doyle, M. R. (2001). Meanings of wealth in European and Chinese fairy tales. *American Behavioral Scientist, 45*, 191–204.

Drukker, J. W., & Tassenaar, V. (1997). Paradoxes of modernization and material well-being in the Netherlands during the nineteenth century. In R. H. Steckel & R. Floud (Eds.), *Health and welfare during industrialization* (pp. 331–378). Chicago: University of Chicago Press.

Du Bois, W. E. B. (1903/1989). *The souls of Black folk.* New York: Penguin.

Ducci, L., Arcuri, L. W., Georgis, T., & Sineshaw, T. (1982). Emotion recognition in Ethiopia. *Journal of Cross-Cultural Psychology, 13*, 340–351.

Dunbar, R. I. M. (1992). Neocortex size as a constraint on group size in primates. *Journal of Human Evolution, 20*, 469–493.

Dunbar, R. I. M. (1993). The co-evolution of neocortical size, group size and language in humans. *Behavioural and Brain Sciences, 16*, 681–735.

Dunbar, R. I. M. (1996). *Grooming, gossip, and the evolution of language.* London: Faber and Faber.

Dunbar, R. I. M. (1998). The social brain hypothesis. *Evolutionary Anthropology, 6*, 178–190.

Dunbar, R. I. M., Marriott, A., & Duncan, N. D. C. (1997). Human conversational behavior. *Human Nature, 8*, 231–246.

Dunning, D., Meyerowitz, J. A., & Holzberg, A. D. (1989). Ambiguity and self-evaluation: The role of idiosyncratic trait definition in self-serving assessments of ability. *Journal of Personality and Social Psychology, 57*, 1082–1090.

Durham, W. H. (1991). *Coevolution: Genes, culture and human diversity.* Stanford, CA: Stanford University Press.

Dutton, D. G., & Aron, A. P. (1974). Some evidence for heightened sexual attraction under conditions of high anxiety. *Journal of Personality and Social Psychology, 30*, 510–517.

Duval, S. & Wicklund, R. (1972). *A theory of objective self-awareness.* New York: Academic Press.

Dweck, C. S., & Leggett, E. L. (1988). A social-cognitive approach to motivation and personality. *Psychological Review, 95*, 256–273.

Earley, P. C. (1993). East meets West meets Mideast: Further explorations of collectivistic and individualistic work groups. *Academy of Management Journal, 36*, 319–348.

Earleywine, M. (2001). Cannabis-induced Koro in Americans. *Addiction, 96*, 1663–1666.

Edgerton, R. B. (1971). *The individual in cultural adaptation: A study of four East African peoples.* Berkeley, CA: University of California Press.

Educational Testing Service. (2003). Test of English as a Foreign Language. Test and score data summary, 2002–2003 edition.

Edwards, C. P. (1994, April). *Cultural relativity meets best practice, or anthropology and early education, a promising friendship.* Paper presented at the meetings of the American Educational Research Association, New Orleans, LA.

Einstein, A. (1954). *Ideas and opinions.* New York: Crown.

Ekman, P. (1972). Universal and cultural differences in facial expression of emotion. In J. R. Cole (Ed.), *Nebraska symposium on motivation*, pp. 207–283. Lincoln: University of Nebraska Press.

Ekman, P. (1973). Universal facial expressions in emotion. *Studia Psychologica, 15*, 140–147.

Ekman, P., & Friesen, W. V. (1969). The repertoire of nonverbal behavior: Categories, origins, usage, and coding. *Semiotica, 1*, 49–98.

Ekman, P., & Friesen, W. V. (1971). Constants across cultures in the face and emotion. *Journal of Personality and Social Psychology, 17*, 124–129.

Ekman, P., Levenson, R. W., & Friesen, W. V. (1983). Autonomic nervous system activity distinguishes among emotions. *Science, 221*, 1208–1210.

Ekman, P., Sorenson, E. R., & Friesen, W. V. (1969). Pan-cultural elements in the facial displays of emotions. *Science, 164*, 86–88.

Elfenbein, H. A., & Ambady, N. (2002). On the universality and cultural specificity of emotion recognition: A meta-analysis. *Psychological Bulletin, 128*, 203–235.

Elias, N. (1939/1994). *The civilizing process.* Oxford: Blackwell.

Elliot, A. J., Chirkov, V. I., Kim, Y., & Sheldon, K. M. (2001). A cross-cultural analysis of avoidance (relative to approach) personal goals. *Psychological Science, 12,* 505–510.

Ellsworth, P. C. (1992). Sense, culture, and sensibility. In S. Kitayama & H. R. Markus (Eds.), *Emotion and Culture: Empirical studies of mutual influence.* (pp. 23–50). Washington, DC: APA.

Endo, Y., Heine, S. J., & Lehman, D. R. (2000). Culture and positive illusions in relationships: How my relationships are better than yours. *Personality and Social Psychology Bulletin, 26,* 1571–1586.

Endo, Y. & Meijer, Z. (2004). Autobiographical memory of success and failure experiences. In Y. Kashima, Y. Endo, E. S. Kashima, C. Leung, & J. McClure (Eds.), *Progress in Asian Social Psychology, Vol. 4* (pp. 67–84). Seoul, Korea: Kyoyook-Kwahak-Sa Publishing Company.

Evans-Pritchard, E. E. (1976). *Witchcraft, oracles, and magic among the Azande.* Oxford, UK: Clarendon Press.

Falbo, T., Poston, D. L., Jr., Triscari, R. S., & Zhang, X. (1997). Self-enhancing illusions among Chinese schoolchildren. *Journal of Cross-Cultural Psychology, 28,* 172–191.

Feather, N. (1966). Effects of prior success and failure on expectations of success and subsequent performance. *Journal of Personality and Social Psychology, 3,* 287–298.

Feinman, S. (1981).Why is cross-sex-role behavior more approved for girls than boys? A status characteristic approach. *Sex Roles, 7,* 289–300.

Feldman, P. J. & Steptoe, A. (2004). How neighborhoods and physical functioning are related: The roles of neighborhood socioeconomic status, perceived neighborhood strain, and individual health risk factors. *Annals of Behavioral Medicine, 27,* 91–99.

Ferber, R. (1985). *Solve your child's sleep problems.* New York: Simon & Schuster.

Ferguson, N. (2003, June 8). The world; Why America outpaces Europe (Clue: The God factor). *The New York Times.*

Fernandez-Dols, J.-M., & Ruiz-Belda, M.-A. (1995). Are smiles a sign of happiness? Gold medal winners at the Olympic Games. *Journal of Personality and Social Psychology, 69,* 1113–1119.

Fessler, D. M. T. (2002). Windfall and socially distributed willpower: The psychocultural dynamics of rotating savings and credit associations in a Bengkulu village. *Ethos, 30,* 25–48.

Festinger, L. (1954). A theory of social comparison processes. *Human Relations, 7,* 117–140.

Festinger, L. (1957). *A theory of cognitive dissonance.* Stanford, CA: Stanford University Press.

Festinger, L., Schacter, S., & Back, K. (1950). *Social pressures in informal groups: A study of human factors in housing.* Stanford, CA: Stanford University Press.

Fischer, D. H. (1989). *Albion's seed: Four British folkways in America.* New York: Oxford University Press.

Fisher, H. (2004). *Why we love: The nature and chemistry of romantic love.* New York: Henry Holt.

Fishman, J. A. (1980). The Whorfian hypothesis: Varieties of valuation, confirmation, and disconfirmation: 1. *International Journal of the Sociology of Language, 26,* 25–40.

Fiske, A. P. (1991). *Structures of social life.* New York: Free Press.

Fiske, A. P. (1992). The four elementary forms of sociality: Framework for a unified theory of social relations. *Psychological Review, 99,* 689–723.

Flaherty, J. A, Gavira, F. M., & Val, E. R. (1982). Diagnostic considerations. In E. R. Val, F. M. Gavira, & J. A. Flaherty (Eds.), *Affective disorders: Psychopathology and treatment. Chicago: Year Book Medical Publishers.*

Floud, R. (1994). The heights of Europeans since 1750: A new source for European economic history. In J. Komlos (Ed.), *Stature, living standards, and economic development,* pp. 9–24. Chicago: University of Chicago Press.

Floud, R., & Harris, B. (1997). Health, height, and welfare: Britain, 1700–1980. In R. H. Steckel & R. Floud (Eds.), *Health and welfare during industrialization* (pp. 91–126). Chicago: University of Chicago Press.

Flynn, J. R. (1987). Massive IQ gains in 14 nations: What IQ tests really measure. *Psychological Bulletin, 101,* 171–191.

Flynn, J. R. (1994). IQ gains over time. In R. J. Sternberg (Ed.), *The encyclopedia of human intelligence* (pp. 617–623). New York: Macmillan.

Flynn, J. R. (1999). Searching for justice: The discovery of IQ gains over time. *American Psychologist, 54,* 5–20.

Ford, C. S., & Beach, F. A. (1951). *Patterns of sexual behavior.* New York: Harper and Row.

Forman, T. A., Williams, D. R., & Jackson, J. S. (1997). Race, place, and discrimination. In C. Gardner (Ed.), *Perspectives on social problems* (Vol. 9, pp. 231–261). New York: JAI Press.

Fox, J. A. (1978). Forecasting crime data: An econometric analysis. Lanham, MD: Lexington Books.

Frager, R. (1970). Conformity and anti-conformity in Japan. *Journal of Personality and Social Psychology, 15,* 203–210.

Freeman, D. (1983). *Margaret Mead and Samoa. The making and unmaking of an anthropological myth.* Cambridge, MA: Harvard University Press.

Freedman, J. L., & Fraser, S. C. (1966). Compliance without pressure: The foot-in-the-door technique. *Journal of Personality and Social Psychology, 4,* 195–202.

Freud, S. (1976). The interpretation of dreams. In J. Strachey (Ed. & Trans.), *The complete psychological works.* New York: Norton. (Original work published in 1900)

Fridlund, A. J. (1991). Sociality of solitary smiling: Potentiation by an implicit audience. *Journal of Personality and Social Psychology, 60,* 229–240.

Friesen, W. V. (1972). *Cultural differences in facial expressions in a social situation: An experimental test of the concept of display rules.* Unpublished doctoral dissertation. University of California, San Francisco.

Fryberg, S. A., & Markus, H. R. (2003). On being American Indian: Current and possible selves. *Self and Identity, 2,* 325–344.

Fuentes-Afflick, E., & Lurie, P. (1997). Low birth weight and Latino ethnicity. *Archives of Pediatric Adolescent Medicine, 151,* 665–674.

Furnham, A. (1990). *The Protestant work ethic: The psychology of work-related beliefs and behaviors.* London: Routledge.

Furnham, A., & Bochner, S. (1982). Social difficulty in a foreign culture: An empirical analysis of culture shock. In S. Bochner (Ed.), *Cultures in contact: Studies in cross-cultural interactions* (pp. 161–198). Elmsford, NY: Pergamon.

Furnham, A., & Bochner, S. (1986). *Culture shock.* London: Methuen.

Furnham, A., Bond, M. H., & Heaven, P. (1993). A comparison of Protestant work ethic beliefs in thirteen nations. *Journal of Social Psychology, 133,* 185–197.

Funder, D. C. (2007). *The Personality Puzzle (4th Edition).* New York: Norton.

Gabrenya, W. K., Wang, Y., & Latane, B. (1985). Social loafing on an optimizing task: Cross-cultural differences among Chinese and Americans. *Journal of Cross-Cultural Psychology, 16,* 223–242.

Gabriel, S., & Gardner, W. (1999). Are there "his" and "hers" types of interdependence? The implications of gender differences in collective versus relational interdependence for affect, behavior, and cognition. *Journal of Personality and Social Psychology, 77,* 642–655.

Galanter, M. (1986). "Moonies" get married: A psychiatric follow-up study of a charismatic religious sect. *American Journal of Psychiatry, 143,* 1245–1249.

Galaty, J. G., & Bonte, P. (Eds). (1991). *Herders, warriors, and traders: Pastoralism in Africa.* Boulder, CO: Westview Press.

Gangestad, S. W., Haselton, M. G., & Buss, D. M. (2006). Evolutionary foundations of cultural variation: Evoked culture and mate preference. *Psychological Inquiry, 17,* 75–95.

Gangestad, S. W., Thornhill, R., & Yeo, R. A. (1994). Facial attractiveness, developmental stability, and fluctuating asymmetry. *Ethology and Sociobiology, 15,* 73–85.

Gardner, G. H. (1962). Cross-cultural communication. *Journal of Social Psychology, 58,* 241–256.

Gardner, W. L., Gabriel, S., & Dean, K. K. (2004). The individual as "melting pot": The flexibility of bicultural self-construals. *Cahiers de Psychologie Cognitive/Current Psychology of Cognition, 22,* 181–201.

Garner, D. M., Garfinkel, P. E., Schwartz, D., & Thompson, M. (1980). Cultural expectations of thinness in women. *Psychological Reports, 47,* 483–491.

Gastil, R. D. (1989). Violence, crime, and punishment. In C. R. Wilson & W. Ferris (Eds.) *Encyclopedia of southern culture.* Chapel Hill: University of North Carolina Press.

Geertz, C. (1973). *The interpretation of cultures.* New York: Basic Books.

Geertz, C. (1975). On the nature of anthropological understanding. *American Scientist, 63,* 4–53.

Geertz, C. (1983). *Local knowledge: Further essays in interpretive anthropology.* New York: Basic Books.

Geertz, H. (1959). The vocabulary of emotion: A study of Javanese socialization processes. *Psychiatry, 22,* 225–237.

Gellantly, A. (1995). Colourful Whorfian ideas: Linguistic and cultural influences on the perception and cognition of colour, and on the investigation of them. *Mind and Language, 10,* 119–125.

Gelman, R., & Gallistel, C. R. (2004). Language and the origin of number concepts. *Science, 306,* 441–443.

Gentner, D. (1982). Why nouns are learned before verbs: Linguistic relativity versus natural partitioning. In S. Kuczaj (Ed.), *Language development: Language, cognition and culture.* Hillsdale, NJ: Erlbaum.

Gibbons, F.X., & Wicklund, R.A. (1976). Selective exposure to self. *Journal of Research in Personality, 10,* 98–106.

Giddens, A. (1992). Introduction in M. Weber (1904/1992). *The Protestant ethic and the spirit of capitalism.* London: Routledge.

Gillette, J., Gleitman, H., Gleitman, L., & Lederer, A. (1999). Human simulations of vocabulary learning. *Cognition, 73,* 135–176.

Gilligan, C. (1977). In a different voice: Women's conceptions of the self and of morality. *Harvard Educational Review, 47,* 481–517.

Gilligan, C., & Attanucci, J. (1988). Two moral orientations: Gender differences and similarities. *Merill-Palmer Quarterly, 34,* 223–237.

Gilmore, D. D. (1990). *Manhood in the making.* New Haven, CT: Yale University Press.

Gilovich, G., Keltner, D., & Nisbett, R. (2006). *Social psychology.* New York: Norton.

Giorgi, L., & Marsh, C. (1990). The Protestant work ethic as a cultural phenomenon. *European Journal of Social Psychology, 20,* 499–517.

Gislen, A., Dacke, M., Kroger, R. H. H., Abrahamson, M., Nilsson, D. E., & Warrant, E. J. (2003). Superior underwater vision in a human population of sea-gypsies. *Current Biology, 13,* 833–836.

Gislen, A., & Gislen, L. (2004). On the optical theory of underwater vision in humans. *Journal of the Optical Society of America A, 21,* 2061–2064.

Gislen, A., Warrant, E. J., & Kroger, R. H. H. (2005). *Voluntary accommodation improves underwater vision in humans.* Manuscript available from the authors (anna.gislen@cob.lu.se).

Gladwell, M. (2000). *The tipping point: How little things can make a big difference.* Boston: Little, Brown.

Gleick, J. (1987). *Chaos: Making a new science.* New York: Penguin Books.

Gleitman, L. (1990). The structural sources of verb meaning. *Language Acquisition: A Journal of Developmental Linguistics, 1,* 3–55.

Gobster, P. H., & Delgado, A. (1992). Ethnicity and recreation use in Chicago's Lincoln Park: In-park user survey findings. In P. Gobster (Ed.), *Managing urban and high-use recreation settings* (pp. 75–81). General Technical Report NC-163: United States Department of Agriculture.

Goel, M. S., McCarthy, E. P., Phillips, R. S., & Wee, C. C. (2004). Obesity among U.S. immigrant subgroups by duration of residence. *Journal of the American Medical Association, 292,* 2860–2867.

Goldin, C. (1998). America's graduation from high school: The evolution and spread of secondary schooling in the twentieth century. *Journal of Economic History, 58,* 345–374.

Good, C., Aronson, J., & Inzlicht, M. (2003). Improving adolescents' standardized test performance: An intervention to reduce the effects of stereotype threat. *Journal of Applied Developmental Psychology, 24,* 645–662.

Goode, W. J. (1959). The theoretical importance of love. *American Sociological Review, 24,* 38–47.

Goodenough, W. H. (1970). *Description and comparison in cultural anthropology.* Chicago: Aldine.

Goody, J. (1977). *The domestication of the savage mind.* Cambridge, UK: Cambridge University Press.

Gordon, A. (2000). Cultural identity and illness: Fulani views. *Culture, Medicine, and Psychiatry, 24,* 297–330.

Gordon, P. (2004). Numerical cognition without words: Evidence from Amazonia. *Science, 306,* 496–499.

Gordon, R. A. (1990). *Anorexia and bulimia: Anatomy of a social epidemic.* Cambridge, UK: Basil/Blackwell.

Gosling, S. D. (1998). Personality dimensions in spotted hyenas (Crocuta crocuta). *Journal of Comparative Psychology, 112,* 107–118.

Gosling, S. D., & John, O. P. (1999). Personality dimensions in nonhuman animals: A cross-species review. *Current Direction in Psychological Science, 8,* 69–75.

Gottesman, I. I. (1991). *Schizophrenia. The origins of madness.* New York: Holt.

Gould, A. B. (1999). *The Dutch are the world's tallest people.* Radio Netherlands. Available: http://www.rnw.nl/health/html/tall_dutch.html

Gould, S. J. (1981). *The mismeasure of man.* New York: Norton.

Greeley, A. M. (1991). *Religion around the world: A preliminary report.* Chicago: National Opinion Research Center.

Greeley, A. M., & Hout, M. (1999). Americans' increasing belief in life after death: Religious competition and acculturation. *American Sociological Review, 64,* 813–835.

Greenberg, J. H. (1963). *Universals of language.* Cambridge, MA: MIT Press.

Greenfield, P. M. (1997). Culture as process: Empirical methods for cultural psychology. In J. W. Berry, Y. H. Poortinga, & J. Pandey (Eds.), *Handbook of Cross-Cultural Psychology, Vol. 1,* 301–346. Boston: Allyn & Bacon.

Greenfield, P. M. (1998). The cultural evolution of IQ. In U. Neisser (Ed.), *The rising curve: Long term gains in IQ and related measures* (pp. 81–123). Washington, DC: American Psychological Association.

Grossmann, K., Grossmann, K. E., Spangler, G., Suess, G., & Unzner, L. (1985). Maternal sensitivity and newborns' orientation responses as related to quality of attachment in Northern Germany. In I. Bretherton & E. Waters (Eds.), *Growing point in attachment theory. Monographs of the Society for Research in Child Development, 50* (1–2 Serial No. 209), 233–256.

Grimm, S. D., & Church, A. T. (1999). A cross-cultural study of response biases in personality measures. *Journal of Research in Personality, 33,* 415–441.

Guarniccia, P. J., Canino, G., Rubio-Stipec, M., & Bravo, M. (1993). The prevalence of ataques de nervios in the Puerto Rico Disaster Study: The role of culture in psychiatric epidemiology. *Journal of Nervous and Mental Disease, 181*(3), 157–165.

Gullahorn, J. T., & Gullahorn, J. E. (1963). An extension of the U-curve hypothesis, *Journal of Social Issues, 19,* 33–47.

Gupta, U., & Singh, P. (1982). Exploratory study of love and liking and type of marriages. *Indian Journal of Applied Psychology, 19,* 92–97.

Gussow, Z. (1985). Pibloktoz (hysteria) among the Polar Eskimo: An ethnopsychiatric study. In R. C. Simons & C. C. Hughes (Eds.), *The culture-bound syndromes* (pp. 271–287). Dordrecht, The Netherlands: Reidel. (Original work published 1960)

Guthrie, G. M., & Zektick, I. N. (1967). Predicting performance in the Peace Corps. *Journal of Social Psychology, 71,* 1–21.

Haidt, J. (2001). The emotional dog and its rational tail: A social intuitionist approach to moral judgment. *Psychological Review, 108,* 814–834.

Haidt, J., & Joseph, C. (2004). Intuitive ethics: How innately prepared intuitions generate culturally variable virtues. Deadalus, 55–66.

Haidt, J., & Keltner, D. (1999). Culture and facial expression: Open-ended methods find more expressions and a gradient of recognition. *Cognition and Emotion, 13,* 225–266.

Haidt, J., Koller, S. H., & Dias, M. G. (1993). Affect, culture, and morality, or Is it wrong to eat your dog? *Journal of Personality and Social Psychology, 65,* 613–628.

Haight, W. L. (1999). The pragmatics of caregiver-child pretending at home: Understanding culturally specific socialization practices. In A. Goncu (Ed.), *Children's engagement in the world: Sociocultural perspectives* (pp. 128–147). New York: Cambridge University Press.

Hall, E. T. (1976). *Beyond culture.* New York: Anchor Books.

Hall, G. S. (1916). *Adolescence.* New York: Appleton.

Halmi, K. A., Falk, J. R., & Schwartz, E. (1981). Binge-eating and vomiting: A survey of a college population. *Psychological Medicine, 11,* 697–706.

Hamamura, T. (2006). *How do cultures change? A case of Japanese collectivism.* Unpublished paper, University of British Columbia.

Hamamura, T., & Heine, S. J. (2007). Self-enhancement, self-improvement, and face among Japanese. In E. C. Chang (Ed.), *Self-criticism and self-enhancement: theory, research, and clinical implications.* Washington, DC: American Psychological Association.

Hamamura, T., Heine, S. J., & Paulhus, D. L. (2007). *Cultural differences in response styles: The role of dialectical thinking.* Unpublished manuscript, University of British Columbia.

Hamilton, D. L., & Gifford, R. K. (1976). Illusory correlation in interpersonal perception: A cognitive basis of stereotypic judgments. *Journal of Experimental Social Psychology, 12,* 392–407.

Hamilton, V. L., & Sanders, J. (1992). *Everyday justice: Responsibility and the individual in Japan and the United States.* New Haven, CT: Yale University Press.

Hampden-Turner, C., & Trompenaars, A. (1993). *The seven cultures of capitalism: Value systems for creating wealth in the United States, Japan, Germany, France, Britain, Sweden, and the Netherlands.* New York: Doubleday.

Han, S., & Shavit, S. (1994). Persuasion and culture: Advertising appeals in individualistic and collectivist societies. *Journal of Experimental Social Psychology, 30,* 326–350.

Hanning, R. W. (1977). *The individual in twelfth-century romance.* New Haven, CT: Yale University Press.

Hansen, I. G. (2005). *The psychological confluence and divergence of religion and culture and the implications for tolerance.* Unpublished manuscript, University of British Columbia.

Hare, R. D. (1999). *Without conscience: The disturbing world of the psychopaths among us.* New York: Guilford.

Harrington, L., & Liu, J. H. (2002). Self-enhancement and attitudes toward high achievers: A bicultural view of the independent and interdependent self. *Journal of Cross-Cultural Psychology, 33,* 37–55.

Hart, D., Lucca-Irizarry, N., & Damon, W. (1986). The development of self-understanding in Puerto Rico and the United States. *Journal of Early Adolescence, 6,* 293–304.

Harton, H. C., & Bourgeois, M. J. (2004). Cultural elements emerge from dynamic social impact. In M. Schaller & C. Crandall (Eds.), *The psychological foundations of culture.* Hillsdale, NJ: Lawrence Erlbaum.

Haun, D. B. M., Rapold, C. J., Call, J., Janzen, G., & Levinson, S. C. (2006). Cognitive cladistics and cultural override in Hominid spatial cognition. *Proceedings of the National Academy of Sciences, 103,* 17568–17573.

Hazan, C., & Shaver, P. (1987), Romantic love conceptualized as an attachment process. *Journal of Personality and Social Psychology, 52,* 511–524.

Healy, J. M. (1990). *Endangered minds: Why children don't think and what we can do about it.* New York: Simon & Schuster.

Heath, C., Bell, C., & Sternberg, E. (2001). Emotional selection in memes: The case of urban legends. *Journal of Personality and Social Psychology, 81,* 1028–1041.

Heatherton, T. F., Nichols, P. A., Mahamedi, F., & Keel, P. (1995). Body weight, dieting, and eating disorder symptoms among college students, 1982–1992. *American Journal of Psychiatry, 152,* 1623–1629.

Heine, S. J. (2003). An exploration of cultural variation in self-enhancing and self-improving motivations. *Nebraska Symposium of Motivation.*

Heine, S. J. (2005). Constructing good selves in Japan and North America. In R. M. Sorrentino, D. Cohen, J. M. Olson, & M. P. Zanna (Eds.), *Culture and social behavior: The Tenth Ontario Symposium.* (pp. 115–143). Hillsdale, NJ: Lawrence Erlbaum.

Heine, S. J., Buchtel, E., & Norenzayan, A. (2007). What do cross-national comparisons of mean levels of personality traits tell us? Unpublished manuscript. University of British Columbia.

Heine, S. J., Foster, J., & Spina, R. (2007). *Do birds of a feather universally flock together? Cultural variation in the similarity-attraction effect.* Manuscript submitted for publication.

Heine, S. J., & Hamamura, T. (2007). In search of East Asian self-enhancement. *Personality and Social Psychology Review, 11,* 1–24.

Heine, S. J., Kitayama, S., & Lehman, D. R. (2001a). Cultural differences in self-evaluation: Japanese readily accept negative self-relevant information. *Journal of Cross-Cultural Psychology, 32,* 434–443.

Heine, S. J., Kitayama, S., Lehman, D. R., Takata, T., Ide, E., Leung, C., & Matsumoto, H. (2001b). Divergent consequences of success and failure in Japan and North America: An investigation of self-improving motivations and malleable selves. *Journal of Personality and Social Psychology, 81,* 599–615.

Heine, S. J., Kitayama, S., & Hamamura, T. (in press). Different meta-analyses, different conclusions: A reply to Sedikides, Gaertner, & Vevea (2005), JPSP. *Asian Journal of Social Psychology.*

Heine, S. J., & Lehman, D. R. (1997a). The cultural construction of self-enhancement: An examination of group-serving biases. *Journal of Personality and Social Psychology, 72,* 1268–1283.

Heine, S. J., & Lehman, D. R. (1997b). Culture, dissonance, and self-affirmation. *Personality and Social Psychology Bulletin, 23,* 389–400.

Heine, S. J., & Lehman, D. R. (2004). Move the body, change the self: Acculturative effects on the self-concept. In M. Schaller & C. Crandall (Eds.), *Psychological foundations of culture,* (pp. 305–331). Mahwah, NJ: Lawrence Erlbaum.

Heine, S. J., Lehman, D. R., Markus, H. R., & Kitayama, S. (1999). Is there a universal need for positive self-regard? *Psychological Review, 106,* 766–794.

Heine, S. J., Lehman, D. R., Peng, K., & Greenholtz, J. (2002). What's wrong with cross-cultural comparisons of subjective Likert scales? The reference-group problem. *Journal of Personality and Social Psychology, 82,* 903–918.

Heine, S. J., & Renshaw, K. (2002). Interjudge agreement, self-enhancement, and liking: Cross-cultural divergences. *Personality and Social Psychology Bulletin, 28,* 442–451, 578–587.

Heine, S. J., Takemoto, T., Moskalenko, S., & Lasaleta, J. (2007). Mirrors in the head: Cultural variation in objective self-awareness. Manuscript submitted for publication. University of British Columbia.

Henderson, V., & Dweck, C. S. (1990). Motivation and achievement. In S. S. Feldman & G. R. Elliott

(Eds.), *At the threshold: The developing adolescent* (pp. 308–329). Cambridge, MA: Harvard University Press.

Henrich, J. et al. (2006). Costly punishment across human societies. *Science, 312,* 1767–1170.

Henrich, J., & Gil-White, F. J. (2001). The evolution of prestige: Freely conferred deference as a mechanism for enhancing the benefits of cultural transmission. *Evolution and Human Behavior, 22,* 165–196.

Herdt, B. (2006). *The Sambia: Ritual, sexuality, and change in Papua New Guinea.* Belmont, CA: Thomson Wadsworth.

Hess, T. M., Auman, C., & Colcombe, S. J. (2003). The impact of stereotype threat on age differences in memory performance. *Journals of Gerontology: Series B: Psychological Sciences & Social Sciences, 58,* 3–11.

Hewlett, B. S. (1992). The parent-infant relationship and social-emotional development among Aka Pygmies. In J. L. Roopmarine & D. B. Carter (Eds.), *Parent-child socialization in diverse cultures* (pp. 223–243). Norwood, NJ: Ablex.

Hezel, F. X. (1987). Truk suicide epidemic and social change. *Human Organization, 46,* 283–291.

Higgins, E. T. (1996). The "self-digest": Self-knowledge serving self-regulatory functions. *Journal of Personality and Social Psychology, 71,* 1062–1083.

Ho, D. Y. F. (1976). On the concept of face. *American Journal of Sociology, 81,* 867–884.

Hock, H. W., van Harten, P. N., van Hoeken, D., & Susser, E. (1998). Lack of relation between culture and anorexia nervosa—Results of an incidence study on Curacao. *New England Journal of Medicine, 338,* 1231–1232.

Hofstede, G. (1980). *Culture's consequences: International differences in work-related values.* Beverly Hills, CA: Sage.

Hofstede, G. (1983). *Dimensions of national cultures in fifty countries and three regions.* In J. Deregowski, S. Dzuirawiec, and R. Annis (Eds.), Expiscations in Cross-Cultural Psychology, Lisse, Netherlands: Swets and Zeitlinger.

Holden, C., & Mace, R. (1997). Phylogenetic analysis of the evolution of lactose digestion in adults. *Human Biology, 69,* 605–628.

Hollingshead, A. B., & Redlich, R. C. (1958). *Social class and mental illness: A community study.* New York: Wiley.

Hollox, E. (2005). Genetics of lactase persistence—fresh lessons in the history of milk drinking. *European Journal of Human Genetics, 13,* 267–269.

Holmes, T. H., & Rahe, R. H. (1967). The social readjustment rating scale. Journal of *Psychosomatic Research, 11,* 213–218

Hong, J. J. (2005). *Social values and self-construal in the expression of social anxiety: A cross-cultural comparison.* Unpublished doctoral dissertation, University of British Columbia.

Hong, Y., Chiu, C., Dweck, C. S., Lin, D. M., & Wan, W. (1999). Implicit theories, attributions, and coping: A meaning system approach. *Journal of Personality and Social Psychology, 77,* 588–599.

Hong, Y., Morris, M. W., Chiu, C., & Benet-Martinez, V. (2000). Multicultural minds: A dynamic constructivist approach to culture and cognition. *American Psychologist, 55,* 705–720.

Hortacsu, N. (1999). The first year of family- and couple-initiated marriages of a Turkish sample: A longitudinal investigation. *International Journal of Psychology, 34,* 29–41.

Hosey, G. R., Wood, M., & Thompson, R. J. (1985). Social facilitation in a "non-social" animal, the centipede Lithobius forficatus. *Behavioural Processes, 10,* 123–130.

Hoshino-Browne, E., & Spencer, S. J. (2000). *Cross-cultural differences in attribution and perseverance.* Poster presented at the 1st Convention of the Society for Personality and Social Psychology, Nashville, TN. February 2–6, 2000.

Hoshino-Browne, E., Zanna, A. S., Spencer, S. J., Zanna, M. P., Kitayama, S., & Lackenbauer, S. (2005). On the cultural guises of cognitive dissonance: The case of Easterners and Westerners. *Journal of Personality and Social Psychology, 89,* 294–310.

Hough, W. (1922). Synoptic series of objects in the United States National Museum illustrating the history of inventions, *Proceedings of the United States National Museum, 60,* art. 9, p. 2, pl. 16.

House, J. S., Landis, K. R., & Umberson, D. (1988). Social relationships and health. *Science, 241,* 540–545.

Hsiao-Ying, T. (1995). Sojourner adjustment: The case of foreigners in Japan. *Journal of Cross-Cultural Psychology, 26,* 523–536.

Hsu, L. (2004). *Patterns of social anxiety in Chinese and European-Canadian students.* Unpublished Master's thesis. University of British Columbia.

Hughes, C. C. (1996). The culture-bound syndromes and psychiatric diagnosis. In J. E. Mezzich, A. Kleinman, H. Fabrega, Jr., & D. L. Parron (Eds.), *Culture and psychiatric diagnosis: A DSM-IV perspective* (pp. 289–307). Washington, DC: American Psychiatric Press.

Hui, C.H., & Triandis, H. C. (1989). Effects of culture and response format on extreme response style. *Journal of Cross-Cultural Psychology, 20,* 296–309.

Human Development Reports. (2005, September 7). *Human development report 2005.* Retrieved October 10, 2006, from http://hdr.undp.org/reports/global/2005/pdf/hdr05_HDI.pdf

Humphrey, N. K. (1976). The social function of intellect. In P. P. G. Bateson & R. A. Hinde (Eds.), *Growing points in ethology* (pp. 303–317). Cambridge, UK: University of Cambridge Press.

Hunt, E., & Agnoli, F. (1991). The Whorfian hypothesis: A cognitive psychology perspective. *Psychological Review, 98,* 377–389.

Hunter, J. D. (1991). *Culture wars: The struggle to define America.* New York: Basic Books.

Huntington, S. P. (1998). The clash of civilizations and the remaking of world order. New York: Simon & Schuster.

Huttenlocher, J., & Smiley, P. (1987). Early word meaning: The case of object names. *Cognitive Psychology, 19,* 63–89.

Hwu, H. G,, Yeh, E. K., & Chang, L. Y. (1989). Prevalence of psychiatric disorders in Taiwan defined by the Chinese Diagnostic Interview Schedule. *Acta Psychiatrica Scandinavica, 79,* 136–147.

Hypertension Detection and Follow-Up Program Cooperative Group. (1977). Race, education, and prevalence of hypertension. *American Journal of Epidemiology, 106,* 351–361.

I-Ching. (1991). (J. N. Wu, Trans.). Washington, DC: Taoist Center.

Ickes, W., Wicklund, R., & Ferris, C. (1973). Objective self-awareness and self-esteem. *Journal of Experimental Social Psychology, 9,* 202–219.

Ignatieff, M. (1994). *Blood and belonging: Journeys into the new nationalism.* New York: Farrar, Straus, & Giroux.

Ingham, A. G., Levinger, G., Graves, J., & Peckham, V. (1974). The Ringelmann effect: Studies of group size and group performance. *Journal of Experimental Social Psychology, 10,* 371–384.

Inglehart, R., & Klingemann, H. (2000). Genes, culture, democracy, and happiness. In E. Diener & E. Suh (Eds.), *Culture and subjective well-being* (pp. 165–184). Cambridge, MA: MIT Press.

Inglehart, R. F. (2004). *Human beliefs and values: A cross-cultural sourcebook based on the 1999–2002 values surveys.* Mexico City: Siglo XXI.

Ingram, R. E., Scott, W., & Siegle, G. (1999). Depression: Social and cognitive aspects. In T. Millon, P. H. Blaney, & R. D. Davis (Eds.), *Oxford textbook of psychopathology* (pp. 203–226). New York: Oxford University Press.

Inkeles, A. (1953). Some sociological observations on culture and personality studies. In C. Kluckhohn, H. A. Murray, & D. M. Schneider (Eds.), *Personality in nature, society, and culture* (pp. 577–592). New York: Knopf.

Ip, G. W., & Chiu, C. (2002, June 21). *Assessing prevention pride and promotion pride in Chinese and American cultures: Validity of the regulatory focus questionnaire.* Paper presented at the conference on Culture and Social Behavior: The Tenth Ontario Symposium, London, ON.

Ishii, K., Reyes, J. A., & Kitayama, S. (2003). Spontaneous attention to word content versus emotional tone: Differences among three cultures. *Psychological Science, 14,* 39–46.

Iyengar, S. S., & Lepper, M. R. (1999). Rethinking the value of choice: A cultural perspective on intrinsic motivation. *Journal of Personality and Social Psychology, 76,* 349–366.

Iyengar, S. S., & Lepper, M. R. (2000). When choice is demotivating: Can one desire too much of a good thing? *Journal of Personality & Social Psychology, 79,* 995–1006.

Iyengar, S. S., Lepper, M. R., & Ross, L. (1999). Independence from whom? Interdependence with whom? Cultural perspectives on ingroups versus outgroups. In D. Miller & D. Prentice (Eds.), *Cultural divides: Understanding and overcoming group conflict* (pp. 273–301). New York: Sage.

Izard, C. E. (1994). Innate and universal facial expressions: Evidence from developmental and cross-cultural research. *Psychological Bulletin, 115,* 288–299.

Jablensky, A., Sartorius, N., Ernberg, G., Anker, M., Korten, A., Cooper, J. E., Day, R., & Bertelsen, A. (1991). *Schizophrenia: Manifestations, incidence and course in different cultures: A World Health Organization ten-country study* (Psychological Medicine, Monograph Supplement No. 20). Cambridge, UK: Cambridge University Press.

Jablonski, N. G., & Chaplin, G. (2000). The evolution of human skin coloration. *Journal of Human Evolution, 39*, 57–106.

Jackson, E. F., Fox, W. S., & Crockett, H. J. (1957). Religion and occupational achievement. *American Sociological Review, 35*, 48–63.

Jackson, J. M., & Williams, K. D. (1985). Social loafing on difficult tasks: Working collectively can improve performance. *Journal of Personality and Social Psychology, 49*, 937–942.

Jacobs, R. C., & Campbell, D. T. (1961). The perpetuation of an arbitrary tradition through several generations of a laboratory microculture. *Journal of Abnormal and Social Psychology, 62*, 649–658.

James, S. (2002). *Agonias*: The social and sacred suffering of Azorean immigrants. *Culture, Medicine, and Psychiatry, 26*, 87–110.

James, S. A. (1994). John Henryism and the health of African-Americans. *Culture, Medicine, and Psychiatry, 18*, 163–182.

James, W. (1950/1890). *The principles of psychology.* New York: Dover.

Jankowiak, W. R., & Fischer, E. F. (1992). A cross-cultural perspective on romantic love. *Ethnology, 31*, 149–155.

Jenkins, P. (2002). *The next Christendom: The coming of global Christianity.* New York: Oxford University Press.

Jensen, L. A. (1997a). Culture wars: American moral divisions across the adult lifespan. *Journal of Adult Development, 4*, 107–121.

Jensen, L. A. (1997b). Different worldviews, different morals: America's culture war divide. Human Development, 40, 325–344.

Jensen, L. A. (1998). Moral divisions within countries between orthodoxy and progressivism: India and the United States. *Journal for the Scientific Study of Religion, 37,* 90–107.

Ji, L. (2005, January 26). *Culture and thinking across time.* Paper presented at the Cultural Psychology Preconference, New Orleans, La. January 26, 2005.

Ji, L. J. (2005). Culture and lay theories of change. In R. M. Sorrentino, D. Cohen, J. M. Olson, & M. P. Zanna (Eds.), *Culture and social behavior: The tenth Ontario symposium,* (pp. 117–136). Hillsdale, NJ: Lawrence Erlbaum.

Ji, L. J., Nisbett, R. E., & Su, Y. (2001). Culture, change, and prediction. *Psychological Science, 12,* 450–456.

Ji, L. J., Peng, K., & Nisbett, R. E. (2000). Culture, control, and perception of relationships in the environment. *Journal of Personality and Social Psychology, 78*, 943–955.

Ji, L. J., Zhang, Z., & Nisbett, R. E. (2004). Is it culture or is it language? Examination of language effects in cross-cultural research on categorization. *Journal of Personality and Social Psychology, 87*, 57–65.

Johnson, J., & Newport, E. L. (1989). Critical period effects in second language learning: The influence of maturational state on the acquisition of English as a second language. *Cognitive Psychology, 21,* 60–99.

Johnson, S. (2005). *Everything bad is good for you.* New York: Riverhead Books.

Jones, E. E., & Harris, V. A. (1967). The attribution of attitudes. *Journal of Experimental Social Psychology, 3,* 1–24.

Jones, R. B., Larkins, C., & Hughes, B. O. (1996). Approach/avoidance responses of domestic chicks to familiar and unfamiliar video images of biologically neutral stimuli. *Applied Animal Behaviour Science, 48,* 81–98.

Kagamimori, S., Iibuchi, Y., & Fox, A. J. (1983). A comparison of socioeconomic differences between Japan and England and Wales. *World Health Statistics Quarterly, 36,* 119–128.

Kagan, J., Kearsley, R. B., & Zelazo, P. R. (1977). The effects of infant day care on psychological development. *Evaluation Quarterly, 1,* 109–142.

Kalin, R., & Tilby, P. (1978). Development and validation of a sex-role ideology scale. *Psychological Reports, 42,* 731–738.

Kanagawa, C., Cross, S. E., & Markus, H. R. (2001). "Who am I?": The cultural psychology of the conceptual self. *Personality and Social Psychology Bulletin, 27,* 90–103.

Kaplan, G. A. (1985). *Twenty years of health in Alameda County: The human population laboratory analyses.* Paper presented at the annual meeting of the Society for Prospective Medicine, San Francisco, CA.

Kaplan, G. A., & Keil, J. E. (1993). Socioeconomic factors and cardiovascular disease: A review of the literature. *Circulation, 88,* 1973–1998.

Karau, S. J., & Williams, K. D. (1993). Social loafing: A meta-analytic review and theoretical integration.

Journal of Personality and Social Psychology, 65, 681–706.

Karno, M., & Edgerton, R. B. (1969). Perception of mental illness in a Mexican-American community. *Archives of General Psychiatry, 20,* 233–238.

Kasahara, Y. (1986). Fear of eye-to-eye confrontation among neurotic patients in Japan. In T. Lebra & W. P. Lebra (Eds.), *Japanese culture and behavior* (pp. 379–387). Honolulu: University of Hawaii Press.

Kashima, E. S., & Kashima, Y. (1998). Culture and language: The case of cultural dimensions and personal pronoun use. *Journal of Cross-Cultural Psychology. 29,* 461–486.

Kashima, Y., Siegal, M., Tanaka, K., & Kashima, E. S. (1992). Do people believe behaviors are consistent with attitudes? Towards a cultural psychology of attribution processes. *British Journal of Social Psychology, 31,* 111–124.

Kashima, Y., Siegal, M., Tanaka, K., & Isaka, H. (1988). Universalism in lay conceptions of distributive justice: A cross-cultural examination. *International Journal of Psychology, 23,* 51–64.

Kashima, Y., Yamaguchi, S., Kim, U., Choi, S., Gelfand, M., & Yuki, M. (1995). Culture, gender, and self: A perspective from individualism-collectivism research. *Journal of Personality and Social Psychology, 69,* 925–937.

Katz, D., & Schnack, R. L. (1938). *Social psychology.* New York: Wiley.

Kawamura, S. (1959). The process of sub-culture propagation among Japanese macaques, *Primates, 2,* 43–60.

Keel, P. K., & Klump, K. L. (2003). Are eating disorders culture-bound syndromes? Implications for conceptualizing their etiology. *Psychological Bulletin, 129,* 747–769.

Keltner, D. (1995). Signs of appeasement: Evidence for the distinct display of embarrassment, amusement, and shame. *Journal of Personality and Social Psychology, 68,* 441–454.

Kenrick, D. T., Li, N. P., & Butner, J. (2003). Dynamical evolutionary psychology: Individual decision-rules and emergent social norms. *Psychological Review, 1,* 3–28.

Kephart, W. M. (1967). Some correlates of romantic love. *Journal of Marriage and the Family, 29,* 470–474.

Kessler, R. C., McGonagle, K. A., Zhao, S., Nelson, C. B., Hughes, N., Eshleman, S., Wittchen, H.-U., & Kendler, K. S. (1994). Lifetime and 12–month prevalence of DSM-III-R psychiatric disorders in the United States: Results from the National Comorbidity Survey. *Archives of General Psychiatry, 51,* 8–19.

Kitayama, S., Markus, H. R., Matsumoto, H., & Norasakkunkit, V. (1997). Individual and collective processes in the construction of the self: Self-enhancement in the United States and self-criticism in Japan. *Journal of Personality and Social Psychology, 72,* 1245–1267.

Kim, H. S. (2002). We talk, therefore we think? A cultural analysis of the effect of talking on thinking. *Journal of Personality and Social Psychology, 83,* 828–842.

Kim, H. S., & Drolet, A. (2003). Choice and self-expression: A cultural analysis of variety seeking. *Journal of Personality and Social Psychology, 85,* 373–382.

Kim, H. S., & Markus, H. R. (1999). Deviance or uniqueness, harmony or conformity? A cultural analysis. *Journal of Personality and Social Psychology, 77,* 785–800.

Kim, H. S., & Sherman, D. K. (in press). "Express yourself": Culture and the effect of self-expression on choice. *Journal of Personality and Social Psychology, 92,* 1–11.

Kim, J., & Hatfield, E. (2004). Love types and subjective well-being: A cross cultural study. *Social Behavior and Personality, 32,* 173–182.

Kim, K. H. S., Relkin, N., & Lee, K. (1997). Distinct cortical areas associated with native and second languages. *Nature, 388,* 171–174.

King, J. E., & Figueredo, A. J. (1997). The Five-Factor Model plus dominance in chimpanzee personality. *Journal of Research in Personality, 31,* 257–271.

Kishwar, M. (1994). Love and marriage. *Manushi, 80,* 11–19.

Kitayama, S., Duffy, S., Kawamura, T., & Larsen, J. T. (2003). Perceiving an object and its context in different cultures: A cultural look at New Look. *Psychological Science, 14,* 201–206.

Kitayama, S., Ishii, K. (2002). Word and voice: Spontaneous attention to emotional utterances in two languages. *Cognition and Emotion, 16,* 29–59.

Kitayama, S., Ishii, K., Imada, T., Takemura, K., & Ramaswamy, J. (2006). Voluntary settlement and the spirit of independence: Evidence from Japan's "Northern Frontier." *Journal of Personality and Social Psychology, 91,* 369–384.

Kitayama, S., Markus, H. R., & Kurokawa, M. (2000). Culture, emotion, and well-being: Good feelings in

Japan and the United States. *Cognition and Emotion, 14*, 93–124.

Kitayama, S., Markus, H. R., Matsumoto, H., & Norasakkunkit, V. (1997). Individual and collective processes in the construction of the self: Self-enhancement in the United States and self-criticism in Japan. *Journal of Personality and Social Psychology, 72*, 1245–1267.

Kitayama, S., Mesquita, B., & Karasawa, M. (2006). Emotional basis of independent and interdependent selves: Intensity of experiencing engaging and disengaging emotions in the US and Japan. *Journal of Personality and Social Psychology, 91*, 890–903.

Kitayama, S., Snibbe, A. C., & Markus, H. R. (2004). Is there any "Free" choice?: Self and dissonance in two cultures. *Psychological Science, 15*, 527–533.

Kitayama, S., & Uchida, Y. (2003). Explicit self-criticism and implicit self-regard: Evaluating self and friend in two cultures. *Journal of Experimental Social Psychology, 39*, 476–482.

Kleinman, A. (1982). Neurasthenia and depression: A study of somatization and culture in China. *Culture, Medicine, and Psychiatry, 6*, 117–190.

Kleinman, A. (1988). *Rethinking psychiatry: From cultural category to personal experience*. New York: Free Press.

Kluckhohn, C. (1949). *Mirror for man: The relation of anthropology to modern life*: New York: McGraw-Hill.

Knapp, R. H. (1944). A psychology of rumor. *Public Opinion Quarterly, 8*, 22–37.

Knight, N., Varnum, M. E. W., & Nisbett, R. E. (2005). *Culture, class, and categorization*. Manuscript submitted for publication.

Kohlberg, L. (1971). From is to ought: How to commit the naturalistic fallacy and get away with it in the study of moral development. In L. Mischel (Ed.), *Cognitive development and epistemology* (pp. 151–284). New York: Academic Press.

Komlos, J. (1998). Shrinking in a growing economy? The mystery of physical stature during the Industrial Revolution. *Journal of Economic History, 58*, 779–802.

Koopman, C., Eisenthal, S., & Stoeckle, J. D. (1984). Ethnicity in the reported pain, emotional distress and requests of medical outpatients. *Social Science Medicine, 18*, 487–490.

Koskenvuo, M., Kaprio, J., Kesaniemi, A., & Sarna, S. (1978). Differences in mortality from ischemic heart disease by marital status and social class. *Journal of Chronic Diseases, 33*, 95–106.

Kosic, A., Kruglanski, A. W., Pierro, A., & Mannetti, L. (2004). The social cognition of immigrants' acculturation: Effects of the need for closure and the reference group at entry. *Journal of Personality and Social Psychology, 86*, 796–813.

Kraut, R. E., & Johnston, R. E. (1979). Social and emotional messages of smiling: An ethological approach. *Journal of Personality and Social Psychology, 37*, 1539–1553.

Kuczynski, L., & Kochanska, G. (1990). Development of children's noncompliance strategies from toddlerhood to age 5. *Developmental Psychology, 26*, 398–408.

Kuhn, M. T., & McPartland, T. (1954). An empirical investigation of self-attitudes. *American Sociological Review, 19*, 68–76.

Kühnen, U., Hannover, B., & Schubert, B. (2001). The semantic-procedural interface model of the self: The role of self-knowledge for context-dependent versus context-independent modes of thinking. *Journal of Personality and Social Psychology, 80*, 397–409.

Kühnen, U., & Oyserman, D. (2002). Thinking about the self influences thinking in general: Cognitive consequences of salient self-concept. *Journal of Experimental Social Psychology, 38*, 492–499.

Kumanyika, S. K., Wilson, J. F., & Guilford-Davenport, M. (1993). Weight related attitudes and behaviors of black women. *Journal of the American Dietetic Association, 93*, 416–422.

Kunda, Z. (1990). The case for motivated reasoning. *Psychological Bulletin, 108*, 480–498.

Kurman, J. (2001). Self-enhancement: Is it restricted to individualistic cultures? *Personality and Social Psychology Bulletin, 12*, 1705–1716.

Kurman, J. (2003). Why is self-enhancement low in certain collectivist cultures? An investigation of two competing explanations. *Journal of Cross-Cultural Psychology, 34*, 496–510.

Kurman, J., Yoshihara-Tanaka, C., & Elkohsi, T. (2003). Is self-enhancement negatively related to constructive self-criticism? Self-enhancement in Israel and in Japan. *Journal of Cross-Cultural Psychology, 34*, 24–37.

Kuroda, Y., Hayashi, C., & Suzuki, T. (1986). The role of language in cross-national surveys: American and Japanese respondents. *Applied Stochastic Model and Data Analysis, 2*, 43–59.

Kyei, K. G., & Schreckenbach, H. (1975). *No time to die*. Accra, Ghana: Catholic Press.

Lachlan, R. F., Crooks, L., & Laland, K. N. (1998). Who follows whom? Shoaling preferences and social learning of foraging information in guppies. *Animal Behavior, 56*, 181–190.

Lachman, M. E., & Weaver, S. L. (1998). The sense of control as a moderator of social class differences in health and well-being. *Journal of Personality and Social Psychology, 74*, 763–773.

LaFromboise, T., Coleman, H. L. K., & Gerton, J. (1993). Psychological impact of biculturalism: Evidence and theory. *Psychological Bulletin, 114*, 395–412.

Lalonde, R. N., & Cameron, J. E. (1993). An intergroup perspective on immigrant acculturation with a focus on collective strategies. *International Journal of Psychology, 28*, 57–74.

Lambert, T. A., Kahn, A. S., & Apple, K. J. (2003). Pluralistic ignorance and hooking up. *Journal of Sex Research, 40*, 129–133.

Landes, D. S. (1999). *The wealth and poverty of nations.* New York: Norton.

Langer, E. J., & Rodin, J. (1976). The effects of choice and enhanced personal responsibility for the aged: A field experiment in an institutional setting. *Journal of Personality and Social Psychology, 34*, 191–198.

Lao Tzu. (2000). *Tao te ching.* Washington, DC: Counterpoint.

Larson, J. R., Foster-Fishman, P. G., & Keys, C. B. (1994). Discussion of shared and unshared information in decision-making groups. *Journal of Personality and Social Psychology, 67*, 446–461.

Latané, B. 1996. Dynamic social impact: The creation of culture by communication. *Journal of Communication, 46*(4), 13–25.

Lavin, T., Hall, D. G., & Leung, D. (2006). *Culture and the acquisition of nouns and verbs.* Manuscript submitted for publication.

Lavin, T., Hall, D. G., & Waxman, S. R. (2006). Culture and verb learning. In K. Hirsh-Pasek and R. Golinkoff (Eds.), *Action Meets Word: How Children Learn Verbs.* (pp. 525–543). Oxford, UK: Oxford University Press.

Lebra, T. S. (1994). Mother and child in Japanese socialization: A Japan-US comparison. In P. Greenfield & R. Cocking (Eds.), *Cross-cultural roots of minority child development* (pp. 259–274). Hillsdale, NJ: Erlbaum.

Leclerc, A., Lert, F., & Goldberg, M. (1984). Les inegalities sociales devant la mort en Grande-Bretagne et en France. *Social Science and Medicine, 19*, 479–487.

Lederer, R. (1987). Anguished English. New York: Dell.

LeDoux, J. E. (1996). *The emotional brain: The mysterious underpinnings of emotional life.* New York: Simon & Schuster.

Lee, A. Y., Aaker, J. L., & Gardner, W. L. (2000). The pleasures and pains of distinct self-construals: The role of interdependence in regulatory focus. *Journal of Personality and Social Psychology, 78*, 1122–1134.

Lee, C. K., Kwak, Y. S., Rhee, H., Kim, Y. S., Han, J. H., Choi, J. O., & Lee, Y. H. (1987). The nationwide epidemiological study of mental disorders in Korea. *Journal of Korean Medical Science, 2*, 19–34.

Lee, F., Hallahan, M., & Herzog, T. (1996). Explaining real life events: How culture and domain shape attributions. *Personality and Social Psychology Bulletin, 22*, 732–741.

Lee, G. R., & Stone, L. H. (1980). Mate-selection systems and criteria: Variation according to family structure. *Journal of Marriage and the Family, 42*, 319–326.

Lee, S. H. (1987). Social phobia in Korea. In *Social phobia in Japan and Korea: Proceedings of the first cultural psychiatry symposium between Japan and Korea* (pp. 24–52). Seoul: East Asian Academy of Cultural Psychiatry.

Lefebvre, L., & Giraldeau, L. A. (1994). Cultural transmission in pigeons is affected by the number of tutors and bystanders present. *Animal Behaviour, 47*, 331–337.

Leff, J., Sartorius, N., Jablensky, A., Korten, A., & Ernberg, G. (1992). The International Pilot Study of Schizophrenia: Five-year follow-up findings. *Psychological Medicine, 22*, 131–145.

Lenneberg, E. H. (1967). *Biological foundations of language.* New York: Wiley.

Lenski, G., & Lenski, J. (1987). *Human societies. 5th ed.* New York: McGraw-Hill.

Leor, J., Poole, W. K., & Kloner, R. A. (1996). Sudden cardiac death triggered by an earthquake. *New England Journal of Medicine, 334*, 413–419.

Leroi, A. M. (2003). *Mutants: On genetic variety and the human body.* New York: Penguin Books.

Leuers, T. R. S., & Sonoda, N. (1999). Independent Self Bias. In Sugiman, T., Karasawa, M., Liu, J. H., & Ward, C., (Eds.), *Progress in Asian Social Psychology, Volume II: Theoretical and Empirical Contributions* (p. 87–104). Seoul, Korea: Kyoyook-Kwahak-Sa Publishing Company.

Leulliette, P. (1976, October 10–11). Au nom de la loi. *Le Monde.*

Leung, K., Au, Y., Fernandez-Dols, J. M., & Iwawaki, S. (1992). Preference for methods of conflict processing in two collectivist cultures. *International Journal of Psychology, 27,* 195–209.

Leung, K., & Bond, M. H. (2004). Social axioms: A model for social beliefs in multicultural perspective. In M. P. Zanna (Ed.), *Advances in Experimental Social Psychology, Vol. 36,* (pp. 119–197). San Diego, CA: Elsevier.

Leung, K., Bond, M. H., Carment, D. W., Krishnan, L., & Liebrand, W. B. G. (1990). Effects of cultural femininity on preference for methods of conflict processing: A cross-cultural study. *Journal of Experimental Social Psychology, 26,* 373–388.

Levenson, R. W. (1992). Autonomic nervous system differences among emotions. *Psychological Science, 3,* 23–27.

Levenson, R. W., Ekman, P., Heider, K., & Friesen, W. V. (1992). Emotion and autonomic nervous system activity in the Minangkabau of West Sumatra. *Journal of Personality and Social Psychology, 62,* 972–988.

Leventhal, T., & Brooks-Gunn, J. (2000). The neighborhoods they live in: The effects of neighborhood residence on child and adolescent outcomes. *Psychological Bulletin, 126,* 309–337.

Levine, R., Sato, S., Hashimoto, T., & Verma, J. (1995). Love and marriage in eleven cultures. *Journal of Cross-Cultural Psychology, 26,* 554–571.

Levine, R. A. (2001). Culture and personality studies, 1918–1960: Myth and history. *Journal of Personality, 69,* 803–818.

Levine, R. V., & Norenzayan, A. (1999). The pace of life in 31 countries. *Journal of Cross-Cultural Psychology, 30,* 178–205.

Levinson, S. C. (1997). Language and cognition: The cognitive consequences of spatial description in Guugu Yimithirr. *Journal of Linguistic Anthropology, 7,* 98–131.

Lewis, C. C. (1995). *Educating hearts and minds.* New York: Cambridge University Press.

Lewontin, R. C. (1972). The apportionment of human diversity. In T. H. Dobzhansky, M. K. Hecht, & W. C. Steere (Eds.), *Evolutionary biology* (Vol. 6, pp. 381–398). New York: Appleton-Century-Crofts.

Lim, T. W. (n.d.). Changes in the physiques of Japanese women: Much closer to their American Sisters. Retrieved November 29, 2005, from http://www.mynippon.com/nao/discover.htm.

Lin, R. Y., Rin, H., Yeh, E. K., Hsu, C. C., & Chu, H. M. (1969). Mental disorders in Taiwan, fifteen years later: A preliminary report. In W. Caudill & T. Y. Lin (Eds.), *Mental health research in Asia and the Pacific* (pp. 66–91). Honolulu: East-West Center Press.

Lin, T.-Y., & Lin, M. C. (1981). Love, denial and rejection: Responses of Chinese families to mental illness. In A. Kleinman & T.-Y. Lin, *Normal and abnormal behavior in Chinese culture* (pp. 387–401). Boston: D. Reidel.

Lipset, S. M. (1996). *American exceptionalism: A double-edged sword.* New York: W. W. Norton.

Littlewood, R., & Lipsedge, M. (1987). The butterfly and the serpent: Culture, psychopathology, and biomedicine. *Culture, Medicine, and Psychiatry, 11,* 289–335.

Lockwood, P., & Kunda, Z. (1997). Superstars and me: Predicting the impact of role models on the self. *Journal of Personality and Social Psychology, 73,* 91–103.

Lockwood, P., Marshall, T. C., & Sadler, P. (2005). Promoting success or preventing failure: Cultural differences in motivation by positive and negative role models. *Personality and Social Psychology Bulletin, 31*(3), 379–392.

Loftus, E. F. (1993). The reality of repressed memories. *American Psychologist, 48,* 518–537.

Lopez, S. R., & Guarnaccia, P. J. J. (2000). Cultural psychopathology: Uncovering the social world of mental illness. *Annual Review of Psychology, 51,* 571–598.

Lord, C., Ross, L., & Lepper, M. (1979). Biased assimilation and attitude polarization: The effects of prior theories on subsequently considered evidence. *Journal of Personality and Social Psychology, 37,* 2098–2109.

Lubman, S. (1998, February 23). Some students must learn to question. *San Jose Mercury News,* A1–A12.

Lucy, J. A., & Shweder, R. A. (1979). Whorf and his critics: Linguistic and nonlinguistic influences on color memory. *American Anthropologist, 81,* 581–605.

Lundberg, O. (1991). Causal explanations for class inequality in health—an empirical analysis. *Social Science and Medicine, 32,* 385–393.

Luria, A. R. (1928). The problem of the cultural development of the child. *Journal of Genetic Psychology, 35,* 493–506.

Luria, A. R. (1971). Towards the problem of the historical nature of psychological processes. *International Journal of Psychology, 6*, 259–272.

Lutz, C. (1988). *Unnatural emotions.* Chicago: University of Chicago Press.

Lydon, J. E., Jamieson, D. W., & Zanna, M. P. (1988). Interpersonal similarity and the social and intellectual dimension of first impressions. *Social Cognition, 6*, 269–286.

Lynge, E. (1984). Socioeconomic occupational mortality differentials in Europe. *Sozial-und Praventivmedizin, 29*, 265–267.

Lynn, R. (1989). Positive correlation between height, head size, and IQ: A nutrition theory of the secular increases in intelligence. *British Journal of Educational Psychology, 59*, 372–377.

Lysgaard, S. (1955). Adjustment in a foreign society: Norwegian Fulbright grantees visiting the United States. *International Social Science Bulletin, 7*, 45–51.

Lyubomirsky, S., King, L., & Diener, E. (2005). The benefits of frequent positive affect: Does happiness lead to success? *Psychological Bulletin, 131*, 803–855.

Ma, V., & Schoeneman, T. J. (1997). Individualism versus collectivism: A comparison of Kenyan and American self-concepts. *Basic and Applied Social Psychology, 19*, 261–273.

Maass, A., Karasawa, M., Politi, F., & Suga, S. (2005). *Do verbs and adjectives play different roles in different cultures? A cross-linguistic analysis of person representation.* Manuscript submitted for publication.

Macmillan, N. A. (1987). Beyond the categorical/continuous distinction: A psychophysical approach to processing modes. In S. Harnad (Ed.), *Categorical perception: The groundwork of cognition* (pp. 53–85). Cambridge, UK: Cambridge University Press.

Macpherson, C., & Macpherson, L. (1987). Towards an explanation of recent trends in suicide in Western Samoa. *Man, 22*, 305–330.

Madsen, M. C. (1971). Developmental and cross-cultural differences in the cooperative and competitive behavior of young children. *Journal of Cross-Cultural Psychology*, 365–371.

Mahalingam, R. (2003). Essentialism, culture and beliefs about gender among the Aravanis of Tamil Nadu, India. *Sex Roles, 49*, 489–496.

Mahalingam, R., & Rodriguez, J. (2003). Essentialism, power and cultural psychology of gender. *Journal of Cognition and Culture, 3*, 157–174. Marmot, M. G., & Syme, S. L. (1976). Acculturation and coronary heart disease in Japanese-Americans. *American Journal of Epidemiology, 104*, 225–247.

Mahler, I. (1974). A comparative study of locus of control. *Psychologia, 17*, 135–139.

Major, B., Spencer, S., Schmader, T., Wolfe, C., & Crocker, J. (1998). Coping with negative stereotypes about intellectual performance: The role of psychological disengagement. *Personality and Social Psychology Bulletin, 24*, 34–50.

Malcolm, L. A. (1974). Ecological factors relating to child growth and nutritional status. In A. F. Roche & R. Falkner (Eds.), *Nutrition and malnutrition: Identification and measurement* (pp. 329–352). New York: Plenum Press.

Malinowski, B. (1922/1965). *Argonauts of the Western Pacific: An account of native enterprise and adventure in the archipelagoes of Melanesian New Guinea.* New York: Dutton.

Mandel, N. (2003). Shifting selves and decision making: The effects of self construal priming on consumer risk taking. *Journal of Consumer Research, 30*, 30–40.

Mandelbaum, D. G. (1951). *Selected writings of Edward Sapir in language, culture, and personality.* Berkeley, CA: University of California Press.

Mann, A. H. (1977). Psychiatric morbidity and hostility in hypertension. *Psychological Medicine, 7*, 653–659.

Marin, G., Gamba, R. J., & Marin, G. V. (1992). Extreme response style and acquiescence among Hispanics. *Journal of Cross-Cultural Psychology, 23*, 498–509.

Mark, N. (1998). Birds of a feather sing together: Relation of social positions to musical preferences. *Social Forces, 77*, 253–277.

Markides, K. S., & Coreil, J. (1986). The health of Hispanics in the southwestern United States: An epidemiologic paradox. *Public Health Reports, 101*, 253–265.

Marmot, M. G. (2004). *The status syndrome: How social standing affects our health and longevity.* New York: Henry Holt.

Marmot, M. G., Bosma, H., Hemingway, H., Brunner, E., & Stansfeld, S. (1997). Contribution of job control and other risk factors to social variations in coronary heart disease incidence. *Lancet, 350*, 235–239.

Marmot, M. G., & Davey Smith, G. (1989). Why are the Japanese living longer? *British Medical Journal, 299*, 1547–1551.

Marmot, M. G., Kogevinas, M., & Elston, M. A. (1987). Social/economic status and disease. *Annual Review of Public Health, 8*, 111–135.

Marmot, M. G., Shipley, M. J., & Rose, G. (1984). Inequalities in death: Specific explanations of a general pattern? *Lancet, 1984*(1), 1003–1006.

Markus, H. R., & Kitayama, S. (1991). Culture and the self: Implications for cognition, emotion, and motivation. *Psychological Review, 98*, 224–253.

Markus, H. R., & Kitayama, S. (1998). The cultural psychology of personality. *Journal of Cross-Cultural Psychology, 29*, 63–87.

Markus, H. R., Uchida, Y., Omoregie, H., Townsend, S. S. M., & Kitayama, S. (2006). Going for the gold: Models of agency in Japanese and American contexts. *Psychological Science, 17*, 103–112.

Martin, R. D. (1981). Relative brain size and basal metabolic rate in terrestrial vertebrates. *Nature, 293*, 57–60.

Masson, J. L., & Padwardhan, M. W. (1970). *Aesthetic rapture: The Rasadhyaya of the Natyasastra*. Poona, India: Deccan College.

Masuda, T., Ellsworth, P. C., Mesquita, B., Leu, J., Tanida, S., & van de Veerdonk, E. (2005). *Placing the face in context: Cultural differences in the perception of facial emotion*. Manuscript under review.

Masuda, T., Gonzalez, R., Kwan, L. Y., & Nisbett, R. E. (2005). *Culture and esthetic preference: Comparing the attention to context of East Asians and Americans*. Manuscript under review.

Masuda, T., & Nisbett, R. E. (2001). Attending holistically vs. analytically: Comparing the context sensitivity of Japanese and Americans. *Journal of Personality and Social Psychology, 81*, 922–934.

Masuda, T., & Nisbett, R. E. (2006). Culture and change blindness. *Cognitive Science, 30*, 381–399.

Mather, J. A., & Anderson, R. C. (1993). Personalities of octopuses (Octopus rubescens). *Journal of Comparative Psychology, 107*, 336–340.

Matsumoto, D., & Ekman, P. (1989). American-Japanese cultural differences in intensity ratings of facial expressions of emotion. *Motivation and Emotion, 13*, 143–157.

Matsumoto, D., Kudoh, T., Scherer, K., & Wallbott, H. (1988). Antecedents of and reactions to emotions in the United States and Japan. *Journal of Cross-Cultural Psychology, 19*, 267–286.

Matsumoto, D., & Willingham, B. (2006). The thrill of victory and the agony of defeat: Spontaneous expressions of medal winners of the 2004 Athens Olympic Games. *Journal of Personality and Social Psychology, 91*, 568–581.

Mayberry, R. I. (1993). First-language acquisition after childhood differs from second-language acquisition: The case of American Sign Language. *Journal of Speech and Hearing Research, 36*, 1258–1270.

Mazur, A. (1985). A biosocial model of status in face-to-face primate groups. *Social Forces, 64*, 377–402.

McAdams, D. P. (1992). The five-factor model of personality: A critical appraisal. *Journal of Personality, 60*, 329–361.

McCauley, R. N., & Henrich, J. (2006). Susceptibility to the Muller-Lyer Illusion, theory-neutral observation, and the diachronic penetrability of the visual input system. *Philosophical Psychology, 19*, 1–23.

McClelland, D. (1961). *The achieving society*. Princeton, NJ: Van Nostrand.

McCrae, R. R. (2002). NEO-PI-R data from 36 cultures: Further intercultural comparisons. In R. R. McCrae & J. Allik (Eds.), *The Five-Factor Model of personality across cultures* (pp. 105–126). New York: Kluwer.

McCrae, R. R., Terraciano, A., & 78 members of the Personality Profiles of Cultures Project. (2005). Universal features of personality traits from the observer's perspective: Data from 50 cultures. *Journal of Personality and Social Psychology, 88*, 547–561.

McCrae, R. R., Yik, M. S. M., Trapnell, P. D., Bond, M. H., & Paulhus, D. L. (1998). Interpreting personality profiles across cultures: Bilingual, acculturation, and peer rating studies of Chinese undergraduates. *Journal of Personality and Social Psychology, 74*, 1041–1055.

McWhiney, G. (1988). *Cracker culture: Celtic ways in the old South*. Tuscaloosa: University of Alabama Press.

Mead, M. (1928). *Coming of age in Samoa: A psychological study of primitive youth for Western civilization*. New York: Blue Ribbon Books.

Mehler, J., Jusczyk, P., & Lambertz, G. (1988). A precursor of language acquisition in young infants. *Cognition, 29*, 143–178.

Meijer, Z., Heine, S. J., & Yamagami, M. (1999, August 4–7). *Remember those good old days? Culture, self-discrepancies, and biographical memory*. Symposium presentation at the 3rd Conference of the Asian Association of Social Psychology, Taipei, Taiwan.

Menon, T., Morris, M. W., Chiu, C., & Hong, Y. (1999). Culture and the construal of agency:

Attribution to individual versus group dispositions. *Journal of Personality and Social Psychology, 76,* 701–717.

Mesoudi, A., Whiten, A., & Laland, K.N. (2006). Towards a unified science of cultural evolution. *Behavioral and Brain Sciences, 29,* 329–383.

Mesquita, B. (2001). Emotions in collectivist and individualist contexts. *Journal of Personality and Social Psychology, 80,* 68–74.

Mesquita, B., & Frijda, N. H. (1992). Cultural variation in emotion: A review. *Psychological Bulletin, 112,* 179–204.

Mesquita, B., & Karasawa, M. (2002). Different emotional lives. *Cognition and Emotion, 17,* 127–141.

Miller, G. E., & Cohen, S. (2005). Infectious disease and psychoneuroimmunology. In K.Vedhara & M. Irwin (Eds.), *Human psychoneuroimmunology* (pp. 219–242). New York: Oxford University Press.

Miller, J. G., (1984). Culture and the development of everyday social explanation. *Journal of Personality and Social Psychology, 46,* 961–978.

Miller, J. G., & Bersoff, D. M. (1992). Culture and moral judgment: How are conflicts between justice and interpersonal responsibilities resolved? *Journal of Personality and Social Psychology, 62,* 541–554.

Miller, J. G., Bersoff, D. M., & Harwood, R. L. (1990). Perceptions of social responsibilities in India and the United States: Moral imperatives or personal decisions? *Journal of Personality and Social Psychology, 58,* 33–47.

Miller, K. F., & Paredes, D. R. (1996). On the shoulders of giants: Cultural tools and mathematical development. In R. J. Sternberg & T. Ben-Zeev (Eds.), *The nature of mathematical thinking* (pp. 83–117). Mahwah, NJ: Lawrence Erlbaum.

Miller, P. J., Wang, S., Sandel, T., & Cho, G. E. (2002). Self-esteem as folk theory: A comparison of European American and Taiwanese mothers' beliefs. *Parenting: Science and Practice, 2,* 209–239.

Miller, P. J., Wiley, A. R., Fung H., & Liang, C. H. (1997). Personal storytelling as a medium of socialization in Chinese and American families. *Child Development, 68,* 557–568.

Minami, M. (1994). English and Japanese: A cross-cultural comparison of parental styles of narrative elicitation. *Issues in Applied Linguistics, 5,* 383–407.

Minoura, Y. (1992). A sensitive period for the incorporation of a cultural meaning system: A study of Japanese children growing up in the United States. *Ethos, 20,* 304–339.

Mittleman, M. A., Malone, M. A., Maclure, M., Sherwood, J. B., & Muller, J. E. (1998). Workplace stress as a trigger of acute myocardial infarction. *Circulation, 97,* 15.

Miyake, K. (1993). Temperament, mother-infant interaction, and early development. *The Japanese Journal of Research on Emotions, 1,* 48–55.

Miyake, K., Cheng, S., & Campos, J. J. (1985). Infant temperament, mother's mode of interaction, and attachment in Japan: An interim report. In I. Bretherton & E. Waters (Eds.), *Growing point in attachment theory. Monographs of the Society for Research in Child Development, 50* (1–2 Serial No. 209), 276–297.

Miyamoto, T., & Onizawa, C. (1985). Taijin kyoufushou to seishin bunretsubyou [Taijin kyoufushou and schizophrenia]. *Seishinka MOOK, 12,* 51–60.

Miyamoto, Y., & Nisbett, R. E. (2006). Culture and the physical environment: Holistic versus analytic perceptual affordances. *Psychological Science, 17,* 113–119.

Miyamoto, Y., & Schwarz, N. (2006). When conveying a message may hurt the relationship: Cultural differences in the difficulty of using an answering machine. *Journal of Experimental Social Psychology, 42,* 540–547.

Modiano, D., et al. (2001). The lower susceptibility to *Plasmodium falciparum* malaria of Fulani of Burkina Faso (west Africa) is associated with low frequencies of classic malaria-resistance genes. *Transactions of the Royal Society of Tropical Medicine and Hygiene, 95,* 149–152.

Modiano, D., Petrarca, V., Sirma, B., Nebie, I., Diallo, D., Esposito, F., & Coluzzi, M. (1996). Different response to *Plasmodium falciparum* malaria in West African sympatric ethnic groups. *Proceedings of the National Academy of Science, 93,* 13206–13211.

Montagu, A. (1986). *Touching: The human significance of skin.* New York: Harper and Row.

Mori, A., Kitanishi, K., & Fujimoto, H. (1989). 15nenkan no chiryou taishou to chiryou seiseki [Therapeutic subjects and their progress over a 15-year period]. In A. Mori & K. Kitanishi (Eds.), *Morita ryouhou no kenkyuu: Arata na tenkai o mezashite [Research on Morita treatment: Toward a new development]* (pp. 17–52). Tokyo: Kongo Shuppan.

Morikawa, H., Shand, N., & Kosawa, Y. (1988). Maternal speech to prelingual infants in Japan and the United States: Relationships among functions, forms and referents. *Journal of Child Language, 15,* 237–256.

Morita, S. (1917). The true nature of shinkeishitsu and its treatment. In *Anthology of theses commemorating the 25th anniversary of Professor Kure's appointment to his chair.* Tokyo: Jikei University.

Morling. B. (2000). "Taking" an aerobics class in the U.S. and "entering" an aerobics class in Japan: Primary and secondary control in a fitness context. *Asian Journal of Social Psychology, 3,* 73–85.

Morling, B., & Evered, S. (2006). Secondary control reviewed and defined. *Psychological Bulletin, 132,* 269–296.

Morling, B., Kitayama, S., & Miyamoto, Y. (2002). Cultural practices emphasize influence in the United States and adjustment in Japan. *Personality and Social Psychology Bulletin, 28,* 311–323.

Morris, D. (1997). *The human sexes.* London, UK: BBC Books.

Morris, M., & Peng, K. (1994). Culture and cause: American and Chinese attributions for social and physical events. *Journal of Personality and Social Psychology, 67,* 949–971.

Moskalenko, S., & Heine, S. J. (2003). Watching your troubles away: Television viewing as a stimulus for subjective self-awareness. *Personality and Social Psychology Bulletin, 29,* 76–85.

Mumford, D. B., Whitehouse, A. M., & Choudry, I. Y. (1992). Survey of eating disorders in English-medium schools in Lahore, Pakistan. *International Journal of Eating Disorders, 11,* 173–184.

Murdock, G. P. (1980). *Theories of illness: A world survey.* Pittsburgh: University of Pittsburgh Press.

Murphy, F. C., Nimmo-Smith, I., & Lawrence, A. D. (2003). Functional neuroanatomy of emotion: A meta-analysis. *Cognitive, Affective, and Behavioral Neuroscience, 3,* 207–233.

Murphy-Berman, V., Berman, J. J., Singh, P., Pachauri, A., & Kuman, P. (1984). Factors affecting allocation to needy and meritorious recipients: A cross-cultural comparison. *Journal of Personality and Social Psychology, 46,* 1267–1272.

Murray, S. L., Holmes, J. G., & Griffin, D. W. (1996). The benefits of positive illusions: Idealization and the construction of satisfaction in close relationships. *Journal of Personality and Social Psychology, 70,* 79–98.

Murstein, B. I., Merighi, J. R., & Vyse, S. A. (1991). Love styles in the United States and France: A cross-cultural comparison. *Journal of Social and Clinical Psychology, 10,* 37–46.

Myers, I. B. (1962). *The Myers-Briggs Type Indicator.* Princeton, NJ: Educational Testing Service.

Nagell, K., Olguin, K., & Tomasello, M. (1993). Processes of social learning in the tool use of chimpanzees (Pan troglodytes) and human children (Homo sapiens). *Journal of Comparative Psychology, 107,* 174–186.

National Center for Health Statistics (NCHS). (1993). *Health, United States, 1992.* Hyattsville, MD: U.S. Public Health Service.

Neff, L. J. Sargent, R. G., McKeown, R. E., & Jackson, K. L. (1997). Black-White differences in body size perceptions and weight management practices among adolescent females. *Journal of Adolescent Health, 20,* 459–465.

Neto, F., Mullet, E., & Deschamps, J. (2000). Cross-cultural variations in attitudes toward love. *Journal of Cross-Cultural Psychology, 31,* 626–635.

Newcomb, T. M. (1961). *The acquaintance process.* New York: Holt, Rinehart & Winston.

Newport, E. L. (1991). Contrasting concepts of the critical period for language. In S. Carey & R. Gelman, (Eds.), *The epigenesis of mind: Essays on biology and cognition. The Jean Piaget Symposium series* (pp. 111–130). Hillsdale, NJ: Erlbaum.

Newton, M. (2002). *Savage girls and wild boys: A history of feral children.* New York, NY: Picador.

Ngui, P. W. (1969). The koro epidemic in Singapore. *Australian New Zealand Journal of Psychiatry, 3,* 263–266.

Nisbett, R. E. (1993). Violence and U.S. regional culture. *American Psychologist, 48,* 441–449.

Nisbett, R. E. (2003). *The geography of thought.* New York: Free Press.

Nisbett, R. E., & Cohen, D. (1996). *Culture of honor: The psychology of violence in the South.* Boulder, CO: Westview Press.

Nisbett, R. E., Peng, K., Choi, I., & Norenzayan, A. (2001). Culture and systems of thought: Holistic vs. analytic cognition. *Psychological Review, 108,* 291–310.

Nisbett, R. E., & Wilson, T. D. (1977). Telling more than we can know: Verbal reports on mental processes. *Psychological Review, 84,* 231–259.

Nobakht, M., & Dezhkam, M. (2000). An epidemiological study of eating disorders in Iran. *International Journal of Eating Disorders, 28,* 265–271.

Noels, K. A., Pon, G., & Clement, R. (1996). Language, identity, and adjustment: The role of linguistic self-confidence in the acculturation process. *Journal of Language and Social Psychology, 15,* 246–264.

Norasakkunkit, V., & Kalick, M. S. (2002). Culture, ethnicity, and emotional distress measures: The role of self-construal and self-enhancement. *Journal of Cross-Cultural Psychology, 33,* 56–70.

Norenzayan, A. (2005). *Middle Eastern cognition in cross-cultural context.* Unpublished manuscript, University of British Columbia.

Norenzayan, A. (2006). Evolution and transmitted culture. *Psychological Inquiry, 17,* 123–128.

Norenzayan, A., Atran, S., Faulkner, J., & Schaller, M. (2006). Memory and mystery: The cultural selection of minimally counterintuitive narratives. *Cognitive Science, 30,* 531–553.

Norenzayan, A., Choi, I., & Nisbett, R. E. (2002a). Cultural similarities and differences in social inference: Evidence from behavioral predictions and lay theories of behavior. *Personality and Social Psychology Bulletin, 28,* 109–120.

Norenzayan, A., Choi, I., & Nisbett, R. E. (2002b). Eastern and Western folk psychology and the prediction of behavior. *Personality and Social Psychology Bulletin, 28,* 109–120.

Norenzayan, A., & Heine, S. J., (2005). Psychological universals: What are they, and how can we know? *Psychological Bulletin, 131,* 763–784.

Norenzayan, A., Smith, E. E., Kim, B. J., & Nisbett, R. E. (2002). Cultural preferences for formal versus intuitive reasoning. *Cognitive Science, 26,* 653–684.

Nwaefuna, A. (1981). Anorexia nervosa in a developing country [Letter to the editor]. *British Journal of Psychiatry, 138,* 270.

Oberg, K. (1960). Cultural shock: Adjustment to new cultural environments, *Practical Anthropology, 7,* 177–182.

Obeyesekere, G. (1985). Depression, Buddhism and the work of culture in Sri Lanka. In A. Kleinman & B. Good (Eds.), *Culture and depression,* (pp. 134–152). Berkeley, CA: University of California Press.

Oettingen, G., Little, T. D., Lindenberger, U., & Baltes, P. B. (1994). Causality, agency, and control beliefs in East versus West Berlin children: A natural experiment on the role of context. *Journal of Personality and Social Psychology, 66,* 579–595.

Oettingen, G., & Seligman, M. E. P. (1990). Pessimism and behavioral signs of depression in East versus West Berlin. *European Journal of Social Psychology, 20,* 207–220.

Oishi, S. (2002). The experiencing and remembering of well-being: A cross-cultural analysis. *Personality and Social Psychology Bulletin, 28,* 1398–1406.

Oishi, S., & Diener, E. (2003). Culture and well-being: The cycle of action, evaluation, and decision. *Personality and Social Psychology Bulletin, 29,* 939–949.

Oishi, S., Diener, E., Scollon, C. N., & Biswas-Diener, R. (2004). Cross-situational consistency of affective experiences across cultures. *Journal of Personality and Social Psychology, 86,* 460–472.

Oishi, S., Lun, J., Sherman, G. D. (2006). *Residential mobility, self-concept, and well-being: What happens when you move?* Unpublished manuscript.

Okazaki, S. (1997). Sources of ethic differences between Asian American and White American college students on measures of depression and social anxiety. *Journal of Abnormal Psychology, 106,* 52–60.

Okazaki, S., Liu, J. F., Longworth, S. L., & Minn, J. Y. (2002). Asian American-White American differences in expressions of social anxiety: A replication and extension. *Cultural Diversity and Ethnic Minority Psychology, 8,* 234–247.

Organisation for Economic Co-operation and Development (OECD). (2004, February 22). *Health at a glance: OECD indicators 2003*: Chart 8. Increasing obesity rates among the adult population in OECD countries. Retrieved October 6, 2005, from http://www.oecd.org/LongAbstract/0,2546, en_2649_201185_16361657_1_1_1_1,00.html.

Orwell, G. (1990). Nineteen eighty-four. London, UK: Penguin. (Original work published 1848)

Ostir, G. V., Ottenbacher, K. J., & Markides, K. S. (2004). Onset of frailty in older adults and the protective role of positive affect. *Psychology and Aging, 19,* 402–408.

Ouchi, W. G., & Jaeger, A. M. (1978). Type Z organization: Stability in the midst of mobility. *Academy of Management Review, 3,* 305–314.

Oxford English Dictionary. (1989). Second edition.

Oyserman, D., Coon, H. M., & Kemmelmeier, M. (2002). Rethinking individualism and collectivism: Evaluation of theoretical assumptions and meta-analyses *Psychological Bulletin, 128,* 3–72.

Pablos-Mendez, A. (1994). Letter to the editor. *Journal of the American Medical Association, 271,* 1237–1238.

Pagsberg, A. K., & Wang, A. R. (1994). Epidemiology of anorexia and bulimia nervosa in Bornholm

County, Denmark, 1970–1989. *Acta Psychiatrica Scandinavica, 90,* 259–265.

Pamuk, E., Makuk, D., Heck, K., & Reuben, C. (1998). *Health, United States, 1998, with socioeconomic status and health chartbook.* Hyattsville, MD: National Center for Health Statistics.

Panksepp, J. (1998). *Affective neuroscience: The foundations of human and animal emotions.* New York: Oxford University Press.

Parekh, R., & Beresin, E. V. (2001). Looking for love? Take a cross-cultural walk through the personals. *Academic Psychiatry, 25,* 223–233.

Parker, G., Cheah, Y. C., & Roy, K. (2001). Do the Chinese somatize depression? A cross-cultural study. *Social Psychiatry and Psychiatric Epidemiology, 36,* 287–293.

Parker, G., Gladstone, G., & Chee, K. T. (2001). Depression in the planet's largest ethnic group: The Chinese. *American Journal of Psychiatry, 158,* 857–864.

Parker, S. T., & Gibson, K. R. (1977). object manipulation, tool use and sensorimotor intelligence as feeding adaptations in great apes and cebus monkeys. *Journal of Human Evolution, 6,* 623–641.

Parkinson, B. (2005). Do facial movements express emotions or communicate motives? *Personality and Social Psychology Review, 9,* 278–311.

Payer, L. (1996). *Medicine and Culture.* New York: Owl Books.

Pearce, N. E., Davis, P. B., Smith, A. H., & Foster, F. H. (1985). Social class, ethnic group, and male mortality in New Zealand, 1974–8. *Journal of Epidemiology and Community Health, 39,* 9–14.

Peng, K., & Nisbett, R. E. (1999). Culture, dialectics, and reasoning about contradiction. *American Psychologist, 54,* 741–754.

Peng, K., Nisbett, R. E., & Wong, N. Y. C. (1997). Validity problems comparing values across cultures and possible solutions. *Psychological Methods, 2,* 329–344.

Perani, D., Paulesu, E., & Galles, N. S. (1998). The bilingual brain: Proficiency and age of acquisition of the second language. *Brain, 121,* 1841–1852.

Perez-Stable, E. J., Marin, G., & Marin, B. V. (1994). Behavioral risk factors: A comparison of Latinos and non-Latino Whites in San Francisco. *American Journal of Public Health, 84,* 971–976.

Phan, K. L., Wager, T. D., Taylor, S. F., & Liberzon, I. (2002). Functional neuroanatomy of emotion: A meta-analysis of emotion activation studies in PET and fMRI. *Neuroimage, 16,* 331–348.

Philbrick, J. L., & Opolot, J. A. (1980). Love style: Comparison of African and American attitudes. *Psychological Reports, 46,* 286.

Pica, P., Lerner, C., Izard, V., & Dehaene, S. (2004). Exact and approximate arithmetic in an Amazonian indigenous group. *Science, 306,* 499–501.

Pike, K. L. (1967). *Language in relation to a unified theory of the structure of human behavior.* The Hague: Mouton.

Pinker, S. (1994). *The language instinct.* New York: William Morrow.

Plaut, V. C., Markus, H. R., & Lachman, M. E. (2002). Place matters: Consensual features and regional variation in American well-being and self. *Journal of Personality and Social Psychology, 83,* 160–184.

Poma, P. A. (1983). Hispanic cultural influences on medical practice. *Journal of the National Medical Association, 75,* 941–946.

Poortinga, Y. H., & Van Hemert, D. A. (2001). Personality and culture: Demarcating the common and the unique. *Journal of Personality, 69,* 1033–1060.

Population Reference Bureau. (2006, August). *2006 World population data sheet.* Retrieved October 10, 2006, from http://www.prb.org/pdf06/06 WorldDataSheet.pdf.

Povinelli, D. J., Perilloux, H. K., Reaux, J. E., & Bierschwale, D. T. (1998). Young and juvenile chimpanzees' (Pan troglodytes) reactions to intentional versus accidental and inadvertent actions. *Behavioural Processes, 42,* 205–218.

Prentice, D., & Miller, D. (1996). Pluralistic ignorance and the perpetuation of social norms by unwitting actors. In M. Zanna (Ed.), *Advances in experimental social psychology* (pp. 161–209). San Diego, CA: Academic Press.

Prince, R. (1960). The "brain fag" syndrome in Nigerian students. *Journal of Mental Science, 104,* 559–570.

Putnam, R. D. (2000). *Bowling alone: The collapse and revival of American community.* New York: Simon & Schuster.

Putnam, R. D., Leonardi, R., & Nanetti, R. Y. (1993). *Making democracy work.* Princeton, NJ: Princeton University Press.

Pyszczynski, T., & Greenberg, J. (1983). Determinants of reduction in intended effort as a strategy for coping with anticipated failure. *Journal of Research in Personality, 17,* 412–422.

Quinn, D. M., & Crocker, J. (1999). When ideology hurts: Effects of belief in the Protestant ethic and feeling overweight on the psychological well-being of women. *Journal of Personality and Social Psychology, 77*, 402–414.

Quinones-Vidal, E., Lopez-Garcia, J. J., Penaranda-Ortega, M., & Tortosa-Gil, F. (2004). The nature of social and personality psychology as reflected in JPSP, 1965–2000. *Journal of Personality and Social Psychology, 86*, 435–452.

Ratner, C. (1989). A sociohistorical critique of naturalistic theories of color perception. *Journal of Mind and Behavior, 10*, 361–373.

Redelmeier, D. A., & Singh, S. M. (2001). Survival in academy award-winning actors and actresses. *Annals of Internal Medicine, 134*, 955–962.

Rees, P. (2002, October 20). Japan: The missing million. *BBC News.* Retrieved November 29, 2005, from http://news.bbc.co.uk/2/hi/programmes/correspondent/2334893.stm.

Reisenzein, R., Bordgen, S., Holtbernd, T., & Matz, D. (2006). Evidence for strong disassociation between emotion and facial displays: The case of surprise. *Journal of Personality and Social Psychology, 91*, 295–315.

Renaud, S., & de Lorgeril, M. (1992). Wine, alcohol, platelets, and the French paradox for coronary heart disease. *The Lancet, 339*, 1523–1526.

Rendell, L., & Whitehead, H. (2001). Culture in whales and dolphins. *Behavioral and Brain Sciences, 24*, 309–382.

Rensink, R. A., O'Regan, J. K., & Clark, J. J. (1997). To see or not to see: The need for attention to perceive changes in scenes. *Psychological Science, 8*, 368–373.

Reykowski, J. (1994). Collectivism and individualism as dimensions of social change. In U. Kim, H. Triandis, C. Kagitcibasi, S.-C. Choi, & G. Yoon (Eds.), Individualism and collectivism: Theory, method, and applications. Thousand Oaks, CA: Sage.

Rhee, E., Uleman, J. S., Lee, H. K., & Roman, R. J. (1995). Spontaneous self-descriptions and ethnic identities in individualistic and collectivistic cultures. *Journal of Personality & Social Psychology, 69*, 142–152.

Rhodes, G., Lee, K., Palermo, R., Weiss, M., Yoshikawa, S., Clissa, P., Williams, T., Peters, M., Winkler, C., & Jeffery, L. (2005). Attractiveness of own-race, other-race, and mixed-race faces. *Perception, 34*, 319–340.

Rhodes, G., Zebrowitz, L. A., Clark, A., Kalick, S. M., Hightower, A., & McKay, R. (2001). Do facial averageness and symmetry signal health? *Evolution and Human Behavior, 22*, 31–46.

Rice, T. W., & Steele, B. J. (2004). Subjective well-being and culture across time and space. *Journal of Cross-Cultural Psychology, 35*, 633–647.

Richard, J. L. (1987, April). Les facteurs de risqué coronarien: Le paradoxe français. *Archives des Maladies du Coeur et des Vaisseaux, 80*, 17–21.

Richardson, A. (1974). *British immigrants and Australia: A psycho-social inquiry.* Canberra: Australian National University Press.

Richerson, P. J., & Boyd, R. (2005). *Not by genes alone: How culture transformed human evolution.* Chicago: University of Chicago Press.

Rivera-Sinclair, E. A. (1997). Acculturation/biculturalism and its relationship to adjustment in Cuban-Americans. *International Journal of Intercultural Relations, 21*, 379–391.

Roberson, D., Davidoff, J., Davies, I., & Shapiro, L. (2005). Colour categories in Himba: Evidence for the cultural relativity hypothesis. *Cognitive Psychology, 50*, 378–411.

Roberson, D., Davies, I., & Davidoff, J. (2000). Color categories are not universal: Replications and new evidence from a stone-age culture. *Journal of Experimental Psychology: General, 129*, pp. 369–398.

Robins, L. N., & Regier, D. A. (1991). *Psychiatric disorders in America: The Epidemiological Catchment Area study.* New York: Free Press.

Robinson, M. D., & Clore, G. L. (2002). Belief and feeling: Evidence for an accessibility model of emotional self-report. *Psychological Bulletin, 128*, 934–960.

Rodgers, J. S., Peng, K., Wang, L., & Hou, Y. (2004). Dialectical self-esteem and East-West differences in psychological well-being. *Personality and Social Psychology Bulletin, 30*, 1416–1432.

Rodin, J., & Langer, E. J. (1977). Long-term effects of a control-relevant intervention with institutionalized aged. *Journal of Personality and Social Psychology, 35*, 897–902.

Rogoff, B. (1981). Schooling and the development of cognitive skills. In H. C. Triansis & A. Heron (Eds.), *Handbook of cross-cultural psychology* (Vol. 4, pp. 233–294). Rockleigh, NJ: Allyn & Bacon.

Rogoff, B. (2003). *The cultural nature of human development.* Oxford, UK: Oxford University Press.

Rosaldo, M. Z. (1980). *Knowledge and passion: Ilongot notions of self and social life.* Cambridge, UK: Cambridge University Press.

Rosch Heider, E. (1972). Universals in color naming and memory. *Journal of Experimental Psychology, 93,* 10–20.

Rosch Heider, E., & Olivier, D. C. (1972). The structure of the color space in naming and memory for two languages. *Cognitive Psychology, 3,* 337–354.

Rosen, B. C. (1998). *Winners and losers of the information revolution: Psychosocial change and its discontents.* Westport, CT: Praeger.

Rosen, D. S. (2003). Eating disorders in children and young adolescents: Etiology, classification, clinical features, and treatment. *Adolescent Medicine, 14,* 49–59.

Rosenberg, M. (1965). *Society and the adolescent self-image.* Princeton, NJ: Princeton University Press.

Rosenthal, D. (Ed.) (2004). *Variety International Film Guide.* Los Angeles: Silman-James Press.

Ross, C. E., & Mirowsky, J. (1984). Socially-desirable response and acquiescence in a cross-cultural survey of mental health. *Journal of Health and Social Behavior, 25,* 189–197.

Ross, M., Xun, W. Q. E., & Wilson, A. E. (2002). Language and the bicultural self. *Personality and Social Psychology Bulletin, 28,* 1040–1050.

Ross, N., Medin, D., Coley, J., & Atran, S. (2003). Cultural and experiential differences in the development of folkbiological induction. *Cognitive Development, 18,* 25–47.

Rothbaum, F., Pott, M., Azuma, H., Miyake, K., & Weisz, J. (2000). The development of close relationships in Japan and the US: Paths of symbiotic harmony and generative tension. *Child Development, 71,* 1121–1142.

Rothbaum, F., Weisz, J., Pott, M., Miyake, K., & Morelli, G. (2000). Attachment and culture: Security in the United States and Japan. *American Psychologist, 55,* 1093–1104.

Rothbaum, F., Weisz, J. R., & Snyder, S. S. (1982). Changing the world and changing the self: A two-process model of perceived control. *Journal of Personality and Social Psychology, 42,* 5–37.

Rotimi, C., Puras, A., Cooper, R., McFarlane-Anderson, N., Forrester, T., Ogunbiyi, O., & Ward, L. M. R. (1996). Polymorphisms of rennin-angiotensin genes among Nigerians, Jamicans, and African Americans. *Hypertension, 27,* 558–563.

Rozin, P., Bauer, R., & Catanese, D. (2003). Food and life: Pleasure and worry, among American college students: Gender differences and regional similarities. *Journal of Personality and Social Psychology, 85,* 132–141.

Rozin, P., Fischler, C., Imada, S., Sarubin, A., & Wrzesniewski, A. (1999). Attitudes to food and the role of food in life in the USA, Japan, Flemish Belgium, and France: Possible implications for the diet-health debate. *Appetite, 33,* 163–180.

Rozin, P., Fischler, C., Shields, C., & Masson, E. (2006). Attitudes towards large numbers of choices in the food domain: A cross-cultural study of five countries in Europe and the USA. Manuscript under review.

Rozin, P., Kabnick, K., Pete, E., Fischler, C., & Shields, C. (2003). The ecology of eating: Smaller portion sizes in France than in the United States help explain the French Paradox. *Psychological Science, 14,* 450–454.

Rozin, P., Kurzer, N., & Cohen, A. B. (2002). Free associations to "food:" The effects of gender, generation, and culture. *Journal of Research in Personality, 36,* 419–441.

Rozin, P., Leeman, R. F., Fischler, C., & Shields, C. (2006). *Doctors in each of five countries resemble their countrymen more than doctors in other countries in attitudes toward food and health.* Unpublished manuscript, University of Pennsylvania.

Rozin, P., Lowery, L., Imada, S., & Haidt, J. (1999). The CAD triad hypothesis: A mapping between three moral emotions (contempt, anger, disgust) and three moral codes (community, autonomy, divinity). *Journal of Personality and Social Psychology, 76,* 574–586.

Rubel, A. J., O'Nell, C. W., & Collado, R. (1985). The folk illness called susto. In R. C. Simons & C. C. Hughes (Eds.), *The culture-bound syndromes* (pp. 333–350). Dordrecht, The Netherlands: Reidel.

Rubinstein, D. H. (1983). Epidemic suicide among Micronesian adolescents. *Social Science and Medicine, 17,* 657–665.

Rubinstein, D. H. (1992). Suicidal behavior in Micronesia. In L. P. Kok & W. S. Tseng (Eds.), *Suicidal behavior in the Asia-Pacific region* (pp. 199–230). Singapore: Singapore University.

Rudmin, F. W. (2003). Critical history of the acculturation psychology of assimilation, separation, integration, and marginalization. *Review of General Psychology, 7,* 3–37.

Ruiz-Belda, M.-A., Fernandez-Dols, J.-.M, Carrera, P., & Barchard, K. (2003). Spontaneous facial expressions of happy bowlers and soccer fans. *Cognition and Emotion, 17,* 315–326.

Russell, J. A. (1991). Culture and the categorization of emotions. *Psychological Bulletin, 110,* 426–450.

Russell, J. A. (1994). Is there universal recognition of emotion from facial expression? A review of the cross-cultural studies. *Psychological Bulletin, 115,* 102–141.

Ryder, A. G. (2004). *Cross-cultural differences in the presentation of depression: Chinese somatization and Western psychologization.* Unpublished doctoral dissertation, University of British Columbia.

Ryder, A. G., Alden, L. E., & Paulhus, D. L. (2000). Is acculturation unidimensional or bidimensional? A head-to-head comparison in the prediction of personality, self-identity, and adjustment. *Journal of Personality and Social Psychology, 79,* 49–65.

Ryder, A. G., Bean, G., & Dion, K. L. (2000). Caregiver responses to symptoms of first-onset psychosis: A comparative study of Chinese- and Euro-Canadian families. *Transcultural Psychiatry, 37,* 225–236.

Ryder, A. G., Yang, J., Zhu, X., Yao, S., Yi, J., Heine, S. J., & Bagby, R. M. (2007). *Culture and depression: Are there differences in Chinese and North American symptom presentation?* Unpublished manuscript, Concordia University.

Sagi, A., Lamb, M. E., Lewkowicz, K. S., Shoham, R., Dvir, R., & Estes, D. (1985). Security of infant-mother, -father, and metapelet attachments among kibbutz reared Israeli children. In I. Bretherton & E. Waters (Eds.), *Growing point in attachment theory. Monographs of the Society for Research in Child Development, 50* (1–2 Serial No. 209), 257–275.

Sakai, M., Ishikawa, S., Takizawa, M., Sato, H., & Sakano, Y. (2004). The state of hikikomori from a family's point of view: Statistical survey and the role of psychological intervention. *Japanese Journal of Counseling Science, 37,* 168–179.

Sampson, R. J., & Groves, W. B. (1989). Community structure and crime: Testing social-disorganization theory. *American Journal of Sociology, 94,* 774–780.

Samuels, B. (1986). Infant mortality and low birth weight among minority groups in the United States: A review of the literature. In *Report of the Secretary's Task Force on Black and Minority Health* (Vol. 6, pp. 33–85). Washington, DC: U.S. Department of Health and Human Services, Government Printing Office.

Sanchez-Burks, J. (2002). Protestant relational ideology and (in)attention to relational work settings. *Journal of Personality and Social Psychology, 83,* 919–929.

Sanchez-Burks, J., Lee, F., Choi, I., Nisbett, R., Zhao, S., & Koo, J. (2003). Conversing across cultures: East-West communication styles in work and nonwork contexts. *Journal of Personality and Social Psychology, 85,* 363–372.

Sanchez-Burks, J., Nisbett, R. E., & Ybarra, O. (2000). Cultural styles, relational schemas and prejudice against outgroups. *Journal of Personality and Social Psychology, 79,* 174–189.

Sapolsky, R. M. (2005). The influence of social hierarchy on primate health. *Science, 308,* 648–652.

Saucier, G., & Goldberg, L. R. (1998). What is beyond the big five? *Journal of Personality, 66,* 495–524.

Saunders, B. A. C., & Van Brakel, J. (1997). Are there non-trivial constraints on colour categorization? *Behavioral and Brain Sciences, 20,* 167–178.

Savage-Rumbaugh, E. S., McDonald, K., Sevcik, R. A., Hopkins, W. D., & Rubert, E. (1986). Spontaneous symbol acquisition and communicative use by pygmy chimpanzees (Pan paniscus). *Journal of Experimental Psychology: General 115,* 211–235.

Schacter, S. (1951). Deviation, rejection, and communication. *Journal of Abnormal and Social Psychology, 62,* 356–363.

Schacter, S., & Singer, J. E. (1962). Cognitive, social, and psychological determinants of emotional state. *Psychological Review, 69,* 379–399.

Schaffer, H. R., & Emerson, P. E. (1964). The development of social attachments in infancy. *Monographs of the Society for Research in Child Development, 29* (Serial No. 94).

Schaller, M., Conway, L. G., III, & Tanchuk, T. L. (2002). Selective pressures on the once and future contents of ethnic stereotypes: Effects of the communicability of traits. *Journal of Personality and Social Psychology, 82,* 861–877.

Scherer, K. R., Wallbott, H. G., & Summerfield, A. B. (Eds.). (1986). *Experiencing emotion: A cross-cultural study.* Cambridge, UK: Cambridge University Press.

Schieffelin, E. L. (1979). Mediators as metaphors: Moving a man to tears in Papua New Guinea. In A. L. Becker & A. Yengoyan (Eds.), *The imagination of reality: Essays in Southeast Asian Conference Systems.* Norwood, NJ: Ablex.

Schlegel, A., & Barry, H., III. (1991). *Adolescence: An anthropological inquiry*. New York: Free Press.

Schmidt, K., Hill, L., & Guthrie, G. (1977). Running amok. *International Journal of Psychiatry, 23*(4), 264–274.

Schmidtke, A., Weinacker, B., Apter, A., Batt, A., Berman, A., Bille-Brahe, U., et al. (1998). *Suicide rates in the world (update)*. Retrieved October 10, 2006 from University of Würzburg, International Academy for Suicide Research website: http://wwwalt.uni-wuerzburg.de/IASR/suicide-rates.htm

Schmidtke, A., Weinacker, B., Apter, A., Batt, A., Berman, A., Bille-Brahe, U., et al. (1998). *Suicide rates in the world (update)*. Retrieved November 29, 2005, from http://www.uni-wuerzburg.de/IASR/suicide-rates.htm.

Schmitt, E. (2001, August 6). Census data show a sharp increase in living standard. *New York Times*. www.nytimnes.com/2001/08/06/national/06CENS.html.

Schooler, J. W., & Engstler-Schooler, T. Y. (1990). Verbal overshadowing of visual memories: Some things are better left unsaid. *Cognitive Psychology, 22*, 36–71.

Schwartz, B. (2004). *The paradox of choice: Why more is less*. New York: HarperCollins.

Schwartz, S. H. (1994). Beyond individualism/collectivism: New cultural dimensions of values. In U. Kim, H. C. Triandis, C. Kagitcibasi, S.-C. Choi, & G. Yoon (Eds.), *Individualism and collectivism: Theory, method, and applications*. (pp. 85–119). Thousand Oaks, CA: Sage.

Schwartz, S. H., & Bilsky, W. (1990). Toward a theory of the universal content and structure of values: Extensions and cross-cultural replications. *Journal of Personality and Social Psychology, 58*, 878–891.

Schwartz, S. H., & Sagiv, L. (1995). Identifying culture specifics in the content and structure of values. *Journal of Cross-Cultural Psychology, 26*, 92–116.

Scribner, S., & Cole, M. (1973). Cognitive consequences of formal and informal education. *Science, 182*, 553–559.

Scribner, S., & Cole, M. (1981). *The psychology of literacy*. Cambridge, MA: Harvard University Press.

Searle, W., & Ward, C. (1990). The prediction of psychological and socio-cultural adjustment during cross-cultural transitions. *International Journal of Intercultural Relations, 14*, 449–464.

Sears, D. (1986). College sophomores in the laboratory: Influences of a narrow data base on social

psychology's view of human nature. *Journal of Personality and Social Psychology, 51*, 515–530.

Sedikides, C., Gaertner, L., & Toguchi, Y. (2003). Pancultural self-enhancement. *Journal of Personality and Social Psychology, 84*, 60–79.

Seeman, M., & Seeman, T. E. (1983). Health behavior and personal autonomy—A longitudinal study of the sense of control in illness. *Journal of Health and Social Behavior, 24*, 144–160.

Segal, M. W. (1974). Alphabet and attraction: An unobtrusive measure of the effect of propinquity in a field setting. *Journal of Personality and Social Psychology, 30*, 654–657.

Segall, M. H., Campbell, D. T., & Herskiovits, M. J. (1963). Cultural differences in the perception of geometric illusions. *Science, 193*, 769–771.

Segerstrom, S. C., & Miller, G. E. (2004). Psychological stress and the immune system: A meta-analytic study of 30 years of inquiry. *Psychological Bulletin, 130*, 601–630.

Seginer, R., Trommsdorff, G., & Essau, C. (1993). Adolescent control beliefs: Cross-cultural variations of primary and secondary orientations. *International Journal of Behavioral Development, 16*, 243–260.

Sen, A. K. *Development as freedom*. Oxford, UK: Oxford University Press.

Seyfarth, R. M., Cheney, D. L., & Marler, P. (1980). Monkey responses to three different alarm calls: evidence of predator classification and semantic communication, *Science, 210*, 801–803.

Shachar, R. (1991). His and her marital satisfaction: The double standard. *Sex Roles, 25*, 451–467.

Shay, T. (1994). The level of living in Japan, 1885–1938. In J. Komlos (Ed.), *Stature, living standards, and economic development* (pp. 173–204). Chicago: University of Chicago Press.

Shih, M., Pittinsky, T. L., & Ambady, N. (1999). Stereotype susceptibility: Identity salience and shifts in quantitative performance. *Psychological Science, 10*, 80–83.

Shweder, R. (1997). The surprise of ethnography. *Ethos, 25*, 152–163.

Shweder, R. (2000). Moral maps, "first world" conceits, and the new evangelists. In L. E. Harrison & S. P. Huntington (Eds.), *Culture matters: How values shape human progress* (pp. 158–176). New York: Basic Books.

Shweder, R. A. (1990). Cultural psychology: What is it? In J. W. Stigler, R. A. Shweder, & G. Herdt (Eds.), *Cultural psychology: Essays on comparative human development* (pp. 1–43).Cambridge: Cambridge University Press.

Shweder, R. A. (1994). You're not sick, you're just in love: Emotion as an interpretative system. In P. Ekman & R. J. Davidson (Eds.), *The Nature of Emotion: Fundamental Questions.* (pp. 32–44). Oxford, UK: Oxford University Press.

Shweder, R. A., & Bourne, E. J. (1982). Does the concept of the person vary cross-culturally? In A. J. Marsella & G. M. White (Eds.), *Cultural conceptions of mental health and therapy.* New York: Kluwer.

Shweder, R. A., & Bourne, E. J. (1984). Does the concept of the person vary cross-culturally? In R. A. Shweder & R. A. LeVine (Eds.), *Culture theory: Essays on mind, self and emotion* (pp. 158–199). Cambridge, UK: Cambridge University Press.

Shweder, R. A., & Haidt, J. (2000). The cultural psychology of the emotions: Ancient and new. In M. Lewis & J. M. Haviland-Jones (Eds), *Handbook of emotions.* (2nd ed., pp. 397–414). New York: Guilford.

Shweder, R. A., Jensen, L. A., & Goldstein, W. M. (1995). Who sleeps by whom revisited: A method for extracting the moral goods implicit in practice. In Goodnow et al. (Eds.), *Cultural practices as contexts for development. New Directions in Child Development,* 67, (pp. 21–39). San Francisco: Jossey Bass.

Shweder, R. A., Much, N. C., Mahapatra, M., & Park, L. (1997). The "big three" of morality (autonomy, community, and divinity), and the "big three" explanations of suffering. In A. Brandt & P. Rozin (Eds.), *Morality and Health* (pp. 119–169). New York: Routledge.

Siegrist, J., & Marmot, M. (2004). Health inequalities and the psychosocial environment—Two scientific challenges. *Social Science and Medicine, 58,* 1463–1473.

Simon, L., Greenberg, J., & Brehm, J. (1995). Trivialization: the forgotten mode of dissonance reduction. *Journal of Personality and Social Psychology, 68,* 247–260.

Singelis, T. M., Bond, M. H., Lai, S. Y., & Sharkey, W. F. (1999). Unpackaging culture's influence on self-esteem and embarrassability: The role of self-construals. *Journal of Cross-Cultural Psychology, 30,* 315–331.

Skolnick, A. S. (1987). *The intimate environment: Exploring marriage and family.* Boston: Little, Brown.

Smith, P. B., Trompenaars, F., & Dugan, S. (1995). The Rotter locus of control scale in 43 countries: A test of cultural relativity. *International Journal of Psychology, 30,* 377–400.

Snarey, J. (1985). The cross-cultural universality of social-moral development: A critical review of Kohlbergian research. *Psychological Bulletin, 97,* 202–232.

Snarey, J., & Keljo, K. (1991). In a Gemeinschaft voice: The cross-cultural expansion of moral development theory. In W. M. Kurtines & J. L. Gewitz (Eds.), *Handbook of moral behavior and development,* (Vol.1, pp. 395–424). Hillsdale, NJ: Erlbaum.

Snibbe, A. C., Kitayama, S., Markus, H. R., & Suzuki, T. (2003). "They saw a game": Self and group enhancement in Japan and the U.S. *Journal of Cross-Cultural Psychology, 34,* 581–595.

Snibbe, A. C., & Markus, H. R. (2005). You can't always get what you want: Social class, agency, and choice. *Journal of Personality and Social Psychology, 88,* 703–720.

Sorlie, P. D., Backlund, E., Johnson, N. J., & Rogot, E. (1993). Mortality by Hispanic status in the United States, *Journal of the American Medical Association, 270,* 2464–2469.

Spencer-Rodgers, J., Peng, K., Wang, L., & Hou, Y. (2004). Dialectical self-esteem and East-West differences in psychological well-being. *Personality and Social Psychology Bulletin, 30,* 1416–1432.

Sperber, D. (1996). *Explaining culture: A naturalistic approach.* Oxford: Blackwell Press.

Sprecher, S., & Chandak, R. (1992). Attitudes about arranged marriages and dating among men and women from India. *Free Inquiry in Creative Sociology, 20,* 1–11.

Sroufe, L. A. (1979). The coherence of individual development: Early care, attachment, and subsequent developmental issues. *American Psychologist, 34,* 834–841.

Statistics Canada. (2001). *Education in Canada 2000* (Cat. No. 81–229-XIB). Ottawa, ON.

Steckel, R. H. (1983). *Height and per capita income.* NBER Working Paper No. W0880. http://ssrn.com/abstract=233738.

Steckel, R. H. (1994) Heights and health in the United States, 1710–1950. In J. Komlos (Ed.), *Stature, living standards, and economic development* (pp. 153–172). Chicago: University of Chicago Press.

Steele, C. M. (1992, April). Race and the schooling of Black Americans. *The Atlantic Monthly,* 68–80.

Steele, C. M., & Aronson, J. (1995). Stereotype threat and the intellectual test performance of African

Americans. *Journal of Personality and Social Psychology, 69,* 797–811.

Steele, C. M., Spencer, S. J., & Lynch, M. (1993). Self-image resilience and dissonance: The role of affirmational resources. *Journal of Personality and Social Psychology, 64,* 885–896.

Stevenson, H. W. (1982). Influences of schooling on cognitive development. In D. A. Wagner & H. W. Stevenson (Eds.), *Cultural perspectives on child development* (pp. 208–224). San Francisco, CA: W. H. Freeman.

Stevenson, H. W. (1992). A long way to being number one: What we have to learn from East Asia. *Federation of Behavioral, Psychological and cognitive sciences, Science and Public Policy Seminars,* 1–17.

Stevenson, H. W., & Stigler, J. W. (1992). *The learning gap: Why our schools are failing and what we can learn from Japanese and Chinese education.* New York: Summit Books.

Stigler, J. W., Shweder, R. A., & Herdt, G. (1990). *Cultural psychology: Essays on comparative human development.* Cambridge, UK: Cambridge University Press.

Stone, J., Lynch, C. I., & Sjomeling, M. (1999). Stereotype threat effects on Black and White athletic performance. *Journal of Personality and Social Psychology, 77,* 1213–1227.

Stouffer, S. A., Suchman, E. A., DeVinney, L. C., Star, S. A., & Williams, R. M., Jr. (1949). *The American soldier: Adjustment during army life.* Princeton, NJ: Princeton University Press.

Strack, F., Martin, L. L., & Stepper, S. (1988). Inhibiting and facilitating conditions of the human smile: A nonobtrusive test of the facial feedback hypothesis. *Journal of Personality and Social Psychology, 54,* 768–777.

Su, S. K., Chiu, C.-Y., Hong, Y.-Y., Leung, K., Peng, K., & Morris, M. W. (1999). Self organization and social organization: American and Chinese constructions. In T. R. Tyler, R. Kramer, & O. John (Eds.), *The psychology of the social self* (pp. 193–222). Mahwah, NJ: Lawrence Erlbaum.

Suarez-Orozco, C., & Suarez-Orozco, M. M. (1995). *Transformations: Migration, family life, and achievement motivation among Latino Adolescents.* Stanford, CA: Stanford University Press.

Suarez-Orozco, C., & Suarez-Orozco, M. (2001). *Children of immigration.* Cambridge, MA: Harvard University Press.

Suh, E., Diener, E., Oishi, S., & Triandis, H. C. (1998). The shifting basis of life satisfaction judgments across cultures: Emotions versus norms. *Journal of Personality and Social Psychology, 74,* 482–493.

Suh, E. M. (2002). Culture, identity consistency, and subjective well-being. *Journal of Personality and Social Psychology, 83,* 1378–1391.

Sussman, N. M., & Rosenfeld, H. M. (1982). Influence of culture, language, and sex of conversational distance. *Journal of Personality and Social Psychology, 42,* 66–74.

Suwanlert, S. (1988). A study of latah in Thailand. *Journal of the Psychiatric Association of Thailand, 33(3),* 129–133.

Tafarodi, R. W., & Swann, W. B., Jr. (1996). Individualism-collectivism and global self-esteem: Evidence for a cultural trade-off. *Journal of Cross-Cultural Psychology, 27,* 651–672.

Tagliacozzo, R. (1979). Smokers' self-categorization and the reduction of cognitive dissonance. *Addictive Behaviors, 4,* 393–399.

Tajfel, H. (1970). Experiments in intergroup discrimination. *Scientific American, 223*(5), 96–102.

Takata, T. (2003). Self-enhancement and self-criticism in Japanese culture: An experimental analysis. *Journal of Cross-Cultural Psychology, 34,* 542–551.

Takemura, K., Yuki, M., Kashima, E. S., & Halloran, M. (2004). A cross-cultural comparison of behaviors and independent/interdependent self-views. *Progress in Asian Psychology, 5.*

Tamis-LeMonda, C. S., Bornstein, M. H., & Cyphers, L. (1992). Language and play at one year: A comparison of toddlers and mothers in the United States and Japan. *International Journal of Behavioral Development, 15,* 19–42.

Tardif, T. (1996). Nouns are not always learned before verbs: Evidence from Mandarin speakers' early vocabularies. *Developmental Psychology, 32,* 492–504.

Taylor, S. E., & Brown, J. D. (1988). Illusion and well-being: A social psychological perspective on mental health. *Psychological Bulletin, 103,* 193–210.

Teoh, J.-I. (1972). The changing psychopathology of amok. *Psychiatry, 35,* 345–351.

Thornhill, R. (1992). Fluctuating asymmetry and the mating system of the Japanese scorpionfly Panorpa japonica. *Animal Behavior, 44,* 867–879.

Tobin, J. J., Wu, D. Y. H., & Davidson, D. (1989). *Preschool in three cultures.* New Haven, CT: Yale University Press.

Tocqueville, A. (1835/1969). In J. P. Mayer (Ed.) *Democracy in America*, trans. George Lawrence. Garden City, NY: University of Chicago Press.

Tomasello, M. (1996). Do apes ape? In C. M. Heyes & B. G. Galef (Eds.), *Social learning in animals: The roots of culture*, (pp. 319–346). New York: Academic Press.

Tomasello, M. (1999). *The cultural origins of human cognition.* Cambridge, MA: Harvard University Press.

Tomasello, M., Carpenter, M., Call, J., Behne, T., & Moll, H. (2005). Understanding and sharing intentions: The origins of cultural cognition. *Behavioral and Brain Sciences, 28,* 675–735.

Tomasello, M., Kruger, A. C., & Ratner, H. H. (1993). Cultural learning. *Behavioral and Brain Sciences, 16,* 495–552.

Tonnies, F. (1957). *Community and society* (C. P. Loomis, Trans.). New York: Harper & Row. (Original work published in 1887)

Tooby, J., & Cosmides, L. (1992). The psychological foundations of culture. In J. H. Barkow, L. Cosmides, & J. Tooby (Eds.), *The adapted mind: Evolutionary psychology and the generation of culture* (pp. 19–136). New York: Oxford University Press.

Tracy, J. L., & Robins, R. W. (2006a). Appraisal antecedents of shame and guilt: Support for a theoretical model. *Personality and Social Psychology Bulletin, 32,* 1339–1351.

Tracy, J. L., & Robins, R. W. (2006b). *The nonverbal expression of pride: Evidence for cross-cultural recognition.* Unpublished manuscript. University of British Columbia.

Trafimow, D., Triandis, H. C., & Goto, S. G. (1991). Some tests of the distinction between the private self and the collective self. *Journal of Personality and Social Psychology, 60,* 649–655.

Triandis, H. C. (1989a). Cross-cultural studies of individualism and collectivism. *Nebraska Symposium of Motivation, 37,* 41–133.

Triandis, H. C. (1989b). The self and social behavior in differing cultural contexts. *Psychological Review, 96,* 506–520.

Triandis, H. C. (1994). *Culture and social behavior.* New York: McGraw Hill.

Triandis, H. C. (1996). The psychological measurement of cultural syndromes. *American Psychologist, 51,* 407–415.

Triandis, H. C., McCusker, C., & Hui, C. H. (1990). Multimethod probes of individualism and collectivism. *Journal of Personality and Social Psychology, 59,* 1006–1020.

Trommsdorff, G. (1995). Parent-adolescent relations in changing societies: A cross-cultural study. In P. Noack, M. Hofer, & J. Youniss (Eds.), *Psychological responses to social change. Human development in changing environments* (pp. 189–218). Berlin: Walter de Gruyter.

Tropp, L. R., & Wright, S. C. (2003). Evaluations and perceptions of self, ingroup, and outgroup: Comparisons between Mexican-American and European-American children. *Self and Identity, 2,* 203–221.

True, M. M., Pisani, L., & Oumar, F. (2001). Infant-mother attachment among the Dogon of Mali. *Child Development, 72,* 1451–1466.

Tsai, J., Ying, Y., & Lee, P. (2000). The meaning of "Being Chinese" and "Being American": Variation among Chinese American young adults. *Journal of Cross-Cultural Psychology, 31,* 302–332.

Tsai, J. L., Chentsova-Dutton, Y., & Freire-Bebeau, L. (2002). Emotional expression and physiology in European Americans and Hmong Americans. *Emotion, 2,* 380–397.

Tsai, J. L., Knutson, B. K., & Fung, H. H. (2006). Cultural variation in affect valuation. *Journal of Personality and Social Psychology, 90,* 288–307.

Tsai, J. L., Louie, J., Chen, E., & Uchida, Y. (in press). Learning what feelings to desire: Socialization of ideal affect through children's storybooks. *Personality and Social Psychology Bulletin.*

Tsai, J. L., Miao, F. F., & Seppala, E. (2007). Good feelings in Christianity and Buddhism: Religious differences in ideal affect. *Personality and Social Psychology Bulletin, 33*(3), 409–421.

Tsai, J. L., Simeonova, D. I., & Watanabe, J. T. (2004). Somatic and social: Chinese Americans talk about emotion. *Personality and Social Psychology Bulletin, 30,* 1226–1238.

Tsai, J. L., Ying, Y., & Lee, P. A. (2000). The meaning of "being Chinese" and "being American": Variation among Chinese American young adults. *Journal of Cross-Cultural Psychology, 31,* 302–332.

Tseng, W. (2001). *Handbook of cultural psychiatry.* New York: Academic Press.

Tucker, D. M., & Williamson, P. A. (1984). Asymmetric neural control systems in human self-regulation. *Psychological Review, 91,* 185–215.

Turiel, E., Killen, M., & Helwig, C. C. (1987). Morality: Its structure, function, and vagaries. In J.

Kagan & S. Lamb (Eds.), *The emergence of morality in young children* (pp. 155–243). Chicago: University of Chicago Press.

Tweed, R. G., & Lehman, D. R. (2002). Learning considered within a cultural context: Confucian and Socratic approaches. *American Psychologist, 57,* 89–99.

Twenge, J. M., & Campbell, W. K. (2001). Age and birth cohort differences in self-esteem: A cross-temporal meta-analysis. *Personality and Social Psychology Review, 5,* 321–344.

U.S. Census Bureau. (2000). *"Census 2000 Summary File 3 (SF3)—Sample Data, Table PCT 25 Sex by Age by Educational Attainment for the Population 18 Years and Over."* Retrieved 21 August 2006 from U.S. Census http://factfinder.census.gov.

Vagero, D., & Lundberg, O. (1989). Health inequalities in Britain and Sweden. *Lancet, 1989(2),* 35–36.

Van Boven, L. (2000). Pluralistic ignorance and political correctness: The case of affirmative action. *Political Psychology, 21,* 267–276.

Vandello, J. (2004, January 30–31). *Fewer women, more violence? Examining geographic sex ratios across the United States.* Paper presented at the 5th Annual conference of the Society of Personality and Social Psychology, Austin, TX.

Vandello, J. A., & Cohen, D. (1999). Patterns of individualism and collectivism across the United States. *Journal of Personality and Social Psychology, 77,* 279–292.

Vandello, J. A., & Cohen, D. (2003). Male honor and female fidelity: Implicit cultural scripts that perpetuate domestic violence. *Journal of Personality and Social Psychology, 84,* 997–1010.

Vaughn, C. E., & Leff, J. P. (1976). The influence of family and social factors on the course of psychiatric illness. *British Journal of Psychiatry, 129,* 125–137.

Vayda, E., Mindell, W. R., & Rutkow, I. M. (1982). A decade of surgery in Canada, England and Wales, and the United States. *Archives of Surgery, 117,* 846–853.

Veenhoven, R. (1993). *Happiness in nations.* Rotterdam, Netherlands: Risbo.

Verkuyten, M., & Masson, K. (1996). Culture and gender differences in the perception of friendship by adolescents. *International Journal of Psychology, 31,* 207–217.

Vouloumanos, A., & Werker, J. F. (2004). Tuned to the signal: The special status of speech for young infants, *Developmental Science, 7,* 270–276.

Vygotsky, L. S. (1929). The problem of the cultural development of the child II. *Journal of Genetic Psychology, 36,* 414–434.

Vygotsky, L. S. (1978). *Mind in society.* Cambridge: Harvard University Press.

de Waal, F. (2001). *The ape and the sushi master: Cultural reflections of a primatologist.* New York: Basic Books.

Walker, L. J. (1984). Sex differences in the development of moral reasoning: A critical review. *Child Development, 55,* 677–691.

Wallace, R., & Wallace, R. G. (2002). Immune cognition and vaccine strategy: Beyond genomics. *Microbes and Infection, 4,* 521–527.

Wang, Q. (2001). "Did you have fun?" American and Chinese mother-child conversations about shared emotional experiences. *Cognitive Development, 16,* 693–715.

Wang, Q. (2004). The emergence of cultural self-constructs: Autobiographical memory and self-description in European American and Chinese children. *Developmental Psychology, 40,* 3–15.

Wang, Q., & Conway, M. A. (2004). The stories we keep: Autobiographical memory in American and Chinese middle-aged adults. *Journal of Personality, 72,* 911–938.

Wang, Q., Leichtman, M. D., & Davies, K. (2000). Sharing memories and telling stories: American and Chinese mothers and their 3-year-olds. *Memory, 8,* 159–177.

Ward, C. (1996). Acculturation. In D. Landis & R. S. Bhagat (Eds)., *Handbook of intercultural training,* (2nd ed., pp. 124–147). Thousand Oaks, CA: Sage.

Ward, C., & Kennedy, A. (1995). Crossing-cultures: The relationship between psychological and sociocultural dimensions of cross-cultural adjustment. In J. Pandey, D. Sinha, & P. S. Bhawuk (Eds.), *Asian contributions to cross-cultural psychology* (pp. 289–306). New Delhi, India: Sage.

Ward, C., Leong, C., & Low, M. (2004). Personality and sojourner adjustment: An exploration of the Big Five and the cultural fit proposition. *Journal of Cross-Cultural Psychology, 35,* 137–151.

Warner, R. (1985). *Recovery from schizophrenia: Psychiatry and political economy.* New York: Routledge & Kegan Paul.

Watkins, D., Yau, J., Dahlin, B., & Wondimu, H. (1997). The Twenty Statements Test: Some measurement issues. *Journal of Cross-Cultural Psychology, 28,* 626–633.

Weber, M. (1904/ 1992). *The Protestant ethic and the spirit of capitalism.* London: Routledge.

Weber, M. (1947). *The theory of social and economic organization* (T. Parsons, Trans.). New York: Free Press.

Weintraub, K. J. (1978). *The value of the individual: Self and circumstance in autobiography.* Chicago: University of Chicago Press.

Weiss, M. J. (1994). *Latitudes and attitudes: An atlas of American tastes, trends, politics, and passions.* Boston: Little, Brown.

Weisz, J. R., Rothbaum, F. M., & Blackburn, T. C. (1984). Standing out and standing in: The psychology of control in America and Japan. *American Psychologist, 39,* 955–969.

Welch, M. (2005, December). They shoot helicopters, don't they? How journalists spread rumors during Katrina. *Reasononline.* Retrieved August 21, 2006, from http://www.reason.com/0512/co.mw.they.shtml

Wen, J. K. (1995). Sexual beliefs and problems in contemporary Taiwan. In T.-Y. Lin, W. S. Tseng, & E. K. Yeh (Eds.), *Chinese societies and mental health* (pp. 219–230). Hong Kong: Oxford University Press.

Wenar, C. (1982). On negativism. *Human Development, 25,* 1–23.

Werker, J. F., & Tees, R. C. (1984). Cross-language speech perception: Evidence for perceptual reorganization during the first year of life. *Infant Behavior and Development, 7,* 49–63.

Wertsch, J. V. (1998). *Mind as action.* New York: Oxford University Press.

Westermarck, E. (1922). *The history of human marriage.* 5th Ed. Vol. II. New York: Allerton.

Wheatley, T., & Haidt, M. (2005). Hypnotic disgust makes moral judgments more severe. *Psychological Science, 16,* 780–784.

White, K., & Lehman, D. R. (2005). Culture and social comparison seeking: The role of self-motives. *Personality and Social Psychology Bulletin, 31,* 232–242.

Whiten, A. (1998). Imitation of the sequential structure of actions by chimpanzees. *Journal of Comparative Psychology, 112,* 270–281.

Whiten, A., Goodall, J., McGrew, W. C., Nishida, T., Reynolds, V., Sugiyama, Y., Tutin, C. E. G., Wrangham, R. W., & Boesch, C. (1999). Cultures in chimpanzees. *Nature, 399,* 682–685.

Whiting, B. B. (1976). Unpackaging variables. In K. F. Riegel & J. A. Meacham (Eds.), *The changing individual in a changing world* (Vol. 1, pp. 303–309). Chicago: Aldine.

Whiting, J. W. M. (1964). The effects of climate on certain cultural practices. In W. H. Goodenough (Ed.), *Explorations in cultural anthropology: Essays in honor of George Peter Murdock* (pp. 511–544). New York: McGraw-Hill.

Whiting, J. W. M., & Whiting, B. B. (1979). Aloofness and intimacy of husbands and wives: A cross-cultural study. *Ethos, 3,* 183–207.

Whiting, R. (1990). *You gotta have wa.* New York: Vintage Departures.

Whitwell, G., de Souza, C., & Nicholas, S. (1997). Height, health, and economic growth in Australia, 1860–1940. In R. H. Steckel & R. Floud (Eds.), *Health and welfare during industrialization* (pp. 379–422). Chicago: University of Chicago Press.

Whorf, B. L. (1956). *Language, thought, and reality.* Cambridge, MA: MIT Press.

Wierzbicka, A. (1986). Human emotions: Universal or culture specific? *American Anthropologist, 88,* 584–594.

Wilkinson, R. G. (1994). The epidemiological transition: From material scarcity to social disadvantage? *Daedalus, 123,* 61–77.

Williams, D. R. (2003). The health of men: Structured inequalities and opportunities. *American Journal of Public Health, 93,* 724–731.

Williams, D. R. (2005, May 6). *Understanding the relationship between race and health: Patterns, paradoxes, and prospects.* Presentation at the Canadian Institute for Advanced Research. Theme: Successful Societies, Cambridge, MA.

Williams, D. R., Yu, Y., Jackson, J. S., & Anderson, N. B. (1997). Racial differences in physical and mental health: Socio-economic status, stress, and discrimination. *Journal of Health Psychology, 2,* 335–351.

Williams, J., & Best, D. (1990a). *Measuring sex stereotypes: A multination study.* Beverly Hills, CA: Sage.

Williams, J., & Best, D. (1990b). *Sex and psyche: Gender and self viewed cross-culturally.* Beverly Hills, CA: Sage.

Williams, T. P. & Sogon, S. (1984). Group composition and conforming behavior in Japanese students. *Japanese Psychological Research, 26,* 231–234.

Wilss, W. (1982). *The science of translation: Problems and methods*. Tuebingen: Narr.

Winkielman, P. & Cacioppo, J. T. (2001). Mind at ease puts a smile on the face: Psychophysiological evidence that processing facilitation elicits positive affect. *Journal of Personality and Social Psychology, 81*, 989–1000.

Wise, P. (1993). Confronting racial disparities in infant mortality: Reconciling science and politics. *American Journal of Preventive Medicine, 9*(supplement), 7–16.

Wiseman, C. V., Gray, J. J., Mosimann, J. E., & Ahrens, A. H. (1992). Cultural expectations of thinness in women: An update. *International Journal of Eating Disorders, 11*, 85–89.

Witkin, H. A. (1969). *Social influences in the development of cognitive style*. New York: Rand McNally.

Witkin, H. A., & Berry, J. W. (1975). Psychological differentiation in cross-cultural perspective. *Journal of Cross-Cultural Psychology, 6*, 4–87.

Wittchen, H. U., & Fehm, L. (2003). Epidemiology and natural course of social fears and social phobia. *Acta Psychiatrica Scandinavica, 108*, 4–18.

Wong, R. Y. M., & Hong, Y. (2005). Dynamic influences of culture on cooperation in the Prisoner's Dilemma. *Psychological Science, 16*, 429–434.

World Heath Organization (WHO). (1973). *The international pilot study of schizophrenia*. Geneva: WHO.

World Health Organization. (2004). *Country reports and charts*. Retrieved October 18, 2005, from http://www.who.int/mental_health/prevention/suicide/country_reports/en/index.html.

World Health Organization. (2005). *WHO global comparable estimates*. Retrieved October 18, 2005, from http://www.who.int/ncd_surveillance/infobase/web/InfoBaseCommon.

Worthman, C. M., & Melby, M. K. (2002). Toward a comparative developmental ecology of human sleep. In M. A. Carskadon (Ed.), *Adolescent sleep patterns*, 69–117. Cambridge, UK: Cambridge University Press.

Wundt, W. (1921). *Elements of folk psychology*. London: Allen & Unwin.

Xu, X., & Whyte, M. K. (1990). Love matches and arranged marriages: A Chinese replication. *Journal of Marriage and the Family, 52*, 709–722.

Yamada, A., & Singelis, T. M. (1999). Biculturalism and self-construal. *International Journal of Intercultural Relations, 23*, 697–709.

Yamagishi, T., Cook, K. S., & Watabe, M. (1998). Uncertainty, trust, and commitment formation in the United States and Japan, *American Journal of Sociology, 104*, 165–194.

Yamagishi, T., & Yamagishi, M. (1994) Trust and commitment in the United States and Japan. *Motivation and Emotion, 18*, 9–66.

Yamaguchi, S., Gelfand, M., Ohashi, M. M., & Zemba, Y. (2003). *The cultural psychology of control: Illusions of personal versus collective control in the U.S. and Japan*. Unpublished manuscript.

Yamashita, I. (1977/1993). *Taijin-Kyoufu or delusional social phobia*. Sapporo: Hokkaido University Press. (English translation of Japanese book originally published in 1977, Tokyo: Kanehara)

Yap, P. M. (1951). Mental diseases peculiar to certain cultures: A survey of comparative psychiatry. *Journal of Mental Science, 97*, 313–327.

Yelsma, P., & Athappilly, K. (1988). Marital satisfaction and communication practices: Comparisons among Indian and American couples. *Journal of Comparative Family Studies, 19*, 37–54.

Yik, M. S. M., Russell, J. A., Ahn, C., Fernandez-Dols, J. M., & Suzuki, N. (2002). Relating the five-factor model of personality to a circumplex model of affect: A five language study. In R. R. McCrae & J. Allik (Eds.), *The Five-Factor Model of personality across cultures* (pp. 79–104). New York: Kluwer.

Yuki, M. (2003). Intergroup comparison versus intragroup relationships: A cross-cultural examination of social identity theory in North American and East Asian cultural contexts. *Social Psychology Quarterly, 66*, 166–183.

Yuki, M., Maddux, W. W., Brewer, M. B., & Takemura, K. (2005). Cross-cultural differences in relationship- and group-based trust. *Personality and Social Psychology Bulletin, 31*, 48–62.

Ying, Y., & Liese, L. H. (1991). Emotional well-being of Taiwan students in the U.S.: An examination of pre- to post-arrival differential. *International Journal of Intercultural Relations, 15*, 345–366.

Zajonc, R. B. (1968). Attitudinal effects of mere exposure. *Journal of Personality and Social Psychology Monograph Supplement, 9* (2, pt. 2), 1–27.

Zajonc, R. B. (2005). *Preferences*. Invited address at the 6th Convention of the Society for Personality and Social Psychology, New Orleans, LA.

Zajonc, R. B., Heingartner, A., & Herman, E. M. (1969). Social enhancement and impairment of performance in the cockroach. *Journal of Personality and Social Psychology, 13*, 83–92.

Zajonc, R. B., Wilson, W. R., & Rajecki, D. W. (1975). Affiliation and social discrimination produced by brief exposure in day old domestic chicks. *Animal Behavior, 23*, 131–138.

Zarate, M. A.., Uleman, J. S., & Voils, C. I. (2001). Effects of culture and processing goals on the activation and binding of trait concepts. *Social Cognition, 19*, 295–323.

Zatzick, D. F., & Dimsdale, J. E. (1990). Cultural variation in response to painful stimuli. *Psychosomatic Medicine, 52*, 544–557.

Zax, M., & Takahashi, S. (1967). Cultural influences on response style: Comparisons of Japanese and American college students. *Journal of Social Psychology, 71*, 3–10.

Zborowski, M. (1969). *People in pain*. San Francisco: Jossey-Bass.

Zhang, F. C., Mitchell, J. E., Kuang, L., Wang, M. Y., Yang, D. L., Zheng, J., Zhau, Y. R., Zhang, Z. H., Filice, G. A., Pomeroy, C., & Pyle, R. L. (1992). The prevalence of anorexia nervosa and bulimia nervosa among freshman medical college students in China. *International Journal of Eating Disorders, 12*, 209–214.

Zhang, M. (1989). The diagnosis and phenomenology of neurasthenia: A Shanghai study. *Culture, Medicine and Psychiatry, 13*, 147–161.

Zheng, X., & Berry, J. W. (1991). Psychological adaptation of Chinese sojourners in Canada. *International Journal of Psychology, 26*, 451–470.

Zhou, M. (1997). Growing up American: The challenge confronting immigrant children and children of immigrants. *Annual Review of Sociology, 23*, 63–95.

Zhou, M., & Bankston, C. L. (1998). *Growing up American: How Vietnamese children adapt to life in the United States*. New York: Sage.

Zillmann, D. (1978). Attribution and misattribution of excitatory reactions. In J. H. Harvey, W. J. Ickes, & R. F. Kidd (Eds.), *New directions in attribution research* (Vol. 2., pp. 335–370). Hillsdale, NJ: Erlbaum.

Zola, I. K. (1966). Culture and symptoms: An analysis of patients' presenting complaints. *American Sociological Review, 31*, 615–630.

Zuckerman, M. (1979). Attribution of success and failure revisited, or the motivational bias is alive and well in attribution theory. *Journal of Personality, 47*, 245–287.

Credits

Chapter 1

p.2: © The New Yorker Collection, 2001, Donald Reilly, from cartoonbank.com. All Rights Reserved; **p. 6:** Anup Shah/Nature Picture Library; **p. 9:** © The New Yorker Collection, 2001, David Sipress, from cartoonbank.com. **p. 11, 1.1:** After Nagell, K., Olguin, K., & Tomasello, M. (1994). Processes of social learning in the tool use of chimpanzees (*Pan troglodytes*) and human children (*Homo sapiens*). *Journal of Comparative Psychology, 107,* 174–186. All Rights Reserved; **p. 13:** © The New Yorker Collection, 1995, Leo Cullum, from cartoonbank.com. All Rights Reserved; **p. 15, 1.2:** From Hough, W. (1922). Synoptic series of objects in the United States National Museum illustrating the history of inventions, *Proceedings of the United States National Museum, 60,* art. 9, p. 2, pl. 16; **p. 20, 1.3:** "The relation between average group size and neocortex ratio of various primates," "The relation of neocortex ratio to extract vs. non extract foraging techniques," and "The relation of the neocortex ratio to percentage of fruit in the diet." This article was published in the Journal of Human Evolution, Vol. 20, R. I. M. Dunbar, Neocortex Size as a Constraint on Group Size in Primates, Copyright © Elsevier 1992; **p. 29:** Figure 4.12, p. 97 from Herdt, B. (2006). *The Sambia: Ritual, sexuality, and change in Papua New Guinea.* Thomson Wadsworth. Reprinted with permission; **p. 32, 1.4:** Psychological universals: What are they and how can we know?, *Psychological Bulletin,* Vol. 131, No. 5, p. 773, 2005, Copyright © American Psychological Association. Reprinted with permission; **p. 34:** © Bettmann/CORBIS; **p. 40:** © The New Yorker Collection, 2005, Robert Weber, from cartoonbank.com. All Rights Reserved.

Chapter 2

p. 44: © The New Yorker Collection, 2002, Peter Steiner, from cartoonbank.com. All Rights Reserved;
p. 45: © CORBIS; **p. 46:** © The New Yorker Collection, 1994, Mick Stevens, from cartoonbank.com. All Rights Reserved; **p. 49, 2.1:** Figure 10.1, Major Axes of the Continents from *Guns, Germs and Steel: The Fate of Human Societies.* Copyright © 1997 by Jared Diamond. Used by permission of W. W. Norton & Company, Inc.; **p. 53 (top):** National Geographic/Getty Images; **p. 53 (bottom):** Getty Images; **p. 63:** © CORBIS; **p. 69:** Illustration by H. J. Ford in *The yellow fairy book.* (1966/1894). Ed. Andrew Lang. Dover Publications. **p. 46; p. 57:** © The New Yorker Collection, 2004, Carolita Johnson, from cartoonbank.com. All Rights Reserved; **p. 75:** Chris Ware/The New Yorker, © Condé Nast Publications, Inc.; **p. 78, 2.3:** Simulated item similar to those in the Raven's Progressive Matrices—Standard Progressive Matrices. Copyright 1998 by Harcourt Assessment, Inc. Reproduced with permission. All rights reserved; **p. 79, 2.4:** Data from U.S. Census Bureau. (2005). Table A-2. "Percent of people 25 years and over who have completed high school or college by race, Hispanic origin, and sex: selected years 1940 to 2005." Retrieved December 14, 2006 from www.census.gov/population/www/socdemo/educ-attn.html; **p. 84:** Whiting, R. (1990). *You gotta have wa.* New York: Vintage Departures.

Chapter 3

p. 109: © David Wall/Alamy; **p. 111:** © The New Yorker Collection, 1987, Mick Stevens, from cartoonbank.com. All Rights Reserved; **p. 124:** Data from Snibbe, A. C., & Markus, H. R. (2005). You can't always get what you want: Social class, agency, and choice. *Journal of Personality and Social Psychology, 88,* 703–720; **p. 127:** © CORBIS; **p. 131, 3.2:** "Change in testosterone levels, tracked in Northern and Southern participants" (Figure 4.2, p. 47) from *Culture of honor: The* *psychology of violence in the south.* Copyright © 1996 West-view Press; **p. 132, 3.3:** "Distance at which subject gave way in 'chicken' game" (Figure 4.3, p. 51) from *Culture of honor: The psychology of violence in the south.* Copyright © 1996 Westview Press.

Chapter 4

p. 141, 4.1: Data from Werker, J. F., & Tees, R. C. (1984). Cross-language speech perception: Evidence for perceptual reorganization during the first year of life. *Infant Behavior and Development, 7,* 49-63; **p. 143 (left):** Courtesy of HarperCollins; **p. 148, 4.2:** Data from Ji, L. (2005). Culture and thinking across time. Paper presented at the Cultural Psychology Preconference, New Orleans, LA. January 26, 2005; **p. 150:** Ann Landers: "Letter from Wondering," January 14, 1992. Reprinted by permission of Esther P. Lederer Trust and Creators Syndicate, Inc.; Dear Prudence: "Bringing Up Baby," Slate Magazine, June 2, 2005. Slate.com and Washingtonpost.com. Newsweek Interactive. All rights reserved. Reprinted with permission; **p. 153, 4.3:** Data from Shweder, R. A., Jensen, L. A., & Goldstein, W. M. (1995). Who sleeps by whom revisited: A method for extracting the moral goods implicit in practice. In Goodnow et al. (Eds.). Cultural practices as contexts for development. *New Directions in Child Development, 67,* 21-39. San Francisco: Jossey Bass; **p. 159, 4.4:** Data from Grossmann, K., Grossmann, K. E., Spangler, G., Suess, G., & Unzner, L. (1985). Maternal sensitivity and newborns' orientation responses as related to quality of attachment in Northern Germany. In I. Bretherton & E. Waters (Eds.), *Growing point in attachment theory.* Monographs of the Society for Research in Child Development, 50 (1-2 Serial No. 209), 233-256; and Sagi, A., Lamb, M. E., Lewkowicz, K. S., Shoham, R., Dvir, R., & Estes, D. (1985). Security of infant-mother, -father, and metapelet attachments among kibbutz reared Israeli children. In I. Bretherton & E. Waters (Eds.), *Growing point in attachment theory.* Monographs of the Society for Research in Child Development, 50 (1-2 Serial No. 209), 257-275; and Campos, J. J., Barrett, K. C., Lamb, M. E., Goldsmith, H. H., & Stenberg, C. (1983). Socioemotional development. In M. M. Haith & J. J. Campos (Eds.), *Handbook of child psychology: Vol. 2. Infancy and psychobiology,* 783-915. New York: Wiley; **p. 161:** Illustration and translation from Gilovich, T., Keltner, D., & Nisbett, R. E. (2006). *Social psychology.* New York: W. W. Norton & Company; **(left):** McCain Library and Archives, University of Southern Mississippi;

(right): Hong Kong Educational Publishing Co.; **p. 166:** © The New Yorker Collection, 2006, Robert Weber, from cartoonbank.com. All Rights Reserved; **p. 171, 4.5:** Reprinted with the permission of James Stigler and Simon & Schuster Adult Publishing Group and James Stigler, from THE LEARNING GAP: Why Schools are Failing and What We Can Learn from Japanese and Chinese Education by Harold W. Stevenson and James W. Stigler. Copyright © 1993 by Harold W. Stevenson and James W. Stigler. All rights reserved; **p. 172:** © The New Yorker Collection, 1998, Mike Twohy from cartoon-bank.com. All Rights Reserved.

Chapter 5

p. 179: © Reuters/CORBIS; **p. 181, 5.1:** Data from Ma, V., & Schoeneman, T. J. (1997). Individualism versus collectivism: A comparison of Kenyan and American self-concepts. *Basic and Applied Social Psychology, 19,* 261-273; **p. 184, 5.2:** After Markus, H. R., & Kitayama, S. (1991). Culture and the self: Implications for cognition, emotion, and motivation. *Psychological Review, 98,* 224-253; **p. 185, 5.3:** After Markus, H. R., & Kitayama, S. (1991). Culture and the self: Implications for cognition, emotion, and motivation. *Psychological Review, 98,* 224-253; **p. 188, 5.4:** Data from Hofstede, G. (1980). *Culture's consequences: International differences in work-related values.* Beverly Hills, CA: Sage; **p. 193, Table 5.1:** Data from Williams, J., & Best, D. (1990a). Measuring sex stereotypes: A multination study. Beverly Hills, CA: Sage; **p. 194:** © The New Yorker Collection 2001 Bruce Eric Kaplan from cartoonbank.com. All Rights Reserved; **p. 195, Table 5.2:** Data from Williams, J., & Best, D. (1990b). Sex and psyche: Gender and self viewed cross-culturally. Beverly Hills, CA: Sage; **p. 199, Table 5.3:** Data from Kanagawa, C., Cross, S. E., & Markus, H. R. (2001). "Who am I?": The cultural psychology of the conceptual self. *Personality and Social Psychology Bulletin, 27,* 90-103; **p. 205, 5.5:** Data from Cialdini, R. B., Wosinka, W., Barrett, D. W., Butner, J., & Gornik-Durose, M. (1999). Compliance with a request in two cultures: The differential influence of social proof and commitment/consistency on collectivists and individualists. *Personality and Social Psychology Bulletin, 25,* 1242-1253; **p. 206, Table 5.4:** Data from Suh, E. M. (2002). Culture, identity consistency, and subjective well-being. *Journal of Personality and Social Psychology, 83,* 1378-1391; **p. 211, 5.6:** Data from Cohen, D., & Gunz, A. (2002). As seen by the other . . . The self from the "outside in" and the "inside out" in the memories and emotional perceptions of Easterners and Westerners. *Psychological Science, 13,* 55-59; **p. 212, 5.7:** Data from Heine, S. J., Takemoto, T., Moskalenko, S., & Lasaleta, J. (2006). Mirrors in the head: Cultural variation in objective self-awareness. Manuscript submitted for publication. University of British Columbia; **p. 213:** Photos courtesy of Timothy Takemoto and Naoko Sonoda; **p. 218, 5.8:** Data from Oishi, S., Lun, J., Sherman, G. D. (2006). Residential mobility, self-concept, and well-being: What happens when you move? Unpublished manuscript; **p. 224, Table 5.5:** Data from McCrae, R. R. (2002). NEO-PI-R data from 36 cultures: Further intercultural comparisons. In R. R. McCrae & J. Allik (Eds.), *The Five-Factor Model of personality across cultures* (pp. 105-126). New York: Kluwer.

Chapter 6

p. 230: Rosenberg Self Esteem Scale from *Society and the Adolescent Self-Image,* revised edition. Middletown, CT: Wesleyan University Press (1989). Reprinted with permission of Dr. Florence Rosenberg and the Morris Rosenberg Foundation; **p. 236:** © The New Yorker Collection, 2002, Barbara Smaller, from cartoonbank.com. All Rights Reserved; **p. 239, 6.1:** Data from Twenge, J. M., & Campbell, W. K. (2001). Age and birth cohort differences in self-esteem: A cross-temporal meta-analysis. *Personality and Social Psychology Review, 5,* 321-344; **p. 242, 6.2:** Data from Heine, S. J., Kitayama, S., Lehman, D. R., Takata, T., Ide, E., Leung, C., & Matsumoto, H. (2001b). Divergent consequences of success and failure in Japan and North America: An investigation of self-improving motivations and malleable selves. *Journal of Personality and Social Psychology, 81,* 599-615; **p. 245:** Time & Life Pictures/Getty Images; **p. 250, 6.3:** Data from Sanchez-Burks, J. (2002). Protestant relational ideology and (in)attention to relational work settings. *Journal of Personality and Social Psychology, 83,* 919-929; **p. 254, 6.4:** Data from Morling, B., Kitayama, S., & Miyamoto, Y. (2002). Cultural practices emphasize influence in the United States and adjustment in Japan. *Personality and Social Psychology Bulletin, 28,* 311-323; **p. 256, 6.5:** Data from Menon, T., Morris, M. W., Chiu, C., & Hong, Y. (1999). Culture and the construal of agency: Attribution to individual versus group dispositions. *Journal of Personality and Social Psychology, 76,* 701-717; **p. 260, 6.6:** Data from Iyengar, S. S., & Lepper, M. R. (1999). Rethinking the value of choice: A cultural per-

spective on intrinsic motivation. *Journal of Personality and Social Psychology, 76,* 349-366; **p. 264, 6.7:** Data from Oettingen, G., & Seligman, M. E. P. (1990). Pessimism and behavioral signs of depression in East versus West Berlin. *European Journal of Social Psychology, 20,* 207-220; **p. 265, 6.8:** Data from Snibbe, A. C., & Markus, H. R. (2005). You can't always get what you want: Social class, agency, and choice. *Journal of Personality and Social Psychology, 88,* 703-720; **p. 267 (top):** © The New Yorker Collection 2000 Jack Ziegler from cartoonbank.com. All Rights Reserved; **(bottom), 6.9:** Picture of Asch Stimulus Cards from "Effects of Group Pressure on the Modification and Distortion of Judgment" (1951) in G. Guetzkow (ed) *Groups, Leadership & Men.* We have made diligent efforts to contact the copyright holder to obtain permission to reprint this selection. If you have information that would help us, please write to Permissions Department, W. W. Norton & Company, Inc., 500 Fifth Avenue, New York, NY 10110; **p. 270, 6.10:** Data from Kim, H. S., & Markus, H. R. (1999). Deviance or uniqueness, harmony or conformity? A cultural analysis. *Journal of Personality and Social Psychology, 77,* 785-800; **p. 271, 6.11:** Data from Kim, H. S., & Markus, H. R. (1999). Deviance or uniqueness, harmony or conformity? A cultural analysis. *Journal of Personality and Social Psychology, 77,* 785-800.

Chapter 7

p. 275: © The New Yorker Collection, 1995, Charles Barsotti, from cartoonbank.com. All Rights Reserved; **p. 280:** © The New Yorker Collection, 1992, Leo Cullum, from cartoonbank.com. All Rights Reserved; **p. 286:** © The New Yorker Collection, 2000, David Sipress, from cartoonbank.com. All Rights Reserved; **p. 290, 7.2:** Data from Miller, J. G., Bersoff, D. M., & Harwood, R. L. (1990). Perceptions of social responsibilities in India and the United States: Moral imperatives or personal decisions? *Journal of Personality and Social Psychology, 58,* 33-47; **p. 292, 7.3:** Miller, J. G., & Bersoff, D. M. (1992). Culture and moral judgment: How are conflicts between justice and interpersonal responsibilities resolved? *Journal of Personality and Social Psychology, 62,* 541-554; **p. 298, 7.4:** Jensen, L. A. (1997). Culture wars: American moral divisions across the adult lifespan. *Journal of Adult Development, 4,* 107-121; **p. 302, Table 7.1:** Data from Rozin, P., Lowery, L., Imada, S., & Haidt, J. (1999). The CAD triad hypothesis: A mapping between three moral emotions (contempt, anger, disgust) and three moral codes

Chapter 10

p. 416: Courtesy of Mo Gan-Ming, M. D.; **p. 4.17:** Drawing by George Cohen from Spores, J. C. (1988). *Running amok: A historical inquiry.* Ohio University Press; **p. 427, 10.1:** Data from World Health Organization. (2004). Country reports and charts. Retrieved October 18, 2005, from http://www.who.int/mental_health/prevention/suicide/country_reports/en/index.html; **p. 433 (left):** Chlaus Lotscher/Peter Arnold, Inc.; **(center):** © Michael Prince/CORBIS; **(right):** © Catherine Wessel/CORBIS; **p. 436, 10.2:** Data from World Health Organization. (2005). WHO global comparable estimates. Retrieved October 18, 2005, from http://www.who.int/ncd_surveillance/infobase/web/InfoBaseCommon; **p. 437, 10.3:** Data from Organisation for Economic Co-operation and Development. (2004, February 22). Health at a glance: OECD indicators 2003: Chart 8. Increasing obesity rates among the adult population in OECD countries. Retrieved October 6, 2005, from http://www.oecd.org/LongAbstract/0,2546,en_2649_201185_16361657_1_1_1_1,00.html; **p. 438:** © The New Yorker Collection, 2005, Lee Lorenz, from cartoonbank.com. All Rights Reserved; **p. 439, 10.4:** Figure: "Chernoff face representation of attitudes towards food." This article was published in *Appetite*, Vol. 33, Paul Rozin, et.al., Attitudes Toward Food and The Role of Food in Life in the U.S.A., Japan, Flemish Belgium, and France: Possible Implications for the Diet-Health Debate, p. 175, Copyright © Elsevier 1999. Reprinted with permission; **p. 443, 10.5:** Data from Wilkinson, R. G. (1994). The epidemiological transition: From material scarcity to social disadvantage? *Daedalus, 123,* 61-77; **p. 446:** © The New Yorker Collection, 2001, Sam Gross, from cartoonbank.com. All Rights Reserved; **p. 448, 10.6:** Data from United Nations Development Program. (2003). Human development report. New York: Oxford University Press; **p. 451, Table 10.1:** Data from National Center for Health Statistics (NCHS). (1993). Health, United States, 1992. Hyattsville, MD: U.S. Public Health Service. As cited in Williams, D. R. (2005). Understanding the relationship between race and health: Patterns, paradoxes, and prospects. Presentation at the Canadian Institute for Advanced Research. Theme: Successful Societies. Cambridge, MA. May 6, 2005; **p. 457:** © The New Yorker Collection, 1998, Mick Stevens, from cartoonbank.com; **p. 458, 10.7:** Data from Rozin, P., Leeman, R. F., Fischler, C., & Shields, C. (2006). Doctors in each of five countries resemble their countrymen more than doctors in other countries in attitudes toward food and health. Unpublished manuscript. University of Pennsylvania.

Chapter 11

p. 463: © Associated Press; **p. 464 (a):** © Kevin R. Morris/CORBIS; **(b)** Gavin Hellier/JAI/ CORBIS; **(c)** © Hulton-Deutsch Collection/CORBIS; **(d)** © Associated Press; **p.** Images from Figure 4a and 4b in Rhodes, G., Lee, K., Palermo, R., Weiss, M., Yoshikawa, S., Clissa, P., Williams, T., Peters, M., Winkler, C., & Jeffery, L. (2005). Attractiveness of own-race, other-race, and mixed-race faces. *Perception, 34,* 319-340; Courtesy of Gillian Rhodes; **p. 468 (left):** Scala / Art Resource, NY; **(center):** Pushkin Museum of Fine Arts, Moscow, Russia/Scala/Art Resource, NY; **(right):** © Associated Press; **p. 470, 11.1:** Data from Segal, M. W. (1974). Alphabet and attraction: An unobtrusive measure of the effect of propinquity in a field setting. *Journal of Personality and Social Psychology, 30,* 654-657; **p. 473, 11.2:** Data from Heine, S. J., Foster, J., & Spina, R. (2006). Do birds of a feather universally flock together? Cultural variation in the similarity-attraction effect. Manuscript submitted for publication; **p. 475:** Courtesy of Glenn Adams; **p. 481, Table 11.1:** Data from Broude, G. J., & Green, S. J. (1983). Cross-cultural codes on husband–wife relationships. *Ethology, 22,* 273-274; **p. 483, 11.3:** Data from Endo, Y., Heine, S. J., & Lehman, D. R. (2000). Culture and positive illusions in relationships: How my relationships are better than yours. *Personality and Social Psychology Bulletin, 26,* 1571-1586; **486:** © The New Yorker Collection, 2003, Roz Chast, from cartoonbank.com. All Rights Reserved; **p. 487, 11.4:** Data from Gupta, U., & Singh, P. (1982). Exploratory study of love and liking and type of marriages. *Indian Journal of Applied Psychology, 19,* 92-97; **p. 490, 11.5:** Data from Iyengar, S. S., Lepper, M. R., & Ross, L. (1999). Independence from whom? Interdependence with whom? Cultural perspectives on ingroups versus outgroups. In D. Miller & D. Prentice (Eds.), *Cultural Divides: Understanding and overcoming group conflict* (pp. 273-301). New York: Sage; **p. 492, 11.6:** Courtesy of Masaki Yuki; **p. 494, 11.7:** Data from Yuki, M., Maddux, W. W., Brewer, M. B., & Takemura, K. (2005). Cross-cultural differences in relationship- and group-based trust. *Personality and Social Psychology Bulletin, 31*, 48-62; **p. 500, 11.8:** Data from Earley, P. C. (1993). East meets West meets Mideast: Further explorations of collectivistic and individualistic work groups. *Academy of Management Journal, 36,* 319-348; **p. 501, 11.9:** Adapted from Madsen, M.C.

(1971). Developmental and cross-cultural differences in the cooperative and competitive behavior of young children. *Journal of Cross-Cultural Psychology,* 365-371; **p. 502, 11.10:** Data from Madsen, M.C. (1971). Developmental and cross-cultural differences in the cooperative and competitive behavior of young children. *Journal of Cross-Cultural Psychology,* 365-371.

Chapter 12

p. 509: © CHRIS WATTIE/Reuters/CORBIS; **p. 510:** © Peter Turnley/CORBIS; **p. 513, 12.1:** Adapted from Lysgaard, S. (1955). Adjustment in a foreign society: Norwegian Fulbright grantees visiting the United States. *International Social Science Bulletin, 7,* 45-51; **p. 515, Table 12.1:** Data from the TOEFL Test and Data Summary, 2002-03; **p. 521, 12.2** Adapted from Berry, J. W., Kim, U., Power, S., Young, M., & Bujaki, M. (1989). Acculturation attitudes in plural societies. *Applied psychology: An international review, 38,* 185-206; **p. 522:** From Ryder, A. G., Alden, L. E., & Paulhus, D. L. (2000). Is acculturation unidimensional or bidimensional? A head-to-head comparison in the prediction of personality, self-identity, and adjustment. *Journal of Personality and Social Psychology, 79,* 49-65; **p. 525, 12.3:** The social cog-

nition of immigrants' acculturation: Effects of the need for closure and the reference group at entry. *Journal of Personality and Social Psychology,* Vol. 86, No. 6, 2004. Copyright © American Psychological Association. Reprinted with permission; **p. 529, 12.4:** Data from Heine, S. J., & Lehman, D. R. (2004). Move the body, change the self: Acculturative effects on the self-concept. In M. Schaller & C. Crandall (Eds.), *Psychological Foundations of Culture,* (pp. 305-331). Mahwah, NJ: Erlbaum; **p. 531, 12.5:** Data from Heine, S. J., & Lehman, D. R. (2004). Move the body, change the self: Acculturative effects on the self-concept. In M. Schaller & C. Crandall (Eds.), *Psychological Foundations of Culture,* (pp. 305-331). Mahwah, NJ: Erlbaum; **p. 536, 12.6:** Hong, Y., Morris, M. W., Chiu, C., & Benet-Mart°nez, V. (2000). Multicultural minds: A dynamic constructivist approach to culture and cognition. *American Psychologist, 55,* 705-720; **p. 541, 12.7:** Gardner, W. L.; Gabriel, S., & Dean, K. K. (2004). The individual as "melting pot": The flexibility of bicultural self-construals. *Cahiers de Psychologie Cognitive/Current Psychology of Cognition, 22,* 181-201; **p. 544, 12.8:** Steele, C. M., & Aronson, J. (1995). Stereotype threat and the intellectual test performance of African Americans. *Journal of Personality and Social Psychology, 69,* 797-811.

Name index

Aaker, J. L., 121, 241, 538
Abel, T. M., 361
Abraido-Lanza, A. F., 527
Abramson, L. Y., 263
Abu-Lughod, L., 332, 338
Adams, G., 475, 476, 477, 478
Adler, N. E., 448
Adonu, J. K., 476, 477
Agiobu-Kemmer, I., 154
Agnoli, F., 392
Ahn, C., 221
Ahrens, A. H., 414
Aiello, L. C., 17, 18
Ainsworth, M. D. S., 156
Akhtar, S., 411
Akinkugbe, O. O., 452
Alden, L. E., 522, 526
Allan, G. A., 264
Allik, J., 221
Allport, G. W., 66, 217, 219
Altrocchi, J., 182
Altrocchi, L., 182
Ambady, N., 328, 544
American Psychiatric Association, 430
Anderson, C. A., 127
Anderson, E., 532, 533
Anderson, J. C., 337, 338
Anderson, K. O., 333
Anderson, N. B., 452
Anderson, R. C., 222
Anderson, S. L., 476, 477
Angel, R., 455
Annis, R. C., 519
Apfel, N., 545
Apple, K. J., 90
Arcuri, L. W., 329

Arendt, H., 90
Argyle, M., 372
Armes, K., 520
Aron, A. P., 318
Aron-Brunetiere, R., 457
Aronson, J., 543, 545
Asch, S., 37, 266, 267, 268, 490
Athappilly, K., 486
Atran, S., 68, 69
Attanucci, J., 287
Au, Y., 504
Auman, C., 545
Averill, J. R., 483
Avis, J., 96
Azuma, H., 157, 158–59, 163, 384

Babiker, I. E., 518
Bachman, J. G., 105
Bachnik, J. M., 489
Back, K., 469
Bagozzi, R. Wong, N., 382
Baillargeon, R., 32
Bakan, D., 191
Baltes, P. B., 262
Baltzell, E. D., 86
Bankston, C. L., 527
Barber, B. R., 70, 71
Barchard, K., 331
Bargh, J. A., 249, 533
Barkee, A. P., 466
Barrett, D. W., 204
Barrett, J. L., 68
Barrett, K. C., 157
Barrett, L. F., 314, 315, 318
Barry, H., III, 165
Bates, M. S., 333
Bauer, R., 439

Baumeister, R. F., 232, 237
Beach, F. A., 31, 465, 467, 468
Bean, G., 422
Beard, G. M., 421
Behne, T., 10
Beja-Pereira, A., 434
Bell, C., 66
Bell, R. M., 415
Bemporad, J. R., 415
Bendix, R., 248
Benedict, R., 37
Benet-Martínez, V., 223, 537
Beresin, E. V., 122
Berger, P. L., 275
Berkman, L. F., 447
Berlin, B., 394, 401
Berman, J. J., 308
Berntson, G. G., 314
Berry, J. W., 102, 363, 512, 515, 519, 521, 523, 525, 526
Bersoff, D. M., 289, 291
Best, D., 192, 195
Best, J., 66
Bhalla, S. K., 468
Biernat, M., 110
Bierschwale, D. T., 9
Bilger, B., 440, 441
Bilsky, W., 226
Biswas-Diener, R., 199–200, 347
Blackburn, T. C., 253
Blackmore, S., 59
Blascovich, J., 543
Blehar, M. C., 156
Block, J., 219
Blood, R. O., 486
Bochner, S., 182, 511, 512, 518
Boland, J. E., 366

Bond, M. H., 102, 106, 124, 182, 190, 233, 247, 255, 504, 531
Bond, R., 269, 491
Bonte, P., 128
Bordgen, S., 331
Bornstein, M. H., 162, 359
Boroditsky, L., 400
Bosma, H., 446–47
Boucher, J. D., 320
Bourgeois, M. J., 64
Bourne, E. J., 276, 372
Bowdle, B. F., 111, 126, 130, 131
Bowlby, J., 156
Boyd, R., 3, 17, 22, 54, 81
Boyer, P., 68
Brandt, M. E., 320
Bravo, M., 419
Brehm, J., 203, 232
Breslow, L., 447
Briggs, J. L., 321, 332
Brislin, R. W., 104
Brooks-Gunn, J., 445
Brosschot, J. F., 337
Broude, G. J., 480, 481
Brown, D. E., 23, 139
Brown, J. D., 231, 236
Bruner, J., 25, 38, 39
Brunner, E., 446–47
Buchtel, E., 111, 225
Budaev, S. V., 222
Bugental, D. B., 446
Bujaki, M., 523, 526
Bunker, J. P., 444
Burrows, L., 249, 533
Burton, R., 149
Bushnell, J. A., 413
Buss, D. M., 51, 277
Butler, J. C., 219
Butner, J., 204, 225
Byrne, D., 38, 472

Cacioppo, J. T., 314, 466, 471
Call, J., 10, 400
Callaghan, T., 9
Cameron, J. E., 523, 541
Campbell, D. T., 86, 279
Campbell, J. D., 207
Campbell, W. K., 239
Campos, J. J., 157, 158
Canino, G., 419

Cannon, T. D., 430
Carey, S., 34, 404
Carlyle, T., 345
Carment, D. W., 504
Carnegie, D., 474
Carpenter, M., 10
Carr, J. E., 417
Carrera, P., 331
Carroll, J. M., 331
Cassidy, C. M., 468
Castellazzo, G., 448
Catanese, D., 439
Caudill, W., 384
Caudill, W. A., 163
Cavalli-Sforza, F., 108–9, 434
Cavalli-Sforza, L. L., 60, 108–9, 434, 451
Cawte, J. E., 418
Central Intelligence Agency, 280
Chandak, R., 480
Chandler, M., 428
Chandra, S., 491
Chang, L. Y., 425
Chang, W. C., 255, 421
Chang, Y. H., 418
Chao, M. T., 527
Chaplin, G., 433
Chartrand, T. L., 249
Chase-Lansdale, L. P., 445
Cheah, Y. C., 421
Chee, K. T., 420
Chee, M. W., 142
Chen, C., 105
Chen, C. C., 418
Chen, E., 351, 445
Chen, M., 249, 533
Cheney, D. L., 13, 21, 139
Cheng, S., 158
Chentsova-Dutton, Y., 318
Chernoff, H., 439
Cheung, F. M., 222, 223
Cheung, S. F., 223
Cheung, T., 182
Chirkov, V. I., 241
Chiu, C., 214, 215, 252, 255, 257, 320
Chiu, L. H., 358
Cho, G. E., 102, 236, 237
Choi, I., 81, 108, 110, 162, 216, 358, 374, 377, 382, 528

Choi, S., 160, 191, 249
Choi, Y., 108, 110, 382
Chomsky, N., 276
Choudry, I. Y., 414
Christenfeld, N., 446
Chua, H. F., 366
Chua, W. L., 255
Church, A. T., 107, 223, 512, 514, 515
Cialdini, R. B., 204, 233
Clancy, P. M., 384
Clark, D. M., 424
Clark, J. J., 370
Clement, R., 516
Clements, F. E., 454
Clore, G. L., 38, 350
Clutton-Brock, T. H., 18
Cogan, J. C., 468
Cohen, A. B., 304, 305, 306, 439
Cohen, D., 47, 81, 88, 90, 93, 94, 111, 122, 126, 127, 128, 129, 130, 131, 133, 134, 189, 210, 211
Cohen, G. L., 545
Cohen, S., 445
Colcombe, S. J., 545
Cole, M., 37, 102, 168
Coleman, H. L. K., 512
Collado, R., 418
Collard, M., 56
Collins, J., 452
Conway, L. G., III, 62, 63
Conway, M. A., 359
Cook, K. S., 490
Coon, H. M., 233
Coreil, J., 452
Cornell, S., 451
Cortez, V. L., 446
Cosmides, L., 50, 276
Costa, P. T., Jr., 221
Cousins, S. D., 199, 375, 423, 425
Cox, J. L., 518
Crespo, C. J., 445
Crocker, J., 234, 247
Crockett, H. J., 247
Crooks, L., 7
Cross, P., 230
Cross, S. E., 198, 206, 520
Csikszentmihalyi, M., 474
Cullum, J. G., 64

Cunningham, M. R., 466
Custance, D., 12
Cyphers, L., 162, 359

Dahlin, B., 182
Dalal, R., 377
Damon, W., 182
Dar-Nimrod, I., 545
Darwin, C., 268, 323, 324, 464
Dasen, P., 102
Dasen, P. R., 166
Davey Smith, G., 449
David, R., 452
Davidoff, J., 342, 395, 396, 397
Davidson, D., 216
Davies, I., 342, 395, 396, 397
Davies, I. R. L., 395
Davies, K., 155
Davis, P. B., 443
Dawkins, R., 58, 59
Deacon, T. W., 5
Dean, K. K., 540
Dehaene, S., 402, 403
Delgado, A., 351
de Lorgeril, M., 437
Desai, S. R., 480
Deschamps, J., 480
de Souza, C., 441
DeVinney, L. C., 110
DeVos, J., 32
Dezhkam, M., 415
Dhawan, N., 182
Diamond, E. L., 337
Diamond, J., 48, 49, 434
Dias, M. G., 293
Diener, C., 346, 347, 348
Diener, E., 33, 199–200, 217, 242,
    344, 346, 347, 348
Diener, M., 346, 347, 348
Diez-Roux, A. V., 450
Dimsdale, J. E., 333
Dion, K. K., 482, 485
Dion, K. L., 422, 482, 485
Doi, T., 341
Douglas-Hamilton, I., 7
Douglas-Hamilton, O., 7
Doyle, K. O., 122
Doyle, M. R., 122
Drolet, A., 270
Drukker, J. W., 441

Du Bois, W. E. B., 532
Ducci, L., 329
Duffy, S., 363
Dunbar, R. I. M., 19, 20, 21, 22,
    474
Duncan, N. D. C., 474
Dungan, S., 255
Dunning, D., 231
Durham, W. H., 60
Dutton, D. G., 318
Duval, S., 208
Dweck, C. S., 214, 215, 252, 320

Earleywine, M., 416
Edgerton, R. B., 452
Educational Testing System, 517
Edwards, C. P., 163
Edwards, W. T., 333
Einstein, A., 392
Eisenthal, S., 333
Ekman, P., 111, 314, 315, 318, 323,
    324, 325, 326, 327, 328, 330,
    331, 332, 334, 340
Elfenbein, H. A., 328
Elias, N., 43
Elkoshi, T., 234
Elliot, A. J., 241
Ellsworth, P. C., 315, 320, 322, 364
Elston, M. A., 447
Emerson, P. E., 156
Endo, Y., 234, 235, 483
Engstler-Schooler, T. Y., 386
Epel, E. S., 448
Ernberg, G., 431
Essau, C., 255
Evans-Pritchard, E. E., 455
Evered, S., 252

Falbo, T., 147
Falk, J. R., 413
Faulkner, J., 69
Feather, N., 33, 241
Fehm, L., 425
Feinman, S., 197
Feldman, M. W., 60
Feldman, P. J., 447
Ferber, R., 149–50
Ferguson, N., 246
Fernandez-Dols, J. M., 221, 504
Fernandez-Dols, J.-M., 331

Ferris, C., 208, 209, 212
Fessler, D. M. T., 495
Festinger, L., 93, 200, 232, 469
Figueredo, A., 221
Fischer, D. H., 85, 126, 128
Fischer, E. F., 480
Fischler, C., 261, 437, 438, 439,
    457
Fisher, H., 479
Fishman, J. A., 392
Fiske, A. P., 190, 494, 496
Flaherty, J. A., 420
Florez, K. R., 527
Floud, R., 440, 441
Flynn, J. R., 76, 79
Ford, C. S., 31, 465, 467, 468
Forman, T. A., 452
Foster, F. H., 443
Foster, J., 472, 473
Foster-Fishman, P. G., 491
Fox, A. J., 443
Fox, J. A., 164
Fox, W. S., 247
Frager, R., 491
Fraser, S. C., 204
Fredman, T., 12
Freedman, J. L., 204
Freeman, D., 97, 165
Freire-Bebeau, L., 318
Freud, S., 300
Fridlund, A. J., 331
Friesen, W. V., 111, 314, 318,
    324–25, 327, 331, 332, 334, 340
Frijda, N. H., 315, 322
Fryberg, S. A., 182, 234
Fu, J. H., 214, 252, 320
Fujimoto, H., 425
Funder, D., 94
Fung, H., 156, 236, 237
Fung, H. H., 319, 351
Furnham, A., 246, 247, 511, 512,
    518

Gabrenya, W. K., 147, 499
Gabriel, S., 249, 540
Gaby, A., 400
Gaeddert, W. P., 480
Gaertner, L., 236
Galanter, M., 485
Galaty, J. G., 128

Galles, N. S., 142
Gallistel, C. R., 404
Gamba, R. J., 107
Gangestad, S. W., 51, 465
Garcia, J., 545
Gardner, G. H., 520
Gardner, W., 249
Gardner, W. L., 121, 241, 538, 540
Garfinkel, P. E., 414
Garner, D. M., 414
Gastil, R. D., 126
Gavira, F. M., 420
Gay, J., 37, 168
Geertz, C., 22, 26, 138, 339, 372
Geertz, H., 341
Gelfand, M., 191, 249, 257
Gellantly, A., 395
Gelman, R., 404
Gentner, D., 159, 160
Georgis, T., 329
Gerton, J., 512
Gibbons, F. X., 208
Gibson, K. R., 18
Giddens, A., 246
Gifford, R. K., 37
Gillette, J., 160
Gilligan, C., 191, 287
Gilmore, D. D., 47
Gil-White, F. J., 8
Giorgi, L., 247
Giraldeau, L. A., 7
Gislen, A., 435
Gislen, L., 435
Gladstone, G., 420
Gladwell, M., 22, 427, 428
Gleick, J., 88
Gleitman, H., 160
Gleitman, L., 160
Glick, J. A., 37, 168
Glynn, L. M., 446
Gobster, P. H., 351
Goddard, H. H., 169
Goel, M. S., 526
Goldberg, L. R., 221
Goldberg, M., 443
Goldin, C., 79
Goldsmith, H. H., 157
Goldstein, W. M., 150, 152
Gomby, D. S., 444
Gonzalez, R., 355, 357, 366, 367

Good, C., 545
Goode, W. J., 482
Goodenough, W. H., 31
Goody, J., 168
Gopnik, A., 160
Gordon, A., 444
Gordon, P., 34, 402
Gordon, R. A., 414, 445
Gornik-Durose, M., 204
Gosling, S. D., 221
Goto, S. G., 121, 539
Gottesman, I. I., 430
Gould, A. B., 109
Gould, S. J., 169
Graves, J., 498
Gray, J. J., 414
Greeley, A. M., 274, 275
Green, S. J., 480, 481
Greenberg, J., 232, 241
Greenberg, J. H., 276
Greenfield, P. M., 78, 92, 99
Greenholtz, J., 109
Griffin, D. W., 482
Grimm, S. D., 107, 223
Grossman, K. E., 33, 158
Grossmann, K., 33, 158
Groves, W. B., 445
Guarnaccia, P. J. J., 410
Guarniccia, P. J., 419
Guilford-Davenport, M., 468–69
Gullahorn, J. E., 514, 516
Gullahorn, J. T., 514, 516
Gunz, A., 210
Gupta, U., 259, 486
Gussow, Z., 419
Guthrie, G., 418
Guthrie, G. M., 515

Haidt, J., 293, 295, 299, 300, 301,
   302, 320, 329, 334, 340
Haidt, M., 300
Haight, W. L., 155
Hall, D. G., 160, 162, 359
Hall, E. T., 190, 389
Hall, G. S., 164
Hallahan, M., 374
Hallett, D., 428
Halloran, M., 110
Halmi, K. A., 413

Hamamura, T., 74, 234, 235, 236,
   240, 382, 528
Hamilton, D. L., 37
Hamilton, V. L., 374
Hampden-Turner, C., 248
Han, S., 122
Hanning, R. W., 237
Hannover, B., 121, 359, 539
Hansen, I. G., 35
Hare, R. D., 301
Harrington, L., 234
Harris, B., 441
Harris, P. L., 96
Harris, V. A., 371
Hart, D., 182
Hartmann, D., 451
Harton, H. C., 64
Harvey, P. H., 18
Harwood, R. L., 289
Haselton, M. G., 51
Hashimoto, T., 481
Hatfield, E., 480
Haun, D. B. M., 400
Hayashi, C., 105
Hazan, C., 157
Healy, J. M., 78
Heath, C., 66
Heatherton, T. F., 413
Heaven, P., 247
Heck, K., 450
Heider, K., 111, 318
Heine, S. J., 31, 32, 33, 109, 110,
   111, 120, 137, 202, 208, 209,
   212, 216, 225, 230, 234, 235,
   236, 238, 240, 241, 277, 382,
   471, 472, 473, 483, 528, 529,
   530, 539, 545
Heingartner, A., 32, 498
Heinrich, J., 8, 33
Helwig, C. C., 300
Heminway, H., 446–47
Henderson, V., 215
Henrich, J., 146, 279
Herdt, B., 28
Herdt, G., 39
Herman, E. M., 32, 498
Herskiovits, M. J., 279
Herzog, T., 374
Hess, T. M., 545
Hewlett, B. S., 163

Hezel, F. X., 428
Higgins, E. T., 240
Hill, L., 418
Ho, D. Y. F., 240
Hock, H. W., 415
Hofstede, G., 188, 190, 196, 247
Holden, C., 434
Hollingshead, A. B., 431
Hollox, E., 434
Holmes, J. G., 482
Holmes, T. H., 474
Holtbernd, T., 331
Holzberg, A. D., 231
Hong, J. J., 424
Hong, Y., 215, 255, 257, 533, 534, 535
Hopkins, W. D., 9, 13
Horiuchi, G. T., 66
Hornblow, A. R., 413
Hortacsu, N., 480, 485
Hosey, G. R., 498
Hoshino-Browne, E., 33, 203, 211, 242
Hou, Y., 350, 381
Hough, W., 15
House, J. S., 474
Hout, M., 275
Hsiao-Ying, T., 515
Hsu, C. C. Chu, H. M., 430
Hsu, F. I., 361
Hsu, L., 424, 425
Hughes, B. O., 240
Hughes, C. C., 418
Hui, C. H., 105, 117, 182
Human Development Reports, 280
Humphrey, N. K., 19
Hunt, E., 392
Hunter, J., 474
Hunter, J. D., 295, 296, 297
Huttenlocher, J., 159
Hwu, H. G., 425
Hypertension Detection and Follow-up Program Cooperative Group, 450

Ickes, W., 208, 209, 212
Ickovics, J. R., 448
Ignatieff, M., 71
Iibuchi, Y., 443

Imada, S., 300, 301, 302, 320, 438, 439
Imada, T., 189, 344
Ingham, A. G., 498
Inglehart, R., 346
Inglehart, R. F., 280
Ingram, R. E., 420
Inkeles, A., 482
Inzlicht, M., 545
Isaka, H., 309
Ishii, K., 189, 344, 391, 392
Ishikawa, S., 409
Ito, T. A., 314
Iwawaki, S., 504
Iyengar, S. S., 259, 262, 489, 528
Izard, C. E., 323
Izard, V., 402

Jablensky, A., 430, 431
Jablonski, N. G., 433
Jackson, E. F., 247
Jackson, J. M., 499
Jackson, J. S., 452
Jackson, K. L., 469
Jacobs, R. C., 86
Jaeger, A. M., 308
James, S., 418
James, S. A., 452
James, W., 314
Jamieson, D. W., 472
Jankowiak, W. R., 480
Janzen, G., 400
Jenkins, P., 275
Jensen, L. A., 150, 152, 296, 297, 298, 299
Ji, L. J., 147, 358, 362, 363, 382, 383
John, O. P., 221
Johnson, J., 141, 146
Johnson, S., 80
Johnston, R. E., 331
Jones, E. E., 232, 371
Jones, R. B., 240
Joseph, C., 300
Joyce, P., 413
Jusczyk, P., 140

Kabnick, K., 437, 438
Kagamimori, S., 443
Kagan, J., 384

Kahn, A. S., 90
Kalick, M. S., 234, 424
Kalin, R., 195
Kanagawa, C., 198, 206
Kaplan, G. A., 445
Kaprio, J., 443
Karasawa, M., 319, 336, 372, 422
Karau, S. J., 499
Karno, M., 452
Kasahara, Y., 425, 426
Kashima, E. S., 110, 161, 203
Kashima, Y., 161, 191, 203, 249, 309
Katigbak, M. S., 223
Katz, D., 90
Kawamura, S., 5
Kawamura, T., 363
Kay, P., 394, 401
Kearsley, R. B., 384
Keel, P., 413
Keel, P. K., 414, 415
Keil, J. E., 445
Keljo, K., 287, 288
Keltner, D., 327, 329, 334
Kemmelmeier, M., 233
Kennedy, A., 515, 518
Kenrick, D. T., 225
Kephart, W. M., 481
Kesaniemi, A., 443
Kessler, R. C., 420
Keys, C. B., 491
Killen, M., 300
Kim, B. J., 33, 376
Kim, H. S., 269, 270, 271, 383, 384, 388
Kim, J., 480
Kim, K. H. S., 142
Kim, U., 191, 249, 512, 523, 526
Kim, Y., 241
Kim-Prieto, C., 377
King, J. E., 221
King, L., 344
Kishwar, M., 485
Kitanishi, K., 425
Kitayama, S., 39, 98, 118, 122, 125, 176, 183, 185, 187, 189, 198, 203, 217, 230, 234, 235, 236, 238, 242, 254, 257, 319, 336, 343, 344, 345, 363, 391, 392, 473, 528, 539

Kleinman, A., 33, 410, 412, 420, 421, 423, 431
Klingemann, H., 346
Kloner, R. A., 446
Kluckhohn, C., 40
Klump, K. L., 414, 415
Knapp, R. H., 55, 66
Knight, N., 360
Knutson, B. K., 319, 351
Kobayashi, C., 236
Kochanska, G., 163
Kogevinas, M., 447
Kohlberg, L., 281–85, 300
Koller, S. H., 293
Komlos, J., 441
Koopman, C., 333
Korten, A., 431
Kosawa, Y., 162
Kosic, A., 523, 524
Koskenvuo, M., 443
Kraut, R. E., 331
Krishnan, L., 504
Kroger, R. H. H., 435
Kruger, A., 9, 10, 13
Kruglanski, A. W., 523, 524
Kuczynski, L., 163
Kudoh, T., 336, 422
Kuhn, M. T., 177
Kühnen, U., 121, 359, 539
Kuman, P., 308
Kumanyika, S. K., 468–69
Kunda, Z., 231, 232
Kurman, J., 234, 236
Kuroda, Y., 105
Kurokawa, M., 336, 343, 345
Kurzer, N., 439
Kwan, L. Y., 355, 357, 366, 367
Kyei, K. G., 474

Lachlan, R. F., 7
Lachman, M. E., 64, 346, 447
LaFromboise, T., 512
Lai, S. Y., 124, 233
Laland, K. N., 7, 56, 60
Lalonde, C., 428
Lalonde, R. N., 523, 541
Lamb, M. E., 157
Lambert, T. A., 90
Lambertz, G., 140
Landes, D. S., 245, 246

Landis, K. R., 474
Langer, E. J., 447
Lao Tzu, 378, 379
Larkins, C., 240
Larsen, H. T., 314
Larsen, J. T., 363
Larson, J. R., 491
Lasaleta, J., 212
Latane, B., 147, 499
Latané, B., 64
Lavin, T., 160, 162, 359
Lawrence, A. D., 314
Lebra, T. S., 163
Leclerc, A., 443
Lederer, A., 160
Lederer, R., 103
LeDoux, J. E., 315
Lee, A. Y., 121, 241, 538
Lee, C. K., 415, 425
Lee, F., 374, 537
Lee, G. R., 482
Lee, H. K., 182, 516
Lee, K., 142
Lee, P., 541
Lee, P. A., 146
Lee, S.-Y., 105
Leeman, R. F., 457
Lefebvre, L., 7
Leff, J., 431
Leff, J. P., 431
Leggett, E. L., 214
Lehman, D. R., 109, 137, 202, 230, 234, 235, 383, 473, 483, 529, 530, 539
Leichtman, M. D., 155
Lenneberg, E. H., 141
Lenski, G., 15
Lenski, J., 15
Leonardi, R., 82
Leong, C., 520
Leong, F., 223
Leor, J., 446
Lepper, M., 381
Lepper, M. R., 259, 262, 489, 528
Lerner, C., 402
Leroi, A. M., 58
Lert, F., 443
Leu, J., 537
Leuers, T. R. S., 182, 213
Leulliette, P., 456

Leung, D., 162
Leung, K., 190, 223, 504
Levenson, R. W., 111, 314, 318, 342
Leventhal, T., 445
Levine, R., 481
Levine, R. A., 37
Levine, R. V., 111
Levinger, G., 498
Levinson, S. C., 398, 400
Lewis, C. C., 237
Lewontin, R. C., 451
Li, N. P., 225
Li, S. R., 420
Liang, C. H., 156, 236, 237
Liberzon, I., 314
Liebrand, W. B. G., 504
Liese, L. H., 516
Lim, T. W., 441
Lin, D. M., 215
Lin, M. C., 422
Lin, R. Y., 430
Lin, T.-Y., 422
Linden, W., 337, 338
Lindenberger, U., 262
Lipsedge, M., 419
Lipset, S. M., 526
Little, B., 372
Little, T. D., 262
Littlewood, R., 419
Liu, J. F., 424
Liu, J. H., 234
Lockwood, P., 232, 241
Loftus, E. F., 93
Longworth, S. L., 424
Lopez, S. R., 410
Lopez-Garcia, J. J., 35
Lord, C., 381
Louie, J., 351
Low, M., 520
Lowery, L., 300, 301, 302, 320
Lubman, S., 383
Lucca-Irizarry, N., 182
Lucy, J. A., 395
Lun, J., 217, 218
Lundberg, O., 449
Luria, A. R., 16, 37, 168
Lutz, C., 340
Lydon, J. E., 472
Lynch, C. I., 545

Lynch, M., 203
Lynge, E., 443
Lynn, R., 79
Lysgaard, S., 512, 514, 515
Lyubomirsky, S., 344

Ma, V., 180, 182
Maass, A., 372
Mace, R., 434
Maclure, M., 446
MacMillan, N. A., 396
Macpherson, C., 428
Macpherson, L., 428
Madsen, M. C., 501
Mahalingam, R., 197
Mahamedi, F., 413
Mahapatra, M., 285
Mahler, I., 255
Major, B., 234
Makuc, D., 450
Malcolm, L. A., 440
Malinowski, B., 497
Malone, M. A., 446
Mandel, N., 539
Mandelbaum, D. G., 144
Manis, M., 110
Mann, A. H., 337
Mannetti, L., 523, 524
Marcus, H. R., 269, 270, 271
Marin, G., 107
Marin, G. V., 107
Mark, N., 64
Markides, K. S., 452
Markus, H., 39, 98, 125, 183, 185,
    187, 198, 217
Markus, H. R., 64, 118, 122, 176,
    182, 198, 203, 206, 230, 234,
    235, 238, 242, 257, 265, 266,
    319, 336, 343, 345, 346, 473,
    528
Marler, P., 139
Marmot, M., 445
Marmot, M. G., 442, 445, 446–47,
    449, 527
Marriott, A., 474
Marsh, C., 247
Marshall, T. C., 241
Martin, L. L., 335
Martin, R. D., 17
Masson, E., 261

Masson, J. L., 340
Masson, K., 188
Master, A., 545
Masuda, T., 355, 357, 363, 364,
    366, 367, 370
Mather, J. A., 222
Matsumoto, D., 331, 336, 422
Matsumoto, H., 118, 234, 242, 528
Matz, D., 331
Mayberry, R. I., 141
Mazur, A., 130
McAdams, D. P., 219
McCarthy, E. P., 526
McCauley, R. N., 146, 279
McClelland, D., 122, 247
McCormick, N. B., 480
McCrae, R. R., 219, 221, 223, 531
McCusker, C., 117, 182
McDonald, K., 9, 13
McKeown, R. E., 469
McPartland, T., 177
McWhiney, G., 126
Mead, M., 97, 164
Mehler, J., 140
Meijer, Z., 234, 235
Melby, M. K., 149
Menon, T., 255, 257
Menozzi, P., 451
Merighi, J. R., 480
Mesoudi, A., 56, 60
Mesquita, B., 315, 319, 322, 336,
    343, 422
Meyerowitz, J. A., 231
Miao, F. F., 351
Miller, D., 88
Miller, G. E., 445
Miller, J. G., 147, 289, 291, 372
Miller, K. F., 34
Miller, P. J., 102, 156, 236, 237
Miller, P. M. C., 518
Millteman, M. A., 446
Minami, M., 384
Mindell, W. R., 457
Minn, J. Y., 424
Minoura, Y., 145
Mirowsky, J., 107
Miyake, K., 154, 157, 158–59, 163
Miyamoto, T., 425
Miyamoto, Y., 118, 254, 368, 390,
    391

Modiano, D., 444
Moll, H., 10
Montagu, A., 465
Morelli, G., 154, 159
Mori, A., 425
Morikawa, H., 162
Morita, S., 425
Morling, B., 118, 252, 253, 254
Morris, M., 122, 374, 534
Morris, M. W., 255, 257, 537
Mosimann, J. E., 414
Moskalenko, S., 208, 209, 212
Much, N. C., 285
Muller, J. E., 446
Mullet, E., 480
Mumford, D. B., 414
Murdock, G. P., 454
Murphy, F. C., 314
Murphy-Berman, V., 308
Murray, S. L., 482
Murstein, B. I., 480

Nagell, K., 11
Naidu, R. K., 182
Nanetti, R. Y., 82
National Center for Health Statistics
    (NCHS), 450, 452
Neff, L. J., 469
Neto, F., 480
Newcomb, T. M., 472
Newport, E. L., 139, 141, 146
Newton, M., 143, 144
Ngui, P. W., 416
Nicholas, S., 441
Nichols, P. A., 413
Nimmo-Smith, I., 314
Nisbett, R. E., 33, 81, 93, 109,
    110, 111, 112, 126, 127, 128,
    129, 130, 131, 133, 134, 162,
    216, 248, 249, 355, 357, 358,
    359, 360, 362, 363, 366, 367,
    368, 370, 374, 376, 379, 383,
    528
Nobakht, M., 415
Noels, K. A., 516
Norasakkunkit, V., 118, 234, 242,
    424, 528
Norenzayan, A., 31, 32, 33, 52, 68,
    69, 81, 111, 120, 162, 216, 225,
    358, 360, 376, 528

Nwaefuna, A., 415
Nyhof, M. A., 68

Oakley-Browne, M. A., 413
Oberg, K., 512, 513, 515
Obeyesekere, G., 411
Odbert, H. S., 217, 219
Oettingen, G., 262, 263
Ohashi, M. M., 257
Oishi, S., 33, 199–200, 217, 218, 242, 348, 349
Okazaki, S., 424
Olguin, K., 11
Olivier, D. C., 395
O'Malley, P. M., 105
Omoregie, H., 122, 176, 257
O'Nell, C. W., 418
Onizawa, C., 425
Opolot, J. A., 480
O'Regan, J. K., 370
Organisation for Economic Co-operation and Development (OECD), 436
Ouchi, W. G., 308
Oumar, F., 158–59
Oxford English Dictionary, 240
Oyserman, D., 233, 359

Pachauri, A., 308
Pagsberg, A. K., 414
Pamuk, E., 450
Panksepp, J., 315
Paredes, D. R., 34
Parekh, R., 122
Park, H., 377
Park, L., 285
Parker, G., 420, 421
Parker, S. T., 18
Parkinson, B., 330, 331
Patwardhan, M. W., 340
Paulesu, E., 142
Paulhus, D. L., 382, 522, 526, 531
Payer, L., 454, 456, 457
Pearce, N. E., 443
Peckham, V., 498
Penaranda-Ortega, M., 35
Peng, K., 81, 109, 110, 111, 112, 122, 162, 350, 358, 362, 363, 374, 379, 381, 534
Perani, D., 142

Perilloux, H. K., 9
Pete, E., 437, 438
Phan, K. L., 314
Philbrick, J. L., 480
Phillips, D. P., 446
Phillips, R. S., 526
Piazza, A., 451
Pica, P., 402
Pierro, A., 523, 524
Pike, C. L., 466
Pinker, S., 13, 277, 342, 393, 402
Pisani, L., 158–59
Pittinsky, T. L., 544
Plaut, V. C., 64, 346, 475, 478
Poehlmann, K. M., 314
Politi, F., 372
Pon, G., 516
Poole, W. K., 446
Poortinga, Y. H., 277
Population Reference Bureau, 281
Postman, L. J., 66
Poston, D. L., Jr., 147
Pott, M., 154, 157, 158–59, 163
Povinelli, D. J., 9
Power, S., 523, 526
Prentice, D., 88
Prince, R., 419
Puente, S., 126
Putnam, R., 72
Putnam, R. D., 82, 239
Pyszczynski, T., 241

Quinn, D., 543
Quinn, D. M., 247
Quinones-Vidal, E., 35

Rahe, R. H., 474
Rajecki, D. W., 471
Ramaswamy, J., 189, 344
Ramble, C., 68
Rantilla, A., 126
Rapold, C. J., 400
Ratner, C., 395
Ratner, H. H., 9, 10, 13
Reaux, J. E., 9
Redelmeier, D. A., 450
Redlich, R. C., 431
Rees, P., 409
Regier, D. A., 420
Reisenzein, R., 331

Relkin, N., 142
Renaud, S., 437
Rendell, L., 7
Renshaw, K., 33, 471, 473
Rensink, R. A., 370
Rettek, S. I., 182
Reuben, C., 450
Reyes, J. A., 391, 392
Reyes, J. A. S., 223
Reykowski, J., 204
Rhee, E., 182, 516
Rhodes, G., 466, 467
Rice, T. W., 82
Richard, J. L., 437
Richardson, A., 515
Richerson, P. J., 3, 17, 22, 54, 81
Rin, H., 418, 430
Rivera-Sinclair, E. A., 526
Roberson, D., 342, 395, 396, 397
Robins, L. N., 420
Robins, R. W., 320, 327
Robinson, M. D., 350
Rodgers, J. S., 350
Rodin, J., 447
Rodriguez, J., 197
Rogoff, B., 37, 163, 168
Roman, R. J., 182, 516
Rosaldo, M. Z., 311
Rosch Heider, E., 395, 396, 403
Rose, G., 442, 445
Roseman, I. J., 182
Rosen, B. C., 239
Rosen, D. S., 414
Rosenberg, M., 230
Rosenfeld, H. M., 102, 111, 136
Rosenthal, D., 71
Ross, C. E., 107
Ross, L., 381, 489, 528
Ross, M., 102, 537
Rothbaum, F., 154, 157, 158–59, 163, 252
Rothbaum, F. M., 253
Rothblum, E. D., 468
Rotomi, C., 452
Roy, K., 421
Rozin, P., 261, 300, 301, 302, 304, 305, 306, 320, 437, 438, 439, 457
Rubel, A. J., 418
Rubert, E., 9, 13

Rubinstein, D. H., 427, 428
Rubio-Stipec, M., 419
Rudmin, F. W., 511, 522, 526
Ruiz-Belda, M.-A., 331
Russell, J. A., 221, 314, 327, 328, 331, 340, 342
Rutkow, I. M., 457
Ryder, A. G., 420, 421, 422, 424, 522, 526

Sadler, P., 241
Sagi, A., 158
Sagiv, L., 281
Sakai, M., 409
Sakano, Y., 409
Sam, D., 521
Sampson, R. J., 445
Samuels, B., 452
Sanchez-Burks, J., 248, 249
Sandel, T., 102, 236, 237
Sanders, J., 374
Sapolsky, R. M., 445, 448
Sargent, R. G., 469
Sarna, S., 443
Sartorius, N., 431
Sarubin, A., 438, 439
Sato, H., 409
Sato, S., 481
Saucier, G., 221
Saunders, B. A. C., 395
Savage-Rumbaugh, E. S., 9, 13
Schacter, S., 93, 268, 315–17, 469
Schaffer, H. R., 156
Schaller, M., 62, 63, 69
Scherer, K., 336, 422
Scherer, K. R., 321
Schieffelin, E. L., 338
Schlegel, A., 165
Schmader, T., 234
Schmidt, K., 418
Schmidte, A., 426
Schmidtke, A., 280
Schmitt, E., 218
Schnack, R. L., 90
Schoeneman, T. J., 180, 182
Schooler, C., 163
Schooler, J. W., 386
Schreckenbach, H., 474
Schubert, B., 121, 359, 539
Schwartz, D., 414

Schwartz, E., 413
Schwartz, S. H., 112, 188, 190, 226, 262, 281, 319, 320
Schwarz, N., 111, 126, 130, 131, 390, 391
Scollon, C. N., 199–200
Scott, W., 420
Scribner, M., 102
Scribner, S., 37, 168
Searle, W., 520
Sears, D., 35
Sedikides, C., 236
Seeman, M., 447
Seeman, T. E., 447
Sefa-Dedeh, A., 468
Segal, M. W., 470
Segall, M. H., 279
Segerstrom, S. C., 445
Seginer, R., 255
Seligman, M. E. P., 262, 263
Sen, A. K., 449
Seppala, E., 351
Sevcik, R. A., 9, 13
Seyfarth, R. M., 13, 21, 139
Shachar, R., 485
Shand, N., 162
Shao, L., 348
Shapiro, L., 395, 396, 397
Sharkey, W. F., 124, 233
Sharp, D. W., 37, 168
Shaver, P., 157
Shavit, S., 122
Shay, T., 440
Sheldon, K. M., 241
Shen, Y. C., 420
Shennan, S., 56
Sherman, D. K., 388
Sherman, G. D., 217, 218
Sherwood, J. B., 446
Shields, C., 261, 437, 438, 457
Shih, M., 544
Shimoda, K., 372
Shipley, M. J., 442, 445
Shrira, I., 446
Shweder, R., 96, 277, 293, 296, 301
Shweder, R. A., 23, 24, 27, 36, 39, 150, 152, 187, 276, 285, 322, 340, 372, 395
Siegal, M., 203, 309

Siegel, J. I., 305
Siegle, G., 420
Siegrist, J., 445
Simeonova, D. I., 528
Simon, L., 232
Sineshaw, T., 329
Singelis, T. M., 124, 233, 526
Singer, J. E., 93, 315–17
Singh, P., 259, 308, 486
Singh, S. M., 450
Sjomeling, M., 545
Skolnick, A. S., 480
Smiley, P., 159
Smith, A. H., 443
Smith, E. E., 33, 376
Smith, H., 348
Smith, P. B., 255, 269, 491
Snarey, J., 284, 287, 288
Snibbe, A. C., 122, 203, 235, 265, 266
Snyder, S. S., 252
Sogon, S., 491
Sokol, B., 428
Sonoda, N., 182, 213
Sorenson, E. R., 327
Spangler, G., 33, 158
Spencer, S., 234
Spencer, S. J., 33, 203, 242, 543
Spencer-Rodgers, J., 381
Sperber, D., 61
Spina, R., 472, 473
Sprecher, S., 480
Sroufe, L. A., 163
Stansfeld, S., 446–47
Star, S. A., 110
Statistics Canada, 79
Steckel, R. H., 441
Steele, B. J., 82
Steele, C. M., 203, 542, 543
Stenberg, C., 157
Stepper, S., 335
Steptoe, A., 447
Sternberg, E., 66
Stevenson, H. W., 105, 170, 171, 172, 173, 216, 237
Stigler, J. W., 39, 171, 172, 216, 237
Stoeckle, J. D., 333
Stone, J., 545
Stone, L. H., 482

Stouffer, S. A., 110
Strack, F., 335
Su, S. K., 251, 253
Su, Y., 383
Suarez-Orazco, M. M., 509, 527
Suarez-Orozco, C., 509, 527
Suchman, E. A., 110
Suess, G., 33, 158
Suga, S., 372
Suh, E., 348
Suh, E. M., 206, 348, 375
Summerfield, A. B., 321
Susser, E., 415
Sussman, N. M., 102, 111, 136
Suwanlert, S., 418
Suzuki, N., 221
Suzuki, T., 105, 235
Swann, W. B., Jr., 236
Syme, S. L., 527

Tafarodi, R. W., 236
Tagliacozzo, R., 201
Tajfel, H., 37, 491
Takahashi, S., 105
Takata, T., 236
Takemoto, T., 212
Takemura, K., 110, 189, 344
Takizawa, M., 409
Tamis-LeMonda, C. S., 162, 359
Tanaka, K., 203, 309
Tanchuk, T. L., 62, 63
Tardif, T., 160
Tassenaar, V., 441
Taylor, S. E., 231
Taylor, S. F., 314
Teasdale, J. D., 263
Tees, R. C., 140
Tehrani, J. J., 56
Teoh, J.-I., 417
Terraciano, A., 219, 221
Thayer, J. F., 337
Thoits, P., 455
Thompson, M., 414
Thompson, R. J., 498
Thornhill, R., 465
Tilby, P., 195
Tobin, J. J., 216
Tocqueville, A., 126, 127
Toguchi, Y., 236
Toh, Y., 255

Tomasello, M., 9, 10, 11, 12, 13
Tong, J. U., 214, 252, 320
Tonnies, F., 287
Tooby, J., 50, 276
Tornatzky, L. G., 255
Tortosa-Gil, F., 35
Townsend, S. S. M., 122, 176, 257
Tracy, J. L., 320, 327
Trafimow, D., 121, 539
Trapnell, P. D., 531
Triandis, H. C., 38, 72, 88, 100,
    105, 117, 121, 182, 190, 348,
    539
Triscari, R. S., 147
Trommsdorf, G., 165
Trommsdorff, G., 255
Trompenaars, A., 248
Trompenaars, F., 255
Tropp, L. R., 233
True, M. M., 158–59
Tsai, J., 318, 541
Tsai, J. L., 146, 319, 351, 528
Tseng, W., 418, 426
Tucker, D. M., 240
Turiel, E., 300
Tweed, R. G., 383
Twenge, J. M., 239

Uchida, Y., 122, 176, 236, 257, 351
Uleman, J. S., 182, 372, 516
Umberson, D., 474
Unzner, L., 33, 158
U.S. Census Bureau, 79

Vagero, D., 449
Val, E. R., 420
Van Boven, L., 90
Van Brakel, J., 395
Vandello, J., 126, 164
Vandello, J. A., 111, 189
van Harten, P. N., 415
Van Hemert, D. A., 277
van Hoeken, D., 415
Varnum, M. E. W., 360
Vaughn, C. E., 431
Vayda, E., 457
Veenhoven, R., 345
Verkuyten, M., 188
Verma, J., 481
Voils, C. I., 372

Vouloumanos, A., 140
Vygotsky, L. S., 37
Vyse, S. A., 480

de Waal, F., 10
Wager, T. D., 314
Walker, L. J., 287
Wall, S., 156
Wallace, R., 444
Wallace, R. G., 444
Wallbott, H., 336, 422
Wallbott, H. G., 321
Waller, N. G., 223
Wan, W., 215
Wang, A. R., 414
Wang, L., 350, 381
Wang, Q., 155, 156, 182, 237, 336,
    359
Wang, S., 102, 236, 237
Wang, Y., 147, 499
Ward, C., 223, 511, 515, 518, 520
Warner, R., 431
Warrant, E. J., 435
Watabe, M., 490
Watanabe, J. T., 528
Waters, E., 156
Watkins, D., 182
Waxman, S. R., 160, 162, 359
Weaver, S. L., 447
Weber, M., 81, 244, 246, 248
Wee, C. C., 526
Weinstein, H., 384
Weintraub, K. J., 238
Weiss, M. J., 64
Weisz, J., 154, 157, 158–59, 163
Weisz, J. R., 252, 253
Welch, M., 55
Wells, A., 424
Wells, J. E., 413
Wen, J. K., 419
Wenar, C., 162
Werker, J. F., 140
Wertsch, J. V., 37, 169
Westermarck, E., 153
Wheatley, T., 300
Wheeler, P., 17, 18
White, K., 235
Whitehead, H., 7
Whitehouse, A. M., 414
Whiten, A., 6, 10, 12, 56, 60

Whiting, B. B., 124, 153
Whiting, J., 149
Whiting, J. W. M., 149, 153
Whiting, R., 84
Whitwell, G., 441
Whorf, B. L., 392
Whyte, M. K., 480, 486
Wicklund, R., 208, 209, 212
Wicklund, R. A., 208
Wierzabicka, A., 339
Wiley, A. R., 156, 236, 237
Wilkinson, R. G., 443, 449
Williams, D. R., 451, 452
Williams, J., 192, 195
Williams, K. D., 499
Williams, R. M., Jr., 110
Williams, T. P., 491
Williamson, P. A., 240
Willingham, B., 331
Wilson, A. E., 102, 537
Wilson, J. F., 468–69
Wilson, T. D., 93
Wilson, W. R., 471
Wilss, W., 104
Winkielman, P., 466, 471
Wise, P., 451
Wiseman, C. V., 414
Witkin, H. A., 363
Wittchen, H. U., 425

Wolfe, C., 234
Wondimu, H., 182
Wong, N. Y. C., 109, 110, 111, 112
Wood, M., 498
Worchel, P., 38
World Health Organization, 427, 430, 431, 435
Worthman, C. M., 149
Wosinka, W., 204
Wright, S. C., 233
Wrzesniewski, A., 438, 439
Wu, D. Y. H., 216
Wundt, W., 36

Xu, X., 480, 486
Xun, W. Q. E., 102, 537

Yamada, A., 526
Yamagishi, M., 490
Yamagishi, T., 490
Yamaguchi, S., 191, 249, 257
Yamashita, I., 426
Yap, P. M., 417
Yau, J., 182
Ybarra, O., 248, 249
Yeh, E. K., 425, 430
Yelsma, P., 486
Yeo, R. A., 465

Yi, Y., 382
Yik, M. S. M., 221, 531
Ying, Y., 146, 516, 541
Yoshihara-Tanaka, C., 234
Young, M., 523, 526
Yu, Y., 452
Yuki, M., 110, 191, 249, 491, 492, 494

Zajonc, R. B., 32, 471, 498
Zanna, M. P., 472
Zarate, M. A., 372
Zatzick, D. F., 333
Zax, M., 105
Zborowski, M., 333
Zektick, I. N., 515
Zelazo, P. R., 384
Zemba, Y., 257
Zhang, F. C., 414
Zhang, M., 421
Zhang, W. X., 420
Zhang, X., 147
Zhang, Z., 358
Zheng, X., 515
Zhou, M., 509, 527
Zillman, D., 318
Zola, I. K., 333
Zuckerman, M., 232

Subject Index

abacus, 34
abortion, 296–97
accessibility universal, 32
acculturation
  changes in attitude with, 511–16
  on cultural differences, 137
  cultural fit, 519–21
  frame-switching, 531–41
  pitfalls of, 526–27
  of self-esteem, 528–31
  stereotype threat and, 542–45
  strategies for, 521–26
  studying, 511–12
  success in, 516–26
achievement motivation, 242–50
acquiescence bias, 107–8
actions, see behaviors
actor-observer bias, 489–90
Adams, Glenn, 475–76
adaptations, cultural persistence and, 83–85
adjustment
  cultural distance and, 516–19
  as secondary control, 252, 254
  U-shaped pattern of, 513–15
adolescent rebellion, 164–66
advertisements, conformity and, 271
affirmative action, 542
Afghanistan, 178–79
Africa/Africans
  attachment styles in, 158
  brain fag syndrome, 418–19
  butterfly effect in, 88
  cartoon controversy and, 273
  collectivism in, 188
  continental axes and, 49
  control strategies in, 255

cultural differences in, 54
cultural learning among animals
  in, 6–7
culture of honor in, 128
describing emotions, 340
developmental transitions in, 163
eating disorders in, 414
equality matching and, 495
genetic variations among, 451
health and income, 449
hypertension in, 452
interpersonal attraction and, 468
mortality and income, 443
Müller-Lyer illusion and, 279
Pygmies in, 108–9
skin color in, 433
sleeping arrangements in, 149
subjective well-being and, 346
voodoo death, 418
on witchcraft, 455
see also South Africa
African-Americans
  causes of death among, 451
  co-sleeping and, 149
  education and, 542–44
  extremity bias, 105
  frame-switching and, 532–33,
    536
  health and income, 449
  hypertension in, 451–52
  interpersonal attraction and, 468
  reference-group effects, 110
  self-views of, 234
  socioeconomic status of, 450
  stereotype threat and, 542–45
agency
  defined, 192

motivation and, 250–66
  progressive religions on, 296
agonias disorder, 418
agreeableness (OCEAN), 220
agriculture, continental axes and, 49
Ah-Q mentality, 222
Ainu people (Japan), 418, 463–64
Aka Pygmies (Africa), 163
alcohol abuse, 410, 417
altruistic phobia, 425
amae, 341
Amazon, 403
American College Testing Program
  (ACT), 542
American Psychiatric Association,
  409
Americans, see United
  States/Americans
amok phenomenon, 417–18
AMS (Acute Mediterranean
  Syndrome), 332–33
amusement, 340
analytic thinking
  attention in, 361–70
  overview, 358–61
  reasoning styles, 375–78
  toleration of contradiction,
    378–83
  understanding other's behaviors,
    370–75
anger
  Chewong people and, 340
  cultural display rules for, 332
  culture of honor and, 131
  ethic of autonomy and, 301–2
  expressing, 337–39
  facial expressions of, 324, 327

anger (*continued*)
liget and, 311–12
suppressing, 337–39
two-factor theory of emotions
and, 316–18
animal domestication, 49–50
Ann Landers advice column, 150
anorexia nervosa, 413–15
answering machines, 390–91
anthropocentric ways, 404–5
antibiotics, 457
anxious-ambivalent attachment,
157–59
appraisals
role in emotions, 319–22
variations in experiencing
emotions, 342–43
Arab cultures, 332, 338, 360
Arakaki, Nagisa, 429
Arawak people, 508
archival data, 128–29
Arctic hysteria, 419
Argentina, 71, 324–25
argument-related murders, 129
Aristotle, 360, 379
arranged marriages, 480–82, 484
Asahi Shinbun, 256
Asch, Solomon, 266–68, 491
Asia
calculation tools in, 34
cartoon controversy and, 273
collectivism in, 188
conformity and, 269
equality matching and, 495
self-awareness in, 210–11
self-concept measures and, 192
theories on nature of self, 216
see also East Asia; South Asia
Asian-Americans
co-sleeping and, 149
group membership and, 490
happiness and, 351
immigration and, 509
life satisfaction and, 349–50
making choices, 259–61
positive emotions and, 351
reasoning styles in, 376–77
self-improvement motivation, 242
talking and thinking, 383–89
value endorsement by, 540–41

Asian-Canadians
acculturation and, 530–31
on romantic love, 483–84
self-awareness in, 210–11
self-enhancing tendencies in, 235
assertiveness (measure), 192
assimilation strategy, 522–23, 525,
527
asymmetry, 495
Atahuallpa, Incan emperor, 48
ataques de nervios condition, 419
attachment styles, 156–59
attachment theory, 156–59
attention, 361–70
attributions
dispositional, 371–72
explaining behaviors through,
534–35
fundamental attribution error,
371–75
situational, 371–72
Australia
arranged marriages and, 481
gender identity in, 191
Gidjingali aborigines of, 340
height in, 440
immigration and, 509
individualism in, 188
interpersonal attraction and,
466–67
linguistic relativity in, 398, 400
malgri syndrome, 418
resource distribution and, 309
skin color in, 433
views of self in, 182
Austria, 194
authority ranking, 495
autokinetic effect, 87
autonomy
developmental transitions and,
163
ethic of, 285, 297, 301–2
self-concept and, 190
autonomy ideal (sleeping
arrangement), 154
Aveyron, wild boy of, 143
avoidant attachment, 156, 158–59
Ayurvedic medicine, 219
Azande tribe, 320, 455
Aztec people, 402

Babylonians, 402
back-translation method, 104
Baka people, 95–96
balance and reciprocity, 495–96
Bali/Balinese, 338–39, 372
Baptists, 244, 297–98, 303–4
Barber, Benjamin, 71
Baring's Bank, 256
baseball, 84–85
bask in the reflected glory, 233,
235
Baxter, Richard, 245
behavioral measures, 111, 131
behaviorism, psychology and, 38
behaviors
cultural context of, 25
explaining, 534–35
healthy outcomes and, 453
making sense of, 374–75
morality and, 305–6
stages of moral development,
281–85
understanding others', 370–75
Belgium/Belgians
attitudes toward food, 439–40
happiness and, 321
painting styles in, 356
Benedict XVI, Pope, 244
Benin, 508
Berckhyde (Flemish artist), 356
Berinmo language, 396–97
Berlin Wall, 262
Bernard, St., 244
Berry, John, 38
between-groups manipulation,
114–16
Bible, 303–4, 351
bicultural people, 528, 537–41
Big Five Traits, 219–25
bilateral symmetry, 465
bilinguals and languages, 142
bin Laden, Osama, 275
biological evolution, 56–62
bisexuality, 28–30
Blanche (French painter), 356–57
blending cultures, 528–31
blood pressure, 338–39, 542
blood types, 219
blowing noses, 43–44
Bolivia, 33, 194

Bonaparte, Josephine, 457
Bonaparte, Napoleon, 457
Bond, Michael, 38
The Book of Changes, 379
Boroditsky, Lera, 400
Bowling Alone (Putnam), 72
brain fag syndrome, 418–19
brain size, cultural learning and, 17–21
Brazil
    cultural learning from warfare in, 7
    facial expressions for emotions, 324–25
    gender identity in, 194
    Piraha tribe, 403
Britain, *see* Great Britain
Broca's area (brain), 142
Buddhism, 351, 360
Buganda people (Uganda), 340
bulimia nervosa, 413–15
Burma, 435
Bush, George W., 64, 207, 217
Butch Cassidy and the Sundance Kid (film), 325
butterfly effect, 88
Buzkashi sport (Afghanistan), 178–79

calling (purpose), 243–44
Calvinism, 244–45, 248
Cambodia, 434
Cameroon, 96
Canada/Canadians
    acculturation and, 518–19, 528–31
    beliefs about future, 147–48
    Hutterites in, 22
    individualism in, 188
    Jean and, 508–9
    negotiation and, 504
    obesity rates in, 438
    pursuit of happiness in, 345
    Quebec's independence movement, 71
    on romantic love, 483
    self-improvement motivation, 241–42
    similarity-attraction effect and, 472
    somatization in, 421–22

suicide rates in, 428–29
    views of self in, 182
Cannon, Walter, 315
capitalism, 242–45, 262, 533
cardiovascular disease, 337
Caribbean, 415, 495
Carlyle, Thomas, 345
Carrier tribe, 519
Carter, Jimmy, 302–4
cartoon controversy, 273–74, 286
Castro, Fidel, 371
categorical perception, 396–97
Catholicism
    attitudes toward work, 244
    individualism and, 247
    political issues and, 296
    response to illness, 320
    self-starvation and, 415
    Weber on, 246
    work ethic and, 246–47
chess (game), 501
Chewong people (Malaysia), 340
child-rearing styles, 236, 368
Chile, 324–25, 360–61
chimpanzees
    Big Five traits in, 221–22
    brain size of, 18
    creative invention in, 14
    cultural learning in, 5–6
    emulative learning in, 11–12
    imitative learning in, 10
    language abilities of, 13
    theory of mind and, 9–10
China/Chinese
    acculturation, 520
    analytic thinking and, 359
    anger responses in, 337–39
    arranged marriages, 486
    attention to stimuli in, 366
    beliefs about future, 147–48
    brain fag syndrome, 418–19
    Cultural Revolution in, 61
    eating disorders in, 414–15
    emotion words and, 102
    on explaining behaviors, 534–36
    frame-switching and, 540
    frigophobia in, 418
    holistic thinking and, 360, 362
    koro syndrome, 415–16
    making choices, 259

making sense of behavior, 374
    math education in, 171, 173–74
    medical practices in, 456
    mental health and, 420–23
    noun biases and, 160
    obesity rates in, 435–36
    painting styles in, 356–57
    parenting styles in, 155–56
    personality traits and, 222–23, 225
    prevention orientation, 538–39
    response to illness in, 320
    self-esteem in, 234
    self-improvement motivation, 241
    social loafing and, 499–500
    on talking and thinking, 384
    theories on nature of self, 216
    TKS disorder in, 426
    toleration of contradiction, 379–83
    views of self in, 182
Chinese-Americans, 361–62, 534, 540
Chinese Personality Assessment Inventory (CPAI), 222–23
choices
    ethic of autonomy, 285
    making, 257–66
Chomsky, Noam, 276
Christianity
    cartoon controversy, 274
    on creation myth, 66–67
    encouragement for enthusiasm, 351
    gender identity and, 196
    growth of, 275
    on morality, 303–6
    self-esteem and, 237
    on talking and thinking, 384
    views of Islam, 275
Chuushingura, legend of, 429
cigarette smoking, 200–201, 442, 444–45, 453
Civilization (game), 80
The Civilizing Process (Elias), 43
clans, social properties of, 21–22
The Clash of Civilization (Huntington), 274
Clinton, Bill, 201

close relationships
    friends and enemies, 474–78
    groups and, 487–88
    love, 479–87
clustering technique, 167–68, 170
Coca-Cola, 204
code-switching, 532–33, 536
cognition
    cultural differences in, 358
    methods for studying, 94
    in primates, 18–19, 21
    see also analytic thinking; holistic
        thinking
cognitive dissonance, 200, 202–3
cognitive tools, universality of,
    31–34
Cohen, Dov, 126–34
Cold War, 262
Cole, Michael, 38
collaboration, 98, 104
collectivism
    acculturation and, 520
    childhood experiences and,
        154–56
    conformity and, 268–69
    control and, 255
    cooperation and, 503
    cultural evolution and, 72–76
    defined, 192
    experiencing emotions and,
        343–44
    friendship and, 475
    group membership and, 490–91
    making choices and, 258–59, 262
    negotiation and, 504
    principle of equality, 307
    reading primers and, 161
    self-concept and, 187–90, 192
    subjective well-being and,
        348–49
    thinking styles and, 359
    value endorsement for, 540–41
color
    perception of, 393–97
    skin, 432–35
Columbine High School
    (Colorado), 164
Columbus, Christopher, 508
commitment, 490
communal sharing, 494–95

communicable ideas, spread of,
    62–65
communication
    explicit vs. implicit, 389–92
    language facilitating, 12–13
communism, 262
community, ethic of, see ethic of
    community
compensatory self-enhancement, 232
competition vs. cooperation,
    500–505
complexion, 465
computers
    Moore's Law on, 15–16
    obtaining information from, 78
conformity, motivation for, 266–71,
    491
Confucianism, 360
Congo, Democratic Republic of,
    281
conscientiousness (OCEAN), 220
considerateness, 231
contemporary legends, 66–67
contempt, 301, 327
contentment, 222
contradiction, 378–83
control
    exercising, 257–66
    health and, 447
    over facial expressions, 331
    perceptions of, 250–52
    primary, 252–57
    secondary, 252–57
conventional moral reasoning, 282
Cook Islands, 182
cooperation vs. competition,
    500–505
co-sleeping, 149–51
CPAI (Chinese Personality
    Assessment Inventory), 222–23
CPU (central processing unit),
    24–26
creative invention, 14
creativity
    self and, 180
    self-evaluation on, 231
Creole languages, 277
crime rates
    adolescence and, 164
    as quality of life standard, 281

Croats, 524–25
Cromartie, Warren, 85
Cruise, Tom, 386–87
CTMM IQ test, 78
cultural differences
    acculturation on, 137
    in attachment styles, 156–59
    beliefs about future, 147–48
    in cognition, 358
    in control, 252–53
    dealing with social withdrawal,
        409
    in depression, 421
    in describing emotions, 339–42
    in display rules, 332–34
    ecological, 46–54
    emerging with age, 146–48
    in emotions, 320–39
    ethnocentrism and, 279–81
    in experiencing emotions,
        342–44
    in eye movement, 364–66
    in facial expressions, 328–30
    in gender identity, 191–97
    geographic, 46–54
    with group membership, 489
    in happiness, 344–52
    individualism vs. collectivism,
        154–56
    in intensity of emotions, 336–39
    in medical practices, 454–56
    models of diversity, 276–79
    in moral reasoning, 283, 288–93,
        295–99
    in motivation, 228–29
    in nonverbal communications,
        389–92
    in noun biases, 159–62
    in obesity rates, 436–37
    in perception, 358
    in personality traits, 217–25
    priming and, 121
    in response to illness, 320–21
    Sambia case study, 27–30
    with self-awareness, 207–14
    with self-concept, 182–86
    with self-consistency, 198–207
    in similarity-attraction effect,
        472–73
    situation sampling and, 119

in sleeping arrangements, 148–54
in spatial perception, 397–401
in stigma of mental illness, 422
in subjective well-being, 344–52
in suicide rates, 427
in talking and thinking, 387–88
theories on nature of self,
    214–17
unpackaging findings, 124–25
view of self as, 182
in weight, 435–42
cultural distance, 516–19
cultural evolution
    biological evolution and, 56–62
    changes in cultures, 70–76
    changing nature of manners,
        43–46
    cultural persistence and, 81–90
    as cumulative process, 13–17
    factors for spreading of ideas,
        62–70
    influences on, 85–88
    origin of cultural variations,
        46–56
    pluralistic ignorance and, 88–90
    trends in intelligence, 76–81
cultural fit, 519–21
cultural innovation, 83–85
cultural knowledge, 137–38
cultural learning
    in animals, 5–8
    cumulative cultural evolution
        and, 13–17
    human adeptness at, 17–23
    language and, 12–13
    theory of mind and, 9–12
    from warfare, 7
cultural messages, 122–23
cultural norms, see norms
cultural persistence, 81–90
cultural priming, 120–21
cultural psychology, 1–3, 36–39
Cultural Revolution (China), 61
cultural variation, see cultural
    differences
culture(s)
    acquired physical variation,
        435–42
    blending, 528–31
    changing nature of, 4

defined, 3–5
distributive justice and, 306–9
evoked vs. transmitted, 50–54
gender and, 191–97
health and, 442–53
height and, 440–42
heterogeneity with individuals,
    190–91
high context, 389–91
ideological conflicts and, 274
immersion in, 98
individualistic, 72–76
as individuals, 3–4
as information, 3
interconnected, 70–71
justice and, 306–9
learning about, 96–98
low context, 389–90
manners and, 43
medicine and, 453–59
mind independence from, 23–27
priming, 120–21, 533–41
reliance on, 1
sensitive periods for acquiring,
    144–46
shaping norms, 136
uniqueness in humans, 5–7
universals in, 23–24, 30–34, 323
unpackaging, 123–26
see also methods for studying
    cultures
culture-bound syndromes
    agonias disorder, 418
    amok phenomenon, 417–18
    Arctic hysteria, 419
    ataques de nervios condition, 419
    brain fag syndrome, 418–19
    defined, 412–13
    dhat syndrome, 411–413
    eating disorders, 413–15
    frigophobia, 418
    koro syndrome, 415–16
    latah condition, 418
    malgri syndrome, 418
    susto condition, 418
    TKS disorder as, 426
    voodoo death, 418
culture of honor, 126–34
culture shock, 513–15
Curacao (island), 415

D'Andrade, Roy, 38
Dani people (New Guinea), 328,
    395
Darwin, Charles, 268, 323–24, 464
Dawkins, Richard, 59
Declaration of Independence, 345
democracy, 262–63
demotivation, failure and, 33
Denmark/Danes
    cartoon controversy and, 273
    eating disorders in, 414
    mortality and income, 443
    quality of life and, 280
dependability, 223, 231
dependent variable, 101, 113–14
depression
    amok phenomenon and, 418
    as basic category, 412
    hikikomori and, 409
    learned helplessness and, 263–64
    negative affect in, 33
    as universal syndrome, 419–23
deprivation effects, 112–13
Descartes, René, 423
development
    attachment styles and, 154–56
    evolutionism on, 278
developmental transitions, 162–66
dhat syndrome, 411–13
Diamond, Jared, 48–49
diet, see nutrition
Dinka culture, 52–54
discounting, 232
discrimination, 452, 511, 527, 542
diseases
    among Fore people, 60
    animal domestication and, 50
    spread of ideas compared to, 56
disgust
    cultural display rules for, 332
    ethic of divinity and, 301
    facial expressions of, 324, 327
    language for, 339
display rules, 331
dispositional attributions, 371–72
distal causes, 48–49
distributive justice, culture and,
    306–9
divinity, ethic of, see ethic of
    divinity

divorce rates, 485
Dogon people (West Africa), 158
dolphins, cultural learning in, 7
"The Donkey Lettuce" (Grimm Brothers), 69
downward social comparison, 232, 235
Dragnet (TV series), 80
driving ability, 231
Druze people, 234
DSM-IV, 409, 419–20
Duchenne smiles, 331
Dutch, *see* Netherlands/Dutch
dynamic social impact theory, 64

East Asia
    acculturation, 520, 528–31
    acquiescence bias and, 107
    analytic thinking and, 359
    attention to stimuli, 361–62
    beliefs about future, 147
    child-rearing styles, 368
    comparisons with North America, 100
    conformity and, 269–70
    control strategies in, 255
    dissonance reduction and, 203
    eating disorders in, 414
    eye movement in, 364–66
    face and, 277
    failure and motivation, 33
    field dependence in, 363
    group membership and, 489, 491–94
    happiness and, 352
    height in, 441
    as high context culture, 390
    holistic thinking and, 359, 362
    koro syndrome, 415–16
    life satisfaction and, 349–50
    making choices, 259
    making sense of behavior, 374–75
    math education and, 170–74
    moderacy biases and, 105
    motivation in, 235–36
    noun biases and, 160–61
    painting styles in, 356
    positive emotions and, 351
    power and agency in, 252–53

rationalizing decisions, 203
reasoning styles in, 376–78
relationships and, 162
self-awareness in, 209–11
self-esteem in, 234
self-improvement orientation, 242
social anxiety disorder in, 424–25
subjective well-being and, 348
talking and thinking in, 384–85
theories on nature of self, 216
toleration of contradiction, 379–83
Eastern Cree tribe, 518–19
eating disorders, 413–15, 466
ecological cultural variation, 46–54
Edgerton, Robert, 54
education
    African-Americans and, 542
    East Asia and, 170–74
    physical health and, 450
    as quality of life standard, 281
    socialization through, 166–74
    trends in obtaining, 79–80
Efe people (Zaire), 149
Egypt
    Fertile Crescent and, 49
    linguistic relativity and, 392
    quality of life and, 280
    suicide in, 426–27
Einstein, Albert, 402
Ekman, Paul, 324–25, 331–32
Elements of Folk Psychology (Wundt), 36
elephants, cultural learning in, 6–7
elitism, 86
embarrassment, 327, 333–34
emotions
    basic vs. nonbasic, 329–30, 339–40
    cultural context of, 25
    cultural display rules, 331–34
    displaying vs. experiencing, 330–31
    facial expressions and, 323–30
    facial feedback hypothesis, 334–36
    intensity of, 336–39
    James-Lange theory of, 313–15, 318

language and, 339–42
    liget as, 311–12, 341
    moral violations and, 299–302
    as quality of life standard, 280
    role of appraisals in, 319–22
    schadenfreude as, 341, 393, 402
    spread of ideas, 65–67
    translating words for, 102
    two-factor theory of, 315–19
    variations in experiencing, 342–44
emulative learning, 10–12
encephalization quotient, 17–18
enemies, 474–78
energy, 311
Enlightenment, 345
enthusiasm, 340
entity theory of self, 214–15, 251
entity theory of the world, 251
environment
    physiological responses to, 319
    as quality of life standard, 281
epidemiology of ideas, 61–62
equality
    of income, 449
    principle of, 306–8
    as quality of life standard, 280
equality matching, 495–96
equity, principle of, 307
Eskimos, 321–22, 332, 340
ethic of autonomy
    defined, 285
    overview, 297
    violations of, 301–2
ethic of community
    defined, 285, 297
    overview, 286–93
    violations of, 301–2
ethic of divinity
    defined, 285–86
    overview, 293–95
    religious orientation and, 298–99
    violations of, 301–2
Ethiopia, 463–64
ethnic groups
    causes of death among, 451
    health and, 450–53
    trait words about, 63–64
ethnocentrism, 41, 279–81
ethnographies, 97, 480

Eurasia/Eurasians
  continental axes and, 49
  interpersonal attraction and, 467
  population density and, 50
European-Americans
  acculturation and, 527
  actor-observer bias, 489
  anthropocentric ways of, 405
  attention to stimuli, 361–62
  causes of death among, 451
  child-rearing styles, 237
  conformity and, 269–70
  education and, 542–44
  facial expressions and, 328
  happiness and, 352
  health outcomes of, 452
  individualism and, 155
  interpersonal attraction and, 468
  life satisfaction and, 349
  making choices, 259–60
  moderacy bias in, 105
  as monoculturals, 540
  positive emotions and, 351
  Protestantism and, 248
  reasoning styles in, 376–77
  self-improvement motivation,
    242
  self views of, 233–34
  sleeping arrangements in,
    148–49, 151
  social anxiety disorder and, 424
  socioeconomic status of, 450
  talking and thinking, 384–89
  value endorsement by, 540–41
European-Australians, 466
European-Canadians
  acculturation and, 530–32
  anger responses in, 337–39
  dissonance reduction and, 202–3
  on romantic love, 483–84
  self-awareness in, 210–11
  self-enhancing tendencies in, 235
  self-esteem in, 230, 234
Europe/Europeans
  cartoon controversy and, 273
  collectivism in, 188
  eating disorders in, 415
  gender identity in, 196
  height in, 441
  holistic thinking and, 360

immigration and, 509
individualism in, 188
making choices, 261
medical practices in, 457
Müller-Lyer illusion and, 279
Protestantism and, 246
self-awareness in, 210–11
skin color in, 434
social anxiety disorder in, 425
subjective well-being in, 82–83
underwater visual acuity, 435
euthanasia, 296
evoked culture, transmitted vs.,
  50–54
evolutionism, 278–79, 281–85
existential universal, 33
experimental method, cross-cultural
  research with, 113–16
explicit communication, 389–92
external attribution, 232–33, 235
external locus of control, 252
extraversion (OCEAN), 220, 225,
  519–20
extremity biases, 105–7
Exxon, 70
eye-tracker device, 364–66

face
  cultural diversity regarding, 277
  defined, 239
  motivation for, 239–42
  as personality trait, 222
facial expressions
  attitudes toward food, 439–40
  communication and, 389
  controlling, 331
  display rules for, 331–34
  emotions and, 323–30
  feedback hypothesis, 334–36
facial feedback hypothesis, 334–36
factor analysis, 220
failure as demotivating, 33
faith, 304
fear
  Chewong people and, 340
  defined, 314–15
  facial expressions of, 324, 327
  as useful signal, 299, 319–20
fecundity, 59
feelings, see emotions

female chastity anxiety (sleeping
  arrangement), 153
Ferber, Richard, 149–50
Fertile Crescent, 49–50
Festinger, Leon, 200
fidelity, 58–59
field dependence, 363–64
field experiments, 133
field independence, 363–64
Finland, 196, 437, 443
First Nations (Canada), 428–29
fitting in, see conformity
Five Factor Model of Personality,
  219–25
fMRI (functional magnetic
  resonance imaging), 19, 142
folk tales, 69–70
Fore people (New Guinea), 60,
  325–28, 497
frame-switching, 531–41
France
  acculturation and, 517
  attitudes toward food, 439–40
  Haiti and, 508
  on health and nutrition, 458
  height in, 440
  making choices, 261
  medical practices in, 456–57
  mortality and income, 443
  obesity rates in, 437–39
  wild boy of Aveyron, 143
Franklin, Benjamin, 245
free choice, 265
freedom
  ethic of autonomy, 285
  independence and, 533
  Muslims on, 274
Freeman, Derek, 165
French Paradox, 437
Freud, Sigmund, 303
friends, 474–78, 517
frigophobia, 418
fruit, brain size and, 18, 20
Fulani people, 66, 443–44
functional universal, 33
fundamental attribution error,
  371–75

Gaby, Alice, 400
Galileo, Galilei, 268, 360

gander-pulling, 126
Gandhi, Mahatma, 268
GDP, 347, 448
Geertz, Clifford, 138, 372
Gemeinschaft, 287–88
gender, self-concept measures and,
    191–97
generalizability, 100
genetic variation
    across populations, 432–35
    among ethnic groups, 451
    biological evolution and, 57–59
    in height, 440
    memes and, 59–60
Genie case study, 143–44
geographic cultural variation, 46–54
Gergen, Ken, 38
Germany/Germans
    acculturation and, 517
    achievement motivation and, 247
    attachment styles in, 158–59
    describing emotions, 341
    emotion words and, 102, 393
    gender identity in, 194, 196
    on health and nutrition, 458
    making choices, 261–64
    National Socialism in, 60–61, 90
    pronouncing shibboleths, 142
    Protestantism and, 246
    secularization theory and, 274
Gesellschaft, 287–88
Ghana, 475–78, 508
Gidjingali aborigines, 340
Gilligan, Carol, 286–87
Gini coefficient, 449
globalization, trend toward, 71
Goddard, H. H., 169
Google, folk tales search on, 69–70
Gore Associates, 22
gorillas, language abilities of, 13
Gould, Glenn, 411
Graduate Record Examination, 543
Graham, Franklin, 275
Grand Theft Auto III (game), 80–81
Great Britain
    arranged marriages and, 481
    color terms in, 396
    Haiti and, 508
    health and income, 449
    on health and nutrition, 458

height in, 440
individualism in, 188
making choices, 261
mortality study, 442–45
obesity rates in, 437–38
Protestantism and, 246
schizophrenia and, 431
views of self in, 182
Greece/Greeks
    analytic thinking and, 360
    facial expressions and, 328
    linguistic relativity and, 392
    taking and thinking, 384
Greenfield, Patricia, 38, 92–93
Greenland, 434
Grimm Brothers, 69
groups
    acculturation and, 518
    ancestral population size, 21–23
    bases of identification, 491–94
    brain size and, 18–19, 21
    control strategies in, 252–53, 255
    ethic of community and, 287–88
    forms of relationships, 494–97
    making choices and, 259–60
    principle of equality, 306
    references to scandals, 256
    relations with, 487–91
    working with others, 497–505
    see also ethnic groups; ingroups;
        outgroups
Guns, Gems, and Steel (Diamond), 48
Guugu Ymthirr, 398–400

Haiti, 508
Half-Life (game), 80
Hall, Edward, 389
Halloween candy scare, 65–66
happiness
    cultural differences in, 321, 323,
        328, 344–52
    emotions associated with, 343
    facial expressions of, 324–25,
        327–28
    life satisfaction and, 349
    pursuit of, 345
harmony, 222
Harris, Eric, 164
Harvard University, 86
Hatfield clan, 127

Hawaii, hunting traditions in, 47
head-hunting ritual, 311–12
health, see mental health; physical
    health
healthy migrant hypothesis, 452
Hebrew Bible, 303–4
Hehe tribe, 54
height, culture and, 440–42
Henrich, Joe, 360–61
Herodotus, 392
heterosexuality, 28–30
high context culture, 389–91
hikikomori, 408–9, 413
Himba language, 396–97
Hindi language, 140–41
Hindu religion
    gender identity and, 197
    moral reasoning and, 299
    on semen production, 411
Hippocrates, 219
Hispanic-Americans
    acculturation and, 527
    causes of death among, 451
    co-sleeping and, 149
    extremity bias and, 105
    health outcomes of, 452–53
    immigration and, 509
    positivity of self-view, 233
Hofstede, Geert, 38, 187–88
Hokusal (Japanese artist), 356
holistic thinking
    attention in, 361–70
    overview, 358–61
    reasoning styles, 375–78
    toleration of contradiction,
        378–83
    understanding other's behaviors,
        370–75
Holland, see Netherlands/Dutch
holy anorexia, 415
Homer, 384
homosexuality, 28–30
honeymoon stage, 512–13
Hong Kong, 225, 241, 536–38
honor, culture of, 126–34
host culture, 512–16, 521–25
human rights
    independence and, 533
    subjective well-being and,
        347–48

humans
    ancestral population size, 21–23
    biological variability of, 432–42
    brain size of, 17–21
    cultural learning and, 7–9,
        17–23
    cumulative cultural evolution
        and, 13–17
    language and, 12–13
    place in the world, 404–5
    on prestige, 8
    reliance on culture, 1, 3
    theory of mind and, 9–12
    uniqueness of culture, 5–7
    Van Doren on, 30
    variations in skin color, 432–35
Hungary, 427
Huntington, Samuel, 274
hunting traditions in Hawaii, 47
Hurricane Katrina, 54–55
Hussein, Saddam, 128
Hutterites, 22
Hyman, Misty, 176
hypertension, 450–51
hypotheses, testing, 121–23

IBM, 187–88
I Ching, 379
idealization, 482–84
ideas
    epidemiology of, 61–62
    factors for spread of, 62–70
    as replicators, 58–61
    studying rumors, 54–56
Ifaluk (Micronesia), 102, 340
Ignatieff, Michael, 71
IKEA, 70
iklas, 341
illness, responses to, 320–21
Ilongot tribe, 311–12
imitating mechanisms, 8–9
imitative learning, 10–11
immersion in cultures, 98
immigration
    changing attitudes toward host
        culture, 512–16
    cultural persistence and, 82
    defined, 512
    healthy migrant hypothesis, 453
    height and, 441

influxes of, 509
    weight gains, 526–27
Imo (macaque), 5, 7
implicit communication, 389–92
Incan people, 48–49
incest avoidance (sleeping
    arrangement), 152
income, see per capita income
incremental theory of self, 214–16,
    251
incremental theory of the world,
    251
independence prime, 121, 540–41
independent self-concepts
    acculturation and, 520–21
    analytic thinking and, 360
    close relationships and, 487–88
    conformity and, 269
    consistency and, 205–6
    cultural context for, 190–91
    frame-switching and, 533
    individualistic cultures and,
        187–88, 359
    interdependent vs., 182–84
    measures of, 191–92
    relationships and, 477–78
independent variable, 100–101,
    113–15
India/Indians
    arranged marriages, 480–81,
        484–87
    cultural display rules for, 334
    eating disorders in, 414
    ethic of community in, 288–93
    fundamental attribution error,
        372–74
    gender identity in, 196–97
    health and income, 449
    moral reasoning and, 299
    Natyashastra and, 340
    resource distribution and,
        308–9
    sleeping arrangements in, 151–54
    viewing people with status,
        115–16
    views of self in, 182
individualism
    acculturation and, 520
    childhood experiences and,
        154–56

conformity and, 268
control and, 253, 255
cooperation and, 503
as CPAI factor, 223
cultural evolution and, 72–76
culture and, 3–4
developmental transitions and,
    163
experiencing emotions and,
    343–44
group membership and, 490
heterogeneity with culture,
    190–91
love marriages and, 482, 484–85
making choices and, 258, 261–62
negotiation and, 504
reading primers and, 161
religion and, 243, 247
self-concept and, 187–90, 192
subjective well-being and,
    348–49
thinking styles and, 359
value endorsement for, 540–41
Indonesia, 517, 532
Industrial Revolution, 441
influence, 254–55
information
    culture as, 3
    emotional ideas and, 66
    memes and, 59
    from television viewing, 78
Ingalik people, 455
ingroups
    bases of identification, 491–94
    independent view of self and,
        183
    making choices, 260
    relations with, 487–91
    social loafing and, 500
initiation rituals, 28–30
innovation, cultural, 83–85
insults, culture of honor and,
    129–33
integration strategy, 522, 525
intelligence
    measuring, 19, 169, 216
    trends in, 76–81
interconnected cultures, 70–71
interdependence prime, 121,
    540–41

interdependent self-concepts
    acculturation and, 520–21
    collectivistic cultures and,
        187–88, 359
    conformity and, 269
    consistency and, 204
    cultural context for, 190–91
    frame-switching and, 533
    holistic thinking and, 360
    independent vs., 185–86
    measures of, 191–92
    prevention orientation and,
        538–39
    relationships and, 477–78
    social anxiety disorder and, 424
interest (emotion), 327
International Olympic Organization,
    176
Internet
    interconnection of cultures and,
        71
    obtaining information from, 78
    relationships on, 469
interpersonal attraction
    other bases for, 469–71
    similarity-attraction effect,
        471–73
    universal standards of, 463–69
interpersonal relatedness, 223
interpersonal space, 136–37
introversion, 520
intuition, moral violations and, 300
Inuit people, 419, 434
IQ scores, 76–81, 216, 385–87
Iran, 49, 415
Ireland/Irish
    cultural display rules, 333
    culture of honor in, 128
    stereotypes about, 62–63
Islam
    cartoon controversy and, 273–74
    Christian views of, 275
    ethic of divinity, 286
    Fulani and, 443
    gender identity and, 196
    growth of, 275
    suicide and, 426
Israel/Israelis
    arranged marriages, 485
    attachment styles in, 158–59

    self-views of, 234
    social loafing and, 500
Italy/Italians
    acculturation and, 524–25
    cultural display rules, 333
    cultural persistence and, 81–82
    eating disorders in, 415
    gender identity in, 194
    on health and nutrition, 458
    height in, 441
    holistic thinking and, 360
    making choices, 261
Itami, Juzo, 429
Ivory Coast, 508

Jamaica, 115–16
James, William, 313–15
James-Lange theory of emotions,
    313–15, 318
Japan/Japanese
    acculturation and, 515, 517, 520,
        527, 529–31
    analytic thinking and, 359
    arranged marriages, 485–86
    attachment styles in, 158–59
    attitudes toward food, 439
    baseball in, 84–85
    on blood types, 219
    collectivism in, 189
    color terms and, 394–95
    control strategies in, 253–57
    on creation myth, 66
    cultural difference considerations,
        124–25
    cultural display rules, 332–33
    cultural learning among animals
        in, 5, 7
    daily emotions of, 345
    developmental transitions in, 163
    dissonance reduction and, 202–3
    emotion of amae, 341
    experiencing emotions, 343–44
    external attributions for success,
        235
    eye movement in, 364–66
    facial expressions and, 324–25,
        328
    field dependence and, 363–64
    gender identity in, 191, 194
    group membership and, 490–94

    happiness in, 323
    height in, 441
    as high context culture, 390–91
    hikikomori condition, 408–9, 413
    immersion in, 98
    individualism and, 74–76
    ingroups and, 489
    intensity of emotions, 336
    interconnection of cultures and,
        70
    interpersonal attraction and,
        463–64, 466–67, 471
    interpersonal space in, 136–37
    latah condition in, 418
    life expectancy in, 449, 527
    making choices, 259
    making sense of behavior, 374
    math education in, 171–74
    moral violations and, 302
    mortality and income, 443
    motivations for, 228–29
    negotiation and, 504
    noun biases and, 160
    obesity rates in, 437–38
    Olympic Games and, 176
    painting styles in, 356, 367–68,
        370
    personality traits in, 225
    phonemes in language, 140
    pronouncing shibboleths, 141–42
    quality of life and, 280
    references to scandals, 256–57
    resource distribution and, 309
    on romantic love, 483–84
    self-awareness in, 212–14
    self-consistency in, 198–200
    self-esteem in, 234
    self-improvement motivation,
        241–42
    seniority systems and, 308
    similarity-attraction effect and,
        472–73
    situation-sampling example,
        119–20
    suicide in, 427, 429
    surveys and, 102
    taijin kyoufushou disorder, 425–26
    on talking and thinking, 384
    theories on nature of self, 216
    tolerance of contradiction, 382

views of self in, 182
WWII rumors against, 55
Javanese people, 341, 455
Jean, Michelle, 508–9
jerungdu, 28–30
Jihad vs. McWorld (Barber), 71
Johnson, Steven, 80
Jolie, Angelina, 462–63, 469
Journal of Personality and Social Psychology, 35
Judaism
    on creation myth, 66–67
    cultural display rules, 333
    on morality, 303–6
    political issues and, 296
    on talking and thinking, 384
justice, culture and, 306–9

Kalahari, 47, 279
Kaluli people (New Guinea), 338
Kamba tribe, 54
Kazakhstan, 71
Kenya, 180–82
Kerry, John, 64, 206–7, 217
Kim, Heejung, 384, 387
King, Martin Luther, 268
Kissinger, Henry, 142
Kissinger, Walter, 142
Kitayama, Shinobu, 98
Klebold, Dylan, 164
Kleinman, Arthur, 421
knowledge, holistic thinking and, 359
Kohlberg, Lawrence, 281–85
Korea/Koreans
    acculturation and, 520
    analytic thinking and, 359
    eating disorders in, 415
    gender identity in, 191
    noun biases and, 160
    reasoning styles in, 378
    self-consistency in, 206–7
    self-esteem in, 234
    on talking and thinking, 384
    TKS disorder in, 426
    views of self in, 182
koro syndrome, 415–16
!Kung tribe, 47

lactase nonpersistence, 434
bin Laden, Osama, 275

Lange, Carl, 313–15
language
    accents in, 40
    acculturation success and, 516–19, 532
    bilinguals' brains, 142
    color terms in, 394
    cultural learning and, 12–13
    cultural universals, 23–24
    emotions and, 339–42
    group membership and, 489
    noun biases, 159–62
    Sapir-Whorf hypothesis, 392–404
    sensitive periods for acquiring, 139–44
    socialization and, 144
    talking and thinking, 383–89
    translating emotional words, 102
    translating survey questions, 101–2
    universalism on, 276–77
Lao Tzu, 378–79, 384
latah condition, 418
Latin America
    arranged marriages and, 481
    collectivism in, 188
    subjective well-being and, 346, 348
    susto condition in, 418
learned helplessness, 263
Leeson, Nick, 256
Le Monde, 456
Leontiev, Aleksei. N., 37
life expectancy
    GDP and, 448
    Gini coefficient and, 449
    in Japan, 449, 527
life satisfaction, 349–50
liget (emotion), 311–12, 341
linguistic relativity, 342, 392–404
Lithuania, 426
"Little Red Riding Hood" (Grimm Brothers), 69
longevity
    defined, 58–59
    happiness and, 344
    as quality of life standard, 280
Lonner, Walter, 38
Lotus Sutra, 351
Louix XIV, King of France, 457

love, 340, 479–87
love marriages, 480–82
low context culture, 389–90
loyalty, 231
Luther, Martin, 243–44, 268

macaques, cultural learning in, 5, 7–8
major depressive disorder (MDD), 419–23
Malaysia/Malaysians
    acculturation and, 518, 520
    amok phenomenon in, 417
    Chewong people of, 340
    facial expressions and, 328
    gender identity in, 196
    Moken tribe and, 435
    personality traits in, 225
    views of self in, 182
malgri syndrome, 418
manners, changing nature of, 43–46
Maori people, 234
Mapuche (Chile), 360–61
marginalization strategy, 522–23
marking pricing, 496–97
Markus, Hazel, 98
marriage
    arranged vs. love, 480–87
    universal nature of, 31
Martin, Steve, 276
Marxism, 243
Maryland Police Academy, 470–71
Masai people, 181–82, 184
masculinity, cultural differences in, 47
Masuda, Taka, 355
math education, East Asia and, 170–74
mathematics, 402–3
Mayan people, 49, 402, 405
McCartney, Paul, 23
McCoy clan, 127
MDD (major depressive disorder), 419–23
Mead, Margaret, 164–65
medicine
    culture and, 453–59
    holistic thinking and, 360
meditation, 351, 384
Melanesians, 433

memes, 59–60
Menominee tribe, 405
mental health
    cultural differences with, 422
    culture-bound syndromes,
        412–19
    depression, 419–23
    psychological disorders, 410–12
    social anxiety disorder, 423–26
    social withdrawal, 408–10
mere exposure effect, 471
meritocracy, 307
Methodism, 244, 246
methodological equivalence, 99
methods for studying cultures
    challenge of unpacking,
        123–26
    considerations, 92–94
    cultural priming, 120–21
    culture-level measures, 121–23
    culture of honor case study,
        126–34
    experiments, 113–16
    meaningful comparisons across,
        96–101
    multiple, 116–17
    selecting cultures to study, 94–96
    situation sampling, 117–20
    surveys, 101–13
Mexican-Americans, 233
Mexico
    anthropocentric ways and, 405
    continental axes and, 49
    cooperation and, 502–3
    height in, 441
    quality of life and, 280
    Zinacantecans in, 92, 99, 163
Micronesia, 102, 340, 427–28
Middle East
    calculation tools in, 34
    cartoon controversy and, 273
    culture of honor in, 128
    eating disorders in, 414
    Fertile Crescent and, 49
    gender identity in, 194
    tribalism in, 71
migrants, 512
military, 495
Miller, George, 421
mimicry, 249–50

Minangkabau people, 111
mind
    independence from culture,
        23–27
    theory of, 9–12, 95
minimally counterintuitive ideas,
    67–70
Minoura, Yasuko, 145–46
Miss America pageant, 414
Miwata, Katsutoshi, 429
moderacy biases, 105–7
modernization, 222
Moken tribe, 435
monocultural people, 528, 538–41
Moon, Sung Myung, 485
Moore's Law, 15
morality of thought, 302–6
moral reasoning
    conventional, 282
    cultural differences in, 283,
        288–93, 295–99
    emotions and, 299–302
    ethic of autonomy, 285, 297,
        301–2
    ethic of community, 285–93,
        297, 301–2
    ethic of divinity, 285–86,
        293–95, 298–99, 301–2
    postconventional, 282–83
    preconventional, 281–82
    role of emotions in, 299–302
    stages of moral development,
        281–85
moral violations, 299–302
mortality
    among ethnic groups, 451
    income and, 442–43
Moss, Kate, 468
Mossi people, 443–44
motivation
    agency and control, 250–66
    behind self-starvation, 415
    for conformity, 266–71
    defined, 227
    for face, 239–42
    religion and, 242–50
    for self-enhancement, 227–39
    for self-esteem, 227–39
    for self-improvement, 239–42
    success and, 33

MTV, 70–71
Müller-Lyer illusion, 278–79
multicultural worlds
    acculturation in, 512–27
    changing attitudes toward host
        culture, 512–16
    evidence for blending, 528–31
    example of, 508–9
    frame-switching in, 531–41
    stereotype threat, 542–45
    studying acculturation, 511–12
Mundrukuku tribe (Amazon), 403
Mursi people, 463–64
Muslims, see Islam
mutations, 58
myths, evolution of cultural ideas
    and, 66

naïve dialectism, 379
Namibia, 396
National Socialism, 60–61, 90
Native Americans
    anthropocentric ways and, 405
    positivity of self-view, 234
    views of self among, 182
natural selection, 56
Natyashastra, 340
need, principle of, 306, 309
need for cognitive closure (NCC),
    523–25
negative valence, 223
negotiation, 503–4
neocortex ratio, 19–21
NEO-PI-R questionnaire, 221–22
Netherlands/Dutch
    acculturation and, 517
    experiencing emotions, 343
    gender identity in, 196
    Haiti and, 508
    height in, 440–41
    linguistic relativity and, 398–400
    negotiation and, 504
    obesity rates in, 437
    Protestantism and, 246
    reference-group effects example,
        109
neurasthenia, 421
neuroticism (OCEAN), 220–22, 225
New Guinea
    color terms in, 395

cultural learning from warfare in, 7
Dani people, 328, 395
Fore people, 60, 325–28, 497
Kaluli people, 338
Papua New Guinea, 28–30
Newman, Paul, 325
newspapers
    making sense of behavior, 374–75
    references to scandals, 255–57
Newsweek, 65
New Testament (Bible), 304
New Yorker magazine, 75
New York Times, 256, 374
New Zealand
    acculturation and, 518, 520
    gender identity in, 194
    individualism in, 188
    mortality and income, 443
Nicklaus, Jack, 8
Nietzche, Friedrich, 274
Nigeria
    depression in, 420
    eating disorders in, 415
    gender identity in, 194, 196
    Haiti and, 508
1984 (Orwell), 393
Nisbett, Richard, 126–34, 355, 361
nonuniversals, 34
nonverbal communication, 314, 389–92
norms
    culture shaping, 136
    dynamic social impact theory on, 64
    effects of initial conditions on, 86–87
    of interpersonal space, 136–37
    transmitted culture and, 52
North America
    acculturation and, 530–32
    beliefs about future, 147
    cartoon controversy and, 273
    comparisons with East Asia, 100
    depression in, 420
    developmental transitions in, 163
    dhat syndrome in, 411–13
    dissonance reduction and, 202–3
    fundamental attribution error, 372

group membership and, 489
immigration and, 509
as low context culture, 390
motivations for, 228–29
noun biases and, 160
psychological studies and, 35
pursuit of happiness in, 345
self-awareness in, 208–10
similarity-attraction effect and, 472–73
sleeping arrangements in, 148–54
social anxiety disorder and, 424
social anxiety disorder in, 425
theories on nature of self, 216
tolerance of contradiction, 382
Norway
    Fulbright scholar study, 512–16
    health and income, 449
    height in, 440
    mortality and income, 443
    quality of life and, 280
noun biases, 159–62
Nuer culture, 52–54
number systems, 248–49
nutrition
    brain size and, 18, 20
    health and, 458–59
    height and, 441
    illness and, 454
    obesity and, 435–40

obesity
    diet and, 435–40
    immigrants and, 453, 526–27
objective self-awareness, 207–8, 211–12
obligations, moral, 288–93
obsessive-compulsive disorder, 409
Occam's Razor, 117
OCEAN acronym, 220–21
Old Testament (Bible), 304
O'Neil, Suzy, 176
openness to experiences (OCEAN), 220
orthodox religions, 296–97
Orwell, George, 392–93
Otis IQ test, 78
outgroups
    bases of identification, 492–94
    independent view of self and, 183

making choices, 259–60
relations with, 487–91
social loafing and, 500

Paduang people, 463–64, 469
pain expression, cultural display rules for, 333
Pakistan
    arranged marriages, 480–81
    eating disorders in, 414
    gender identity in, 195–96
Palestinian Territory, 281
Papua New Guinea, 28–30
parasite prevalence, 51–52
Pascal, Blaise, 402
passion, 311
Patterns of Culture (Benedict), 37
Patterns of Sexual Behavior (Ford and Beach), 467
Pearl Harbor, 55
People.com, 462
per capita income
    height and, 441
    mortality and, 442–43
    as quality of life standard, 280
    subjective well-being and, 346–47
perception
    about gender identity, 193
    categorical, 396–97
    of color, 393–97
    cultural differences in, 358
    primary control and, 252
    spatial, 397–401
personal choice, 259–60, 285
personality
    acculturation and, 511
    actor-observer bias and, 489–90
    categorizing by traits, 217–19
    Five Factor Model of Personality, 219–25
    gender-related traits and, 192–94
    methods for studying, 94
    self-description of, 181–82
    understanding behaviors via, 370–75
perspective of others, 9–12
Peru
    continental axes and, 49
    effects of schooling, 170

Peru (*continued*)
  gender identity in, 194
  quality of life and, 280
Philippines
  Ilongot tribe, 311–12
  interconnection of cultures and, 71
  linguistic relativity and, 392
  nonverbal communication and, 392
  skin color in, 434
phonemes, 139–41, 323, 396
physical health
  acculturation and, 526–27
  acquired across cultures, 435–42
  anger and, 337
  biological variability of humans, 432
  culture and, 442–53
  ethnicity and, 450–53
  genetic variation across populations, 432–35
  height variations, 440–42
  intelligence and, 78–79
  medicine and culture, 453–59
  nutrition and, 458–59
  socioeconomic status and, 442–53
physiological responses
  culture of honor theory, 130
  for emotions, 314
  to environment, 319
  reference-group effects and, 111
pidgin language, 276
Pietism, 244
pigeons, cultural learning in, 7
Piraha tribe, 403
Pitt, Brad, 462–63, 469
Pizarro, Francisco, 48–49
Plato, 360
Playboy magazine, 414
pluralistic ignorance, 88–90
Pokot tribe, 54
Poland/Poles
  collectivism in, 204
  self-consistency in, 204–5
  term for disgust, 339
political issues, differences of opinion on, 296
pop culture, intelligence and, 80–81

Pope, Alexander, 345
populations
  ancestral size, 21–23
  in Eurasia, 50
  food surplus and, 50
  generalizability of, 100
  genetic variation across, 432–35
  spread of ideas through, 55–56
Portugal, 323, 418
postconventional moral reasoning, 282–83
poverty
  culture of honor and, 127
  health and, 448
power
  Protestant Reformation and, 246
  self-concept and, 189
  of studies, 100
preconventional moral reasoning, 281–82
predestination, 238, 244–45
prejudice, 542
prestige, humans and, 8–9
prevention orientation, 240–42, 538–39
pride, 327
primary control, 252–57
primates
  brain size of, 18, 20–21
  cultural learning in, 6–7
  emotional expressions in, 323–24
  emulative learning in, 12
  language abilities of, 13
  social groups and, 18–19
priming cultures, 120–21, 533–41
Princeton University, 88
principle of equality, 306–8
principle of equity, 307
principle of need, 306, 309
progressive religions, 296–98
Prohibition, 89
promotion orientation, 240–42, 538–39
propinquity effect, 469–71
protection of the vulnerable (sleeping arrangement), 152
The Protestant Ethic and the Spirit of Capitalism (Weber), 242
Protestantism
  capitalism and, 244–45

  on faith, 304
  gender identity and, 196
  ideas emerging from, 243
  individualism and, 243, 247
  on morality, 305–6
  political issues and, 296
  predestination and, 238, 244–45
Protestant Reformation, 243–44, 246
Protestant work ethic, 244, 246–48
proximal causes, 48
Prudence advice column, 150–51
psycholinguistics, 393
psychological disorders, 410–12
psychologization, 421
psychopaths, 300–301
Puerto Rico, 280, 419
punishment, cultural universality of, 33
Puritanism
  baseball and, 126
  on predestination, 244
  Quakerism and, 85–86
  Weber on, 246
Putnam, Robert, 72–75
Pygmies (Africa), 108–9

Quakerism, 85–86
quality of life standards, 280–81
quantity estimator, 32
Quebec (Canada), 71
questionnaires, 101–4, 115, 221–22

racism, 452
random assignment, 114
ratchet effect, 13
rationalizations
  about cigarette smoking, 201
  about decisions for others, 203
Raven's Matrices IQ test, 78, 385–87
reasoning styles, 375–78
Rebel Without a Cause (film), 164
reference-group effects, 108–12
relatedness (measure), 192
relationships
  attachment styles, 156–59
  Chinese and, 161
  close, 474–88
  East Asia and, 162

elementary forms of, 494–97
emotion of *amae*, 341
ethic of community and, 287
friends and enemies, 474–78
independent self-concepts and, 359
interdependent self-concepts and, 359
Internet-based, 469
love in, 479–87
personality and, 218
self-concept and, 190
relativism, 277–79
religion
    achievement motivation and, 242–50
    cartoon controversy, 273–74, 286
    ethic of divinity, 285–86, 293–95, 298–99, 301–2
    evolution of cultural ideas and, 66
    gender identity and, 196–97
    growth of, 275
    holistic thinking and, 360
    ideological conflicts and, 274
    individualism and, 243, 247
    influences on cultural evolution, 85–86
    medical practices and, 454–55
    meditation and, 351, 384
    political issues and, 296
    secularization theory and, 274
    self-starvation and, 415
    on suicide, 426
    tribalism and, 71
    work ethic and, 244, 246–48
Renoir, Auguste, 468
ren qin, 222
resource distribution, 307–9
respect for hierarchy (sleeping arrangement), 153
response biases, 105, 115
reverse-scoring, 108
Rimaibe people, 443–44
ritualized displays, 334
Rod and Frame task, 362–63
Romans, 402
romantic love, 479–87
Rorshach ink blots, 361–62

Rosaldo, Michelle, 311
Rosch Heider, E., 395–96, 404
Rosenberg self-esteem scale, 230
rotating credit association, 495–96
Rubens, Peter Paul, 468
rumors, studying, 54–56
Russia, 37, 71, 262
Russian cultural-historical school, 37

saccades, 366
sacred couple (sleeping arrangement), 153
sadness, 324, 327
Saito, Tamaki, 409
salmon bias, 453
Sambia case study, 27–30
Samburu people, 181–82, 184
Samoa/Samoans, 164–65, 340, 435–36
samples/sampling, 95, 117–20
Sanchez-Burks, J., 248–49
San Jose Mercury, 383
Sapir, Edward, 144, 392
Sapir-Whorf hypothesis, 392–404
SAT (Scholastic Aptitude Test), 77, 216, 542
Scandinavia
    family meal study in, 96–97
    Protestantism and, 246
    subjective well-being and, 82, 346, 348
Schacter, Stanley, 315–18
schadenfreude, 341, 393, 402
schizophrenia, 409, 412, 429–32
Scholastic Aptitude Test (SAT), 77, 216, 542
scientific method, 455
Scotland, 128, 194
Scribner, Sylvia, 38
Sebei tribe, 54
secondary control, 252–57
secularization theory, 274–75
secure attachment, 156, 158–59
Segall, Marshall, 38
self
    awareness of, 207–14
    collectivism and, 187–90
    consistency with, 198–207
    creativity and, 180

    cultural gender identity and, 191–97
    entity theory of, 214–15
    identifying, 177–82
    incremental theory of, 214–16
    independent view of, 182–84
    individualism and, 187–90
    interdependent view of, 184–86
    theories regarding nature of, 214–17
    Triandis on, 38–39
self-awareness, 207–14
self-consistency, 198–207
self-discipline, 84
self-enhancement, 227–39
self-esteem, 102, 227–39, 528–31
self-expression, 387–88
self-improvement, 239–42
self-serving biases, 230–31
self-starvation, 415
Senegal, 6
seniority system, 308
sensitive periods
    for acquiring culture, 144–46
    for cultural socialization, 138–44
    defined, 138
    for language acquisition, 139–44
separation strategy, 522–23, 525
seppuku, 429
September 11, 2007 attacks, 275
Sex Role Ideology (SRI), 195
sex roles
    cultural differences in, 47
    Sex Role Ideology scale, 195
sexual identity
    debate over, 296
    Sambia case study, 28–30
sexual selection, 56–57
shame, 327, 340
Shaw, George Bernard, 482
shibboleths, 141
Siamese people, 455
Siberia, 418
sign language, 13, 141
similarity-attraction effect, 471–73
Simpson, Jessica, 464
Singapore
    acculturation and, 518, 520
    koro syndrome in, 416
    quality of life and, 280

Singer, James, 315–18
situational attributions, 371–72
situation-sampling methodology, 117–20
skin color, 432–35
sleeping arrangements, cultural differences in, 148–54
Smith, Reggie, 84
social anxiety disorder, 409, 412, 423–26
social brain hypothesis, 19, 22
social class, *see* socioeconomic status
social facilitation, 497–98
socialization
    attachment styles, 156–59
    childhood experiences and, 148–62
    cultural differences and, 146–48
    developmental transitions and, 162–66
    individualism vs. collectivism, 154–56, 359
    language and, 144
    making choices and, 258
    noun biases, 159–62
    parenting styles and, 155–56
    sensitive periods for, 138–46
    sleeping arrangements and, 148–54
    social withdrawal and, 409
    through education, 166–74
social loafing, 498–500
social phobia, *see* social anxiety disorder
social potency, 223
social striving, 500
social withdrawal, 408–10
socioeconomic status
    acculturation strategies and, 523
    ethic of divinity and, 294–95
    health and, 442–53
    hypertension and, 452
    making choices across, 264–66
    social withdrawal and, 408–9
somatization, 222, 421
Sony, 70
The Sopranos (TV series), 80
South Africa
    cultural learning among animals in, 7

gender identity in, 194
interconnection of cultures and, 71
South Asia
    amok phenomenon, 417–18
    dhat syndrome in, 411–13
    eating disorders in, 414
    koro syndrome, 415–16
    latah condition, 418
    Moken tribe and, 435
    subjective well-being and, 346
    tribalism in, 71
South Pacific
    cartoon controversy and, 273
    collectivism in, 188
    color terms and, 394
    sex roles in, 47
Soviet Union, 37, 71, 262
Space Invaders (game), 80
Space Quest math game, 259–60
Spain/Spanish
    acculturation and, 517
    facial expressions and, 328
    Haiti and, 508
    negotiation and, 504
    personality traits in, 223, 225
    Pizarro defeating Incans, 48–49
    Protestantism and, 246
spatial perception, 397–401
spitting, 44–45
standardized scores (Z-scores), 106–7
stereotypes
    about gender identity, 193–94
    about Irish, 62–63
    communicable ideas and, 63
stereotype threat, 542–45
Stevenson, Harold, 38
sticking out, 266–71
stress
    amok phenomenon and, 417
    health and, 449–50
    hypertension and, 452
    interdependence and, 520–21
    socioeconomic status and, 445–46
studying cultures, *see* methods for studying cultures
subjective self-awareness, 207–8, 211
subjective well-being, 82, 344–52
success as motivation, 33

Sudan, 52–54
suicide
    quality of life and, 280
    social withdrawal and, 409
    as universal syndrome, 426–29
Surinamese, 343
surprise, 324, 327
surveys
    acquiescence bias, 107–8
    deprivation effects, 112–13
    extremity biases, 105–7
    moderacy biases, 105–7
    reference-group effects, 108–12
    response biases, 105
    survey data, 129
    translating questionnaire items, 101–4
    Zinacantecan people and, 92
susto condition, 418
Suzuki, Ichiro, 429
Sweden/Swedish
    facial expressions and, 328
    gender identity in, 194
    health and income, 449
    interconnection of cultures and, 70
    views of self in, 182
Switzerland, 261

Tahiti, 47
Tai Chi, 378
taijin kyoufushou (TKS) disorder, 425–26
Taiwan
    child-rearing styles, 236–37
    math education in, 171–73
    positive emotions and, 351
    social loafing and, 499
Takahashi, Naoko, 176
talking, thinking and, 383–89
Talmud, 303
Tampopo (film), 429
Tanzania, 6
Taoism, 360
Tao Te Ching, 378
television viewing, 78
temperamentalness, 223
terrain, 456
terrible twos, 162–63
testing hypotheses, 121–23

Thailand, 435, 463–64
thematic categorization, 358
theory of mind, 9–12, 95
thinking aloud, 385–86
third-person imagery, 210–11
thought
    analytic thinking, 358–61
    education and, 169–70
    holistic thinking, 358–61
    measuring, 121–23
    mind independence and, 25
    morality of, 302–6
    talk and, 383–89
thrift, 222
TOEFL (Test of English as a
    Foreign Language), 517
Togo, 508
Tonnies, Ferdinand, 287
tools
    cultural learning with, 6, 8
    cumulative cultural evolution,
        14–16
trait words about ethnic groups,
    63–64
transitions, developmental, 162–66
translation of questionnaire items,
    101–4
transmitted culture, evoked vs.,
    50–54
tribalism, trend toward, 71
Truk (island), 47
trust, 490
trustworthiness, 222
Tsai, Jeanne, 351
Tsimshian tribe, 518–19
Turkey/Turks
    arranged marriages, 485
    experiencing emotions, 343
    facial expressions and, 328
    Fertile Crescent and, 49
Twenty-Statements Test, 180–82,
    198, 213
two-factor theory of emotions,
    315–19

Uganda, 340
Ukraine, 320
ultraviolet radiation (UVR), 433–34
uncertainty avoidance, 189–90
Unification Church, 485

United Kingdom, see Great Britain
United States/Americans
    acculturation and, 520, 526–27,
        532–33
    adaptation and, 83–85
    arranged marriages and, 481, 485
    attachment styles in, 158–59
    attention to stimuli in, 366
    attitudes toward food, 439
    bask in the reflected glory, 235
    collectivism in, 189
    color terms and, 395
    conformity and, 270
    control strategies in, 253–57, 262
    cooperation and, 502–3
    cultural difference considerations,
        124–25
    cultural display rules, 332–34
    culture of honor in, 126–34
    daily emotions of, 345
    depression in, 420
    displaying emotions, 331
    experiencing emotions, 343–44
    on explaining behaviors, 535–36
    facial expressions for emotions,
        324–25
    field independence and, 363–64
    friendship in, 475–78
    fundamental attribution error,
        372–74
    gender identity in, 191, 194, 197
    group membership and, 491–94
    health and income, 449
    on health and nutrition, 458
    height in, 440–41
    holistic thinking and, 362
    immigration and, 509
    individualism and, 72–76, 188
    influences on cultural evolution,
        85–86
    intensity of emotions, 336
    interconnection of cultures and,
        70
    interpersonal attraction and, 464,
        468, 471
    interpersonal space in, 136–37
    koro syndrome in, 416
    making choices, 260–61
    making sense of behavior, 374
    math education in, 171, 173

    medical practices in, 456–57
    moral reasoning and, 283,
        295–96
    moral violations and, 302
    mortality and income, 443
    Müller-Lyer illusion and, 279
    neurasthenia in, 421
    obesity rates in, 437–39
    Olympic Games and, 176
    painting styles in, 367–68, 370
    parenting styles in, 155–56
    prevention orientation, 539
    Protestantism and, 246–47
    pursuit of happiness in, 345
    quality of life and, 280
    reasoning styles in, 376–78
    references to scandals, 256–57
    religion in, 274–75
    resource distribution and, 308–9
    response to illness in, 320
    schizophrenia and, 431
    self-awareness in, 212–14
    self-concept measures and, 192
    self-consistency in, 198–99,
        204–7
    seniority systems and, 308
    situation-sampling example,
        119–20
    social loafing and, 499–500
    subjective well-being and, 346
    subjective well-being in, 82
    suicide in, 427
    surveys and, 102
    talking and thinking in, 384
    theories on nature of self, 216
    toleration of contradiction,
        379–83
    Twenty-Statements Test and,
        180–81
universal health insurance, 308
universalism, 276–77
universals
    in cultures, 23–24, 30–34, 323
    of sexuality, 30
universal syndromes
    depression, 419–23
    schizophrenia, 429–32
    social anxiety disorder, 423–26
    suicide, 426–29
University of Michigan, 130, 134

University of Pennsylvania, 86,
    294–95
unpackaging culture, 123–26
upward social comparison, 232, 235
U.S. Patent and Trademark Office, 15
U.S. Public Health Service, 169
usurped choice, 265
Utku Eskimos, 321–22, 332, 340

values
    cultural differences in, 320
    deprivation effects and, 112
Vancouver Index of Acculturation,
    522
Van Doren, Mark, 30
Van Gogh, Vincent, 268
Venezuela, 102, 136–37
vervet monkeys, 13, 21
Vietnam/Vietnamese
    acculturation and, 527
    making choices, 259
    skin color in, 434
violations, moral, 299–302
violence
    adolescence and, 164
    amok phenomenon and, 417–18
    cartoon controversy and, 273–74
    culture of honor and, 126–34
    social withdrawal and, 409

Vitamin D, 433–34
vocabulary, television viewing and,
    78
Volkerspsychologie (Wundt), 36
voodoo death, 418

warfare, 7, 47
Weber, Max, 242–46
Wechsler IQ test, 78
weight
    cultural differences in, 435–42
    immigration and, 526
    interpersonal attraction and,
        466–69
welfare system, 308
Wesley, John, 246
West Sumatra, 111
whales
    cultural learning in, 7
    language abilities of, 13
Whiting, Roger, 84
Whorf, Benjamin, 392
Whorfian hypothesis, 392–404
Wierzabicka, Anna, 339
wild boy of Aveyron, 143
witchcraft, 455
within-groups manipulation, 114–16
wonder, 340
Wonder, Stevie, 23

Woods, Tiger, 8
work ethic, Protestant, 244,
    246–48
workforce
    education and, 79–80
    mortality and income, 442–43
working with others
    competing vs. cooperating,
        500–505
    social facilitation, 497–98
    social loafing, 498–500
    social striving, 500
World Journal, 374
World War II
    individualism after, 74, 76
    pronouncing shibboleths, 141
    rumors during, 55

yang, 378, 456
yin, 378, 456
You Gotta Have Wa (Whiting), 84

Zaire, 149
Zambia, 283
Zelda (game), 80
Zinacantecan people (Mexico), 92,
    99, 163
Z-scores, 106–7, 346